CAMBRIDGE LIBRARY COLLECTION

Books of enduring scholarly value

Fiction and Poetry

Reading became an increasingly popular entertainment in eighteenth-and nineteenth-century Britain, Europe and America, reaching an ever wider spectrum of society as the cost of printing came down and levels of literacy rose. The novels avidly consumed in this period were not merely escapist fiction. Many of them drew attention to serious social issues such as slavery, child labour and other forms of exploitation that blighted the age of revolutions and empire, some were thinly disguised autobiographies, while others had clear educational aims: thus the line between fiction and non-fiction was a fluid one. Poetry too flourished across a wide range of genres, and the political and social agendas of the Romantic movement in particular led to its being read and appreciated at all levels of society. In this series, the Cambridge Library Collection offers the texts of fiction and poetry as these works were first published and received by an eager reading public.

Wuthering Heights and Agnes Grey

The tragic lives of the Brontë sisters hold a romantic fascination as great as that of the stories into which they poured their rich imaginations and experiences. Following their first appearance in 1847 and the deaths of Emily (1818–48) and Anne (1820–49), these two classics of English literature – one an impassioned tale of doomed love, the other a quietly intense portrait of the governess in Victorian society – were published together with poems and a biographical notice in this revised 1851 edition. It was prepared by the authors' sister and fellow novelist, Charlotte (1816–55). *Wuthering Heights* was Emily's only novel, and although it received mixed reviews upon first publication because of its stark depiction of mental and physical cruelty, it has since become an icon of its genre. *Agnes Grey*, Anne's debut novel, astutely shows the governess to be an often invisible and abused member of the household.

Cambridge University Press has long been a pioneer in the reissuing of out-of-print titles from its own backlist, producing digital reprints of books that are still sought after by scholars and students but could not be reprinted economically using traditional technology. The Cambridge Library Collection extends this activity to a wider range of books which are still of importance to researchers and professionals, either for the source material they contain, or as landmarks in the history of their academic discipline.

Drawing from the world-renowned collections in the Cambridge University Library and other partner libraries, and guided by the advice of experts in each subject area, Cambridge University Press is using state-of-the-art scanning machines in its own Printing House to capture the content of each book selected for inclusion. The files are processed to give a consistently clear, crisp image, and the books finished to the high quality standard for which the Press is recognised around the world. The latest print-on-demand technology ensures that the books will remain available indefinitely, and that orders for single or multiple copies can quickly be supplied.

The Cambridge Library Collection brings back to life books of enduring scholarly value (including out-of-copyright works originally issued by other publishers) across a wide range of disciplines in the humanities and social sciences and in science and technology.

Wuthering Heights
and
Agnes Grey

EMILY BRONTË
ANNE BRONTË

CAMBRIDGE UNIVERSITY PRESS

Cambridge, New York, Melbourne, Madrid, Cape Town,
Singapore, São Paolo, Delhi, Mexico City

Published in the United States of America by Cambridge University Press, New York

www.cambridge.org
Information on this title: www.cambridge.org/9781108057066

© in this compilation Cambridge University Press 2013

This edition first published 1851
This digitally printed version 2013

ISBN 978-1-108-06035-6 Hardback
ISBN 978-1-108-05706-6 Paperback

EXTRACTS FROM REVIEWS OF "WUTHERING HEIGHTS,"

"THE PALLADIUM."

"We look upon 'Wuthering Heights' as the flight of an impatient fancy, fluttering in the very exultation of young wings; sometimes beating against its solitary bars, but turning rather to exhaust, in a circumscribed space, the energy and agility which it may not yet spend in the heavens. In this thought let the critic take up the book; lay it down in what thought he will, there are some things in it he can lay down no more.

"That Catherine Earnshaw—at once so wonderfully fresh, so fearfully natural—new 'as if brought from other spheres,' and familiar as the recollection of some woful experience, what can surpass the compatibility of her simultaneous loves; the involuntary art with which her two natures are so made to co-exist, that in the very arms of her lover we dare not doubt her purity; the inevitable belief with which we watch the oscillations of the old and new elements in her mind, and the exquisite truth of the last victory of nature over education, when the past returns to her as a flood, sweeping every modern landmark from within her, and the soul of the child expanding, fills the woman? Found at last by her husband, insensible, on the breast of her lover, and dying of the agony of their parting, one looks back upon her, like that husband, without one thought of accusation or absolution; her memory is chaste as the loyalty of love, pure as the air of the 'Heights' on which she dwelt.

"Not a subordinate place or person in this novel but bears more or less the stamp of high genius. Ellen Dean is the ideal of the peasant playmate and servant of 'the family.' The substratum in which her mind moves is finely preserved. Joseph, as a specimen of the sixty years' servitor of 'the house,' is worthy a museum case. We feel that if Catherine Earnshaw bore her husband a child it must be that Cathy Linton and no other. What terrible truth, what nicety of touch, what 'uncanny' capacity for mental aberration in the first symptoms of Catherine's delirium!

"We repeat, that there are passages in this book of 'Wuthering Heights of which any novelist, past or present, might be proud. Open the volume at the first page and read to the twelfth. There are few things in modern prose to surpass these pages for native power. We cannot praise too warmly the brave simplicity, the unaffected air of intense belief, the admirable combination of extreme likelihood with the rarest originality, the nice provision of the possible, even in the highest effects of the supernatural, the easy strength and instinct of keeping with which the accessory circumstances are grouped, the exquisite but unconscious art with which the chiaro-scuro of the whole is managed, and the ungenial frigidity of time, place, weather, and persons, is made to heighten the unspeakable pathos of one ungovernable outburst.

"The *thinking-out* of some of these pages — of pp. 9 and 10 — is the masterpiece of a poet, rather than the hybrid creation of a novelist. The mass of readers will probably yawn over the whole; but, *in the memory of those whose remembrance makes fame*, the images in these pages will live when every word that conveyed them is forgotten—as a recollection of *things heard and seen*. This is the highest triumph of description.

"Let this author rejoice if he can again give us such an elaboration of a rare and fearful form of mental disease—so terribly strong, so exquisitely subtle—with such nicety in its transitions, such symptomatic truth in its details as to be at once a psychological and medical study. It has been said of Shakspeare that he drew cases which the physician might study; *Ellis* Bell has done no less."

a

REVIEWS OF "WUTHERING HEIGHTS."

"The Britannia."

"There are scenes of savage wildness in nature which, though they inspire no pleasurable sensation, we are yet well satisfied to have seen. In the rugged rock, the gnarled roots which cling to it, the dark screen of overhanging vegetation, the dank, moist ground, and tangled network of weeds and bushes; even in the harsh cry of solitary birds, the yells of wild animals, and the startling motion of the snake as it springs away, scared by the intruder's foot, there is an image of primeval rudeness which has much to fascinate, though nothing to charm the mind. The elements of beauty are round us in the midst of gloom and danger, and some forms are the more picturesque from their distorted growth amidst so many obstacles.

"The principle may, to some extent, be applied to life. The uncultured freedom of native character presents more rugged aspects than we meet with in educated society. Its manners are not only more rough, but its passions are more violent. Its knows nothing of those breakwaters to the fury of the tempest which civilized training establishes to subdue the harsher markings of the soul. Its wrath is unrestrained by reflection; the lips curse and the hand strikes with the first impulse of anger. It is more subject to brutal instinct than to divine reason.

"It is humanity in this wild state that the author of 'Wuthering Heights' essays to depict. His work is strangely original. It bears a resemblance to some of those irregular German tales in which the writers, giving the reins to their fancy, represent personages as swayed and impelled to evil by supernatural influences. But *they* give spiritual identity to evil impulses, while Ellis Bell more naturally shows them as the offspring of the unregenerated heart. He displays considerable power in his creations. They have all the angularity of misshapen growth, and form in this respect a striking contrast to those regular forms we are accustomed to meet with in English fiction. They exhibit nothing of the composite character. There is in them no trace of ideal models. They are so new, so wildly grotesque, so entirely without art, that they strike us as proceeding from a mind of limited experience, but of original energy, and of a singular and distinctive cast.

"We do not know whether the author writes with any purpose; but we can speak of one effect of his production. It strongly shows the brutalizing influence of unchecked passion. His characters are a commentary on the truth that there is no tyranny in the world like that which thoughts of evil exercise in the daring and reckless breast. Another reflection springing from the narrative is—that temper is often spoiled in the years of childhood. 'The child is father to the man.' The pains and crosses of its youthful years are engrafted in its blood and form a sullen and a violent disposition. Grooms know how often the tempers of horses are irremediably spoiled in training. But parents are less wise regarding their children. The intellect in its growth has the faculty of accommodating itself to adverse circumstances. To violence it sometimes opposes violence, sometimes dogged obstinacy. The consequence in either case is fatal to the tranquillity of life."

"The Atlas."

"To estimate this work aright, the reader must have all the scenic accompaniment before him. He must not fancy himself in a London mansion, but in an old north country manor-house, situated in 'the dreary, dreamy moorland,' far from the haunts of civilized men. There is, at all events, keeping in the book: the groups of figures and the scenery are in harmony with each other. There is a touch of Salvator Rosa in all."

WUTHERING HEIGHTS:

BY ELLIS BELL.

WUTHERING HEIGHTS

AND

AGNES GREY.

BY

ELLIS AND ACTON BELL.

A NEW EDITION REVISED, WITH

A BIOGRAPHICAL NOTICE OF THE AUTHORS,
A SELECTION FROM THEIR LITERARY REMAINS,
AND A PREFACE,

By CURRER BELL.

LONDON:
SMITH, ELDER AND CO., 65, CORNHILL.

1851.

London
Printed by STEWART and MURRAY,
Old Bailey.

CONTENTS.

BIOGRAPHICAL NOTICE

OF

ELLIS AND ACTON BELL.

It has been thought that all the works published under the names of Currer, Ellis, and Acton Bell, were, in reality, the production of one person. This mistake I endeavoured to rectify by a few words of disclaimer prefixed to the third edition of *Jane Eyre*. These, too, it appears, failed to gain general credence, and now, on the occasion of a reprint of *Wuthering Heights* and *Agnes Grey*, I am advised distinctly to state how the case really stands.

Indeed, I feel myself that it is time the obscurity attending those two names — Ellis and Acton — was done away. The little mystery, which formerly yielded some harmless pleasure, has lost its interest; circumstances are changed. It becomes, then, my duty to explain briefly the origin and authorship of the books written by Currer, Ellis, and Acton Bell.

About five years ago, my two sisters and myself, after a somewhat prolonged period of separation, found ourselves reunited, and at home. Resident in a remote district where education had made little progress, and where, consequently, there was no inducement to seek social intercourse beyond our own domestic circle, we were wholly dependent on ourselves and each other, on books and study, for the enjoyments and occupations of life. The highest stimulus, as well as the liveliest pleasure we had known from childhood upwards, lay in attempts at literary composition; formerly we used to show each other what we wrote, but of late years this habit of communication and consultation had been discontinued; hence it ensued, that we were mutually ignorant of the progress we might respectively have made.

One day, in the autumn of 1845, I accidentally lighted on a MS. volume of verse in my sister Emily's handwriting. Of course, I was not surprised, knowing that she could and did write verse: I looked it over, and something more than surprise seized me,—a deep conviction that these were not common effusions, nor at all like the poetry women generally write. I thought them condensed and terse, vigorous and genuine. To my ear, they had also a peculiar music—wild, melancholy, and elevating.

My sister Emily was not a person of demonstrative character, nor one, on the recesses of whose mind and feelings, even those nearest and dearest to her could, with impunity, intrude unlicensed; it took hours to reconcile her to the discovery I had made, and days to persuade her that such poems merited publication. I knew, however, that a mind like hers could not be without some latent spark of honourable ambition, and refused to be discouraged in my attempts to fan that spark to flame.

Meantime, my younger sister quietly produced some of her own compositions, intimating that since Emily's had given me pleasure, I might like to look at hers. I could not but be a partial judge, yet I thought that these verses too had a sweet sincere pathos of their own.

We had very early cherished the dream of one day becoming authors. This dream, never relinquished even when distance divided and absorbing tasks occupied us, now suddenly acquired strength and consistency: it took the character of a resolve. We agreed to arrange a small selection of our poems, and, if possible, get them printed. Averse to personal publicity, we veiled our own names under those of Currer, Ellis, and Acton Bell; the ambiguous choice being dictated by a sort of conscientious scruple at assuming Christian names positively masculine, while we did not like to declare ourselves women, because—without at that time suspecting that our mode of writing and thinking was not what is called " feminine"—we had a vague impression that authoresses are liable to be looked on with prejudice; we had noticed how critics sometimes use for their chastisement the weapon of personality, and for their reward, a flattery, which is not true praise.

The bringing out of our little book was hard work. As was to be expected, neither we nor our poems wore at all wanted; but for this we had been prepared at the outset; though inexperienced ourselves, we had read the experience of others. The great puzzle lay in the difficulty of getting answers of any kind from the publishers to whom we applied. Being greatly harassed by this obstacle, I ventured to apply to the Messrs Chambers, of Edinburgh, for a word of advice; *they* may have forgotten the circumstance, but *I* have not, for from them I received a brief and business-like but, civil and sensible reply, on which we acted, and at last made a way.

The book was printed: it is scarcely known, and all of it that merits to be known are the poems of Ellis Bell. The fixed conviction I held, and hold, of the worth of these poems has not indeed received the confirmation of much favourable criticism; but I must retain it notwithstanding.

Ill-success failed to crush us: the mere effort to succeed had given a wonderful zest to existence; it must be pursued. We each set to work on a prose tale: Ellis Bell produced *Wuthering Heights*, Acton Bell *Agnes Grey*, and Currer Bell also wrote a narrative in one volume. These MSS. were perseveringly obtruded upon various publishers for the space of a year and a half; usually, their fate was an ignominious and abrupt dismissal.

At last *Wuthering Heights* and *Agnes Grey* were accepted on terms somewhat impoverishing to the two authors; Currer Bell's book found acceptance nowhere, nor any acknowledgment of merit, so that something like the chill of despair began to invade his heart. As a forlorn hope, he tried one publishing house more—Messrs. Smith and Elder. Ere long, in a much shorter space than that on which experience had taught him to calculate—there came a letter, which he opened in the dreary expectation of finding two hard hopeless lines, intimating that Messrs. Smith and Elder were not disposed to publish the MS.," and, instead, he took out of the envelope a letter of two pages. He read it trembling. It declined, indeed, to publish that tale, for business reasons, but it discussed its merits and demerits so courteously, so considerately, in a spirit so rational, with a discrimination so enlightened, that this very refusal cheered the author better than a vulgarly-expressed acceptance would have done. It was added, that a work in three volumes would meet with careful attention.

I was then just completing *Jane Eyre*, at which I had been working while the one volume tale was plodding its weary round in London: in three weeks I sent it off; friendly and skilful hands took it in. This was in the commencement of September 1847; it came out before the close of October following, while *Wuthering Heights* and *Agnes Grey*, my sisters' works, which had already been in the press for months, still lingered under a different management.

They appeared at last. Critics failed to do them justice. The immature but very real powers revealed in *Wuthering Heights* were scarcely recognised; its import and nature were misunderstood; the identity of its author was misrepresented; it was said that this was an earlier and ruder attempt of the same pen which had produced *Jane Eyre*. Unjust and grievous error! We laughed at it at first, but I deeply lament it now. Hence, I fear, arose a prejudice against the book. That writer who could attempt to palm off an inferior and immature production under cover of one successful effort, must indeed be unduly eager after the secondary and sordid result of authorship, and pitiably indifferent to its true and honourable meed. If reviewers and the public truly believed this, no wonder that they looked darkly on the cheat.

Yet I must not be understood to make these things subject for reproach or complaint; I dare not do so; respect for my sister's memory forbids me. By her any such querulous manifestation would have been regarded as an unworthy, and offensive weakness.

It is my duty, as well as my pleasure, to acknowledge one exception to the general rule of criticism.   One writer,* endowed with the keen vision and fine sympathies of genius, has discerned the real nature of *Wuthering Heights*, and has, with equal accuracy, noted its beauties and touched on its faults.   Too often do reviewers remind us of the mob of Astrologers, Chaldeans, and Soothsayers gathered before the " writing on the wall," and unable to read the characters or make known the interpretation.   We have a right to rejoice when a true seer comes at last, some man in whom is an excellent spirit, to whom have been given light, wisdom, and understanding; who can accurately read the " Mene, Mene, Tekel, Upharsin" of an original mind (however unripe, however inefficiently cultured and partially expanded that mind may be); and who can say with confidence, " This is the interpretation thereof."

Yet even the writer to whom I allude shares the mistake about the authorship, and does me the injustice to suppose that there was equivoque in my former rejection of this honour (as an honour, I regard it).   May I assure him that I would scorn in this and in every other case to deal in equivoque ; I believe language to have been given us to make our meaning clear, and not to wrap it in dishonest doubt.

The Tenant of Wildfell Hall by Acton Bell, had likewise an unfavourable reception.   At this I cannot wonder.   The choice of subject was an entire mistake. Nothing less congruous with the writer's nature could be conceived.   The motives which dictated this choice

* See the *Palladium* for September 1850.

were pure, but, I think, slightly morbid. She had, in the course of her life, been called on to contemplate, near at hand and for a long time, the terrible effects of talents misused and faculties abused; hers was naturally a sensitive, reserved, and dejected nature; what she saw sank very deeply into her mind; it did her harm. She brooded over it till she believed it to be a duty to reproduce every detail (of course with fictitious characters, incidents, and situations) as a warning to others. She hated her work, but would pursue it. When reasoned with on the subject, she regarded such reasonings as a temptation to self-indulgence. She must be honest; she must not varnish, soften, or conceal. This wellmeant resolution brought on her misconstruction and some abuse, which she bore, as it was her custom to bear whatever was unpleasant, with mild, steady patience. She was a very sincere and practical Christian, but the tinge of religious melancholy communicated a sad shade to her brief, blameless life.

Neither Ellis nor Acton allowed herself for one moment to sink under want of encouragement; energy nerved the one, and endurance upheld the other. They were both prepared to try again; I would fain think that hope and the sense of power was yet strong within them. But a great change approached: affliction came in that shape which to anticipate is dread; to look back on, grief. In the very heat and burden of the day, the labourers failed over their work.

My sister Emily first declined. The details of her illness are deep-branded in my memory, but to dwell on them, either in thought or narrative, is not in my power. Never in all her life had she lingered over any task that lay before her, and she did not linger now.

She sank rapidly. She made haste to leave us. Yet, while physically she perished, mentally, she grew stronger than we had yet known her. Day by day, when I saw with what a front she met suffering, I looked on her with an anguish of wonder and love. I have seen nothing like it; but, indeed, I have never seen her parallel in anything. Stronger than a man, simpler than a child, her nature stood alone. The awful point was, that, while full of ruth for others, on herself she had no pity; the spirit was inexorable to the flesh; from the trembling hand, the unnerved limbs, the faded eyes, the same service was exacted as they had rendered in health. To stand by and witness this, and not dare to remonstrate, was a pain no words can render.

Two cruel months of hope and fear passed painfully by, and the day came at last when the terrors and pains of death were to be undergone by this treasure, which had grown dearer and dearer to our hearts as it wasted before our eyes. Towards the decline of that day, we had nothing of Emily but her mortal remains as consumption left them. She died December 19, 1848.

We thought this enough; but we were utterly and presumptuously wrong. She was not buried ere Anne fell ill. She had not been committed to the grave a fortnight, before we received distinct intimation that it was necessary to prepare our minds to see the younger sister go after the elder. Accordingly, she followed in the same path with slower step, and with a patience that equalled the other's fortitude. I have said that she was religious, and it was by leaning on those Christian doctrines in which she firmly believed, that she found support through her most painful journey. I witnessed their efficacy in her latest hour and greatest trial, and must bear my testimony to the calm triumph with which they brought her through. She died May 28, 1849.

What more shall I say about them? I cannot and need not say much more. In externals, they were two unobtrusive women; a perfectly secluded life gave them retiring manners and habits. In Emily's nature the extremes of vigour and simplicity seemed to meet. Under an unsophisticated culture, inartificial tastes, and an unpretending outside, lay a secret power and fire that might have informed the brain and kindled the veins of a hero; but she had no worldly wisdom; her powers were unadapted to the practical business of life; she would fail to defend her most manifest rights, to consult her most legitimate advantage. An interpreter ought always to have stood between her and the world. Her will was not very flexible, and it generally opposed her interest. Her temper was magnanimous, but warm and sudden; her spirit altogether unbending.

Anne's character was milder and more subdued; she wanted the power, the fire, the originality of her sister, but was well-endowed with quiet virtues of her own. Long-suffering, self-denying, reflective, and intelligent, a constitutional reserve and taciturnity placed and kept her in the shade, and covered her mind, and especially her feelings, with a sort of nun-like veil, which was rarely lifted. Neither Emily nor Anne was learned; they had no thought of filling their pitchers at the well-spring of other minds; they always wrote from the impulse of nature, the dictates of intuition, and from such stores of observation as their limited experience had enabled them to amass. I may sum up all by saying, that for strangers they were nothing, for superficial observers less than nothing; but for those who had known them all their lives in the intimacy of close relationship, they were genuinely good and truly great.

This notice has been written, because I felt it a sacred duty to wipe the dust off their gravestones, and leave their dear names free from soil.

CURRER BELL.

September 19, 1850.

EDITOR'S PREFACE

TO THE NEW EDITION OF

WUTHERING HEIGHTS.

I HAVE just read over "Wuthering Heights," and, for
the first time, have obtained a clear glimpse of what
are termed (and, perhaps, really are) its faults; have gained
a definite notion of how it appears to other people—to
strangers who knew nothing of the author; who are
unacquainted with the locality where the scenes of the
story are laid; to whom the inhabitants, the customs, the
natural characteristics of the outlying hills and hamlets
in the West-Riding of Yorkshire are things alien and
unfamiliar.

To all such "Wuthering Heights" must appear a rude
and strange production. The wild moors of the north
of England can for them have no interest; the language,
The manners, the very dwellings and household customs
of the scattered inhabitants of those districts, must be to
such readers in a great measure unintelligible, and—
where intelligible—repulsive. Men and women who,
perhaps, naturally very calm, and with feelings moderate
in degree, and little marked in kind, have been trained
from their cradle to observe the utmost evenness of manner
and guardedness of language, will hardly know what to
make of the rough, strong utterance, the harshly manifested
passions, the unbridled aversions, and headlong partialities

b 2

of unlettered moorland hinds and rugged moorland squires, who have grown up untaught and unchecked, except by mentors as harsh as themselves. A large class of readers, likewise, will suffer greatly from the introduction into the pages of this work of words printed with all their letters, which it has become the custom to represent by the initial and final letter only—a blank line filling the interval. I may as well say at once that, for this circumstance, it is out of my power to apologize; deeming it, myself, a rational plan to write words at full length. The practice of hinting by single letters those expletives with which profane and violent persons are wont to garnish their discourse, strikes me as a proceeding which, however well meant, is weak and futile. I cannot tell what good it does—what feeling it spares—what horror it conceals.

With regard to the rusticity of "Wuthering Heights," I admit the charge, for I feel the quality. It is rustic all through. It is moorish, and wild, and knotty as a root of heath. Nor was it natural that it should be otherwise; the author being herself a native and nursling of the moors. Doubtless, had her lot been cast in a town, her writings, if she had written at all, would have possessed another character. Even had chance or taste led her to choose a similar subject, she would have treated it otherwise. Had Ellis Bell been a lady or a gentleman accustomed to what is called "the world," her view of a remote and unreclaimed region, as well as of the dwellers therein, would have differed greatly from that actually taken by the homebred country girl. Doubtless it would have been wider—more comprehensive: whether it would have been more original or more truthful is not so certain. As far as the scenery and locality are concerned, it could scarcely have been so sympathetic: Ellis Bell did not describe as one whose eye and taste alone found pleasure in the prospect; her native hills were far more to her than a spectacle; they were what she lived in, and by, as much as the wild birds, their tenants, or as the heather, their produce. Her descriptions, then, of natural scenery, are what they should be, and all they should be.

Where delineation of human character is concerned, the case is different. I am bound to avow that she had scarcely more practical knowledge of the peasantry amongst whom she lived, than a nun has of the country people who sometimes pass her convent gates. My sister's disposition was not naturally gregarious; circumstances favoured and fostered her tendency to seclusion; except to go to church or take a walk on the hills, she rarely crossed the threshold of home. Though her feeling for the people round was benevolent, intercourse with them she never sought; nor, with very few exceptions, ever experienced. And yet she knew them : knew their ways, their language, their family histories; she could hear of them with interest, and talk of them with detail, minute, graphic, and accurate; but *with* them, she rarely exchanged a word. Hence it ensued that what her mind had gathered of the real concerning them, was too exclusively confined to those tragic and terrible traits of which, in listening to the secret annals of every rude vicinage, the memory is sometimes compelled to receive the impress. Her imagination, which was a spirit more sombre than sunny, more powerful than sportive, found in such traits material whence it wrought creations like Heathcliff, like Earnshaw, like Catherine. Having formed these beings, she did not know what she had done. If the auditor of her work when read in manuscript, shuddered under the grinding influence of natures so relentless and implacable, of spirits so lost and fallen; if it was complained that the mere hearing of certain vivid and fearful scenes banished sleep by night, and disturbed mental peace by day, Ellis Bell would wonder what was meant, and suspect the complainant of affectation. Had she but lived, her mind would of itself have grown like a strong tree, loftier, straighter, wider-spreading, and its matured fruits would have attained a mellower ripeness and sunnier bloom; but on that mind time and experience alone could work : to the influence of other intellects, it was not amenable.

Having avowed that over much of " Wuthering Heights" there broods " a horror of great darkness;" that, in its storm-heated and electrical atmosphere, we seem at times to breathe lightning, let me point to those spots where clouded daylight and the eclipsed sun still attest their existence. For a specimen of true benevolence and homely fidelity, look at the character of Nelly Dean; for an example of constancy and tenderness, remark that of Edgar Linton. (Some people will think these qualities do not shine so well incarnate in a man as they would do in a woman, but Ellis Bell could never be brought to comprehend this notion : nothing moved her more than any insinuation that the faithfulness and clemency, the long-suffering and loving-kindness which are esteemed virtues in the daughters of Eve, become foibles in the sons of Adam. She held that mercy and forgiveness are the divinest attributes of the Great Being who made both man and woman, and that what clothes the Godhead in glory, can disgrace no form of feeble humanity.) There is a dry saturnine humour in the delineation of old Joseph, and some glimpses of grace and gaiety animate the younger Catherine. Nor is even the first heroine of the name destitute of a certain strange beauty in her fierceness, or of honesty in the midst of perverted passion and passionate perversity.

Heathcliff, indeed, stands unredeemed; never once swerving in his arrow-straight course to perdition, from the time when " the little black-haired, swarthy thing, as dark as if it came from the Devil," was first unrolled out of the bundle and set on its feet in the farm-house kitchen, to the hour when Nelly Dean found the grim, stalwart corpse laid on its back in the panel-enclosed bed, with wide-gazing eyes that seemed " to sneer at her attempt to close them, and parted lips and sharp white teeth that sneered too."

Heathcliff betrays one solitary human feeling, and that is *not* his love for Catherine; which is a sentiment fierce and inhuman: a passion such as might boil and glow in the bad essence of some evil genius; a fire that might form the tormented centre—the ever-suffering soul of a magnate of the infernal world: and by its quenchless and ceaseless ravage effect the execution of the decree which dooms him to carry Hell with him wherever he wanders. No; the single link that connects Heathcliff with humanity is his rudely confessed regard for Hareton Earnshaw—the young man whom he has ruined; and then his half-implied esteem for Nelly Dean. These solitary traits omitted, we should say he was child neither of Lascar nor gipsy, but a man's shape animated by demon life—a Ghoul—an Afreet.

Whether it is right or advisable to create beings like Heathcliff, I do not know: I scarcely think it is. But this I know; the writer who possesses the creative gift owns something of which he is not always master—something that at times strangely wills and works for itself. He may lay down rules and devise principles, and to rules and principles it will perhaps for years lie in subjection; and then, haply without any warning of revolt, there comes a time when it will no longer consent " to harrow tne vallies, or be bound with a band in the furrow"—when it " laughs at the multitude of the city, and regards not the crying of the driver"—when, refusing absolutely to make ropes out of sea-sand any longer, it sets to work on statue-hewing, and you have a Pluto or a Jove, a Tisiphone or a Psyche, a Mermaid or a Madonna, as Fate or Inspiration direct.   Be the work grim or glorious, dread or divine, you have little choice left but quiescent adoption. As for you—the nominal artist—your share in it has been to work passively under dictates you neither delivered nor could question—that would not be uttered at your prayer, nor suppressed nor changed at your caprice.   If the result be attractive, the World will praise you, who little deserve praise ; if it be repulsive, the same World will blame you, who almost as little deserve blame.

" Wuthering Heights" was hewn in a wild workshop, with simple tools, out of homely materials.   The statuary found a granite block on a solitary moor : gazing thereon, he saw how from thc crag might be elicited a head, savage, swart, sinister ; a form moulded with at least one element of grandeur—power.   He wrought with a rude chisel, and from no model but the vision of his meditations.   With time and labour, the crag took human shape ; and there it stands colossal, dark, and frowning, half statue, half rock : in the former sense, terrible and goblin-like ; in the latter, almost beautiful, for its colouring is of mellow grey, and moorland moss clothes it ; and heath, with its blooming bells and balmy fragrance, grows faithfully close to the giant's foot.

CURRER BELL.

WUTHERING HEIGHTS:

BY ELLIS BELL.

CHAPTER I.

1801.——I have just returned from a visit to my landlord—
the solitary neighbour that I shall be troubled with. This is
certainly a beautiful country! In all England, I do not
believe that I could have fixed on a situation so completely
removed from the stir of society. A perfect misanthropist's
heaven: and Mr. Heathcliff and I are such a suitable pair
to divide the desolation between us. A capital fellow! He
little imagined how my heart warmed towards him when I
beheld his black eyes withdraw so suspiciously under their
brows, as I rode up, and when his fingers sheltered themselves, with a jealous resolution, still further in his waistcoat,
as I announced my name.

"Mr. Heathcliff?" I said.

A nod was the answer.

"Mr. Lockwood your new tenant, sir. I do myself the
honour of calling as soon as possible after my arrival, to
express the hope that I have not inconvenienced you by
my perseverance in soliciting the occupation of Thrushcross
Grange: I heard yesterday you had had some thoughts——"

"Thrushcross Grange is my own, sir," he interrupted,
wincing. "I should not allow any one to inconvenience me,
if I could hinder it—walk in!"

The "walk in" was uttered with closed teeth, and expressed the sentiment, "Go to the Deuce:" even the gate
over which he leant manifested no sympathizing movement
to the words; and I think that circumstance determined me
to accept the invitation: I felt interested in a man who
seemed more exaggeratedly reserved than myself.

B

When he saw my horse's breast fairly pushing the barrier, he did pull out his hand to unchain it, and then sullenly preceded me up the causeway, calling, as we entered the court,—" Joseph, take Mr. Lockwood's horse; and bring up some wine."

"Here we have the whole establishment of domestics, I suppose," was the reflection, suggested by this compound order. "No wonder the grass grows up between the flags, and cattle are the only hedge-cutters."

Joseph was an elderly, nay, an old man : very old, perhaps, though hale and sinewy. "The Lord help us!" he soliloquized in an undertone of peevish displeasure, while relieving me of my horse : looking, meantime, in my face so sourly that I charitably conjectured he must have need of divine aid to digest his dinner, and his pious ejaculation had no reference to my unexpected advent.

Wuthering Heights is the name of Mr. Heathcliff's dwelling. "Wuthering" being a significant provincial adjective, descriptive of the atmospheric tumult to which its station is exposed in stormy weather. Pure, bracing ventilation they must have up there at all times, indeed : one may guess the power of the north wind blowing over the edge, by the excessive slant of a few stunted firs at the end of the house; and by a range of gaunt thorns all stretching their limbs one way, as if craving alms of the sun. Happily, the architect had foresight to build it strong : the narrow windows are deeply set in the wall, and the corners defended with large jutting stones.

Before passing the threshold, I paused to admire a quantity of grotesque carving lavished over the front, and especially about the principal door; above which, among a wilderness of crumbling griffins and shameless little boys, I detected the date "1500," and the name "Hareton Earnshaw." I would have made a few comments, and requested a short history of the place from the surly owner; but his attitude at the door appeared to demand my speedy entrance, or complete departure, and I had no desire to aggravate his impatience previous to inspecting the penetralium.

One step brought us into the family sitting-room, without any introductory lobby or passage : they call it here "the house" pre-eminently. It includes kitchen and parlour, generally; but I believe at Wuthering Heights the kitchen is

forced to retreat altogether into another quarter : at least I
distinguished a chatter of tongues, and a clatter of culinary
utensils, deep within; and I observed no signs of roasting,
boiling, or baking, about the huge fire-place ; nor any glitter
of copper saucepans and tin cullenders on the walls.   One
end, indeed, reflected splendidly both light and heat from
ranks of immense pewter dishes, interspersed with silver jugs
and tankards, towering row after row, on a vast oak dresser,
to the very roof.   The latter had never been underdrawn: its
entire anatomy lay bare to an inquiring eye, except where a
frame of wood laden with oatcakes and clusters of legs of
beef, mutton, and ham, concealed it.   Above the chimney
were sundry villainous old guns, and a couple of horse-pistols ;
and, by way of ornament, three gaudily painted canisters disposed along its ledge.   The floor was of smooth, white stone ;
the chairs, high-backed, primitive structures, painted green :
one or two heavy black ones lurking in the shade.   In an
arch under the dresser, reposed a huge, liver-coloured bitch
pointer, surrounded by a swarm of squealing puppies; and
other dogs haunted other recesses.

The apartment and furniture would have been nothing
extraordinary as belonging to a homely, northern farmer, with
a stubborn countenance, and stalwart limbs set out to advantage in knee-breeches and gaiters.   Such an individual
seated in his arm-chair, his mug of ale frothing on the round
table before him, is to be seen in any circuit of five or six
miles among these hills, if you go at the right time after
dinner.   But Mr. Heathcliff forms a singular contrast to his
abode and style of living.   He is a dark-skinned gipsy in
aspect, in dress and manners a gentleman : that is, as much
a gentleman as many a country squire : rather slovenly, perhaps, yet not looking amiss with his negligence, because he
has an erect and handsome figure ; and rather morose.   Possibly, some people might suspect him of a degree of under-
bred pride ; I have a sympathetic chord within that tells me
it is nothing of the sort : I know, by instinct, his reserve
springs from an aversion to showy displays of feeling—to
manifestations of mutual kindliness.   He 'll love and hate
equally under cover, and esteem it a species of impertinence
to be loved or hated again.   No, I 'm running on too fast :
I bestow my own attributes over liberally on him.   Mr.
Heathcliff may have entirely dissimilar reasons for keeping

his hand out of the way when he meets a would-be acquaintance, to those which actuate me. Let me hope my constitution is almost peculiar: my dear mother used to say I should never have a comfortable home; and only last summer I proved myself perfectly unworthy of one.

While enjoying a month of fine weather at the sea-coast, I was thrown into the company of a most fascinating creature: a real goddess in my eyes, as long as she took no notice of me. I "never told my love" vocally; still, if looks have language, the merest idiot might have guessed I was over head and ears: she understood me at last, and looked a return—the sweetest of all imaginable looks. And what did I do? I confess it with shame—shrunk icily into myself, like a snail; at every glance retired colder and farther; till finally the poor innocent was led to doubt her own senses, and, overwhelmed with confusion at her supposed mistake, persuaded her mamma to decamp. By this curious turn of disposition I have gained the reputation of deliberate heartlessness; how undeserved, I alone can appreciate.

I took a seat at the end of the hearthstone opposite that towards which my landlord advanced, and filled up an interval of silence by attempting to caress the canine mother; who had left her nursery, and was sneaking wolfishly to the back of my legs, her lip curled up, and her white teeth watering for a snatch. My caress provoked a long, guttural gnarl.

"You'd better let the dog alone," growled Mr. Heathcliff in unison, checking fiercer demonstrations with a punch of his foot. "She's not accustomed to be spoiled—not kept for a pet." Then, striding to a side-door, he shouted again, "Joseph!"

Joseph mumbled indistinctly in the depths of the cellar, but gave no intimation of ascending; so his master dived down to him, leaving me *vis-à-vis* the ruffianly bitch and a pair of grim shaggy sheep dogs, who shared with her a jealous guardianship over all my movements. Not anxious to come in contact with their fangs, I sat still; but, imagining they would scarcely understand tacit insults, I unfortunately indulged in winking and making faces at the trio, and some turn of my physiognomy so irritated madam, that she suddenly broke into a fury and leapt on my knees. I flung her back, and hastened to interpose the table between us.

This proceeding roused the whole hive : half a dozen four-footed fiends, of various sizes and ages, issued from hidden dens to the common centre. I felt my heels and coat-laps peculiar subjects of assault; and, parrying off the larger combatants as effectually as I could with the poker, I was constrained to demand, aloud, assistance from some of the household in re-establishing peace.

Mr. Heathcliff and his man climbed the cellar steps with vexatious phlegm : I don't think they moved one second faster than usual, though the hearth was an absolute tempest of worrying and yelping. Happily, an inhabitant of the kitchen made more despatch : a lusty dame, with tucked-up gown, bare arms, and fire-flushed cheeks, rushed into the midst of us flourishing a frying-pan; and used that weapon, and her tongue, to such purpose, that the storm subsided magically, and she only remained, heaving like a sea after a high wind, when her master entered on the scene.

"What the devil is the matter?" he asked, eyeing me in a manner that I could ill endure after this inhospitable treatment.

"What the devil, indeed!" I muttered. "The herd of possessed swine could have had no worse spirits in them than those animals of yours, sir. You might as well leave a stranger with a brood of tigers!"

"They won't meddle with persons who touch nothing," he remarked, putting the bottle before me and restoring the displaced table. "The dogs do right to be vigilant. Take a glass of wine?"

"No, thank you."

"Not bitten, are you?"

"If I had been, I would have set my signet on the biter."

Heathcliff's countenance relaxed into a grin.

"Come, come," he said, "you are flurried, Mr. Lockwood. Here, take a little wine. Guests are so exceedingly rare in this house that I and my dogs, I am willing to own, hardly know how to receive them. Your health, sir!"

I bowed and returned the pledge; beginning to perceive that it would be foolish to sit sulking for the misbehaviour of a pack of curs : besides, I felt loath to yield the fellow further amusement at my expense; since his humour took that turn. He—probably swayed by prudential considerations of the folly of offending a good tenant—relaxed a little in the laconic style of chipping off his pronouns and auxiliary verbs, and introduced what he supposed would be a subject of interest to me,—a discourse on the advantages and disadvantages of my present place of retirement. I found him very intelligent on the topics we touched; and before I went home, I was encouraged so far as to volunteer another visit to-morrow. He evidently wished no repetition of my intrusion. I shall go, notwithstanding. It is astonishing how sociable I feel myself compared with him.

CHAPTER II.

YESTERDAY afternoon set in misty and cold. I had half a mind to spend it by my study fire, instead of wading through heath and mud to Wuthering Heights. On coming up from dinner, however (N. B.—I dine between twelve and one o'clock; the housekeeper, a matronly lady, taken as a fixture along with the house, could not, or would not, comprehend my request that I might be served at five), on mounting the stairs with this lazy intention, and stepping into the room, I saw a servant-girl on her knees surrounded by brushes and coal-scuttles, and raising an infernal dust as she extinguished the flames with heaps of cinders. This spectacle drove me back immediately; I took my hat, and, after a four miles' walk, arrived at Heathcliff's garden gate just in time to escape the first feathery flakes of a snow shower.

On that bleak hill-top the earth was hard with a black frost, and the air made me shiver through every limb. Being unable to remove the chain, I jumped over, and, running up the flagged causeway bordered with straggling gooseberry bushes, knocked vainly for admittance, till my knuckles tingled and the dogs howled.

"Wretched inmates!" I ejaculated, mentally, "you deserve perpetual isolation from your species for your churlish inhospitality. At least, I would not keep my doors barred in the day-time. I don't care—I will get in!" So resolved, I grasped the latch, and shook it vehemently. Vinegar-faced Joseph projected his head from a round window of the barn.

"What are ye for?" he shouted. "T' maister's down i' t' fowld. Go round by th' end ot' laith, if ye went to spake to him."

"Is there nobody inside to open the door?" I hallooed, responsively.

"There's nobbut t' missis; and shoo'll not oppen't an ye mak yer flaysome dins till neeght."

"Why? Cannot you tell her who I am, eh, Joseph?"

"Nor-ne me! I'll hae no hend wi't,"muttered the head vanishing.

The snow began to drive thickly. I seized the handle to essay another trial; when a young man without coat, and shouldering a pitchfork, appeared in the yard behind. He hailed me to follow him, and, after marching through a washhouse, and a paved area containing a coal-shed, pump, and pigeon-cot, we at length arrived in the huge, warm, cheerful apartment, where I was formerly received. It glowed delightfully in the radiance of an immense fire, compounded of coal, peat, and wood; and near the table, laid for a plentiful evening meal, I was pleased to observe the "missis," an individual whose existence I had never previously suspected. I bowed and waited, thinking she would bid me take a seat. She looked at me, leaning back in her chair, and remained motionless and mute.

"Rough weather!" I remarked. "I'm afraid, Mrs. Heathcliff, the door must bear the consequence of your servants' leisure attendance: I had hard work to make them hear me."

She never opened her mouth. I stared—she stared also: at any rate, she kept her eyes on me in a cool, regardless manner, exceedingly embarrassing and disagreeable.

"Sit down," said the young man, gruffly. "He'll be in soon."

I obeyed; and hemmed, and called the villain Juno, who deigned, at this second interview, to move the extreme tip of her tail, in token of owning my acquaintance.

"A beautiful animal!" I commenced again. "Do you intend parting with the little ones, madam?"

"They are not mine," said the amiable hostess, more repellingly than Heathcliff himself could have replied.

"Ah, your favourites are among these?" I continued, turning to an obscure cushion full of something like cats.

"A strange choice of favourites!" she observed scornfully.

Unluckily, it was a heap of dead rabbits. I hemmed once more, and drew closer to the hearth, repeating my comment on the wildness of the evening.

"You should not have come out," she said, rising and reaching from the chimney-piece two of the painted canisters.

Her position before was sheltered from the light; now, I had a distinct view of her whole figure and countenance. She was slender, and apparently scarcely past girlhood: an admirable form, and the most exquisite little face that I have ever had the pleasure of beholding; small features, very fair; flaxen ringlets, or rather golden, hanging loose on her delicate neck; and eyes, had they been agreeable in expression, that would have been irresistible: fortunately for my susceptible heart, the only sentiment they evinced hovered between scorn and a kind of desperation, singularly unnatural to be detected there. The canisters were almost out of her reach; I made a motion to aid her; she turned upon me as a miser might turn if any one attempted to assist him in counting his gold.

"I don't want your help," she snapped; "I can get them for myself."

"I beg your pardon!" I hastened to reply.

"Were you asked to tea?" she demanded, tying an apron over her neat black frock, and standing with a spoonful of the leaf poised over the pot.

"I shall be glad to have a cup," I answered.

"Were you asked?" she repeated.

"No," I said, half smiling. "You are the proper person to ask me."

She flung the tea back, spoon and all, and resumed her chair in a pet; her forehead corrugated, and her red underlip pushed out, like a child's ready to cry.

Meanwhile, the young man had slung on to his person a decidedly shabby upper garment, and, erecting himself before the blaze, looked down on me from the corner of his eyes, for all the world as if there were some mortal feud unavenged between us. I began to doubt whether he were a servant or not: his dress and speech were both rude, entirely devoid of the superiority observable in Mr. and Mrs. Heathcliff; his thick, brown curls were rough and uncultivated, his whiskers encroached bearishly over his cheeks, and his hands were embrowned like those of a common labourer: still his bearing was free, almost haughty, and he showed none of a domestic's assiduity in attending on the lady of the house. In the absence of clear proofs of his condition, I deemed it best to abstain from noticing his curious conduct; and, five minutes afterwards, the entrance of Heathcliff relieved me, in some measure, from my uncomfortable state.

"You see, sir, I am come, according to promise!" I exclaimed, assuming the cheerful; "and I fear I shall be weather-bound for half an hour, if you can afford me shelter during that space."

"Half an hour?" he said, shaking the white flakes from his clothes; "I wonder you should select the thick of a snow-storm to ramble about in. Do you know that you run a risk of being lost in the marshes? People familiar with these moors often miss their road on such evenings; and I can tell you there is no chance of a change at present."

"Perhaps I can get a guide among your lads, and he might stay at the Grange till morning—could you spare me one?"

"No, I could not."

"Oh, indeed! Well, then, I must trust to my own sagacity."

"Umph!"

"Are you going to mak th' tea?" demanded he of the shabby coat, shifting his ferocious gaze from me to the young lady.

"Is he to have any?" she asked, appealing to Heathcliff.

"Get it ready, will you?" was the answer, uttered so savagely that I started. The tone in which the words were said revealed a genuine bad nature. I no longer felt inclined to call Heathcliff a capital fellow. When the preparations were finished, he invited me with—"Now, sir, bring forward your chair." And we all, including the rustic youth, drew round the table; an austere silence prevailing while we discussed our meal.

I thought, if I had caused the cloud, it was my duty to make an effort to dispel it. They could not every day sit so grim and taciturn; and it was impossible, however ill-tempered they might be, that the universal scowl they wore was their everyday countenance.

"It is strange," I began, in the interval of swallowing one cup of tea and receiving another,—"it is strange how custom can mould our tastes and ideas: many could not imagine the existence of happiness in a life of such complete exile from the world as you spend, Mr. Heathcliff; yet, I'll venture to say, that, surrounded by your family, and with your amiable lady as the presiding genius over your home and heart——"

"My amiable lady!" he interrupted, with an almost diabolical sneer on his face. "Where is she—my amiable lady?"

"Mrs. Heathcliff, your wife, I mean."

"Well, yes—Oh, you would intimate that her spirit has taken the post of ministering angel, and guards the fortunes of Wuthering Heights even when her body is gone. Is that it?"

Perceiving myself in a blunder, I attempted to correct it. I might have seen there was too great a disparity between the ages of the parties to make it likely that they were man and wife. One was about forty; a period of mental vigour at which men seldom cherish the delusion of being married for love by girls: that dream is reserved for the solace of our declining years. The other did not look seventeen.

Then it flashed upon me,—"The clown at my elbow, who is drinking his tea out of a basin and eating his bread with unwashed hands, may be her husband: Heathcliff junior, of course. Here is the consequence of being buried alive: she has thrown herself away upon that boor from sheer ignorance that better individuals existed! A sad pity—I must beware how I cause her to regret her choice." The last reflection may seem conceited; it was not. My neighbour struck me as bordering on repulsive; I knew, through experience, that I was tolerably attractive.

"Mrs. Heathcliff is my daughter-in-law," said Heathcliff, corroborating my surmise. He turned, as he spoke, a peculiar look in her direction: a look of hatred; unless he has a most perverse set of facial muscles that will not, like those of other people, interpret the language of his soul.

"Ah, certainly—I see now: you are the favoured possessor of the beneficent fairy," I remarked, turning to my neighbour.

This was worse than before: the youth grew crimson, and clenched his fist with every appearance of a meditated assault. But he seemed to recollect himself presently, and smothered the storm in a brutal curse, muttered on my behalf: which, however, I took care not to notice.

"Unhappy in your conjectures, sir," observed my host; "we neither of us have the privilege of owning your good fairy; her mate is dead. I said she was my daughter-in-law, therefore, she must have married my son."

"And this young man is——"

"Not my son, assuredly."

Heathcliff smiled again, as if it were rather too bold a jest to attribute the paternity of that bear to him.

"My name is Hareton Earnshaw," growled the other; "and I'd counsel you to respect it!"

"I've shown no disrespect," was my reply, laughing internally at the dignity with which he announced himself.

He fixed his eye on me longer than I cared to return the stare, for fear I might be tempted either to box his ears or render my hilarity audible. I began to feel unmistakeably out of place in that pleasant family circle. The dismal spiritual atmosphere overcame, and more than neutralized, the glowing physical comforts round me; and I resolved to be cautious how I ventured under those rafters a third time.

The business of eating being concluded, and no one uttering a word of sociable conversation, I approached a window to examine the weather. A sorrowful sight I saw: dark night coming down prematurely, and sky and hills mingled in one bitter whirl of wind and suffocating snow.

"I don't think it possible for me to get home now without a guide," I could not help exclaiming. "The roads will be buried already; and, if they were bare, I could scarcely distinguish a foot in advance."

"Hareton, drive those dozen sheep into the barn porch. They'll be covered if left in the fold all night: and put a plank before them," said Heathcliff.

"How must I do?" I continued, with rising irritation.

There was no reply to my question; and on looking round I saw only Joseph bringing in a pail of porridge for the dogs, and Mrs. Heathcliff leaning over the fire, diverting herself with burning a bundle of matches which had fallen from the chimney-piece as she restored the tea-canister to its place. The former, when he had deposited his burden, took a critical survey of the room, and, in cracked tones, grated out,—

"Aw wonder how yah can faishion to stand thear i' idleness un war, when all on 'em's goan out! Bud yah're a nowt, and it's no use talking—yah'll niver mend o' yer ill ways; but goa raight to t' divil, like yer mother afore ye!"

I imagined, for a moment, that this piece of eloquence was addressed to me; and, sufficiently enraged, stepped towards the aged rascal with an intention of kicking him out of the door. Mrs. Heathcliff, however, checked me by her answer.

"You scandalous old hypocrite!" she replied. "Are you not afraid of being carried away bodily, whenever you mention the devil's name? I warn you to refrain from provoking me, or I'll ask your abduction as a special favour. Stop! look here, Joseph," she continued, taking a long, dark book from a shelf; "I'll show you how far I've progressed in the Black Art: I shall soon be competent to make a clear house of it. The red cow didn't die by chance; and your rheumatism can hardly be reckoned among providential visitations!"

"Oh, wicked, wicked!" gasped the elder; "may the Lord deliver us from evil!"

"No, reprobate! you are a castaway—be off, or I'll hurt you seriously! I'll have you all modelled in wax and clay; and the first who passes the limits I fix, shall—I'll not say what he shall be done to—but, you'll see! Go, I'm looking at you!"

The little witch put a mock malignity into her beautiful eyes, and Joseph, trembling with sincere horror, hurried out praying and ejaculating "wicked" as he went. I thought her conduct must be prompted by a species of dreary fun; and, now that we were alone, I endeavoured to interest her in my distress.

"Mrs. Heathcliff," I said earnestly, "you must excuse

me for troubling you. I presume, because, with that face, I'm sure you cannot help being good-hearted. Do point out some landmarks by which I may know my way home: I have no more idea how to get there than you would have how to get to London!"

"Take the road you came," she answered, ensconcing herself in a chair, with a candle, and the long book open before her. "It is brief advice, but as sound as I can give."

"Then, if you hear of me being discovered dead in a bog or a pit full of snow, your conscience won't whisper that it is partly your fault?"

"How so? I cannot escort you. They wouldn't let me go to the end of the garden-wall."

"*You!* I should be sorry to ask you to cross the threshold, for my convenience, on such a night," I cried. "I want you to *tell* me my way, not to *show* it; or else to persuade Mr. Heathcliff to give me a guide."

"Who? There is himself, Earnshaw, Zillah, Joseph, and I. Which would you have?"

"Are there no boys at the farm?"

"No; those are all."

"Then, it follows that I am compelled to stay."

"That you may settle with your host. I have nothing to do with it."

"I hope it will be a lesson to you to make no more rash journeys on these hills," cried Heathcliff's stern voice from the kitchen entrance. "As to staying here, I don't keep accommodations for visitors: you must share a bed with Hareton or Joseph, if you do."

"I can sleep on a chair in this room," I replied.

"No, no! A stranger is a stranger, be he rich or poor: it will not suit me to permit any one the range of the place while I am off guard!" said the unmannerly wretch.

With this insult, my patience was at an end. I uttered an expression of disgust, and pushed past him into the yard, running against Earnshaw in my haste. It was so dark that I could not see the means of exit; and, as I wandered round, I heard another specimen of their civil behaviour amongst each other. At first the young man appeared about to befriend me.

"I'll go with him as far as the park," he said.

"You'll go with him to hell!" exclaimed his master, or

whatever relation he bore. "And who is to look after the horses, eh?"

"A man's life is of more consequence than one evening's neglect of the horses: somebody must go," murmured Mrs. Heathcliff, more kindly than I expected.

"Not at your command!" retorted Hareton. "If you set store on him, you'd better be quiet."

"Then I hope his ghost will haunt you; and I hope Mr. Heathcliff will never get another tenant till the Grange is a ruin!" she answered sharply.

"Hearken, hearken, shoo's cursing on em!" muttered Joseph, towards whom I had been steering.

He sat within earshot, milking the cows by the light of a lantern, which I seized unceremoniously, and, calling out that I would send it back on the morrow, rushed to the nearest postern.

"Maister, maister, he's staling t' lantern!" shouted the ancient, pursuing my retreat. "Hey, Gnasher! Hey, dog! Hey, Wolf, holld him, holld him!"

On opening the little door, two hairy monsters flew at my throat, bearing me down and extinguishing the light; while a mingled guffaw from Heathcliff and Hareton, put the copestone on my rage and humiliation. Fortunately, the beasts seemed more bent on stretching their paws and yawning, and flourishing their tails, than devouring me alive; but they would suffer no resurrection, and I was forced to lie till their malignant masters pleased to deliver me: then, hatless and trembling with wrath, I ordered the miscreants to let me out—on their peril to keep me one minute longer—with several incoherent threats of retaliation that, in their indefinite depth of virulency, smacked of King Lear.

The vehemence of my agitation brought on a copious bleeding at the nose, and still Heathcliff laughed, and still I scolded. I don't know what would have concluded the scene, had there not been one person at hand rather more rational than myself, and more benevolent than my entertainer. This was Zillah, the stout housewife; who at length issued forth to inquire into the nature of the uproar. She thought that some of them had been laying violent hands on me; and, not daring to attack her master, she turned her vocal artillery against the younger scoundrel.

" Well, Mr. Earnshaw," she cried, " I wonder what you'll have agait next! Are we going to murder folk on our very door-stones? I see this house will never do for me—look at t' poor lad, he's fair choking! Wisht, wisht! you mun'n't go on so. Come in, and I'll cure that: there now, hold ye still."

With these words she suddenly splashed a pint of icy water down my neck, and pulled me into the kitchen. Mr. Heathcliff followed, his accidental merriment expiring quickly in his habitual moroseness.

I was sick exceedingly, and dizzy and faint; and thus compelled perforce to accept lodgings under his roof. He told Zillah to give me a glass of brandy, and then passed on to the inner room; while she condoled with me on my sorry predicament, and having obeyed his orders, whereby I was somewhat revived, ushered me to bed.

CHAPTER III.

WHILE leading the way up-stairs, she recommended that I should hide the candle, and not make a noise; for her master had an odd notion about the chamber she would put me in, and never let anybody lodge there willingly. I asked the reason. She did not know, she answered: she had only lived there a year or two; and they had so many queer goings on, she could not begin to be curious.

Too stupified to be curious myself, I fastened my door and glanced round for the bed. The whole furniture consisted of a chair, a clothes-press, and a large oak case, with squares cut out near the top resembling coach windows. Having approached this structure, I looked inside, and perceived it to be a singular sort of old-fashioned couch, very conveniently designed to obviate the necessity for every member of the family having a room to himself. In fact, it formed a little closet, and the ledge of a window, which it enclosed, served as a table. I slid back the panelled sides, got in with my light, pulled them together again, and felt secure against the vigilance of Heathcliff, and every one else.

The ledge, where I placed my candle, had a few mildewed

books piled up in one corner; and it was covered with writing scratched on the paint. This writing, however, was nothing but a name repeated in all kinds of characters, large and small—*Catherine Earnshaw*, here and there varied to *Catherine Heathcliff*, and then again to *Catherine Linton*.

In vapid listlessness I leant my head against the window, and continued spelling over Catherine Earnshaw—Heathcliff —Linton, till my eyes closed; but they had not rested five minutes when a glare of white letters started from the dark, as vivid as spectres—the air swarmed with Catherines; and rousing myself to dispel the obtrusive name, I discovered my candle-wick reclining on one of the antique volumes, and perfuming the place with an odour of roasted calf-skin. I snuffed it off, and, very ill at ease under the influence of cold and lingering nausea, sat up and spread open the injured tome on my knee. It was a Testament, in lean type, and smelling dreadfully musty: a fly-leaf bore the inscription— "Catherine Earnshaw, her book," and a date some quarter of a century back. I shut it, and took up another, and another, till I had examined all. Catherine's library was select, and its state of dilapidation proved it to have been well used; though not altogether for a legitimate purpose: scarcely one chapter had escaped a pen-and-ink commentary —at least, the appearance of one—covering every morsel of blank that the printer had left. Some were detached sentences; other parts took the form of a regular diary, scrawled in an unformed, childish hand. At the top of an extra page (quite a treasure, probably, when first lighted on) I was greatly amused to behold an excellent caricature of my friend Joseph, —rudely yet powerfully sketched. An immediate interest kindled within me for the unknown Catherine, and I began forthwith to decypher her faded hieroglyphics.

"An awful Sunday!" commenced the paragraph beneath. "I wish my father were back again. Hindley is a detestable substitute—his conduct to Heathcliff is atrocious—H. and I are going to rebel—we took our initiatory step this evening.

"All day had been flooding with rain; we could not go to church, so Joseph must needs get up a congregation in the garret; and, while Hindley and his wife basked down stairs before a comfortable fire—doing anything but reading their bibles, I'll answer for it—Heathcliff, myself, and the unhappy plough-boy, were commanded to take our Prayer-books, and mount: we were ranged in a row, on a sack of corn, groaning and shivering, and hoping that Joseph would shiver too, so that he might give us a short homily for his own sake. A vain idea! The service lasted precisely three hours; and yet my brother had the face to exclaim, when he saw us descending, 'What! done already?' On Sunday evenings we used to be permitted to play, if we did not make much noise; now a mere titter is sufficient to send us into corners!

"'You forget you have a master here,' says the tyrant. 'I'll demolish the first who puts me out of temper! I insist on perfect sobriety and silence. Oh, boy! was that you? Frances, darling, pull his hair as you go by: I heard him snap his fingers.' Frances pulled his hair heartily, and then went and seated herself on her husband's knee; and there they were, like two babies, kissing and talking nonsense by the hour—foolish palaver that we should be ashamed of. We made ourselves as snug as our means allowed in the arch of the dresser. I had just fastened our pinafores together, and hung them up for a curtain, when in comes Joseph, on an errand from the stables. He tears down my handywork, boxes my ears, and croaks:

"'T' maister nobbut just buried, and Sabbath not oe'red, und t' sound o' t' gospel still i' yer lugs, and ye darr be laiking! shame on ye! sit ye down, ill childer! there's good books eneugh if ye'll read 'em: sit ye down, and think o' yer sowls!'

Saying this, he compelled us so to square our positions that we might receive from the far-off fire a dull ray to show us the text of the lumber he thrust upon us. I could not bear the employment. I took my dingy volume by the scroop, and hurled it into the dog-kennel, vowing I hated a good book. Heathcliff kicked his to the same place. Then there was a hubbub!

"'Maister Hindley!' shouted our chaplain. 'Maister, coom hither! Miss Cathy's riven th' back off 'Th' Helmet o' Salvation,' un' Heathcliff's pawsed his fit into t' first part o' 'T' Brooad Way to Destruction!' It's fair flaysome that ye let 'em go on this gait. Ech! th' owd man wad ha' laced 'em properly—but he's goan!'

" Hindley hurried up from his paradise on the hearth, and

C

seizing one of us by the collar, and the other by the arm, hurled both into the back-kitchen; where, Joseph asseverated, "owd Nick" would fetch us as sure as we were living: and, so comforted, we each sought a separate nook to await his advent. I reached this book, and a pot of ink from a shelf, and pushed the house-door ajar to give me light, and I have got the time on with writing for twenty minutes; but my companion is impatient, and proposes that we should appropriate the dairy woman's cloak, and have a scamper on the moors, under its shelter. A pleasant suggestion—and then, if the surly old man come in, he may believe his prophecy verified—we cannot be damper, or colder, in the rain than we are here."

    *   *   *   *   *   *

I suppose Catherine fulfilled her project, for the next sentence took up another subject: she waxed lachrymose.

"How little did I dream that Hindley would ever make me cry so!" she wrote. "My head aches, till I cannot keep it on the pillow; and still I can't give over. Poor Heathcliff! Hindley calls him a vagabond, and won't let him sit with us, nor eat with us any more; and, he says, he and I must not play together, and threatens to turn him out of the house if we break his orders. He has been blaming our father (how dared he?) for treating H. too liberally; and swears he will reduce him to his right place—"

    *   *   *   *   *   *

I began to nod drowsily over the dim page: my eye wandered from manuscript to print. I saw a red ornamented title—"Seventy Times Seven, and the First of the Seventy First. A Pious Discourse delivered by the Reverend Jabes Branderham, in the Chapel of Gimmerden Sough." And while I was, half consciously, worrying my brain to guess what Jabes Branderham would make of his subject, I sank back in bed, and fell asleep. Alas, for the effects of bad tea and bad temper! what else could it be that made me pass such a terrible night? I don't remember another that I can at all compare with it since I was capable of suffering.

I began to dream, almost before I ceased to be sensible of my locality. I thought it was morning; and I had set out on my way home, with Joseph for a guide. The snow lay yards deep in our road; and, as we floundered on, my companion wearied me with constant reproaches that I had not orought a pilgrim's staff: telling me I could never get into the house without one, and boastfully flourishing a heavy-headed cudgel, which I understood to be so denominated. For a moment I considered it absurd that I should need such a weapon to gain admittance into my own residence. Then, a new idea flashed across me. I was not going there: we were journeying to hear the famous Jabes Branderham preach from the text—"Seventy Times Seven"; and either Joseph, the preacher, or I had committed the "First of the Seventy First," and were to be publicly exposed and excommunicated.

We came to the chapel. I have passed it really in my walks, twice or thrice; it lies in a hollow, between two hills: an elevated hollow, near a swamp, whose peaty moisture is said to answer all the purposes of embalming on the few corpses deposited there. The roof has been kept whole hitherto; but, as the clergyman's stipend is only twenty pounds per annum, and a house with two rooms, threatening speedily to determine into one, no clergyman will undertake the duties of pastor: especially as it is currently reported that his flock would rather let him starve than increase the living by one penny from their own pockets. However, in my dream, Jabes had a full and attentive congregation; and he preached—good God! what a sermon: divided into *four hundred and ninety* parts, each fully equal to an ordinary address from the pulpit, and each discussing a separate sin! Where he searched for them, I cannot tell. He had his private manner of interpreting the phrase, and it seemed necessary the brother should sin different sins on every occasion. They were of the most curious character: odd transgressions that I never imagined previously.

Oh, how weary I grew. How I writhed, and yawned, and nodded, and revived! How I pinched and pricked myself, and rubbed my eyes, and stood up, and sat down again, and nudged Joseph to inform me if he would *ever* have done. I was condemned to hear all out: finally, he reached the "*First of the Seventy-First*." At that crisis, a sudden inspiration descended on me; I was moved to rise and denounce Jabes Branderham as the sinner of the sin that no Christian need pardon.

"Sir," I exclaimed, "sitting here, within these four walls, at one stretch, I have endured and forgiven the four hundred and ninety heads of your discourse. Seventy times seven times have I plucked up my hat, and been about to depart —Seventy times seven times have you preposterously forced me to resume my seat. The four hundred and ninety-first is too much. Fellow-martyrs, have at him! Drag him down, and crush him to atoms, that the place which knows him may know him no more!"

"*Thou art the Man!*" cried Jabes, after a solemn pause, leaning over his cushion. "Seventy times seven times didst thou gapingly contort thy visage—seventy times seven did I take counsel with my soul—Lo, this is human weakness: this also may be absolved! The First of the Seventy-First is come. Brethren, execute upon him the judgment written! Such honour have all His saints!"

With that concluding word, the whole assembly, exalting their pilgrim's staves, rushed round me in a body; and I, having no weapon to raise in self-defence, commenced grappling with Joseph, my nearest and most ferocious assailant, for his. In the confluence of the multitude, several clubs crossed; blows, aimed at me, fell on other sconces. Presently the whole chapel resounded with rappings and counter-rappings: every man's hand was against his neighbour; and Branderham, unwilling to remain idle, poured forth his zeal in a shower of loud taps on the boards of the pulpit, which responded so smartly that, at last, to my unspeakable relief, they woke me. And what was it that had suggested the tremendous tumult? What had played Jabes's part in the row? Merely, the branch of a fir-tree that touched my lattice, as the blast wailed by, and rattled its dry cones against the panes! I listened doubtingly an instant; detected the disturber, then turned and dozed, and dreamt again: if possible, still more disagreeably than before.

This time, I remembered I was lying in the oak closet, and I heard distinctly the gusty wind, and the driving of the snow; I heard, also, the fir-bough repeat its teasing sound, and ascribed it to the right cause: but it annoyed me so much that I resolved to silence it, if possible; and, I thought, I rose and endeavoured to unhasp the casement. The hook was soldered into the staple: a circumstance observed by me when awake, but forgotten. "I must stop it, nevertheless!" I muttered, knocking my knuckles through the glass, and stretching an arm out to seize the importunate branch; instead of which, my fingers closed on the fingers of a little, ice-cold hand! The intense horror of nightmare came over me: I tried to draw back my arm, but the hand clung to it, and a most melancholy voice sobbed, " Let me in—let me in!" "Who are you?" I asked struggling, meanwhile, to disengage myself. "Catherine Linton," it replied, shiveringly (why did I think of *Linton?* I had read *Earnshaw* twenty times for Linton) "I'm come home: I'd lost my way on the moor!" As it spoke, I discerned, obscurely, a child's face looking through the window. Terror made me cruel; and, finding it useless to attempt shaking the creature off, I pulled its wrist on to the broken pane, and rubbed it to and fro till the blood ran down and soaked the bedclothes: still it wailed, " Let me in!" and maintained its tenacious gripe, almost maddening me with fear. "How can I?" I said at length. " Let *me* go, if you want me to let you in!" The fingers relaxed, I snatched mine through the hole, hurriedly piled the books up in a pyramid against it, and stopped my ears to exclude the lamentable prayer. I seemed to keep them closed above a quarter of an hour; yet, the instant I listened again, there was the doleful cry moaning on! "Begone!" I shouted, "I'll never let you in, not if you beg for twenty years!" "It is twenty years," mourned the voice: "twenty years. I've been a waif for twenty years!" Thereat began a feeble scratching outside, and the pile of books moved as if thrust forward. I tried to jump up; but could not stir a limb; and so yelled aloud, in a frenzy of fright. To my confusion, I discovered the yell was not ideal: hasty footsteps approached my chamber door; somebody pushed it open, with a vigorous hand, and a light glimmered through the squares at the top of the bed. I sat shuddering yet, and wiping the perspiration from my forehead: the intruder appeared to hesitate and muttered to himself. At last, he said in a half-whisper, plainly not expecting an answer, " Is any one here?" I considered it best to confess my presence; for I knew Heathcliff's accents, and feared he might search further, if I kept quiet. With this intention, I turned and opened the panels. I shall not soon forget the effect my action produced.

Heathcliff stood near the entrance, in his shirt and trousers; with a candle dripping over his fingers, and his face as white as the wall behind him. The first creak of the

oak startled him like an electric shock: the light leaped from
his hold to a distance of some feet, and his agitation was so
extreme, that he could hardly pick it up.

"It is only your guest, sir," I called out, desirous to spare
him the humiliation of exposing his cowardice further. "I
had the misfortune to scream in my sleep, owing to a frightful nightmare. I'm sorry I disturbed you."

"Oh, God confound you, Mr. Lockwood! I wish you
were at the—" commenced my host, setting the candle on a
chair, because he found it impossible to hold it steady.
"And who showed you up to this room?" he continued,
crushing his nails into his palms, and grinding his teeth to
subdue the maxillary convulsions. "Who was it? I've
a good mind to turn them out of the house this moment!"

"It was your servant, Zillah," I replied, flinging myself
on to the floor, and rapidly resuming my garments. "I
should not care if you did, Mr. Heathcliff; she richly deserves it. I suppose that she wanted to get another proof
that the place was haunted, at my expense. Well, it is—
swarming with ghosts and goblins! You have reason in
shutting it up, I assure you. No one will thank you for a
doze in such a den!"

"What do you mean?" asked Heathcliff, "and what are
you doing? Lie down and finish out the night, since you *are*
here; but, for Heaven's sake! don't repeat that horrid noise:
nothing could excuse it, unless you were having your throat
cut!"

"If the little fiend had got in at the window, she probably would have strangled me!" I returned. "I'm not
going to endure the persecutions of your hospitable ancestors
again. Was not the Reverend Jabes Branderham akin to
you on the mother's side? And that minx, Catherine Linton, or Earnshaw, or however she was called—she must have
been a changeling—wicked little soul! She told me she
had been walking the earth these twenty years: a just
punishment for her mortal transgressions, I've no doubt!"

Scarcely were these words uttered, when I recollected the
association of Heathcliff's with Catherine's name in the book,
which had completely slipped from my memory till thus
awakened. I blushed at my inconsideration; but, without
showing further consciousness of the offence, I hastened to
add,—"The truth is, sir, I passed the first part of the night

in—" Here I stopped afresh—I was about to say "perusing those old volumes," then it would have revealed my knowledge of their written, as well as their printed contents; so correcting myself, I went on, " In spelling over the name scratched on that window-ledge. A monotonous occupation, calculated to set me asleep, like counting, or ——"

"What *can* you mean by talking in this way to *me!*" thundered Heathcliff with savage vehemence. "How—how *dare* you, under my roof?—God! he 's mad to speak so!" And he struck his forehead with rage.

I did not know whether to resent this language or pursue my explanation; but he seemed so powerfully affected that I took pity and proceeded with my dreams; affirming I had never heard the appellation of "Catherine Linton" before, but reading it often over produced an impression which personified itself when I had no longer my imagination under control. Heathcliff gradually fell back into the shelter of the bed, as I spoke; finally sitting down almost concealed behind it. I guessed, however, by his irregular and intercepted breathing, that he struggled to vanquish an excess of violent emotion. Not liking to show him that I had heard the conflict, I continued my toilette rather noisily, looked at my watch, and soliloquised on the length of the night: "Not three o'clock, yet! I could have taken oath it had been six. Time stagnates here: we must surely have retired to rest at eight!"

" Always at nine in winter, and rise at four," said my host, suppressing a groan: and, as I fancied, by the motion of his arm's shadow, dashing a tear from his eyes. " Mr. Lockwood," he added, " you may go into my room: you 'll only be in the way coming down stairs so early; and your childish outcry has sent sleep to the devil for me."

" And for me too," I replied. " I 'll walk in the yard till daylight, and then I 'll be off; and you need not dread a repetition of my intrusion. I am now quite cured of seeking pleasure in society, be it country or town. A sensible man ought to find sufficient company in himself."

" Delightful company!" muttered Heathcliff. " Take the candle, and go where you please. I shall join you directly. Keep out of the yard, though, the dogs are unchained; and the house—Juno mounts sentinel there, and—

nay, you can only ramble about the steps and passages. But, away with you! I'll come in two minutes."

I obeyed, so far as to quit the chamber; when, ignorant where the narrow lobbies led, I stood still, and was witness, involuntarily, to a piece of superstition on the part of my landlord, which belied, oddly, his apparent sense. He got on to the bed, and wrenched open the lattice, bursting, as he pulled at it, into an uncontrollable passion of tears. " Come in! come in!" he sobbed. "Cathy, do come. Oh do—*once* more! Oh! my heart's darling! hear me *this* time, Catherine, at last!" The spectre showed a spectre's ordinary caprice: it gave no sign of being; but the snow and wind whirled wildly through, even reaching my station, and blowing out the light.

There was such anguish in the gush of grief that accompanied this raving, that my compassion made me overlook its folly, and I drew off, half angry to have listened at all, and vexed at having related my ridiculous nightmare, since it produced that agony; though *why*, was beyond my comprehension. I descended cautiously to the lower regions, and landed in the back-kitchen, where a gleam of fire, raked compactly together, enabled me to rekindle my candle. Nothing was stirring except a brindled, grey cat, which crept from the ashes, and saluted me with a querulous mew.

Two benches, shaped in sections of a circle, nearly enclosed the hearth; on one of these I stretched myself, and Grimalkin mounted the other. We were both of us nodding, ere any one invaded our retreat; and then it was Joseph, shuffling down a wooden ladder that vanished in the roof, through a trap: the ascent to his garret, I suppose. He cast a sinister look at the little flame which I had enticed to play between the ribs, swept the cat from its elevation, and bestowing himself in the vacancy, commenced the operation of stuffing a three-inch pipe with tobacco. My presence in his sanctum was evidently esteemed a piece of impudence too shameful for remark: he silently applied the tube to his lips, folded his arms, and puffed away. I let him enjoy the luxury, unannoyed, and after smoking out the last wreath, and heaving a profound sigh, he got up, and departed as solemnly as he came.

A more elastic footstep entered next; and now I opened

my mouth for a " good-morning," but closed it again, the salutation unachieved; for Hareton Earnshaw was performing his orisons, *sotto voce*, in a series of curses directed against every object he touched, while he rummaged a corner for a spade or shovel to dig through the drifts. He glanced over the back of the bench, dilating his nostrils, and thought as little of exchanging civilities with me as with my companion, the cat. I guessed, by his preparations, that egress was allowed, and, leaving my hard couch, made a movement to follow him. He noticed this, and thrust at an inner door with the end of his spade, intimating by an inarticulate sound that there was the place where I must go, if I changed my locality.

It opened into the house, where the females were already astir. Zillah urging flakes of flame up the chimney with a colossal bellows; and Mrs. Heathcliff, kneeling on the hearth, reading a book by the aid of the blaze. She held her hand interposed between the furnace-heat and her eyes, and seemed absorbed in her occupation; desisting from it only to chide the servant for covering her with sparks, or to push away a dog, now and then, that snoozled its nose over-forwardly into her face. I was surprised to see Heathcliff there also. He stood by the fire, his back towards me, just finishing a stormy scene to poor Zillah; who ever and anon interrupted her labour to pluck up the corner of her apron, and heave an indignant groan.

" And you, you worthless—" he broke out as I entered, turning to his daughter-in-law, and employing an epithet as harmless as duck, or sheep, but generally represented by a dash —— " There you are, at your idle tricks again! The rest of them do earn their bread—you live on my charity! Put your trash away, and find something to do. You shall pay me for the plague of having you eternally in my sight—do you hear, damnable jade?"

" I'll put my trash away, because you can make me, if I refuse," answered the young lady, closing her book, and throwing it on a chair. " But I'll not do anything, though you should swear your tongue out, except what I please!"

Heathcliff lifted his hand, and the speaker sprang to a safer distance, obviously acquainted with its weight. Having no desire to be entertained by a cat-and-dog combat, I stepped forward briskly, as if eager to partake the warmth

of the hearth, and innocent of any knowledge of the interrupted dispute. Each had enough decorum to suspend further hostilities: Heathcliff placed his fists, out of temptation, in his pockets; Mrs. Heathcliff curled her lip, and
walked to a seat far off, where she kept her word by playing
the part of a statue during the remainder of my stay. That
was not long. I declined joining their breakfast, and, at
the first gleam of dawn, took an opportunity of escaping
into the free air, now clear, and still, and cold as impal-
pable ice.

My landlord hallooed for me to stop, ere I reached the
bottom of the garden, and offered to accompany me across
the moor. It was well he did, for the whole hill-back was
one billowy, white ocean; the swells and falls not indicating
corresponding rises and depressions in the ground: many
pits, at least, were filled to a level; and entire ranges of
mounds, the refuse of the quarries, blotted from the chart
which my yesterday's walk left pictured in my mind. I had
remarked on one side of the road, at intervals of six or seven
yards, a line of upright stones, continued through the whole
length of the barren: these were erected, and daubed with
lime on purpose to serve as guides in the dark; and also
when a fall, like the present, confounded the deep swamps on
either hand with the firmer path: but, excepting a dirty dot
pointing up here and there, all traces of their existence had
vanished; and my companion found it necessary to warn me
frequently to steer to the right or left, when I imagined I
was following, correctly, the windings of the road.

We exchanged little conversation, and he halted at the
entrance of Thrushcross-park, saying, I could make no error
there. Our adieux were limited to a hasty bow, and then
I pushed forward, trusting to my own resources; for the
porter's lodge is untenanted as yet. The distance from the
gate to the Grange is two miles: I believe I managed to make
it four; what with losing myself among the trees, and
sinking up to the neck in snow: a predicament which only
those who have experienced it can appreciate. At any rate,
whatever were my wanderings, the clock chimed twelve as I
entered the house; and that gave exactly an hour for every
mile of the usual way from Wuthering Heights.

My human fixture and her satellites rushed to welcome
me; exclaiming, tumultuously, they had completely given

me up: everybody conjectured that I perished last night; and they were wondering how they must set about the search for my remains. I bid them be quiet, now that they saw me returned, and, benumbed to my very heart, I dragged up-stairs; whence, after putting on dry clothes, and pacing to and fro thirty or forty minutes, to restore the animal heat, I am adjourned to my study, feeble as a kitten: almost too much so to enjoy the cheerful fire and smoking coffee which the servant has prepared for my refreshment.

CHAPTER IV.

WHAT vain weather-cocks we are! I, who had determined to hold myself independent of all social intercourse, and thanked my stars that, at length, I had lighted on a spot where it was next to impracticable—I, weak wretch, after maintaining till dusk a struggle with low spirits and solitude, was finally compelled to strike my colours; and, under pretence of gaining information concerning the necessities of my establishment, I desired Mrs. Dean, when she brought in supper, to sit down while I ate it; hoping sincerely she would prove a regular gossip, and either rouse me to animation or lull me to sleep by her talk.

"You have lived here a considerable time," I commenced; "did you not say sixteen years?"

"Eighteen, sir: I came, when the mistress was married, to wait on her; after she died, the master retained me for his house-keeper."

"Indeed."

There ensued a pause. She was not a gossip, I feared; unless about her own affairs, and those could hardly interest me. However, having studied for an interval, with a fist on either knee, and a cloud of meditation over her ruddy countenance, she ejaculated—

"Ah, times are greatly changed since then!"

"Yes," I remarked, "you've seen a good many alterations, I suppose?"

"I have: and troubles too," she said.

"Oh, I'll turn the talk on my landlord's family!" I thought to myself. "A good subject to start! And that pretty girl-widow, I should like to know her history: whether she be a native of the country, or, as is more probable, an exotic that the surly *indigenæ* will not recognise for kin." With this intention I asked Mrs. Dean why Heathcliff let Thrushcross Grange, and preferred living in a situation and residence so much inferior. "Is he not rich enough to keep the estate in good order?" I inquired.

"Rich sir!" she returned. "He has, nobody knows what money, and every year it increases. Yes, yes, he's rich enough to live in a finer house than this: but he's very near—close-handed; and, if he had meant to flit to Thrushcross Grange, as soon as he heard of a good tenant he could not have borne to miss the chance of getting a few hundreds more. It is strange people should be so greedy, when they are alone in the world!"

"He had a son, it seems?"

"Yes, he had one—he is dead."

"And that young lady, Mrs. Heathcliff, is his widow?"

"Yes."

"Where did she come from originally?"

"Why, sir, she is my late master's daughter: Catherine Linton was her maiden name. I nursed her, poor thing! I did wish Mr. Heathcliff would remove here, and then we might have been together again."

"What! Catherine Linton?" I exclaimed, astonished. But a minute's reflection convinced me it was not my ghostly Catherine. "Then," I continued, "my predecessor's name was Linton?"

"It was."

"And who is that Earnshaw: Hareton Earnshaw, who lives with Mr. Heathcliff? are they relations?"

"No; he is the late Mrs. Linton's nephew."

"The young lady's cousin then?"

"Yes; and her husband was her cousin also: one on the mother's, the other on the father's side: Heathcliff married Mr. Linton's sister."

"I see the house at Wuthering Heights has 'Earnshaw' carved over the front door. Are they an old family?"

"Very old, sir; and Hareton is the last of them, as our Miss Cathy is of us—I mean, of the Lintons. Have you been to Wuthering Heights? I beg pardon for asking; but I should like to hear how she is!"

"Mrs. Heathcliff? she looked very well, and very handsome; yet, I think, not very happy."

"Oh dear, I don't wonder! And how did you like the master?"

"A rough fellow, rather, Mrs. Dean. Is not that his character?"

"Rough as a saw-edge, and hard as whinstone! The less you meddle with him the better."

"He must have had some ups and downs in life to make him such a churl. Do you know anything of his history?"

"It's a cuckoo's, sir—I know all about it: except where he was born, and who were his parents, and how he got his money, at first. And Hareton has been cast out like an unfledged dunnock! The unfortunate lad is the only one in all this parish that does not guess how he has been cheated."

"Well, Mrs. Dean, it will be a charitable deed to tell me something of my neighbours: I feel I shall not rest, if I go to bed; so be good enough to sit and chat an hour."

"Oh, certainly, sir! I'll just fetch a little sewing, and then I'll sit as long as you please. But you've caught cold: I saw you shivering, and you must have some gruel to drive it out."

The worthy woman bustled off, and I crouched nearer the fire; my head felt hot, and the rest of me chill: moreover, I was excited, almost to a pitch of foolishness, through my nerves and brain. This caused me to feel, not uncomfortable, but rather fearful (as I am still) of serious effects from the incidents of to-day and yesterday. She returned presently, bringing a smoking basin and a basket of work; and, having placed the former on the hob, drew in her seat, evidently pleased to find me so companionable.

Before I came to live here, she commenced—waiting no farther invitation to her story—I was almost always at Wuthering Heights; because my mother had nursed Mr. Hindley Earnshaw, that was Hareton's father, and I got used to playing with the children: I ran errands too, and helped to make hay, and hung about the farm ready for anything that anybody would set me to. One fine summer morning—it was the beginning of harvest, I remember—Mr. Earnshaw, the old master, came down stairs, dressed for a journey; and after he had told Joseph what was to be done during the day, he turned to Hindley, and Cathy, and me— for I sat eating my porridge with them—and he said, speaking to his son, 'Now my bonny man, I'm going to Liverpool, to-day, what shall I bring you? You may choose what you like: only let it be little, for I shall walk there and back: sixty miles each way, that is a long spell!' Hindley named a fiddle, and then he asked Miss Cathy; she was hardly six years old, but she could ride any horse in the stable, and she chose a whip. He did not forget me; for he had a kind heart, though he was rather severe sometimes. He promised to bring me a pocketful of apples and pears, and then he kissed his children, said good-bye, and set off.

It seemed a long while to us all—the three days of his absence—and often did little Cathy ask when he would be home. Mrs. Earnshaw, expected him by supper-time, on the third evening, and she put the meal off hour after hour; there were no signs of his coming, however, and at last the children got tired of running down to the gate to look. Then it grew dark; she would have had them to bed, but they begged sadly to be allowed to stay up; and, just about eleven o'clock, the door-latch was raised quietly and in stept the master. He threw himself into a chair, laughing and groaning, and bid them all stand off, for he was nearly killed —he would not have such another walk for the three kingdoms.

"And at the end of it, to be flighted to death! he said opening his great coat, which he held bundled up in his arms. "See here, wife! I was never so beaten with anything in my life: but you must e'en take it as a gift of God; though it's as dark almost as if it came from the devil."

We crowded round, and over Miss Cathy's head, I had a peep at a dirty, ragged, black-haired child; big enough both to walk and talk: indeed, its face looked older than Catherine's; yet, when it was set on its feet, it only stared round, and repeated over and over again some gibberish, that nobody could understand. I was frightened, and Mrs. Earnshaw was ready to fling it out of doors: she did fly up, asking how he could fashion to bring that gipsy brat into the house, when they had their own bairns to feed and fend for? What he meant to do with it, and whether he were mad? The master tried to explain the matter; but he was really half dead with fatigue, and all that I could make out, amongst her scolding, was a tale of his seeing it starving, and houseless, and as good as dumb, in the streets of Liverpool; where he picked it up and inquired for its owner. Not a soul knew to whom it belonged, he said; and his money and time being both limited, he thought it better to take it home with him at once, than run into vain expenses there: because he was determined he would not leave it as he found it. Well, the conclusion was that my mistress grumbled herself calm; and Mr. Earnshaw told me to wash it, and give it clean things, and let it sleep with the children.

Hindley and Cathy contented themselves with looking and listening till peace was restored: then, both began searching their father's pockets for the presents he had promised them. The former was a boy of fourteen, but when he drew out what had been a fiddle, crushed to morsels in the great coat, he blubbered aloud; and Cathy, when she learned the master had lost her whip in attending on the stranger, showed her humour by grinning and spitting at the stupid little thing; earning for her pains, a sound blow from her father to teach her cleaner manners. They entirely refused to have it in bed with them, or even in their room; and I had no more sense, so I put it on the landing of the stairs, hoping it might be gone on the morrow. By chance, or else attracted by hearing his voice, it crept to Mr. Earnshaw's door, and there he found it on quitting his chamber. Inquiries were made as to how it got there; I was obliged to confess, and in recompense for my cowardice and inhumanity was sent out of the house.

This was Heathcliff's first introduction to the family. On coming back a few days afterwards (for I did not consider my banishment perpetual) I found they had christened him "Heathcliff:" it was the name of a son who died in childhood, and it has served him ever since, both for Christian and surname. Miss Cathy and he were now very thick; but Hindley hated him: and to say the truth I did the same; and we plagued and went on with him shamefully: for I wasn't reasonable enough to feel my injustice, and the mistress never put in a word on his behalf when she saw him wronged.

He seemed a sullen, patient child; hardened, perhaps, to ill-treatment: he would stand Hindley's blows without winking or shedding a tear, and my pinches moved him only to draw in a breath and open his eyes, as if he had hurt himself by accident and nobody was to blame. This endurance made old Earnshaw furious, when he discovered his son persecuting the poor, fatherless child, as he called him. He took to Heathcliff strangely, believing all he said (for that matter, he said precious little, and generally the truth), and petting him up far above Cathy, who was too mischievous and wayward for a favourite.

So, from the very beginning, he bred bad feeling in the house; and at Mrs. Earnshaw's death, which happened in less than two years after, the young master had learned to regard his father as an oppressor rather than a friend, and Heathcliff as a usurper of his parent's affections and his privileges; and he grew bitter with brooding over these injuries. I sympathized a while; but when the children fell ill of the measles, and I had to tend them, and take on me the cares of a woman at once, I changed my ideas. Heathcliff was dangerously sick; and while he lay at the worst he would have me constantly by his pillow: I suppose he felt I did a good deal for him, and he hadn't wit to guess that I was compelled to do it. However, I will say this, he was the quietest child that ever nurse watched over. The difference between him and the others forced me to be less partial. Cathy and her brother harassed me terribly; *he* was as uncomplaining as a lamb; though hardness, not gentleness, made him give little trouble.

He got through, and the doctor affirmed it was in a great measure owing to me, and praised me for my care. I was vain of his commendations, and softened towards the being by whose means I earned them, and thus Hindley lost his last ally: still I couldn't dote on Heathcliff, and I wondered often what my master saw to admire so much in the sullen boy; who never, to my recollection, repaid his indulgence by any sign of gratitude. He was not insolent to his benefactor, he was simply insensible; though knowing perfectly the hold he had on his heart, and conscious he had only to speak and all the house would be obliged to bend to his wishes. As an instance, I remember Mr. Earnshaw once bought a couple of colts at the parish fair, and gave the lads each one. Heathcliff took the handsomest, but it soon fell lame, and when he discovered it, he said to Hindley,

"You must exchange horses with me: I don't like mine; and if you won't I shall tell your father of the three thrashings you've given me this week, and show him my arm, which is black to the shoulder." Hindley put out his tongue, and cuffed him over the ears. "You'd better do it at once," he persisted, escaping to the porch (they were in the stable): "you will have to; and if I speak of these blows, you'll get them again with interest." "Off, dog!" cried Hindley, threatening him with an iron weight used for weighing potatoes and hay. "Throw it," he replied, standing still, "and then I'll tell how you boasted that you would turn me out of doors as soon as he died, and see whether he will not turn you out directly." Hindley threw it, hitting him on the breast, and down he fell, but staggered up immediately, breathless and white; and, had not I prevented it, he would have gone just so to the master, and got full revenge by letting his condition plead for him, intimating who had caused it. "Take my colt, gipsy, then!" said young Earnshaw, "And I pray that he may break your neck: take him, and be damned, you beggarly interloper! and wheedle my father out of all he has: only afterwards show him what you are, imp of Satan—And take that, I hope he'll kick out your brains!"

Heathcliff had gone to loose the beast, and shift it to his own stall; he was passing behind it, when Hindley finished his speech by knocking him under its feet, and without stopping to examine whether his hopes were fulfilled, ran away as fast as he could. I was surprised to witness how coolly the child gathered himself up, and went on with his intention; exchanging saddles and all, and then sitting down on a bundle of hay to overcome the qualm which the violent blow occasioned, before he entered the house. I persuaded him easily to let me lay the blame of his bruises on the horse: he minded little what tale was told since he had what he wanted. He complained so seldom, indeed, of such stirs as these, that I really thought him not vindictive: I was deceived completely, as you will hear.

CHAPTER V.

In the course of time, Mr. Earnshaw began to fail. He had been active and healthy, yet his strength left him suddenly; and when he was confined to the chimney-corner he grew grievously irritable. A nothing vexed him; and suspected slights of his authority nearly threw him into fits. This was especially to be remarked if any one attempted to impose upon, or domineer over, his favourite : he was painfully jealous lest a word should be spoken amiss to him; seeming to have got into his head the notion that, because he liked Heathcliff, all hated, and longed to do him an ill-turn. It was a disadvantage to the lad; for the kinder among us did not wish to fret the master, so we humoured his partiality; and that humouring was rich nourishment to the child's pride and black tempers. Still it became in a manner necessary; twice, or thrice, Hindley's manifestations of scorn, while his father was near, roused the old man to a fury : he seized his stick to strike him, and shook with rage that he could not do it.

At last, our curate (we had a curate then who made the living answer by teaching the little Lintons and Earnshaws, and farming his bit of land himself) advised that the young man should be sent to college; and Mr. Earnshaw agreed, though with a heavy spirit, for he said—" Hindley was naught, and would never thrive as where he wandered."

I hoped heartily we should have peace now. It hurt me to think the master should be made uncomfortable by his own good deed. I fancied the discontent of age and disease arose from his family disagreements; as he would have it that it did : really, you know, sir, it was in his sinking frame. We might have got on tolerably, notwithstanding, but for two people, Miss Cathy and Joseph, the servant : you saw him, I dare say, up yonder. He was, and is yet most likely, the wearisomest, self-righteous pharisee that ever ransacked a Bible to rake the promises to himself and fling the curses to his neighbours. By his knack of sermonizing and pious discoursing, he contrived to make a great impression on Mr. Earnshaw; and the more feeble the master became, the more influence he gained. He was relentless in worrying him about his soul's concerns, and about ruling his children rigidly. He encouraged him to regard Hindley as a reprobate; and, night after night, he regularly grumbled out a long string of tales against Heathcliff and Catherine: always minding to flatter Earnshaw's weakness by heaping the heaviest blame on the latter.

Certainly, she had ways with her such as I never saw a child take up before; and she put all of us past our patience fifty times and oftener in a day: from the hour she came down stairs till the hour she went to bed, we had not a minute's security that she wouldn't be in mischief. Her spirits were always at high-water mark, her tongue always going—singing, laughing, and plaguing everybody who would not do the same. A wild, wicked slip she was—but, she had the bonniest eye, and sweetest smile, and lightest foot in the parish: and, after all, I believe she meant no harm; for when once she made you cry in good earnest, it seldom happened that she would not keep you company, and oblige you to be quiet that you might comfort her. She was much too fond of Heathcliff. The greatest punishment we could invent for her was to keep her separate from him: yet she got chided more than any of us on his account. In play, she liked exceedingly to act the little mistress; using her hands freely, and commanding her companions: she did so to me, but I would not bear slapping and ordering; and so I let her know.

Now, Mr. Earnshaw did not understand jokes from his children: he had always been strict and grave with them; and Catherine, on her part, had no idea why her father should be crosser and less patient in his ailing condition, than he was in his prime. His peevish reproofs wakened in her a naughty delight to provoke him: she was never so happy as when we were all scolding her at once, and she defying us with her bold, saucy look, and her ready words; turning Joseph's religious curses into ridicule, baiting me, and doing just what her father hated most—showing how her pretended insolence, which he thought real, had more power over Heathcliff than his kindness: how the boy would do *her* bidding in anything, and *his* only when it suited his own inclination. After behaving as badly as possible all day, she sometimes came fondling to make it up at night. "Nay, Cathy," the old man would say, "I cannot

love thee; thou 'rt worse than thy brother. Go, say thy
prayers, child, and ask God's pardon. I doubt thy mother
and I must rue that we ever reared thee!" That made her
cry, at first; and then being repulsed continually hardened
her, and she laughed if I told her to say she was sorry for
her faults, and beg to be forgiven.

But the hour came, at last, that ended Mr. Earnshaw's
troubles on earth. He died quietly in his chair one October
evening, seated by the fire-side. A high wind blustered
round the house, and roared in the chimney: it sounded
wild and stormy, yet it was not cold, and we were all
together—I, a little removed from the hearth, busy at my
knitting, and Joseph reading his Bible near the table (for
the servants generally sat in the house then, after their work
was done). Miss Cathy had been sick, and that made her
still; she leant against her father's knee, and Heathcliff was
lying on the floor with his head in her lap. I remember the
master, before he fell into a doze, stroking her bonny hair—
it pleased him rarely to see her gentle—and saying—"Why
canst thou not always be a good lass, Cathy?" And she
turned her face up to his, and laughed, and answered,
"Why cannot you always be a good man, father?" But as
soon as she saw him vexed again, she kissed his hand, and
said she would sing him to sleep. She began singing very
low, till his fingers dropped from hers, and his head sank on
his breast. Then I told her to hush, and not stir, for fear she
should wake him. We all kept as mute as mice a full half-
hour, and should have done so longer, only Joseph, having
finished his chapter, got up and said that he must rouse the
master for prayers and bed. He stepped forward, and called
him by name, and touched his shoulder; but he would not
move, so he took the candle and looked at him. I thought
there was something wrong as he set down the light; and
seizing the children each by an arm, whispered them to
"frame up stairs, and make little din—they might pray
alone that evening—he had summut to do."

"I shall bid father good-night first," said Catherine,
putting her arms round his neck, before we could hinder her.
The poor thing discovered her loss directly—she screamed
out—"Oh, he 's dead, Heathcliff! he 's dead!" And they
both set up a heart-breaking cry.

I joined my wail to theirs, loud and bitter; but Joseph,

asked what we could be thinking of to roar in that way over a saint in heaven. He told me to put on my cloak and run to Gimmerton for the doctor and the parson. I could not guess the use that either would be of, then. However, I went, through wind and rain, and brought one, the doctor, back with me; the other said he would come in the morning. Leaving Joseph to explain matters, I ran to the children's room: their door was ajar, I saw they had never laid down, though it was past midnight; but they were calmer, and did not need me to console them. The little souls were comforting each other with better thoughts than I could have hit on: no parson in the world ever pictured heaven so beautifully as they did, in their innocent talk; and, while I sobbed and listened, I could not help wishing we were all there safe together.

CHAPTER VI.

MR. HINDLEY came home to the funeral; and—a thing that amazed us, and set the neighbours gossiping right and left —he brought a wife with him. What she was, and where she was born, he never informed us: probably, she had neither money nor name to recommend her, or he would scarcely have kept the union from his father.

She was not one that would have disturbed the house much on her own account. Every object she saw, the moment she crossed the threshold, appeared to delight her; and every circumstance that took place about her: except the preparing for the burial, and the presence of the mourners. I thought she was half silly, from her behaviour while that went on: she ran into her chamber, and made me come with her, though I should have been dressing the children; and there she sat shivering and clasping her hands, and asking repeatedly—"Are they gone yet?" Then she began describing with hysterical emotion the effect it produced on her to see black; and started, and trembled, and, at last, fell a weeping — and when I asked what was the matter? answered, she didn't know; but she felt so afraid of dying!

I imagined her as little likely to die as myself. She was rather thin, but young, and fresh complexioned, and her eyes sparkled as bright as diamonds. I did remark, to be sure, that mounting the stairs made her breathe very quick; that the least sudden noise set her all in a quiver, and that she coughed troublesomely sometimes: but, I knew nothing of what these symptoms portended, and had no impulse to sympathize with her. We don't in general take to foreigners here, Mr. Lockwood, unless they take to us first.

Young Earnshaw was altered considerably in the three years of his absence. He had grown sparer, and lost his colour, and spoke and dressed quite differently; and, on the very day of his return, he told Joseph and me we must thenceforth quarter ourselves in the back-kitchen, and leave the house for him. Indeed, he would have carpeted and papered a small spare room for a parlour; but his wife expressed such pleasure at the white floor and huge glowing fire-place, at the pewter dishes and delf-case, and dog-kennel, and the wide space there was to move about in where they usually sat, that he thought it unnecessary to her comfort, and so dropped the intention.

She expressed pleasure, too, at finding a sister among her new acquaintance; and she prattled to Catherine, and kissed her, and ran about with her, and gave her quantities of presents, at the beginning. Her affection tired very soon, however, and when she grew peevish, Hindley became tyrannical A few words from her, evincing a dislike to Heathcliff, were enough to rouse in him all his old hatred of the boy. He drove him from their company to the servants, deprived him of the instructions of the curate, and insisted that he should labour out of doors instead; compelling him to do so as hard as any other lad on the farm.

Heathcliff bore his degradation pretty well at first, because Cathy taught him what she learnt, and worked or played with him in the fields. They both promised fair to grow up as rude as savages; the young master being entirely negligent how they behaved, and what they did, so they kept clear of him. He would not even have seen after their going to church on Sundays, only Joseph and the curate reprimanded his carelessness when they absented themselves; and that reminded him to order Heathcliff a flogging, and Catherine a fast from dinner or supper. But it was one of their chief amusements to run away to the moors in the morning and remain there all day, and the after punishment grew a mere thing to laugh at. The curate might set as many chapters as he pleased for Catherine to get by heart, and Joseph might thrash Heathcliff till his arm ached; they forgot everything the minute they were together again : at least the minute they had contrived some naughty plan of revenge; and many a time I've cried to myself to watch them growing more reckless daily, and I not daring to speak a syllable, for fear of losing the small power I still retained over the unfriended creatures. One Sunday evening, it chanced that they were banished from the sitting-room, for making a noise, or a light offence of the kind; and when I went to call them to supper, I could discover them nowhere. We searched the house, above and below, and the yard and stables; they were invisible : and, at last, Hindley in a passion told us to bolt the doors, and swore nobody should let them in that night. The household went to bed; and I, too, anxious to lie down, opened my lattice and put my head out to hearken, though it rained : determined to admit them in spite of the prohibition, should they return. In a while, I distinguished steps coming up the road, and the light of a lantern glimmered through the gate. I threw a shawl over my head and ran to prevent them from waking Mr. Earnshaw by knocking. There was Heathcliff, by himself: it gave me a start to see him alone.

"Where is Miss Catherine?" I cried hurriedly. "No accident, I hope?" "At Thrushcross Grange," he answered; "and I would have been there too, but they had not the manners to ask me to stay." "Well, you will catch it !" I said : "you'll never be content till you're sent about your business. What in the world led you wandering to Thrushcross Grange?" "Let me get off my wet clothes, and I'll tell you all about it, Nelly," he replied. I bid him beware of rousing the master, and while he undressed and I waited to put out the candle, he continued—"Cathy and I escaped from the wash-house to have a ramble at liberty, and getting a glimpse of the Grange lights, we thought we would just go and see whether the Lintons passed their Sunday evenings standing shivering in corners, while their father and mother sat eating and drinking, and singing and laughing, and burning their eyes out before the fire. Do you think they

do? Or reading sermons, and being catechised by their
man-servant, and set to learn a column of Scripture names,
if they don't answer properly?" "Probably not," I responded. "They are good children, no doubt, and don't
deserve the treatment you receive, for your bad conduct."
"Don't cant, Nelly," he said: "nonsense! We ran from
the top of the Heights to the park, without stopping—
Catherine completely beaten in the race, because she was
barefoot. You'll have to seek for her shoes in the bog to-
morrow. We crept through a broken hedge, groped our
way up the path, and planted ourselves on a flower-plot
under the drawing-room window. The light came from
thence; they had not put up the shutters, and the curtains
were only half closed. Both of us were able to look in by
standing on the basement, and clinging to the ledge, and we
saw—ah! it was beautiful—a splendid place carpeted with
crimson, and crimson-covered chairs and tables, and a pure
white ceiling bordered by gold, a shower of glass-drops
hanging in silver chains from the centre, and shimmering
with little soft tapers. Old Mr. and Mrs. Linton were not
there; Edgar and his sister had it entirely to themselves.
Shouldn't they have been happy? We should have thought
ourselves in heaven! And now, guess what your good children were doing? Isabella—I believe she is eleven, a year
younger than Cathy—lay screaming at the farther end of the
room, shrieking as if witches were running red hot needles
into her. Edgar stood on the hearth weeping silently, and in
the middle of the table sat a little dog, shaking its paw and
yelping; which, from their mutual accusations, we understood they had nearly pulled in two between them. The
idiots! That was their pleasure! to quarrel who should
hold a heap of warm hair, and each begin to cry because
both, after struggling to get it, refused to take it. We
laughed outright at the petted things; we did despise them!
When would you catch me wishing to have what Catherine
wanted? or find us by ourselves, seeking entertainment in
yelling, and sobbing, and rolling on the ground, divided by
the whole room? I'd not exchange, for a thousand lives,
my condition here, for Edgar Linton's at Thrushcross
Grange — not if I might have the privilege of flinging
Joseph off the highest gable, and painting the house-front
with Hindley's blood!"

"Hush, hush!" I interrupted. "Still you have not told me, Heathcliff, how Catherine is left behind?"

"I told you we laughed," he answered. "The Lintons heard us, and with one accord, they shot like arrows to the door; there was silence, and then a cry, 'Oh, mamma, mamma! Oh, papa! Oh, mamma, come here. Oh, papa, oh!' They really did howl out something in that way. We made frightful noises to terrify them still more, and then we dropped off the ledge, because somebody was drawing the bars, and we felt we had better flee. I had Cathy by the hand, and was urging her on, when all at once she fell down. 'Run, Heathcliff, run!' she whispered. 'They have let the bull-dog loose, and he holds me!' The devil had seized her ankle, Nelly: I heard his abominable snorting. She did not yell out—no! She would have scorned to do it, if she had been spitted on the horns of a mad cow. I did, though: I vociferated curses enough to annihilate any fiend in Christendom; and I got a stone and thrust it between his jaws, and tried with all my might to cram it down his throat. A beast of a servant came up with a lantern, at last, shouting —'Keep fast, Skulker, keep fast!' He changed his note, however, when he saw Skulker's game. The dog was throttled off; his huge, purple tongue hanging half a foot out of his mouth, and his pendent lips streaming with bloody slaver. The man took Cathy up; she was sick: not from fear, I'm certain, but from pain. He carried her in; I followed, grumbling execrations and vengeance. 'What prey, Robert?' hallooed Linton from the entrance. 'Skulker has caught a little girl, sir,' he replied; 'and there's a lad here,' he added, making a clutch at me, 'who looks an out-and-outer! Very like, the robbers were for putting them through the window, to open the doors to the gang after all were asleep, that they might murder us at their ease. Hold your tongue, you foul-mouthed thief, you! you shall go to the gallows for this. Mr. Linton, sir, don't lay by your gun.' 'No, no, Robert,' said the old fool. 'The rascals knew that yesterday was my rent-day: they thought to have me cleverly. Come in; I'll furnish them a reception. There, John, fasten the chain. Give Skulker some water, Jenny. To beard a magistrate in his stronghold, and on the Sabbath, too!

Where will their insolence stop? Oh, my dear Mary, look here! Don't be afraid, it is but a boy—yet the villain scowls so plainly in his face, would it not be a kindness to the country to hang him at once, before he shows his nature in acts as well as features?' He pulled me under the chandelier, and Mrs. Linton placed her spectacles on her nose and raised her hands in horror. The cowardly children crept nearer also, Isabella lisping—'Frightful thing! Put him in the cellar, papa. He's exactly like the son of the fortune-teller, that stole my tame pheasant. Isn't he, Edgar?'

"While they examined me, Cathy came round; she heard the last speech, and laughed. Edgar Linton, after an inquisitive stare, collected sufficient wit to recognise her. They see us at church, you know, though we seldom meet them elsewhere. 'That's Miss Earnshaw!' he whispered to his mother, 'and look how Skulker has bitten her—how her foot bleeds!'"

"'Miss Earnshaw? Nonsense!' cried the dame, 'Miss Earnshaw scouring the country with a gipsy! And yet, my dear, the child is in mourning—surely it is—and she may be lamed for life!'

"'What culpable carelessness in her brother!'" exclaimed Mr. Linton, turning from me to Catherine. 'I've understood from Shielders' (that was the curate, sir) 'that he lets her grow up in absolute heathenism. But who is this? Where did she pick up this companion? Oho! I declare he is that strange acquisition my late neighbour made in his journey to Liverpool—a little Lascar, or an American or Spanish castaway.'

"'A wicked boy, at all events,' remarked the old lady, 'and quite unfit for a decent house! Did you notice his language, Linton? I'm shocked that my children should have heard it.'

"I recommended cursing—don't be angry, Nelly—and so Robert was ordered to take me off. I refused to go without Cathy; he dragged me into the garden, pushed the lantern into my hand, assured me that Mr. Earnshaw should be informed of my behaviour, and, bidding me march directly, secured the door again. The curtains were still looped up at one corner, and I resumed my station as spy; because, if Catherine had wished to return, I intended shattering their great glass panes to a million fragments, unless they let her out. She sat on the sofa quietly. Mrs. Linton took off the grey cloak of the dairy-maid which we had borrowed for our excursion, shaking her head and expostulating with her, I suppose : she was a young lady, and they made a distinction between her treatment and mine. Then the woman servant brought a basin of warm water, and washed her feet; and Mr. Linton mixed a tumbler of negus, and Isabella emptied a plateful of cakes into her lap, and Edgar stood gaping at a distance. Afterwards, they dried and combed her beautiful hair, and gave her a pair of enormous slippers, and wheeled her to the fire; and I left her, as merry as she could be, dividing her food between the little dog and Skulker, whose nose she pinched as he ate; and kindling a spark of spirit in the vacant blue eyes of the Lintons—a dim reflection from her own enchanting face. I saw they were full of stupid admiration; she is so immeasurably superior to them—to everybody on earth, is she not, Nelly?"

"There will more come of this business than you reckon on," I answered, covering him up and extinguishing the light. "You are incurable, Heathcliff, and Mr. Hindley will have to proceed to extremities, see if he won't." My words came truer than I desired. The luckless adventure made Earnshaw furious. And then, Mr. Linton, to mend matters, paid us a visit himself, on the morrow; and read the young master such a lecture on the road he guided his family, that he was stirred to look about him, in earnest. Heathcliff received no flogging, but he was told that the first word he spoke to Miss Catherine should ensure a dismissal; and Mrs. Earnshaw undertook to keep her sister-in-law in due restraint when she returned home; employing art, not force : with force she would have found it impossible.

CHAPTER VII.

CATHY stayed at Thrushcross Grange five weeks: till Christmas. By that time her ankle was thoroughly cured, and her manners much improved. The mistress visited her often in the interval, and commenced her plan of reform by trying to raise her self-respect with fine clothes and flattery, which she took readily; so that, instead of a wild, hatless little savage jumping into the house, and rushing to squeeze us all breathless, there 'lighted from a handsome black pony a very dignified person, with brown ringlets falling from the cover of a feathered beaver, and a long cloth habit, which she was obliged to hold up with both hands that she might sail in. Hindley lifted her from her horse, exclaiming delightedly, " Why, Cathy, you are quite a beauty ! I should scarcely have known you : you look like a lady now. Isabella Linton is not to be compared with her, is she Frances ?" " Isabella has not her natural advantages," replied his wife : " but she must mind and not grow wild again here. Ellen, help Miss Catherine off with her things — Stay, dear, you will disarrange your curls—let me untie your hat."

I removed the habit, and there shone forth beneath, a grand plaid silk frock, white trousers, and burnished shoes ; and, while her eyes sparkled joyfully when the dogs came bounding up to welcome her, she dare hardly touch them lest they should fawn upon her splendid garments. She kissed me gently : I was all flour making the Christmas cake, and it would not have done to give me a hug ; and, then, she looked round for Heathcliff. Mr. and Mrs. Earnshaw watched anxiously their meeting ; thinking it would enable them to judge, in some measure, what grounds they had for hoping to succeed in separating the two friends.

Heathcliff was hard to discover, at first. If he were careless, and uncared for, before Catherine's absence, he had been ten times more so, since. Nobody but I even did him the kindness to call him a dirty boy, and bid him wash himself, once a week ; and children of his age, seldom have a natural pleasure in soap and water. Therefore, not to mention his clothes, which had seen three months' service in mire and dust, and his thick uncombed hair, the surface of his face and hands was dismally beclouded. He might well skulk behind the settle, on beholding such a bright, graceful damsel enter the house, instead of a rough-headed counterpart to himself, as he expected. " Is Heathcliff not here ?" she demanded, pulling off her gloves, and displaying fingers wonderfully whitened with doing nothing and staying in doors.

" Heathcliff, you may come forward," cried Mr. Hindley, enjoying his discomfiture, and gratified to see what a forbiding young blackguard he would be compelled to present himself. "You may come and wish Miss Catherine welcome, like the other servants."

Cathy, catching a glimpse of her friend in his concealment, flew to embrace him; she bestowed seven or eight kisses on his cheek within the second, and then stopped, and drawing back, burst into a laugh, exclaiming, "Why, how very black and cross you look! and how—how funny and grim! But that's because I'm used to Edgar and Isabella Linton. Well, Heathcliff, have you forgotten me?"

She had some reason to put the question, for shame and pride threw double gloom over his countenance, and kept him immoveable.

"Shake hands, Heathcliff," said Mr. Earnshaw, condescendingly; "once in a way, that is permitted."

"I shall not," replied the boy, finding his tongue at last; "I shall not stand to be laughed at. I shall not bear it!"

And he would have broken from the circle, but Miss Cathy seized him again.

"I did not mean to laugh at you," she said; "I could not hinder myself: Heathcliff, shake hands at least! What are you sulky for? It was only that you looked odd. If you wash your face, and brush your hair it will be all right: but you are so dirty!"

She gazed concernedly at the dusky fingers she held in her own, and also at her dress; which she feared had gained no embellishment from its contact with his.

"You needn't have touched me!" he answered, following her eye and snatching away his hand. I shall be as dirty as I please: and I like to be dirty, and I will be dirty."

With that he dashed head foremost out of the room, amid the merriment of the master and mistress, and to the serious disturbance of Catherine; who could not comprehend how her remarks should have produced such an exhibition of bad temper.

After playing lady's maid to the new comer, and putting my cakes in the oven, and making the house and kitchen cheerful with great fires, befitting Christmas eve, I prepared to sit down and amuse myself by singing carols, all alone; regardless of Joseph's affirmations that he considered the merry tunes I chose as next door to songs. He had retired to private prayer in his chamber, and Mr. and Mrs. Earnshaw were engaging Missy's attention by sundry gay trifles

bought for her to present to the little Lintons, as an acknowledgment of their kindness. They had invited them to spend
the morrow at Wuthering Heights, and the invitation had
been accepted, on one condition : Mrs. Linton begged that
her darlings might be kept carefully apart from that
"naughty swearing boy.'

Under these circumstances I remained solitary. I smelt
the rich scent of the heating spices; and admired the shining
kitchen utensils, the polished clock, decked in holly, the silver
mugs ranged on a tray ready to be filled with mulled ale for
supper ; and above all, the speckless purity of my particular
care—the scoured and well-swept floor. I gave due inward
applause to every object, and then I remembered how old
Earnshaw used to come in when all was tidied, and call me
a cant lass, and slip a shilling into my hand as a Christmas
box ; and from that I went on to think of his fondness for
Heathcliff, and his dread lest he should suffer neglect after
death had removed him ; and that naturally led me to consider the poor lad's situation now, and from singing I changed
my mind to crying. It struck me soon, however, there would
be more sense in endeavouring to repair some of his wrongs
than shedding tears over them: I got up and walked into
the court to seek him. He was not far : I found him smoothing the glossy coat of the new pony in the stable, and feeding the other beasts, according to custom.

"Make haste, Heathcliff!" I said, "the kitchen is so
comfortable; and Joseph is up stairs: make haste, and let me
dress you smart before Miss Cathy comes out, and then you
can sit together, with the whole hearth to yourselves, and
have a long chatter till bedtime."

He proceeded with his task and never turned his head towards me.

"Come—are you coming?" I continued. "There's a
little cake for each of you, nearly enough; and you'll need
half-an-hour's donning."

I waited five minutes, but getting no answer left him.
Catherine supped with her brother and sister-in-law : Joseph
and I joined at an unsociable meal, seasoned with reproofs
on one side and sauciness on the other. His cake and cheese
remained on the table all night for the fairies. He managed
to continue work till nine o'clock, and then marched dumb
and dour to his chamber. Cathy sat up late, having a world

of things to order for the reception of her new friends: she came into the kitchen once to speak to her old one; but he was gone, and she only staid to ask what was the matter with him, and then went back. In the morning he rose early; and as it was a holiday, carried his ill-humour on to the moors; not reappearing till the family were departed for church. Fasting and reflection seemed to have brought him to a better spirit. He hung about me for a while, and having screwed up his courage, exclaimed abruptly,—

"Nelly, make me decent, I'm going to be good."

"High time, Heathcliff," I said; "you *have* grieved Catherine: she's sorry she ever came home, I dare say! It looks as if you envied her, because she is more thought of than you."

The notion of *envying* Catherine was incomprehensible to him, but the notion of grieving her he understood clearly enough.

"Did she say she was grieved?" he inquired, looking very serious.

"She cried when I told her you were off again this morning."

"Well, *I* cried last night," he returned, "and I had more reason to cry than she."

"Yes; you had the reason of going to bed with a proud heart and an empty stomach," said I. "Proud people breed sad sorrows for themselves. But, if you be ashamed of your touchiness, you must ask pardon, mind, when she comes in. You must go up and offer to kiss her, and say—you know best what to say; only do it heartily, and not as if you thought her converted into a stranger by her grand dress. And now, though I have dinner to get ready, I'll steal time to arrange you so that Edgar Linton shall look quite a doll beside you: and that he does. You are younger, and yet, I'll be bound, you are taller and twice as broad across the shoulders: you could knock him down in a twinkling? don't you feel that you could?"

Heathcliff's face brightened a moment; then it was over-cast afresh, and he sighed.

"But, Nelly, if I knocked him down twenty times, that wouldn't make him less handsome or me more so. I wish I had light hair and a fair skin, and was dressed and behaved as well, and had a chance of being as rich as he will be!"

"And cried for mama at every turn," I added, "and trembled if a country lad heaved his fist against you, and sat at home all day for a shower of rain. Oh, Heathcliff, you are showing a poor spirit! Come to the glass, and I'll let you see what you should wish. Do you mark those two lines between your eyes; and those thick brows, that instead of rising arched, sink in the middle; and that couple of black fiends, so deeply buried, who never open their windows boldly, but lurk glinting under them, like devil's spies? Wish and learn to smooth away the surly wrinkles, to raise your lids frankly, and change the fiends to confidant, innocent angels, suspecting and doubting nothing, and always seeing friends where they are not sure of foes. Don't get the expression of a vicious cur that appears to know the kicks it gets are its dessert, and yet hates all the world, as well as the kicker, for what it suffers."

"In other words, I must wish for Edgar Linton's great blue eyes and even forehead," he replied. "I do—and that won't help me to them."

"A good heart will help you to a bonny face, my lad," I continued, "if you were a regular black; and a bad one will turn the bonniest into something worse than ugly. And now that we've done washing, and combing, and sulking— tell me whether you don't think yourself rather handsome? I'll tell you, I do. You're fit for a prince in disguise. Who knows but your father was Emperor of China, and your mother an Indian queen, each of them able to buy up, with one week's income, Wuthering Heights and Thrushcross Grange together? And you were kidnapped by wicked sailors and brought to England. Were I in your place, I would frame high notions of my birth; and the thoughts of what I was should give me courage and dignity to support the oppressions of a little farmer!"

So I chattered on; and Heathcliff gradually lost his frown and began to look quite pleasant, when all at once our conversation was interrupted by a rumbling sound moving up the road and entering the court. He ran to the window and I to the door, just in time to behold the two Lintons descend from the family carriage, smothered in cloaks and furs, and the Earnshaws dismount from their horses: they often rode to church in winter. Catherine took a hand of each of the children, and brought them into the house and set them before the fire, which quickly put colour into their white faces.

I urged my companion to hasten now and show his amiable humour, and he willingly obeyed; but ill-luck would have it that, as he opened the door leading from the kitchen on one side, Hindley opened it on the other. They met, and the master irritated at seeing him clean and cheerful; or, perhaps, eager to keep his promise to Mrs. Linton, shoved him back with a sudden thrust, and angrily bade Joseph " keep the fellow out of the room—send him into the garret till dinner is over. He'll be cramming his fingers in the tarts and stealing the fruit, if left alone with them a minute."

" Nay, sir," I could not avoid answering, " he'll touch nothing, not he: and I suppose he must have his share of the dainties as well as we."

" He shall have his share of my hand, if I catch him down stairs till dark," cried Hindley. " Begone, you vaga-bond! What! you are attempting the coxcomb, are you? Wait till I get hold of those elegant locks—see if I won't pull them a bit longer!"

" They are long enough already," observed Master Linton, peeping from the doorway; " I wonder they don't make his head ache. It's like a colt's mane over his eyes!"

He ventured this remark without any intention to insult; but Heathcliff's violent nature was not prepared to endure the appearance of impertinence from one whom he seemed to hate, even then, as a rival. He seized a tureen of hot apple sauce (the first thing that came under his gripe) and dashed it full against the speaker's face and neck; who instantly commenced a lament that brought Isabella and Catherine hurrying to the place. Mr. Earnshaw snatched up the cul-prit directly and conveyed him to his chamber; where, doubtless, he administered a rough remedy to cool the fit of passion, for he appeared red and breathless. I got the dish-cloth, and rather spitefully scrubbed Edgar's nose and mouth, affirming it served him right for meddling. His sister began weeping to go home, and Cathy stood by confounded, blush-ing for all.

" You should not have spoken to him!" she expostulated with Master Linton. " He was in a bad temper, and now you've spoilt your visit; and he'll be flogged: I hate him to

E

be flogged! I can't eat my dinner. Why did you speak to him, Edgar?"

"I didn't," sobbed the youth, escaping from my hands, and finishing the remainder of the purification with his cambric pocket-handkerchief. "I promised mama that I wouldn't say one word to him, and I didn't."

"Well, don't cry," replied Catherine, contemptuously; "you're not killed. Don't make more mischief; my brother is coming: be quiet! Hush! Isabella! Has anybody hurt *you?*"

"There, there, children—to your seats!" cried Hindley, bustling in. "That brute of a lad has warmed me nicely. Next time, Master Edgar, take the law into your own fists— it will give you an appetite!"

The little party recovered its equanimity at sight of the fragrant feast. They were hungry after their ride, and easily consoled, since no real harm had befallen them. Mr. Earnshaw carved bountiful platefuls, and the mistress made them merry with lively talk. I waited behind her chair, and was pained to behold Catherine, with dry eyes and an indifferent air, commence cutting up the wing of a goose before her. "An unfeeling child," I thought to myself; "how lightly she dismisses her old playmate's troubles. I could not have imagined her to be so selfish." She lifted a mouthful to her lips; then she set it down again: her cheeks flushed, and the tears gushed over them. She slipped her fork to the floor, and hastily dived under the cloth to conceal her emotion. I did not call her unfeeling long; for I perceived she was in purgatory throughout the day, and wearying to find an opportunity of getting by herself, or paying a visit to Heathcliff, who had been locked up by the master: as I discovered, on endeavouring to introduce to him a private mess of victuals.

In the evening we had a dance. Cathy begged that he might be liberated then, as Isabella Linton had no partner; her entreaties were vain, and I was appointed to supply the deficiency. We got rid of all gloom in the excitement of the exercise, and our pleasure was increased by the arrival of the Gimmerton band, mustering fifteen strong: a trumpet, a trombone, clarionets, bassoons, French horns, and a bass viol, besides singers. They go the rounds of all the respectable houses, and receive contributions every Christmas, and we esteemed it a first-rate treat to hear them. After the usual carols had been sung, we set them to songs and glees. Mrs. Earnshaw loved the music, and so they gave us plenty.

Catherine loved it too; but she said it sounded sweetest at the top of the steps, and she went up in the dark: I followed. They shut the house door below, never noting our absence, it was so full of people. She made no stay at the stairs' head, but mounted farther, to the garret where Heathcliff was confined, and called him. He stubbornly declined answering for a while; she persevered, and finally persuaded him to hold communion with her through the boards. I let the poor things converse unmolested, till I supposed the songs were going to cease, and the singers to get some refreshment; then, I clambered up the ladder to warn her. Instead of finding her outside, I heard her voice within. The little monkey had crept by the skylight of one garret, along the roof, into the skylight of the other, and it was with the utmost difficulty I could coax her out again. When she did come, Heathcliff came with her, and she insisted that I should take him into the kitchen, as my fellow-servant had gone to a neighbour's to be removed from the sound of our "devil's psalmody," as it pleased him to call it. I told them I intended by no means to encourage their tricks; but as the prisoner had never broken his fast since yesterday's dinner, I would wink at his cheating Mr. Hindley that once. He went down; I set him a stool by the fire, and offered him a quantity of good things; but he was sick and could eat little, and my attempts to entertain him were thrown away. He leant his two elbows on his knees, and his chin on his hands, and remained wrapt in dumb meditation. On my inquiring the subject of his thoughts, he answered gravely—

"I'm trying to settle how I shall pay Hindley back. I don't care how long I wait, if I can only do it at last. I hope he will not die before I do!"

"For shame, Heathcliff!" said I. "It is for God to punish wicked people; we should learn to forgive."

"No, God won't have the satisfaction that I shall," he returned. "I only wish I knew the best way! Let me alone, and I'll plan it out: while I'm thinking of that I don't feel pain."

But, Mr. Lockwood, I forget these tales cannot divert

you. I'm annoyed how I should dream of chattering on at such a rate; and your gruel cold, and you nodding for bed! I could have told Heathcliff's history, all that you need hear, in half a dozen words. Thus interrupting herself, the housekeeper rose, and proceeded to lay aside her sewing; but I felt incapable of moving from the hearth, and I was very far from nodding. "Sit still, Mrs. Dean," I cried, "do sit still, another half hour! You've done just right to tell the story leisurely. That is the method I like; and you must finish in the same style. I am interested in every character you have mentioned, more or less."

"The clock is on the stroke of eleven, sir."

"No matter—I'm not accustomed to go to bed in the long hours. One or two is early enough for a person who lies till ten."

"You shouldn't lie till ten. There's the very prime of the morning gone long before that time. A person who has not done one half his day's work by ten o'clock, runs a chance of leaving the other half undone."

"Nevertheless, Mrs. Dean, resume your chair; because to-morrow I intend lengthening the night till afternoon. I prognosticate for myself an obstinate cold, at least."

"I hope not, sir. Well, you must allow me to leap over some three years, during that space Mrs. Earnshaw——"

"No, no, I'll allow nothing of the sort! Are you acquainted with the mood of mind in which, if you were seated alone, and the cat licking its kitten on the rug before you, you would watch the operation so intently that puss's neglect of one ear would put you seriously out of temper?"

"A terribly lazy mood, I should say."

"On the contrary, a tiresomely active one. It is mine, at present; and, therefore, continue minutely. I perceive that people in these regions acquire over people in towns the value that a spider in a dungeon does over a spider in a cottage, to their various occupants; and yet the deepened attraction is not entirely owing to the situation of the looker-on. They *do* live more in earnest, more in themselves, and less in surface, change, and frivolous external things. I could fancy a love for life here almost possible; and I was a fixed unbeliever in any love of a year's standing. One state resembles setting a hungry man down to a single dish, on which he may concentrate his entire appetite and do it justice; the other, introducing him to a table laid out by French cooks: he can perhaps extract as much enjoyment from the whole; but each part is a mere atom in his regard and remembrance."

" Oh! here we are the same as anywhere else, when you get to know us," observed Mrs. Dean, somewhat puzzled at my speech.

" Excuse me," I responded; " you, my good friend, are a striking evidence against that assertion. Excepting a few provincialisms of slight consequence, you have no marks of the manners which I am habituated to consider as peculiar to your class. I am sure you have thought a great deal more than the generality of servants think. You have been compelled to cultivate your reflective faculties for want of occasions for frittering your life away in silly trifles."

Mrs. Dean laughed.

" I certainly esteem myself a steady, reasonable kind of body," she said; " not exactly from living among the hills, and seeing one set of faces, and one series of actions, from year's end to year's end; but I have undergone sharp discipline, which has taught me wisdom: and then, I have read more than you would fancy, Mr. Lockwood. You could not open a book in this library that I have not looked into, and got something out of also: unless it be that range of Greek and Latin, and that of French; and those I know one from another: it is as much as you can expect of a poor man's daughter. However, if I am to follow my story in true gossip's fashion, I had better go on; and instead of leaping three years, I will be content to pass to the next summer— the summer of 1778, that is nearly twenty-three years ago."

CHAPTER VIII.

On the morning of a fine June day, my first bonny little nursling, and the last of the ancient Earnshaw stock was born. We were busy with the hay in a far away field, when the girl that usually brought our breakfasts, came running an hour too soon, across the meadow and up the lane, calling me as she ran.

"Oh, such a grand bairn!" she panted out. "The finest lad that ever breathed! But the doctor says missis must go: he says she's been in a consumption these many months. I heard him tell Mr. Hindley: and now she has nothing to keep her, and she'll be dead before winter. You must come home directly. You're to nurse it, Nelly: to feed it with sugar and milk, and take care of it day and night. I wish I were you, because it will be all yours when there is no missis!"

"But is she very ill?" I asked, flinging down my rake, and tying my bonnet.

"I guess she is; yet she looks bravely," replied the girl, "and she talks as if she thought of living to see it grow a man. She's out of her head for joy, it's such a beauty! If I were her, I'm certain I should not die: I should get better at the bare sight of it, in spite of Kenneth. I was fairly mad at him. Dame Archer brought the cherub down to master, in the house, and his face just began to light up, when the old croaker steps forward, and says he,—'Earnshaw, it's a blessing your wife has been spared to leave you this son. When she came, I felt convinced we shouldn't keep her long; and now, I must tell you, the winter will probably finish her. Don't take on, and fret about it too much: it can't be helped. And besides, you should have known better than to choose such a rush of a lass!'"

"And what did the master answer?" I inquired.

"I think he swore: but I didn't mind him, I was straining to see the bairn," and she began again to describe it rapturously. I, as zealous as herself, hurried eagerly home to admire, on my part; though I was very sad for Hindley's sake. He had room in his heart only for two idols—his wife and himself: he doted on both, and adored one, and I couldn't conceive how he would bear the loss.

When we got to Wuthering Heights, there he stood at the front door; and, as I passed in, I asked, how was the baby?"

"Nearly ready to run about, Nell!" he replied, putting on a cheerful smile.

"And the mistress?" I ventured to inquire; "the doctor says she's—"

"Damn the doctor!" he interrupted, reddening. "Frances is quite right: she'll be perfectly well by this time next week. Are you going up stairs? will you tell her that I'll come, if she'll promise not to talk. I left her because she would not hold her tongue; and she must—tell her Mr. Kenneth says she must be quiet."

I delivered this message to Mrs. Earnshaw; she seemed in flighty spirits, and replied merrily—

"I hardly spoke a word, Ellen, and there he has gone out twice, crying. Well, say I promise I won't speak: but that does not bind me not to laugh at him!"

Poor soul! Till within a week of her death that gay heart never failed her; and her husband persisted doggedly, nay, furiously, in affirming her health improved every day. When Kenneth warned him that his medicines were useless at that stage of the malady, and he needn't put him to further expense by attending her, he retorted—

"I know you need not—she's well—she does not want any more attendance from you! She never was in a consumption. It was a fever; and it is gone: her pulse is as slow as mine now, and her cheek as cool."

He told his wife the same story, and she seemed to believe him; but one night, while leaning on his shoulder, in the act of saying she thought she should be able to get up to-morrow, a fit of coughing took her—a very slight one—he raised her in his arms; she put her two hands about his neck, her face changed, and she was dead.

As the girl had anticipated, the child Hareton, fell wholly into my hands. Mr. Earnshaw, provided he saw him healthy and never heard him cry, was contented, as far as regarded him. For himself, he grew desperate: his sorrow was of that kind that will not lament. He neither wept nor prayed; he cursed and defied: execrated God and man, and gave himself up to reckless dissipation. The servants could not bear his tyrannical and evil conduct long: Joseph and I were the only two that would stay. I had not the heart to leave my charge; and besides, you know, I had been his foster-sister, and excused his behaviour more readily than a stranger would. Joseph remained to hector over tenants and labourers; and because it was his vocation to be where he had plenty of wickedness to reprove.

The master's bad ways and bad companions formed a pretty example for Catherine and Heathcliff. His treatment of the latter was enough to make a fiend of a saint. And, truly, it

appeared as if the lad *were* possessed of something diabolical
at that period. He delighted to witness Hindley degrading
himself past redemption; and became daily more notable for
savage sullenness and ferocity. I could not half tell what an
infernal house we had. The curate dropped calling, and
nobody decent came near us, at last; unless Edgar Linton's
visits to Miss Cathy might be an exception. At fifteen she
was the queen of the country-side: she had no peer; and she
did turn out a haughty, headstrong creature! I own I did
not like her, after her infancy was past; and I vexed her frequently by trying to bring down her arrogance: she never
took an aversion to me, though. She had a wondrous constancy to old attachments: even Heathcliff kept his hold on
her affections unalterably; and young Linton, with all his
superiority, found it difficult to make an equally deep impression. He was my late master: that is his portrait over the
fireplace. It used to hang on one side, and his wife's on the
other; but her's has been removed, or else you might see
something of what she was. Can you make that out?

Mrs. Dean raised the candle, and I discerned a soft-
featured face, exceedingly resembling the young lady at the
Heights, but more pensive and amiable in expression. It
formed a sweet picture. The long light hair curled slightly
on the temples; the eyes were large and serious; the figure
almost too graceful. I did not marvel how Catherine Earnshaw could forget her first friend for such an individual. I
marvelled much how he, with a mind to correspond with his
person, could fancy my idea of Catherine Earnshaw.

"A very agreeable portrait," I observed to the housekeeper. "Is it like?"

"Yes," she answered; "but he looked better when he was
animated; that is his everyday countenance: he wanted
spirit in general."

Catherine had kept up her acquaintance with the Lintons
since her five weeks' residence among them; and as she had
no temptation to show her rough side in their company, and
had the sense to be ashamed of being rude where she experienced such invariable courtesy, she imposed unwittingly on
the old lady and gentleman, by her ingenious cordiality;
gained the admiration of Isabella, and the heart and soul of
her brother: acquisitions that flattered her from the first,
for she was full of ambition, and led her to adopt a double

character without exactly intending to deceive any one. In the place where she heard Heathcliff termed a "vulgar young ruffian," and "worse than a brute," she took care not to act like him; but at home she had small inclination to practise politeness that would only be laughed at, and restrain an unruly nature when it would bring her neither credit nor praise.

Mr. Edgar seldom mustered courage to visit Wuthering Heights openly. He had a terror of Earnshaw's reputation, and shrunk from encountering him; and yet he was always received with our best attempts at civility: the master himself avoided offending him—knowing why he came; and if he could not be gracious, kept out of the way. I rather think his appearance there was distasteful to Catherine : she was not artful, never played the coquette, and had evidently an objection to her two friends meeting at all; for when Heathcliff expressed contempt of Linton in his presence, she could not half coincide, as she did in his absence; and when Linton evinced disgust and antipathy to Heathcliff, she dare not treat his sentiments with indifference, as if depreciation of her playmate were of scarcely any consequence to her. I've had many a laugh at her perplexities and untold troubles, which she vainly strove to hide from my mockery. That sounds ill-natured : but she was so proud, it became really impossible to pity her distresses, till she should be chastened into more humility. She did bring herself, finally, to confess, and to confide in me : there was not a soul else that she might fashion into an adviser.

Mr. Hindley had gone from home one afternoon, and Heathcliff presumed to give himself a holiday on the strength of it. He had reached the age of sixteen then, I think, and without having bad features or being deficient in intellect, he contrived to convey an impression of inward and outward repulsiveness that his present aspect retains no traces of. In the first place, he had, by that time, lost the benefit of his early education : continual hard work, begun soon and concluded late, had extinguished any curiosity he once possessed in pursuit of knowledge, and any love for books or learning. His childhood's sense of superiority, instilled into him by the favours of old Mr. Earnshaw, was faded away. He struggled long to keep up an equality with Catherine in her studies, and yielded with poignant though silent regret: but he yielded completely; and there was no prevailing on him to take a step in the way of moving upward, when he found he must, necessarily, sink beneath his former level. Then personal appearance sympathised with mental deterioration: he acquired a slouching gait, and ignoble look; his naturally reserved disposition was exaggerated into an almost idiotic excess of unsociable moroseness; and he took a grim pleasure, apparently, in exciting the aversion rather than the esteem of his few acquaintance.

Catherine and he were constant companions still at his seasons of respite from labour; but he had ceased to express his fondness for her in words, and recoiled with angry suspicion from her girlish caresses, as if conscious there could be no gratification in lavishing such marks of affection on him. On the before-named occasion he came into the house to announce his intention of doing nothing, while I was assisting Miss Cathy to arrange her dress: she had not reckoned on his taking it into his head to be idle; and, imagining she would have the whole place to herself, she managed, by some means, to inform Mr. Edgar of her brother's absence, and was then preparing to receive him.

"Cathy, are you busy, this afternoon?" asked Heathcliff. "Are you going anywhere?"

"No, it is raining," she answered.

"Why have you that silk frock on then?" he said. "Nobody coming here, I hope?"

"Not that I know of," stammered Miss: "but you should be in the field now, Heathcliff. It is an hour past dinner time: I thought you were gone."

"Hindley does not often free us from his accursed presence," observed the boy. "I'll not work any more to-day: I'll stay with you."

"Oh, but Joseph will tell," she suggested; "you'd better go!"

"Joseph is loading lime on the farther side of Pennistow Crag; it will take him till dark, and he'll never know."

So saying, he lounged to the fire, and sat down. Catherine reflected an instant, with knitted brows—she found it needful to smooth the way for an intrusion. "Isabella and Edgar Linton talked of calling this afternoon," she said, at the conclusion of a minute's silence. "As it rains, I hardly expect them ; but they may come, and if they do, you run the risk of being scolded for no good."

" Order Ellen to say you are engaged, Cathy," he persisted ; " don't turn me out for those pitiful, silly friends of yours! I 'm on the point, sometimes, of complaining that they—but I 'll not——"

" That they what ? " cried Catherine, gazing at him with a troubled countenance. " Oh, Nelly ! " she added petulantly, jerking her head away from my hands, " you 've combed my hair quite out of curl! That 's enough, let me alone. What are you on the point of complaining about, Heathcliff ? "

" Nothing—only look at the almanack on that wall ; " he pointed to a framed sheet hanging near the window, and continued—" The crosses are for the evenings you have spent with the Lintons, the dots for those spent with me. Do you see? I 've marked every day."

" Yes—very foolish : as if I took notice ! " replied Catherine, in a peevish tone. " And where is the sense of that ? "

" To show that I *do* take notice," said Heathcliff.

" And should I always be sitting with you ? " she demanded, growing more irritated. " What good do I get? What do you talk about? You might be dumb, or a baby, for anything you say to amuse me, or for anything you do, either ! "

" You never told me before that I talked too little, or that you disliked my company, Cathy ! " exclaimed Heathcliff in much agitation.

" It is no company at all, when people know nothing and say nothing," she muttered.

Her companion rose up, but he hadn't time to express his feelings further, for a horse's feet were heard on the flags, and, having knocked gently, young Linton entered, his face brilliant with delight at the unexpected summons he had received. Doubtless Catherine marked the difference between her friends, as one came in and the other went out. The contrast resembled what you see in exchanging a bleak, hilly, coal country for a beautiful fertile valley ; and his voice and greeting were as opposite as his aspect. He had a sweet, low manner of speaking, and pronounced his words as you do : that's less gruff than we talk here, and softer.

" I 'm not come too soon, am I ? " he said, casting a look

at me: I had begun to wipe the plate, and tidy some drawers at the far end in the dresser.

" No," answered Catherine. " What are you doing there, Nelly?"

" My work, Miss," I replied. (Mr. Hindley had given me directions to make a third party in any private visits Linton chose to pay.)

She stepped behind me and whispered crossly, " Take yourself and your dusters off; when company are in the house, servants don't commence scouring and cleaning in the room where they are!"

" It's a good opportunity, now that master is away," I answered aloud: " he hates me to be fidgeting over these things in his presence. I'm sure Mr. Edgar will excuse me."

" I hate you to be fidgeting in *my* presence," exclaimed the young lady imperiously, not allowing her guest time to speak: she had failed to recover her equanimity since the little dispute with Heathcliff.

" I'm sorry for it, Miss Catherine!" was my response; and I proceeded assiduously with my occupation.

She, supposing Edgar could not see her, snatched the cloth from my hand, and pinched me, with a prolonged wrench, very spitefully on the arm. I've said I did not love her, and rather relished mortifying her vanity now and then: besides, she hurt me extremely; so I started up from my knees, and screamed out, " Oh, Miss, that's a nasty trick! You have no right to nip me, and I'm not going to bear it."

" I didn't touch you, you lying creature!" cried she, her fingers tingling to repeat the act, and her ears red with rage. She never had power to conceal her passion, it always set her whole complexion in a blaze.

" What's that, then?" I retorted, showing a decided purple witness to refute her.

She stamped her foot, wavered a moment, and then, irresistibly impelled by the naughty spirit within her, slapped me on the cheek: a stinging blow that filled both eyes with water.

" Catherine, love! Catherine!" interposed Linton, greatly shocked at the double fault of falsehood and violence which his idol had committed.

"Leave the room, Ellen!" she repeated trembling all over.

Little Hareton, who followed me everywhere, and was sitting near me on the floor, at seeing my tears commenced crying himself, and sobbed out complaints against "wicked aunt Cathy," which drew her fury on to his unlucky head: she seized his shoulders, and shook him till the poor child waxed livid, and Edgar thoughtlessly laid hold of her hands to deliver him. In an instant one was wrung free, and the astonished young man felt it applied over his own ear in a way that could not be mistaken for jest. He drew back in consternation. I lifted Hareton in my arms, and walked off to the kitchen with him, leaving the door of communication open, for I was curious to watch how they would settle their disagreement. The insulted visitor moved to the spot where he had laid his hat, pale and with a quivering lip.

"That's right!" I said to myself. "Take warning and begone! It's a kindness to let you have a glimpse of her genuine disposition."

"Where are you going?" demanded Catherine, advancing to the door.

He swerved aside, and attempted to pass.

"You must not go!" she exclaimed, energetically.

"I must and shall!" he replied in a subdued voice.

"No," she persisted, grasping the handle; "not yet, Edgar Linton: sit down, you shall not leave me in that temper. I should be miserable all night, and I won't be miserable for you!"

"Can I stay after you have struck me?" asked Linton.

Catherine was mute.

"You've made me afraid and ashamed of you," he continued; "I'll not come here again!"

Her eyes began to glisten, and her lids to twinkle.

"And you told a deliberate untruth!" he said.

"I didn't!" she cried, recovering her speech; "I did nothing deliberately. Well, go, if you please—get away! And now I'll cry—I'll cry myself sick!"

She dropped down on her knees by a chair, and set to weeping in serious earnest. Edgar persevered in his resolution as far as the court; there he lingered. I resolved to encourage him.

"Miss is dreadfully wayward, sir," I called out. "As

bad as any marred child : you'd better be riding home, or
else she will be sick, only to grieve us."

The soft thing looked askance through the window : he
possessed the power to depart, as much as a cat possesses
the power to leave a mouse half killed, or a bird half eaten.
Ah, I thought, there will be no saving him : he's doomed,
and flies to his fate ! And so it was : he turned abruptly,
hastened into the house again, shut the door behind him ;
and when I went in a while after to inform them that Earnshaw had come home rabid drunk, ready to pull the old
place about our ears (his ordinary frame of mind in that
condition), I saw the quarrel had merely effected a closer
intimacy—had broken the outworks of youthful timidity,
and enabled them to forsake the disguise of friendship, and
confess themselves lovers.

Intelligence of Mr. Hindley's arrival drove Linton speedily
to his horse, and Catherine to her chamber. I went to
hide little Hareton, and to take the shot out of the master's
fowling-piece ; which he was fond of playing with in his
insane excitement, to the hazard of the lives of any who
provoked, or even attracted his notice too much ; and I had
hit upon the plan of removing it, that he might do less mischief if he did go the length of firing the gun.

CHAPTER IX.

HE entered, vociferating oaths dreadful to hear ; and caught
me in the act of stowing his son away in the kitchen cupboard. Hareton was impressed with a wholesome terror of
encountering either his wild-beast's fondness or his madman's
rage ; for in one he ran a chance of being squeezed and
kissed to death, and in the other of being flung into the fire,
or dashed against the wall ; and the poor thing remained
perfectly quiet wherever I chose to put him.

"There, I've found it out at last !" cried Hindley, pulling
me back by the skin of my neck, like a dog. "By heaven
and hell, you've sworn between you to murder that child !
I know how it is, now, that he is always out of my way.

But, with the help of Satan, I shall make you swallow the carving knife, Nelly! You needn't laugh; for I've just crammed Kenneth, head-downmost, in the Blackhorse marsh; and two is the same as one—and I want to kill some of you: I shall have no rest till I do!"

"But I don't like the carving knife, Mr. Hindley," I answered; "it has been cutting red herrings. I'd rather be shot, if you please."

"You'd rather be damned!" he said; "and so you shall. No law in England can hinder a man from keeping his house decent, and mine's abominable! open your mouth."

He held the knife in his hand, and pushed its point between my teeth: but, for my part, I was never much afraid of his vagaries. I spat out, and affirmed it tasted detestably—I would not take it on any account.

"Oh!" said he, releasing me, "I see that hideous little villain is not Hareton: I beg your pardon, Nell. If it be, he deserves flaying alive for not running to welcome me, and for screaming as if I were a goblin. Unnatural cub, come hither! I'll teach thee to impose on a good-hearted, deluded father. Now, don't you think the lad would be handsomer cropped? It makes a dog fiercer, and I love something fierce—get me a scissors—something fierce and trim! Besides, it's infernal affectation—devilish conceit it is, to cherish our ears—we're asses enough without them. Hush, child, hush! Well then, it is my darling! wisht, dry thy eyes—there's a joy; kiss me. What! it won't? Kiss me, Hareton! Damn thee, kiss me! By God, as if I would rear such a monster! As sure as I'm living, I'll break the brat's neck."

Poor Hareton was squalling and kicking in his father's arms with all his might, and redoubled his yells when he carried him up stairs and lifted him over the banister. I cried out that he would frighten the child into fits, and ran to rescue him. As I reached them, Hindley leant forward on the rails to listen to a noise below; almost forgetting what he had in his hands. "Who is that?" he asked, hearing some one approaching the stair's foot. I leant forward also, for the purpose of signing to Heathcliff, whose step I recognised, not to come further; and, at the instant when my eye quitted Hareton, he gave a sudden spring, delivered himself from the careless grasp that held him, and fell.

There was scarcely time to experience a thrill of horror before we saw that the little wretch was safe. Heathcliff arrived underneath just at the critical moment; by a natural impulse, he arrested his descent, and setting him on his feet, looked up to discover the author of the accident. A miser who has parted with a lucky lottery ticket for five shillings, and finds next day he has lost in the bargain five thousand pounds, could not show a blanker countenance than he did on beholding the figure of Mr. Earnshaw above. It expressed, plainer than words could do, the intensest anguish at having made himself the instrument of thwarting his own revenge. Had it been dark, I dare say, he would have tried to remedy the mistake by smashing Hareton's skull on the steps; but, we witnessed his salvation; and I was presently below with my precious charge pressed to my heart. Hindley descended more leisurely, sobered and abashed.

"It is your fault, Ellen," he said; "you should have kept him out of sight: you should have taken him from me! Is he injured anywhere?"

"Injured!" I cried angrily; "if he's not killed, he'll be an idiot! Oh! I wonder his mother does not rise from her grave to see how you use him. You're worse than a heathen—treating your own flesh and blood in that manner!"

He attempted to touch the child, who, on finding himself with me, sobbed off his terror directly. At the first finger his father laid on him, however, he shrieked again louder than before, and struggled as if he would go into convulsions.

"You shall not meddle with him!" I continued, "He hates you—they all hate you—that's the truth! A happy family you have; and a pretty state you're come to!"

"I shall come to a prettier, yet! Nelly," laughed the misguided man, recovering his hardness. "At present, convey yourself and him away. And, hark you, Heathcliff! clear you too, quite from my reach and hearing. I wouldn't murder you to-night; unless, perhaps, I set the house on fire: but that's as my fancy goes."

While saying this he took a pint bottle of brandy from the dresser, and poured some into a tumbler.

"Nay, don't!" I entreated. "Mr. Hindley, do take warning. Have mercy on this unfortunate boy, if you care nothing for yourself!"

"Any one will do better for him, than I shall," he answered.

"Have mercy on your own soul!" I said, endeavouring to snatch the glass from his hand.

"Not I! On the contrary, I shall have great pleasure in sending it to perdition, to punish its Maker," exclaimed the blasphemer. "Here's to its hearty damnation!"

He drank the spirits, and impatiently bade us go; terminating his command with a sequel of horrid imprecations, too bad to repeat or remember.

"It's a pity he cannot kill himself with drink," observed Heathcliff, muttering an echo of curses back when the door was shut. "He's doing his very utmost; but his constitution defies him. Mr. Kenneth says, he would wager his mare, that he'll outlive any man on this side Gimmerton, and go to the grave a hoary sinner; unless some happy chance out of the common course befall him."

I went into the kitchen and sat down to lull my little lamb to sleep. Heathcliff, as I thought, walked through to the barn. It turned out afterwards that he only got as far as the other side the settle, when he flung himself on a bench by the wall, removed from the fire, and remained silent.

I was rocking Hareton on my knee, and humming a song that began,—

> "It was far in the night, and the bairnies grat,
> The mither beneath the mools heard that,"

when Miss Cathy, who had listened to the hubbub from her room, put her head in, and whispered,—

"Are you alone, Nelly?"

"Yes, Miss," I replied.

She entered and approached the hearth. I, supposing she was going to say something, looked up. The expression of her face seemed disturbed and anxious. Her lips were half asunder, as if she meant to speak, and she drew a breath; but it escaped in a sigh instead of a sentence. I resumed my song; not having forgotten her recent behaviour.

"Where's Heathcliff?" she said, interrupting me.

"About his work in the stable," was my answer.

He did not contradict me; perhaps he had fallen into a

F

doze. There followed another long pause, during which I perceived a drop or two trickle from Catherine's cheek to the flags. Is she sorry for her shameful conduct? I asked myself. That will be a novelty : but she may come to the point as she will—I sha'n't help her! No, she felt small trouble regarding any subject, save her own concerns.

"Oh, dear!" she cried at last. "I'm very unhappy!"

"A pity," observed I. "You're hard to please : so many friends and so few cares, and can't make yourself content!"

"Nelly, will you keep a secret for me?" she pursued, kneeling down by me, and lifting her winsome eyes to my face with that sort of look which turns off bad temper, even when one has all the right in the world to indulge it.

"Is it worth keeping?" I inquired, less sulkily.

"Yes, and it worries me, and I must let it out! I want to know what I should do. To-day, Edgar Linton has asked me to marry him, and I've given him an answer. Now, before I tell you whether it was a consent or denial, you tell me which it ought to have been."

"Really, Miss Catherine, how can I know?" I replied. "To be sure, considering the exhibition you performed in his presence this afternoon, I might say it would be wise to refuse him : since he asked you after that, he must either be hopelessly stupid or a venturesome fool."

"If you talk so, I won't tell you any more," she returned peevishly, rising to her feet. "I accepted him, Nelly. Be quick, and say whether I was wrong!"

"You accepted him! then, what good is it discussing the matter? You have pledged your word, and cannot retract."

"But, say whether I should have done so—do!" she exclaimed in an irritated tone; chafing her hands together, and frowning.

"There are many things to be considered before that question can be answered properly," I said, sententiously. "First and foremost, do you love Mr. Edgar?"

"Who can help it? Of course I do," she answered.

Then I put her through the following catechism : for a girl of twenty-two, it was not injudicious.

"Why do you love him, Miss Cathy?"

"Nonsense, I do—that's sufficient."

"By no means; you must say why?"

"Well, because he is handsome, and pleasant to be with."

" Bad ! was my commentary."

" And because he is young and cheerful."

" Bad, still."

" And because he loves me."

" Indifferent, coming there."

" And he will be rich, and I shall like to be the greatest woman of the neighbourhood, and I shall be proud of having such a husband."

" Worst of all !   And now, say how you love him ?"

" As everybody loves—You 're silly, Nelly."

" Not at all—Answer."

" I love the ground under his feet, and the air over his head, and everything he touches, and every word he says. I love all his looks, and all his actions, and him entirely and altogether.   There now !"

" And why ?"

" Nay ; you are making a jest of it : it is exceedingly ill-natured !   It 's no jest to me !" said the young lady scowling, and turning her face to the fire.

" I 'm very far from jesting, Miss Catherine," I replied. " You love Mr. Edgar because he is handsome, and young, and cheerful, and rich, and loves you.   The last, however, goes for nothing : you would love him without that, probably ; and with it you wouldn't, unless he possessed the four former attractions."

" No, to be sure not : I should only pity him—hate him, perhaps, if he were ugly, and a clown."

" But there are several other handsome, rich young men in the world : handsomer, possibly, and richer than he is. What should hinder you from loving them ?"

" If there be any, they are out of my way : I 've seen none like Edgar."

" You may see some ; and he won't always be handsome, and young, and may not always be rich."

" He is now ; and I have only to do with the present.   I wish you would speak rationally."

" Well, that settles it : if you have only to do with the present, marry Mr. Linton."

" I don't want your permission for that—I *shall* marry him : and yet you have not told me whether I 'm right."

" Perfectly right ; if people be right to marry only for the present.   And now, let us hear what you are unhappy about.

Your brother will be pleased; the old lady and gentleman will not object, I think; you will escape from a disorderly, comfortless home into a wealthy respectable one; and you love Edgar, and Edgar loves you. All seems smooth and easy : where is the obstacle?"

"*Here!* and *here!*" replied Catherine, striking one hand on her forehead, and the other on her breast: "in whichever place the soul lives. In my soul and in my heart, I 'm convinced I 'm wrong!"

"That 's very strange! I cannot make it out."

"It 's my secret. But if you will not mock at me, I 'll explain it: I can't do it distinctly; but I 'll give you a feeling of how I feel."

She seated herself by me again: her countenance grew sadder and graver, and her clasped hands trembled.

"Nelly, do you never dream queer dreams?" she said, suddenly, after some minutes' reflection.

"Yes, now and then," I answered.

"And so do I. I 've dreamt in my life dreams that have stayed with me ever after, and changed my ideas: they 've gone through and through me, like wine through water, and altered the colour of my mind. And this is one : I 'm going to tell it—but take care not to smile at any part of it."

"Oh! don't, Miss Catherine!" I cried. "We 're dismal enough without conjuring up ghosts and visions to perplex us. Come, come, be merry and like yourself! Look at little Hareton! *he 's* dreaming nothing dreary. How sweetly he smiles in his sleep!"

"Yes; and how sweetly his father curses in his solitude! You remember him, I dare say, when he was just such another as that chubby thing: nearly as young and innocent. However, Nelly, I shall oblige you to listen: it 's not long; and I 've no power to be merry to-night."

"I won't hear it, I won't hear it!" I repeated, hastily.

I was superstitious about dreams then, and am still; and Catherine had an unusual gloom in her aspect, that made me dread something from which I might shape a prophecy, and foresee a fearful catastrophe. She was vexed, but she did not proceed. Apparently taking up another subject, she recommenced in a short time.

"If I were in heaven, Nelly, I should be extremely miserable."

"Because you are not fit to go there," I answered. "All sinners would be miserable in heaven."

"But it is not for that. I dreamt once that I was there."

"I tell you I won't hearken to your dreams, Miss Catherine! I'll go to bed," I interrupted again.

She laughed, and held me down; for I made a motion to leave my chair.

"This is nothing," cried she: "I was only going to say that heaven did not seem to be my home; and I broke my heart with weeping to come back to earth; and the angels were so angry that they flung me out into the middle of the heath on the top of Wuthering Heights; where I woke sobbing for joy. That will do to explain my secret, as well as the other. I've no more business to marry Edgar Linton than I have to be in heaven; and if the wicked man in there had not brought Heathcliff so low, I shouldn't have thought of it. It would degrade me to marry Heathcliff now; so he shall never know how I love him: and that, no, because he's handsome, Nelly, but because he's more myself than I am. Whatever our souls are made of, his and mine are the same; and Linton's is as different as a moonbeam from lightning, or frost from fire."

Ere this speech ended, I became sensible of Heathcliff's presence. Having noticed a slight movement, I turned my head, and saw him rise from the bench, and steal out noiselessly. He had listened till he heard Catherine say it would degrade her to marry him, and then he staid to hear no farther. My companion, sitting on the ground, was prevented by the back of the settle from remarking his presence or departure; but I started, and bade her hush!

"Why?" she asked, gazing nervously round.

"Joseph is here," I answered, catching opportunely the roll of his cartwheels up the road; "and Heathcliff will come in with him. I'm not sure whether he were not at the door this moment."

"Oh, he couldn't overhear me at the door!" said she. "Give me Hareton, while you get the supper, and when it is ready ask me to sup with you. I want to cheat my uncomfortable conscience, and be convinced that Heathcliff has no notion of these things. He has not, has he? He does not know what being in love is?"

"I see no reason that he should not know, as well as you," I returned; "and if *you* are his choice, he'll be the most unfortunate creature that ever was born! As soon as you become Mrs. Linton, he loses friend, and love, and all! Have you considered how you'll bear the separation, and how he'll bear to be quite deserted in the world? Because, Miss Catherine——"

"He quite deserted! we separated!" she exclaimed, with an accent of indignation. "Who is to separate us, pray? They'll meet the fate of Milo! Not as long as I live, Ellen: for no mortal creature. Every Linton on the face of the earth might melt into nothing, before I could consent to forsake Heathcliff. Oh, that's not what I intend— that's not what I mean! I shouldn't be Mrs. Linton were such a price demanded! He'll be as much to me as he has been all his lifetime. Edgar must shake off his antipathy, and tolerate him, at least. He will, when he learns my true feelings towards him. Nelly, I see now, you think me a selfish wretch; but did it never strike you that if Heathcliff and I married, we should be beggars? whereas, if I marry Linton, I can aid Heathcliff to rise, and place him out of my brother's power."

"With your husband's money, Miss Catherine?" I asked. "You'll find him not so pliable as you calculate upon: and, though I'm hardly a judge, I think that's the worst motive you've given yet for being the wife of young Linton."

"It is not," retorted she; "it is the best! The others were the satisfaction of my whims; and for Edgar's sake, too, to satisfy him. This is for the sake of one who comprehends in his person my feelings to Edgar and myself. I cannot express it; but surely you and everybody have a notion that there is or should be an existence of yours beyond you. What were the use of my creation if I were entirely contained here? My great miseries in this world have been Heathcliff's miseries, and I watched and felt each from the beginning: my great thought in living is himself. If all else perished, and *he* remained, *I* should still continue to be; and if all else remained, and he were annihilated, the universe would turn to a mighty stranger: I should not seem a part of it. My love for Linton is like the foliage in the woods: time will change it, I'm well aware, as winter changes the trees. My love for Heathcliff resembles the eternal rocks beneath: a source of little visible delight, but necessary. Nelly, I *am* Heathcliff! He's always, always in my mind: not as a pleasure, any more than I am always a pleasure to myself, but as my own being. So don't talk of our separation again: it is impracticable; and——"

She paused, and hid her face in the folds of my gown; but I jerked it forcibly away. I was out of patience with her folly!

"If I can make any sense of your nonsense, Miss," I said, "it only goes to convince me that you are ignorant of the duties you undertake in marrying; or else that you are a wicked, unprincipled girl. But trouble me with no more secrets: I'll not promise to keep them."

"You'll keep that?" she asked, eagerly.

"No, I'll not promise," I repeated.

She was about to insist, when the entrance of Joseph finished our conversation; and Catherine removed her seat to a corner, and nursed Hareton, while I made the supper. After it was cooked, my fellow-servant and I began to quarrel who should carry some to Mr. Hindley; and we didn't settle it till all was nearly cold. Then we came to the agreement that we would let him ask, if he wanted any; for we feared particularly to go into his presence when he had been some time alone.

"And how isn't that nowt comed in fro' th' field, be this time? What is he about? girt idle seeght!" demanded the old man, looking round for Heathcliff.

"I'll call him," I replied. "He's in the barn, I've no doubt."

I went and called, but got no answer. On returning, I whispered to Catherine that he had heard a good part of what she said, I was sure; and told how I saw him quit the kitchen just as she complained of her brother's conduct regarding him. She jumped up in a fine fright, flung Hareton on to the settle, and ran to seek for her friend herself; not taking leisure to consider why she was so flurried, or how her talk would have affected him. She was absent such a while that Joseph proposed we should wait no longer. He cunningly conjectured they were staying away in order to avoid hearing his protracted blessing. They were "ill eneugh for ony fahl manners," he affirmed. And on their behalf he added that night a special prayer to the usual quarter of an hour's supplication before meat, and would have tacked another to the end of the grace, had not his young mistress broken in upon him with a hurried command that he must run down the road, and, wherever Heathcliff had rambled, find and make him re-enter directly!"

"I want to speak to him, and I *must*, before I go up stairs," she said. "And the gate is open: he is somewhere out of hearing; for he would not reply, though I shouted at the top of the fold as loud as I could."

Joseph objected at first; she was too much in earnest, however, to suffer contradiction; and at last he placed his hat on his head, and walked grumbling forth. Meantime, Catherine paced up and down the floor, exclaiming—

"I wonder where he is—I wonder where he *can* be! What did I say, Nelly? I've forgotten. Was he vexed at my bad humour this afternoon? Dear! tell me what I've said to grieve him? I do wish he'd come. I do wish he would!"

"What a noise for nothing!" I cried, though rather uneasy myself. "What a trifle scares you! It's surely no great cause of alarm that Heathcliff should take a moonlight saunter on the moors, or even lie too sulky to speak to us in the hay-loft. I'll engage he's lurking there. See if I don't ferret him out!"

I departed to renew my search; its result was disappointment, and Joseph's quest ended in the same.

"Yon lad gets war un war!" observed he on re-entering. "He's left th' yate at t' full swing, and Miss's pony has trodden dahn two rigs o' corn, and plottered through, raight o'er into t' meadow! Hahsomdiver, t' maister 'ull play t' divil to-morn, and he'll do weel. He's patience itsseln wi' sich careless, offald craters—patience itsseln he is! Bud he'll not be soa allus—yah's see, all on ye! Yah mumn't drive him out of his heead for nowt!"

"Have you found Heathcliff, you ass?" interrupted Catherine. "Have you been looking for him, as I ordered?"

"I sud more likker look for th' horse," he replied. "It 'ud be to more sense. Bud, I can look for norther horse nur man of a neeght loike this—as black as t' chimbley! und

Heathcliff's noan t' chap to coom at *my* whistle—happen he'll be less hard o' hearing wi' *ye !*"

It *was* a very dark evening for summer: the clouds appeared inclined to thunder, and I said we had better all sit down; the approaching rain would be certain to bring him home without further trouble. However, Catherine would not be persuaded into tranquillity. She kept wandering to and fro, from the gate to the door, in a state of agitation which permitted no repose ; and at length took up a permanent situation on one side of the wall, near the road: where, heedless of my expostulations and the growling thunder, and the great drops that began to plash around her, she remained, calling at intervals, and then listening, and then crying outright. She beat Hareton, or any child, at a good passionate fit of crying.

About midnight, while we still sat up, the storm came rattling over the Heights in full fury. There was a violent wind, as well as thunder, and either one or the other split a tree off at the corner of the building: a huge bough fell across the roof, and knocked down a portion of the east chimney-stack, sending a clatter of stones and soot into the kitchen fire. We thought a bolt had fallen in the middle of us ; and Joseph swung on to his knees, beseeching the Lord to remember the patriarchs Noah and Lot, and, as in former times, spare the righteous, though he smote the ungodly. I felt some sentiment that it must be a judgment on us also. The Jonah, in my mind, was Mr. Earnshaw ; and I shook the handle of his den that I might ascertain if he were yet living. He replied audibly enough, in a fashion which made my companion vociferate, more clamorously than before, that a wide distinction might be drawn between saints like himself and sinners like his master. But the uproar passed away in twenty minutes, leaving us all unharmed : excepting Cathy, who got thoroughly drenched for her obstinacy in refusing to take shelter, and standing bonnetless and shawlless to catch as much water as she could with her hair and clothes. She came in and lay down on the settle, all soaked as she was, turning her face to the back, and putting her hands before it.

" Well, Miss !" I exclaimed, touching her shoulder ; " you are not bent on getting your death, are you ? Do you know what o'clock it is ? Half-past twelve. Come, come to bed !

there's no use waiting longer on that foolish boy : he'll be
gone to Gimmerton, and he'll stay there now. He guesses
we shouldn't wake for him till this late hour : at least, he
guesses that only Mr. Hindley would be up ; and he'd rather
avoid having the door opened by the master."

" Nay, nay, he's noan at Gimmerton," said Joseph.
" I 's niver wonder but he's at t' bothom of a bog-hoile.
This visitation worn't for nowt, and I wod hev ye to look
out, Miss—yah muh be t' next. Thank Hivin for all ! All
warks togither for gooid to them as is chozzen, and piked
out fro' th' rubbidge ! Yah knaw whet t' Scripture ses."
And he began quoting several texts, referring us to chapters
and verses where we might find them.

I, having vainly begged the wilful girl to rise and remove
her wet things, left him preaching and her shivering, and
betook myself to bed with little Hareton, who slept as fast
as if every one had been sleeping round him. I heard
Joseph read on a while afterwards ; then I distinguished his
slow step on the ladder, and then I dropped asleep.

Coming down somewhat later than usual, I saw, by the
sunbeams piercing the chinks of the shutters, Miss Catherine
still seated near the fire-place. The house door was ajar,
too ; light entered from its unclosed windows ; Hindley had
come out, and stood on the kitchen hearth, haggard and
drowsy.

" What ails you, Cathy ?" he was saying when I entered :
" You look as dismal as a drowned whelp. Why are you
so damp and pale, child ?"

" I've been wet," she answered reluctantly, " and I'm
cold, that's all."

" Oh, she is naughty !" I cried, perceiving the master to
be tolerably sober. " She got steeped in the shower of yesterday evening, and there she has sat the night through, and
I couldn't prevail on her to stir."

Mr. Earnshaw stared at us in surprise. " The night
through," he repeated. " What kept her up ? not fear of
the thunder, surely ? That was over hours since."

Neither of us wished to mention Heathcliff's absence, as
long as we could conceal it ; so I replied, I didn't know
how she took it into her head to sit up ; and she said
nothing. The morning was fresh and cool ; I threw back
the lattice, and presently the room filled with sweet scents

from the garden; but Catherine called peevishly to me, " Ellen, shut the window. I'm starving!" And her teeth chattered as she shrunk closer to the almost extinguished embers.

" She's ill," said Hindley, taking her wrist; " I suppose that's the reason she would not go to bed. Damn it! I don't want to be troubled with more sickness here. What took you into the rain?"

" Running after t'lads, as usuald!" croaked Joseph, catching an opportunity, from our hesitation, to thrust in his evil tongue. " If I war yah, maister, I'd just slam t'boards i' their faces all on 'em, gentle and simple! Never a day ut yah're off, but yon cat o' Linton comes sneaking hither; and Miss Nelly, shoo's a fine lass! shoo sits watching for ye i' t'kitchen; and as yah're in at one door, he's out at t'other; and, then, wer grand lady goes a coorting of her side? It's bonny behaviour, lurking amang t'fields, after twelve ot' night, wi that fahl, flaysome divil of a gipsy, Heathcliff! They think *I'm* blind; but I'm noan: no'wt ut t'soart! —I seed young Linton boath coming and going, and I seed *yah* (directing his discourse to me), yah gooid fur nowt, slattenly witch! nip up and bolt into th' house, t' minute yah heard t'maister's horse fit clatter up t' road."

" Silence, eavesdropper!" cried Catherine; " none of your insolence before me! Edgar Linton came yesterday by chance, Hindley; and it was *I* who told him to be off: because I knew you would not like to have met him as you were."

" You lie, Cathy, no doubt," answered her brother, " and you are a confounded simpleton! But never mind Linton at present: tell me, were you not with Heathcliff last night? Speak the truth, now. You need not be afraid of harming him: though I hate him as much as ever, he did me a good turn a short time since, that will make my conscience tender of breaking his neck. To prevent it, I shall send him about his business, this very morning; and after he's gone, I'd advise you all to look sharp: I shall only have the more humour for you."

" I never saw Heathcliff last night," answered Catherine, beginning to sob bitterly: " and if you do turn him out of doors, I'll go with him. But, perhaps, you'll never have an opportunity: perhaps, he's gone." Here she burst into uncontrollable grief, and the remainder of her words were inarticulate.

Hindley lavished on her a torrent of scornful abuse, and bade her get to her room immediately, or she shouldn't cry for nothing! I obliged her to obey; and I shall never forget what a scene she acted when we reached her chamber: it terrified me. I thought she was going mad, and I begged Joseph to run for the doctor. It proved the commencement of delirium: Mr. Kenneth, as soon as he saw her, pronounced her dangerously ill; she had a fever. He bled her, and he told me to let her live on whey and water gruel, and take care she did not throw herself down stairs or out of the window; and then he left: for he had enough to do in the parish, where two or three miles was the ordinary distance between cottage and cottage.

Though I cannot say I made a gentle nurse, and Joseph and the master were no better; and though our patient was as wearisome and headstrong as a patient could be, she weathered it through. Old Mrs. Linton paid us several visits, to be sure, and set things to rights, and scolded and ordered us all; and when Catherine was convalescent, she insisted on conveying her to Thrushcross Grange: for which deliverance we were very grateful. But the poor dame had reason to repent of her kindness: she and her husband both took the fever, and died within a few days of each other.

Our young lady returned to us, saucier and more passionate, and haughtier than ever. Heathcliff had never been heard of since the evening of the thunder-storm; and, one day I had the misfortune, when she had provoked me exceedingly, to lay the blame of his disappearance on her: where indeed it belonged, as she well knew. From that period, for several months, she ceased to hold any communication with me, save in the relation of a mere servant. Joseph fell under a ban also: he *would* speak his mind, and lecture her all the same as if she were a little girl; and she esteemed herself a woman, and our mistress, and thought that her recent illness gave her a claim to be treated with consideration. Then the doctor had said that she would not bear crossing much; she ought to have her own way; and it was nothing less than murder, in her eyes, for any one to presume to stand up and contradict her. From Mr. Earnshaw and his companions she kept aloof; and tutored by

Kenneth, and serious threats of a fit that often attended her rages, her brother allowed her whatever she pleased to demand, and generally avoided aggravating her fiery temper. He was rather *too* indulgent in humouring her caprices; not from affection, but from pride : he wished earnestly to see her bring honour to the family by an alliance with the Lintons, and as long as she let him alone she might trample on us like slaves, for aught he cared ! Edgar Linton, as multitudes have been before and will be after him, was infatuated; and believed himself the happiest man alive on the day he led her to Gimmerton chapel, three years subsequent to his father's death.

Much against my inclination, I was persuaded to leave Wuthering Heights and accompany her here. Little Hareton was nearly five years old, and I had just begun to teach him his letters. We made a sad parting; but Catherine's tears were more powerful than ours. When I refused to go, and when she found her entreaties did not move me, she went lamenting to her husband and brother. The former offered me munificent wages; the latter ordered me to pack up: he wanted no women in the house, he said, now that there was no mistress; and as to Hareton, the curate should take him in hand, by-and-bye. And so I had but one choice left: to do as I was ordered. I told the master he got rid of all decent people only to run to ruin a little faster; I kissed Hareton, said good-bye; and since then he has been a stranger : and it's very queer to think it, but I've no doubt he has completely forgotten all about Ellen Dean, and that he was ever more than all the world to her, and she to him !

At this point of the housekeeper's story, she chanced to glance towards the time-piece over the chimney; and was in amazement on seeing the minute-hand measure half-past one. She would not hear of staying a second longer : in truth, I felt rather disposed to defer the sequel of her narrative, myself. And now that she is vanished to her rest, and I have meditated for another hour or two, I shall summon courage to go, also, in spite of aching laziness of head and limbs.

CHAPTER X.

A CHARMING introduction to a hermit's life! Four weeks' torture, tossing and sickness! Oh, these bleak winds and bitter northern skies, and impassable roads, and dilatory country surgeons! And, oh, this dearth of the human physiognomy! and, worse than all, the terrible intimation of Kenneth that I need not expect to be out of doors till spring!

Mr. Heathcliff has just honoured me with a call. About seven days ago he sent me a brace of grouse—the last of the season. Scoundrel! He is not altogether guiltless in this illness of mine; and that I had a great mind to tell him. But, alas! how could I offend a man who was charitable enough to sit at my bedside a good hour, and talk on some other subject than pills, and draughts, blisters, and leeches? This is quite an easy interval. I am too weak to read, yet I feel as if I could enjoy something interesting. Why not have up Mrs. Dean to finish her tale? I can recollect its chief incidents, as far as she had gone. Yes: I remember her hero had run off, and never been heard of for three years; and the heroine was married. I'll ring: she'll be delighted to find me capable of talking cheerfully. Mrs. Dean came.

" It wants twenty minutes, sir, to taking the medicine," she commenced.

" Away, away with it!" I replied; " I desire to have——"

" The doctor says you must drop the powders."

" With all my heart! Don't interrupt me. Come and take your seat here. Keep your fingers from that bitter phalanx of vials. Draw your knitting out of your pocket—that will do—now continue the history of Mr. Heathcliff, from where you left off, to the present day. Did he finish his education on the Continent, and come back a gentleman? or did he get a sizer's place at college, or escape to America and earn honours by drawing blood from his foster country? Or make a fortune more promptly, on the English high-ways?"

" He may have done a little in all these vocations, Mr. Lockwood; but I couldn't give my word for any. I stated

before that I didn't know how he gained his money ; neither
am I aware of the means he took to raise his mind from the
savage ignorance into which it was sunk : but, with your
leave, I'll proceed in my own fashion, if you think it will
amuse and not weary you. Are you feeling better this
morning ? "

" Much."

" That's good news. I got Miss Catherine and myself to
Thrushcross Grange ; and, to my agreeable disappointment,
she behaved infinitely better than I dared to expect. She
seemed almost over fond of Mr. Linton ; and even to his
sister, she showed plenty of affection. They were both very
attentive to her comfort, certainly. It was not the thorn
bending to the honeysuckles, but the honeysuckles em-
bracing the thorn. There were no mutual concessions : one
stood erect, and the others yielded ; and who *can* be ill-
natured and bad-tempered when they encounter neither opposition nor indifference ? I observed that Mr. Edgar had
a deep-rooted fear of ruffling her humour. He concealed it
from her ; but if ever he heard me answer sharply, or saw
any other servant grow cloudy at some imperious order of
hers, he would show his trouble by a frown of displeasure
that never darkened on his own account. He many a time
spoke sternly to me about my pertness, and averred that the
stab of a knife could not inflict a worse pang than he suffered
at seeing his lady vexed. Not to grieve a kind master, I
learned to be less touchy ; and, for the space of half a year,
the gunpowder lay as harmless as sand, because no fire came
near to explode it. Catherine had seasons of gloom and
silence, now and then : they were respected with sympathizing
silence by her husband, who ascribed them to an alteration
in her constitution, produced by her perilous illness ; as she
was never subject to depression of spirits before. The return
of sunshine was welcomed by answering sunshine from him.
I believe I may assert that they were really in possession of
deep and growing happiness.

It ended. Well, we *must* be for ourselves in the long
run ; the mild and generous are only more justly selfish than
the domineering ; and it ended when circumstances caused
each to feel that the one's interest was not the chief consideration in the other's thoughts. On a mellow evening in
September, I was coming from the garden with a heavy

basket of apples which I had been gathering. It had got dusk, and the moon looked over the high wall of the court, causing undefined shadows to lurk in the corners of the numerous projecting portions of the building. I set my burden on the house steps by the kitchen door, and lingered to rest, and drew in a few more breaths of the soft, sweet air; my eyes were on the moon, and my back to the entrance, when I heard a voice behind me say,—

"Nelly, is that you?"

It was a deep voice, and foreign in tone; yet there was something in the manner of pronouncing my name which made it sound familiar. I turned about to discover who spoke, fearfully; for the doors were shut, and I had seen nobody on approaching the steps. Something stirred in the porch; and, moving nearer, I distinguished a tall man dressed in dark clothes, with dark face and hair. He leant against the side, and held his fingers on the latch as if intending to open for himself. 'Who can it be?' I thought. 'Mr. Earnshaw? Oh, no! The voice has no resemblance to his.'

"I have waited here an hour," he resumed, while I continued staring; "and the whole of that time all round has been as still as death. I dared not enter. You do not know me? Look, I'm not a stranger!"

A ray fell on his features; the cheeks were sallow, and half covered with black whiskers; the brows lowering, the eyes deep set and singular. I remembered the eyes.

"What!" I cried, uncertain whether to regard him as a worldly visitor, and I raised my hands in amazement. "What! you come back? Is it really you? Is it?"

"Yes, Heathcliff," he replied, glancing from me up to the windows, which reflected a score of glittering moons, but showed no lights from within. Are they at home? where is she? Nelly, you are not glad! you needn't be so disturbed. Is she here? Speak! I want to have one word with her— your mistress. Go, and say some person from Gimmerton desires to see her."

"How will she take it?" I exclaimed, "what will she do? The surprise bewilders me—it will put her out of her head! And you are Heathcliff! But altered! Nay, there's no comprehending it. Have you been for a soldier?"

"Go, and carry my message," he interrupted, impatiently; "I'm in hell till you do!"

He lifted the latch, and I entered; but when I got to the parlour where Mr. and Mrs. Linton were, I could not persuade myself to proceed. At length, I resolved on making an excuse to ask if they would have the candles lighted, and I opened the door.

They sat together in a window whose lattice lay back against the wall, and displayed, beyond the garden trees and the wild green park, the valley of Gimmerton, with a long line of mist winding nearly to its top (for very soon after you pass the chapel, as you may have noticed, the sough that runs from the marshes joins a beck which follows the bend of the glen). Wuthering Heights rose above this silvery vapour; but our old house was invisible; it rather dips down on the other side. Both the room and its occupants, and the scene they gazed on, looked wondrously peaceful. I shrank reluctantly from performing my errand; and was actually going away leaving it unsaid, after having put my question about the candles, when a sense of my folly compelled me to return, and mutter:—"A person from Gimmerton wishes to see you, ma'am."

"What does he want?" asked Mrs. Linton.

"I did not question him," I answered.

"Well, close the curtains, Nelly," she said; "and bring up tea. I'll be back again directly."

She quitted the apartment; Mr. Edgar inquired, carelessly, who it was.

"Some one mistress does not expect," I replied. "That Heathcliff, you recollect him, sir, who used to live at Mr. Earnshaw's."

"What! the gipsy—the plough-boy?" he cried. "Why did you not say so to Catherine?"

"Hush! you must not call him by those names, master," I said. "She'd be sadly grieved to hear you. She was nearly heartbroken when he ran off. I guess his return will make a jubilee to her."

Mr. Linton walked to a window on the other side of the room that overlooked the court. He unfastened it, and leant out. I suppose they were below, for he exclaimed quickly:—"Don't stand there, love! Bring the person in, if it be any one particular." Ere long, I heard the click of the latch,

and Catherine flew up stairs, breathless and wild; too excited to show gladness: indeed, by her face, you would
rather have surmised an awful calamity.

"Oh, Edgar, Edgar!" she panted, flinging her arms
round his neck. "Oh, Edgar, darling! Heathcliff's come
back—he is!" And she tightened her embrace to a squeeze.

"Well, well," cried her husband, crossly, "don't strangle
me for that! He never struck me as such a marvellous treasure. There is no need to be frantic!"

"I know you didn't like him," she answered, repressing a
little the intensity of her delight. "Yet, for my sake, you
must be friends now. Shall I tell him to come up?"

"Here?" he said, "into the parlour?"

"Where else?" she asked.

He looked vexed, and suggested the kitchen as a more
suitable place for him. Mrs. Linton eyed him with a droll
expression—half angry, half laughing at his fastidiousness.

"No," she added, after a while; "I cannot sit in the
kitchen. Set two tables here, Ellen: one for your master
and Miss Isabella, being gentry; the other for Heathcliff and
myself, being of the lower orders. Will that please you,
dear? Or must I have a fire lighted elsewhere? If so, give
directions. I'll run down and secure my guest. I'm afraid
the joy is too great to be real!"

She was about to dart off again; but Edgar arrested her.

"*You* bid him step up," he said, addressing me; "and,
Catherine, try to be glad, without being absurd! The whole
household need not witness the sight of your welcoming a
runaway servant as a brother."

I descended, and found Heathcliff waiting under the porch,
evidently anticipating an invitation to enter. He followed
my guidance without waste of words, and I ushered him into
the presence of the master and mistress, whose flushed cheeks
betrayed signs of warm talking. But the lady's glowed
with another feeling when her friend appeared at the door:
she sprang forward, took both his hands, and led him to
Linton; and then she seized Linton's reluctant fingers and
crushed them into his. Now fully revealed by the fire and
candlelight, I was amazed, more than ever, to behold the
transformation of Heathcliff. He had grown a tall, athletic,
well-formed man; beside whom, my master seemed quite
slender and youth-like. His upright carriage suggested the

idea of his having been in the army. His countenance was much older in expression and decision of feature than Mr. Linton's: it looked intelligent, and retained no marks of former degradation. A half-civilized ferocity lurked yet in the depressed brows and eyes full of black fire, but it was subdued; and his manner was even dignified: quite divested of roughness, though too stern for grace. My master's surprise equalled or exceeded mine: he remained for a minute at a loss how to address the ploughboy, as he had called him. Heathcliff dropped his slight hand, and stood looking at him coolly till he chose to speak.

"Sit down, sir," he said, at length. "Mrs. Linton, recalling old times, would have me give you a cordial reception; and, of course, I am gratified when anything occurs to please her."

"And I also," answered Heathcliff, "especially if it be anything in which I have a part. I shall stay an hour or two willingly."

He took a seat opposite Catherine, who kept her gaze fixed on him as if she feared he would vanish were she to remove it. He did not raise his to her often: a quick glance now and then sufficed; but it flashed back, each time more confidently, the undisguised delight he drank from hers. They were too much absorbed in their mutual joy to suffer embarrassment. Not so Mr. Edgar: he grew pale with pure annoyance: a feeling that reached its climax when his lady rose, and stepping across the rug, seized Heathcliff's hands again, and laughed like one beside herself.

"I shall think it a dream to-morrow!" she cried. "I shall not be able to believe that I have seen, and touched, and spoken to you once more. And yet, cruel Heathcliff! you don't deserve this welcome. To be absent and silent for three years, and never to think of me!"

"A little more than you have thought of me," he murmured. "I heard of your marriage, Cathy, not long since; and, while waiting in the yard below, I meditated this plan, just to have one glimpse of your face: a stare of surprise, perhaps, and pretended pleasure; afterwards settle my score with Hindley; and then prevent the law by doing execution on myself. Your welcome has put these ideas out of my mind: but beware of meeting me with another aspect next time! Nay, you'll not drive me off again. You were really sorry for me, were you? Well, there was cause. I've fought through a bitter life since I last heard your voice; and you must forgive me, for I struggled only for you!"

"Catherine, unless we are to have cold tea, please to come to the table," interrupted Linton, striving to preserve his ordinary tone, and a due measure of politeness. "Mr. Heathcliff will have a long walk, wherever he may lodge to-night; and I'm thirsty."

She took her post before the urn; and Miss Isabella came, summoned by the bell; then, having handed their chairs forward, I left the room. The meal hardly endured ten minutes. Catherine's cup was never filled: she could neither eat nor drink. Edgar had made a slop in his saucer, and scarcely swallowed a mouthful. Their guest did not protract his stay that evening above an hour longer. I asked, as he departed, if he went to Gimmerton?

"No, to Wuthering Heights," he answered: "Mr. Earnshaw invited me, when I called this morning."

Mr. Earnshaw invited *him!* and *he* called on Mr. Earnshaw! I pondered this sentence painfully, after he was gone. Is he turning out a bit of a hypocrite, and coming into the country to work mischief under a cloak? I mused: I had a presentiment in the bottom of my heart, that he had better have remained away.

About the middle of the night, I was wakened from my first nap by Mrs. Linton gliding into my chamber, taking a seat on my bedside, and pulling me by the hair to rouse me.

"I cannot rest, Ellen," she said by way of apology. "And I want some living creature to keep me company in my happiness! Edgar is sulky, because I'm glad of a thing that does not interest him: he refuses to open his mouth, except to utter pettish, silly speeches; and he affirmed I was cruel and selfish for wishing to talk when he was so sick and sleepy. He always contrives to be sick at the least cross! I gave a few sentences of commendation to Heathcliff, and he, either for a headache or a pang of envy, began to cry: so I got up and left him."

"What use is it praising Heathcliff to him?" I answered. "As lads they had an aversion to each other, and Heathcliff would hate just as much to hear him praised: it's human nature. Let Mr. Linton alone about him, unless you would like an open quarrel between them."

"But does it not show great weakness?" pursued she.
"I'm not envious: I never feel hurt at the brightness of
Isabella's yellow hair and the whiteness of her skin, at her
dainty elegance, and the fondness all the family exhibit for
her. Even you, Nelly, if we have a dispute sometimes, you
back Isabella at once; and I yield like a foolish mother: I
call her a darling, and flatter her into a good temper. It
pleases her brother to see us cordial, and that pleases me.
But they are very much alike: they are spoiled children,
and fancy the world was made for their accommodation;
and, though I humour both, I think a smart chastisement
might improve them, all the same."

"You're mistaken, Mrs. Linton," said I. "They humour
you: I know what there would be to do if they did not.
You can well afford to indulge their passing whims as long
as their business is to anticipate all your desires. You may,
however, fall out, at last, over something of equal consequence to both sides; and then those you term weak are
very capable of being as obstinate as you."

"And then we shall fight to the death, sha'n't we, Nelly?"
she returned, laughing. "No! I tell you, I have such faith
in Linton's love, that I believe I might kill him, and he
wouldn't wish to retaliate."

I advised her to value him the more for his affection.

"I do:" she answered, "but he needn't resort to whining
for trifles. It is childish; and, instead of melting into tears
because I said that Heathcliff was now worthy of any one's
regard, and it would honour the first gentleman in the country to be his friend, he ought to have said it for me, and
been delighted from sympathy. He must get accustomed to
him, and he may as well like him: considering how Heathcliff has reason to object to him, I'm sure he behaved ex-
cellently!"

"What do you think of his going to Wuthering
Heights?" I inquired. "He is reformed in every respect,
apparently: quite a Christian: offering the right hand of
fellowship to his enemies all around!"

"He explained it," she replied. "I wonder as much as
you. He said he called to gather information concerning
me from you, supposing you resided there still; and Joseph
told Hindley, who came out and fell to questioning him of
what he had been doing, and how he had been living; and

finally, desired him to walk in. There were some persons sitting at cards; Heathcliff joined them; my brother lost some money to him, and, finding him plentifully supplied, he requested that he would come again in the evening: to which he consented. Hindley is too reckless to select his acquaintance prudently: he doesn't trouble himself to reflect on the causes he might have for mistrusting one whom he has basely injured. But Heathcliff affirms his principal reason for resuming a connection with his ancient persecutor is a wish to install himself in quarters at walking distance from the Grange, and an attachment to the house where we lived together; and likewise a hope that I shall have more opportunities of seeing him there than I could have if he settled in Gimmerton. He means to offer liberal payment for permission to lodge at the Heights; and doubtless my brother's covetousness will prompt him to accept the terms: he was always greedy; though what he grasps with one hand he flings away with the other."

" It 's a nice place for a young man to fix his dwelling in !" said I. " Have you no fear of the consequences, Mrs. Linton ?"

" None for my friend," she replied: " his strong head will keep him from danger; a little for Hindley: but he can't be made morally worse than he is; and I stand between him and bodily harm. The event of this evening has reconciled me to God and humanity! I had risen in angry rebellion against Providence. Oh, I 've endured very, very bitter misery, Nelly! If that creature knew how bitter, he 'd be ashamed to cloud its removal with idle petulance. It was kindness for him which induced me to bear it alone: had I expressed the agony I frequently felt, he would have been taught to long for its alleviation as ardently as I. However, it 's over, and I 'll take no revenge on his folly: I can afford to suffer anything, hereafter! Should the meanest thing alive slap me on the cheek, I 'd not only turn the other, but, I 'd ask pardon for provoking it; and, as a proof, I 'll go make my peace with Edgar instantly.—Good-night—I 'm an angel!"

In this self complacent conviction she departed; and the success of her fulfilled resolution was obvious on the morrow: Mr. Linton had not only abjured his peevishness (though his spirits seemed still subdued by Catherine's exuberance of vivacity) but he ventured no objection to her taking Isabella with her to Wuthering Heights in the afternoon; and she rewarded him with such a summer of sweetness and affection in return, as made the house a paradise for several days; both master and servants profiting from the perpetual sunshine.

Heathcliff—Mr. Heathcliff I should say in future—used the liberty of visiting at Thrushcross Grange cautiously, at first: he seemed estimating how far its owner would bear his intrusion. Catherine, also, deemed it judicious to moderate her expressions of pleasure in receiving him; and he gradually established his right to be expected. He retained a great deal of the reserve for which his boyhood was remarkable; and that served to repress all startling demonstrations of feeling. My master's uneasiness experienced a lull, and further circumstances diverted it into another channel for a space.

His new source of trouble sprang from the not anticipated misfortune of Isabella Linton evincing a sudden and irresistible attraction towards the tolerated guest. She was at that time a charming young lady of eighteen; infantile in manners, though possessed of keen wit, keen feelings, and a keen temper, too, if irritated. Her brother, who loved her tenderly, was appalled at this fantastic preference. Leaving aside the degradation of an alliance with a nameless man, and the possible fact that his property, in default of heirs male, might pass into such a one's power, he had sense to comprehend Heathcliff's disposition: to know that, though his exterior was altered, his mind was unchangeable, and unchanged. And he dreaded that mind: it revolted him: he shrank forebodingly from the idea of committing Isabella to its keeping. He would have recoiled still more had he been aware that her attachment rose unsolicited, and was bestowed where it awakened no reciprocation of sentiment; for the minute he discovered its existence, he laid the blame on Heathcliff's deliberate designing.

We had all remarked, during some time, that Miss Linton fretted and pined over something. She grew cross and wearisome; snapping at and teazing Catherine continually, at the imminent risk of exhausting her limited patience. We excused her to a certain extent, on the plea of ill health:

she was dwindling and fading before our eyes. But one day, when she had been peculiarly wayward, rejecting her breakfast, complaining that the servants did not do what she. told them; that the mistress would allow her to be nothing in the house, and Edgar neglected her; that she had caught a cold with the doors being left open, and we let the parlour fire go out on purpose to vex her; with a hundred yet more frivolous accusations, Mrs. Linton peremptorily insisted that she should get to bed; and, having scolded her heartily, threatened to send for the doctor. Mention of Kenneth, caused her to exclaim, instantly, that her health was perfect, and it was only Catherine's harshness which made her unhappy.

"How can you say I am harsh, you naughty fondling?" cried the mistress, amazed at the unreasonable assertion. 'You are surely losing your reason. When have I been harsh, tell me?"

"Yesterday," sobbed Isabella, "and now!"

"Yesterday!" said her sister-in-law. "On what occasion?"

"In our walk along the moor: you told me to ramble where I pleased, while you sauntered on with Mr. Heathcliff?"

"And that's your notion of harshness?" said Catherine, laughing. "It was no hint that your company was superfluous: we didn't care whether you kept with us or not; I merely thought Heathcliff's talk would have nothing entertaining for your ears."

"Oh, no," wept the young lady; "you wished me away, because you knew I liked to be there!"

"Is she sane?" asked Mrs. Linton, appealing to me. "I'll repeat our conversation, word for word, Isabella; and you point out any charm it could have had for you."

"I don't mind the conversation," she answered: "I wanted to be with——"

"Well!" said Catherine, perceiving her hesitate to complete the sentence.

"With him: and I won't be always sent off!" she continued, kindling up. "You are a dog in the manger, Cathy, and desire as one to be loved but yourself!"

"You are an impertinent little monkey!" exclaimed Mrs. Linton, in surprise. "But I'll not believe this idiocy! It

is impossible that you can covet the admiration of Heathcliff
—that you can consider him an agreeable person! I hope I
have misunderstood you, Isabella?"

"No, you have not," said the infatuated girl. "I love
him more than ever you loved Edgar; and he might love
me, if you would let him!"

"I wouldn't be you for a kingdom, then!" Catherine
declared, emphatically: and she seemed to speak sincerely.
"Nelly, help me to convince her of her madness. Tell her
what Heathcliff is: an unreclaimed creature, without refine-
ment, without cultivation: an arid wilderness of furze and
whinstone. I'd as soon put that little canary into the park
on a winter's day, as recommend you to bestow your heart on
him! It is deplorable ignorance of his character, child, and
nothing else, which makes that dream enter your head.
Pray, don't imagine that he conceals depths of benevolence
and affection beneath a stern exterior! He's not a rough
diamond—a pearl-containing oyster of a rustic: he's a fierce,
pitiless, wolfish man. I never say to him 'let this or that
enemy alone, because it would be ungenerous or cruel to
harm them;' I say 'let them alone, because _I_ should hate
them to be wronged:' and he'd crush you, like a sparrow's
egg, Isabella, if he found you a troublesome charge. I
know he couldn't love a Linton; and yet he'd be quite
capable of marrying your fortune and expectations: avarice
is growing with him a besetting sin. There's my picture:
and I'm his friend—so much so, that had he thought seriously
to catch you, I should, perhaps, have held my tongue, and
let you fall into his trap."

Miss Linton regarded her sister-in-law with indignation.

"For shame! for shame!" she repeated, angrily. "You
are worse than twenty foes, you poisonous friend!"

"Ah! you won't believe me, then?" said Catherine.
"You think I speak from wicked selfishness?"

"I'm certain you do," retorted Isabella; "and I shudder
at you!"

"Good!" cried the other. "Try for yourself, if that be
your spirit: I have done, and yield the argument to your
saucy insolence."

"And I must suffer for her egotism!" she sobbed, as
Mrs. Linton left the room. "All, all is against me: she
has blighted my single consolation. But she uttered false-

hoods, didn't she? Mr. Heathcliff is not a fiend: he has an honourable soul, and a true one, or how could he remember her?"

"Banish him from your thoughts, miss," I said. "He's a bird of bad omen: no mate for you. Mrs. Linton spoke strongly, and yet I can't contradict her. She is better acquainted with his heart than I, or any one besides; and she never would represent him as worse than he is. Honest people don't hide their deeds. How has he been living? how has he got rich? why is he staying at Wuthering Heights, the house of a man whom he abhors? They say Mr. Earnshaw is worse and worse since he came. They sit up all night together continually, and Hindley has been borrowing money on his land, and does nothing but play and drink: I heard only a week ago—it was Joseph who told me —I met him at Gimmerton: "Nelly," he said, "we's hae a crowner's 'quest enow, at ahr folks. One on 'em's a'most getten his finger cut off wi' hauding t'other fro' sticking hisseln loike a cawlf. That's maister, yah knaw, 'at's soa up o' going tuh t'grand 'sizes. He's noan feared o' t' bench o' judges, norther Paul, nur Peter, nur John, nur Mathew, nor noan on 'em, not he!' He fair like's he langs to set his brazened face agean 'em! And yon bonny lad Heathcliff, yah mind, he's a rare un? He can girn a laugh as weel's onybody at a raight divil's jest. Does he niver say nowt of his fine living amang us, when he goes to t' Grange? This is t' way on't — up at sun-down; dice, brandy, cloised shutters, und can'le light till next day at noon: then, t' fooil gangs banning un raving to his cham'er, makking dacent fowks dig thur fingers i' thur lugs fur varry shame; un' the knave, why he can caint his brass, un ate, un sleep, un off to his neighbour's to gossip wi' t' wife. I' course, he tells Dame Catherine how her father's goold runs into his pocket, and her fathur's son gallops down t' broad road, while he flees afore to oppen t' pikes?" Now, Miss Linton, Joseph is an old rascal, but no liar; and, if his account of Heathcliff's conduct be true, you would never think of desiring such a husband, would you!"

"You are leagued with the rest, Ellen!" she replied "I'll not listen to your slanders. What malevolence you must have to wish to convince me that there is no happiness in the world!"

Whether she would have got over this fancy if left to herself, or persevered in nursing it perpetually, I cannot say: she had little time to reflect. The day after, there was a justice-meeting at the next town; my master was obliged to attend; and Mr. Heathcliff, aware of his absence, called rather earlier than usual. Catherine and Isabella were sitting in the library, on hostile terms, but silent. The latter alarmed at her recent indiscretion, and the disclosure she had made of her secret feelings in a transient fit of passion; the former, on mature consideration, really offended with her companion; and, if she laughed again at her pertness, inclined to make it no laughing matter to *her*. She did laugh as she saw Heathcliff pass the window. I was sweeping the hearth, and I noticed a mischievous smile on her lips. Isabella, absorbed in her meditations, or a book, remained till the door opened; and it was too late to attempt an escape, which she would gladly have done had it been practicable.

" Come in, that's right!" exclaimed the mistress, gaily, pulling a chair to the fire. " Here are two people sadly in need of a third to thaw the ice between them; and you are the very one we should both of us choose. Heathcliff, I'm proud to show you, at last, somebody that dotes on you more than myself. I expect you to feel flattered. Nay, it's not Nelly; don't look at her! My poor little sister-in-law is breaking her heart by mere contemplation of your physical and moral beauty. It lies in your own power to be Edgar's brother! No, no, Isabella, you sha'n't run off," she continued, arresting, with feigned playfulness, the confounded girl, who had risen indignantly. " We were quarrelling like cats about you, Heathcliff; and I was fairly beaten in protestations of devotion and admiration : and, moreover, I was informed that if I would but have the manners to stand aside, my rival, as she will have herself to be, would shoot a shaft into your soul that would fix you for ever, and send my image into eternal oblivion!"

" Catherine!" said Isabella, calling up her dignity, and disdaining to struggle from the tight grasp that held her. " I'd thank you to adhere to the truth and not slander me, even in joke! Mr. Heathcliff, be kind enough to bid this friend of yours release me : she forgets that you and I are not intimate acquaintances; and what amuses her is painful to me beyond expression."

As the guest answered nothing, but took his seat, and looked thoroughly indifferent what sentiments she cherished concerning him, she turned and whispered an earnest appeal for liberty to her tormentor.

"By no means!" cried Mrs. Linton in answer. "I won't be named a dog in the manger again. You *shall* stay: now then! Heathcliff, why don't you evince satisfaction at my pleasant news? Isabella swears that the love Edgar has for me is nothing to that she entertains for you. I'm sure she made some speech of the kind; did she not, Ellen? And she has fasted ever since the day before yesterday's walk, from sorrow and rage that I despatched her out of your society under the idea of its being unacceptable."

"I think you belie her," said Heathcliff, twisting his chair to face them. "She wishes to be out of my society now, at any rate!"

And he stared hard at the object of discourse, as one might do at a strange repulsive animal: a centipede from the Indies, for instance, which curiosity leads one to examine in spite of the aversion it raises. The poor thing couldn't bear that: she grew white and red in rapid succession, and, while tears beaded her lashes, bent the strength of her small fingers to loosen the firm clutch of Catherine; and perceiving that as fast as she raised one finger off her arm another closed down, and she could not remove the whole together, she began to make use of her nails; and their sharpness presently ornamented the detainer's with crescents of red.

"There's a tigress!" exclaimed Mrs. Linton, setting her free, and shaking her hand with pain. "Begone, for God's sake, and hide your vixen face! How foolish to reveal those talons to *him*. Can't you fancy the conclusions he'll draw? Look, Heathcliff! they are instruments that will do execution—you must beware of your eyes."

"I'd wrench them off her fingers, if they ever menaced me," he answered, brutally, when the door had closed after her. "But what did you mean by teasing the creature in that manner, Cathy? You were not speaking the truth, were you?"

"I assure you I was," she returned. "She has been dining for your sake several weeks; and raving about you this morning, and pouring forth a deluge of abuse, because

I represented your failings in a plain light, for the purpose
of mitigating her adoration. But don't notice it further: I
wished to punish her sauciness, that's all. I like her too
well, my dear Heathcliff, to let you absolutely seize and
devour her up."

"And I like her too ill to attempt it," said he, "except
in a very ghoulish fashion. You'd hear of odd things if I
lived alone with that mawkish, waxen face: the most ordinary would be painting on its white the colours of the rain-
bow, and turning the blue eyes black, every day or two:
they detestably resemble Linton's."

"Delectably!" observed Catherine. "They are dove's
eyes—angel's!"

"She's her brother's heir, is she not?" he asked, after a
brief silence.

"I should be sorry to think so," returned his companion.
"Half a dozen nephews shall erase her title, please Heaven!
Abstract your mind from the subject at present: you are
too prone to covet your neighbour's goods; remember *this*
neighbour's goods are mine."

"If they were *mine*, they would be none the less that,"
said Heathcliff; "but though Isabella Linton may be silly,
she is scarcely mad; and, in short, we'll dismiss the matter,
as you advise."

From their tongues, they did dismiss it; and Catherine,
probably, from her thoughts. The other, I felt certain,
recalled it often in the course of the evening. I saw him
smile to himself—grin rather—and lapse into ominous musing whenever Mrs. Linton had occasion to be absent from
the apartment.

I determined to watch his movements. My heart invariably cleaved to the master's, in preference to Catherine's
side: with reason I imagined, for he was kind, and trustful,
and honourable; and she—she could not be called the *opposite*, yet she seemed to allow herself such wide latitude, that
I had little faith in her principles, and still less sympathy
for her feelings. I wanted something to happen which
might have the effect of freeing both Wuthering Heights
and the Grange of Mr. Heathcliff, quietly; leaving us as we
had been prior to his advent. His visits were a continual
nightmare to me; and, I suspected, to my master also.
His abode at the Heights was an oppression past explaining.

I felt that God had forsaken the stray sheep there to its own wicked wanderings, and an evil beast prowled between it and the fold, waiting his time to spring and destroy.

CHAPTER XI.

SOMETIMES, while meditating on these things in solitude, I've got up in a sudden terror, and put on my bonnet to go see how all was at the farm. I've persuaded my conscience that it was a duty to warn him how people talked regarding his ways; and then I've recollected his confirmed bad habits, and, hopeless of benefiting him, have flinched from re-entering the dismal house, doubting if I could bear to be taken at my word.

One time I passed the old gate, going out of my way, on a journey to Gimmerton. It was about the period that my narrative has reached: a bright frosty afternoon; the ground bare, and the road hard and dry. I came to a stone where the highway branches off on to the moor at your left hand; a rough sand-pillar, with the letters W. H. cut on its north side, on the east, G., and on the south-west, T. G. It serves as a guide-post to the Grange, and Heights, and village. The sun shone yellow on its grey head, reminding me of summer; and I cannot say why, but all at once, a gush of child's sensations flowed into my heart. Hindley and I held it a favourite spot twenty years before. I gazed long at the weather-worn block; and, stooping down, perceived a hole near the bottom still full of snail-shells and pebbles, which we were fond of storing there with more perishable things; and, as fresh as reality, it appeared that I beheld my early playmate seated on the withered turf: his dark, square head bent forward, and his little hand scooping out the earth with a piece of slate. "Poor Hindley!" I exclaimed, involuntarily. I started; my bodily eye was cheated into a momentary belief that the child lifted its face and stared straight into mine! It vanished in a twinkling; but immediately I felt an irresistible yearning to be at the Heights.

Superstition urged me to comply with this impulse : supposing he should be dead ! I thought—or should die soon ! —supposing it were a sign of death ! The nearer I got to the house the more agitated I grew ; and on catching sight of it I trembled every limb. The apparition had outstripped me : it stood looking through the gate. That was my first idea on observing an elf-locked, brown-eyed boy setting his ruddy countenance against the bars. Further reflection suggested this must be Hareton, *my* Hareton, not altered greatly since I left him, ten months since.

"God bless thee, darling !" I cried, forgetting instantaneously my foolish fears. "Hareton, it's Nelly ! Nelly, thy nurse."

He retreated out of arm's length, and picked up a large flint.

"I am come to see thy father, Hareton," I added, guessing from the action that Nelly, if she lived in his memory at all, was not recognised as one with me.

He raised his missile to hurl it; I commenced a soothing speech, but could not stay his hand: the stone struck my bonnet ; and then ensued, from the stammering lips of the little fellow, a string of curses, which, whether he comprehended them or not, were delivered with practised emphasis, and distorted his baby features into a shocking expression of malignity. You may be certain this grieved more than angered me. Fit to cry, I took an orange from my pocket, and offered it to propitiate him. He hesitated, and then snatched it from my hold; as if he fancied I only intended to tempt and disappoint him. I showed another, keeping it out of his reach.

"Who has taught you those fine words, my bairn," I inquired. "The curate ?"

"Damn the curate, and thee ! Gie me that," he replied.

"Tell us where you got your lessons, and you shall have it," said I. "Who's your master?"

"Devil daddy," was his answer.

"And what do you learn from daddy ?" I continued.

He jumped at the fruit; I raised it higher. "What does he teach you ?" I asked.

"Naught," said he, "but to keep out of his gait. Daddy cannot bide me, because I swear at him."

"Ah! and the devil teaches you to swear at daddy?" I observed.

"Ay—nay," he drawled.

"Who, then?"

"Heathcliff."

"I asked if he liked Mr. Heathcliff?"

"Ay!" he answered again.

Desiring to have his reasons for liking him, I could only gather the sentences—" I known't : he pays dad back what he gies to me—he curses daddy for cursing me. He says I mun do as I will."

"And the curate does not teach you to read and write then?" I pursued.

"No, I was told the curate should have his —— teeth dashed down his —— throat, if he stepped over the threshold —Heathcliff had promised that!"

I put the orange in his hand, and bade him tell his father that a woman called Nelly Dean was waiting to speak with him, by the garden gate. He went up the walk, and entered the house; but, instead of Hindley, Heathcliff appeared on the door stones; and I turned directly and ran down the road as hard as ever I could race, making no halt till I gained the guide post, and feeling as scared as if I had raised a goblin. This is not much connected with Miss Isabella's affair; except that it urged me to resolve further on mounting vigilant guard, and doing my utmost to check the spread of such bad influence at the Grange : even though I should wake a domestic storm, by thwarting Mrs. Linton's pleasure.

The next time Heathcliff came, my young lady chanced to be feeding some pigeons in the court. She had never spoken a word to her sister-in-law for three days; but she had like- wise dropped her fretful complaining, and we found it a great comfort. Heathcliff had not the habit of bestowing a single unnecessary civility on Miss Linton, I knew. Now, as soon as he beheld her, his first precaution was to take a sweeping survey of the house-front. I was standing by the kitchen window, but I drew out of sight. He then stept across the pavement to her, and said something : she seemed embarrassed, and desirous of getting away; to prevent it, he laid his hand on her arm. She averted her face : he apparently put some question which she had no mind to answer. There was another rapid glance at the house, and supposing himself unseen, the scoundrel had the impudence to embrace her.

"Judas! Traitor!" I ejaculated. "You are a hypocrite, too, are you? A deliberate deceiver."

"Who is, Nelly?" said Catherine's voice at my elbow: I had been over intent on watching the pair outside to mark her entrance.

"Your worthless friend!" I answered, warmly; "the sneaking rascal yonder. Ah, he has caught a glimpse of us—he is coming in! I wonder will he have the art to find a plausible excuse for making love to Miss, when he told you he hated her?"

Mrs. Linton saw Isabella tear herself free, and run into the garden; and a minute after, Heathcliff opened the door. I couldn't withhold giving some loose to my indignation; but Catherine angrily insisted on silence, and threatened to order me out of the kitchen, if I dared to be so presumptuous as to put in my insolent tongue.

"To hear you, people might think you were the mistress!" she cried. "You want setting down in your right place! Heathcliff, what are you about raising this stir? I said you must let Isabella alone!—I beg you will, unless you are tired of being received here, and wish Linton to draw the bolts against you!"

"God forbid that he should try!" answered the black villain. I detested him just then. "God keep him meek and patient! Every day I grow madder after sending him to heaven!"

"Hush!" said Catherine shutting the inner door! "Don't vex me. Why have you disregarded my request? Did she come across you on purpose?"

"What is it to you?" he growled. "I have a right to kiss her, if she chooses; and you have no right to object. I am not *your* husband: *you* needn't be jealous of me!"

"I'm not jealous *of* you;" replied the mistress, "I'm jealous *for* you. Clear your face: you shan't scowl at me! If you like Isabella, you shall marry her. But do you like her? Tell the truth, Heathcliff! There, you won't answer. I'm certain you don't!"

"And would Mr. Linton approve of his sister marrying that man?" I inquired.

H

"Mr. Linton should approve," returned my lady, decisively.

"He might spare himself the trouble," said Heathcliff: "I could do as well without his approbation. And as to you, Catherine, I have a mind to speak a few words, now, while we are at it. I want you to be aware that I *know* you have treated me infernally — infernally! Do you hear? And, if you flatter yourself that I don't perceive it, you are a fool; and if you think I can be consoled by sweet words, you are an idiot; and if you fancy I'll suffer unrevenged, I'll convince you of the contrary, in a very little while! Meantime, thank you for telling me your sister-in-law's secret: I swear I'll make the most of it. And stand you aside!"

"What new phase of his character is this?" exclaimed Mrs. Linton, in amazement. "I've treated you infernally— and you'll take revenge! How will you take it, ungrateful brute? How have I treated you infernally?"

"I seek no revenge on you," replied Heathcliff less vehemently. "That's not the plan. The tyrant grinds down his slaves and they don't turn against him; they crush those beneath them. You are welcome to torture me to death for your amusement, only allow me to amuse myself a little in the same style, and refrain from insult as much as you are able. Having levelled my palace, don't erect a hovel and complacently admire your own charity in giving me that for a home. If I imagined you really wished me to marry Isabell, I'd cut my throat!"

"Oh, the evil is that I am *not* jealous, is it?" cried Catherine. "Well, I won't repeat my offer of a wife: it is as bad as offering Satan a lost soul. Your bliss lies, like his, in inflicting misery. You prove it. Edgar is restored from the ill-temper he gave way to at your coming; I begin to be secure and tranquil; and you, restless to know us at peace, appear resolved on exciting a quarrel. Quarrel with Edgar if you please, Heathcliff, and deceive his sister: you'll hit on exactly the most efficient method of revenging yourself on me."

The conversation ceased. Mrs. Linton sat down by the fire, flushed and gloomy. The spirit which served her was growing intractable: she could neither lay nor control it. He stood on the hearth with folded arms, brooding on his evil thoughts; and in this position I left them to seek the master, who was wondering what kept Catherine below so long.

"Ellen," said he, when I entered, "have you seen your mistress?"

"Yes; she's in the kitchen, sir," I answered. "She's sadly put out by Mr. Heathcliff's behaviour: and, indeed, I do think it's time to arrange his visits on another footing. There's harm in being too soft, and now it's come to this——." And I related the scene in the court, and, as near as I dared, the whole subsequent dispute. I fancied it could not be very prejudicial to Mrs. Linton; unless she made it so afterwards, by assuming the defensive for her guest. Edgar Linton had difficulty in hearing me to the close. His first words revealed that he did not clear his wife of blame.

"This is insufferable!" he exclaimed. "It is disgraceful that she should own him for a friend, and force his company on me! Call me two men out of the hall, Ellen. Catherine shall linger no longer to argue with the low ruffian—I have humoured her enough."

He descended, and bidding the servants wait in the passage, went, followed by me, to the kitchen. Its occupants had recommenced their angry discussion: Mrs. Linton, at least, was scolding with renewed vigour; Heathcliff had moved to the window, and hung his head, somewhat cowed by her violent rating, apparently. He saw the master first, and made a hasty motion that she should be silent; which she obeyed, abruptly, on discovering the reason of his intimation.

"How is this?" said Linton, addressing her; "what notion of propriety must you have to remain here, after the language which has been held to you by that blackguard? I suppose, because it is his ordinary talk, you think nothing of it: you are habituated to his baseness, and perhaps, imagine I can get used to it too!"

"Have you been listening at the door, Edgar?" asked the mistress, in a tone particularly calculated to provoke her husband, implying both carelessness and contempt of his irritation. Heathcliff, who had raised his eyes at the former speech, gave a sneering laugh at the latter; on purpose, it seemed, to draw Mr. Linton's attention to him. He succeeded; but Edgar did not mean to entertain him with any high flights of passion.

"I have been so far forbearing with you, sir," he said quietly; "not that I was ignorant of your miserable, degraded character, but I felt you were only partly responsible for that; and Catherine wishing to keep up your acquaintance, I acquiesced — foolishly. Your presence is a moral poison that would contaminate the most virtuous: for that cause, and to prevent worse consequences, I shall deny you hereafter admission into this house, and give notice now that I require your instant departure. Three minutes' delay will render it involuntary and ignominious."

Heathcliff measured the height and breadth of the speaker with an eye full of derision.

"Cathy, this lamb of yours threatens like a bull!" he said. "It is in danger of splitting its skull against my knuckles. By God! Mr. Linton, I'm mortally sorry that you are not worth knocking down!"

My master glanced towards the passage, and signed me to fetch the men: he had no intention of hazarding a personal encounter. I obeyed the hint; but Mrs. Linton, suspecting something, followed; and when I attempted to call them, she pulled me back, slammed the door to, and locked it.

"Fair means!" she said, in answer to her husband's look of angry surprise. If you have not courage to attack him, make an apology, or allow yourself to be beaten. It will correct you of feigning more valour than you possess. No, I'll swallow the key before you shall get it! I'm delightfully rewarded for my kindness to each! After constant indulgence of one's weak nature, and the other's bad one, I earn for thanks, two samples of blind ingratitude, stupid to absurdity! Edgar, I was defending you and yours; and I wish Heathcliff may flog you sick, for daring to think an evil thought of me!"

It did not need the medium of a flogging to produce that effect on the master. He tried to wrest the key from Catherine's grasp, and for safety she flung it into the hottest part of the fire; whereupon Mr. Edgar was taken with a nervous trembling, and his countenance grew deadly pale. For his life he could not avert that excess of emotion: mingled anguish and humiliation overcame him completely. He leant on the back of a chair, and covered his face.

"Oh! heavens! In old days this would win you knighthood!" exclaimed Mrs. Linton. "We are vanquished! we

are vanquished! Heathcliff would as soon lift a finger at
you as the king would march his army against a colony of
mice. Cheer up! you sha'n't be hurt! Your type is not a
lamb, it's a sucking leveret."

"I wish you joy of the milk-blooded coward, Cathy!"
said her friend. "I compliment you on your taste. And
that is the slavering, shivering thing you preferred to me!
I would not strike him with my fist, but I'd kick him with
my foot, and experience considerable satisfaction. Is he
weeping, or is he going to faint for fear?"

The fellow approached and gave the chair on which
Linton rested a push. He'd better have kept his distance;
my master quickly sprang erect, and struck him full on the
throat a blow that would have levelled a slighter man. It
took his breath for a minute; and, while he choked, Mr.
Linton walked out by the back door into the yard, and from
thence, to the front entrance.

"There! you've done with coming here," cried Catherine,
"Get away, now; he'll return with a brace of pistols, and
half a dozen assistants. If he did overhear us, of course,
he'd never forgive you. You've played me an ill turn,
Heathcliff! But, go—make haste! I'd rather see Edgar at
bay than you."

"Do you suppose I'm going with that blow burning in
my gullet?" he thundered. "By hell, no! I'll crush his
ribs in like a rotten hazel-nut, before I cross the threshold!
If I don't floor him now, I shall murder him some time, so,
as you value his existence, let me get at him!"

"He is not coming," I interposed, framing a bit of a
lie. "There's the coachman, and the two gardeners; you'll
surely not wait to be thrust into the road by them! Each
has a bludgeon; and master will, very likely, be watching from the parlour windows to see that they fulfil his
orders."

The gardeners and coachman *were* there; but Linton was
with them. They had already entered the court. Heathcliff, on the second thoughts, resolved to avoid a struggle
against three underlings; he seized the poker, smashed the
lock from the inner door, and made his escape as they
tramped in.

Mrs. Linton, who was very much excited, bade me accompany her up stairs. She did not know my share in contri-

buting to the disturbance, and I was anxious to keep her in ignorance.

"I'm nearly distracted, Nelly!" she exclaimed, throwing herself on the sofa. "A thousand smiths' hammers are beating in my head! Tell Isabella to shun me; this uproar is owing to her; and should she or any one else aggravate my anger at present, I shall get wild. And, Nelly, say to Edgar, if you see him again to-night, that I'm in danger of being seriously ill. I wish it may prove true. He has startled and distressed me shockingly! I want to frighten him. Besides, he might come and begin a string of abuse, or complainings; I'm certain I should recriminate, and God knows where we should end! Will you do so, my good Nelly? You are aware that I am no way blameable in this matter. What possessed him to turn listener? Heathcliff's talk was outrageous, after you left us; but I could soon have diverted him from Isabella, and the rest meant nothing. Now, all is dashed wrong; by the fool's craving to hear evil of self, that haunts some people like a demon! Had Edgar never gathered our conversation, he would never have been the worse for it. Really, when he opened on me in that unreasonable tone of displeasure, after I had scolded Heathcliff till I was hoarse for *him*, I did not care, hardly, what they did to each other; especially as I felt that, however the scene closed, we should all be driven asunder for nobody knows how long! Well, if I cannot keep Heathcliff for my friend—if Edgar will be mean and jealous, I'll try to break their hearts by breaking my own. That will be a prompt way of finishing all, when I am pushed to extremity! But it's a deed to be reserved for a forlorn hope; I'd not take Linton by surprise with it. To this point he has been discreet in dreading to provoke me; you must represent the peril of quitting that policy, and remind him of my passionate temper, verging, when kindled, on frenzy. I wish you could dismiss that apathy out of that countenance, and look rather more anxious about me!"

The stolidity with which I received these instructions was, no doubt, rather exasperating; for they were delivered in perfect sincerity, but I believed a person who could plan the turning of her fits of passion to account, beforehand, might, by exerting her will, manage to control herself tolerably, even while under their influence; and I did not wish to "frighten" her husband, as she said, and multiply his annoyances for the purpose of serving her selfishness. Therefore I said nothing when I met the master coming towards the parlour; but I took the liberty of turning back to listen whether they would resume their quarrel together. He began to speak first.

"Remain where you are, Catherine," he said; without any anger in his voice, but with much sorrowful despondency. "I shall not stay. I am neither come to wrangle nor be reconciled; but I wish just to learn whether, after this evening's events, you intend to continue your intimacy with——"

"Oh, for mercy's sake," interrupted the mistress, stamping her foot, "for mercy's sake, let us hear no more of it now! Your cold blood cannot be worked into a fever: your veins are full of ice-water; but mine are boiling, and the sight of such chillness makes them dance."

"To get rid of me, answer my question," persevered Mr. Linton: "You *must* answer it; and that violence does not alarm me. I have found that you can be as stoical as any one, when you please. Will you give up Heathcliff hereafter, or will you give up me? It is impossible for you to be *my* friend and *his* at the same time; and I absolutely *require* to know which you choose."

"I require to be let alone!" exclaimed Catherine, furiously. "I demand it! Don't you see I can scarcely stand? Edgar, you—you leave me!"

She rang the bell till it broke with a twang; I entered leisurely. It was enough to try the temper of a saint, such senseless, wicked rages! There she lay dashing her head against the arm of the sofa, and grinding her teeth, so that you might fancy she would crash them to splinters! Mr. Linton stood looking at her in sudden compunction and fear. He told me to fetch some water. She had no breath for speaking. I brought a glass full; and, as she would not drink, I sprinkled it on her face. In a few seconds she stretched herself out stiff, and turned up her eyes, while her cheeks, at once blanched and livid, assumed the aspect of death. Linton looked terrified.

"There is nothing in the world the matter," I whispered. I did not want him to yield, though I could not help being afraid in my heart.

"She has blood on her lips!" he said shuddering.

"Never mind!" I answered, tartly. And I told him how she had resolved, previous to his coming, on exhibiting a fit of frenzy. I incautiously gave the account aloud, and she heard me; for she started up—her hair flying over her shoulders, her eyes flashing, the muscles of her neck and arms standing out preternaturally. I made up my mind for broken bones, at least; but she only glared about her for an instant, and then rushed from the room. The master directed me to follow; I did, to her chamber door: she hindered me from going further by securing it against me.

As she never offered to descend to breakfast next morning, I went to ask whether she would have some carried up. "No!" she replied, peremptorily. The same question was repeated at dinner and tea; and again on the morrow after, and received the same answer. Mr. Linton, on his part, spent his time in the library, and did not inquire concerning his wife's occupations. Isabella and he had had an hour's interview, during which he tried to elicit from her some sentiment of proper horror for Heathcliff's advances: but he could make nothing of her evasive replies, and was obliged to close the examination unsatisfactorily; adding, however, a solemn warning, that if she were so insane as to encourage that worthless suitor, it would dissolve all bonds of relationship between herself and him.

CHAPTER XII.

WHILE Miss Linton moped about the park and garden, always silent, and almost always in tears; and her brother shut himself up among books that he never opened—wearying, I guessed, with a continual vague expectation that Catherine, repenting her conduct, would come of her own accord to ask pardon, and seek a reconciliation—and *she* fasted pertinaciously, under the idea, probably, that at every meal, Edgar was ready to choke for her absence, and pride alone held him from running to cast himself at her feet; I went about my household duties, convinced that the Grange had but one sensible soul in its walls, and that lodged in my body. I wasted no condolences on miss, nor any expostulations on my mistress; nor did I pay attention to the sighs of my master, who yearned to hear his lady's name, since he might not hear her voice. I determined they should come about as they pleased for me; and though it was a tiresomely slow process, I began to rejoice at length in a faint dawn of its progress: as I thought at first.

Mrs. Linton, on the third day, unbarred her door; and, having finished the water in her pitcher and decanter, desired a renewed supply, and a basin of gruel, for she believed she was dying. That I set down as a speech meant for Edgar's ears; I believed no such thing, so I kept it to myself, and brought her some tea and dry toast. She ate and drank eagerly; and sank back on her pillow again clenching her hands and groaning. "Oh, I will die," she exclaimed, " since no one cares anything about me. I wish I had not taken that." Then a good while after I heard her murmur, " No, I'll not die—he'd be glad—he does not love me at all —he would never miss me!"

" Did you want anything, ma'am?" I inquired, still preserving my external composure, in spite of her ghastly countenance and strange exaggerated manner.

" What is that apathetic being doing?" she demanded, pushing the thick entangled locks from her wasted face. " Has he fallen into a lethargy, or is he dead?"

" Neither," replied I; "if you mean Mr. Linton. He's tolerably well, I think; though his studies occupy him rather more than they ought: he is continually among his books, since he has no other society."

I should not have spoken so, if I had known her true condition, but I could not get rid of the notion that she acted a part of her disorder.

" Among his books!" she cried, confounded. " And I dying! I on the brink of the grave! My God! does he know how I'm altered?" continued she, staring at her reflection in a mirror hanging against the opposite wall. " Is that Catherine Linton? He imagines me in a pet—in play, perhaps. Cannot you inform him that it is frightful earnest? Nelly, if it be not too late, as soon as I learn how he feels, I'll choose between these two; either to starve at

once—that would be no punishment unless he had a heart—
or to recover and leave the country. Are you speaking the
truth about him now? Take care. Is he actually so utterly
indifferent for my life?"

"Why, ma'am," I answered, "the master has no idea of
your being deranged; and, of course, he does not fear that
you will let yourself die of hunger."

"You think not? Cannot you tell him I will?" she
returned. "Persuade him! speak of your own mind: say
you are certain I will!"

"No, you forget, Mrs. Linton," I suggested, "that you
have eaten some food with a relish this evening, and to-
morrow you will perceive its good effects."

"If I were only sure it would kill him," she interrupted,
"I'd kill myself directly! These three awful nights, I've
never closed my lids—and oh, I've been tormented! I've
been haunted, Nelly! But I begin to fancy you don't like
me. How strange! I thought, though everybody hated
and despised each other, they could not avoid loving me.
And they have 'all turned to enemies in a few hours: *they*
have, I'm positive; the people *here*. How dreary to meet
death, surrounded by their cold faces! Isabella, terrified
and repelled, afraid to enter the room, it would be so dreadful to watch Catherine go. And Edgar standing solemnly
by to see it over; then offering prayers of thanks to God for
restoring peace to his house, and going back to his *books!*
What in the name of all that feels, has he to do with *books,*
when I am dying?"

She could not bear the notion which I had put into her
head of Mr. Linton's philosophical resignation. Tossing
about, she increased her feverish bewilderment to madness,
and tore the pillow with her teeth; then raising herself up
all burning, desired that I would open the window. We
were in the middle of winter, the wind blew strong from the
north-east, and I objected. Both the expressions flitting
over her face, and the changes of her moods, began to alarm
me terribly; and brought to my recollection her former
illness, and the doctor's injunction that she should not be
aroused. A minute previously she was violent; now, supported on one arm, and not noticing my refusal to obey her,
she seemed to find childish diversion in pulling the feathers
from the rents she had just made, and ranging them on the

sheet according to their different species: her mind had strayed to other associations.

"That's a turkey's," she murmured to herself; "and this is a wild duck's; and this is a pigeon's. Ah, they put pigeons' feathers in the pillows—no wonder I couldn't die! Let me take care to throw it on the floor when I lie down. And here is a moor-cock's; and this—I should know it among a thousand—it's a lapwing's. Bonny bird; wheeling over our heads in the middle of the moor. It wanted to get to its nest, for the clouds had touched the swells, and it felt rain coming. This feather was picked up from the heath, the bird was not shot: we saw its nest in the winter, full of little skeletons. Heathcliff set a trap over it, and the old ones dare not come. I made him promise he'd never shoot a lapwing after that, and he didn't. Yes, here are more! Did he shoot my lapwings, Nelly? Are they red, any of them? Let me look."

"Give over with that baby-work!" I interrupted, dragging the pillow away, and turning the holes towards the mattress, for she was removing its contents by handfuls. "Lie down and shut your eyes: you're wandering. There's a mess! The down is flying about like snow."

I went here and there collecting it.

"I see in you, Nelly," she continued, dreamily, "an aged woman: you have grey hair and bent shoulders. This bed is the fairy cave under Peniston Crag, and you are gathering elf-bolts to hurt our heifers; pretending, while I am near, that they are only locks of wool. That's what you'll come to fifty years hence: I know you are not so now. I'm not wandering: you're mistaken, or else I should believe you really *were* that withered hag, and I should think I *was* under Peniston Crag; and I'm conscious it's night, and there are two candles on the table making the black press shine like jet."

"The black press? where is that?" I asked. "You are talking in your sleep!"

"It's against the wall, as it always is," she replied. "It *does* appear odd—I see a face in it!"

"There is no press in the room, and never was," said I, resuming my seat, and looping up the curtain that I might watch her.

"Don't *you* see that face?" she inquired, gazing earnestly at the mirror.

And say what I could, I was incapable of making her comprehend it to be her own; so I rose and covered it with a shawl.

"It's behind there still!" she pursued, anxiously. "And it stirred. Who is it?" I hope it will not come out when you are gone! Oh! Nelly, the room is haunted! I'm afraid of being alone!"

I took her hand in mine, and bid her be composed; for a succession of shudders convulsed her frame, and she *would* keep straining her gaze towards the glass.

"There's nobody here!" I insisted. "It was *yourself*, Mrs. Linton: you knew it a while since."

"Myself!" she gasped, "and the clock is striking twelve! It's true, then! that's dreadful!"

Her fingers clutched the clothes, and gathered them over her eyes. I attempted to steal to the door with an intention of calling her husband; but I was summoned back by a piercing shriek—the shawl had dropped from the frame.

"Why, what *is* the matter?" cried I. "Who is coward now? Wake up! That is the glass—the mirror, Mrs. Linton; and you see yourself in it, and there am I, too, by your side."

Trembling and bewildered, she held me fast, but the horror gradually passed from her countenance; its paleness gave place to a glow of shame.

"Oh, dear! I thought I was at home," she sighed. "I thought I was lying in my chamber at Wuthering Heights. Because I'm weak, my brain got confused, and I screamed unconsciously. Don't say anything; but stay with me. I dread sleeping: my dreams appal me."

"A sound sleep would do you good, ma'am," I answered; "and I hope this suffering will prevent your trying starving again."

"Oh, if I were but in my own bed in the old house!" she went on bitterly, wringing her hands. "And that wind sounding in the firs by the lattice. Do let me feel it—it comes straight down the moor—do let me have one breath!"

To pacify her, I held the casement ajar a few seconds. A cold blast rushed through; I closed it, and returned to my post. She lay still now, her face bathed in tears. Exhaustion of body had entirely subdued her spirit: our fiery Catherine was no better than a wailing child.

" How long is it since I shut myself in here ? " she asked, suddenly reviving.

" It was Monday evening," I replied, " and this is Thursday night, or rather Friday morning, at present."

" What ! of the same week ? " she exclaimed. " Only that brief time ? "

" Long enough to live on nothing but cold water and ill-temper," observed I.

" Well, it seems a weary number of hours," she muttered doubtfully : " it must be more. I remember being in the parlour, after they had quarrelled, and Edgar being cruelly provoking, and me running into this room desperate. As soon as ever I had barred the door, utter blackness overwhelmed me, and I fell on the floor. I couldn't explain to Edgar how certain I felt of having a fit, or going raging mad, if he persisted in teasing me ! I had no command of tongue, or brain, and he did not guess my agony, perhaps : it barely left me sense to try to escape from him and his voice. Before I recovered sufficiently to see and hear, it began to be dawn, and, Nelly, I'll tell you what I thought, and what has kept recurring and recurring till I feared for my reason. I thought as I lay there, with my head against that table leg, and my eyes dimly discerning the grey square of the window, that I was enclosed in the oak-panelled bed at home ; and my heart ached with some great grief which, just waking, I could not recollect. I pondered, and worried myself to discover what it could be, and, most strangely, the whole last seven years of my life grew a blank ! I did not recall that they had been at all. I was a child ; my father was just buried, and my misery arose from the separation that Hindley had ordered between me and Heathcliff. I was laid alone, for the first time ; and, rousing from a dismal doze after a night of weeping, I lifted my hand to push the panels aside : it struck the table-top ! I swept it along the carpet, and then memory burst in : my late anguish was swallowed in a paroxysm of despair. I cannot say why I felt so wildly wretched : it must have been temporary derangement ; for there is scarcely cause. But, supposing at twelve years old I had been wrenched from the Heights, and every early association, and my all in all, as Heathcliff was at that time, and been converted at a stroke into Mrs. Linton, the lady of Thrushcross Grange, and the wife of a stranger: an exile, and outcast, thenceforth, from what had been my world.   You may fancy a glimpse of the abyss where I grovelled! Shake your head as you will, Nelly, *you* have helped to unsettle me! You should have spoken to Edgar, indeed you should, and compelled him to leave me quiet! Oh, I 'm burning! I wish I were out of doors! I wish I were a girl again, half savage and hardy, and free; and laughing at injuries, not maddening under them! Why am I so changed? why does my blood rush into a hell of tumult at a few words? I 'm sure I should be myself were I once among the heather on those hills. Open the window again wide: fasten it open! Quick, why don't you move?"

"Because I won't give you your death of cold," I answered.

"You won't give me a chance of life, you mean," she said sullenly. "However, I'm not helpless yet; I'll open it myself."

And sliding from the bed, before I could hinder her, she crossed the room, walking very uncertainly, threw it back, and bent out, careless of the frosty air that cut about her shoulders as keen as a knife. I entreated, and finally attempted to force her to retire. But I soon found her delirious strength much surpassed mine (she *was* delirious, I became convinced by her subsequent actions and ravings). There was no moon, and everything beneath lay in misty darkness: not a light gleamed from any house, far or near—all had been extinguished long ago; and those at Wuthering Heights were never visible—still she asserted she caught their shining.

"Look!" she cried eagerly, "that's my room with the candle in it, and the trees swaying before it; and the other candle is in Joseph's garret. Joseph sits up late, doesn't he? He's waiting till I come home, that he may lock the gate. Well, he'll wait a while yet. It's a rough journey, and a sad heart to travel it; and we must pass by Gimmerton Kirk, to go that journey! We've braved it's ghosts often together, and dared each other to stand among the graves and ask them to come. But Heathcliff, if I dare you now, will you venture? If you do, I'll keep you. I'll not lie there by myself: they may bury me twelve feet deep, and throw the church down over me, but I won't rest till you are with me. I never will!"

She paused, and resumed with a strange smile. " He's considering—he'd rather I'd come to him! Find a way, then! not through that kirkyard. You are slow! Be content, you always followed me!"

Perceiving it vain to argue against her insanity, I was planning how I could reach something to wrap about her, without quitting my hold of herself (for I could not trust her alone by the gaping lattice), when, to my consternation, I heard the rattle of the door-handle, and Mr. Linton entered. He had only then come from the library; and, in passing through the lobby, had noticed our talking and been attracted by curiosity, or fear, to examine what it signified, at that late hour.

" Oh, sir!" I cried, checking the exclamation risen to his lips at the sight which met him, and the bleak atmosphere of the chamber. " My poor mistress is ill, and she quite masters me: I cannot manage her at all; pray, come and persuade her to go to bed. Forget your anger, for she's hard to guide any way but her own."

" Catherine ill?" he said, hastening to us. " Shut the window, Ellen! Catherine! why—"

He was silent. The haggardness of Mrs. Linton's appearance smote him speechless, and he could only glance from her to me in horrified astonishment.

" She's been fretting here," I continued, " and eating scarcely anything, and never complaining: she would admit none of us till this evening, and so we couldn't inform you of her state, as we were not aware of it ourselves; but it is nothing."

I felt I uttered my explanations awkwardly; the master frowned. " It is nothing, is it, Ellen Dean?" he said sternly. " You shall account more clearly for keeping me ignorant of this!" And he took his wife in his arms, and looked at her with anguish.

At first she gave him no glance of recognition: he was invisible to her abstracted gaze. The delirium was not fixed, however; having weaned her eyes from contemplating the outer darkness, by degrees she centred her attention on him, and discovered who it was that held her.

"Ah! you are come, are you, Edgar Linton?" she said, with angry animation. "You are one of those things that are ever found when least wanted, and when you are wanted, never! I suppose we shall have plenty of lamentations now —I see we shall—but they can't keep me from my narrow home out yonder: my resting-place, where I'm bound before spring is over! There it is: not among the Lintons, mind, under the chapel-roof, but in the open air, with a head-stone; and you may please yourself, whether you go to them or come to me!"

"Catherine, what have you done?" commenced the master. "Am I nothing to you any more? Do you love that wretch Heath—"

"Hush!" cried Mrs. Linton. "Hush, this moment! You mention that name and I end the matter instantly, by a spring from the window! What you touch at present, you may have; but my soul will be on that hill-top before you lay hands on me again. I don't want you, Edgar: I'm past wanting you. Return to your books. I'm glad you possess a consolation, for all you had in me is gone."

"Her mind wanders, sir," I interposed. "She has been talking nonsense the whole evening; but let her have quiet, and proper attendance, and she'll rally. Hereafter, we must be cautious how we vex her."

"I desire no further advice from you," answered Mr. Linton. "You knew your mistress's nature, and you encouraged me to harass her. And not to give me one hint of how she has been these three days! It was heartless! Months of sickness could not cause such a change!"

I began to defend myself, thinking it too bad to be blamed for another's wicked waywardness. "I knew Mrs. Linton's nature to be headstrong and domineering," cried I; "but I didn't know that you wished to foster her fierce temper! I didn't know that, to humour her, I should wink at Mr. Heathcliff. I performed the duty of a faithful servant in telling you, and I have got a faithful servant's wages! Well, it will teach me to be careful next time. Next time you may gather intelligence for yourself!"

"The next time you bring a tale to me, you shall quit my service, Ellen Dean," he replied.

"You'd rather hear nothing about it, I suppose, then, Mr. Linton?" said I. "Heathcliff has your permission to come a courting to miss, and to drop in at every opportunity your absence offers, on purpose to poison the mistress against you?"

Confused as Catherine was, her wits were alert at applying our conversation.

"Ah! Nelly has played traitor," she exclaimed, passionately. "Nelly is my hidden enemy. You witch! So you do seek elf-bolts to hurt us! Let me go, and I'll make her rue! I'll make her howl a recantation!"

A maniac's fury kindled under her brows; she struggled desperately to disengage herself from Linton's arms. I felt no inclination to tarry the event; and, resolving to seek medical aid on my own responsibility, I quitted the chamber.

In passing the garden to reach the road, at a place where a bridle hook is driven into the wall, I saw something white moved irregularly, evidently by another agent than the wind. Notwithstanding my hurry, I staid to examine it, lest ever after I should have the conviction impressed on my imagination that it was a creature of the other world. My surprise and perplexity were great on discovering, by touch more than vision, Miss Isabella's springer, Fanny suspended by a handkerchief, and nearly at its last gasp. I quickly released the animal, and lifted it into the garden. I had seen it follow its mistress up-stairs when she went to bed; and wondered much how it could have got out there, and what mischievous person had treated it so. While untying the knot round the hook, it seemed to me that I repeatedly caught the beat of horses' feet galloping at some distance; but there were such a number of things to occupy my reflections that I hardly gave the circumstance a thought: though it was a strange sound, in that place, at two o'clock in the morning.

Mr. Kenneth was fortunately just issuing from his house to see a patient in the village as I came up the street; and my account of Catherine Linton's malady induced him to accompany me back immediately. He was a plain rough man; and he made no scruple to speak his doubts of her surviving this second attack; unless she were more submissive to his directions than she had shown herself before.

"Nelly Dean," said he, "I can't help fancying there's an extra cause for this. What has there been to do at the Grange? We've odd reports up here. A stout, hearty lass like Catherine, does not fall ill for a trifle; and that sort of people should not either. It's hard work bringing them through fevers, and such things. How did it begin?"

"The master will inform you," I answered; "but you are acquainted with the Earnshaws' violent dispositions, and Mrs. Linton caps them all. I may say this; it commenced in a quarrel. She was struck during a tempest of passion with a kind of fit. That's her account, at least; for she flew off in the height of it, and locked herself up. Afterwards, she refused to eat, and now she alternately raves and remains in a half dream; knowing those about her, but having her mind filled with all sorts of strange ideas and illusions."

"Mr. Linton will be sorry?" observed Kenneth, interrogatively.

"Sorry? he'll break his heart should anything happen!" I replied. "Don't alarm him more than necessary."

"Well, I told him to beware," said my companion; "and he must bide the consequences of neglecting my warning! Hasn't he been intimate with Mr. Heathcliff lately?"

"Heathcliff frequently visits at the Grange," answered I, "though more on the strength of the mistress having known him when a boy, than because the master likes his company. At present, he's discharged from the trouble of calling; owing to some presumptuous aspirations after Miss Linton which he manifested. I hardly think he'll be taken in again."

"And does Miss Linton turn a cold shoulder on him?" was the doctor's next question.

"I'm not in her confidence," returned I, reluctant to continue the subject.

"No, she's a sly one," he remarked, shaking his head. "She keeps her own counsel! But she's a real little fool. I have it from good authority, that, last night (and a pretty night it was!) she and Heathcliff were walking in the plantation at the back of your house, above two hours; and he pressed her not to go in again, but just mount his horse and away with him! My informant said she could only put him off by pledging her word of honour to be prepared on their first meeting after that: when it was to be, he didn't hear; but you urge Mr. Linton to look sharp!"

This news filled me with fresh fears; I outstripped Kenneth, and ran most of the way back. The little dog was yelping in the garden yet. I spared a minute to open the gate for it, but instead of going to the house door, it coursed up and down snuffing the grass, and would have escaped to the road, had I not seized and conveyed it in with me. On ascending to Isabella's room, my suspicions were confirmed: it was empty. Had I been a few hours sooner, Mrs. Linton's illness might have arrested her rash step. But what could be done now? There was a bare possibility of overtaking them if pursued instantly. *I* could not pursue them, however; and I dare not rouse the family, and fill the place with confusion; still less unfold the business to my master, absorbed as he was in his present calamity, and having no heart to spare for a second grief! I saw nothing for it but to hold my tongue, and suffer matters to take their course; and Kenneth being arrived, I went with a badly composed countenance to announce him. Catherine lay in a troubled sleep: her husband had succeeded in soothing the excess of frenzy; he now hung over her pillow, watching every shade, and every change of her painfully expressive features.

The doctor, on examining the case for himself, spoke hopefully to him of its having a favourable termination, if we could only preserve around her, perfect and constant tranquillity. To me, he signified the threatening danger was not so much death, as permanent alienation of intellect.

I did not close my eyes that night, nor did Mr. Linton: indeed, we never went to bed; and the servants were all up long before the usual hour, moving through the house with stealthy tread, and exchanging whispers as they encountered each other in their vocations. Every one was active, but Miss Isabella; and they began to remark how sound she slept: her brother, too, asked if she had risen, and seemed impatient for her presence, and hurt that she showed so little anxiety for her sister-in-law. I trembled lest he should send me to call her; but I was spared the pain of being the first proclaimant of her flight. One of the maids, a thoughtless girl, who had been on an early errand to Gimmerton, came panting up stairs, open mouthed, and dashed into the chamber, crying——

"Oh, dear, dear! What mun we have next? Master, master, our young lady——"

"Hold your noise!" cried I hastily, enraged at her clamorous manner.

"Speak lower, Mary—What is the matter?" said Mr. Linton. "What ails your young lady?"

"She's gone, she's gone! Yon' Heathcliff's run off wi' her!" gasped the girl.

"That is not true!" exclaimed Linton, rising in agitation. "It cannot be: how has the idea entered your head? Ellen Dean, go and seek her. It is incredible: it cannot be."

As he spoke he took the servant to the door, and then repeated his demand to know her reasons for such an assertion.

"Why, I met on the road a lad that fetches milk here," she stammered, "and he asked whether we wern't in trouble at the Grange. I thought he meant for missis's sickness, so I answered, yes. Then says he, 'there's somebody gone after 'em, I guess?'" I stared. He saw I knew nought about it, and he told how a gentleman and lady had stopped to have a horse's shoe fastened at a blacksmith's shop, two miles out of Gimmerton, not very long after midnight! and how the blacksmith's lass had got up to spy who they were: she knew them both directly. And she noticed the man—Heathcliff it was, she felt certain: nob'dy could mistake him, besides—put a sovereign in her father's hand for payment. The lady had a cloak about her face; but having desired a sup of water, while she drank, it fell back, and she saw her very plain. Heathcliff held both bridles as they rode on, and they set their faces from the village, and went as fast as the rough roads would let them. The lass said nothing to her father, but she told it all over Gimmerton this morning."

I ran and peeped, for form's sake, into Isabella's room; confirming, when I returned, the servant's statement. Mr. Linton had resumed his seat by the bed; on my re-entrance, he raised his eyes, read the meaning of my blank aspect, and dropped them without giving an order, or uttering a word.

"Are we to try any measures for overtaking and bringing her back," I inquired. "How should we do?"

"She went of her own accord," answered the master; "she had a right to go if she pleased. Trouble me no more about her. Hereafter she is only my sister in name: not because I disown her, but because she has disowned me."

And that was all he said on the subject: he did not make a single inquiry further, or mention her in any way, except directing me to send what property she had in the house to her fresh home, wherever it was, when I knew it.

CHAPTER XIII.

FOR two months the fugitives remained absent; in those two months, Mrs. Linton encountered and conquered the worst shock of what was denominated a brain fever. No mother could have nursed an only child more devotedly than Edgar tended her. Day and night he was watching, and patiently enduring all the annoyances that irritable nerves and a shaken reason could inflict; and, though Kenneth remarked that what he saved from the grave would only recompense his care by forming the source of constant future anxiety—in fact, that his health and strength were being sacrificed to preserve a mere ruin of humanity—he knew no limits in gratitude and joy when Catherine's life was declared out of danger; and hour after hour he would sit beside her, tracing the gradual return to bodily health, and flattering his too sanguine hopes with the illusion that her mind would settle back to its right balance also, and she would soon be entirely her former self.

The first time she left her chamber was at the commencement of the following March. Mr. Linton had put on her pillow, in the morning, a handful of golden crocuses; her eye, long stranger to any gleam of pleasure, caught them in waking, and shone delighted as she gathered them eagerly together.

"These are the earliest flowers at the Heights," she exclaimed. "They remind me of soft thaw winds, and warm sunshine, and nearly melted snow. Edgar, is there not a south wind, and is not the snow almost gone?"

"The snow is quite gone down here, darling," replied her husband; "and I only see two white spots on the whole range of moors: the sky is blue, and the larks are singing, and the becks and brooks are all brim full. Catherine, last spring at this time, I was longing to have you under this roof; now, I wish you were a mile or two up those hills: the air blows so sweetly, I feel that it would cure you."

" I shall never be there, but once more," said the invalid: " and then you'll leave me, and I shall remain for ever. Next spring you'll long again to have me under this roof, and you'll look back and think you were happy to-day."

Linton lavished on her the kindest caresses, and tried to cheer her by the fondest words; but, vaguely regarding the flowers, she let the tears collect on her lashes and stream down her cheeks unheeding. We knew she was really better, and, therefore, decided that long confinement to a single place produced much of this despondency, and it might be partially removed by a change of scene. The master told me to light a fire in the many-weeks deserted parlour, and to set an easy-chair in the sunshine by the window; and then he brought her down, and she sat a long while enjoying the genial heat, and, as we expected, revived by the objects round her: which, though familiar, were free from the dreary associations investing her hated sick-chamber. By evening, she seemed greatly exhausted; yet no arguments could persuade her to return to that apart-ment, and I had to arrange the parlour sofa for her bed, till another room could be prepared. To obviate the fatigue of mounting and descending the stairs, we fitted up this, where you lie at present: on the same floor with the parlour; and she was soon strong enough to move from one to the other, leaning on Edgar's arm. Ah, I thought myself, she might recover, so waited on as she was. And there was double cause to desire it, for on her existence depended that of another: we cherished the hope that in a little while, Mr. Linton's heart would be gladdened, and his lands secured from a stranger's gripe, by the birth of an heir.

I should mention that Isabella sent to her brother, some six weeks from her departure a short note, announcing her marriage with Heathcliff. It appeared dry and cold; but at the bottom was dotted in with pencil an obscure apology, and an entreaty for kind remembrance and reconciliation, if her proceeding had offended him: asserting that she could not help it then, and being done, she had now no power to repeal it. Linton did not reply to this, I believe; and, in a fortnight more, I got a long letter which I considered odd, coming from the pen of a bride just out of the honeymoon. I'll read it: for I keep it yet. Any relic of the dead is precious, if they were valued living.

DEAR ELLEN, it begins.

I came last night to Wuthering Heights, and heard, for the first time, that Catherine has been, and is yet, very ill. I must not write to her I suppose, and my brother is either too angry or too distressed to answer what I send him. Still, I must write to somebody, and the only choice left me is you.

Inform Edgar that I'd give the world to see his face again—that my heart returned to Thrushcross Grange in twenty-four hours after I left it, and is there at this moment, full of warm feelings for him, and Catherine! *I can't follow it, though*—(those words are underlined) they need not expect me, and they may draw what conclusions they please; taking care, however, to lay nothing at the door of my weak will or deficient affection.

The remainder of the letter is for yourself alone. I want to ask you two questions: the first is,—How did you contrive to preserve the common sympathies of human nature when you resided here? I cannot recognise any sentiment which those around share with me.

The second question, I have great interest in; it is this— Is Mr. Heathcliff a man? If so, is he mad? And if not, is he a devil? I sha'n't tell my reasons for making this inquiry; but, I beseech you to explain, if you can, what I have married: that is, when you call to see me; and you must call, Ellen, very soon. Don't write, but come, and bring me something from Edgar.

Now, you shall hear how I have been received in my new home, as I am led to imagine the Heights will be. It is to amuse myself that I dwell on such subjects as the lack of external comforts: they never occupy my thoughts, except at the moment when I miss them. I should laugh and dance for joy, if I found their absence was the total of my miseries, and the rest was an unnatural dream!

The sun set behind the Grange, as we turned on to the moors; by that, I judged it to be six o'clock; and my companion halted half an hour, to inspect the park, and the gardens, and, probably, the place itself, as well as he could;

so it was dark when we dismounted in the paved yard of the farm-house, and your old fellow-servant, Joseph, issued out to receive us by the light of a dip candle. He did it with a courtesy that redounded to his credit. His first act was to elevate his torch to a level with my face, squint malignantly, project his under lip, and turn away. Then he took the two horses, and led them into the stables; reappearing for the purpose of locking the outer gate, as if we lived in an ancient castle.

Heathcliff stayed to speak to him, and I entered the kitchen—a dingy, untidy hole: I dare say you would not know it, it is so changed since it was in your charge. By the fire stood a ruffianly child, strong in limb and dirty in garb, with a look of Catherine in his eyes and about his mouth.

"This is Edgar's legal nephew," I reflected—"mine in a manner; I must shake hands, and—yes—I must kiss him. It is right to establish a good understanding at the beginning."

I approached, and, attempting to take his chubby fist, said—

"How do you do, my dear?"

He replied in a jargon I did not comprehend.

"Shall you and I be friends, Hareton?" was my next essay at conversation.

An oath, and a threat to set Throttler on me if I did not "frame off" rewarded my perseverance.

"Hey, Throttler, lad!" whispered the little wretch, rousing a half-bred bull-dog from its lair in a corner. "Now, wilt thou be ganging?" he asked authoritatively.

Love for my life urged a compliance; I stepped over the threshold to wait till the others should enter. Mr. Heathcliff was nowhere visible; and Joseph, whom I followed to the stables, and requested to accompany me in, after staring and muttering to himself, screwed up his nose and replied—

"Mim! mim! mim! Did iver Christian body hear aught like it? Minching un' munching! How can I tell whet ye say?"

"I say, I wish you to come with me into the house!" I cried, thinking him deaf, yet highly disgusted at his rudeness.

"None o' me! I getten summut else to do," he answered, and continued his work; moving his lantern jaws meanwhile, and surveying my dress and countenance (the former a great deal too fine, but the latter, I'm sure, as sad as he could desire) with sovereign contempt.

I walked round the yard, and through a wicket, to another door, at which I took the liberty of knocking, in hopes some more civil servant might shew himself. After a short suspense, it was opened by a tall, gaunt man, without neckerchief, and otherwise extremely slovenly; his features were lost in masses of shaggy hair that hung on his shoulders; and *his* eyes, too, were like a ghostly Catherine's with all their beauty annihilated.

" What's your business here?" he demanded grimly. " Who are you?"

" My name *was* Isabella Linton," I replied. " You've seen me before, sir. I'm lately married to Mr. Heathcliff, and he has brought me here—I suppose by your permission."

" Is he come back, then?" asked the hermit, glaring like a hungry wolf.

" Yes—we came just now," I said; "but he left me by the kitchen door; and when I would have gone in, your little boy played sentinel over the place, and frightened me off by the help of a bull-dog."

" It's well the hellish villain has kept his word!" growled my future host, searching the darkness beyond me in expectation of discovering Heathcliff; and then he indulged in a soliloquy of execrations, and threats of what he would have done had the " fiend" deceived him.

I repented having tried this second entrance, and was almost inclined to slip away before he finished cursing, but ere I could execute that intention, he ordered me in, and shut and re-fastened the door. There was a great fire, and that was all the light in the huge apartment, whose floor had grown a uniform grey; and the once brilliant pewter dishes, which used to attract my gaze when I was a girl, partook of a similar obscurity, created by tarnish and dust. I inquired whether I might call the maid, and be conducted to a bed-room? Mr. Earnshaw vouchsafed no answer. He walked up and down, with his hands in his pockets, apparently quite forgetting my presence; and his abstraction was evidently so deep, and his whole aspect so misanthropical, that I shrank from disturbing him again.

"You'll not be surprised, Ellen, at my feeling particularly cheerless, seated in worse than solitude on that inhospitable hearth, and remembering that four miles distant lay my delightful home, containing the only people I loved on earth; and there might as well be the Atlantic to part us, instead of those four miles: I could not overpass them! I questioned with myself—where must I turn for comfort? and—mind you don't tell Edgar, or Catherine—above every sorrow beside, this rose pre-eminent: despair at finding nobody who could or would be my ally against Heathcliff! I had sought shelter at Wuthering Heights, almost gladly, because I was secured by that arrangement from living alone with him; but he knew the people we were coming amongst, and he did not fear their intermeddling.

I sat and thought a doleful time: the clock struck eight, and nine, and still my companion paced to and fro, his head bent on his breast, and perfectly silent, unless a groan or a bitter ejaculation forced itself out at intervals. I listened to detect a woman's voice in the house, and filled the interim with wild regrets and dismal anticipations, which, at last, spoke audibly in irrepressible sighing and weeping. I was not aware how openly I grieved, till Earnshaw halted opposite, in his measured walk, and gave me a stare of newly-awakened surprise. Taking advantage of his recovered attention, I exclaimed—

"I'm tired with my journey, and I want to go to bed! Where is the maid-servant? Direct me to her, as she won't come to me!"

"We have none," he answered; "you must wait on yourself!"

"Where must I sleep, then?" I sobbed; I was beyond regarding self-respect, weighed down by fatigue and wretchedness.

"Joseph will show you Heathcliff's chamber," said he; "open that door—he's in there."

I was going to obey, but he suddenly arrested me, and added in the strangest tone—

"Be so good as to turn your lock, and draw your bolt—don't omit it!"

"Well!" I said. "But why, Mr. Earnshaw?" I did not relish the notion of deliberately fastening myself in with Heathcliff.

"Look here!" he replied, pulling from his waistcoat a curiously constructed pistol, having a double-edged spring knife attached to the barrel. "That's a great tempter to a desperate man, is it not? I cannot resist going up with this every night, and trying his door. If once I find it open he's done for! I do it invariably, even though the minute before I have been recalling a hundred reasons that should make me refrain: it is some devil that urges me to thwart my own schemes by killing him. You fight against that devil for love as long as you may; when the time comes, not all the angels in heaven shall save him!"

I surveyed the weapon inquisitively. A hideous notion struck me: how powerful I should be possessing such an instrument! I took it from his hand, and touched the blade. He looked astonished at the expression my face assumed during a brief second: it was not horror, it was covetousness. He snatched the pistol back, jealously; shut the knife, and returned it to its concealment.

"I don't care if you tell him," said he. "Put him on his guard, and watch for him. You know the terms we are on, I see: his danger does not shock you."

"What has Heathcliff done to you?" I asked. "In what has he wronged you, to warrant this appalling hatred? Wouldn't it be wiser to bid him quit the house?"

"No!" thundered Earnshaw, "should he offer to leave me, he's a dead man: persuade him to attempt it, and you are a murderess! Am I to lose *all*, without a chance of retrieval? Is Hareton to be a beggar? Oh, damnation! I *will* have it back: and I'll have *his* gold too; and then his blood; and hell shall have his soul! It will be ten times blacker with that guest than ever it was before!"

You 've acquainted me, Ellen, with your old master's habits. He is clearly on the verge of madness: he was so last night at least. I shuddered to be near him, and thought on the servant's ill-bred moroseness as comparatively agreeable. He now recommenced his moody walk, and I raised the latch, and escaped into the kitchen. Joseph was bending over the fire, peering into a large pan that swung above it; and a wooden bowl of oatmeal stood on the settle close by. The contents of the pan began to boil, and he turned to plunge his hand into the bowl; I conjectured that this preparation was probably for our supper, and, being hungry, I resolved it should be eatable; so crying out, sharply "*I'll* make the porridge!" I removed the vessel out of his reach, and proceeded to take off my hat and riding habit. "Mr. Earnshaw," I continued, "directs me to wait on myself: I will. I'm not going to act the lady among you, for fear I should starve."

"Gooid Lord!" he muttered, sitting down, and stroking his ribbed stockings from the knee to the ankle. "If there's to be fresh ortherings—just when I getten used to two maisters, if I mun hev a *mistress* set o'er my heead, it's like time to be flitting. I niver *did* think to see t' day that I mud lave th' owld place—but I doubt it's nigh at hand!"

This lamentation drew no notice from me: I went briskly to work, sighing to remember a period when it would have been all merry fun; but compelled speedily to drive off the remembrance. It racked me to recall past happiness, and the greater peril there was of conjuring up its apparition, the quicker the thible ran round, and the faster the handfuls of meal fell into the water. Joseph beheld my style of cookery with growing indignation.

"Thear!" he ejaculated. "Hareton, thou willn't sup thy porridge to-neeght; they'll be naught but lumps as big as my neive. Thear, agean! I'd fling in bowl un all, if I wer ye! There, pale t' guilp off, un' then ye'll hae done wi't. Bang, bang. It's a mercy t' bothom isn't deaved out!"

It *was* rather a rough mess, I own, when poured into the basins; four had been provided, and a gallon pitcher of new milk was brought from the dairy, which Hareton seized and commenced drinking and spilling from the expansive lip. I expostulated, and desired that he should have his in a mug; affirming that I could not taste the liquid treated so dirtily. The old cynic chose to be vastly offended at this nicety; assuring me, repeatedly, that "the barn was every bit as good" as I, "and every bit as wollsome," and wondering how I could fashion to be so conceited. Meanwhile, the infant ruffian continued sucking; and glowered up at me defyingly, as he slavered into the jug.

"I shall have my supper in another room," I said. "Have you no place you call a parlour?"

"*Parlour!*" he echoed, sneeringly, "*parlour!* Nay, we've noa *parlours.* If yah dunnut loike wer company, there's maister's; un' if yah dunnut loike maister, there's us."

"Then I shall go up stairs," I answered; "show me a chamber."

I put my basin on a tray, and went myself to fetch some more milk. With great grumblings, the fellow rose, and preceded me in my ascent: we mounted to the garrets; he opened a door, now and then, to look into the apartments we passed.

"Here's a rahm," he said, at last, flinging back a cranky board on hinges. "It's weel eneugh to ate a few porridge in. There's a pack o' corn i' t' corner, thear, meeterly clane; if ye're feared o' muckying yer grand silk cloes, spread yer hankerchir o' t' top on 't."

The "rahm" was a kind of lumber-hole smelling strong of malt and grain; various sacks of which articles were piled around, leaving a wide, bare space in the middle.

"Why, man!" I exclaimed, facing him angrily, "this is not a place to sleep in. I wish to see my bed-room."

"*Bed-rume!*" he repeated, in a tone of mockery. "Yah's see all t' *bed-rumes* thear is—yon's mine."

He pointed into the second garret, only differing from the first in being more naked about the walls, and having a large, low, curtainless bed, with an indigo-coloured quilt, at one end.

"What do I want with yours?" I retorted. "I suppose Mr. Heathcliff does not lodge at the top of the house, does he?"

"Oh! it's Maister *Hathecliff's* ye're wanting?" cried he, as if making a new discovery. "Couldn't ye ha' said soa, at onst? un then, I mud ha' telled ye, baht all this wark, that that's just one ye cannut see—he allas keeps it locked, un' nob'dy iver mells on't but hisseln."

"You've a nice house, Joseph," I could not refrain from observing, "and pleasant inmates; and I think the concentrated essence of all the madness in the world took up its abode in my brain the day I linked my fate with theirs! However, that is not to the present purpose—there are other rooms. For Heaven's sake, be quick, and let me settle some-where !"

He made no reply to this adjuration; only plodding dog-gedly down the wooden steps, and halting before an apart-ment which, from that halt and the superior quality of its furniture, I conjectured to be the best one. There was a carpet: a good one, but the pattern was obliterated by dust; a fireplace hung with cut paper dropping to pieces; a hand-some oak-bedstead with ample crimson curtains of rather expensive material and modern make; but they had evi-dently experienced rough usage : the valances hung in fes-toons, wrenched from their rings, and the iron rod supporting them was bent in an arc, on one side, causing the drapery to trail upon the floor. The chairs were also damaged, many of them severely ; and deep indentations deformed the panels of the walls. I was endeavouring to gather resolution for entering, and taking possession, when my fool of a guide announced. "This here is t' maister's." My supper by this time was cold, my appetite gone, and my patience exhausted. I insisted on being provided instantly with a place of refuge, and means of repose.

"Whear the divil?" began the religious elder. "The Lord bless us ! The Lord forgie us ! Whear the *hell*, wold ye gang ? ye marred, wearisome nowt ! Ye've seen all but Hareton's bit of a cham'er. There's not another hoile to lig down in i' th' hahse !"

I was so vexed, I flung my tray and its contents on the ground ; and then seated myself at the stairs-head, hid my face in my hands, and cried.

"Ech ! ech !" exclaimed Joseph. "Weel done, Miss Cathy ! weel done, Miss Cathy ! Howsiver, t' maister sall just tum'le o'er them brocken pots ; un' then we's hear sum-mut ; we's hear how it's to be. Gooid-for-naught madling ! ye desarve pining fro' this to Churstmas, flinging t' pre-cious gifts o' God under fooit i' yer flaysome rages ! But, I'm mista'en if ye shew yer sperrit lang. Will Hathecliff bide sich bonny ways, think ye ? I nobbut wish he may catch ye i' that plisky. I nobbut wish he may."

And so he went scolding to his den beneath, taking the candle with him ; and I remained in the dark. The period of reflection succeeding this silly action, compelled me to admit the necessity of smothering my pride and choking my wrath, and bestirring myself to remove its effects. An unexpected aid presently appeared in the shape of Throttler, whom I now recognised as a son of our old Skulker: it had spent its whelphood at the Grange, and was given by my father to Mr. Hindley. I fancy it knew me: it pushed its nose against mine by way of salute, and then hastened to devour the porridge; while I groped from step to step, collecting the shattered earthenware, and drying the spatters of milk from the banister with my pocket-handkerchief. Our labours were scarcely over when I heard Earnshaw's tread in the passage; my assistant tucked in his tail, and pressed to the wall; I stole into the nearest doorway. The dog's endeavour to avoid him was unsuccessful; as I guessed by a scutter down stairs, and a prolonged, piteous yelping. I had better luck: he passed on, entered his chamber, and shut the door. Directly after Joseph came up with Hareton, to put him to bed. I had found shelter in Hareton's room, and the old man on seeing me, said—

"They's rahm fur boath ye un yer pride, now, I sud think i' the hahse. It's empty; ye may hev it all to yerseln, un Him as allas maks a third, i' sich ill company!"

Gladly did I take advantage of this intimation; and the minute I flung myself into a chair, by the fire, I nodded, and slept. My slumber was deep and sweet, though over far too soon. Mr. Heathcliff awoke me; he had just come in, and demanded, in his loving manner, what I was doing there? I told him the cause of my staying up so late—that he had the key of our room in his pocket. The adjective *our* gave mortal offence. He swore it was not, nor ever should be mine; and he'd—But I'll not repeat his language, nor describe his habitual conduct: he is ingenious and unresting in seeking to gain my abhorrence! I sometimes wonder at him with an intensity that deadens my fear: yet, I assure you, a tiger or a venomous serpent could not rouse terror in me equal to that which he wakens. He told me of Catherine's illness, and accused my brother of causing it; promising that I should be Edgar's proxy in suffering, till he could get hold of him.

I do hate him—I am wretched—I have been a fool! Beware of uttering one breath of this to any one at the Grange. I shall expect you every day—don't disappoint me!" ISABELLA.

CHAPTER XIV.

As soon as I had perused this epistle, I went to the master, and informed him that his sister had arrived at the Heights, and sent me a letter expressing her sorrow for Mrs. Linton's situation, and her ardent-desire to see him; with a wish that he would transmit to her, as early as possible, some token of forgiveness by me.

"Forgiveness!" said Linton. "I have nothing to forgive her, Ellen. You may call at Wuthering Heights this afternoon, if you like, and say that I am not *angry*, but I'm *sorry* to have lost her; especially as I can never think she'll be happy. It is out of the question my going to see her, however: we are eternally divided; and should she really wish to oblige me, let her persuade the villain she has married to leave the country."

"And you won't write her a little note, sir?" I asked, imploringly.

"No," he answered. "It is needless. My communication with Heathcliff's family shall be as sparing as his with mine. It shall not exist!"

Mr. Edgar's coldness depressed me exceedingly; and all the way from the Grange I puzzled my brains how to put more heart into what he said, when I repeated it; and how to soften his refusal of even a few lines to console Isabella. I dare say she had been on the watch for me since morning: I saw her looking through the lattice, as I came up the garden causeway, and I nodded to her; but she drew back, as if afraid of being observed. I entered without knocking. There never was such a dreary, dismal scene as the formerly cheerful house presented! I must confess, that if I had been in the young lady's place, I would, at least, have swept the hearth, and wiped the tables with a duster. But she already partook of the pervading spirit of neglect which encompassed her. Her pretty face was wan and listless; her hair uncurled: some locks hanging lankly down, and some carelessly twisted round her head. Probably she had not touched her dress since yester evening. Hindley was not there. Mr. Heathcliff sat at a table, turning over some papers in his pocket-book; but he rose when I appeared, asked me how I did, quite friendly, and offered me a chair.

He was the only thing there that seemed decent; and I thought he never looked better. So much had circumstances altered their positions, that he would certainly have struck a stranger as a born and bred gentleman; and his wife as a thorough little slattern! She came forward eagerly to greet me; and held out one hand to take the expected letter. I shook my head. She wouldn't understand the hint, but followed me to a sideboard, where I went to lay my bonnet, and importuned me in a whisper to give her directly what I had brought. Heathcliff guessed the meaning of her manœuvres, and said—

" If you have got anything for Isabella (as no doubt you have, Nelly), give it to her. You needn't make a secret of it: we have no secrets between us."

" Oh, I have nothing," I replied, thinking it best to speak the truth at once. " My master bid me tell his sister that she must not expect either a letter or a visit from him at present. He sends his love, ma'am, and his wishes for your happiness, and his pardon for the grief you have occasioned; but he thinks that after this time, his household and the household here should drop intercommunication, as nothing could come of keeping it up."

Mrs. Heathcliff's lip quivered slightly, and she returned to her seat in the window. Her husband took his stand on the hearthstone, near me, and began to put questions concerning Catherine. I told him as much as I thought proper of her illness, and he extorted from me, by cross-examination, most of the facts connected with its origin. I blamed her, as she deserved, for bringing it all on herself; and ended by hoping that he would follow Mr. Linton's example, and avoid future interference with his family, for good or evil.

" Mrs. Linton is now just recovering," I said, " she'll never be like she was, but her life is spared; and if you really have a regard for her, you'll shun crossing her way again: nay, you'll move out of this country entirely; and that you may not regret it, I'll inform you Catherine Linton is as different now from your old friend Catherine Earnshaw, as that young lady is different from me. Her appearance is changed greatly, her character much more so; and the person who is compelled, of necessity, to be her companion, will only sustain his affection hereafter by the remembrance

K

of what she once was, by common humanity, and a sense of
duty !"

"That is quite possible," remarked Heathcliff, forcing
himself to seem calm: "quite possible that your master
should have nothing but common humanity and a sense of
duty to fall back upon. But do you imagine that I shall
leave Catherine to his *duty* and *humanity*? and can you
compare my feelings respecting Catherine to his? Before
you leave this house, I must exact a promise from you, that
you'll get me an interview with her: consent, or refuse,
I *will* see her! What do you say?"

" I say, Mr. Heathcliff," I replied, "you must not: you
never shall, through my means. Another encounter between
you and the master would kill her altogether."

"With your aid, that may be avoided," he continued;
" and should there be danger of such an event—should he be
the cause of adding a single trouble more to her existence—
why, I think, I shall be justified in going to extremes!
I wish you had sincerity enough to tell me whether Catherine would suffer greatly from his loss: the fear that she
would restrains me. And there you see the distinction between our feelings: had he been in my place and I in
his, though I hated him with a hatred that turned my
life to gall, I never would have raised a hand against him.
You may look incredulous, if you please! I never would
have banished him from her society as long as she desired
his. The moment her regard ceased, I would have torn
his heart out, and drank his blood! But, till then — if
you don't believe me, you don't know me—till then, I would
have died by inches before I touched a single hair of his
head !"

"And yet," I interrupted, "you have no scruples in
completely ruining all hopes of her perfect restoration, by
thrusting yourself into her remembrance now, when she
has nearly forgotten you, and involving her in a new tumult
of discord and distress."

"You suppose she has nearly forgotten me?" he said.
"Oh, Nelly! you know she has not! You know as well
as I do, that for every thought she spends on Linton,
she spends a thousand on me! At a most miserable period
of my life, I had a notion of the kind: it haunted me
on my return to the neighbourhood last summer; but only

her own assurance could make me admit the horrible idea again. And then, Linton would be nothing, nor Hindley, nor all the dreams that ever I dreamt. Two words would comprehend my future—*death* and *hell*: existence, after losing her, would be hell. Yet I was a fool to fancy for a moment that she valued Edgar Linton's attachment more than mine. If he loved with all the powers of his puny being, he couldn't love as much in eighty years as I could in a day. And Catherine has a heart as deep as I have: the sea could be as readily contained in that horse-trough, as her whole affection be monopolized by him. Tush! He is scarcely a degree dearer to her than her dog, or her horse. It is not in him to be loved like me: how can she love in him what he has not?

"Catherine and Edgar are as fond of each other as any two people can be," cried Isabella, with sudden vivacity. "No one has a right to talk in that manner, and I won't hear my brother depreciated in silence!"

"Your brother is wondrous fond of you too, isn't he?" observed Heathcliff, scornfully. "He turns you adrift on the world with surprising alacrity."

"He is not aware of what I suffer," she replied. "I didn't tell him that."

"You have been telling him something, then: you have written, have you?"

"To say that I was married, I did write—you saw the note."

"And nothing since?"

"No."

"My young lady is looking sadly the worse for her change of condition," I remarked. "Somebody's love comes short in her case, obviously: whose, I may guess; but, perhaps, I shouldn't say."

"I should guess it was her own," said Heathcliff. "She degenerates into a mere slut! She is tired of trying to please me uncommonly early. You'd hardly credit it, but the very morrow of our wedding, she was weeping to go home. However, she'll suit this house so much the better for not being over nice, and I'll take care she does not disgrace me by rambling abroad."

"Well, sir," returned I, "I hope you'll consider that Mrs. Heathcliff is accustomed to be looked after and waited on; and that she has been brought up like an only daughter, whom every one was ready to serve. You must let her have a maid to keep things tidy about her, and you must treat her kindly. Whatever be your notion of Mr. Edgar, you cannot doubt that she has a capacity for strong attachments, or she wouldn't have abandoned the elegances and comforts, and friends of her former home, to fix contentedly, in such a wilderness as this, with you."

"She abandoned them under a delusion," he answered; "picturing in me a hero of romance, and expecting unlimited indulgences from my chivalrous devotion. I can hardly regard her in the light of a rational creature, so obstinately has she persisted in forming a fabulous notion of my character, and acting on the false impressions she cherished. But, at last, I think she begins to know me: I don't perceive the silly smiles and grimaces that provoked me at first; and the senseless incapability of discerning that I was in earnest when I gave her my opinion of her infatuation and herself. It was a marvellous effort of perspicacity to discover that I did not love her. I believed, at one time, no lessons could teach her that! And yet it is poorly learnt; for this morning she announced, as a piece of appalling intelligence, that I had actually succeeded in making her hate me! A positive labour of Hercules, I assure you! If it be achieved, I have cause to return thanks. Can I trust your assertion, Isabella? Are you sure you hate me? If I let you alone for half a day, won't you come sighing and wheedling to me again? I dare say she would rather I had seemed all tenderness before you: it wounds her vanity to have the truth exposed. But I don't care who knows that the passion was wholly on one side; and I never told her a lie about it. She cannot accuse me of showing one bit of deceitful softness. The first thing she saw me do, on coming out of the Grange, was to hang up her little dog; and when she pleaded for it, the first words I uttered were a wish that I had the hanging of every being belonging to her, except one: possibly she took that exception for herself. But no brutality disgusted her: I suppose she has an innate admiration of it, if only her precious person were secure from injury! Now, was it not the depth of absurdity—of genuine idiocy, for that pitiful, slavish, mean-minded brach to dream that I could love her? Tell

your master, Nelly, that I never, in all my life, met with
such an abject thing as she is. She even disgraces the
name of Linton; and I've sometimes relented, from pure
lack of invention in my experiments on what she could
endure, and still creep shamefully cringing back! But tell
him, also, to set his fraternal and magisterial heart at ease:
that I keep strictly within the limits of the law. I have
avoided, up to this period, giving her the slightest right
to claim a separation; and what's more, she'd thank nobody for dividing us. If she desired to go, she might: the
nuisance of her presence outweighs the gratification to be
derived from tormenting her!"

"Mr. Heathcliff," said I, "this is the talk of a madman;
your wife, most likely is convinced you are mad; and, for
that reason, she has borne with you hitherto: but now that
you say she may go, she'll doubtless avail herself of the permission. You are not so bewitched, ma'am, are you, as to
remain with him of your own accord?"

"Take care, Ellen!" answered Isabella, her eyes sparkling
irefully! there was no misdoubting by their expression, the full
success of her partner's endeavours to make himself detested.
"Don't put faith in a single word he speaks. He's a lying
fiend! a monster, and not a human being! I've been told I
might leave him before; and I've made the attempt, but I
dare not repeat it! Only Ellen, promise you'll not mention
a syllable of his infamous conversation to my brother or
Catherine. Whatever he may pretend, he wishes to provoke
Edgar to desperation: he says he has married me on purpose
to obtain power over him; and he sha'n't obtain it—I'll die
first! I just hope, I pray, that he may forget his diabolical
prudence and kill me! The single pleasure I can imagine,
is to die, or to see him dead!"

"There—that will do for the present!" said Heathcliff.
"If you are called upon in a court of law, you'll remember
her language, Nelly! And take a good look at that countenance: she's near the point which would suit me. No;
you're not fit to be your own guardian, Isabella now; and I,
being your legal protector, must retain you in my custody,
however distasteful the obligation may be. Go up stairs; I
have something to say to Ellen Dean in private. That's not
the way: up stairs, I tell you! Why this is the road up-
stairs, child!"

He seized, and thrust her from the room; and returned muttering,—

"I have no pity! I have no pity! The more the worms writhe, the more I yearn to crush out their entrails! It is a moral teething; and I grind with greater energy, in proportion to the increase of pain."

"Do you understand what the word pity means?" I said hastening to resume my bonnet. "Did you ever feel a touch of it in your life?"

"Put that down!" he interrupted, perceiving my intention to depart. "You are not going yet. Come here now, Nelly: I must either persuade or compel you to aid me in fulfilling my determination to see Catherine, and that without delay. I swear that I meditate no harm: I don't desire to cause any disturbance, or to exasperate, or insult Mr. Linton; I only wish to hear from herself how she is, and why she has been ill; and to ask, if anything that I could do would be of use to her. Last night, I was in the Grange garden six hours, and I'll return there to-night; and every night I'll haunt the place, and every day, till I find an opportunity of entering. If Edgar Linton meets me, I shall not hesitate to knock him down, and give him enough to ensure his quiescence while I stay. If his servants oppose me, I shall threaten them off with these pistols. But wouldn't it be better to prevent my coming in contact with them, or their master? And you could do it so easily. I'd warn you when I came, and then you might let me in unobserved, as soon as she was alone, and watch till I departed, your conscience quite calm: you would be hindering mischief."

I protested against playing that treacherous part in my employer's house: and besides, I urged the cruelty and selfishness of his destroying Mrs. Linton's tranquillity for his satisfaction. "The commonest occurrence startles her painfully," I said. "She's all nerves, and she couldn't bear the surprise, I'm positive. Don't persist, sir! or else, I shall be obliged to inform my master of your designs; and he'll take measures to secure his house and its inmates from any such unwarrantable intrusions!"

"In that case, I'll take measures to secure you, woman!" exclaimed Heathcliff, "you shall not leave Wuthering Heights till to-morrow morning. It is a foolish story to assert that

Catherine could not bear to see me; and as to surprising her, I don't desire it: you must prepare her—ask her if I may come. You say she never mentions my name, and that I am never mentioned to her. To whom should she mention me if I am a forbidden topic in the house? She thinks you are all spies for her husband. Oh, I 've no doubt she's in hell among you! I guess by her silence as much as anything, what she feels. You say she is often restless, and anxious looking: is that a proof of tranquillity? You talk of her mind being unsettled. How the devil could it be otherwise in her frightful isolation. And that insipid, paltry creature attending her from *duty* and *humanity!* From *pity* and *charity!* He might as well plant an oak in a flower-pot and expect it to thrive, as imagine he can restore her to vigour in the soil of his shallow cares! Let us settle it at once: will you stay here, and am I to fight my way to Catherine over Linton and his footman? Or will you be my friend, as you have been hitherto, and do what I request? Decide! because there is no reason for my lingering another minute, if you persist in your stubborn ill-nature!"

Well, Mr. Lockwood, I argued and complained, and flatly refused him fifty times; but in the long run he forced me to an agreement. I engaged to carry a letter from him to my mistress; and should she consent, I promised to let him have intelligence of Linton's next absence from home, when he might come, and get in as he was able: I wouldn't be there, and my fellow-servants should be equally out of the way. Was it right or wrong? I fear it was wrong, though expedient. I thought I prevented another explosion by my compliance; and I thought, too, it might create a favourable crisis in Catherine's mental illness: and then I remembered Mr. Edgar's stern rebuke of my carrying tales; and I tried to smooth away all disquietude on the subject, by affirming, with frequent iteration, that that betrayal of trust, if it merited so harsh an appellation, should be the last. Notwithstanding, my journey homeward was sadder than my journey thither; and many misgivings I had, ere I could prevail on myself to put the missive into Mrs. Linton's hand.

But here is Kenneth; I 'll go down, and tell him how much better you are. My history is *dree*', as we say, and will serve to while away another morning.

Dree, and dreary! I reflected as the good woman descended to receive the doctor; and not exactly of the kind which I should have chosen to amuse me. But never mind! I'll extract wholesome medicines from Mrs. Dean's bitter herbs; and firstly, let me beware the fascination that lurks in Catherine Heathcliff's brilliant eyes. I should be in a curious taking if I surrendered my heart to that young person, and the daughter turned out a second edition of the mother!

CHAPTER XV.

ANOTHER week over—and I am so many days nearer health, and spring! I have now heard all my neighbour's history, at different sittings, as the housekeeper could spare time from more important occupations. I'll continue it in her own words, only a little condensed. She is, on the whole, a very fair narrator, and I don't think I could improve her style.

In the evening, she said, the evening of my visit to the Heights, I knew, as well as if I saw him, that Mr. Heathcliff was about the place; and I shunned going out, because I still carried his letter in my pocket, and didn't want to be threatened or teased any more. I had made up my mind not to give it till my master went somewhere, as I could not guess how its receipt would affect Catherine. The consequence was, that it did not reach her before the lapse of three days. The fourth was Sunday, and I brought it into her room after the family were gone to church. There was a man-servant left to keep the house with me, and we generally made a practice of locking the doors during the hours of service; but on that occasion the weather was so warm and pleasant that I set them wide open, and, to fulfil my engagement, as I knew who would be coming, I told my companion that the mistress wished very much for some oranges, and he must run over to the village and got a few, to be paid for on the morrow. He departed, and I went up stairs.

Mrs. Linton sat in a loose, white dress, with a light shawl over her shoulders, in the recess of the open window, as usual. Her thick, long hair, had been partly removed at the beginning of her illness, and now she wore it simply combed in its natural tresses over her temples and neck. Her appearance was altered, as I had told Heathcliff; but when she was calm, there seemed unearthly beauty in the change. The flash of her eyes had been succeeded by a dreamy and melancholy softness; they no longer gave the impression of looking at the objects around her: they appeared always to gaze beyond, and far beyond—you would have said out of this world. Then, the paleness of her face—its haggard aspect having vanished as she recovered flesh—and the peculiar expression arising from her mental state, though painfully suggestive of their causes, added to the touching interest which she awakened; and—invariably to me, I know, and to any person who saw her, I should think—refuted more tangible proofs of convalescence, and stamped her as one doomed to decay.

A book lay spread on the sill before her, and the scarcely perceptible wind fluttered its leaves at intervals. I believe Linton had laid it there: for she never endeavoured to divert herself with reading, or occupation of any kind, and he would spend many an hour in trying to entice her attention to some subject which had formerly been her amusement. She was conscious of his aim, and in her better moods endured his efforts placidly, only showing their uselessness by now and then suppressing a wearied sigh, and checking him at last with the saddest of smiles and kisses. At other times, she would turn petulantly away, and hide her face in her hands, or even push him off angrily; and then he took care to let her alone, for he was certain of doing no good.

Gimmerton chapel bells were still ringing; and the full, mellow flow of the beck in the valley came soothingly on the ear. It was a sweet substitute for the yet absent murmur of the summer foliage, which drowned that music about the Grange when the trees were in leaf. At Wuthering Heights it always sounded on quiet days following a great thaw or a season of steady rain. And of Wuthering Heights Catherine was thinking as she listened: that is, if she thought or listened at all; but she had the vague, distant look I mentioned before, which expressed no recognition of material things either by ear or eye.

"There's a letter for you, Mrs. Linton," I said, gently inserting it in one hand that rested on her knee. "You must read it immediately, because it wants an answer. Shall I break the seal?" "Yes," she answered, without altering the direction of her eyes. I opened it—it was very short. "Now," I continued, "read it." She drew away her hand, and let it fall. I replaced it in her lap, and stood waiting till it should please her to glance down; but that movement was so long delayed that at last I resumed—

"Must I read it, ma'am? It is from Mr. Heathcliff."

There was a start and a troubled gleam of recollection, and a struggle to arrange her ideas. She lifted the letter, and seemed to peruse it; and when she came to the signature she sighed: yet still I found she had not gathered its import, for, upon my desiring to hear her reply, she merely pointed to the name, and gazed at me with mournful and questioning eagerness.

"Well, he wishes to see you," said I, guessing her need of an interpreter. "He's in the garden by this time, and impatient to know what answer I shall bring."

As I spoke, I observed a large dog lying on the sunny grass beneath raise its ears as if about to bark, and then smoothing them back, announce, by a wag of the tail, that some one approached whom it did not consider a stranger. Mrs. Linton bent forward, and listened breathlessly. The minute after a step traversed the hall; the open house was too tempting for Heathcliff to resist walking in: most likely he supposed that I was inclined to shirk my promise, and so resolved to trust to his own audacity. With straining eagerness Catherine gazed towards the entrance of her chamber. He did not hit the right room directly, she motioned me to admit him, but he found it out ere I could reach the door, and in a stride or two was at her side, and had her grasped in his arms.

He neither spoke nor loosed his hold for some five minutes, during which period he bestowed more kisses than ever he gave in his life before, I dare say: but then my mistress had kissed him first, and I plainly saw that he could hardly bear, for downright agony, to look into her face!

The same conviction had stricken him as me, from the instant
he beheld her, that there was no prospect of ultimate
recovery there—she was fated, sure to die.

" Oh, Cathy ! Oh, my life ! how can I bear it ?" was the
first sentence he uttered, in a tone that did not seek to disguise his despair. And now he stared at her so earnestly
that I thought the very intensity of his gaze would bring
tears into his eyes ; but they burned with anguish : they did
not melt.

" What now ?" said Catherine, leaning back, and returning his look with a suddenly clouded brow : her humour was
a mere vane for constantly varying caprices. " You and
Edgar have broken my heart, Heathcliff ! And you both
come to bewail the deed to me, as if *you* were the people to
be pitied ! I shall not pity you, not I. You have killed
me—and thriven on it, I think. How strong you are !
How many years do you mean to live after I am gone ?"

Heathcliff had knelt on one knee to embrace her ; he attempted to rise, but she seized his hair, and kept him down.

"I wish I could hold you," she continued, bitterly, "till
we were both dead ! I shouldn't care what you suffered. I
care nothing for your sufferings. Why shouldn't *you* suffer?
I do ! Will you forget me ? Will you be happy when I
am in the earth ? Will you say twenty years hence, ' That's
the grave of Catherine Earnshaw. I loved her long ago,
and was wretched to lose her ; but it is past. I've loved
many others since : my children are dearer to me than she
was ; and, at death, I shall not rejoice that I am going to
her : I shall be sorry that I must leave them !' Will you
say so, Heathcliff?"

" Don't torture me till I'm as mad as yourself," cried he,
wrenching his head free, and grinding his teeth.

The two, to a cool spectator, made a strange and fearful
picture. Well might Catherine deem that heaven would
be a land of exile to her, unless with her mortal body she
cast away her moral character also. Her present countenance had a wild vindictiveness in its white cheek, and a
bloodless lip and scintillating eye ; and she retained in her
closed fingers a portion of the locks she had been grasping.
As to her companion, while raising himself with one hand,
he had taken her arm with the other ; and so inadequate
was his stock of gentleness to the requirements of her condi-

tion, that on his letting go I saw four distinct impressions left blue in the colourless skin.

"Are you possessed with a devil," he pursued savagely, "to talk in that manner to me when you are dying? Do you reflect that all those words will be branded in my memory, and eating deeper eternally after you have left me? You know you lie to say I have killed you: and, Catherine, you know that I could as soon forget you as my existence! Is it not sufficient for your infernal selfishness, that while you are at peace I shall writhe in the torments of hell?"

"I shall not be at peace," moaned Catherine, recalled to a sense of physical weakness by the violent, unequal throbbing of her heart, which beat visibly and audibly under this excess of agitation. She said nothing further till the paroxysm was over; then she continued, more kindly—

"I'm not wishing you greater torment than I have, Heathcliff. I only wish us never to be parted: and should a word of mine distress you hereafter, think I feel the same distress underground, and for my own sake, forgive me! Come here and kneel down again! You never harmed me in your life. Nay, if you nurse anger, that will be worse to remember than my harsh words! Won't you come here again? Do!"

Heathcliff went to the back of her chair, and leant over, but not so far as to let her see his face, which was livid with emotion. She bent round to look at him; he would not permit it: turning abruptly, he walked to the fireplace, where he stood, silent, with his back towards us. Mrs. Linton's glance followed him suspiciously: every movement woke a new sentiment in her. After a pause, and a prolonged gaze, she resumed; addressing me in accents of indignant disappointment :—

"Oh, you see, Nelly, he would not relent a moment to keep me out of the grave. *That* is how I'm loved! Well, never mind. That is not *my* Heathcliff. I shall love mine yet; and take him with me : he's in my soul. And," added she musingly, " the thing that irks me most is this shattered prison, after all. I'm tired of being enclosed here. I'm wearying to escape into that glorious world, and to be always there : not seeing it dimly through tears, and yearning for it through the walls of an aching heart; but really with it, and in it. Nelly, you think you are better and more fortunate than I; in full health and strength: you are sorry for me—very soon that will be altered. I shall be sorry for *you*. I shall be incomparably beyond and above you all. I *wonder* he won't be near me!" She went on to herself. "I thought he wished it. Heathcliff, dear! you should not be sullen now. Do come to me, Heathcliff."

In her eagerness she rose, and supported herself on the arm of the chair. At that earnest appeal, he turned to her, looking absolutely desperate. His eyes, wide and wet, at last flashed fiercely on her; his breast heaved convulsively. An instant they held asunder; and then how they met I hardly saw, but Catherine made a spring, and he caught her, and they were locked in an embrace from which I thought my mistress would never be released alive: in fact, to my eyes, she seemed directly insensible. He flung himself into the nearest seat, and on my approaching hurriedly to ascertain if she had fainted, he gnashed at me, and foamed like a mad dog, and gathered her to him with greedy jealousy. I did not feel as if I were in the company of a creature of my own species: it appeared that he would not understand, though I spoke to him; so I stood off, and held my tongue, in great perplexity.

A movement of Catherine's relieved me a little presently: she put up her hand to clasp his neck, and bring her cheek to his as he held her; while he, in return, covering her with frantic caresses, said wildly—

"You teach me now how cruel you 've been—cruel and false. *Why* did you despise me? *Why* did you betray your own heart, Cathy? I have not one word of comfort. You deserve this. You have killed yourself. Yes, you may kiss me, and cry; and wring out my kisses and tears: they 'll blight you—they 'll damn you. You loved me—then what *right* had you to leave me? What right—answer me—for the poor fancy you felt for Linton? Because misery, and degradation, and death, and nothing that God or satan could inflict would have parted us, *you*, of your own will, did it. I have not broken your heart—*you* have broken it; and in breaking it, you have broken mine. So much the worse for me, that I am strong. Do I want to live? What kind of living will it be when you—oh, God! would *you* like to live with your soul in the grave?"

"Let me alone. Let me alone," sobbed Catherine. "If

I've done wrong, I'm dying for it. It is enough! You left me too: but I won't upbraid you! I forgive you. Forgive me!"

"It is hard to forgive, and to look at those eyes, and feel those wasted hands," he answered. "Kiss me again; and don't let me see your eyes! I forgive what you have done to me. I love *my* murderer—but *yours!* How can I?"

They were silent—their faces hid against each other, and washed by each other's tears. At least, I suppose the weeping was on both sides; as it seemed Heathcliff *could* weep on a great occasion like this.

I grew very uncomfortable, meanwhile; for the afternoon wore fast away, the man whom I had sent off returned from his errand, and I could distinguish, by the shine of the western sun up the valley, a concourse thickening outside Gimmerton chapel porch.

"Service is over," I announced. "My master will be here in half an hour."

Heathcliff groaned a curse, and strained Catherine closer: she never moved.

Ere long I perceived a group of the servants passing up the road towards the kitchen wing. Mr. Linton was not far behind; he opened the gate himself, and sauntered slowly up, probably enjoying the lovely afternoon that breathed as soft as summer.

"Now he is here," I exclaimed. "For Heaven's sake, hurry down! "You'll not meet any one on the front stairs. Do be quick; and stay among the trees till he is fairly in."

"I must go, Cathy," said Heathcliff, seeking to extricate himself from his companion's arms. "But, if I live, I'll see you again before you are asleep. I won't stray five yards from your window."

"You must not go!" she answered, holding him as firmly as her strength allowed. "You *shall* not, I tell you."

"For one hour," he pleaded earnestly.

"Not for one minute," she replied.

"I *must*—Linton will be up immediately," persisted the alarmed intruder.

He would have risen, and unfixed her fingers by the act—she clung fast, gasping: there was mad resolution in her face.

"No!" she shrieked. "Oh, don't, don't go. It is the

last time! Edgar will not hurt us. Heathcliff, I shall die! I shall die!"

"Damn the fool! There he is," cried Heathcliff, sinking back into his seat. "Hush, my darling! Hush, hush, Catherine! I'll stay. If he shot me so, I'd expire with a blessing on my lips."

And there they were fast again. I heard my master mounting the stairs—the cold sweat ran from my forehead: I was horrified.

"Are you going to listen to her ravings?" I said, passionately. "She does not know what she says. Will you ruin her, because she has not wit to help herself? Get up! You could be free instantly. That is the most diabolical deed that ever you did. We are all done for—master, mistress, and servant."

I wrung my hands, and cried out; and Mr. Linton hastened his step at the noise. In the midst of my agitation, I was sincerely glad to observe that Catherine's arms had fallen relaxed, and her head hung down.

"She's fainted, or dead," I thought: "so much the better. Far better that she should be dead, than lingering a burden and a misery-maker to all about her."

Edgar sprang to his unbidden guest, blanched with astonishment and rage. What he meant to do, I cannot tell; however, the other stopped all demonstrations, at once, by placing the lifeless-looking form in his arms.

"Look there!" he said, "Unless you be a fiend, help her first—then you shall speak to me!"

He walked into the parlour, and sat down. Mr. Linton summoned me, and with great difficulty, and after resorting to many means, we managed to restore her to sensation; but she was all bewildered: she sighed, and moaned, and knew nobody. Edgar, in his anxiety for her, forgot her hated friend. I did not. I went, at the earliest opportunity, and besought him to depart; affirming that Catherine was better, and he should hear from me in the morning, how she passed the night.

"I shall not refuse to go out of doors," he answered; "but I shall stay in the garden: and, Nelly, mind you keep your word to-morrow. I shall be under those larch trees. Mind! or I pay another visit, whether Linton be in or not."

He sent a rapid glance through the half-open door of the chamber, and, ascertaining that what I stated was apparently true, delivered the house of his luckless presence.

CHAPTER XVI.

About twelve o'clock that night, was born the Catherine you saw at Wuthering Heights: a puny, seven months' child; and two hours after the mother died, having never recovered sufficient consciousness to Miss Heathcliff, or know Edgar. The latter's distraction at his bereavement is a subject too painful to be dwelt on; its after effects showed how deep the sorrow sunk. A great addition, in my eyes, was his being left without an heir. I bemoaned that, as I gazed on the feeble orphan; and I mentally abused old Linton for (what was only natural partiality) the securing his estate to his own daughter, instead of his son's. An unwelcomed infant it was, poor thing! It might have wailed out of life, and nobody cared a morsel, during those first hours of existence. We redeemed the neglect afterwards; but its beginning was as friendless as its end is likely to be.

Next morning—bright and cheerful out of doors—stole softened in through the blinds of the silent room, and suffused the couch and its occupant with a mellow, tender glow. Edgar Linton had his head laid on the pillow, and his eyes shut. His young and fair features were almost as deathlike as those of the form beside him, and almost as fixed: but *his* was the hush of exhausted anguish, and *hers* of perfect peace. Her brow smooth, her lids closed, her lips wearing the expression of a smile; no angel in heaven could be more beautiful than she appeared. And I partook of the infinite calm in which she lay: my mind was never in a holier frame than while I gazed on that untroubled image of Divine rest. I instinctively echoed the words she had uttered a few hours before: "Incomparably beyond and above us all! Whether still on earth or now in heaven, her spirit is at home with God!"

I don't know if it be a peculiarity in me, but I am seldom

otherwise than happy while watching in the chamber of death, should no frenzied or despairing mourner share the duty with me. I see a repose that neither earth nor hell can break, and I feel an assurance of the endless and shadowless hereafter—the Eternity they have entered—where life is boundless in its duration, and love in its sympathy, and joy in its fulness. I noticed on that occasion how much selfishness there is even in a love like Mr. Linton's, when he so regretted Catherine's blessed release! To be sure, one might have doubted, after the wayward and impatient existence she had led, whether she merited a haven of peace at last. One might doubt in seasons of cold reflection; but not then, in the presence of her corpse. It asserted its own tranquillity, which seemed a pledge of equal quiet to its former inhabitants.

Do you believe such people *are* happy in the other world, sir? I'd give a great deal to know.

I declined answering Mrs. Dean's question, which struck me as something heterodox. She proceeded:

Retracing the course of Catherine Linton, I fear we have no right to think she is; but we'll leave her with her Maker.

The master looked asleep, and I ventured soon after sunrise to quit the room and steal out to the pure refreshing air. The servants thought me gone to shake off the drowsiness of my protracted watch; in reality, my chief motive was seeing Mr. Heathcliff. If he had remained among the larches all night, he would have heard nothing of the stir at the Grange: unless, perhaps, he might catch the gallop of the messenger going to Gimmerton. If he had come nearer, he would probably be aware, from the lights flitting to and fro, and the opening and shutting of the outer doors, that all was not right within. I wished, yet feared, to find him. I felt the terrible news must be told, and I longed to get it over; but *how* to do it, I did not know. He was there—at least a few yards further in the park; leant against an old ash tree, his hat off, and his hair soaked with the dew that had gathered on the budded branches, and fell pattering round him. He had been standing a long time in that position, for I saw a pair of ousels passing and repassing scarcely three feet from him, busy in building their nest, and regarding his proximity no more than that of a piece of timber. They flew off at my approach, and he raised his eyes and spoke:—

"She's dead!" he said; "I've not waited for you to learn that. Put your handkerchief away—don't snivel before me. Damn you all! she wants none of *your* tears!"

I was weeping as much for him as her: we do sometimes pity creatures that have none of the feeling either for themselves or others. When I first looked into his face, I perceived that he had got intelligence of the catastrophe; and a foolish notion struck me that his heart was quelled and he prayed, because his lips moved and his gaze was bent on the ground.

"Yes, she's dead!" I answered, checking my sobs and drying my cheeks. "Gone to heaven, I hope; where we may, every one, join her, if we take due warning and leave our evil ways to follow good!"

"Did *she* take due warning, then?" asked Heathcliff, attempting a sneer. "Did she die like a saint? Come, give me a true history of the event. How did ——"

He endeavoured to pronounce the name, but could not manage it; and compressing his mouth he held a silent combat with his inward agony, defying, meanwhile, my sympathy with an unflinching ferocious stare. "How did she die?" he resumed, at last—fain, notwithstanding his hardihood, to have a support behind him; for, after the struggle, he trembled, in spite of himself, to his very finger-ends.

"Poor wretch!" I thought; "you have a heart and nerves the same as your brother men! Why should you be anxious to conceal them? Your pride cannot blind God! You tempt him to wring them, till he forces a cry of humiliation."

"Quietly as a lamb!" I answered, aloud. "She drew a sigh, and stretched herself, like a child reviving, and sinking again to sleep; and five minutes after I felt one little pulse at her heart, and nothing more!"

"And—did she ever mention me?" he asked, hesitating, as if he dreaded the answer to his question would introduce details that he could not bear to hear.

"Her senses never returned: she recognised nobody from the time you left her," I said. "She lies with a sweet smile on her face; and her latest ideas wandered back to pleasant early days. Her life closed in a gentle dream—may she wake as kindly in the other world!"

"May she wake in torment!" he cried, with frightful

vehemence, stamping his foot, and groaning in a sudden paroxysm of ungovernable passion. "Why, she's a liar to the end! Where is she? Not *there*—not in heaven—not perished—where? Oh! you said you cared nothing for my sufferings! And I pray one prayer—I repeat it till my tongue stiffens—Catherine Earnshaw, may you not rest as long as I am living! You said I killed you—haunt me, then! The murdered *do* haunt their murderers, I believe. I know that ghosts *have* wandered on earth. Be with me always—take any form—drive me mad! only *do* not leave me in this abyss, where I cannot find you! Oh, God! it is unutterable! I *cannot* live without my life! I *cannot* live without my soul!"

He dashed his head against the knotted trunk; and, lifting up his eyes, howled, not like a man, but like a savage beast being goaded to death with knives and spears. I observed several splashes of blood about the bark of the tree, and his hand and forehead were both stained; probably the scene I witnessed was a repetition of others acted during the night. It hardly moved my compassion—it appalled me: still, I felt reluctant to quit him so. But the moment he recollected himself enough to notice me watching, he thundered a command for me to go, and I obeyed. He was beyond my skill to quiet or console!

Mrs. Linton's funeral was appointed to take place on the Friday following her decease; and till then her coffin remained uncovered, and strewn with flowers and scented leaves, in the great drawing-room. Linton spent his days and nights there, a sleepless guardian; and—a circumstance concealed from all but me—Heathcliff spent his nights, at least, outside, equally a stranger to repose. I held no communication with him: still, I was conscious of his design to enter, if he could; and on the Tuesday, a little after dark, when my master, from sheer fatigue, had been compelled to retire a couple of hours, I went and opened one of the windows; moved by his perseverance, to give him a chance of bestowing on the fading image of his idol one final adieu. He did not omit to avail himself of the opportunity, cautiously and briefly: too cautiously to betray his presence by the slightest noise. Indeed, I shouldn't have discovered that he had been there, except for the disarrangement of the drapery about the corpse's face, and for observing on the floor a curl of light hair, fastened with a silver thread; which, on examination, I ascertained to have been taken from a locket hung round Catherine's neck. Heathcliff had opened the trinket and cast out its contents, replacing them by a black lock of his own. I twisted the two, and enclosed them together.

Mr. Earnshaw was, of course, invited to attend the remains of his sister to the grave; he sent no excuse, but he never came; so that, besides her husband, the mourners were wholly composed of tenants and servants. Isabella was not asked.

The place of Catherine's interment, to the surprise of the villagers, was neither in the chapel, under the carved monument of the Lintons, nor yet by the tombs of her own relations, outside. It was dug on a green slope in a corner of the kirkyard, where the wall is so low that heath and bilberry plants have climbed over it from the moor; and peat mould almost buries it. Her husband lies in the same spot now; and they have each a simple headstone above, and a plain grey block at their feet, to mark the graves.

CHAPTER XVII.

THAT Friday made the last of our fine days, for a month. In the evening, the weather broke: the wind shifted from south to north-east, and brought rain first, and then sleet and snow. On the morrow one could hardly imagine that there had been three weeks of summer: the primroses and crocuses were hidden under wintry drifts; the larks were silent, the young leaves of the early trees smitten and blackened. And dreary, and chill, and dismal that morrow did creep over! My master kept his room; I took possession of the lonely parlour, converting it into a nursery: and there I was, sitting with the moaning doll of a child laid on my knee; rocking it to and fro, and watching, meanwhile, the still driving flakes build up the uncurtained window, when the door opened, and some person entered, out of breath and laughing! My anger was greater than my astonishment for a minute. I supposed it one of the maids, and I cried—

"Have done! How dare you show your giddiness nere? What would Mr. Linton say if he heard you?"

"Excuse me!" answered a familiar voice; "but I know Edgar is in bed, and I cannot stop myself."

With that the speaker came forward to the fire, panting and holding her hand to her side.

"I have run the whole way from Wuthering Heights!" she continued, after a pause; "except where I've flown. I couldn't count the number of falls I've had. Oh, I'm aching all over! Don't be alarmed! There shall be an explanation as soon as I can give it; only just have the goodness to step out and order the carriage to take me on to Gimmerton, and tell a servant to seek up a few clothes in my wardrobe."

The intruder was Mrs. Heathcliff. She certainly seemed in no laughing predicament: her hair streamed on her shoulders, dripping with snow and water; she was dressed in the girlish dress she commonly wore, befitting her age more than her position: a low frock with short sleeves, and nothing on either head or neck. The frock was of light silk, and clung to her with wet, and her feet were protected merely by thin slippers; add to this a deep cut under one ear, which only the cold prevented from bleeding profusely, a white face scratched and bruised, and a frame hardly able to support itself, through fatigue; and you may fancy my first fright was not much allayed when I had leisure to examine her.

"My dear young lady," I exclaimed, "I'll stir nowhere, and hear nothing, till you have removed every article of your clothes, and put on dry things; and certainly you shall not go to Gimmerton to-night, so it is needless to order the carriage."

"Certainly, I shall," she said; "walking or riding: yet I've no objection to dress myself decently. And—ah, see how it flows down my neck now! The fire does make it smart."

She insisted on my fulfilling her directions, before she would let me touch her; and not till after the coachman had been instructed to get ready, and a maid set to pack up some necessary attire, did I obtain her consent for binding the wound and helping to change her garments.

"Now, Ellen," she said, when my task was finished and she was seated in an easy chair on the hearth, with a cup of tea before her, "you sit down opposite me, and put poor Catherine's baby away: I don't like to see it! You mustn't think I care little for Catherine, because I behaved so foolishly on entering: I've cried too, bitterly—yes, more than any one else has reason to cry. We parted unreconciled, you remember, and I sha'n't forgive myself. But, for all that, I was not going to sympathize with him—the brute beast! O, give me the poker! This is the last thing of his I have about me:" she slipped the gold ring from her third finger, and threw it on the floor. "I'll smash it!" she continued, striking with childish spite, "and then I'll burn it!" and she took and dropped the misused article among the coals. "There! he shall buy another, if he gets me back again. He'd be capable of coming to seek me, to tease Edgar. I dare not stay, lest that notion should possess his wicked head! And besides, Edgar has not been kind, has he? And I won't come suing for his assistance; nor will I bring him into more trouble. Necessity compelled me to seek shelter here; though, if I had not learned he was out of the way, I'd have halted at the kitchen, washed my face, warmed myself, got you to bring what I wanted, and departed again to anywhere out of the reach of my accursed—of that incarnate goblin! Ah, he was in such a fury! If he had caught me! It's a pity Earnshaw is not his match in strength: I wouldn't have run till I'd seen him all but demolished, had Hindley been able to do it!"

"Well, don't talk so fast, miss!" I interrupted, "you'll disorder the handkerchief I have tied round your face, and make the cut bleed again. Drink your tea, and take breath and give over laughing: laughter is sadly out of place under this roof, and in your condition!"

"An undeniable truth," she replied. "Listen to that child! It maintains a constant wail—send it out of my hearing for an hour; I sha'n't stay any longer."

I rang the bell, and committed it to a servant's care; and then I inquired what had urged her to escape from Wuthering Heights in such an unlikely plight, and where she meant to go, as she refused remaining with us.

"I ought, and I wish to remain," answered she, "to cheer Edgar and take care of the baby, for two things, and because the Grange is my right home. But I tell you he wouldn't let me! Do you think he could bear to see me grow fat and merry—could bear to think that we were tranquil, and not resolve on poisoning our comfort? Now, I have the satisfaction of being sure that he detests me, to the point of its annoying him seriously to have me within earshot or eyesight: I notice, when I enter his presence, the muscles of his countenance are involuntarily distorted into an expression of hatred; partly arising from his knowledge of the good causes I have to feel that sentiment for him, and partly from original aversion. It is strong enough to make me feel pretty certain that he would not chase me over England, supposing I contrived a clear escape; and therefore I must get quite away. I've recovered from my first desire to be killed by him: I'd rather he'd kill himself! He has extinguished my love effectually, and so I'm at my ease. I can recollect yet how I loved him; and can dimly imagine that I could still be loving him, if—no, no! Even if he had doted on me, the devilish nature would have revealed its existence somehow. Catherine had an awfully perverted taste to esteem him so dearly, knowing him so well. Monster! would that he could be blotted out of creation, and out of my memory!"

"Hush, hush! He's a human being," I said. "Be more charitable: there are worse men than he is yet!"

"He's not a human being," she retorted; "and he has no claim on my charity. I gave him my heart, and he took and pinched it to death, and flung it back to me. People feel with their hearts, Ellen; and since he has destroyed mine, I have not power to feel for him: and I would not, though he groaned from this to his dying day, and wept tears of blood for Catherine! No, indeed, indeed, I wouldn't!" And here Isabella began to cry; but, immediately dashing the water from her lashes, she recommenced. "You asked, what has driven me to flight at last? I was compelled to attempt it, because I had succeeded in rousing his rage a pitch above his malignity. Pulling out the nerves with red hot pincers requires more coolness than knocking on the head. He was worked up to forget the fiendish prudence he boasted of, and proceeding to murderous violence. I experienced pleasure in being able to exasperate him: the sense of pleasure woke my instinct of self-preservation, so

I fairly broke free; and if ever I come into his hands again he is welcome to a signal revenge.

"Yesterday, you know, Mr. Earnshaw should have been at the funeral. He kept himself sober for the purpose—tolerably sober: not going to bed mad at six o'clock and getting up drunk at twelve. Consequently, he rose, in suicidal low spirits, as fit for the church as for a dance; and instead, he sat down by the fire and swallowed gin or brandy by tumblerfuls.

"Heathcliff—I shudder to name him! has been a stranger in the house from last Sunday till to-day. Whether the angels have fed him, or his kin beneath, I cannot tell; but he has not eaten a meal with us for nearly a week. He has just come home at dawn, and gone up stairs to his chamber; locking himself in—as if anybody dreamt of coveting his company! There he has continued, praying like a methodist: only the deity he implored is senseless dust and ashes; and God, when addressed, was curiously confounded with his own black father! After concluding these precious orisons—and they lasted generally till he grew hoarse and his voice was strangled in his throat—he would be off again; always straight down to the Grange! I wonder Edgar did not send for a constable, and give him into custody! For me, grieved as I was about Catherine, it was impossible to avoid regarding this season of deliverance from degrading oppression as a holiday.

"I recovered spirits sufficient to hear Joseph's eternal lectures without weeping, and to move up and down the house less with the foot of a frightened thief than formerly You wouldn't think that I should cry at anything Joseph could say; but he and Hareton are detestable companions. I'd rather sit with Hindley, and hear his awful talk, than with 't' little maister' and his stanch supporter, that odious old man! When Heathcliff is in, I'm often obliged to seek the kitchen and their society, or starve among the damp uninhabited chambers; when he is not, as was the case this week, I establish a table and chair at one corner of the house fire, and never mind how Mr. Earnshaw may occupy himself; and he does not interfere with my arrangements. He is quieter now than he used to be, if no one provokes him: more sullen and depressed, and less furious. Joseph affirms he's sure he's an altered man: that the Lord has touched his heart, and he is saved 'so as by fire.' I'm puzzled to detect signs of the favourable change: but it is not my business.

"Yester-evening I sat in my nook reading some old books till late on towards twelve. It seemed so dismal to go up stairs, with the wild snow blowing outside, and my thoughts continually reverting to the kirkyard and the new-made grave! I dared hardly lift my eyes from the page before me, that melancholy scene so instantly usurped its place. Hindley sat opposite, his head leant on his hand; perhaps meditating on the same subject. He had ceased drinking at a point below irrationality, and had neither stirred nor spoken during two or three hours. There was no sound through the house but the moaning wind, which shook the windows every now and then, the faint crackling of the coals, and the click of my snuffers as I removed at intervals the long wick of the candle. Hareton and Joseph were probably fast asleep in bed. It was very, very sad: and while I read I sighed, for it seemed as if all joy had vanished from the world, never to be restored.

"The doleful silence was broken at length by the sound of the kitchen latch: Heathcliff had returned from his watch earlier than usual; owing, I suppose, to the sudden storm. That entrance was fastened, and we heard him coming round to get in by the other. I rose with an irrepressible expression of what I felt on my lips, which induced my companion, who had been staring towards the door, to turn and look at me.

"'I'll keep him out five minutes,' he exclaimed. 'You won't object?'

"'No, you may keep him out the whole night for me,' I answered. 'Do! put the key in the lock, and draw the bolts.'

"Earnshaw accomplished this ere his guest reached the front; he then came and brought his chair to the other side of my table, leaning over it, and searching in my eyes for a sympathy with the burning hate that gleamed from his: as he both looked and felt like an assassin, he couldn't exactly find that; but he discovered enough to encourage him to speak.

"'You, and I,' he said, 'have each a great debt to settle with the man out yonder! If we were neither of us cowards, we might combine to discharge it. Are you as soft as your brother? Are you willing to endure to the last, and not once attempt a repayment?'

" 'I'm weary of enduring now,' I replied; 'and I'd be glad of a retaliation that wouldn't recoil on myself; but treachery and violence are spears pointed at both ends : they wound those who resort to them worse than their enemies.'

" 'Treachery and violence are a just return for treachery and violence!' cried Hindley. 'Mrs. Heathcliff, I'll ask you to do nothing; but sit still and be dumb. Tell me now, can you? I'm sure you would have as much pleasure as I in witnessing the conclusion of the fiend's existence: he'll be *your* death unless you overreach him; and he'll be *my* ruin. Damn the hellish villain! He knocks at the door as if he were master here already! Promise to hold your tongue, and before that clock strikes—it wants three minutes of one —you're a free woman!'

"He took the implements which I described to you in my letter from his breast, and would have turned down the candle. I snatched it away, however, and seized his arm.

" 'I'll not hold my tongue!' I said; 'you mustn't touch him. Let the door remain shut, and be quiet!'

" 'No! I've formed my resolution, and by God I'll execute it!' cried the desperate being. 'I'll do you a kindness in spite of yourself, and Hareton justice! And you needn't trouble your head to screen me; Catherine is gone. Nobody alive would regret me, or be ashamed, though I cut my throat this minute—and it's time to make an end!'

"I might as well have struggled with a bear, or reasoned with a lunatic. The only resource left me was to run to a lattice and warn his intended victim of the fate which awaited him.

" 'You'd better seek shelter somewhere else to-night!' I exclaimed, in rather a triumphant tone. 'Mr. Earnshaw has a mind to shoot you, if you persist in endeavouring to enter.'

" 'You'd better open the door, you——' he answered, addressing me by some elegant term that I don't care to repeat.

" 'I shall not meddle in the matter,' I retorted again. 'Come in and get shot, if you please! I've done my duty.'

" With that I shut the window and returned to my place by the fire; having too small a stock of hypocrisy at my command to pretend any anxiety for the danger that menaced him. Earnshaw swore passionately at me : affirming that I loved the villain yet; and calling me all sorts of names for the base spirit I evinced. And I, in my secret heart (and conscience never reproached me), thought what a blessing it would be for *him* should Heathcliff put him out of misery; and what a blessing for *me* should he send Heathcliff to his right abode ! As I sat nursing these reflections, the casement behind me was banged on to the floor by a blow from the latter individual, and his black countenance looked blightingly through. The stanchions stood too close to suffer his shoulders to follow, and I smiled, exulting in my fancied security. His hair and clothes were whitened with snow, and his sharp cannibal teeth, revealed by cold and wrath, gleamed through the dark.

" ' Isabella, let me in, or I 'll make you repent !' he ' girned,' as Joseph calls it.

" ' I cannot commit murder,' I replied. ' Mr. Hindley stands sentinel with a knife and loaded pistol.'

" ' Let me in by the kitchen door,' he said.

" ' Hindley will be there before me,' I answered: ' and that's a poor love of yours that cannot bear a shower of snow ! We were left at peace in our beds as long as the summer moon shone, but the moment a blast of winter returns, you must run for shelter ! Heathcliff, if I were you, I 'd go stretch myself over her grave and die like a faithful dog. The world is surely not worth living in now, is it? You had distinctly impressed on me the idea that Catherine was the whole joy of your life : I can't imagine how you think of surviving her loss.'

" ' He 's there, is he ?' exclaimed my companion, rushing to the gap. ' If I can get my arm out I can hit him !'

" I 'm afraid, Ellen, you 'll set me down as really wicked ; but you don't know all, so don't judge. I wouldn't have aided or abetted an attempt on even *his* life for anything. Wish that he were dead, I must; and therefore I was fearfully disappointed, and unnerved by terror for the consequences of my taunting speech, when he flung himself on Earnshaw's weapon and wrenched it from his grasp.

" The charge exploded, and the knife, in springing back,

closed into its owner's wrist. Heathcliff pulled it away by main force, slitting up the flesh as it passed on, and thrust it dripping into his pocket. He then took a stone, struck down the division between two windows, and sprung in. His adversary had fallen senseless with excessive pain and the flow of blood, that gushed from an artery or a large vein. The ruffian kicked and trampled on him, and dashed his head repeatedly against the flags, holding me with one hand, meantime, to prevent me summoning Joseph. He exerted preterhuman self-denial in abstaining from finishing him completely; but getting out of breath he finally desisted, and dragged the apparently inanimate body on to the settle. There he tore off the sleeve of Earnshaw's coat, and bound up the wound with brutal roughness; spitting and cursing during the operation as energetically as he had kicked before. Being at liberty, I lost no time in seeking the old servant; who, having gathered by degrees the purport of my hasty tale, hurried below, gasping, as he descended the steps two at once.

"'What is ther to do, now? what is ther to do, now?'

"'There's this to do,' thundered Heathcliff, 'that your master's mad; and should he last another month, I'll have him to an asylum. And how the devil did you come to fasten me out, you toothless hound? Don't stand muttering and mumbling there. Come, I'm not going to nurse him. Wash that stuff away; and mind the sparks of your candle —it is more than half brandy!'

"'And so, ye've been murthering on him?' exclaimed Joseph, lifting his hands and eyes in horror. 'If iver I seed a seeght loike this! May the Lord——'

"Heathcliff gave him a push on to his knees in the middle of the blood, and flung a towel to him; but instead of proceeding to dry it up, he joined his hands and began a prayer, which excited my laughter from its odd phraseology. I was in the condition of mind to be shocked at nothing: in fact, I was as reckless as some malefactors show themselves at the foot of the gallows.

"'Oh, I forgot you,' said the tyrant. 'You shall do that. Down with you. And you conspire with him against me, do you, viper? There, that is work fit for you!'

"He shook me till my teeth rattled, and pitched me beside Joseph, who steadily concluded his supplications and then

rose, vowing he would set off for the Grange directly. Mr. Linton was a magistrate, and though he had fifty wives dead he should inquire into this. He was so obstinate in his resolution, that Heathcliff deemed it expedient to compel from my lips a recapitulation of what had taken place; standing over me, heaving with malevolence, as I reluctantly delivered the account in answer to his questions. It required a great deal of labour to satisfy the old man that Heathcliff was not the aggressor; especially with my hardly wrung replies. However, Mr. Earnshaw soon convinced him that he was alive still; Joseph hastened to administer a dose of spirits, and by their succour his master presently regained motion and consciousness. Heathcliff, aware that his opponent was ignorant of the treatment received while insensible, called him deliriously intoxicated; and said he should not notice his atrocious conduct further, but advised him to get to bed. To my joy, he left us, after giving this judicious counsel, and Hindley stretched himself on the hearthstone. I departed to my own room, marvelling that I had escaped so easily.

"This morning, when I came down, about half an hour before noon, Mr. Earnshaw was sitting by the fire, deadly sick; his evil genius, almost as gaunt and ghastly, leant against the chimney. Neither appeared inclined to dine, and, having waited till all was cold on the table, I commenced alone. Nothing hindered me from eating heartily, and I experienced a certain sense of satisfaction and superiority, as, at intervals, I cast a look towards my silent companions, and felt the comfort of a quiet conscience within me. After I had done, I ventured on the unusual liberty of drawing near the fire, going round Earnshaw's seat, and kneeling in the corner beside him.

"Heathcliff did not glance my way, and I gazed up, and contemplated his features almost as confidently as if they had been turned to stone. His forehead, that I once thought so manly, and that I now think so diabolical, was shaded with a heavy cloud; his basilisk eyes were nearly quenched by sleeplessness : and weeping, perhaps, for the lashes were wet then; his lips devoid of their ferocious sneer, and sealed in an expression of unspeakable sadness. Had it been another, I would have covered my face in the presence of such grief. In *his* case, I was gratified; and, ignoble as it seems to insult a fallen enemy, I couldn't miss this chance of sticking in a dart : his weakness was the only time when I could taste the delight of paying wrong for wrong."

"Fie, fie, miss!" I interrupted. "One might suppose you had never opened a Bible in your life. If God afflict your enemies, surely that ought to suffice you. It is both mean and presumptuous to add your torture to his!"

"In general, I'll allow that it would be, Ellen," she continued; "but what misery laid on Heathcliff could content me, unless I have a hand in it? I'd rather he suffered *less*, if I might cause his sufferings and he might *know* that I was the cause. Oh, I owe him so much. On only one condition can I hope to forgive him. It is, if I may take an eye for an eye, a tooth for a tooth; for every wrench of agony, return a wrench : reduce him to my level. As he was the first to injure, make him the first to implore pardon; and then—why then, Ellen, I might show you some generosity. But it is utterly impossible I can ever be revenged, and therefore I cannot forgive him. Hindley wanted some water, and I handed him a glass, and asked him how he was.

"'Not as ill as I wish,' he replied. 'But leaving out my arm, every inch of me is as sore as if I had been fighting with a legion of imps!'

"'Yes, no wonder,' was my next remark. 'Catherine used to boast that she stood between you and bodily harm : she meant that certain persons would not hurt you for fear of offending her. It's well people don't *really* rise from their grave, or, last night, she might have witnessed a repulsive scene! Are not you bruised, and cut over your chest and shoulders?'

"'I can't say,' he answered : 'but what do you mean? Did he dare to strike me when I was down?'

"'He trampled on and kicked you, and dashed you on the ground,' I whispered. 'And his mouth watered to tear you with his teeth; because he's only half man : not so much, and the rest fiend.'

"Mr. Earnshaw looked up, like me, to the countenance of our mutual foe; who, absorbed in his anguish, seemed insensible to anything around him : the longer he stood, the plainer his reflections revealed their blackness through his features.

"'Oh, if God would but give me strength to strangle him

in my last agony, I'd go to hell with joy,' groaned the impatient man, writhing to rise, and sinking back in despair, convinced of his inadequacy for the struggle.

" 'Nay, it's enough that he has murdered one of you,' I observed aloud. 'At the Grange, every one knows your sister would have been living now, had it not been for Mr. Heathcliff. After all, it is preferable to be hated than loved by him. When I recollect how happy we were—how happy Catherine was before he came—I'm fit to curse the day.'

" Most likely, Heathcliff noticed more the truth of what was said, than the spirit of the person who said it. His attention was roused, I saw, for his eyes rained down tears among the ashes, and he drew his breath in suffocating sighs. I stared full at him, and laughed scornfully. The clouded windows of hell flashed a moment towards me ; the fiend which usually looked out, however, was so dimmed and drowned that I did not fear to hazard another sound of derision.

" 'Get up, and begone out of my sight,' said the mourner.

" I guessed he uttered those words, at least, though his voice was hardly intelligible.

" 'I beg your pardon,' I replied. 'But I loved Catherine too ; and her brother requires attendance, which, for her sake, I shall supply. Now that she's dead, I see her in Hindley : Hindley has exactly her eyes, if you had not tried to gouge them out, and made them black and red ; and her ——'

" 'Get up, wretched idiot, before I stamp you to death !' he cried, making a movement that caused me to make one also.

" 'But then,' I continued, holding myself ready to flee ; 'if poor Catherine had trusted you, and assumed the ridiculous, contemptible, degrading title of Mrs. Heathcliff, she would soon have presented a similar picture ! *She* wouldn't have borne your abominable behaviour quietly : her detestation and disgust must have found voice.'

" The back of the settle and Earnshaw's person interposed between me and him ; so instead of endeavouring to reach me, he snatched a dinner knife from the table and flung it at my head. It struck beneath my ear, and stopped the sentence I was uttering ; but, pulling it out, I sprang to the door and delivered another ; which I hope went a little deeper than his missile. The last glimpse I caught of him was a furious rush on his part, checked by the embrace of his host; and both fell locked together on the hearth. In my flight through the kitchen I bid Joseph speed to his master; I knocked over Hareton, who was hanging a litter of puppies from a chair back in the doorway; and, blest as a soul escaped from purgatory, I bounded, leaped, and flew down the steep road; then, quitting its windings, shot direct across the moor, rolling over banks, and wading through marshes: precipitating myself, in fact, towards the beacon light of the Grange. And far rather would I be condemned to a perpetual dwelling in the infernal regions, than, even for one night, abide beneath the roof of Wuthering Heights again."

Isabella ceased speaking, and took a drink of tea; then she rose, and bidding me put on her bonnet, and a great shawl I had brought, and turning a deaf ear to my entreaties for her to remain another hour, she stepped on to a chair, kissed Edgar's and Catherine's portraits, bestowed a similar salute on me, and descended to the carriage, accompanied by Fanny, who yelped wild with joy at recovering her mistress. She was driven away, never to revisit this neighbourhood; but a regular correspondence was established between her and my master when things were more settled. I believe her new abode was in the south, near London; there she had a son born, a few months subsequent to her escape. He was christened Linton, and, from the first, she reported him to be an ailing, peevish creature.

Mr. Heathcliff, meeting me one day in the village, inquired where she lived. I refused to tell. He remarked that it was not of any moment, only she must beware of coming to her brother: she should not be with him, if he had to keep her himself. Though I would give no information, he discovered, through some of the other servants, both her place of residence and the existence of the child. Still he didn't molest her: for which forbearance she might thank his aversion, I suppose. He often asked about the infant, when he saw me; and on hearing its name, smiled grimly, and observed:

"They wish me to hate it too, do they?"

"I don't think they wish you to know anything about it," I answered.

"But I'll have it," he said, "when I want it. They may reckon on that!"

Fortunately, its mother died before the time arrived; some

thirteen years after the decease of Catherine, when Linton was twelve, or a little more.

On the day succeeding Isabella's unexpected visit, I had no opportunity of speaking to my master: he shunned conversation, and was fit for discussing nothing. When I could get him to listen, I saw it pleased him that his sister had left her husband; whom he abhorred with an intensity which the mildness of his nature would scarcely seem to allow. So deep and sensitive was his aversion, that he refrained from going anywhere where he was likely to see or hear of Heathcliff. Grief, and that together, transformed him into a complete hermit: he threw up his office of magistrate, ceased even to attend church, avoided the village on all occasions, and spent a life of entire seclusion within the limits of his park and grounds; only varied by solitary rambles on the moors, and visits to the grave of his wife, mostly at evening, or early morning before other wanderers were abroad. But he was too good to be thoroughly unhappy long. *He* didn't pray for Catherine's soul to haunt him. Time brought resignation, and a melancholy sweeter than common joy. He recalled her memory with ardent, tender love, and hopeful aspiring to the better world; where he doubted not she was gone.

And he had earthly consolation and affections also. For a few days, I said, he seemed regardless of the puny successor to the departed: that coldness melted as fast as snow in April, and ere the tiny thing could stammer a word or totter a step, it wielded a despot's sceptre in his heart. It was named Catherine; but he never called it the name in full, as he had never called the first Catherine short: probably because Heathcliff had a habit of doing so. The little one was always Cathy: it formed to him a distinction from the mother, and yet a connection with her; and his attachment sprang from its relation to her, far more than from its being his own.

I used to draw a comparison between him and Hindley Earnshaw, and perplex myself to explain satisfactorily why their conduct was so opposite in similar circumstances. They had both been fond husbands, and were both attached to their children; and I could not see how they shouldn't both have taken the same road, for good or evil. But, I thought in my mind, Hindley, with apparently the stronger head, has

M

shown himself sadly the worse and the weaker man. When his ship struck, the captain abandoned his post; and the crew, instead of trying to save her, rushed into riot and confusion, leaving no hope for their luckless vessel. Linton, on the contrary, displayed the true courage of a loyal and faithful soul: he trusted God; and God comforted him. One hoped, and the other despaired : they chose their own lots, and were righteously doomed to endure them. But you'll not want to hear my moralizing, Mr. Lockwood ; you'll judge as well as I can, all these things : at least, you'll think you will and that's the same. The end of Earnshaw was what might have been expected; it followed fast on his sister's : there were scarcely six months between them. We, at the Grange, never got a very succinct account of his state preceding it ; all that I did learn, was on occasion of going to aid in the preparations for the funeral. Mr. Kenneth came to announce the event to my master.

"Well, Nelly," said he, riding into the yard one morning, too early not to alarm me with an instant presentiment of bad news, "It's yours and my turn to go into mourning at present. Who's given us the slip now, do you think?"

"Who?" I asked in a flurry.

"Why, guess!" he returned, dismounting, and slinging his bridle on a hook by the door. "And nip up the corner of your apron : I'm certain you'll need it."

"Not Mr. Heathcliff, surely?" I exclaimed.

"What! would you have tears for him?" said the doctor. "No, Heathcliff's a tough young fellow : he looks blooming to-day. I've just seen him. He's rapidly regaining flesh since he lost his better half."

"Who is it then, Mr. Kenneth?" I repeated impatiently.

"Hindley Earnshaw! Your old friend Hindley," he replied, "and my wicked gossip : though he's been too wild for me this long while. There! I said we should draw water. But cheer up! He died true to his character : drunk as a lord. Poor lad; I'm sorry, too. One can't help missing an old companion : though he had the worst tricks with him that ever man imagined, and has done me many a rascally turn. He's barely twenty-seven, it seems ; that's your own age: who would have thought you were born in one year?"

I confess this blow was greater to me than the shock of

Mrs. Linton's death : ancient associations lingered round my heart; I sat down in the porch and wept as for a blood relation, desiring Mr. Kenneth to get another servant to introduce him to the master. I could not hinder myself from pondering on the question—"Had he had fair play?" Whatever I did, that idea would bother me : it was so tiresomely pertinacious that I resolved on requesting leave to go to Wuthering Heights, and assist in the last duties to the dead. Mr. Linton was extremely reluctant to consent, but I pleaded eloquently for the friendless condition in which he lay; and I said my old master and foster-brother had a claim on my services as strong as his own. Besides, I reminded him that the child Hareton was his wife's nephew, and, in the absence of nearer kin, he ought to act as its guardian; and he ought to and must inquire how the property was left, and look over the concerns of his brother-in-law. He was unfit for attending to such matters then, but he bid me speak to his lawyer; and at length permitted me to go. His lawyer had been Earnshaw's also : I called at the village, and asked him to accompany me. He shook his head, and advised that Heathcliff should be let alone; affirming, if the truth were known, Hareton would be found little else than a beggar.

"His father died in debt," he said; "the whole property is mortgaged, and the sole chance for the natural heir is to allow him an opportunity of creating some interest in the creditor's heart, that he may be inclined to deal leniently towards him."

When I reached the Heights, I explained that I had come to see everything carried on decently; and Joseph, who appeared in sufficient distress, expressed satisfaction at my presence. Mr. Heathcliff said he did not perceive that I was wanted; but I might stay and order the arrangements for the funeral, if I chose.

"Correctly," he remarked, "that fool's body should be buried at the cross-roads, without ceremony of any kind. I happened to leave him ten minutes yesterday afternoon, and in that interval he fastened the two doors of the house against me, and he has spent the night in drinking himself to death deliberately! We broke in this morning, for we heard him snorting like a horse; and there he was, laid over the settle : flaying and scalping would not have wakened him. I sent for Kenneth, and he came; but not till the

M 2

beast had changed into carrion: he was both dead and cold, and stark; and so you 'll allow it was useless making more stir about him!"

The old servant confirmed this statement, but muttered,

" I 'd rayther he 'd goan hisseln for t' doctor! I sud ha' taen tent o' t'maister better nor him—and he warn't deead when I left, naught o' t'soart!"

I insisted on the funeral being respectable. Mr. Heathcliff said I might have my own way there too; only, he desired me to remember that the money for the whole affair came out of his pocket. He maintained a hard, careless deport-ment, indicative of neither joy nor sorrow: if anything, it expressed a flinty gratification at a piece of difficult work successfully executed. I observed once, indeed, something like exultation in his aspect: it was just when the people were bearing the coffin from the house. He had the hypo-crisy to represent a mourner; and previous to following with Hareton, he lifted the unfortunate child on to the table and muttered, with peculiar gusto, "Now, my bonny lad you are *mine*! And we 'll see if one tree won't grow as crooked as another, with the same wind to twist it!" The unsuspect-ing thing was pleased at this speech: he played with Heath-cliff's whiskers, and stroked his cheek; but I divined its meaning, and observed tartly, "That boy must go back with me to Thrushcross Grange, sir. There is nothing in the world less yours than he is!"

" Does Linton say so?" he demanded.

" Of course—he has ordered me to take him," I replied.

" Well," said the scoundrel, "We'll not argue the subject now: but·I have a fancy to try my hand at rearing a young one; so intimate to your master that I must supply the place of this with my own, if he attempt to remove it. I don't engage to let Hareton go undisputed; but I'll be pretty sure to make the other come! Remember to tell him."

This hint was enough to bind our hands. I repeated its substance on my return; and Edgar Linton, little interested at the commencement, spoke no more of interfering. I'm not aware that he could have done it to any purpose, had he been ever so willing.

The guest was now the master of Wuthering Heights: he held firm possession, and proved to the attorney—who, in his turn, proved it to Mr. Linton—that Earnshaw had mortgaged every yard of land he owned, for cash to supply his mania for gaming; and he, Heathcliff, was the mortgagee. In that manner Hareton, who should now be the first gentleman in the neighbourhood, was reduced to a state of complete dependence on his father's inveterate enemy; and lives in his own house as a servant, deprived of the advantage of wages: quite unable to right himself, because of his friendlessness, and his ignorance that he has been wronged.

CHAPTER XVIII.

THE twelve years, continued Mrs. Dean, following that dismal period were the happiest of my life: my greatest troubles in their passage rose from our little lady's trifling illnesses, which she had to experience in common with all children, rich and poor. For the rest, after the first six months, she grew like a larch; and could walk and talk too, in her own way, before the heath blossomed a second time over Mrs. Linton's dust. She was the most winning thing that ever brought sunshine into a desolate house: a real beauty in face, with the Earnshaws' handsome dark eyes, but the Lintons' fair skin and small features, and yellow curling hair. Her spirit was high, though not rough, and qualified by a heart sensitive and lively to excess in its affections. That capacity for intense attachments reminded me of her mother: still she did not resemble her; for she could be soft and mild as a dove, and she had a gentle voice and pensive expression: her anger was never furious; her love never fierce: it was deep and tender. However, it must be acknowledged, she had faults to foil her gifts. A propensity to be saucy was one; and a perverse will, that indulged children invariably acquire, whether they be good tempered or cross. If a servant chanced to vex her, it was always—" I shall tell papa!" And if he reproved her, even by a look, you would have thought it a heart-breaking business: I don't believe he ever did

speak a harsh word to her. He took her education entirely on himself, and made it an amusement.   Fortunately, curiosity and a quick intellect made her an apt
scholar : she learned rapidly and eagerly, and did honour to
his teaching.

Till she reached the age of thirteen, she had not once
been beyond the range of the park by herself.   Mr. Linton
would take her with him a mile or so outside, on rare occasions; but he trusted her to no one else.   Gimmerton was an
unsubstantial name in her ears; the chapel, the only building she had approached or entered, except her own home.
Wuthering Heights and Mr. Heathcliff did not exist for
her : she was a perfect recluse ; and, apparently, perfectly
contented.   Sometimes, indeed, while surveying the country
from her nursery window, she would observe—

" Ellen, how long will it be before I can walk to the top
of those hills ?   I wonder what lies on the other side—is it
the sea ?"

" No, Miss Cathy," I would answer ; " it is hills again,
just like these."

" And what are those golden rocks like, when you stand
under them ?" she once asked.

The abrupt descent of Penistone Crags particularly attracted her notice; especially when the setting sun shone on
it and the topmost heights, and the whole extent of landscape besides lay in shadow.   I explained that they were
bare masses of stone, with hardly enough earth in their
clefts to nourish a stunted tree.

" And why are they bright so long after it is evening
here ?" she pursued.

" Because they are a great deal higher up than we are,"
replied I ; " you could not climb them, they are too high
and steep.   In winter the frost is always there before it
comes to us ; and deep into summer I have found snow
under that black hollow on the north-east side !"

" Oh, you have been on them !" she cried, gleefully.
" Then I can go, too, when I am a woman.   Has papa
been, Ellen ?"

" Papa would tell you, miss," I answered, hastily, " that
they are not worth the trouble of visiting.   The moors,
where you ramble with him, are much nicer ; and Thrushcross park is the finest place in the world."

"But I know the park, and I don't know those," she murmured to herself. "And I should delight to look round me from the brow of that tallest point: my little pony Minny shall take me some time."

One of the maids mentioning the Fairy Cave, quite turned her head with a desire to fulfil this project: she teased Mr. Linton about it; and he promised she should have the journey when she got older. But Miss Catherine measured her age by months, and, "Now, am I old enough to go to Penistone Crags?" was the constant question in her mouth. The road thither wound close by Wuthering Heights. Edgar had not the heart to pass it; so she received as constantly the answer, "Not yet, love: not yet."

I said Mrs. Heathcliff lived above a dozen years after quitting her husband. Her family were of a delicate constitution: she and Edgar both lacked the ruddy health that you will generally meet in these parts. What her last illness was, I am not certain: I conjecture, they died of the same thing, a kind of fever, slow at its commencement, but incurable, and rapidly consuming life towards the close. She wrote to inform her brother of the probable conclusion of a four months' indisposition under which she had suffered, and entreated him to come to her, if possible; for she had much to settle, and she wished to bid him adieu, and deliver Linton safely into his hands. Her hope was, that Linton might be left with him, as he had been with her: his father, she would fain convince herself, had no desire to assume the burden of his maintenance or education. My master hesitated not a moment in complying with her request: reluctant as he was to leave home at ordinary calls, he flew to answer this; commending Catherine to my peculiar vigilance, in his absence, with reiterated orders that she must not wander out of the park, even under my escort: he did not calculate on her going unaccompanied.

He was away three weeks. The first day or two, my charge sat in a corner of the library, too sad for either reading or playing: in that quiet state she caused me little trouble; but it was succeeded by an interval of impatient, fretful weariness; and being too busy, and too old then, to run up and down amusing her, I hit on a method by which she might entertain herself. I used to send her on her travels round the grounds—now on foot, and now on a pony; indulging her with a patient audience of all her real and imaginary adventures, when she returned.

The summer shone in full prime; and she took such a taste for this solitary rambling that she often contrived to remain out from breakfast till tea; and then the evenings were spent in recounting her fanciful tales. I did not fear her breaking bounds; because the gates were generally locked, and I thought she would scarcely venture forth alone, if they had stood wide open. Unluckily, my confidence proved misplaced. Catherine came to me, one morning, at eight o'clock, and said she was that day an Arabian merchant, going to cross the Desert with his caravan; and I must give her plenty of provision for herself and beasts: a horse, and three camels, personated by a large hound and a couple of pointers. I got together good store of dainties, and slung them in a basket on one side of the saddle; and she sprang up as gay as a fairy, sheltered by her wide-brimmed hat and gauze veil from the July sun, and trotted off with a merry laugh, mocking my cautious counsel to avoid galloping, and come back early. The naughty thing never made her appearance at tea. One traveller, the hound, being an old dog and fond of its ease, returned; but neither Cathy, nor the pony, nor the two pointers were visible in any direction: I despatched emissaries down this path, and that path, and at last went wandering in search of her myself. There was a labourer working at a fence round a plantation, on the borders of the grounds. I inquired of him if he had seen our young lady.

"I saw her at morn," he replied; "she would have me to cut her a hazel switch, and then she leapt her Galloway over the hedge yonder, where it is lowest, and galloped out of sight."

You may guess how I felt at hearing this news. It struck me directly she must have started for Penistone Crags. "What will become of her?" I ejaculated, pushing through a gap which the man was repairing, and making straight to the high road. I walked as if for a wager, mile after mile, till a turn brought me in view of the Heights; but no Catherine could I detect, far or near. The Crags lie about a mile and a half between Mr. Heathcliff's place, and that is four from the Grange, so I began to fear night would fall ere I could reach them. "And what if she should have slipped in clambering among them," I reflected, "and been killed, or broken some of her bones?" My suspense was truly painful; and, at first, it gave me delightful relief to observe, in hurrying by the farm-house, Charlie, the fiercest of the pointers, lying under a window, with swelled head and bleeding ear. I opened the wicket and ran to the door, knocking vehemently for admittance. A woman whom I knew, and who formerly lived at Gimmerton, answered: she had been servant there since the death of Mr. Earnshaw.

" Ah," said she, " you are come a seeking your little mistress! don't be frightened. She's here safe: but I'm glad it isn't the master."

" He is not at home then, is he?" I panted, quite breathless with quick walking and alarm.

" No, no," she replied: " both he and Joseph are off, and I think they won't return this hour or more. Step in and rest you a bit."

I entered, and beheld my stray lamb seated on the hearth, rocking herself in a little chair that had been her mother's when a child. Her hat was hung against the wall, and she seemed perfectly at home, laughing and chattering, in the best spirits imaginable, to Hareton—now a great, strong lad of eighteen—who stared at her with considerable curiosity and astonishment: comprehending precious little of the fluent succession of remarks and questions which her tongue never ceased pouring forth.

" Very well, miss!" I exclaimed, concealing my joy under an angry countenance. " This is your last ride, till papa comes back. I'll not trust you over the threshold again, you naughty, naughty girl!"

" Aha, Ellen!" she cried, gaily, jumping up and running to my side. " I shall have a pretty story to tell to-night: and so you've found me out. Have you ever been here in your life before?"

" Put that hat on, and home at once," said I. " I'm dreadfully grieved at you, Miss Cathy: you've done extremely wrong! It's no use pouting and crying: that won't repay the trouble I've had, scouring the country after you. To think how Mr. Linton charged me to keep you in; and you stealing off so! it shows you are a cunning little fox, and nobody will put faith in you any more."

" What have I done?" sobbed she, instantly checked.

"Papa charged me nothing: he'll not scold me, Ellen—he's never cross, like you!"

"Come, come!" I repeated. "I'll tie the riband. Now, let us have no petulance. Oh, for shame! You thirteen years old, and such a baby!"

This exclamation was caused by her pushing the hat from her head, and retreating to the chimney out of my reach.

"Nay," said the servant, "don't be hard on the bonny lass, Mrs. Dean. We made her stop: she'd fain have ridden forwards, afeard you should be uneasy. Hareton offered to go with her, and I thought he should: it's a wild road over the hills."

Hareton, during the discussion, stood with his hands in his pockets, too awkward to speak; though he looked as if he did not relish my intrusion.

"How long am I to wait?" I continued, disregarding the woman's interference. "It will be dark in ten minutes. Where is the pony, Miss Cathy? And where is Phœnix? I shall leave you, unless you be quick; so please yourself."

"The pony is in the yard," she replied, "and Phœnix is shut in there. He's bitten—and so is Charlie. I was going to tell you all about it; but you are in a bad temper, and don't deserve to hear."

I picked up her hat, and approached to reinstate it; but perceiving that the people of the house took her part, she commenced capering round the room; and on my giving chase, ran like a mouse over and under and behind the furniture, rendering it ridiculous for me to pursue. Hareton and the woman laughed, and she joined them, and waxed more impertinent still; till I cried, in great irritation,—

"Well, Miss Cathy, if you were aware whose house this is, you'd be glad enough to get out."

"It's *your* father's, isn't it?" said she, turning to Hareton.

"Nay," he replied, looking down, and blushing bashfully. He could not stand a steady gaze from her eyes, though they were just his own.

"Whose then—your master's?" she asked.

He coloured deeper, with a different feeling, muttered an oath, and turned away.

"Who is his master?" continued the tiresome girl, appealing to me. " He talked about 'our house,' and 'our folk.' I thought he had been the owner's son. And he never said, miss : he should have done, shouldn't he, if he's a servant?"

Hareton grew black as a thunder-cloud, at this childish speech. I silently shook my questioner, and at last succeeded in equipping her for departure.

" Now, get my horse," she said, addressing her unknown kinsman as she would one of the stable-boys at the Grange. " And you may come with me. I want to see where the goblin-hunter rises in the marsh, and to hear about the *fairishes,* as you call them : but make haste ! What's the matter? Get my horse, I say."

" I 'll see thee damned before I be *thy* servant !" growled the lad.

" You 'll see me *what?*" asked Catherine in surprise.

" Damned—thou saucy witch !" he replied.

" There, Miss Cathy ! you see you have got into pretty company," I interposed. " Nice words to be used to a young lady ! Pray don't begin to dispute with him. Come, let us seek for Minny ourselves, and begone."

" But Ellen," cried she, staring, fixed in astonishment. " How dare he speak so to me? Mustn't he be made to do as I ask him? You wicked creature, I shall tell papa what you said.—Now, then !"

Hareton did not appear to feel this threat; so the tears sprang into her eyes with indignation. " You bring the pony," she exclaimed, turning to the woman, " and let my dog free this moment !"

" Softly, miss," answered she addressed : " you'll lose nothing by being civil. Though Mr. Hareton, there, be not the master's son, he 's your cousin ; and I was never hired to serve you."

" *He* my cousin !" cried Cathy, with a scornful laugh.

" Yes, indeed," responded her reprover.

" Oh, Ellen ! don't let them say such things," she pursued in great trouble. " Papa is gone to fetch my cousin from London : my cousin is a gentleman's son. That my—" she stopped, and wept outright; upset at the bare notion of relationship with such a clown.

" Hush, hush !" I whispered, " people can have many cousins and of all sorts, Miss Cathy, without being any the worse for it; only they needn't keep their company, if they be disagreeable and bad."

" He's not—he's not my cousin, Ellen!" she went on, gathering fresh grief from reflection, and flinging herself into my arms for refuge from the idea.

I was much vexed at her and the servant for their mutual revelations; having no doubt of Linton's approaching arrival, communicated by the former, being reported to Mr. Heathcliff; and feeling as confident that Catherine's first thought on her father's return, would be to seek an explanation of the latter's assertion concerning her rude-bred kindred. Hareton, recovering from his disgust at being taken for a servant, seemed moved by her distress; and, having fetched the pony round to the door, he took, to propitiate her, a fine crooked-legged terrier whelp from the kennel, and putting it into her hand bid her wisht! for he meant nought. Pausing in her lamentations, she surveyed him with a glance of awe and horror, then burst forth anew.

I could scarcely refrain from smiling at this antipathy to the poor fellow; who was a well-made, athletic youth, good looking in features, and stout and healthy, but attired in garments befitting his daily occupations of working on the farm, and lounging among the moors after rabbits and game. Still, I thought I could detect in his physiognomy a mind owning better qualities than his father ever possessed. Good things lost amid a wilderness of weeds, to be sure, whose rankness far over-topped their neglected growth; yet, notwithstanding, evidence of a wealthy soil, that might yield luxuriant crops under other and favourable circumstances. Mr. Heathcliff, I believe, had not treated him physically ill; thanks to his fearless nature, which offered no temptation to that course of oppression: he had none of the timid susceptibility that would have given zest to ill-treatment, in Heathcliff's judgment. He appeared to have bent his malevolence on making him a brute: he was never taught to read or write; never rebuked for any bad habit which did not annoy his keeper; never led a single step towards virtue, or guarded by a single precept against vice. And from what I heard, Joseph contributed much to his deterioration, by a narrow-minded partiality which prompted him to flatter and pet him, as a boy, because he was the head of the old family. And as he had been in the habit of accusing Catherine Earnshaw and Heathcliff, when children, of putting the master past his patience, and compelling him to seek solace in drink by what he termed their " offalld ways," so at present he laid the whole burden of Hareton's faults on the shoulders of the usurper of his property. If the lad swore, he wouldn't correct him; nor however culpably he behaved. It gave Joseph satisfaction, apparently, to watch him go the worst lengths: he allowed that the lad was ruined: that his soul was abandoned to perdition; but then, he reflected that Heathcliff must answer for it. Hareton's blood would be required at his hands; and there lay immense consolation in that thought. Joseph had instilled into him a pride of name, and of his lineage; he would, had he dared, have fostered hate between him and the present owner of the Heights: but his dread of that owner amounted to superstition; and he confined his feelings regarding him to muttered inuendos and private comminations. I don't pretend to be intimately acquainted with the mode of living customary in those days at Wuthering Heights: I only speak from hearsay; for I saw little. The villagers affirmed Mr. Heathcliff was *near*, and a cruel hard landlord to his tenants; but the house, inside, had regained its ancient aspect of comfort under female management, and the scenes of riot common in Hindley's time were not now enacted within its walls. The master was too gloomy to seek com panionship with any people, good or bad; and he is yet.

This, however, is not making progress with my story. Miss Cathy rejected the peace-offering of the terrier, and demanded her own dogs, Charlie and Phœnix. They came limping, and hanging their heads; and we set out for home, sadly out of sorts, every one of us. I could not wring from my little lady how she had spent the day; except that, as I supposed, the goal of her pilgrimage was Penistone Crags; and she arrived without adventure to the gate of the farmhouse, when Hareton happened to issue forth, attended by some canine followers, who attacked her train. They had a smart battle, before their owners could separate them: that formed an introduction. Catherine told Hareton who she was, and where she was going; and asked him to show her the way: finally, beguiling him to accompany her. He opened the mysteries of the Fairy Cave, and twenty other queer places. But, being in disgrace, I was

not favoured with a description of the interesting objects
she saw. I could gather, however, that her guide had
been a favourite till she hurt his feelings by addressing him
as a servant; and Heathcliff's housekeeper hurt hers by
calling him her cousin. Then the language he had held
to her rankled in her heart; she who was always "love,"
and "darling," and "queen," and "angel," with everybody
at the Grange, to be insulted so shockingly by a stranger!
She did not comprehend it; and hard work I had to obtain
a promise that she would not lay the grievance before her
father. I explained how he objected to the whole household
at the Heights, and how sorry he would be to find she
had been there; but I insisted most on the fact, that if
she revealed my negligence of his orders, he would perhaps
be so angry, that I should have to leave; and Cathy couldn't
bear that prospect: she pledged her word, and kept it, for
my sake. After all, she was a sweet little girl.

CHAPTER XIX.

A LETTER, edged with black, announced the day of my
master's return. Isabella was dead; and he wrote to bid
me get mourning for his daughter, and arrange a room,
and other accommodations, for his youthful nephew. Catherine ran wild with joy at the idea of welcoming her father
back; and indulged most sanguine anticipations of the innumerable excellences of her "real" cousin. The evening
of their expected arrival came. Since early morning, she
had been busy ordering her own small affairs; and now,
attired in her new black frock—poor thing! her aunt's
death impressed her with no definite sorrow—she obliged
me, by constant worrying, to walk with her down through
the grounds to meet them.

"Linton is just six months younger than I am," she
chattered, as we strolled leisurely over the swells and
hollows of mossy turf, under shadow of the trees. "How
delightful it will be to have him for a playfellow! Aunt
Isabella sent papa a beautiful lock of his hair; it was

lighter than mine—more flaxen, and quite as fine. I have it carefully preserved in a little glass box; and I've often thought what pleasure it would be to see its owner. Oh! I am happy—and papa, dear, dear papa! Come, Ellen, let us run! come run!"

She ran, and returned and ran again, many times before my sober footsteps reached the gate, and then she seated herself on the grassy bank beside the path, and tried to wait patiently; but that was impossible: she couldn't be still a minute.

"How long they are!" she exclaimed. "Ah, I see some dust on the road—they are coming! No! When will they be here? May we not go a little way—half a mile, Ellen: only just half a mile? Do say Yes: to that clump of birches at the turn!"

I refused stanchly. At length her suspense was ended: the travelling carriage rolled in sight. Miss Cathy shrieked and stretched out her arms, as soon as she caught her father's face looking from the window. He descended, nearly as eager as herself; and a considerable interval elapsed ere they had a thought to spare for any but themselves. While they exchanged caresses, I 'took a peep in to see after Linton. He was asleep in a corner, wrapped in a warm, fur-lined cloak, as if it had been winter. A pale, delicate, effeminate boy, who might have been taken for my master's younger brother, so strong was the resemblance: but there was a sickly peevishness in his aspect, that Edgar Linton never had. The latter saw me looking; and having shaken hands, advised me to close the door, and leave him undisturbed; for the journey had fatigued him. Cathy would fain have taken one glance, but her father told her to come, and they walked together up the park, while I hastened before to prepare the servants.

"Now, darling," said Mr. Linton, addressing his daughter, as they halted at the bottom of the front steps: "your cousin is not so strong or so merry as you are, and he has lost his mother, remember, a very short time since; therefore, don't expect him to play and run about with you directly. And don't harass him much by talking: let him be quiet this evening at least, will you?"

"Yes, yes, papa," answered Catherine: "but I do want to see him; and he hasn't once looked out."

The carriage stopped; and the sleeper being roused, was lifted to the ground by his uncle.

"This is your cousin Cathy, Linton," he said, putting their little hands together. "She's fond of you already; and mind you don't grieve her by crying to-night. Try to be cheerful now; the travelling is at an end, and you have nothing to do but rest and amuse yourself as you please."

"Let me go to bed, then," answered the boy, shrinking from Catherine's salute; and he put his fingers to remove incipient tears.

"Come, come, there's a good child," I whispered, leading him in. "You'll make her weep too—see how sorry she is for you!"

I do not know whether it was sorrow for him, but his cousin put on as sad a countenance as himself, and returned to her father. All three entered, and mounted to the library, where tea was laid ready. I proceeded to remove Linton's cap and mantle, and placed him on a chair by the table; but he was no sooner seated than he began to cry afresh. My master inquired what was the matter.

"I can't sit on a chair," sobbed the boy.

"Go to the sofa, then, and Ellen shall bring you some tea," answered his uncle, patiently.

He had been greatly tried, during the journey, I felt convinced, by his fretful ailing charge. Linton slowly trailed himself off, and lay down. Cathy carried a foot-stool and her cup to his side. At first she sat silent; but that could not last: she had resolved to make a pet of her little cousin, as she would have him to be; and she commenced stroking his curls, and kissing his cheek, and offering him tea in her saucer, like a baby. This pleased him, for he was not much better: he dried his eyes, and lightened into a faint smile.

"Oh, he'll do very well," said the master to me, after watching them a minute. "Very well, if we can keep him, Ellen. The company of a child of his own age will instil new spirit into him soon, and by wishing for strength he'll gain it."

"Ay, if we can keep him!" I mused to myself; and sore misgivings came over me that there was slight hope of that. And then, I thought, however will that weakling live at Wuthering Heights? Between his father and Hareton, what playmates and instructors they'll be. Our doubts were presently decided—even earlier than I expected. I had just taken the children up stairs, after tea was finished, and seen Linton asleep—he would not suffer me to leave him till that was the case—I had come down, and was standing by the table in the hall, lighting a bedroom candle for Mr. Edgar, when a maid stepped out of the kitchen and informed me that Mr. Heathcliff's servant Joseph was at the door, and wished to speak with the master.

" I shall ask him what he wants first," I said, in considerable trepidation. " A very unlikely hour to be troubling people, and the instant they have returned from a long journey. I don't think the master can see him."

Joseph had advanced through the kitchen as I uttered these words, and now presented himself in the hall. He was donned in his Sunday garments, with his most sanctimonious and sourest face, and, holding his hat in one hand and his stick in the other, he proceeded to clean his shoes on the mat.

" Good-evening, Joseph," I said, coldly. " What business brings you here to-night ? "

" It's Maister Linton I mun spake to," he answered, waving me disdainfully aside.

" Mr. Linton is going to bed ; unless you have something particular to say, I'm sure he won't hear it now," I continued. " You had better sit down in there, and entrust your message to me."

" Which is his rahm ? " pursued the fellow, surveying the range of closed doors.

I perceived he was bent on refusing my mediation, so very reluctantly I went up to the library, and announced the unseasonable visitor, advising that he should be dismissed till next day. Mr. Linton had no time to empower me to do so, for Joseph mounted close at my heels, and, pushing into the apartment, planted himself at the far side of the table, with his two fists clapped on the head of his stick, and began in an elevated tone, as if anticipating opposition,—

" Hathecliff has send me for his lad, and I munn't goa back 'bout him."

Edgar Linton was silent a minute ; an expression of exceeding sorrow overcast his features : he would have pitied the child on his own account ; but, recalling Isabella's

N

hopes and fears, and anxious wishes for her son, and her commendations of him to his care, he grieved bitterly at the prospect of yielding him up, and searched in his heart how it might be avoided. No plan offered itself: the very exhibition of any desire to keep him would have rendered the claimant more peremptory: there was nothing left but to resign him. However, he was not going to rouse him from his sleep.

" Tell Mr. Heathcliff," he answered calmly, " that his son shall come to Wuthering Heights to-morrow. He is in bed, and too tired to go the distance now. You may also tell him that the mother of Linton desired him to remain under my guardianship; and, at present, his health is very precarious."

" Noa!" said Joseph, giving a thud with his prop on the floor, and assuming an authoritative air: " Noa! that means naught. Hathecliff maks noa 'count o' t' mother, nor ye norther; but he'll hev his lad; und I mun tak him—soa now ye knaw!"

" You shall not to-night!" answered Linton decisively. " Walk down stairs at once, and repeat to your master what I have said. Ellen, show him down. Go——"

And, aiding the indignant elder with a lift by the arm, he rid the room of him, and closed the door.

" Varrah weell!" shouted Joseph, as he slowly drew off. " To morn, he's come hisseln, and thrust *him* out, if ye darr!"

CHAPTER XX.

To obviate the danger of this threat being fulfilled, Mr. Linton commissioned me to take the boy home early, on Catherine's pony; and, said he—

" As we shall now have no influence over his destiny, good or bad, you must say nothing of whom he is gone, to my daughter: she cannot associate with him hereafter, and it is better for her to remain in ignorance of his proximity; lest she should be restless, and anxious to visit the Heights.

Merely tell her his father sent for him suddenly, and he has been obliged to leave us."

Linton was very reluctant to be roused from his bed at five o'clock, and astonished to be informed that he must prepare for further travelling; but I softened off the matter by stating that he was going to spend some time with his father, Mr. Heathcliff, who wished to see him so much, he did not like to defer the pleasure till he should recover from his late journey.

"My father!" he cried, in strange perplexity. "Mamma never told me I had a father. Where does he live? I'd rather stay with uncle."

"He lives a little distance from the Grange," I replied; "just beyond those hills: not so far, but you may walk over here when you get hearty. And you should be glad to go home, and to see him. You must try to love him, as you did your mother, and then he will love you."

"But why have I not heard of him before?" asked Linton. "Why didn't mamma and he live together, as other people do?"

"He had business to keep him in the north," I answered, "and your mother's health required her to reside in the south."

"And why didn't mamma speak to me about him?" persevered the child. "She often talked of uncle, and I learnt to love him long ago. How am I to love papa? I don't know him."

"Oh, all children love their parents," I said. "Your mother, perhaps, thought you would want to be with him if she mentioned him often to you. Let us make haste. An early ride on such a beautiful morning is much preferable to an hour's more sleep."

"Is *she* to go with us," he demanded: "the little girl I saw yesterday?"

"Not now," replied I.

"Is uncle?" he continued.

"No, I shall be your companion there," I said.

Linton sank back on his pillow and fell into a brown study.

"I won't go without uncle," he cried at length: "I can't tell where you mean to take me."

I attempted to persuade him of the naughtiness of showing

reluctance to meet his father; still he obstinately resisted
any progress towards dressing, and I had to call for my
master's assistance in coaxing him out of bed. The poor
thing was finally got off, with several delusive assurances
that his absence should be short; that Mr. Edgar and Cathy
would visit him, and other promises, equally ill-founded,
which I invented and reiterated at intervals throughout the
way. The pure heather-scented air, the bright sunshine,
and the gentle canter of Minny, relieved his despondency
after a while. He began to put questions concerning his
new home, and its inhabitants, with greater interest and
liveliness.

" Is Wuthering Heights as pleasant a place as Thrushcross Grange?" he inquired, turning to take a last glance
into the valley, whence a light mist mounted and formed a
fleecy cloud on the skirts of the blue.

" It is not so buried in trees," I replied, " and it is not quite
so large, but you can see the country beautifully all round;
and the air is healthier for you—fresher and dryer. You
will, perhaps, think the building old and dark at first;
though it is a respectable house: the next best in the neighbourhood. And you will have such nice rambles on the
moors. Hareton Earnshaw—that is Miss Cathy's other
cousin, and so yours in a manner—will show you all the
sweetest spots; and you can bring a book in fine weather,
and make a green hollow your study; and, now and then,
your uncle may join you in a walk: he does, frequently,
walk out on the hills."

" And what is my father like?" he asked. " Is he as
young and handsome as uncle?"

" He's as young," said I; " but he has black hair and
eyes, and looks sterner; and he is taller and bigger altogether. He'll not seem to you so gentle and kind at first,
perhaps, because it is not his way: still, mind you, be frank
and cordial with him; and naturally he'll be fonder of you
than any uncle, for you are his own."

" Black hair and eyes!" mused Linton. " I can't fancy
him. Then I am not like him, am I?"

" Not much," I answered. not a morsel, I thought,
surveying with regret the white complexion and slim
frame of my companion, and his large languid eyes—his
mother's eyes, save that, unless a morbid touchiness kindled

them a moment, they had not a vestige of her sparkling spirit.

"How strange that he should never come to see mamma and me!" he murmured. "Has he ever seen me? If he has, I must have been a baby. I remember not a single thing about him!"

"Why, Master Linton," said I, "three hundred miles is a great distance; and ten years seem very different in length to a grown up person compared with what they do to you. It is probable Mr. Heathcliff proposed going from summer to summer, but never found a convenient opportunity; and now it is too late. Don't trouble him with questions on the subject: it will disturb him, for no good."

The boy was fully occupied with his own cogitations for the remainder of the ride, till we halted before the farm-house garden gate. I watched to catch his impressions in his countenance. He surveyed the carved front and low-browed lattices, the straggling gooseberry bushes and crooked firs, with solemn intentness, and then shook his head: his private feelings entirely disapproved of the exterior of his new abode. But he had sense to postpone complaining: there might be compensation within. Before he dismounted, I went and opened the door. It was half-past six; the family had just finished breakfast: the servant was clearing and wiping down the table. Joseph stood by his master's chair telling some tale concerning a lame horse; and Hareton was preparing for the hay-field.

"Hallo, Nelly!" said Mr. Heathcliff, when he saw me. "I feared I should have to come down and fetch my property myself. You've brought it, have you? Let us see what we can make of it."

He got up and strode to the door: Hareton and Joseph followed in gaping curiosity. Poor Linton ran a frightened eye over the faces of the three.

"Sure-ly," said Joseph after a grave inspection, "he's swopped wi' ye, maister, an' yon's his lass!"

Heathcliff, having stared his son into an ague of confusion, uttered a scornful laugh.

"God! what a beauty! what a lovely, charming thing!" he exclaimed. "Hav'n't they reared it on snails and sour milk, Nelly? Oh, damn my soul! but that's worse than I expected—and the devil knows I was not sanguine!"

I bid the trembling and bewildered child get down, and enter. He did not thoroughly comprehend the meaning of his father's speech, or whether it were intended for him: indeed, he was not yet certain that the grim, sneering stranger was his father. But he clung to me with growing trepidation; and on Mr. Heathcliff's taking a seat and bidding him "come hither," he hid his face on my shoulder and wept.

"Tut, tut!" said Heathcliff, stretching out a hand and dragging him roughly between his knees, and then holding up his head by the chin. "None of that nonsense! We're not going to hurt thee, Linton—isn't that thy name? Thou art thy mother's child, entirely! Where is *my* share in thee, puling chicken?"

He took off the boy's cap and pushed back his thick flaxen curls, felt his slender arms and his small fingers; during which examination, Linton ceased crying, and lifted his great blue eyes to inspect the inspector.

"Do you know me?" asked Heathcliff, having satisfied himself that the limbs were all equally frail and feeble.

"No," said Linton, with a gaze of vacant fear.

"You've heard of me, I dare say?"

"No," he replied again.

"No! What a shame of your mother, never to waken your filial regard for me! You are my son, then, I'll tell you; and your mother was a wicked slut to leave you in ignorance of the sort of father you possessed. Now, don't wince, and colour up! Though it *is* something to see you have not white blood. Be a good lad; and I'll do for you. Nelly, if you be tired you may sit down; if not, get home again. I guess you'll report what you hear and see to the cipher at the Grange; and this thing won't be settled while you linger about it."

"Well," replied I, "I hope you'll be kind to the boy, Mr. Heathcliff, or you'll not keep him long; and he's all you have akin in the wide world, that you will ever know— remember."

"I'll be *very* kind to him, you needn't fear," he said, laughing. "Only nobody else must be kind to him: I'm jealous of monopolizing his affection. And, to begin my kindness, Joseph, bring the lad some breakfast. Hareton, you infernal calf, begone to your work. Yes, Nell," he added, when they had departed, "my son is prospective owner of your place, and I should not wish him to die till I was certain of being his successor. Besides, he's *mine*, and I want the triumph of seeing *my* descendant fairly lord of their estates: my child hiring their children to till their fathers' lands for wages. That is the sole consideration which can make me endure the whelp: I despise him for himself, and hate him for the memories he revives! But that consideration is sufficient: he's as safe with me, and shall be tended as carefully as your master tends his own. I have a room up stairs, furnished for him in handsome style; I've engaged a tutor, also, to come three times a week, from twenty miles distance, to teach him what he pleases to learn. I've ordered Hareton to obey him: and in fact I've arranged everything with a view to preserve the superior and the gentleman in him, above his associates. I do regret, however, that he so little deserves the trouble: if I wished any blessing in the world, it was to find him a worthy object of pride; and I'm bitterly disappointed with the whey-faced whining wretch!"

While he was speaking, Joseph returned bearing a basin of milk-porridge, and placed it before Linton; who stirred round the homely mess with a look of aversion, and affirmed he could not eat it. I saw the old man-servant shared largely in his master's scorn of the child; though he was compelled to retain the sentiment in his heart, because Heathcliff plainly meant his underlings to hold him in honour.

"Cannot ate it?" repeated he, peering in Linton's face, and subduing his voice to a whisper, for fear of being overheard. "But Maister Hareton nivir ate naught else, when he wer a little un; and what wer gooid eneugh for him's gooid eneugh for ye, I's rayther think!"

"I *sha'n't* eat it!" answered Linton, snappishly. "Take it away."

Joseph snatched up the food indignantly, and brought it to us.

"Is there aught ails th' victuals?" he asked, thrusting the tray under Heathcliff's nose.

"What should ail them?" he said.

"Wah!" answered Joseph, "yon dainty chap says he cannut ate 'em. But I guess it's raight! His mother wer

just soa—we wer a'most too mucky to sow t' corn for makking her breead."

"Don't mention his mother to me," said the master
angrily. "Get him something that he can eat, that's all.
What is his usual food, Nelly?"

I suggested boiled milk or tea; and the housekeeper received instructions to prepare some. Come, I reflected, his
father's selfishness may contribute to his comfort. He per-
ceives his delicate constitution, and the necessity of treating
him tolerably. I'll console Mr. Edgar by acquainting him
with the turn Heathcliff's humour has taken. Having no
excuse for lingering longer, I slipped out, while Linton was
engaged in timidly rebuffing the advances of a friendly
sheep-dog. But he was too much on the alert to be
cheated: as I closed the door, I heard a cry, and a frantic
repetition of the words—

"Don't leave me! I'll not stay here! I'll not stay
here!"

Then the latch was raised and fell: they did not suffer
him to come forth. I mounted Minny, and urged her to a
trot; and so my brief guardianship ended.

* * *

CHAPTER XXI.

WE had sad work with little Cathy that day: she rose in
high glee, eager to join her cousin, and such passionate tears
and lamentations followed the news of his departure, that
Edgar himself was obliged to sooth her, by affirming he
should come back soon: he added, however, "if I can get
him;" and there were no hopes of that. This promise poorly
pacified her: but time was more potent; and though still at
intervals she inquired of her father when Linton would return, before she did see him again his features had waxed so
dim in her memory that she did not recognise him.

When I chanced to encounter the housekeeper of Wuthering Heights, in paying business-visits to Gimmerton, I used
to ask how the young master got on; for he lived almost as
secluded as Catherine herself, and was never to be seen. I

could gather from her that he continued in weak health, and was a tiresome inmate. She said Mr. Heathcliff seemed to dislike him ever longer and worse, though he took some trouble to conceal it: he had an antipathy to the sound of his voice, and could not do at all with his sitting in the same room with him many minutes together. There seldom passed much talk between them: Linton learnt his lessons and spent his evenings in a small apartment they called the parlour; or else lay in bed all day: for he was constantly getting coughs, and colds, and aches, and pains of some sort.

"And I never knew such a faint-hearted creature," added the woman; "nor one so careful of hisseln. He *will* go on, if I leave the window open a bit late in the evening. Oh! it's killing, a breath of night air! And he must have a fire in the middle of summer; and Joseph's 'bacca pipe is poison; and he must always have sweets and dainties, and always milk, milk for ever—heeding naught how the rest of us are pinched in winter; and there he'll sit, wrapped in his furred cloak in his chair by the fire, with some toast and water or other slop on the hob to sip at; and if Hareton, for pity, comes to amuse him—Hareton is not bad-natured, though he's rough—they're sure to part, one swearing and the other crying. I believe the master would relish Earnshaw's thrashing him to a mummy, if he were not his son; and I'm certain he would be fit to turn him out of doors, if he knew half the nursing he gives hisseln. But then, he won't go into danger of temptation: he never enters the parlour, and should Linton show those ways in the house where he is, he sends him up stairs directly."

I divined, from this account, that utter lack of sympathy had rendered young Heathcliff selfish and disagreeable, if he were not so originally; and my interest in him, consequently, decayed: though still I was moved with a sense of grief at his lot, and a wish that he had been left with us. Mr. Edgar encouraged me to gain information: he thought a great deal about him, I fancy, and would have run some risk to see him; and he told me once to ask the housekeeper whether he ever came into the village? She said he had only been twice, on horseback, accompanying his father; and both times he pretended to be quite knocked up for three or four days afterwards. That housekeeper left, if I recollect rightly, two years after he came; and another, whom I did not know, was her successor: she lives there still.

Time wore on at the Grange in its former pleasant way, till Miss Cathy reached sixteen. On the anniversary of her birth we never manifested any signs of rejoicing, because it was also the anniversary of my late mistress's death. Her father invariably spent that day alone in the library; and walked, at dusk, as far as Gimmerton kirkyard, where he would frequently prolong his stay beyond midnight. Therefore Catherine was thrown on her own resources for amusement. This twentieth of March was a beautiful spring day, and when her father had retired, my young lady came down dressed for going out, and said she asked to have a ramble on the edge of the moor with me: Mr. Linton had given her leave, if we went only a short distance and were back within the hour.

"So make haste, Ellen!" she cried. "I know where I wish to go; where a colony of moor game are settled: I want to see whether they have made their nests yet."

"That must be a good distance up," I answered; "they don't breed on the edge of the moor."

"No, it's not," she said. "I've gone very near with papa."

I put on my bonnet and sallied out, thinking nothing more of the matter. She bounded before me, and returned to my side, and was off again like a young greyhound; and, at first, I found plenty of entertainment in listening to the larks singing far and near, and enjoying the sweet, warm sunshine; and watching her, my pet, and my delight, with her golden ringlets flying loose behind, and her bright cheek, as soft and pure in its bloom as a wild rose, and her eyes radiant with cloudless pleasure. She was a happy creature, and an angel, in those days. It's a pity she could not be content.

"Well," said I, "where are your moor-game, Miss Cathy? We should be at them: the Grange park-fence is a great way off now."

"Oh, a little further—only a little further, Ellen," was her answer, continually. "Climb to that hillock, pass that bank, and by the time you reach the other side I shall have raised the birds."

But there were so many hillocks and banks to climb and pass, that, at length, I began to be weary, and told her we must halt, and retrace our steps. I shouted to her, as she had outstripped me a long way; she either did not hear or did not regard, for she still sprang on, and I was compelled to follow. Finally, she dived into a hollow; and before I came in sight of her again, she was two miles nearer Wuthering Heights than her own home; and I beheld a couple of persons arrest her, one of whom I felt convinced was Mr. Heathcliff himself.

Cathy had been caught in the fact of plundering, or, at least, hunting out the nests of the grouse. The Heights were Heathcliff's land, and he was reproving the poacher.

" I've neither taken any nor found any," she said, as I toiled to them, expanding her hands in corroboration of the statement. " I didn't mean to take them; but papa told me there were quantities up here, and I wished to see the eggs."

Heathcliff glanced at me with an ill-meaning smile, expressing his acquaintance with the party, and, consequently, his malevolence towards it, and demanded who " papa" was?

" Mr. Linton of Thrushcross Grange," she replied. " I thought you did not know me, or you wouldn't have spoken in that way."

" You suppose papa is highly esteemed and respected then ?" he said, sarcastically.

" And what are you ?" inquired Catherine, gazing curiously on the speaker. " That man I've seen before. Is he your son?"

She pointed to Hareton, the other individual, who had gained nothing but increased bulk and strength by the addition of two years to his age: he seemed as awkward and rough as ever.

" Miss Cathy," I interrupted, " it will be three hours instead of one that we are out, presently. We really must go back."

" No, that man is not my son," answered Heathcliff, pushing me aside. " But I have one, and you have seen him before too; and, though your nurse is in a hurry, I think both you and she would be the better for a little rest. Will you just turn this nab of heath, and walk into my house?

You'll get home earlier for the ease; and you shall receive a kind welcome."

I whispered Catherine that she mustn't, on any account, accede to the proposal: it was entirely out of the question.

"Why?" she asked, aloud. "I'm tired of running, and the ground is dewy: I can't sit here. Let us go, Ellen. Besides, he says I have seen his son. He's mistaken, I think; but I guess where he lives: at the farm-house I visited in coming from Penistone Crags. Don't you?"

"I do. Come, Nelly, hold your tongue—it will be a treat for her to look in on us. Hareton, get forwards with the lass. You shall walk with me, Nelly."

"No, she's not going to any such place," I cried, struggling to release my arm, which he had seized; but she was almost at the door-stones already, scampering round the brow at full speed. Her appointed companion did not pretend to escort her: he shied off by the road-side, and vanished.

"Mr. Heathcliff, it's very wrong," I continued: "you know you mean no good. And there she'll see Linton, and all will be told as soon as ever we return; and I shall have the blame."

"I want her to see Linton," he answered; "he's looking better these few days: it's not often he's fit to be seen. And we'll soon persuade her to keep the visit secret: where is the harm of it?"

"The harm of it is, that her father would hate me if he found I suffered her to enter your house; and I am convinced you have a bad design in encouraging her to do so," I replied.

"My design is as honest as possible. I'll inform you of its whole scope," he said. "That the two cousins may fall in love, and get married. I'm acting generously to your master: his young chit has no expectations, and should she second my wishes, she'll be provided for at once as joint successor with Linton."

"If Linton died," I answered, "and his life is quite uncertain, Catherine would be the heir."

"No, she would not," he said. "There is no clause in the will to secure it so: his property would go to me; but, to prevent disputes, I desire their union, and am resolved to bring it about."

" And I'm resolved she shall never approach your house with me again," I returned, as we reached the gate, where Miss Cathy waited our coming.

Heathcliff bade me be quiet ; and, preceding us up the path, hastened to open the door. My young lady gave him several looks, as if she could not exactly make up her mind what to think of him ; but now he smiled when he met her eye, and softened his voice in addressing her ; and I was foolish enough to imagine the memory of her mother might disarm him from desiring her injury. Linton stood on the hearth. He had been out walking in the fields, for his cap was on, and he was calling to Joseph to bring him dry shoes. He had grown tall of his age, still wanting some months of sixteen. His features were pretty yet, and his eye and complexion brighter than I remembered them, though with merely temporary lustre borrowed from the salubrious air and genial sun.

" Now, who is that?" asked Mr. Heathcliff, turning to Cathy. " Can you tell?"

" Your son?" she said, having doubtfully surveyed, first one and then the other.

" Yes, yes," answered he : " but is this the only time you have beheld him? Think! Ah! you have a short memory. Linton, don't you recall your cousin, that you used to tease us so with wishing to see?"

" What, Linton!" cried Cathy, kindling into joyful surprise at the name. " Is that little Linton? He's taller than I am! Are you Linton?"

The youth stepped forward, and acknowledged himself : she kissed him fervently, and they gazed with wonder at the change time had wrought in the appearance of each. Catherine had reached her full height ; her figure was both plump and slender, elastic as steel, and her whole aspect sparkling with health and spirits. Linton's looks and movements were very languid, and his form extremely slight ; but there was a grace in his manner that mitigated these defects, and rendered him not unpleasing. After exchanging numerous marks of fondness with him, his cousin went to Mr. Heathcliff, who lingered by the door, dividing his attention between the objects inside and those that lay without : pretending, that is, to observe the latter, and really noting the former alone.

"And you are my uncle, then!" she cried, reaching up to salute him. "I thought I liked you, though you were cross at first. Why don't you visit at the Grange with Linton? To live all these years such close neighbours, and never see us, is odd: what have you done so for?"

"I visited it once or twice too often before you were born," he answered. "There—damn it! If you have any kisses to spare, give them to Linton: they are thrown away on me."

"Naughty Ellen!" exclaimed Catherine, flying to attack me next with her lavish caresses. "Wicked Ellen! to try to hinder me from entering. But I'll take this walk every morning in future: may I, uncle? and sometimes bring papa. Won't you be glad to see us?"

"Of course!" replied the uncle, with a hardly suppressed grimace, resulting from his deep aversion to both the proposed visitors. "But stay," he continued, turning towards the young lady. "Now I think of it, I'd better tell you. Mr. Linton has a prejudice against me: we quarrelled at one time of our lives, with unchristian ferocity; and, if you mention coming here to him, he'll put a veto on your visits altogether. Therefore, you must not mention it, unless you be careless of seeing your cousin hereafter: you may come, if you will, but you must not mention it."

"Why did you quarrel?" asked Catherine, considerably crest-fallen.

"He thought me too poor to wed his sister," answered Heathcliff, "and was grieved that I got her: his pride was hurt, and he'll never forgive it."

"That's wrong!" said the young lady: "some time, I'll tell him so. But Linton and I have no share in your quarrel. I'll not come here, then; he shall come to the Grange."

"It will be too far for me," murmured her cousin: "to walk four miles would kill me. No, come here, Miss Catherine, now and then: not every morning, but once or twice a week."

The father launched towards his son a glance of bitter contempt.

"I am afraid, Nelly, I shall lose my labour," he muttered to me. "Miss Catherine, as the ninny calls her, will discover his value, and send him to the devil. Now, if it had been Hareton!—Do you know that, twenty times a day, I covet Hareton, with all his degradation? I'd have loved the lad had he been some one else. But I think he's safe from *her* love. I'll pit him against that paltry creature, unless it bestir itself briskly. We calculate it will scarcely last till it is eighteen. Oh, confound the vapid thing! He's absorbed in drying his feet, and never looks at her.—Linton!"

"Yes, father," answered the boy.

"Have you nothing to show your cousin, anywhere about? not even a rabbit, or a weasel's nest? Take her into the garden, before you change your shoes; and into the stable to see your horse."

"Wouldn't you rather sit here?" asked Linton, addressing Cathy in a tone which expressed reluctance to move again.

"I don't know," she replied, casting a longing look to the door, and evidently eager to be active.

He kept his seat, and shrank closer to the fire. Heathcliff rose, and went into the kitchen, and from thence to the yard, calling out for Hareton. Hareton responded, and presently the two re-entered. The young man had been washing himself, as was visible by the glow on his cheeks and his wetted hair.

"Oh, I'll ask *you*, uncle," cried Miss Cathy, recollecting the housekeeper's assertion. "That's not my cousin, is he?"

"Yes," he replied, "your mother's nephew. Don't you like him?"

Catherine looked queer.

"Is he not a handsome lad?" he continued.

The uncivil little thing stood on tiptoe, and whispered a sentence in Heathcliff's ear. He laughed; Hareton darkened: I perceived he was very sensitive to suspected slights, and had obviously a dim notion of his inferiority. But his master or guardian chased the frown by exclaiming—

"You'll be the favourite among us, Hareton! She says you are a—What was it? Well, something very flattering. Here! you go with her round the farm. And behave like a gentleman, mind! Don't use any bad words; and don't stare when the young lady is not looking at you and be ready to hide your face when she is; and, when you speak, say your words slowly, and keep your hands out of your pockets. Be off, and entertain her as nicely as you can."

He watched the couple walking past the window. Earnshaw had his countenance completely averted from his companion. He seemed studying the familiar landscape with a stranger's and an artist's interest. Catherine took a sly look at him, expressing small admiration. She then turned her attention to seeking out objects of amusement for herself, and tripped merrily on, lilting a tune to supply the lack of conversation.

"I've tied his tongue," observed Heathcliff. "He'll not venture a single syllable, all the time! Nelly, you recollect me at his age—nay, some years younger. Did I ever look so stupid : so 'gaumless,' as Joseph calls it?"

"Worse," I replied, "because more sullen with it."

"I've a pleasure in him," he continued reflecting aloud. "He has satisfied my expectations. If he were a born fool I should not enjoy it half so much. But he's no fool ; and I can sympathize with all his feelings, having felt them myself. I know what he suffers now, for instance, exactly : it is merely a beginning of what he shall suffer, though. And he'll never be able to emerge from his bathos of coarseness and ignorance. I've got him faster than his scoundrel of a father secured me, and lower; for he takes a pride in his brutishness. I've taught him to scorn everything extra-animal as silly and weak. Don't you think Hindley would be proud of his son, if he could see him? almost as proud as I am of mine. But there's this difference; one is gold put to the use of paving stones, and the other is tin polished to ape a service of silver. *Mine* has nothing valuable about it ; yet I shall have the merit of making it go as far as such poor stuff can go. *His* had first-rate qualities, and they are lost : rendered worse than unavailing. *I* have nothing to regret; *he* would have more than any but I are aware of. And the best of it is, Hareton is damnably fond of me! You'll own that I've out-matched Hindley there. If the dead villain could rise from his grave to abuse me for his offspring's wrongs, I should have the fun of seeing the said offspring fight him back again; indignant that he should dare to rail at the one friend he has in the world!"

Heathcliff chuckled a fiendish laugh at the idea. I made no reply, because I saw that he expected none. Meantime, our young companion, who sat too removed from us to hear what was said, began to evince symptoms of uneasiness: probably repenting that he had denied himself the treat of

Catherine's society for fear of a little fatigue. His father remarked the restless glances wandering to the window, and the hand irresolutely extended towards his cap.

"Get up, you idle boy!" he exclaimed, with assumed heartiness. "Away after them! they are just at the corner, by the stand of hives."

Linton gathered his energies, and left the hearth. The lattice was open, and, as he stepped out, I heard Cathy inquiring of her unsociable attendant, what was that inscription over the door? Hareton stared up, and scratched his head like a true clown.

"It's some damnable writing," he answered. "I cannot read it."

"Can't read it?" cried Catherine, "I can read it: it's English. But I want to know why it is there."

Linton giggled: the first appearance of mirth he had exhibited.

"He does not know his letters," he said to his cousin. "Could you believe in the existence of such a colossal dunce?"

"Is he all as he should be?" asked Miss Cathy seriously; "or is he simple: not right? I've questioned him twice now, and each time he looked so stupid I think he does not understand me. I can hardly understand *him*, I'm sure!"

Linton repeated his laugh, and glanced at Hareton tauntingly; who certainly did not seem quite clear of comprehension at that moment.

"There's nothing the matter but laziness; is there, Earnshaw?" he said. "My cousin fancies you are an idiot. There you experience the consequence of scorning 'booklarning,' as you would say. Have you noticed, Catherine, his frightful Yorkshire pronunciation?"

"Why, where the devil is the use on't?" growled Hareton, more ready in answering his daily companion. He was about to enlarge further, but the two youngsters broke into a noisy fit of merriment; my giddy miss being delighted to discover that she might turn his strange talk to matter of amusement.

"Where is the use of the devil in that sentence?" tittered Linton. "Papa told you not to say any bad words, and you can't open your mouth without one. Do try to behave like a gentleman, now do!"

o

"If thou wern't more a lass than a lad, I'd fell thee this minute, I would; pitiful lath of a crater!" retorted the angry boor retreating, while his face burnt with mingled rage and mortification; for he was conscious of being insulted, and embarrassed how to resent it.

Mr. Heathcliff having overheard the conversation, as well as I, smiled when he saw him go; but immediately afterwards cast a look of singular aversion on the flippant pair, who remained chattering in the door-way: the boy finding animation enough while discussing Hareton's faults and deficiencies, and relating anecdotes of his goings on; and the girl relishing his pert and spiteful sayings, without considering the ill-nature they evinced. I began to dislike, more than to compassionate, Linton, and to excuse his father, in some measure, for holding him cheap.

We staid till afternoon: I could not tear Miss Cathy away sooner; but happily my master had not quitted his apartment, and remained ignorant of our prolonged absence. As we walked home, I would fain have enlightened my charge on the characters of the people we had quitted; but she got it into her head that I was prejudiced against them.

"Aha!" she cried, "you take papa's side, Ellen: you are partial I know; or else you wouldn't have cheated me so many years into the notion that Linton lived a long way from here. I'm really extremely angry; only I'm so pleased I can't show it! But you must hold your tongue about my uncle: he's *my* uncle remember; and I'll scold papa for quarrelling with him."

And so she ran on, till I relinquished the endeavour to convince her of her mistake. She did not mention the visit that night, because she did not see Mr. Linton. Next day it all came out, sadly to my chagrin; and still I was not altogether sorry: I thought the burden of directing and warning would be more efficiently borne by him than me. But he was too timid in giving satisfactory reasons for his wish that she would shun connection with the household of the Heights, and Catherine liked good reasons for every restraint that harassed her petted will.

"Papa!" she exclaimed after the morning's salutations, "guess whom I saw yesterday, in my walk on the moors. Ah, papa, you started! you've not done right, have you, now? I saw—But listen, and you shall hear how I found you out; and Ellen, who is in league with you, and yet pretended to pity me so, when I kept hoping, and was always disappointed about Linton's coming back!"

She gave a faithful account of her excursion and its consequences; and my master, though he cast more than one reproachful look at me, said nothing till she had concluded. Then he drew her to him, and asked if she knew why he had concealed Linton's near neighbourhood from her? Could she think it was to deny her a pleasure that she might harmlessly enjoy?

"It was because you disliked Mr. Heathcliff," she answered.

"Then you believe I care more for my own feelings than yours, Cathy?" he said. "No, it was not because I disliked Mr. Heathcliff, but because Mr. Heathcliff dislikes me; and is a most diabolical man, delighting to wrong and ruin those he hates, if they give him the slightest opportunity. I knew that you could not keep up an acquaintance with your cousin, without being brought into contact with him; and I knew he would detest you on my account; so for your own good, and nothing else, I took precautions that you should not see Linton again. I meant to explain this some time as you grew older, and I'm sorry I delayed it."

"But Mr. Heathcliff was quite cordial, papa," observed Catherine, not at all convinced; " and *he* didn't object to our seeing each other : he said I might come to his house when I pleased; only I must not tell you, because you had quarrelled with him, and would not forgive him for marrying aunt Isabella. And you won't. *You* are the one to be blamed : he is willing to let *us* be friends, at least; Linton and I; and you are not."

My master, perceiving that she would not take his word for her uncle-in-law's evil disposition, gave a hasty sketch of his conduct to Isabella, and the manner in which Wuthering Heights became his property. He could not bear to discourse long upon the topic; for though he spoke little of it, he still felt the same horror and detestation of his ancient enemy that had occupied his heart ever since Mrs. Linton's death. She might have been living yet, if it had not been for him!" was his constant bitter reflection; and, in his eyes, Heathcliff seemed a murderer. Miss Cathy—conversant with no bad deeds except her own slight acts of disobedience,

o 2

injustice, and passion, arising from hot temper and thought-lessness, and repented of on the day they were committed—was amazed at the blackness of spirit that could brood on and cover revenge for years, and deliberately prosecute its plans without a visitation of remorse. She appeared so deeply impressed and shocked at this new view of human nature—excluded from all her studies and all her ideas till now—that Mr. Edgar deemed it unnecessary to pursue the subject. He merely added,—

"You will know hereafter, darling, why I wish you to avoid his house and family; now return to your old employ-ments and amusements, and think no more about them."

Catherine kissed her father, and sat down quietly to her lessons for a couple of hours, according to custom; then she accompanied him into the grounds, and the whole day passed as usual: but in the evening, when she had retired to her room, and I went to help her to undress, I found her crying, on her knees by the bedside.

"Oh, fie, silly child!" I exclaimed. "If you had any real griefs, you'd be ashamed to waste a tear on this little contrariety. You never had one shadow of substantial sorrow, Miss Catherine. Suppose, for a minute, that master and I were dead, and you were by yourself in the world: how would you feel, then? Compare the present occasion with such an affliction as that, and be thankful for the friends you have, instead of coveting more."

"I'm not crying for myself, Ellen," she answered, "it's for him. He expected to see me again to-morrow, and there he'll be so disappointed: and he'll wait for me, and I sha'n't come!"

"Nonsense!" said I, "do you imagine he has thought as much of you as you have of him? Hasn't he Hareton for a companion? Not one in a hundred would weep at losing a relation they had just seen twice, for two afternoons. Linton will conjecture how it is, and trouble himself no further about you."

"But may I not write a note to tell him why I cannot come?" she asked, rising to her feet. "And just send those books, I promised to lend him? His books are not as nice as mine, and he wanted to have them extremely, when I told him how interesting they were. May I not, Ellen?"

"No, indeed! no, indeed!" replied I with decision.

"Then he would write to you, and there'd never be an end of it. No, Miss Catherine, the acquaintance must be dropped entirely : so papa expects, and I shall see that it is done."

" But how can one little note—" she recommenced, putting on an imploring countenance.

" Silence !" I interrupted. " We'll not begin with your little notes. Get into bed."

She threw at me a very naughty look, so naughty that I would not kiss her good-night at first : I covered her up, and shut her door, in great displeasure; but, repenting half-way, I returned softly, and lo ! there was miss standing at the table with a bit of blank paper before her and a pencil in her hand, which she guiltily slipped out of sight, on my re-entrance.

" You'll get nobody to take that, Catherine," I said, " if you write it; and at present I shall put out your candle."

I set the extinguisher on the flame, receiving as I did so a slap on my hand, and a petulant " cross thing !" I then quitted her again, and she drew the bolt in one of her worst, most peevish humours. The letter was finished and for-warded to its destination by a milk-fetcher who came from the village : but that I didn't learn till some time afterwards. Weeks passed on, and Cathy recovered her temper; though she grew wondrous fond of stealing off to corners by herself; and often, if I came near her suddenly while reading, she would start and bend over the book, evidently desirous to hide it; and I detected edges of loose paper sticking out be-yond the leaves. She also got a trick of coming down early in the morning and lingering about the kitchen, as if she were expecting the arrival of something : and she had a small drawer in a cabinet in the library, which she would trifle over for hours, and whose key she took special care to remove when she left it.

One day, as she inspected this drawer, I observed that the playthings, and trinkets which recently formed its contents, were transmuted into bits of folded paper. My curiosity and suspicions were roused; I determined to take a peep at her mysterious treasures; so, at night, as soon as she and my master were safe up stairs, I searched and readily found among my house keys one that would fit the lock. Having opened, I emptied the whole contents into my apron, and took them with me to examine at leisure in my own chamber.

Though I could not but suspect, I was still surprised to discover that they were a mass of correspondence—daily almost, it must have been—from Linton Heathcliff: answers to documents forwarded by her. The earlier dated were embarrassed and short; gradually, however, they expanded into copious love letters, foolish, as the age of the writer rendered natural, yet with touches here and there which I thought were borrowed from a more experienced source. Some of them struck me as singularly odd compounds of ardour and flatness; commencing in strong feeling, and concluding in the affected, wordy style that a schoolboy might use to a fancied, incorporeal sweetheart. Whether they satisfied Cathy, I don't know; but they appeared very worthless trash to me. After turning over as many as I thought proper, I tied them in a handkerchief and set them aside, re-locking the vacant drawer.

Following her habit, my young lady descended early, and visited the kitchen: I watched her go to the door, on the arrival of a certain little boy; and, while the dairy-maid filled his can, she tucked something into his jacket pocket, and plucked something out. I went round by the garden, and laid wait for the messenger; who fought valorously to defend his trust, and we spilt the milk between us; but I succeeded in abstracting the epistle; and, threatening serious consequences if he did not look sharp home, I remained under the wall and perused Miss Cathy's affectionate composition. It was more simple and more eloquent than her cousin's: very pretty and very silly. I shook my head, and went meditating into the house. The day being wet, she could not divert herself with rambling about the park; so, at the conclusion of her morning studies, she resorted to the solace of the drawer. Her father sat reading at the table; and I, on purpose, had sought a bit of work in some unripped fringes of the window curtain, keeping my eye steadily fixed on her proceedings. Never did any bird flying back to a plundered nest which it had left brimful of chirping young ones, express more complete despair in its anguished cries and flutterings, than she by her single "Oh!" and the change that transfigured her late happy countenance. Mr. Linton looked up.

"What is the matter, love? Have you hurt yourself?" he said.

His tone and look assured her *he* had not been the discoverer of the hoard.

"No, papa—" she gasped. "Ellen! Ellen! come up stairs—I'm sick!"

I obeyed her summons, and accompanied her out.

"Oh, Ellen! you have got them," she commenced immediately, dropping on her knees, when we were enclosed alone. "O, give them to me, and I'll never, never do so again! Don't tell papa. You have not told papa, Ellen? say you have not? I've been exceedingly naughty, but I won't do it any more!"

With a grave severity in my manner, I bade her stand up.

"So," I exclaimed, "Miss Catherine, you are tolerably far on, it seems : you may well be ashamed of them! A fine bundle of trash you study in your leisure hours, to be sure : why it's good enough to be printed! And what do you suppose the master will think, when I display it before him? I hav'n't shown it yet, but you needn't imagine I shall keep your ridiculous secrets. For shame! and you must have led the way in writing such absurdities : he would not have thought of beginning, I'm certain."

"I didn't! I didn't!" sobbed Cathy, fit to break her heart. "I didn't once think of loving him till——"

"*Loving!*" cried I, as scornfully as I could utter the word. "*Loving!* Did anybody ever hear the like! I might just as well talk of loving the miller who comes once a year to buy our corn. Pretty loving, indeed! and both times together you have seen Linton hardly four hours in your life! Now here is the babyish trash. I'm going with it to the library; and we'll see what your father says to such *loving.*"

She sprang at her precious epistles, but I held them above my head; and then she poured out further frantic entreaties that I would burn them—do anything rather than show them. And being really fully as much inclined to laugh as scold—for I esteemed it all girlish vanity—I at length relented in a measure, and asked,—

"If I consent to burn them, will you promise faithfully, neither to send nor receive a letter again, nor a book (for I perceive you have sent him books), nor locks of hair, nor rings, nor playthings?"

" We don't send playthings ! " cried Catherine, her pride overcoming her shame.

" Nor anything at all, then, my lady," I said. " Unless you will, here I go."

" I promise, Ellen ! " she cried, catching my dress. " Oh, put them in the fire, do, do !"

But when I proceeded to open a place with the poker, the sacrifice was too painful to be borne. She earnestly supplicated that I would spare her one or two.

" One or two, Ellen, to keep for Linton's sake ! "

I unknotted the handkerchief, and commenced dropping them in from an angle, and the flame curled up the chimney.

" I will have one, you cruel wretch !" she screamed, darting her hand into the fire, and drawing forth some half consumed fragments, at the expense of her fingers.

" Very well—and I will have some to exhibit to papa !" I answered, shaking back the rest into the bundle, and turning anew to the door.

She emptied her blackened pieces into the flames, and motioned me to finish the immolation. It was done; I stirred up the ashes, and interred them under a shovel-full of coals; and she mutely, and with a sense of intense injury, retired to her private apartment. I descended to tell my master that the young lady's qualm of sickness was almost gone, but I judged it best for her to lie down a while. She wouldn't dine; but she re-appeared at tea, pale, and red about the eyes, and marvellously subdued in outward aspect. Next morning, I answered the letter by a slip of paper, inscribed, " Master Heathcliff is requested to send no more notes to Miss Linton, as she will not receive them." And, thenceforth, the little boy came with vacant pockets.

CHAPTER XXII.

SUMMER drew to an end, and early autumn: it was past
Michaelmas, but the harvest was late that year, and a few
of our fields were still uncleared. Mr. Linton and his
daughter would frequently walk out among the reapers; at
the carrying of the last sheaves, they stayed till dusk, and
the evening happening to be chill and damp, my master
caught a bad cold, that settled obstinately on his lungs, and
confined him in-doors throughout the whole of the winter,
nearly without intermission.

Poor Cathy, frightened from her little romance, had been
considerably sadder and duller since its abandonment; and
her father insisted on her reading less, and taking more
exercise. She had his companionship no longer; I esteemed
it a duty to supply its lack, as much as possible, with mine:
an inefficient substitute; for I could only spare two or three
hours, from my numerous diurnal occupations, to follow her
footsteps, and then my society was obviously less desirable
than his.

On an afternoon in October, or the beginning of November—a fresh watery afternoon, when the turf and paths were
rustling with moist, withered leaves, and the cold, blue sky
was half hidden by clouds—dark grey streamers, rapidly
mounting from the west, and boding abundant rain—I requested my young lady to forego her ramble, because I was
certain of showers. She refused; and I unwillingly donned
a cloak, and took my umbrella to accompany her on a stroll
to the bottom of the park: a formal walk which she generally affected if low-spirited—and that she invariably was
when Mr. Edgar had been worse than ordinary, a thing
never known from his confession, but guessed both by her
and me, from his increased silence and the melancholy of his
countenance. She went sadly on: there was no running or
bounding now, though the chill wind might well have
tempted her to race. And often, from the side of my eye, I
could detect her raising a hand, and brushing something off
her cheek. I gazed round for a means of diverting her
thoughts. On one side of the road rose a high, rough
bank, where hazels and stunted oaks, with their roots half
exposed, held uncertain tenor: the soil was too loose for the

latter; and strong winds had blown some nearly horizontal. In summer, Miss Catherine delighted to climb along these trunks, and sit in the branches, swinging twenty feet above the ground; and I, pleased with her agility and her light, childish heart, still considered it proper to scold every time I caught her at such an elevation, but so that she knew there was no necessity for descending. From dinner to tea she would lie in her breeze-rocked cradle, doing nothing except singing old songs—my nursery lore—to herself, or watching the birds, joint tenants, feed and entice their young ones to fly: or nestling with closed lids, half thinking, half dreaming, happier than words can express.

"Look, miss!" I exclaimed, pointing to a nook under the roots of one twisted tree. "Winter is not here yet. There's a little flower up yonder, the last bud from the multitude of blue-bells that clouded those turf steps in July with a lilac mist. Will you clamber up, and pluck it to show to papa?"

Cathy stared a long time at the lonely blossom trembling in its earthy shelter, and replied, at length—

"No, I'll not touch it: but it looks melancholy, does it not, Ellen?"

"Yes," I observed, "about as starved and sackless as you: your cheeks are bloodless; let us take hold of hands and run. You're so low, I dare say I shall keep up with you."

"No," she repeated, and continued sauntering on, pausing, at intervals, to muse over a bit of moss, or a tuft of blanched grass, or a fungus spreading its bright orange among the heaps of brown foliage; and, ever and anon, her hand was lifted to her averted face.

"Catherine, why are you crying, love?" I asked, approaching and putting my arm over her shoulder. "You mustn't cry, because papa has a cold; be thankful it is nothing worse."

She now put no further restraint on her tears; her breath was stifled by sobs.

"Oh, it *will* be something worse," she said. "And what shall I do when papa and you leave me, and I am by myself? I can't forget your words, Ellen; they are always in my ear. How life will be changed, how dreary the world will be, when papa and you are dead."

"None can tell, whether you won't die before us," I re-

plied. " It's wrong to anticipate evil. We'll hope there
are years and years to come before any of us go: master is
young, and I am strong, and hardly forty-five. My mother
lived till eighty, a canty dame to the last. And suppose
Mr. Linton were spared till he saw sixty, that would be more
years than you have counted, miss. And would it not be
foolish to mourn a calamity above twenty years beforehand?"

" But Aunt Isabella was younger than papa," she remarked, gazing up with timid hope to seek further consolation.

" Aunt Isabella had not you and me to nurse her," I
replied. " She wasn't as happy as master: she hadn't as
much to live for. All you need do is to wait well on your
father, and cheer him by letting him see you cheerful; and
avoid giving him anxiety on any subject: mind that, Cathy!
I'll not disguise but you might kill him, if you were wild
and reckless, and cherished a foolish, fanciful affection for
the son of a person who would be glad to have him in his
grave; and allowed him to discover that you fretted over
the separation he has judged it expedient to make."

" I fret about nothing on earth except papa's illness,"
answered my companion. " I care for nothing in comparison
with papa. And I'll never—never—oh, never, while I have
my senses, do an act or say a word to vex him. I love him
better than myself, Ellen; and I know it by this: I pray
every night that I may live after him; because I would
rather be miserable than that he should be: that proves I
love him better than myself."

" Good words," I replied. " But deeds must prove it
also; and after he is well, remember you don't forget resolutions formed in the hour of fear."

As we talked, we neared a door that opened on the road;
and my young lady, lightening into sunshine again, climbed
up and seated herself on the top of the wall, reaching over
to gather some hips that bloomed scarlet on the summit
branches of the wild rose trees, shadowing the highway
side: the lower fruit had disappeared, but only birds could
touch the upper, except from Cathy's present station. In
stretching to pull them, her hat fell off; and as the door was
locked, she proposed scrambling down to recover it. I bid
her be cautious lest she got a fall, and she nimbly disappeared. But the return was no such easy matter: the

stones were smooth and neatly cemented, and the rosebushes
and blackberry stragglers could yield no assistance in re-
ascending. I, like a fool, didn't recollect that, till I heard
her laughing and exclaiming—

"Ellen! you'll have to fetch the key, or else I must run
round to the porter's lodge. I can't scale the ramparts on
this side!"

"Stay where you are," I answered, "I have my bundle of
keys in my pocket: perhaps I may manage to open it; if
not, I'll go."

Catherine amused herself with dancing to and fro before
the door, while I tried all the large keys in succession. I
had applied the last, and found that none would do; so, repeating my desire that she would remain there, I was about
to hurry home as fast as I could, when an approaching sound
arrested me. It was the trot of a horse; Cathy's dance
stopped also.

"Who is that?" I whispered.

"Ellen, I wish you could open the door," whispered back
my companion, anxiously.

"Ho, Miss Linton!" cried a deep voice (the rider's),
"I'm glad to meet you. Don't be in haste to enter, for I
have an explanation to ask and obtain."

"I sha'n't speak to you, Mr. Heathcliff," answered Catherine. "Papa says you are a wicked man, and you hate both
him and me; and Ellen says the same."

"That is nothing to the purpose," said Heathcliff. (He
it was.) "I don't hate my son, I suppose; and it is concerning him that I demand your attention. Yes; you have
cause to blush. Two or thee months since, were you not in
the habit of writing to Linton? making love in play, eh?
You deserved, both of you, flogging for that! You especially, the elder; and less sensitive, as it turns out. I've got
your letters, and if you give me any pertness I'll send them
to your father. I presume you grew weary of the amusement and dropped it, didn't you? Well, you dropped Linton with it into a Slough of Despond. He was in earnest:
in love, really. As true as I live, he's dying for you;
breaking his heart at your fickleness: not figuratively, but
actually. Though Hareton has made him a standing jest
for six weeks, and I have used more serious measures, and
attempted to frighten him out of his idiocy, he gets worse

daily; and he'll be under the sod before summer, unless you restore him!"

"How can you lie so glaringly to the poor child?" I called from the inside. "Pray ride on! How can you deliberately get up such paltry falsehoods? Miss Cathy, I'll knock the lock off with a stone: you won't believe that vile nonsense. You can feel in yourself, it is impossible that a person should die for love of a stranger."

"I was not aware there were eaves-droppers," muttered the detected villain. "Worthy Mrs. Dean, I like you, but I don't like your double dealing," he added, aloud. "How could *you* lie so glaringly, as to affirm I hated the 'poor child?' and invent bugbear stories to terrify her from my door-stones? Catherine Linton (the very name warms me), my bonny lass, I shall be from home all this week; go and see if I have not spoken truth: do, there's a darling! Just imagine your father in my place, and Linton in yours; then think how you would value your careless lover if he refused to stir a step to comfort you, when your father himself entreated him; and don't, from pure stupidity, fall into the same error. I swear, on my salvation, he's going to his grave, and none but you can save him!"

The lock gave way and I issued out.

"I swear Linton is dying," repeated Heathcliff, looking hard at me. "And grief and disappointment are hastening his death. Nelly, if you won't let her go, you can walk over yourself. But I shall not return till this time next week; and I, think your master himself would scarcely object to her visiting her cousin!"

"Come in," said I, taking Cathy by the arm and half forcing her to re-enter; for she lingered, viewing with troubled eyes the features of the speaker, too stern to express his inward deceit.

He pushed his horse close, and, bending down, observed—

"Miss Catherine, I'll own to you that I have little patience with Linton; and Hareton and Joseph have less. I'll own that he's with a harsh set. He pines for kindness, as well as love; and a kind word from you would be his best medicine. Don't mind Mrs. Dean's cruel cautions; but be generous, and contrive to see him. He dreams of you day and night, and cannot be persuaded that you don't hate him, since you neither write nor call."

I closed the door, and rolled a stone to assist the loosened lock in holding it; and spreading my umbrella, I drew my charge underneath : for the rain began to drive through the moaning branches of the trees, and warned us to avoid delay. Our hurry prevented any comment on the encounter with Heathcliff, as we stretched towards home ; but I divined instinctively that Catherine's heart was clouded now in double darkness. Her features were so sad, they did not seem hers : she evidently regarded what she had heard as every syllable true.

The master had retired to rest before we came in. Cathy stole to his room to inquire how he was; he had fallen asleep. She returned, and asked me to sit with her in the library. We took our tea together ; and afterwards she lay down on the rug, and told me not to talk for she was weary. I got a book, and pretended to read. As soon as she supposed me absorbed in my occupation, she recommenced her silent weeping : it appeared, at present, her favourite diversion. I suffered her to enjoy it a while; then, I expostulated : deriding and ridiculing all Mr. Heathcliff's assertions about his son, as if I were certain she would coincide. Alas ! I hadn't skill to counteract the effect his account had produced : it was just what he intended.

"You may be right, Ellen," she answered; " but I shall never feel at ease till I know. And I must tell Linton it is not my fault that I don't write, and convince him that I shall not change."

What use were anger and protestations against her silly credulity ? We parted that night—hostile ; but next day beheld me on the road to Wuthering Heights, by the side of my wilful young mistress's pony. I couldn't bear to witness her sorrow : to see her pale, dejected countenance, and heavy eyes; and I yielded, in the faint hope that Linton himself might prove, by his reception of us, how little of the tale was founded on fact.

CHAPTER XXIII.

THE rainy night had ushered in a misty morning—half frost, half drizzle—and temporary brooks crossed our path, gurgling from the uplands. My feet were thoroughly wetted; I was cross and low: exactly the humour suited for making the most of these disagreeable things. We entered the farm-house by the kitchen way, to ascertain whether Mr. Heathcliff were really absent; because I put slight faith in his own affirmation.

Joseph seemed sitting in a sort of elysium alone, beside a roaring fire; a quart of ale on the table near him, bristling with large pieces of toasted oat cake; and his black, short pipe in his mouth. Catherine ran to the hearth to warm herself. I asked if the master was in? My question remained so long unanswered, that I thought the old man had grown deaf, and repeated it louder.

" Na—ay!" he snarled, or rather screamed through his nose. " Na—ay! yah muh goa back whear yah coom frough."

" Joseph!" cried a peevish voice, simultaneously with me, from the inner room. " How often am I to call you? There are only a few red ashes now. Joseph! come this moment."

Vigorous puffs, and a resolute stare into the grate declared he had no ear for this appeal. The housekeeper and Hareton were invisible; one gone on an errand, and the other at his work, probably. We knew Linton's tones, and entered.

" Oh, I hope you'll die in a garret! starved to death," said the boy, mistaking our approach for that of his negligent attendant.

He stopped, on observing his error; his cousin flew to him.

" Is that you, Miss Linton?" he said, raising his head from the arm of the great chair, in which he reclined. " No —don't kiss me: it takes my breath. Dear me! Papa said you would call," continued he, after recovering a little from Catherine's embrace; while she stood by looking very contrite. " Will you shut the door, if you please? you left it open; and those—those *detestable* creatures won't bring coals to the fire. It's so cold!"

I stirred up the cinders, and fetched a scuttle full myself.

The invalid complained of being covered with ashes; but he had a tiresome cough, and looked feverish and ill, so I did not rebuke his temper.

"Well, Linton," murmured Catherine, when his corrugated brow relaxed. "Are you glad to see me? Can I do you any good?"

"Why didn't you come before?" he asked. "You should have come, instead of writing. It tired me dreadfully, writing those long letters. I'd far rather have talked to you. Now, I can neither bear to talk, nor anything else. I wonder where Zillah is! Will you (looking at me) step into the kitchen and see?"

I had received no thanks for my other service; and being unwilling to run to and fro at his behest, I replied—

"Nobody is out there but Joseph."

"I want to drink," he exclaimed fretfully, turning away. "Zillah is constantly gadding off to Gimmerton since papa went: it's miserable! And I'm obliged to come down here—they resolved never to hear me up stairs."

"Is your father attentive to you, Master Heathcliff?" I asked, perceiving Catherine to be checked in her friendly advances.

"Attentive? He makes *them* a little more attentive at least," he cried. "The wretches! Do you know, Miss Linton, that brute Hareton laughs at me! I hate him! indeed, I hate them all: they are odious beings."

Cathy began searching for some water; she lighted on a pitcher in the dresser, filled a tumbler, and brought it. He bid her add a spoonful of wine from a bottle on the table; and having swallowed a small portion, appeared more tranquil, and said she was very kind.

"And are you glad to see me?" asked she, reiterating her former question, and pleased to detect the faint dawn of a smile.

"Yes, I am. It's something new to hear a voice like yours!" he replied. "But I have been vexed, because you wouldn't come. And papa swore it was owing to me: he called me a pitiful, shuffling, worthless thing; and said you despised me; and if he had been in my place, he would be more the master of the Grange than your father, by this time. But you don't despise me, do you Miss——"

"I wish you would say Catherine, or Cathy," interrupted my young lady. "Despise you? No! Next to papa, and Ellen, I love you better than anybody living. I don't love Mr. Heathcliff, though; and I dare not come when he returns: will he stay away many days?"

"Not many," answered Linton; "but he goes on to the moors frequently, since the shooting season commenced; and you might spend an hour or two with me, in his absence. Do say you will. I think I should not be peevish with you: you'd not provoke me, and you'd always be ready to help me, wouldn't you?"

"Yes," said Catherine, stroking his long soft hair; "if I could only get papa's consent, I'd spend half my time with you. Pretty Linton! I wish you were my brother."

"And then you would like me as well as your father?" observed he, more cheerfully. "But papa says you would love me better than him and all the world, if you were my wife; so I'd rather you were that."

"No I should never love anybody better than papa," she returned gravely. "And people hate their wives, sometimes; but not their sisters and brothers: and if you were the latter, you would live with us, and papa would be as fond of you as he is of me."

Linton denied that people ever hated their wives; but Cathy affirmed they did, and in her wisdom, instanced his own father's aversion to her aunt. I endeavoured to stop her thoughtless tongue. I couldn't succeed till everything she knew was out. Master Heathcliff, much irritated, asserted her relation was false.

"Papa told me; and papa does not tell falsehoods," she answered pertly.

"*My* papa scorns yours!" cried Linton. "He calls him a sneaking fool."

"Yours is a wicked man," retorted Catherine; "and you are very naughty to dare to repeat what he says. He must be wicked, to have made Aunt Isabella leave him as she did."

"She didn't leave him," said the boy: "you sha'n't contradict me."

"She did," cried my young lady.

"Well, I'll tell *you* something!" said Linton. "Your mother hated your father: now then."

P

"Oh!" exclaimed Catherine, too enraged to continue.

"And she loved mine," added he.

"You little liar! I hate you now!" She panted, and her face grew red with passion.

"She did! she did!" sang Linton, sinking into the recess of his chair, and leaning back his head to enjoy the agitation of the other disputant, who stood behind.

"Hush, Master Heathcliff!" I said; "that's you father's tale too, I suppose."

"It isn't: you hold your tongue!" he answered. "She did, she did, Catherine! she did, she did!"

Cathy, beside herself, gave the chair a violent push, and caused him to fall against one arm. He was immediately seized by a suffocating cough that soon ended his triumph. It lasted so long that it frightened even me. As to his cousin, she wept with all her might; aghast at the mischief she had done: though she said nothing. I held him till the fit exhausted itself. Then he thrust me away, and leant his head down silently. Catherine quelled her lamentations also, took a seat opposite, and looked solemnly into the fire.

"How do you feel now, Master Heathcliff?" I inquired, after waiting ten minutes.

"I wish *she* felt as I do," he replied: "spiteful, cruel thing! Hareton never touches me: he never struck me in his life. And I was better to-day; and there ——" his voice died in a whimper.

"*I* didn't strike you!" muttered Cathy, chewing her lip to prevent another burst of emotion.

He sighed and moaned like one under great suffering, and kept it up for a quarter of an hour; on purpose to distress his cousin apparently, for whenever he caught a stifled sob from her he put renewed pain and pathos into the inflexions of his voice.

"I'm sorry I hurt you, Linton," she said at length, racked beyond endurance. "But *I* couldn't have been hurt by that little push, and I had no idea that you could, either: you're not, much, are you, Linton? Don't let me go home thinking I've done you harm. Answer! speak to me."

"I can't speak to you," he murmured; "you've hurt me so, that I shall lie awake all night choking with this cough.

If you had it you'd know what it was: but *you'll* be comfortably asleep while I'm in agony, and nobody near me. I wonder how you would like to pass those fearful nights!" And he began to wail aloud, for very pity of himself.

" Since you are in the habit of passing dreadful nights," I said, " it won't be miss who spoils your ease : you'd be the same had she never come. However, she shall not disturb you again; and perhaps you'll get quieter when we leave you."

" Must I go?" asked Catherine dolefully, bending over him. " Do you want me to go, Linton?"

" You can't alter what you've done," he replied pettishly, shrinking from her, " unless you alter it for the worse by teasing me into a fever."

" Well, then, I must go?" she repeated.

" Let me alone, at least," said he; " I can't bear your talking."

She lingered, and resisted my persuasions to departure a tiresome while; but as he neither looked up nor spoke, she finally made a movement to the door and I followed. We were recalled by a scream. Linton had slid from his seat on to the hearthstone, and lay writhing in the mere perverseness of an indulged plague of a child, determined to be as grievous and harassing as it can. I thoroughly gauged his disposition from his behaviour, and saw at once it would be folly to attempt humouring him. Not so my companion : she ran back in terror, knelt down, and cried, and soothed, and entreated, till he grew quiet from lack of breath : by no means from compunction at distressing her.

" I shall lift him on to the settle," I said, " and he may roll about as he pleases : we can't stop to watch him. I hope you are satisfied, Miss Cathy, that *you* are not the person to benefit him; and that his condition of health is not occasioned by attachment to you. Now, then, there he is! Come away : as soon as he knows there is nobody by to care for his nonsense, he'll be glad to lie still."

She placed a cushion under his head, and offered him some water; he rejected the latter, and tossed uneasily on the former, as if it were a stone or a block of wood. She tried to put it more comfortably.

" I can't do with that," he said; " it's not high enough."

Catherine brought another to lay above it.

"That's *too* high," murmured the provoking thing.

"How must I arrange it, then?" she asked despairingly.

He twined himself up to her, as she half knelt by the settle, and converted her shoulder into a support.

"No, that won't do," I said. "You'll be content with the cushion, Master Heathcliff. Miss has wasted too much time on you already : we cannot remain five minutes longer."

"Yes, yes, we can!" replied Cathy. "He's good and patient now. He's beginning to think I shall have far greater misery than he will to-night, if I believe he is the worse for my visit; and then I dare not come again. Tell the truth about it, Linton; for I musn't come, if I have hurt you."

"You must come, to cure me," he answered. "You ought to come, because you have hurt me : you know you have, extremely! I was not as ill when you entered as I am at present—was I?"

"But you've made yourself ill by crying and being in a passion."

"I didn't do it all," said his cousin. "However, we'll be friends now. And you want me : you would wish to see me sometimes, really?"

"I told you I did," he replied impatiently. "Sit on the settle and let me lean on your knee. That's as mamma used to do, whole afternoons together. Sit quite still and don't talk : but you may sing a song, if you can sing; or you may say a nice long interesting ballad—one of those you promised to teach me; or a story. I'd rather have a ballad, though : begin."

Catherine repeated the longest she could remember. The employment pleased both mightily. Linton would have another, and after that another, notwithstanding my strenuous objections; and so they went on until the clock struck twelve, and we heard Hareton in the court, returning for his dinner.

"And to-morrow, Catherine, will you be here to-morrow?" asked young Heathcliff, holding her frock as she rose reluctantly.

"No," I answered, "nor next day neither." She, however, gave a different response evidently, for his forehead cleared as she stooped and whispered in his ear.

"You won't go to-morrow, recollect, miss!" I commenced, when we were out of the house. "You are not dreaming of it, are you?"

She smiled.

"Oh, I'll take good care," I continued: "I'll have that lock mended, and you can escape by no way else."

"I can get over the wall," she said, laughing. "The Grange is not a prison, Ellen, and you are not my jailer. And besides, I'm almost seventeen: I'm a woman. And I'm certain Linton would recover quickly if he had me to look after him. I'm older than he is, you know, and wiser: less childish, am I not? And he'll soon do as I direct him, with some slight coaxing. He's a pretty little darling when he's good. I'd make such a pet of him, if he were mine. We should never quarrel, should we, after we were used to each other? Don't you like him, Ellen?"

"Like him!" I exclaimed. "The worst-tempered bit of a sickly slip that ever struggled into its teens. Happily, as Mr. Heathcliff conjectured, he'll not win twenty. I doubt whether he'll see spring, indeed. And small loss to his family whenever he drops off. And lucky it is for us that his father took him: the kinder he was treated, the more tedious and selfish he'd be. I'm glad you have no chance of having him for a husband, Miss Catherine."

My companion waxed serious at hearing this speech. To speak of his death so regardlessly, wounded her feelings.

"He's younger than I," she answered, after a protracted pause of meditation, "and he ought to live the longest: he will—he must live as long as I do. He's as strong now as when he first came into the north; I'm positive of that. It's only a cold that ails him, the same as papa has. You say papa will get better, and why shouldn't he?"

"Well, well," I cried, "after all, we needn't trouble ourselves; for listen, miss,—and mind, I'll keep my word,—if you attempt going to Wuthering Heights again, with or without me, I shall inform Mr. Linton, and, unless he allow it, the intimacy with your cousin must not be revived."

"It has been revived," muttered Cathy, sulkily.

"Must not be continued, then," I said.

"We'll see," was her reply, and she set off at a gallop, leaving me to toil in the rear.

We both reached home before our dinner-time; my mas-

ter supposed we had been wandering through the park, and
therefore he demanded no explanation of our absence. As
soon as I entered, I hastened to change my soaked shoes
and stockings; but sitting such a while at the Heights had
done the mischief. On the succeeding morning I was laid
up, and during three weeks I remained incapacitated for
attending to my duties: a calamity never experienced prior
to that period, and never, I am thankful to say, since.

My little mistress behaved like an angel, in coming to
wait on me, and cheer my solitude: the confinement brought
me exceedingly low. It is wearisome, to a stirring active
body: but few have slighter reasons for complaint than
I had. The moment Catherine left Mr. Linton's room,
she appeared at my bed-side. Her day was divided between
us; no amusement usurped a minute: she neglected her
meals, her studies, and her play; and she was the fondest
nurse that ever watched. She must have had a warm heart,
when she loved her father so, to give so much to me. I said
her days were divided between us; but the master retired
early, and I generally needed nothing after six o'clock, thus
the evening was her own. Poor thing! I never considered
what she did with herself after tea. And though frequently,
when she looked in to bid me good-night, I remarked a
fresh colour in her cheeks and a pinkness over her slender
fingers; instead of fancying the hue borrowed from a cold
ride across the moors, I laid it to the charge of a hot fire in
the library.

CHAPTER XXIV.

At the close of three weeks, I was able to quit my chamber,
and move about the house. And on the first occasion of my
sitting up in the evening, I asked Catherine to read to me,
because my eyes were weak. We were in the library, the
master having gone to bed: she consented, rather unwillingly, I fancied; and imagining my sort of books did
not suit her, I bid her please herself in the choice of what
she perused. She selected one of her own favourites, and

got forward steadily about an hour; then came frequent questions.

"Ellen, are not you tired? Hadn't you better lie down now? You'll be sick, keeping up so long, Ellen."

"No, no, dear, I'm not tired," I returned, continually.

Perceiving me immoveable, she essayed another method of showing her disrelish for her occupation. It changed to yawning, and stretching, and—

"Ellen, I'm tired."

"Give over then and talk," I answered.

That was worse: she fretted and sighed, and looked at her watch till eight, and finally went to her room, completely overdone with sleep; judging by her peevish, heavy look, and the constant rubbing she inflicted on her eyes. The following night she seemed more impatient still; and on the third from recovering my company, she complained of a headache, and left me. I thought her conduct odd; and having remained alone a long while, I resolved on going and inquiring whether she were better, and asking her to come and lie on the sofa, instead of up stairs in the dark. No Catherine could I discover up stairs, and none below. The servants affirmed they had not seen her. I listened at Mr. Edgar's door; all was silence. I returned to her apartment, extinguished my candle, and seated myself in the window.

The moon shone bright; a sprinkling of snow covered the ground, and I reflected that she might, possibly, have taken it into her head to walk about the garden, for refreshment. I did detect a figure creeping along the inner fence of the park; but it was not my young mistress: on its emerging into the light, I recognised one of the grooms. He stood a considerable period, viewing the carriage-road through the grounds; then started off at a brisk pace, as if he had detected something, and reappeared presently, leading miss's pony; and there she was, just dismounted, and walking by its side. The man took his charge stealthily across the grass towards the stable. Cathy entered by the casement-window of the drawing-room, and glided noiselessly up to where I awaited her. She put the door gently to, slipped off her snowy shoes, untied her hat, and was proceeding, unconscious of my espionage, to lay aside her mantle, when I suddenly rose and revealed myself. The surprise petrified her an instant: she uttered an inarticulate exclamation, and stood fixed.

"My dear Miss Catherine," I began, too vividly impressed by her recent kindness to break into a scold, "where have you been riding out at this hour? And why should you try to deceive me, by telling a tale? Where have you been? Speak."

"To the bottom of the park," she stammered. "I didn't tell a tale."

"And nowhere else?" I demanded.

"No," was the muttered reply.

"Oh, Catherine!" I cried, sorrowfully. "You know you have been doing wrong, or you wouldn't be driven to uttering an untruth to me. That does grieve me. I'd rather be three months ill, than hear you frame a deliberate lie."

She sprang forward, and bursting into tears, threw her arms round my neck.

"Well Ellen, I'm so afraid of you being angry," she said. "Promise not to be angry, and you shall know the very truth: I hate to hide it."

We sat down in the window-seat; I assured her I would not scold, whatever her secret might be, and I guessed it, of course; so she commenced—

"I've been to Wuthering Heights, Ellen, and I've never missed going a day since you fell ill; except thrice before, and twice after you left your room. I gave Michael books and pictures to prepare Minny every evening and to put her back in the stable: you mustn't scold *him* either, mind. I was at the Heights by half-past six, and generally stayed till half-past eight, and then galloped home. It was not to amuse myself that I went: I was often wretched all the time. Now and then, I was happy: once in a week perhaps. At first, I expected there would be sad work persuading you to let me keep my word to Linton: for I had engaged to call again next day, when we quitted him; but, as you stayed up stairs on the morrow, I escaped that trouble. While Michael was refastening the lock of the park door in the afternoon, I got possession of the key, and told him how my cousin wished me to visit him, because he was sick, and couldn't come to the Grange; and how papa would object to my going: and then I negotiated with him about the pony. He is fond of reading, and he thinks of leaving soon to get married; so he offered, if I would lend him books out of the library, to do what I wished: but I preferred giving him my own, and that satisfied him better.

" On my second visit, Linton seemed in lively spirits; and Zillah (that is their housekeeper) made us a clean room and a good fire, and told us that, as Joseph was out at a prayer-meeting and Hareton Earnshaw was off with his dogs—robbing our woods of pheasants, as I heard afterwards—we might do what we liked. She brought me some warm wine and gingerbread, and appeared exceedingly good-natured; and Linton sat in the arm chair, and I in the little rocking chair on the hearth-stone, and we laughed and talked so merrily, and found so much to say: we planned where we would go, and what we would do in summer. I needn't repeat that, because you would call it silly.

" One time, however, we were near quarrelling. He said the pleasantest manner of spending a hot July day was lying from morning till evening on a bank of heath in the middle of the moors, with the bees humming dreamily about among the bloom, and the larks singing high up over head, and the blue sky and bright sun shining steadily and cloudlessly. That was his most perfect idea of heaven's happiness: mine was rocking in a rustling green tree, with a west wind blowing, and bright, white clouds flitting rapidly above; and not only larks, but throstles, and blackbirds, and linnets, and cuckoos pouring out music on every side, and the moors seen at a distance, broken into cool dusky dells; but close by great swells of long grass undulating in waves to the breeze; and woods and sounding water, and the whole world awake and wild with joy. He wanted all to lie in an ecstacy of peace; I wanted all to sparkle, and dance in a glorious jubilee. I said his heaven would be only half alive; and he said mine would be drunk: I said I should fall asleep in his; and he said he could not breathe in mine, and began to grow very snappish. At last, we agreed to try both, as soon as the right weather came; and then we kissed each other and were friends.

" After sitting still an hour, I looked at the great room with its smooth uncarpeted floor, and thought how nice it would be to play in, if we removed the table; and I asked Linton to call Zillah in to help us, and we 'd have a game at blind-man's buff; she should try to catch us: you used to, you know, Ellen. He wouldn't: there was no pleasure in it, he said; but he consented to play at ball with me. We found two in a cupboard, among a heap of old toys, tops, and hoops, and battledoors, and shuttlecocks. One was marked C., and the other H.; I wished to have the C., because that stood for Catherine, and the H. might be for Heathcliff, his name; but the bran came out of H., and Linton didn't like it. I beat him constantly: and he got cross again, and coughed, and returned to his chair. That night, though, he easily recovered his good humour : he was charmed with two or three pretty songs—*your* songs, Ellen; and when I was obliged to go, he begged and entreated me to come the following evening; and I promised. Minny and I went flying home as light as air; and I dreamt of Wuthering Heights, and my sweet, darling cousin, till morning.

"On the morrow, I was sad; partly because you were poorly, and partly that I wished my father knew, and approved of my excursions : but it was beautiful moonlight after tea; and, as I rode on, the gloom cleared. I shall have another happy evening, I thought to myself; and what delights me more, my pretty Linton will. I trotted up their garden, and was turning round to the back, when that fellow Earnshaw met me, took my bridle, and bid me go in by the front entrance. He patted Minny's neck, and said she was a bonny beast, and appeared as if he wanted me to speak to him. I only told him to leave my horse alone, or else it would kick him. He answered in his vulgar accent, "It wouldn't do mitch hurt if it did;" and surveyed its legs with a smile. I was half inclined to make it try; however, he moved off to open the door, and, as he raised the latch, he looked up to the inscription above, and said, with a stupid mixture of awkwardness and elation :

"'Miss Catherine! I can read yon, now.'

"'Wonderful,' I exclaimed. 'Pray let us hear you—you *are* grown clever!'

"He spelt, and drawled over by syllables, the name—" Hareton Earnshaw.

"'And the figures?' I cried, encouragingly, perceiving that he came to a dead halt.

"'I cannot tell them yet,' he answered.

" ' Oh, you dunce !' I said, laughing heartily at his failure.

" The fool stared, with a grin hovering about his lips, and a scowl gathering over his eyes, as if uncertain whether he might not join in my mirth : whether it were not pleasant familiarity, or what it really was, contempt. I settled his doubts, by suddenly retrieving my gravity and desiring him to walk away, for I came to see Linton not him. He reddened—I saw that by the moonlight—dropped his hand from the latch, and skulked off, a picture of mortified vanity. He imagined himself to be as accomplished as Linton, I suppose, because he could spell his own name ; and was marvellously discomfited that I didn't think the same."

" Stop, Miss Catherine, dear !" I interrupted. " I shall not scold, but I don't like your conduct there. If you had remembered that Hareton was your cousin as much as Master Heathcliff, you would have felt how improper it was to behave in that way. At least, it was praiseworthy ambition for him to desire to be as accomplished as Linton ; and probably he did not learn merely to show off : you had made him ashamed of his ignorance before, I have no doubt ; and he wished to remedy it and please you. To sneer at his imperfect attempt was very bad breeding. Had *you* been brought up in his circumstances, would you be less rude ? He was as quick and as intelligent a child as ever you were ; and I'm hurt that he should be despised now, because that base Heathcliff has treated him so unjustly."

" Well, Ellen, you won't cry about it, will you?" she exclaimed, surprised at my earnestness. " But wait, and you shall hear if he conned his A B C to please me ; and if it were worth while being civil to the brute. I entered ; Linton was lying on the settle, and half got up to welcome me.

" ' I'm ill to-night, Catherine, love,' he said ; ' and you must have all the talk, and let me listen. Come, and sit by me. I was sure you wouldn't break your word ; and I'll make you promise again, before you go.'

" I knew now that I mustn't tease him, as he was ill ; and I spoke softly and put no questions, and avoided irritating him in any way. I had brought some of my nicest books for him ; he asked me to read a little of one, and I was about to comply, when Earnshaw burst the door open :

having gathered venom with reflection. He advanced direct
to us, seized Linton by the arm, and swung him off the
seat.

" ' Get to thy own room !' he said, in a voice almost inarticulate with passion ; and his face looked swelled and
furious. 'Take her there if she comes to see thee : thou
shalln't keep me out of this. Begone wi' ye both !'

" He swore at us, and left Linton no time to answer, nearly
throwing him into the kitchen ; and he clenched his fist as I
followed, seemingly longing to knock me down. I was
afraid for a moment, and I let one volume fall ; he kicked it
after me, and shut us out. I heard a malignant, crackly
laugh by the fire, and turning, beheld that odious Joseph
standing rubbing his bony hands, and quivering.

" ' I wer sure he'd sarve ye out ! He's a grand lad !
He's getten t'raight sperrit in him ! *He* knaws—Ay, he
knaws, as weel as I do, who sud be t'maister yonder—
Ech, ech, ech ! He made ye skift properly ! Ech, ech,
ech !'

" ' Where must we go ?' I asked of my cousin, disregarding
the old wretch's mockery.

" Linton was white and trembling. He was not pretty
then, Ellen : Oh, no ! he looked frightful ; for his thin face
and large eyes were wrought into an expression of frantic,
powerless fury. He grasped the handle of the door, and
shook it : it was fastened inside.

" ' If you don't let me in I 'll kill you !—If you don't let
me in, I 'll kill you !' he rather shrieked than said. ' Devil !
devil !—I 'll kill you—I 'll kill you !'

" Joseph uttered his croaking laugh again.

" ' Thear, that's t'father !' he cried. ' That's father !
We've allas summut o' either side in us. Niver heed
Hareton, lad—dunnut be 'feard—he cannot get at thee !'

" I took hold of Linton's hands, and tried to pull him
away ; but he shrieked so shockingly that I dared not proceed. At last his cries were choked by a dreadful fit of
coughing ; blood gushed from his mouth, and he fell on the
ground. I ran into the yard, sick with terror ; and called
for Zillah, as loud as I could. She soon heard me : she was
milking the cows in a shed behind the barn, and hurrying
from her work, she inquired what there was to do ? I
hadn't breath to explain ; dragging her in, I looked about

for Linton. Earnshaw had come out to examine the mischief he had caused, and he was then conveying the poor thing up stairs. Zillah and I ascended after him; but he stopped me at the top of the steps, and said I shouldn't go in: I must go home. I exclaimed that he had killed Linton, and I *would* enter. Joseph locked the door, and declared I should do 'no sich stuff,' and asked me whether I were ' bahn to be as mad as him.' I stood crying, till the housekeeper reappeared. She affirmed he would be better in a bit, but he couldn't do with that shrieking and din ; and she took me, and nearly carried me into the house.

" Ellen, I was ready to tear my hair off my head ! I sobbed and wept so that my eyes were almost blind ; and the ruffian you have such sympathy with stood opposite : presuming every now and then to bid me ' wisht,' and denying that it was his fault; and, finally, frightened by my assertions that I would tell papa, and that he should be put in prison and hanged, he commenced blubbering himself, and hurried out to hide his cowardly agitation. Still, I was not rid of him : when at length they compelled me to depart, and I had got some hundred yards off the premises, he suddenly issued from the shadow of the road-side, and checked Minny and took hold of me.

" 'Miss Catherine, I'm ill grieved,' he began, ' but it's rayther too bad ——'

" I gave him a cut with my whip, thinking perhaps he would murder me. He let go, thundering one of his horrid curses, and I galloped home more than half out of my senses.

" I didn't bid you good-night that evening ; and I didn't go to Wuthering Heights the next : I wished to go exceedingly ; but I was strangely excited, and dreaded to hear that Linton was dead, sometimes; and sometimes shuddered at the thought of encountering Hareton. On the third day, I took courage : at least, I couldn't bear longer suspense, and stole off once more. I went at five o'clock, and walked ; fancying I might manage to creep into the house, and up to Linton's room, unobserved. However, the dogs gave notice of my approach. Zillah received me, and saying ' the lad was mending nicely,' showed me into a small, tidy, carpeted apartment ; where, to my inexpressible joy, I beheld Linton laid on a little sofa, reading one of my books. But he

would neither speak to me nor look at me, through a whole
hour, Ellen: he has such an unhappy temper.   And what
quite confounded me, when he did open his mouth it was to
utter the falsehood that I had occasioned the uproar, and
Hareton was not to blame!   Unable to reply, except passionately, I got up and walked from the room.   He sent
after me a faint ' Catherine !'   He did not reckon on being
answered so: but I wouldn't turn back; and the morrow
was the second day on which I stayed at home, nearly determined to visit him no more.   But it was so miserable going
to bed and getting up, and never hearing anything about
him, that my resolution melted into air before it was properly
formed.   It *had* appeared wrong to take the journey once;
now it seemed wrong to refrain.   Michael came to ask if he
must saddle Minny; I said ' Yes,' and considered myself
doing a duty as she bore me over the hills.   I was forced
to pass the front windows to get to the court: it was no
use trying to conceal my presence.

   " ' Young master is in the house,' said Zillah, as she saw
me making for the parlour.   I went in; Earnshaw was there
also, but he quitted the room directly.   Linton sat in the
great arm chair half asleep; walking up to the fire, I began
in a serious tone, partly meaning it to be true—

   " ' As you don't like me, Linton, and as you think I come
on purpose to hurt you, and pretend that I do so every time,
this is our last meeting: let us say good-bye; and tell Mr.
Heathcliff that you have no wish to see me, and that he
mustn't invent any more falsehoods on the subject.'

   " ' Sit down and take your hat off, Catherine,' he answered.
' You are so much happier than I am, you ought to be better.
Papa talks enough of my defects, and shows enough scorn
of me, to make it natural I should doubt myself.   I doubt
whether I am not altogether as worthless as he calls me,
frequently; and then I feel so cross and bitter, I hate everybody!   I *am* worthless, and bad in temper, and bad in spirit,
almost always; and if you choose, you *may* say good-bye:
you'll get rid of an annoyance.   Only, Catherine, do me this
justice: believe that if I might be as sweet, and as kind, and
as good as you are, I would be; as willingly, and more so
than as happy and as healthy.   And believe that your kindness has made me love you deeper than if I deserved your
love; and though I couldn't, and cannot help showing my

nature to you, I regret it and repent it; and shall regret and repent it till I die!'

" I felt he spoke the truth; and I felt I must forgive him : and, though he should quarrel the next moment, I must forgive him again. We were reconciled; but we cried, both of us, the whole time I stayed : not entirely for sorrow; yet I *was* sorry Linton had that distorted nature. He'll never let his friends be at ease, and he'll never be at ease himself! I have always gone to his little parlour, since that night; because his father returned the day after.

" About three times, I think, we have been merry and hopeful, as we were the first evening; the rest of my visits were dreary and troubled : now with his selfishness and spite, and now with his sufferings : but I've learned to endure the former with nearly as little resentment as the latter. Mr. Heathcliff purposely avoids me : I have hardly seen him at all. Last Sunday, indeed, coming earlier than usual, I heard him abusing poor Linton, cruelly, for his conduct of the night before. I can't tell how he knew of it, unless he listened. Linton had certainly behaved provokingly : however, it was the business of nobody but me, and I interrupted Mr. Heathcliff's lecture by entering and telling him so. He burst into a laugh, and went away, saying he was glad I took that view of the matter. Since then, I've told Linton he must whisper his bitter things. Now, Ellen, you have heard all. I can't be prevented from going to Wuthering Heights, except by inflicting misery on two people; whereas, if you'll only not tell papa, my going need disturb the tranquillity of none. You'll not tell, will you? It will be very heartless, if you do."

" I 'll make up my mind on that point by to-morrow, Miss Catherine," I replied. " It requires some study; and so I'll leave you to your rest, and go think it over."

I thought it over aloud, in my master's presence; walking straight from her room to his, and relating the whole story : with the exception of her conversations with her cousin, and any mention of Hareton. Mr. Linton was alarmed and distressed, more than he would acknowledge to me. In the morning, Catherine learnt my betrayal of her confidence, and she learnt also that her secret visits were to end. In vain she wept and writhed against the interdict, and implored her father to have pity on Linton : all she got to comfort

her was a promise that he would write and give him leave
to come to the Grange when he pleased; but explaining that
he must no longer expect to see Catherine at Wuthering
Heights. Perhaps, had he been aware of his nephew's disposition and state of health, he would have seen fit to withhold even that slight consolation.

CHAPTER XXV.

"THESE things happened last winter, sir," said Mrs. Dean;
"hardly more than a year ago. Last winter, I did not think,
at another twelve months' end, I should be amusing a
stranger to the family with relating them! Yet, who knows
how long you'll be a stranger? You're too young to rest
always contented, living by yourself; and I some way fancy
no one could see Catherine Linton and not love her. You
smile; but why do you look so lively and interested, when I
talk about her? and why have you asked me to hang her
picture over your fireplace? and why—"

"Stop, my good friend!" I cried. "It may be very
possible that *I* should love her; but would she love me? I
doubt it too much to venture my tranquillity by running
into temptation: and then my home is not here. I'm of the
busy world, and to its arms I must return. Go on. Was
Catherine obedient to her father's commands?"

"She was," continued the housekeeper. "Her affection
for him was still the chief sentiment in her heart; and he
spoke without anger: he spoke in the deep tenderness of one
about to leave his treasure amid perils and foes, where his
remembered words would be the only aid that he could be-
queath to guide her. He said to me, a few days afterwards,

"'I wish my nephew would write, Ellen, or call. Tell me,
sincerely, what you think of him: is he changed for the
better, or is there a prospect of improvement, as he grows a
man?'"

"'He's very delicate, sir,' I replied; 'and scarcely likely
to reach manhood: but this I can say, he does not resemble
his father; and if Miss Catherine had the misfortune to

marry him, he would not be beyond her control: unless she were extremely and foolishly indulgent. However, master, you'll have plenty of time to get acquainted with him, and see whether he would suit her: it wants four years and more to his being of age."

Edgar sighed; and, walking to the window, looked out towards Gimmerton Kirk. It was a misty afternoon, but the February sun shone dimly, and we could just distinguish the two fir trees in the yard and the sparely scattered grave-stones.

"I've prayed often," he half soliloquized, "for the approach of what is coming; and now I begin to shrink, and fear it. I thought the memory of the hour I came down that glen a bridegroom, would be less sweet than the anticipation that I was soon, in a few months, or possibly, weeks, to be carried up, and laid in its lonely hollow! Ellen, I've been very happy with my little Cathy: through winter nights and summer days she was a living hope at my side But I've been as happy musing by myself among those stones, under that old church: lying, through the long June evenings, on the green mound of her mother's grave, and wishing—yearning for the time when I might lie beneath it. What can I do for Cathy? How must I quit her? I'd not care one moment for Linton being Heathcliff's son; nor for his taking her from me, if he could console her for my loss. I'd not care that Heathcliff gained his ends, and triumphed in robbing me of my last blessing! But should Linton be unworthy—only a feeble tool to his father—I cannot abandon her to him! And, hard though it be to crush her buoyant spirit, I must persevere in making her sad while I live, and leaving her solitary when I die. Darling! I'd rather resign her to God, and lay her in the earth before me."

"Resign her to God, as it is, sir," I answered, "and if we should lose you—which may He forbid—under His providence, I'll stand her friend and counsellor to the last. Miss Catherine is a good girl: I don't fear that she will go wilfully wrong; and people who do their duty are always finally rewarded."

Spring advanced; yet my master gathered no real strength, though he resumed his walks in the grounds with his daughter. To her inexperienced notions, this itself was a sign of convalescence; and then his cheek was often flushed, and his eyes were bright: she felt sure of his recovering. On her seventeenth birthday, he did not visit the church-yard: it was raining, and I observed—

" You'll surely not go out to-night, sir?"

He answered—

" No, I'll defer it this year a little longer."

He wrote again to Linton, expressing his great desire to see him; and, had the invalid been presentable, I've no doubt his father would have permitted him to come. As it was, being instructed, he returned an answer intimating that Mr. Heathcliff objected to his calling at the Grange; but his uncle's kind remembrance delighted him, and he hoped to meet him, sometimes, in his rambles, and personally to petition that his cousin and he might not remain long so utterly divided.

That part of his letter was simple, and probably his own. Heathcliff knew he could plead eloquently for Catherine's company, then.

" I do not ask," he said, " that she may visit here; but, am I never to see her, because my father forbids me to go to her home, and you forbid her to come to mine? Do, now and then, ride with her towards the Heights; and let us exchange a few words, in your presence! We have done nothing to deserve this separation; and you are not angry with me: you have no reason to dislike me, you allow, yourself. Dear uncle! send me a kind note to-morrow, and leave to join you anywhere you please, except at Thrushcross Grange. I believe an interview would convince you that my father's character is not mine: he affirms I am more your nephew than his son; and though I have faults which render me unworthy of Catherine, she has excused them, and, for her sake, you should also. You inquire after my health— it is better; but while I remain cut off from all hope, and doomed to solitude, or the society of those who never did and never will like me, how can I be cheerful and well?"

Edgar, though he felt for the boy, could not consent to grant his request; because he could not accompany Catherine. He said, in summer, perhaps, they might meet: mean time, he wished him to continue writing at intervals, and engaged to give him what advice and comfort he was able by letter; being well aware of his hard position in his family. Linton complied; and had he been unrestrained, would probably have spoiled all by filling his epistles with complaints and lamentations: but his father kept a sharp watch over him; and, of course, insisted on every line that my master sent being shown; so, instead of penning his peculiar personal sufferings and distresses, the themes constantly uppermost in his thoughts, he harped on the cruel obligation of being held asunder from his friend and love; and gently intimated that Mr. Linton must allow an interview soon, or he should fear he was purposely deceiving him with empty promises.

Cathy was a powerful ally at home; and, between them they at length persuaded my master to acquiesce in their having a ride or a walk together about once a week, under my guardianship, and on the moors nearest the Grange: for June found him still declining. Though he had set aside yearly a portion of his income for my young lady's fortune, he had a natural desire that she might retain—or at least return in a short time to—the house of her ancestors; and he considered her only prospect of doing that was by a union with his heir: he had no idea that the latter was failing almost as fast as himself; nor had any one, I believe: no doctor visited the Heights, and no one saw Master Heathcliff to make report of his condition among us. I, for my part, began to fancy my forebodings were false, and that he must be actually rallying, when he mentioned riding and walking on the moors, and seemed so earnest in pursuing his object. I could not picture a father treating a dying child as tyrannically and wickedly as I afterwards learned Heathcliff had treated him, to compel this apparent eagerness: his efforts redoubling the more imminently his avaricious and unfeeling plans were threatened with defeat by death.

CHAPTER XXVI.

SUMMER was already past its prime, when Edgar reluctantly yielded his assent to their entreaties, and Catherine and I set out on our first ride to join her cousin. It was a close, sultry day; devoid of sunshine, but with a sky too dappled

and hazy to threaten rain; and our place of meeting had
been fixed at the guide-stone, by the cross-roads. On arriv-
ing there, however, a little herd-boy, despatched as a messenger told us that,—

"Maister Linton wer just o' this side th' Heights: and
he'd be mitch obleeged to us to gang on a bit further."

"Then Master Linton has forgot the first injunction of
his uncle," I observed: "he bid us keep on the Grange
land, and here we are off at once."

"Well, we'll turn our horses' heads round, when we reach
him," answered my companion, "our excursion shall lie
towards home."

But when we reached him, and that was scarcely a quarter of a mile from his own door, we found he had no horse;
and we were forced to dismount, and leave ours to graze.
He lay on the heath, awaiting our approach, and did not
rise till we came within a few yards. Then he walked so
feebly, and looked so pale, that I immediately exclaimed—

"Why, Master Heathcliff, you are not fit for enjoying a
ramble, this morning. How ill you do look!"

Catherine surveyed him with grief and astonishment: she
changed the ejaculation of joy on her lips, to one of alarm;
and the congratulation on their long postponed meeting, to
an anxious inquiry, whether he were worse than usual?

"No—better—better!" he panted, trembling, and retaining her hand as if he needed its support, while his large blue
eyes wandered timidly over her; the hollowness round them
transforming to haggard wildness the languid expression they
once possessed.

"But you have been worse," persisted his cousin; "worse
than when I saw you last: you are thinner, and—"

"I'm tired," he interrupted, hurriedly. "It is too hot
for walking, let us rest here. And, in the morning, I often
feel sick—papa says I grow so fast."

Badly satisfied, Cathy sat down, and he reclined beside her.

"This is something like your paradise," said she, making
an effort at cheerfulness. "You recollect the two days we
agreed to spend in the place and way each thought pleasantest? This is nearly yours, only there are clouds; but
then they are so soft and mellow: it is nicer than sunshine.
Next week, if you can, we'll ride down to the Grange Park,
and try mine."

Linton did not appear to remember what she talked of; and he had evidently great difficulty in sustaining any kind of conversation. His lack of interest in the subjects she started, and his equal incapacity to contribute to her entertainment, were so obvious that she could not conceal her disappointment. An indefinite alteration had come over his whole person and manner. The pettishness that might be caressed into fondness, had yielded to a listless apathy; there was less of the peevish temper of a child which frets and teases on purpose to be soothed, and more of the self-absorbed moroseness of a confirmed invalid, repelling consolation, and ready to regard the good-humoured mirth of others, as an insult. Catherine perceived, as well as I did, that he held it rather a punishment, than a gratification, to endure our company; and she made no scruple of proposing, presently, to depart. That proposal, unexpectedly, roused Linton from his lethargy, and threw him into a strange state of agitation. He glanced fearfully towards the Heights, begging she would remain another half-hour, at least.

"But, I think," said Cathy, "you'd be more comfortable at home than sitting here; and I cannot amuse you to-day, I see, by my tales, and songs, and chatter: you have grown wiser than I, in these six months; you have little taste for my diversions now; or else, if I could amuse you, I'd willingly stay."

"Stay to rest yourself," he replied. "And Catherine, don't think, or say that I'm *very* unwell: it is the heavy weather and heat that make me dull; and I walked about, before you came, a great deal for me. Tell uncle, I'm in tolerable health, will you?"

"I'll tell him that *you* say so, Linton. I couldn't affirm that you are," observed my young lady, wondering at his pertinacious assertion of what was evidently an untruth.

"And be here again next Thursday," continued he, shunning her puzzled gaze. "And give him my thanks for permitting you to come—my best thanks, Catherine. And—and, if you *did* meet my father, and he asked you about me, don't lead him to suppose that I've been extremely silent and stupid: don't look sad and downcast, as you *are* doing—he'll be angry."

"I care nothing for his anger," exclaimed Cathy, imagining she would be its object.

" But I do," said her cousin, shuddering. " *Don't* provoke him against me, Catherine, for he is very hard."

" Is he severe to you, Master Heathcliff?" I inquired. " Has he grown weary of indulgence, and passed from passive to active hatred?"

Linton looked at me, but did not answer; and, after keeping her seat by his side another ten minutes, during which his head fell drowsily on his breast, and he uttered nothing except suppressed moans of exhaustion or pain, Cathy began to seek solace in looking for bilberries, and sharing the produce of her researches with me: she did not offer them to him, for she saw further notice would only weary and annoy.

" Is it half an hour now, Ellen?" she whispered in my ear, at last. " I can't tell why we should stay. He's asleep, and papa will be wanting us back."

" Well, we must not leave him asleep," I answered; " wait till he wakes, and be patient. You were mighty eager to set off, but your longing to see poor Linton has soon evaporated!"

" Why did *he* wish to see me?" returned Catherine. " In his crossest humours, formerly, I liked him better than I do in his present curious mood. It's just as if it were a task he was compelled to perform—this interview—for fear his father should scold him. But I'm hardly going to come to give Mr. Heathcliff pleasure; whatever reason he may have for ordering Linton to undergo this penance. And, though I'm glad he's better in health, I'm sorry he's so much less pleasant, and so much less affectionate to me."

" You think *he is* better in health, then?" I said.

" Yes," she answered; " because he always made such a great deal of his sufferings, you know. He is not tolerably well, as he told me to tell papa; but he's better, very likely."

" There you differ with me, Miss Cathy," I remarked; " I should conjecture him to be far worse."

Linton here started from his slumber in bewildered terror, and asked if any one had called his name.

" No," said Catherine; " unless in dreams. I cannot conceive how you manage to doze out of doors, in the morning."

" I thought I heard my father," he gasped, glancing up to the frowning nab above us. " You are sure nobody spoke?"

"Quite sure," replied his cousin. "Only Ellen and I were disputing concerning your health. Are you truly stronger, Linton, than when we separated in winter? If you be, I'm certain one thing is not stronger—your regard for me: speak,—are you?"

The tears gushed from Linton's eyes as he answered, "Yes, yes, I am!" And, still under the spell of the imaginary voice, his gaze wandered up and down to detect its owner. Cathy rose. "For to-day we must part," she said. "And I won't conceal that I have been sadly disappointed with our meeting; though I'll mention it to nobody but you: not that I stand in awe of Mr. Heathcliff."

"Hush," murmured Linton; "for God's sake, hush! He's coming." And he clung to Catherine's arm, striving to detain her; but at that announcement she hastily disengaged herself, and whistled to Minny, who obeyed her like a dog.

"I'll be here next Thursday," she cried, springing to the saddle. "Good-bye. Quick, Ellen!"

And so we left him, scarcely conscious of our departure, so absorbed was he in anticipating his father's approach.

Before we reached home, Catherine's displeasure softened into a perplexed sensation of pity and regret, largely blended with vague, uneasy doubts about Linton's actual circumstances, physical and social: in which I partook, though I counselled her not to say much; for a second journey would make us better judges. My master requested an account of our ongoings. His nephew's offering of thanks was duly delivered, Miss Cathy gently touching on the rest: I also threw little light on his inquiries, for I hardly knew what to hide, and what to reveal.

CHAPTER XXVII.

SEVEN days glided away, every one marking its course by the henceforth rapid alteration of Edgar Linton's state. The havoc that months had previously wrought was now emulated by the inroads of hours. Catherine, we would fain have deluded yet; but her own quick spirit refused to delude her : it divined in secret, and brooded on the dreadful probability, gradually ripening into certainty. She had not the heart to mention her ride, when Thursday came round; I mentioned it for her, and obtained permission to order her out of doors: for the library, where her father stopped a short time daily—the brief period he could bear to sit up— and his chamber, had become her whole world. She grudged each moment that did not find her bending over his pillow, or seated by his side. Her countenance grew wan with watching and sorrow, and my master gladly dismissed her to what he flattered himself would be a happy change of scene and society; drawing comfort from the hope that she would not now be left entirely alone after his death.

He had a fixed idea, I guessed by several observations he let fall, that as his nephew resembled him in person he would resemble him in mind; for Linton's letters bore few or no indications of his defective character. And I, through pardonable weakness, refrained from correcting the error; asking myself what good there would be in disturbing his last moments with information that he had neither power nor opportunity to turn to account.

We deferred our excursion till the afternoon; a golden afternoon of August : every breath from the hills so full of life that it seemed whoever respired it, though dying, might revive. Catherine's face was just like the landscape—shadows and sunshine flitting over it in rapid succession; but the shadows rested longer and the sunshine was more transient, and her poor little heart reproached itself for even that passing forgetfulness of its cares.

We discerned Linton watching at the same spot he had selected before. My young mistress alighted, and told me that, as she was resolved to stay a very little while, I had better hold the pony and remain on horseback; but I dissented : I wouldn't risk losing sight of the charge committed to me a minute; so we climbed the slope of heath together. Master Heathcliff received us with greater animation on this occasion : not the animation of high spirits though, nor yet of joy ; it looked more like fear.

"It is late!" he said, speaking short and with difficulty. "Is not your father very ill? I thought you wouldn't come."

"*Why* won't you be candid?" cried Catherine, swallowing her greeting. "Why cannot you say at once you don't want me? It is strange, Linton, that for the second time you have brought me here on purpose, apparently, to distress us both, and for no reason besides!"

Linton shivered, and glanced at her, half supplicating, half ashamed; but his cousin's patience was not sufficient to endure this enigmatical behaviour.

"My father *is* very ill," she said; "and why am I called from his bedside? Why didn't you send to absolve me from my promise, when you wished I wouldn't keep it? Come! I desire an explanation: playing and trifling are completely banished out of my mind; and I can't dance attendance on your affectations now!"

"My affectations!" he murmured; "what are they? For Heaven's sake, Catherine, don't look so angry! Despise me as much as you please; I am a worthless, cowardly wretch: I can't be scorned enough; but I'm too mean for your anger. Hate my father, and spare me for contempt."

"Nonsense!" cried Catherine, in a passion. "Foolish, silly boy! And there! he trembles, as if I were really going to touch him! You needn't bespeak contempt, Linton: anybody will have it spontaneously at your service. Get off! I shall return home: it is folly dragging you from the hearth-stone, and pretending—what do we pretend? Let go my frock! If I pitied you for crying and looking so very frightened, you should spurn such pity. Ellen, tell him how disgraceful this conduct is. Rise, and don't degrade yourself into an abject reptile—*don't!*"

With streaming face and an expression of agony, Linton had thrown his nerveless frame along the ground: he seemed convulsed with exquisite terror.

"Oh!" he sobbed, "I cannot bear it! Catherine, Catherine, I'm a traitor, too, and I dare not tell you! But leave me, and I shall be killed! *Dear* Catherine, my life is in your hands: and you have said you loved me, and if you did, it wouldn't harm you. You'll not go, then? kind, sweet, good Catherine! And perhaps you *will* consent—and he'll let me die with you!"

My young lady, on witnessing his intense anguish, stooped to raise him. The old feeling of indulgent tenderness overcame her vexation, and she grew thoroughly moved and alarmed.

"Consent to what?" she asked. "To stay! Tell me the meaning of this strange talk, and I will. You contradict your own words, and distract me! Be calm and frank, and confess at once all that weighs on your heart. You wouldn't injure me, Linton, would you? You wouldn't let any enemy hurt me, if you could prevent it? I'll believe you are a coward for yourself, but not a cowardly betrayer of your best friend."

"But my father threatened me," gasped the boy, clasping his attenuated fingers, "and I dread him—I dread him! I *dare* not tell!"

"Oh, well!" said Catherine, with scornful compassion, "keep your secret: *I'm* no coward. Save yourself: I'm not afraid!"

Her magnanimity provoked his tears; he wept wildly, kissing her supporting hands, and yet could not summon courage to speak out. I was cogitating what the mystery might be, and determined Catherine should never suffer, to benefit him or any one else, by my good will; when hearing a rustle among the ling, I looked up and saw Mr. Heathcliff almost close upon us, descending the Heights. He didn't cast a glance towards my companions, though they were sufficiently near for Linton's sobs to be audible; but hailing me in the almost hearty tone he assumed to none besides, and the sincerity of which I couldn't avoid doubting, he said—

"It is something to see you so near to my house, Nelly. How are you at the Grange? Let us hear. The rumour goes," he added in a lower tone, "that Edgar Linton is on his deathbed: perhaps they exaggerate his illness?"

"No; my master is dying," I replied: "it is true enough. A sad thing it will be for us all, but a blessing for him!"

"How long will he last, do you think?" he asked.

"I don't know," I said.

"Because," he continued, looking at the two young people, who were fixed under his eye—Linton appeared as if he could not venture to stir, or raise his head, and Catherine could not move, on his account—"because that lad yonder seems determined to beat me; and I'd thank his uncle to be

quick and go before him. Hallo! has the whelp been playing that game long? I *did* give him some lessons about
snivelling. Is he pretty lively with Miss Linton generally?"

"Lively? no — he has shown the greatest distress," I
answered. "To see him, I should say, that instead of
rambling with his sweetheart on the hills, he ought to be in
bed, under the hands of a doctor."

"He shall be, in a day or two," muttered Heathcliff.
"But first — get up, Linton! Get up!" he shouted.
"Don't grovel on the ground there : up, this moment!"

Linton had sunk prostrate again in another paroxysm of
helpless fear, caused by his father's glance towards him, I
suppose : there was nothing else to produce such humiliation.
He made several efforts to obey, but his little strength was
annihilated for the time, and he fell back again with a moan.
Mr. Heathcliff advanced, and lifted him to lean against a
ridge of turf.

"Now," said he, with curbed ferocity, "I'm getting
angry ; and if you don't command that paltry spirit of yours
—*Damn* you! get up directly!"

"I will, father," he panted. "Only, let me alone, or I
shall faint. I've done as you wished, I'm sure. Catherine
will tell you that I—that I—have been cheerful. Ah! keep
by me, Catherine ; give me your hand."

"Take mine," said his father, "stand on your feet.
There now—she'll lend you her arm : that's right, look at
her. You would imagine I was the devil himself, Miss Linton, to excite such horror. Be so kind as to walk home with
him, will you? He shudders if I touch him."

"Linton, dear!" whispered Catherine, "I can't go to
Wuthering Heights : papa has forbidden me. He'll not
harm you : why are you so afraid?"

"I can never re-enter that house," he answered. "I am
not to re-enter it without you!"

"Stop!" cried his father. "We'll respect Catherine's
filial scruples. Nelly, take him in, and I'll follow your
advice concerning the doctor without delay."

"You'll do well," replied I. "But I must remain with
my mistress : to mind your son is not my business."

"You are very stiff," said Heathcliff, "I know that : but
you'll force me to pinch the baby and make it scream before

it moves your charity. Come then, my hero. Are you willing to return, escorted by me?"

He approached once more, and made as if he would seize the fragile being; but, shrinking back, Linton clung to his cousin, and implored her to accompany him, with a frantic importunity that admitted no denial. However I disapproved, I couldn't hinder her: indeed, how could she have refused him herself? What was filling him with dread we had no means of discerning; but there he was, powerless under its gripe, and any addition seemed capable of shocking him into idiocy. We reached the threshold; Catherine walked in, and I stood waiting till she had conducted the invalid to a chair, expecting her out immediately; when Mr. Heathcliff, pushing me forward, exclaimed—

"My house is not stricken with the plague, Nelly; and I have a mind to be hospitable to-day: sit down, and allow me to shut the door."

He shut and locked it also. I started.

"You shall have tea, before you go home," he added. "I am by myself. Hareton is gone with some cattle to the Lees, and Zillah and Joseph are off on a journey of pleasure; and, though I'm used to being alone, I'd rather have some interesting company, if I can get it. Miss Linton, take your seat by *him*. I give you what I have: the present is hardly worth accepting; but, I have nothing else to offer. It is Linton, I mean. How she does stare! It's odd what a savage feeling I have to anything that seems afraid of me! Had I been born where laws are less strict and tastes less dainty, I should treat myself to a slow vivisection of those two, as an evening's amusement."

He drew in his breath, struck the table, and swore to himself, "By hell! I hate them."

"I'm not afraid of you!" exclaimed Catherine, who could not hear the latter part of his speech. She stepped close up; her black eyes flashing with passion and resolution. "Give me that key: I will have it!" she said. "I wouldn't eat or drink here, if I were starving."

Heathcliff had the key in his hand that remained on the table. He looked up, seized with a sort of surprise at her boldness; or, possibly, reminded by her voice and glance, of the person from whom she inherited it. She snatched

at the instrument, and half succeeded in getting it out of
his loosened fingers: but her action recalled him to the
present; he recovered it speedily.

"Now, Catherine Linton," he said, "stand off, or I shall
knock you down; and that will make Mrs. Dean mad."

Regardless of this warning, she captured his closed hand,
and its contents again. "We *will* go!" she repeated, exerting her utmost efforts to cause the iron muscles to relax;
and finding that her nails made no impression, she applied
her teeth pretty sharply. Heathcliff glanced at me a glance
that kept me from interfering a moment. Catherine was
too intent on his fingers to notice his face. He opened
them suddenly, and resigned the object of dispute; but, ere
she had well secured it, he seized her with the liberated
hand, and, pulling her on his knee, administered with the
other a shower of terrific slaps on both sides of the head,
each sufficient to have fulfilled his threat, had she been able
to fall.

At this diabolical violence, I rushed on him furiously.
"You villain!" I began to cry, "you villain!" A touch
on the chest silenced me: I am stout, and soon put out of
breath; and, what with that and the rage, I staggered
dizzily back, and felt ready to suffocate, or to burst a blood-
vessel. The scene was over in two minutes; Catherine,
released, put her two hands to her temples, and looked just
as if she were not sure whether her ears were off or on. She
trembled like a reed, poor thing, and leant against the table
perfectly bewildered.

"I know how to chastise children, you see," said the
scoundrel, grimly, as he stooped to repossess himself of the
key, which had dropped to the floor. "Go to Linton now,
as I told you; and cry at your ease! I shall be your father
to-morrow,—all the father you'll have in a few days—and
you shall have plenty of that. You can bear plenty; you're
no weakling: you shall have a daily taste, if I catch such a
devil of a temper in your eyes again!"

Cathy ran to me instead of Linton, and knelt down and
put her burning cheek on my lap, weeping aloud. Her
cousin had shrunk into a corner of the settle, as quiet as a
mouse; congratulating himself, I dare say, that the correc-
tion had lighted on another than him. Mr. Heathcliff, per-

ceiving us all confounded, rose, and expeditiously made the
tea himself.   The cups and saucers were laid ready.   He
poured it out, and handed me a cup.

"Wash away your spleen," he said.   "And help your
own naughty pet and mine.   It is not poisoned, though I
prepared it.   I'm going out to seek your horses."

Our first thought, on his departure, was to force an exit
somewhere.   We tried the kitchen door, but that was fastened outside : we looked at the windows—they were too
narrow for even Cathy's little figure.

"Master Linton," I cried, seeing we were regularly im-
prisoned ; "you know what your diabolical father is after,
and you shall tell us, or I'll box your ears as he has done
your cousin's."

"Yes, Linton, you must tell," said Catherine.   "It was
for your sake I came: and it will be wickedly ungrateful
if you refuse."

"Give me some tea, I'm thirsty, and then I'll tell you,"
he answered.   "Mrs. Dean, go away.   I don't like you
standing over me.   Now, Catherine, you are letting your
tears fall into my cup.   I won't drink that.   Give me
another."

Catherine pushed another to him, and wiped her face.
I felt disgusted at the little wretch's composure, since he
was no longer in terror for himself.   The anguish he had
exhibited on the moor subsided as soon as ever he entered
Wuthering Heights; so I guessed he had been menaced
with an awful visitation of wrath if he failed in decoying
us there ; and, that accomplished, he had no further immediate fears.

"Papa wants us to be married," he continued, after
sipping some of the liquid.   "And he knows your papa
wouldn't let us marry now; and he's afraid of my dying,
if we wait; so we are to be married in the morning, and
you are to stay here all night; and, if you do as he wishes,
you shall return home next day, and take me with you."

"Take you with her, pitiful changeling ?" I exclaimed.
"*You* marry?   Why the man is mad! or he thinks us
fools, every one.   And, do you imagine that beautiful young
lady, that healthy, hearty girl, will tie herself to a little
perishing monkey like you?   Are you cherishing the notion that *anybody*, let alone Miss Catherine Linton, would

have you for a husband? You want whipping for bringing us in here at all, with your dastardly puling tricks; and— don't look so silly now! I've a very good mind to shake you severely, for your contemptible treachery, and your imbecile conceit."

I did give him a slight shaking; but it brought on the cough, and he took to his ordinary resource of moaning and weeping, and Catherine rebuked me.

"Stay all night? No," she said, looking slowly round. "Ellen, I'll burn that door down, but I'll get out."

And she would have commenced the execution of her threat directly, but Linton was up in alarm for his dear self again. He clasped her in his two feeble arms sobbing—

"Won't you have me, and save me? not let me come to the Grange? Oh! darling Catherine! you mustn't go and leave, after all. You *must* obey my father—you *must!*'

"I must obey my own," she replied, "and relieve him from this cruel suspense. The whole night! What would he think? he'll be distressed already. I'll either break or burn a way out of the house. Be quiet! You're in no danger; but if you hinder me—Linton, I love papa better than you!"

The mortal terror he felt of Mr. Heathcliff's anger, restored to the boy his coward's eloquence. Catherine was near distraught: still, she persisted that she must go home, and tried entreaty in her turn, persuading him to subdue his selfish agony. While they were thus occupied, our jailor re-entered.

"Your beasts have trotted off," he said, "and—now Linton! snivelling again? What has she been doing to you? Come, come—have done, and get to bed. In a month or two, my lad, you'll be able to pay her back her present tyrannies with a vigorous hand. You're pining for pure love, are you not? nothing else in the world: and she shall have you! There to bed! Zillah won't be hear to-night; you must undress yourself. Hush! hold your noise! Once in your own room, I'll not come near you: you needn't fear. By chance, you've managed tolerably. I'll look to the rest."

He spoke these words, holding the door open for his son to pass; and the latter achieved his exit exactly as a spaniel might, which suspected the person who attended on it of designing a spiteful squeeze. The lock was re-secured. Heathcliff approached the fire, where my mistress and I stood silent. Catherine looked up, and instinctively raised her hand to her cheek: his neighbourhood revived a painful sensation. Anybody else would have been incapable of regarding the childish act with sternness, but he scowled on her, and muttered—

"Oh! you are not afraid of me? Your courage is well disguised: you *seem* damnably afraid!"

"I *am* afraid now," she replied "because, if I stay, papa will be miserable; and how can I endure making him miserable—when he—when he— Mr. Heathcliff, *let* me go home! I promise to marry Linton: papa would like me to: and I love him. Why should you wish to force me to do what I'll willingly do of myself?"

"Let him dare to force you!" I cried. "There's law in the land, thank God! there is; though we be in an out-of-the-way place. I'd inform if he were my own son: and its felony without benefit of clergy!"

"Silence!" said the ruffian. "To the devil with your clamour! I don't want *you* to speak. Miss Linton, I shall enjoy myself remarkably in thinking your father will be miserable: I shall not sleep for satisfaction. You could have hit on no surer way of fixing your residence under my roof for the next twenty-four hours, than informing me that such an event would follow. As to your promise to marry Linton, I'll take care you shall keep it; for you shall not quit this place till it is fulfilled."

"Send Ellen, then, to let papa know I'm safe!" exclaimed Catherine, weeping bitterly. "Or marry me now. Poor papa! Ellen, he'll think we're lost. What shall we do?"

"Not he! He'll think you are tired of waiting on him, and run off for a little amusement," answered Heathcliff. "You cannot deny that you entered my house of your own accord, in contempt of his injunctions to the contrary. And it is quite natural that you should desire amusement at your age; and that you would weary of nursing a sick man, and that man *only* your father. Catherine, his happiest days were over when your days began. He cursed you, I dare say, for coming into the world (I did, at least); and it would just do if he cursed you as *he* went out of it. I'd join him. I don't love you! How should I? Weep away. As far as I can see, it will be your chief diversion hereafter; unless Linton make amends for other losses: and your provident parent appears to fancy he may. His letters of advice and consolation entertained me vastly. In his last he recommended my jewel to be careful of his; and kind to her when he got her. Careful and kind—that's paternal. But Linton requires his whole stock of care and kindness for himself. Linton can play the little tyrant well. He'll undertake to torture any number of cats, if their teeth be drawn and their claws pared. You'll be able to tell his uncle fine tales of his *kindness*, when you get home again, I assure you."

"You're right there!" I said; "explain your son's character. Show his resemblance to yourself; and then, I hope, Miss Cathy will think twice before she takes the cockatrice!"

"I don't much mind speaking of his amiable qualities now," he answered; "because she must either accept him or remain a prisoner, and you along with her, till your master dies. I can detain you both, quite concealed, here. If you doubt, encourage her to retract her word, and you'll have an opportunity of judging!"

"I'll not retract my word," said Catherine. "I'll marry him within this hour, if I may go to Thrushcross Grange afterwards. Mr. Heathcliff, you're a cruel man, but you're not a fiend; and you won't, from *mere* malice, destroy irrevocably all my happiness. If papa thought I had left him on purpose, and if he died before I returned, could I bear to live? I've given over crying: but I'm going to kneel here, at your knee; and I'll not get up, and I'll not take my eyes from your face till you look back at me! No, don't turn away! *do* look! You'll see nothing to provoke you. I don't hate you. I'm not angry that you struck me. Have you never loved *anybody* in all your life, uncle? *never?* Ah! you must look once. I'm so wretched, you can't help being sorry and pitying me."

"Keep your eft's fingers off; and move, or I'll kick you!" cried Heathcliff, brutally repulsing her. "I'd rather be hugged by a snake. How the devil can you dream of fawning on me? I *detest* you!"

He shrugged his shoulders: shook himself, indeed, as if

R

his flesh crept with aversion; and thrust back his chair; while I got up, and opened my mouth, to commence a downright torrent of abuse. But I was rendered dumb in the middle of the first sentence, by a threat that I should be shown into a room by myself the very next syllable I uttered. It was growing dark—we heard a sound of voices at the garden gate. Our host hurried out instantly: *he* had his wits about him; *we* had not. There was a talk of two or three minutes, and he returned alone.

" I thought it had been your cousin Hareton," I observed to Catherine. " I wish he would arrive! Who knows but he might take our part?"

" It was three servants sent to seek you from the Grange," said Heathcliff, overhearing me. " You should have opened a lattice and called out: but I could swear that chit is glad you didn't. She's glad to be obliged to stay, I'm certain."

At learning the chance we had missed, we both gave vent to our grief without control; and he allowed us to wail on till nine o'clock. Then he bid us go up stairs, through the kitchen, to Zillah's chamber; and I whispered my companion to obey: perhaps we might contrive to get through the window there, or into a garret, and out by its skylight. The window, however, was narrow, like those below, and the garret trap was safe from our attempts; for we were fastened in as before. We neither of us lay down: Catherine took her station by the lattice, and watched anxiously for morning; a deep sigh being the only answer I could obtain to my frequent entreaties that she would try to rest. I seated myself in a chair, and rocked to and fro, passing harsh judgment on my many derelictions of duty; from which, it struck me then, all the misfortunes of my employers sprang. It was not the case, in reality, I am aware; but it was, in my imagination, that dismal night; and I thought Heathcliff himself less guilty than I.

At seven o'clock he came, and inquired if Miss Linton had risen. She ran to the door immediately, and answered, " Yes." " Here, then," he said, opening it, and pulling her out. I rose to follow, but he turned the lock again. I demanded my release.

" Be patient," he replied; " I'll send up your breakfast in a while."

I thumped on the panels, and rattled the latch angrily;

and Catherine asked why I was still shut up? He answered, I must try to endure it another hour, and they went away. I endured it two or three hours; at length, I heard a foot-step : not Heathcliff's.

" I've brought you something to eat," said a voice ; " oppen t' door ! "

Complying eagerly, I beheld Hareton, laden with food enough to last me all day.

" Tak it," he added, thrusting the tray into my hand.

" Stay one minute," I began.

" Nay," cried he, and retired, regardless of any prayers I could pour forth to detain him.

And there I remained enclosed the whole day, and the whole of the next night; and another, and another. Five nights and four days I remained, altogether, seeing nobody but Hareton, once every morning; and he was a model of a jailer : surly, and dumb, and deaf to every attempt at moving his sense of justice or compassion.

CHAPTER XXVIII.

ON the fifth morning, or rather afternoon, a different step approached—lighter and shorter ; and, this time, the person entered the room. It was Zillah ; donned in her scarlet shawl, with a black silk bonnet on her head, and a willow basket swung to her arm.

" Eh, dear ! Mrs. Dean ! " she exclaimed. " Well ! there is a talk about you at Gimmerton. I never thought but you were sunk in the Blackhorse marsh, and missy with you, till master told me you'd been found, and he'd lodged you here ! What ! and you must have got on an island, sure ? And how long were you in the hole ? Did master save you, Mrs. Dean ? But you're not so thin—you've not been so poorly, have you ? "

" Your master is a true scoundrel ! " I replied. " But he shall answer for it. He needn't have raised that tale : it shall all be laid bare ! "

" What do you mean ? " asked Zillah. " It's not his tale :

they tell that in the village—about your being lost in the marsh; and I calls to Earnshaw, when I come in,—'Eh, they's queer things, Mr. Hareton, happened since I went off. It's a sad pity of that likely young lass, and cant Nelly Dean.' He stared. I thought he had not heard aught, so I told him the rumour. The master listened, and he just smiled to himself, and said, 'If they have been in the marsh, they are out now, Zillah. Nelly Dean is lodged, at this minute, in your room. You can tell her to flit, when you go up; here is the key. The bog-water got into her head, and she would have run home quite flighty; but I fixed her till she came round to her senses. You can bid her go to the Grange at once, if she be able, and carry a message from me, that her young lady will follow in time to attend the squire's funeral.'"

"Mr. Edgar is not dead?" I gasped. "Oh! Zillah, Zillah!"

"No, no; sit you down, my good mistress," she replied, "you're right sickly yet. He's not dead; Doctor Kenneth thinks he may last another day. I met him on the road and asked."

Instead of sitting down, I snatched my outdoor things, and hastened below, for the way was free. On entering the house, I looked about for some one to give information of Catherine. The place was filled with sunshine, and the door stood wide open; but nobody seemed at hand. As I hesitated whether to go off at once, or return and seek my mistress, a slight cough drew my attention to the hearth. Linton lay on the settle, sole tenant, sucking a stick of sugar-candy, and pursuing my movements with apathetic eyes. "Where is Miss Catherine?" I demanded, sternly, supposing I could frighten him into giving intelligence, by catching him thus, alone. He sucked on like an innocent.

"Is she gone?" I said.

"No," he replied; "she's up stairs: she's not to go; we won't let her."

"You won't let her, little idiot!" I exclaimed. "Direct me to her room immediately, or I'll make you sing out sharply."

"Papa would make you sing out, if you attempted to get there," he answered. "He says I'm not to be soft with Catherine: she's my wife, and it's shameful that she should wish to leave me. He says, she hates me and wants me to die, that she may have my money; but she sha'n't have it: and she sha'n't go home! She never shall!—she may cry, and be sick as much as she pleases!"

He resumed his former occupation, closing his lids, as if he meant to drop asleep.

"Master Heathcliff," I resumed, "have you forgotten all Catherine's kindness to you last winter, when you affirmed you loved her, and when she brought you books and sung you songs, and came many a time through wind and snow to see you? She wept to miss one evening, because you would be disappointed; and you felt then that she was a hundred times too good to you: and now you believe the lies your father tells, though you know he detests you both. And you join him against her. That's fine gratitude, is it not?"

The corner of Linton's mouth fell, and he took the sugar-candy from his lips.

"Did she come to Wuthering Heights, because she hated you?" I continued. "Think for yourself! As to your money, she does not even know that you will have any. And you say she's sick; and yet, you leave her alone, up there in a strange house! *You* who have felt what it is to be so neglected! You could pity your own sufferings; and she pitied them, too; but you won't pity hers! I shed tears Master Heathcliff, you see—an elderly woman, and a servant merely—and you, after pretending such affection, and having reason to worship her almost, store every tear you have for yourself, and lie there quite at ease. Ah! you're a heartless, selfish boy!"

"I can't stay with her," he answered crossly. "I'll not stay by myself. She cries so I can't bear it. And she won't give over, though I say I'll call my father. I did call him once, and he threatened to strangle her, if she was not quiet; but she began again the instant he left the room, moaning and grieving all night long, though I screamed for vexation that I couldn't sleep."

"Is Mr. Heathcliff out?" I inquired, perceiving that the wretched creature had no power to sympathize with his cousin's mental tortures.

"He's in the court," he replied, "talking to Doctor Kenneth; who says uncle is dying, truly, at last. I'm glad, for I shall be master of the Grange after him. Catherine always spoke of it as *her* house. It isn't hers! It's mine: papa says everything she has is mine. All her nice books are mine; she offered to give me them, and her pretty birds, and her pony Minny, if I would get the key of our room, and let her out; but I told her she had nothing to give, they were all, all mine. And then she cried, and took a little picture from her neck, and said I should have that; two pictures in a gold case, on one side her mother, and on the other, uncle, when they were young. That was yesterday—I said *they* were mine, too; and tried to get them from her. The spiteful thing wouldn't let me: she pushed me off, and hurt me. I shrieked out—that frightens her—she heard papa coming, and she broke the hinges and divided the case, and gave me her mother's portrait; the other she attempted to hide: but papa asked what was the matter and I explained it. He took the one I had away, and ordered her to resign hers to me; she refused, and he—he struck her down, and wrenched it off the chain, and crushed it with his foot."

"And were you pleased to see her struck?" I asked: having my designs in encouraging his talk.

"I winked," he answered: "I wink to see my father strike a dog or a horse, he does it so hard. Yet I was glad at first—she deserved punishing for pushing me: but when papa was gone, she made me come to the window and showed me her cheek cut on the inside, against her teeth, and her mouth filling with blood; and then she gathered up the bits of the picture, and went and sat down with her face to the wall, and she has never spoken to me since; and I sometimes think she can't speak for pain. I don't like to think so; but she's a naughty thing for crying continually; and she looks so pale and wild, I'm afraid of her."

"And you can get the key if you choose?" I said.

"Yes, when I am up stairs," he answered; "but I can't walk up-stairs now."

"In what apartment is it?" I asked.

"Oh," he cried, "I sha'n't tell *you* where it is! It is our secret. Nobody, neither Hareton nor Zillah, is to know. There! you've tired me—go away, go away!" And he turned his face on to his arm, and shut his eyes again.

I considered it best to depart without seeing Mr. Heathcliff, and bring a rescue for my young lady from the Grange. On reaching it, the astonishment of my fellow-servants to see me, and their joy also, was intense; and when they heard that their little mistress was safe, two or three were about to hurry up and shout the news at Mr. Edgar's door: but I bespoke the announcement of it, myself. How changed I found him, even in those few days! He lay an image of sadness and resignation waiting his death. Very young he looked: though his actual age was thirty-nine, one would have called him ten years younger, at least. He thought of Catherine; for he murmured her name. I touched his hand, and spoke.

"Catherine is coming, dear master!" I whispered; "she is alive and well; and will be here, I hope, to-night."

I trembled at the first effects of this intelligence: he half rose up, looked eagerly round the apartment, and then sank back in a swoon. As soon as he recovered, I related our compulsory visit, and detention at the Heights. I said Heathcliff forced me to go in: which was not quite true. I uttered as little as possible against Linton; nor did I describe all his father's brutal conduct—my intentions being to add no bitterness, if I could help it, to his already over-flowing cup.

He divined that one of his enemy's purposes was to secure the personal property, as well as the estate, to his son: or rather himself; yet why he did not wait till his decease was a puzzle to my master, because ignorant how nearly he and his nephew would quit the world together. However, he felt that his will had better be altered: instead of leaving Catherine's fortune at her own disposal, he determined to put it in the hands of trustees for her use during life, and for her children, if she had any, after her. By that means, it could not fall to Mr. Heathcliff should Linton die.

Having received his orders, I despatched a man to fetch the attorney, and four more, provided with serviceable weapons, to demand my young lady of her jailer. Both parties were delayed very late. The single servant returned first. He said Mr. Green, the lawyer, was out when he arrived at his house, and he had to wait two hours for his re-entrance; and then Mr. Green told him he had a little business in the village that must be done; but he would be at Thrushcross Grange before morning. The four men came back unaccompanied also. They brought word that Catherine was ill: too ill to quit her room; and Heathcliff would not suffer them to see her. I scolded the stupid fellows well for listening to that tale, which I would not carry to my master; resolving to take a whole bevy up to the Heights, at daylight, and storm it literally, unless the prisoner were quietly surrendered to us. Her father *shall* see her, I vowed, and vowed again, if that devil be killed on his own doorstones in trying to prevent it!

Happily, I was spared the journey and the trouble. I had gone down stairs at three o'clock to fetch a jug of water; and was passing through the hall with it in my hand, when a sharp knock at the front door made me jump. "Oh! it is Green," I said, recollecting myself—"only Green," and I went on, intending to send somebody else to open it; but the knock was repeated: not loud, and still importunately. I put the jug on the banister and hastened to admit him myself. The harvest moon shone clear outside. It was not the attorney. My own sweet little mistress sprung on my neck, sobbing,

"Ellen! Ellen! Is papa alive?"

"Yes," I cried: "yes, my angel, he is. God be thanked, you are safe with us again!"

She wanted to run, breathless as she was, up stairs to Mr. Linton's room; but I compelled her to sit down on a chair, and made her drink, and washed her pale face, chafing it into a faint colour with my apron. Then I said I must go first, and tell of her arrival; imploring her to say, she should be happy with young Heathcliff. She stared, but soon comprehending why I counselled her to utter the falsehood, she assured me she would not complain.

I couldn't abide to be present at their meeting. I stood outside the chamber-door a quarter of an hour, and hardly ventured near the bed, then. All was composed, however: Catherine's despair was as silent as her father's joy. She supported him calmly, in appearance; and he fixed on her features his raised eyes, that seemed dilating with ecstasy.

He died blissfully, Mr. Lockwood: he died so. Kissing her cheek, he murmured,—

"I am going to her; and you darling child shall come to us!" and never stirred or spoke again; but continued that rapt, radiant gaze, till his pulse imperceptibly stopped and his soul departed. None could have noticed the exact minute of his death, it was so entirely without a struggle.

Whether Catherine had spent her tears, or whether the grief were too weighty to let them flow, she sat there dry-eyed till the sun rose : she sat till noon, and would still have remained brooding over that deathbed, but I insisted on her coming away and taking some repose. It was well I succeeded in removing her; for at dinnertime appeared the lawyer, having called at Wuthering Heights to get his instructions how to behave. He had sold himself to Mr. Heathcliff: that was the cause of his delay in obeying my master's summons. Fortunately, no thought of worldly affairs crossed the latter's mind, to disturb him, after his daughter's arrival.

Mr. Green took upon himself to order everything and everybody about the place. He gave all the servants but me, notice to quit. He would have carried his delegated authority to the point of insisting that Edgar Linton should not be buried beside his wife, but in the chapel, with his family. There was the will, however, to hinder that, and my loud protestations against any infringement of its directions. The funeral was hurried over; Catherine, Mrs. Linton Heathcliff now, was suffered to stay at the Grange till her father's corpse had quitted it.

She told me that her anguish had at last spurred Linton to incur the risk of liberating her. She heard the men I sent disputing at the door, and she gathered the sense of Heathcliff's answer. It drove her desperate. Linton, who had been conveyed up to the little parlour soon after I left, was terrified into fetching the key before his father re-ascended. He had the cunning to unlock, and re-lock the door, without shutting it; and when he should have gone to bed, he begged to sleep with Hareton; and his petition was granted, for once. Catherine stole out before break of day. She dare not try the doors, lest the dogs should raise an alarm; she visited the empty chambers, and examined their windows; and, luckily, lighting on her mother's, she got easily out of its lattice, and on to the ground, by means of the fir tree close by. Her accomplice suffered for his share in the escape, notwithstanding his timid contrivances.

CHAPTER XXIX.

THE evening after the funeral, my young lady and I were seated in the library; now musing mournfully—one of us despairingly—on our loss, now venturing conjectures as to the gloomy future.

We had just agreed the best destiny which could await Catherine, would be a permission to continue resident at the Grange; at least during Linton's life: he being allowed to join her there, and I to remain as housekeeper. That seemed rather too favourable an arrangement to be hoped for; and yet I did hope, and began to cheer up under the prospect of retaining my home and my employment, and, above all, my beloved young mistress; when a servant—one of the discarded ones, not yet departed—rushed hastily in, and said, "that devil Heathcliff" was coming through the court: should he fasten the door in his face?

If we had been mad enough to order that proceeding, we had not time. He made no ceremony of knocking or announcing his name: he was master, and availed himself of the master's privilege to walk straight in, without saying a word. The sound of our informant's voice directed him to the library; he entered, and motioning him out, shut the door.

It was the same room into which he had been ushered, as a guest, eighteen years before: the same moon shone through the window; and the same autumn landscape lay outside. We had not yet lighted a candle, but all the apartment was visible, even to the portraits on the wall: the splendid head of Mrs. Linton, and the graceful one of her husband. Heathcliff advanced to the hearth. Time had little altered his person either. There was the same man: his dark face rather sallower and more composed, his frame a stone or two heavier, perhaps, and no other difference. Catherine had risen, with an impulse to dash out, when she saw him.

"Stop!" he said, arresting her by the arm. "No more runnings away! Where would you go? I'm come to fetch you home; and I hope you'll be a dutiful daughter, and not encourage my son to further disobedience. I was embarrassed how to punish him when I discovered his part in the business: he's such a cobweb, a pinch would annihilate him; but you'll see by his look that he has received his due!

I brought him down one evening, the day before yesterday, and just set him in a chair, and never touched him afterwards. I sent Hareton out, and we had the room to ourselves. In two hours, I called Joseph to carry him up again; and since then my presence is as potent on his nerves as a ghost; and I fancy he sees me often, though I am not near. Hareton says he wakes and shrieks in the night by the hour together, and calls you to protect him from me; and, whether you like your precious mate or not, you must come: he's your concern now; I yield all my interest in him to you."

"Why not let Catherine continue here?" I pleaded, "and send Master Linton to her. As you hate them both, you'd not miss them: they *can* only be a daily plague to your unnatural heart."

"I'm seeking a tenant for the Grange," he answered; "and I want my children about me, to be sure. Besides that lass owes me her services for her bread. I'm not going to nurture her in luxury and idleness after Linton is gone. Make haste and get ready, now; and don't oblige me to compel you."

"I shall," said Catherine. "Linton is all I have to love in the world, and though you have done what you could to make him hateful to me, and me to him, you *cannot* make us hate each other. And I defy you to hurt him when I am by, and I defy you to frighten me!"

"You are a boastful champion," replied Heathcliff; "but I don't like you well enough to hurt him: you shall get the full benefit of the torment, as long as it lasts. It is not I who will make him hateful to you—it is his own sweet spirit. He's as bitter as gall at your desertion, and its consequences: don't expect thanks for this noble devotion. I heard him draw a pleasant picture to Zillah of what he would do, if he were as strong as I: the inclination is there, and his very weakness will sharpen his wits to find a substitute for strength."

"I know he has a bad nature," said Catherine: "he's your son. But I'm glad I've a better, to forgive it; and I know he loves me, and for that reason I love him. Mr. Heathcliff, *you* have *nobody* to love you; and, however miserable you make us, we shall still have the revenge of thinking that your cruelty arises from your greater misery. You *are* miserable, are you not? Lonely, like the devil, and envious like him? *Nobody* loves you—*nobody* will cry for you when you die! I wouldn't be you!"

Catherine spoke with a kind of dreary triumph: she seemed to have made up her mind to enter into the spirit of her future family, and draw pleasure from the griefs of her enemies.

"You shall be sorry to be yourself presently," said her father-in-law, "if you stand there another minute. Begone, witch, and get your things!"

She scornfully withdrew. In her absence, I began to beg for Zillah's place at the Heights, offering to resign mine to her; but he would suffer it on no account. He bid me be silent; and then, for the first time, allowed himself a glance round the room and a look at the pictures. Having studied Mrs. Linton's, he said—

"I shall have that home. Not because I need it, but—" He turned abruptly to the fire, and continued, with what, for lack of a better word, I must call a smile—"I'll tell you what I did yesterday! I got the sexton, who was digging Linton's grave, to remove the earth off her coffin-lid, and I opened it. I thought, once, I would have stayed there: when I saw her face again—it is hers yet!—he had hard work to stir me; but he said it would change if the air blew on it, and so I struck one side of the coffin loose, and covered it up: not Linton's side, damn him! I wish he'd been soldered in lead. And I bribed the sexton to pull it away when I'm laid there, and slide mine out too; I'll have it made so: and then by the time Linton gets to us he'll not know which is which!"

"You were very wicked, Mr. Heathcliff!" I exclaimed; "were you not ashamed to disturb the dead?"

"I disturbed nobody, Nelly," he replied; "and I gave some ease to myself. I shall be a great deal more comfortable now; and you'll have a better chance of keeping me underground, when I get there. Disturbed her? No! she has disturbed me, night and day, through eighteen years—incessantly—remorselessly—till yesternight; and yesternight I was tranquil. I dreamt I was sleeping the last sleep by that sleeper, with my heart stopped and my cheek frozen against hers."

"And if she had been dissolved into earth, or worse, what would you have dreamt of then?" I said.

" Of dissolving with her, and being more happy still!"
he answered. " Do you suppose I dread any change of that
sort? I expected such a transformation on raising the lid;
but I'm better pleased that it should not commence till I
share it. Besides, unless I had received a distinct impression of her passionless features, that strange feeling would
hardly have been removed. It began oddly. You know
I was wild after she died; and eternally, from dawn to
dawn, praying her to return to me her spirit! I have a
strong faith in ghosts: I have a conviction that they can,
and do, exist among us! The day she was buried, there
came a fall of snow. In the evening I went to the churchyard. It blew bleak as winter—all round was solitary. I
didn't fear that her fool of a husband would wander up the
den so late; and no one else had business to bring them
there. Being alone, and conscious two yards of loose earth
was the sole barrier between us, I said to myself—' I'll
have her in my arms again! If she be cold, I'll think it is
this north wind that chills *me*; and if she be motionless, it is
sleep.' I got a spade from the toolhouse, and began to delve
with all my might—it scraped the coffin; I fell to work
with my hands; the wood commenced cracking about the
screws, I was on the point of attaining my object, when it
seemed that I heard a sigh from some one above, close at
the edge of the grave, and bending down. ' If I can only get
this off,' I muttered, ' I wish they may shovel in the earth
over us both!' and I wrenched at it more desperately still.
There was another sigh, close at my ear. I appeared to feel
the warm breath of it displacing the sleet-laden wind. I
knew no living thing in flesh and blood was by; but, as certainly as you perceive the approach to some substantial body
in the dark, though it cannot be discerned, so certainly I felt
that Cathy was there: not under me, but on the earth. A
sudden sense of relief flowed, from my heart, through every
limb. I relinquished my labour of agony, and turned consoled at once: unspeakably consoled. Her presence was
with me; it remained while I re-filled the grave, and led me
home. You may laugh, if you will; but I was sure I
should see her there. I was sure she was with me, and I
could not help talking to her. Having reached the Heights,
I rushed eagerly to the door. It was fastened; and, I remember, that accursed Earnshaw and my wife opposed my

entrance. I remember stopping to kick the breath out of him, and then hurrying up stairs, to my room and hers. I looked round impatiently—I felt her by me—I could *almost* see her, and yet I *could not!* I ought to have sweat blood then, from the anguish of my yearning—from the fervour of my supplications to have but one glimpse! I had not one. She showed herself, as she often was in life, a devil to me! And, since then, sometimes more and sometimes less, I've been the sport of that intolerable torture! Infernal! keeping my nerves at such a stretch, that, if they had not resembled catgut, they would long ago have relaxed to the feebleness of Linton's. When I sat in the house with Hareton, it seemed that on going out, I should meet her; when I walked on the moors I should meet her coming in. When I went from home, I hastened to return: she *must* be somewhere at the Heights, I was certain! And when I slept in her chamber—I was beaten out of that. I couldn't lie there; for the moment I closed my eyes, she was either outside the window, or sliding back the panels, or entering the room, or even resting her darling head on the same pillow as she did when a child; and I must open my lids to see. And so I opened and closed them a hundred times a-night—to be always disappointed! It racked me! I've often groaned aloud, till that old rascal Joseph no doubt believed that my conscience was playing the fiend inside of me. Now, since I've seen her, I'm pacified—a little. It was a strange way of killing: not by inches, but by fractions of hairbreadths, to beguile me with the spectre of a hope, through eighteen years!"

Mr. Heathcliff paused and wiped his forehead; his hair clung to it, wet with perspiration; his eyes were fixed on the red embers of the fire, the brows not contracted, but raised next the temples; diminishing the grim aspect of his countenance, but imparting a peculiar look of trouble, and a painful appearance of mental tension towards one absorbing subject. He only half addressed me, and I maintained silence. I didn't like to hear him talk! After a short period he resumed his meditation on the picture, took it down and leant it against the sofa to contemplate it at better advantage; and while so occupied Catherine entered, announcing that she was ready, when her pony should be saddled.

" Send that over to-morrow," said Heathcliff to me; then turning to her he added. " You may do without your pony: it is a fine evening, and you'll need no ponies at Wuthering Heights; for what journeys you take, your own feet will serve you. Come along."

" Good-bye, Ellen!" whispered my dear little mistress. As she kissed me, her lips felt like ice. " Come and see me, Ellen, don't forget."

" Take care you do no such thing, Mrs. Dean!" said her new father. " When I wish to speak to you I'll come here. I want none of your prying at my house!"

He signed her to precede him; and casting back a look that cut my heart, she obeyed. I watched them from the window, walk down the garden. Heathcliff fixed Catherine's arm under his: though she disputed the act at first evidently; and with rapid strides, he hurried her into the alley, whose trees concealed them.

CHAPTER XXX.

I HAVE paid a visit to the Heights, but I have not seen her since she left: Joseph held the door in his hand when I called to ask after her, and wouldn't let me pass. He said Mrs. Linton was " thrang," and the master was not in. Zillah has told me something of the way they go on, otherwise I should hardly know who was dead and who living. She thinks Catherine haughty, and does not like her, I can guess by her talk. My young lady asked some aid of her when she first came; but Mr. Heathcliff told her to follow her own business and let his daughter-in-law look after herself; and Zillah willingly acquiesced, being a narrow-minded, selfish woman. Catherine evinced a child's annoyance at this neglect; repaid it with contempt, and thus enlisted my informant among her enemies, as securely as if she had done her some great wrong. I had a long talk with Zillah, about six weeks ago, a little before you came, one day when we foregathered on the moor; and this is what she told me.

"The first thing Mrs. Linton did," she said, "on her

arrival at the Heights, was to run up stairs, without even wishing good-evening to me and Joseph; she shut herself into Linton's room, and remained till morning. Then, while the master and Earnshaw were at breakfast, she entered the house, and asked all in a quiver if the doctor might be sent for? her cousin was very ill.

" 'We know that!' answered Heathcliff; 'but his life is not worth a farthing, and I won't spend a farthing on him.

" 'But I cannot tell how to do,' she said; 'and if nobody will help me, he 'll die!'

" 'Walk out of the room,' cried the master, 'and let me never hear a word more about him! None here care what becomes of him; if you do, act the nurse; if you do not, lock him up and leave him.'

" Then she began to bother me, and I said I 'd had enough plague with the tiresome thing; we each had our tasks, and hers was to wait on Linton, Mr. Heathcliff bid me leave that labour to her.

" How they managed together, I can't tell. I fancy he fretted a great deal, and moaned hisseln night and day; and she had precious little rest: one could guess by her white face and heavy eyes. She sometimes came into the kitchen all wildered like, and looked as if she would fain beg assistance; but I was not going to disobey the master: I never dare disobey him, Mrs. Dean; and, though I thought it wrong that Kenneth should not be sent for, it was no concern of mine either to advise or complain, and I always refused to meddle. Once or twice, after we had gone to bed, I 've happened to open my door again and seen her sitting crying on the stairs' top; and then I 've shut myself in quick, for fear of being moved to interfere. I did pity her then, I 'm sure: still I didn't wish to lose my place, you know.

" At last, one night she came boldly into my chamber, and frightened me out of my wits, by saying,—

" 'Tell Mr. Heathcliff that his son is dying—I 'm sure he is, this time. Get up, instantly, and tell him.'

" Having uttered this speech, she vanished again. I lay a quarter of an hour listening and trembling. Nothing stirred—the house was quiet.

" She's mistaken, I said to myself. He's got over it. I needn't disturb them; and I began to doze. But my sleep

was marred a second time by a sharp ringing of the bell—
the only bell we have, put up on purpose for Linton; and
the master called to me to see what was the matter, and inform them that he wouldn't have that noise repeated.

"I delivered Catherine's message. He cursed to himself,
and in a few minutes came out with a lighted candle, and
proceeded to their room. I followed. Mrs. Heathcliff was
seated by the bedside, with her hands folded on her knees.
Her father-in-law went up, held the light to Linton's face,
looked at him, and touched him; afterwards he turned to her.

"'Now—Catherine' he said, 'how do you feel?'

"She was dumb.

"'How do you feel, Catherine,?' he repeated.

"'He's safe, and I'm free,' she answered: "'I should
feel well—but,' she continued, with a bitterness she couldn't
conceal, 'you have left me so long to struggle against
death alone, that I feel and see only death! I feel like
death!'

"And she looked like it, too! I gave her a little wine.
Hareton and Joseph, who had been wakened by the ringing
and the sound of feet, and heard our talk from outside, now
entered. Joseph was fain, I believe, of the lad's removal;
Hareton seemed a thought bothered: though he was more
taken up with staring at Catherine than thinking of Linton.
But the master bid him get off to bed again: we didn't
want his help. He afterwards made Joseph remove the
body to his chamber, and told me to return to mine, and
Mrs. Heathcliff remained by herself.

"In the morning, he sent me to tell her she must come
down to breakfast: she had undressed, and appeared going
to sleep, and said she was ill; at which I hardly wondered.
I informed Mr. Heathcliff, and he replied,—

"'Well, let her be till after the funeral; and go up now
and then to get her what is needful; and as soon as she
seems better, tell me.'"

Cathy stayed up stairs a fortnight, according to Zillah;
who visited her twice a day, and would have been rather
more friendly, but her attempts at increasing kindness were
proudly and promptly repelled.

Heathcliff went up once, to shew her Linton's will. He had
bequeathed the whole of his, and what had been her, move-
able property to his father: the poor creature was threat-

S

ened, or coaxed, into that act during her week's absence, when his uncle died. The lands, being a minor, he could not meddle with. However, Mr. Heathcliff has claimed and kept them in his wife's right and his also: I suppose legally: at any rate, Catherine, destitute of cash and friends, cannot disturb his possession.

"Nobody," said Zillah, "ever approached her door, except that once, but I; and nobody asked anything about her. The first occasion of her coming down into the house was on a Sunday afternoon. She had cried out, when I carried up her dinner, that she couldn't bear any longer being in the cold; and I told her the master was going to Thrushcross Grange, and Earnshaw and I needn't hinder her from descending; so, as soon as she heard Heathcliff's horse trot off, she made her appearance, donned in black, and her yellow curls combed back behind her ears as plain as a quaker: she couldn't comb them out.

"Joseph and I generally go to chapel on Sundays:" the kirk, you know, has no minister now, explained Mrs. Dean; and they call the Methodists' or Baptists' place (I can't say which it is), at Gimmerton, a chapel. "Joseph had gone," she continued, "but I thought proper to bide at home. Young folks are always the better for an elder's over-looking; and Hareton, with all his bashfulness, isn't a model of nice behaviour. I let him know that his cousin would very likely sit with us, and she had been always used to see the Sabbath respected; so he had as good leave his guns and bits of in-door work alone, while she stayed. He coloured up at the news, and cast his eyes over his hands and clothes. The train-oil and gunpowder were shoved out of sight in a minute. I saw he meant to give her his company; and I guessed, by his way, he wanted to be presentable; so, laughing, as I durst not laugh when the master is by, I offered to help him, if he would, and joked at his confusion. He grew sullen, and began to swear.

"Now, Mrs. Dean," Zillah went on, seeing me not pleased by her manner, "you happen think your young lady too fine for Mr. Hareton; and happen you're right; but I own I should love well to bring her pride a peg lower. And what will all her learning and her daintiness do for her, now? She's as poor as you or I: poorer, I'll be bound: you're saving, and I'm doing my little all that road."

Hareton allowed Zillah to give him her aid; and she flattered him into a good-humour; so, when Catherine came, half forgetting her former insults, he tried to make himself agreeable, by the housekeeper's account.

" Missis walked in," she said, " as chill as an icicle, and as high as a princess. I got up and offered her my seat in the arm-chair. No, she turned up her nose at my civility. Earnshaw rose, too, and bid her come to the settle, and sit close by the fire : he was sure she was starved.

" ' I've been starved a month and more,' she answered, resting on the word as scornful as she could.

" And she got a chair for herself, and placed it at a distance from both of us. Having sat till she was warm, she began to look round, and discovered a number of books in the dresser; she was instantly upon her feet again, stretching to reach them : but they were too high up. Her cousin, after watching her endeavours a while, at last summoned courage to help her; she held her frock, and he filled it with the first that came to hand.

" That was a great advance for the lad. She didn't thank him; still, he felt gratified that she had accepted his assistance, and ventured to stand behind as she examined them, and even to stoop and point out what struck his fancy in certain old pictures which they contained; nor was he daunted by the saucy style in which she jerked the page from his finger : he contented himself with going a bit farther back, and looking at her instead of the book. She continued reading, or seeking for something to read. His attention became, by degrees, quite centred in the study of her thick, silky curls : her face he couldn't see, and she couldn't see him. And, perhaps, not quite awake to what he did, but attracted like a child to a candle, at last he proceeded from staring to touching; he put out his hand and stroked one curl, as gently as if it were a bird. He might have stuck a knife into her neck, she started round in such a taking.

" ' Get away, this moment! How dare you touch me? Why are you stopping there?' she cried, in a tone of disgust. ' I can't endure you! I'll go up stairs again, if you come near me.'

" Mr. Hareton recoiled, looking as foolish as he could do : he sat down in the settle very quiet, and she continued turning over her volumes another half hour; finally, Earnshaw crossed over, and whispered to me.

"'Will you ask her to read to us, Zillah? I'm stalled of doing naught; and I do like—I could like to hear her! Dunnot say I wanted it, but ask of yourseln.'

"'Mr. Hareton wishes you would read to us, ma'am,' I said, immediately. 'He'd take it very kind—he'd be much obliged.'

"She frowned; and looking up, answered—

"'Mr. Hareton, and the whole set of you, will be good enough to understand that I reject any pretence at kindness you have the hypocrisy to offer! I despise you, and will have nothing to say to any of you!· When I would have given my life for one kind word, even to see one of your faces, you all kept off. But I won't complain to you! I'm driven down here by the cold; not either to amuse you or enjoy your society.'

"'What could I ha' done?' began Earnshaw. 'How was I to blame?'

"'Oh! you are an exception,' answered Mrs. Heathcliff. 'I never missed such a concern as you.'

"'But I offered more than once, and asked,' he said, kindling up at her pertness, 'I asked Mr. Heathcliff to let me wake for you—'

"'Be silent! I'll go out of doors, or anywhere, rather than have your disagreeable voice in my ear!' said my lady.

"Hareton muttered she might go to hell, for him! and unslinging his gun, restrained himself from his Sunday occupations no longer. He talked now, freely enough; and she presently saw fit to retreat to her solitude: but the frost had set in, and, in spite of her pride, she was forced to condescend to our company, more and more. However, I took care there should be no further scorning at my good nature: ever since, I've been as stiff as herself; and she has no lover or liker among us: and she does not deserve one; for, let them say the least word to her, and she'll curl back without respect of any one! She'll snap at the master himself, and as good as dares him to thrash her; and the more hurt she gets, the more venomous she grows."

At first, on hearing this account from Zillah, I determined to leave my situation, take a cottage, and get Catherine to come and live with me: but Mr. Heathcliff would as soon permit that as he would set up Hareton in an independent house; and I can see no remedy, at present, unless she could marry again: and that scheme it does not come within my province to arrange.

Thus ended Mrs. Dean's story. Notwithstanding the doctor's prophecy, I am rapidly recovering strength; and, though it be only the second week in January, I propose getting out on horseback in a day or two, and riding over to Wuthering Heights, to inform my landlord that I shall spend the next six months in London; and, if he likes, he may look out for another tenant to take the place after October. I would not pass another winter here for much.

CHAPTER XXXI.

YESTERDAY was bright, calm, and frosty. I went to the Heights as I proposed: my housekeeper entreated me to bear a little note from her to her young lady, and I did not refuse, for the worthy woman was not conscious of anything odd in her request. The front door stood open, but the jealous gate was fastened, as at my last visit; I knocked, and invoked Earnshaw from among the garden beds; he unchained it, and I entered. The fellow is as handsome a rustic as need be seen. I took particular notice of him this time; but then he does his best, apparently, to make the least of his advantages.

I asked if Mr. Heathcliff were at home? He answered, No; but he would be in at dinner-time. It was eleven o'clock, and I announced my intention of going in and waiting for him, at which he immediately flung down his tools and accompanied me, in the office of watchdog, not as a substitute for the host.

We entered together; Catherine was there, making herself useful in preparing some vegetables for the approaching meal; she looked more sulky and less spirited than when I had seen her first. She hardly raised her eyes to notice me, and continued her employment with the same disregard to common forms of politeness as before; never return-—

ing my bow and good-morning by the slightest acknowledgment.

"She does not seem so amiable," I thought, "as Mrs. Dean would persuade me to believe. She's a beauty, it is true; but not an angel."

Earnshaw surlily bid her remove her things to the kitchen. "Remove them yourself," she said, pushing them from her as soon as she had done; and retiring to a stool by the window, where she began to carve figures of birds and beasts out of the turnip parings in her lap. I approached her, pretending to desire a view of the garden; and, as I fancied, adroitly dropped Mrs. Dean's note on to her knee, unnoticed by Hareton—but she asked aloud, "What is that?" And chucked it off.

"A letter from your old acquaintance, the housekeeper at the Grange," I answered; annoyed at her exposing my kind deed, and fearful lest it should be imagined a missive of my own. She would gladly have gathered it up at this information, but Hareton beat her; he seized and put it in his waistcoat, saying Mr. Heathcliff should look at it first. Thereat, Catherine silently turned her face from us, and, very stealthily, drew out her pocket-handkerchief and applied it to her eyes; and her cousin, after struggling a while to keep down his softer feelings, pulled out the letter and flung it on the floor beside her, as ungraciously as he could. Catherine caught and perused it eagerly; then she put a few questions to me concerning the inmates, rational and irrational, of her former home; and gazing towards the hills, murmured in soliloquy:

"I should like to be riding Minny down there! I should like to be climbing up there! Oh! I'm tired—I'm *stalled*, Hareton!" And she leant her pretty head back against the sill, with half a yawn and half a sigh, and lapsed into an aspect of abstracted sadness: neither caring nor knowing whether we remarked her.

"Mrs. Heathcliff," I said, after sitting some time mute, "you are not aware that I am an acquaintance of yours? so intimate that I think it strange you won't come and speak to me My housekeeper never wearies of talking about and praising you; and she'll be greatly disappointed if I return with no news of or from you, except that you received her letter and said nothing!"

She appeared to wonder at this speech and asked,—
" Does Ellen like you ? "

" Yes, very well," I replied hesitatingly.

" You must tell her," she continued, " that I would answer her letter, but I have no materials for writing : not even a book from which I might tear a leaf."

" No books !" I exclaimed. " How do you contrive to live here without them ? if I may take the liberty to inquire. Though provided with a large library, I'm frequently very dull at the Grange ; take my books away, and I should be desperate !"

" I was always reading, when I had them," said Catherine ; " and Mr. Heathcliff never reads ; so he took it into his head to destroy my books. I have not had a glimpse of one for weeks. Only once, I searched through Joseph's store of theology, to his great irritation ; and once, Hareton, I came upon a secret stock in your room—some Latin and Greek, and some tales and poetry : all old friends. I brought the last here—and you gathered them, as a magpie gathers silver spoons, for the mere love of stealing ! They are of no use to you ; or else you concealed them in the bad spirit that as you cannot enjoy them nobody else shall. Perhaps *your* envy counselled Mr. Heathcliff to rob me of my treasures ? But I've most of them written on my brain and printed in my heart, and you cannot deprive me of those !"

Earnshaw blushed crimson when his cousin made this revelation of his private literary accumulations, and stammered an indignant denial of her accusations.

" Mr. Hareton is desirous of increasing his amount of knowledge," I said, coming to his rescue. " He is not *envious* but *emulous* of your attainments. He'll be a clever scholar in a few years."

" And he wants me to sink into a dunce, meantime," answered Catherine. " Yes I hear him trying to spell and read to himself, and pretty blunders he makes ! I wish you would repeat Chevy Chase as you did yesterday : it was extremely funny. I heard you ; and I heard you turning over the dictionary to seek out the hard words, and then cursing because you couldn't read their explanations !"

The young man evidently thought it too bad that he should be laughed at for his ignorance, and then laughed at for trying to remove it. I had a similar notion; and, remembering Mrs. Dean's anecdote of his first attempt at enlightening the darkness in which he had been reared, I observed,—

"But, Mrs. Heathcliff, we have each had a commencement, and each stumbled and tottered on the threshold; had our teachers scorned instead of aiding us, we should stumble and totter yet."

"Oh!" she replied, "I don't wish to limit his acquirements: still, he has no right to appropriate what is mine, and make it ridiculous to me with his vile mistakes and mispronunciations! Those books, both prose and verse, are consecrated to me by other associations; and I hate to have them debased and profaned in his mouth! Besides, of all, he has selected my favourite pieces that I love the most to repeat, as if out of deliberate malice."

Hareton's chest heaved in silence a minute: he laboured under a severe sense of mortification and wrath, which it was no easy task to suppress. I rose, and, from a gentlemanly idea of relieving his embarrassment, took up my station in the doorway, surveying the external prospect as I stood. He followed my example, and left the room; but presently reappeared, bearing half a dozen volumes in his hands, which he threw into Catherine's lap, exclaiming,—

"Take them! I never want to hear, or read, or think of them again!"

"I won't have them now," she answered. "I shall connect them with you, and hate them."

She opened one that had obviously been often turned over, and read a portion in the drawling tone of a beginner; then laughed, and threw it from her. "And listen," she continued, provokingly, commencing a verse of an old ballad in the same fashion.

But his self-love would endure no further torment: I heard, and not altogether disapprovingly, a manual check given to her saucy tongue. The little wretch had done her utmost to hurt her cousin's sensitive though uncultivated feelings, and a physical argument was the only mode he had of balancing the account, and repaying its effects on the inflictor. He afterwards gathered the books and hurled them on the fire. I read in his countenance what anguish it was to offer that sacrifice to spleen. I fancied that as they consumed, he recalled the pleasure they had already imparted, and the triumph and ever-increasing pleasure he had anticipated from them; and I fancied I guessed the incitement to his secret studies also. He had been content with daily labour and rough animal enjoyments, till Catherine crossed his path. Shame at her scorn, and hope of her approval, were his first prompters to higher pursuits; and, instead of guarding him from one and winning him to the other, his endeavours to raise himself had produced just the contrary result.

"Yes; that's all the good that such a brute as you can get from them!" cried Catherine, sucking her damaged lip, and watching the conflagration with indignant eyes.

"You'd *better* hold your tongue, now," he answered, fiercely.

And his agitation precluded further speech; he advanced hastily to the entrance, where I made way for him to pass. But ere he had crossed the door-stones, Mr. Heathcliff, coming up the causeway encountered him, and laying hold of his shoulder asked,—

"What's to do now, my lad?"

"Naught, naught," he said, and broke away to enjoy his grief and anger in solitude.

Heathcliff gazed after him, and sighed.

"It will be odd if I thwart myself," he muttered, unconscious that I was behind him. "But when I look for his father in his face, I find *her* every day more! How the devil is he so like? I can hardly bear to see him."

He bent his eyes to the ground, and walked moodily in. There was a restless, anxious expression in his countenance I had never remarked there before; and he looked sparer in person. His daughter-in-law, on perceiving him through the window, immediately escaped to the kitchen, so that I remained alone.

"I'm glad to see you out of doors again, Mr. Lockwood," he said, in reply to my greeting; "from selfish motives partly: I don't think I could readily supply your loss in this desolation. I've wondered more than once what brought you here."

"An idle whim, I fear, sir," was my answer; "or else an idle whim is going to spirit me away. I shall set out for London, next week; and I must give you warning that

I feel no disposition to retain Thrushcross Grange beyond the twelvemonths I agreed to rent it. I believe I shall not live there any more."

"Oh, indeed; you're tired of being banished from the world, are you?" he said. " But if you be coming to plead off paying for a place you won't occupy, your journey is useless: I never relent in exacting my due from any one."

" I'm coming to plead off nothing about it," I exclaimed, considerably irritated. " Should you wish it, I'll settle with you now," and I drew my note-book from my pocket.

" No, no," he replied coolly; "you'll leave sufficient behind to cover your debts, if you fail to return: I'm not in such a hurry. Sit down and take your dinner with us: a guest that is safe from repeating his visit can generally be made welcome. Catherine, bring the things in: where are you?"

Catherine reappeared, bearing a tray of knives and forks.

" You may get your dinner with Joseph," muttered Heathcliff aside, " and remain in the kitchen till he is gone."

She obeyed his directions very punctually: perhaps she had no temptation to transgress. Living among clowns and misanthropists, she probably cannot appreciate a better class of people when she meets them.

With Mr. Heathcliff, grim and saturnine, on the one hand, and Hareton, absolutely dumb, on the other, I made a somewhat cheerless meal, and bade adieu early. I would have departed by the back way, to get a last glimpse of Catherine and annoy old Joseph; but Hareton received orders to lead up my horse, and my host himself escorted me to the door, so I could not fulfil my wish.

" How dreary life gets over in that house!" I reflected, while riding down the road. " What a realization of something more romantic than a fairy tale it would have been for Mrs. Linton Heathcliff, had she and I struck up an attachment, as her good nurse desired, and migrated together into the stirring atmosphere of the town!"

CHAPTER XXXII.

1802.—This September I was invited to devastate the moors of a friend in the north, and on my journey to his abode, I unexpectedly came within fifteen miles of Gimmerton. The ostler at a roadside public-house was holding a pail of water to refresh my horses, when a cart of very green oats, newly reaped, passed by, and he remarked—

" Yon's frough Gimmerton, nah ! They're allas three wick' after other folk wi' ther harvest."

" Gimmerton?" I repeated—my residence in that locality had already grown dim and dreamy. " Ah! I know. How far is it from this?"

" Happen fourteen mile' o'er th' hills; and a rough road," he answered.

A sudden impulse seized me to visit Thrushcross Grange. It was scarcely noon, and I conceived that I might as well pass the night under my own roof as in an inn. Besides, I could spare a day easily to arrange matters with my landlord, and thus save myself the trouble of invading the neighbourhood again. Having rested a while, I directed my servant to inquire the way to the village; and, with great fatigue to our beasts, we managed the distance in some three hours.

I left him there, and proceeded down the valley alone. The grey church looked greyer, and the lonely churchyard lonelier. I distinguished a moor sheep cropping the short turf on the graves. It was sweet, warm weather—too warm for travelling; but the heat did not hinder me from enjoying the delightful scenery above and below: had I seen it nearer August, I'm sure it would have tempted me to waste a month among its solitudes. In winter nothing more dreary, in summer nothing more divine, than those glens shut in by hills, and those bluff, bold swells of heath.

I reached the Grange before sunset, and knocked for admittance; but the family had retreated into the back premises, I judged, by one thin, blue wreath curling from the kitchen chimney, and they did not hear. I rode into the court. Under the porch, a girl of nine or ten sat knitting, and an old woman reclined on the horse-steps smoking a meditative pipe.

"Is Mrs. Dean within?" I demanded of the dame.

"Mistress Dean? Nay!" she answered, "shoo doesn't bide here: shoo's up at th' Heights."

"Are you the housekeeper, then?" I continued.

"Eea, aw keep th' hause," she replied.

"Well, I'm Mr. Lockwood, the master. Are there any rooms to lodge me in, I wonder? I wish to stay all night."

"T' maister!" she cried in astonishment. "Whet, whoiver knew yah wur coming? Yah sud ha' send word! They's nowt norther dry nor mensful abaht t' place: nowt there isn't!"

She threw down her pipe and bustled in, the girl followed, and I entered too; soon perceiving that her report was true, and, moreover, that I had almost upset her wits by my unwelcome apparition, I bade her be composed. I would go out for a walk; and, meantime, she must try to prepare a corner of a sitting-room for me to sup in, and a bed-room to sleep in. No sweeping and dusting, only good fires and dry sheets were necessary. She seemed willing to do her best; though she thrust the hearth-brush into the grates in mistake for the poker, and mal-appropriated several other articles of her craft: but I retired, confiding in her energy for a resting-place against my return. Wuthering Heights was the goal of my proposed excursion. An after-thought brought me back, when I had quitted the court.

"All well at the Heights?" I inquired of the woman.

"Eea, f'r owt ee knaw!" she answered, skurrying away with a pan of hot cinders.

I would have asked why Mrs. Dean had deserted the Grange, but it was impossible to delay her at such a crisis, so I turned away and made my exit; rambling leisurely along, with the glow of a sinking sun behind, and the mild glory of a rising moon in front—one fading, and the other brightening—as I quitted the park, and climbed the stony by-road branching off to Mr. Heathcliff's dwelling. Before I arrived in sight of it, all that remained of day was a beamless amber light along the west: but I could see every pebble on the path, and every blade of grass, by that splendid moon. I had neither to climb the gate nor to knock—it yielded to my hand. That is an improvement, I thought. And I noticed another, by the aid of my nostrils; a fragrance of stocks and wall flowers, wafted on the air, from amongst the homely fruit trees.

Both doors and lattices were open; and yet, as is usually the case in a coal district, a fine, red fire illumined the chimney: the comfort which the eye derives from it renders the extra heat endurable. But the house of Wuthering Heights is so large, that the inmates have plenty of space for withdrawing out of its influence; and accordingly, what inmates there were had stationed themselves not far from one of the windows. I could both see them and hear them talk before I entered, and looked and listened in consequence; being moved thereto by a mingled sense of curiosity and envy, that grew as I lingered.

" Con-*trary !*" said a voice, as sweet as a silver bell— " That for the third time, you dunce! I'm not going to tell you, again. Recollect, or I'll pull your hair !"

" Contrary, then," answered another, in deep but softened tones. " And now, kiss me, for minding so well."

"No, read it over first correctly, without a single mistake."

The male speaker began to read: he was a young man, respectably dressed and seated at a table, having a book before him. His handsome features glowed with pleasure; and his eyes kept impatiently wandering from the page to a small white hand over his shoulder; which recalled him by a smart slap on the cheek, whenever its owner detected such signs of inattention. Its owner stood behind; her light, shining ringlets blending, at intervals, with his brown locks, as she bent to superintend his studies; and her face—it was lucky he could not see her face, or he would never have been so steady. I could, and I bit my lip, in spite, at having thrown away the chance I might have had of doing something besides staring at its smiting beauty.

The task was done, not free from further blunders; but the pupil claimed a reward, and received at least five kisses: which, however, he generously returned. Then they came to the door, and from their conversation I judged they were about to issue out and have a walk on the moors. I supposed I should be condemned in Hareton Earnshaw's heart, if not by his mouth, to the lowest pit in the infernal regions, if I showed my unfortunate person in his neighbourhood then; and feeling very mean and malignant, I skulked round to seek refuge in the kitchen. There was unobstructed

admittance on that side also; and at the door sat my old
friend Nelly Dean, sewing and singing a song; which was
often interrupted from within by harsh words of scorn and
intolerance, uttered in far from musical accents.

"I'd rayther, by th' haulf, hev 'em swearing i' my lugs
fro'h morn to neeght, nor hearken ye, hahsiver!" said the
tenant of the kitchen, in answer to an unheard speech of
Nelly's. "It's a blazing shame, that I cannot oppen t'
blessed Book, but yah set up them glories to sattan, and
all t' flaysome wickednesses that iver wer born into t'
warld! Oh! ye're a raight nowt; and shoo's another;
and that poor lad 'll be lost, atween ye. Poor lad!" he
added, with a groan; "he's witched: I'm sartin on't! O,
Lord, judge 'em, for there's norther law nor justice amang
wer rullers!"

"No! or we should be sitting in flaming fagots, I suppose," retorted the singer. "But wisht, old man, and read
your Bible like a Christian, and never mind me. This is
'Fairy Annie's Wedding'—a bonny tune—it goes to a
dance."

Mrs. Dean was about to recommence, when I advanced;
and, recognising me directly, she jumped to her feet,
crying—

"Why, bless you, Mr. Lockwood! How could you think
of returning in this way? All's shut up at Thrushcross
Grange. You should have given us notice!"

"I've arranged to be accommodated there, for as long as
I shall stay," I answered. "I depart again to-morrow.
And how are you transplanted here, Mrs. Dean? tell me
that."

"Zillah left, and Mr. Heathcliff wished me to come, soon
after you went to London, and stay till you returned. But,
step in, pray! Have you walked from Gimmerton this
evening?"

"From the Grange," I replied; "and while they make
me lodging room there, I want to finish my business with
your master; because I don't think of having another opportunity in a hurry."

"What business, sir!" said Nelly, conducting me into
the house. "He's gone out at present, and won't return
soon."

"About the rent," I answered.

"Oh! then it is with Mrs. Heathcliff you must settle," she observed; "or rather with me. She has not learnt to manage her affairs yet, and I act for her: there's nobody else."

I looked surprised.

"Ah! you have not heard of Heathcliff's death, I see," she continued.

"Heathcliff dead!" I exclaimed, astonished. "How long ago?"

"Three months since: but sit down, and let me take your hat, and I'll tell you all about it. Stop, you have had nothing to eat, have you?"

"I want nothing: I have ordered supper at home. You sit down too. I never dreamt of his dying! Let me hear how it came to pass. You say you don't expect them back for some time—the young people?"

"No—I have to scold them every evening for their late rambles: but they don't care for me. At least, have a drink of our old ale; it will do you good: you seem weary."

She hastened to fetch it before I could refuse, and I heard Joseph asking whether "it warn't a crying scandal that she should have followers at her time of life? And then, to get them jocks out o' t' maister's cellar! He fair shaamed to 'bide still and see it."

She did not stay to retaliate, but re-entered in a minute, bearing a reaming silver pint, whose contents I lauded with becoming earnestness. And afterwards she furnished me with the sequel of Heathcliff's history. He had a "queer" end, as she expressed it.

I was summoned to Wuthering Heights, within a fortnight of your leaving us, she said; and I obeyed joyfully, for Catherine's sake. My first interview with her grieved and shocked me: she had altered so much since our separation. Mr. Heathcliff did not explain his reasons for taking a new mind about my coming here; he only told me he wanted me, and he was tired of seeing Catherine: I must make the little parlour my sitting room, and keep her with me. It was enough if he were obliged to see her once or twice a day. She seemed pleased at this arrangement; and, by degrees, I smuggled over a great number of books, and other articles, that had formed her amusement at the Grange; and flattered myself we should get on in tolerable comfort. The delusion did not last long. Catherine, contented at first, in a brief space grew irritable and restless. For one thing, she was forbidden to move out of the garden, and it fretted her sadly to be confined to its narrow bounds as spring drew on; for another, in following the house, I was forced to quit her frequently, and she complained of loneliness: she preferred quarrelling with Joseph in the kitchen to sitting at peace in her solitude. I did not mind their skirmishes: but Hareton was often obliged to seek the kitchen also, when the master wanted to have the house to himself; and though in the beginning she either left it at his approach, or quietly joined in my occupations, and shunned remarking or addressing him—and though he was always as sullen and silent as possible—after a while, she changed her behaviour, and became incapable of letting him alone: talking at him; commenting on his stupidity and idleness; expressing her wonder how he could endure the life he lived—how he could sit a whole evening staring into the fire, and dozing.

"He's just like a dog, is he not, Ellen?" she once observed, "or a cart-horse? He does his work, eats his food, and sleeps eternally! What a blank, dreary mind he must have! Do you ever dream, Hareton? And, if you do, what is it about? But you can't speak to me!"

Then she looked at him; but he would neither open his mouth nor look again.

"He's perhaps, dreaming now," she continued. "He twitched his shoulder as Juno twitches hers. Ask him, Ellen."

"Mr. Hareton will ask the master to send you up stairs, if you don't behave!" I said. He had not only twitched his shoulder but clenched his fist, as if tempted to use it.

"I know why Hareton never speaks, when I am in the kitchen," she exclaimed, on another occasion. "He is afraid I shall laugh at him. Ellen, what do you think? He began to teach himself to read once; and, because I laughed, he burned his books, and dropped it: was he not a fool?"

"Were not you naughty?" I said; "answer me that."

"Perhaps I was," she went on, "but I did not expect him to be so silly. Hareton, if I gave you a book, would you take it now? I'll try!"

She placed one she had been perusing on his hand; he

flung it off, and muttered, if she did not give over, he would break her neck.

" Well, I shall put it here," she said, " in the table drawer; and I'm going to bed."

Then she whispered me to watch whether he touched it, and departed. But he would not come near it; and so I informed her in the morning, to her great disappointment. I saw she was sorry for his persevering sulkiness and indolence: her conscience reproved her for frightening him off improving himself: she had done it effectually. But her ingenuity was at work to remedy the injury: while I ironed, or pursued other such stationary employments as I could not well do in the parlour, she would bring some pleasant volume and read it aloud to me. When Hareton was there, she generally paused in an interesting part, and left the book lying about: that she did repeatedly; but he was as obstinate as a mule, and, instead of snatching at her bait, in wet weather he took to smoking with Joseph; and they sat like automatons, one on each side of the fire, the elder happily too deaf to understand her wicked nonsense, as he would have called it, the younger doing his best to seem to disregard it. On fine evenings the latter followed his shooting expeditions, and Catherine yawned and sighed, and teased me to talk to her, and ran off into the court or garden, the moment I began; and, as a last resource, cried and said she was tired of living: her life was useless.

Mr. Heathcliff, who grew more and more disinclined to society, had almost banished Earnshaw from his apartment. Owing to an accident at the commencement of March, he became for some days a fixture in the kitchen. His gun burst while out on the hills by himself; a splinter cut his arm, and he lost a good deal of blood before he could reach home. The consequence was that, perforce, he was condemned to the fireside and tranquillity, till he made it up again. It suited Catherine to have him there: at any rate, it made her hate her room up stairs more than ever; and she would compel me to find out business below, that she might accompany me.

On Easter Monday, Joseph went to Gimmerton fair with some cattle; and, in the afternoon, I was busy getting up linen in the kitchen. Earnshaw sat, morose as usual, at the chimney corner, and my little mistress was beguiling an

T

idle hour with drawing pictures on the window panes;
varying her amusement by smothered bursts of songs, and
whispered ejaculations, and quick glances of annoyance and
impatience in the direction of her cousin, who stedfastly
smoked, and looked into the grate.　At a notice that I
could do with her no longer intercepting my light, she removed to the hearthstone.　I bestowed little attention on
her proceedings, but, presently, I heard her begin—

"I've found out, Hareton, that I want—that I'm glad
—that I should like you to be my cousin now, if you had
not grown so cross to me, and so rough."

Hareton returned no answer.

"Hareton, Hareton, Hareton! do you hear?" she continued.

"Get off wi' ye!" he growled, with uncompromising
gruffness.

"Let me take that pipe," she said, cautiously advancing
her hand and abstracting it from his mouth.

Before he could attempt to recover it, it was broken,
and behind the fire.　He swore at her and seized another.

"Stop," she cried, "you must listen to me first; and I
can't speak while those clouds are floating in my face."

"Will you go to the devil!" he exclaimed, ferociously,
"and let me be!"

"No," she persisted, "I won't: I can't tell what to do
to make you talk to me; and you are determined not to understand.　When I call you stupid, I don't mean anything:
I don't mean that I despise you.　Come, you shall take
notice of me, Hareton: you are my cousin, and you shall
own me."

"I shall have naught to do wi' you and your mucky
pride, and your damned mocking tricks!" he answered.
"I'll go to hell, body and soul, before I look sideways after
you again!　Side out o' t' gate, now; this minute!"

Catherine frowned, and retreated to the window-seat chewing her lip, and endeavouring, by humming an eccentric
tune, to conceal a growing tendency to sob.

"You should be friends with your cousin, Mr. Hareton,"
I interrupted, "since she repents of her sauciness.　It would
do you a great deal of good: it would make you another
man, to have her for a companion."

"A companion!" he cried; "when she hates me, and

does not think me fit to wipe her shoon! Nay, if it made me a king, I'd not be scorned for seeking her good-will any more."

"It is not I who hate you, it is you who hate me!" wept Cathy, no longer disguising her trouble. "You hate me as much as Mr. Heathcliff does, and more."

"You're a damned liar," began Earnshaw: "why have I made him angry, by taking your part, then, a hundred times? and that when you sneered at and despised me, and —Go on plaguing me, and I'll step in yonder, and say you worried me out of the kitchen!"

"I didn't know you took my part," she answered, drying her eyes; "and I was miserable and bitter at everybody; but now I thank you, and beg you to forgive me: what can I do besides?"

She returned to the hearth, and frankly extended her hand. He blackened and scowled like a thunder-cloud, and kept his fists resolutely clenched, and his gaze fixed on the ground. Catherine, by instinct, must have divined it was obdurate perversity, and not dislike, that prompted this dogged conduct; for, after remaining an instant undecided, she stooped and impressed on his cheek a gentle kiss. The little rogue thought I had not seen her, and, drawing back, she took her former station by the window, quite demurely. I shook my head reprovingly, and then she blushed and whispered—

"Well! what should I have done, Ellen? He wouldn't shake hands, and he wouldn't look: I must show him some way that I like him—that I want to be friends."

Whether the kiss convinced Hareton, I cannot tell: he was very careful, for some minutes, that his face should not be seen, and when he did raise it, he was sadly puzzled where to turn his eyes.

Catherine employed herself in wrapping a handsome book neatly in white paper, and having tied it with a bit of ribbon, and addressed it to "Mr. Hareton Earnshaw," she desired me to be her ambassadress, and convey the present to its destined recipient.

"And tell him, if he'll take it I'll come and teach him to read it right," she said; "and, if he refuse it, I'll go up stairs, and never tease him again."

I carried it, and repeated the message; anxiously watched

by my employer. Hareton would not open his fingers, so I laid it on his knee. He did not strike it off, either. I returned to my work. Catherine leaned her head and arms on the table, till she heard the slight rustle of the covering being removed; then she stole away, and quietly seated herself beside her cousin. He trembled, and his face glowed: all his rudeness and all his surly harshness had deserted him: he could not summon courage, at first, to utter a syllable in reply to her questioning look, and her murmured petition.

"Say you forgive me, Hareton, do. You can make me so happy by speaking that little word."

He muttered something inaudible.

"And you'll be my friend?" added Catherine, interrogatively.

"Nay, you'll be ashamed of me every day of your life," he answered; "and the more ashamed, the more you know me; and I cannot bide it."

"So you won't be my friend?" she said, smiling as sweet as honey, and creeping close up.

I overheard no further distinguishable talk, but, on looking round again, I perceived two such radiant countenances bent over the page of the accepted book, that I did not doubt the treaty had been ratified on both sides; and the enemies were, thenceforth, sworn allies.

The work they studied was full of costly pictures; and those and their position had charm enough to keep them unmoved till Joseph came home. He, poor man, was perfectly aghast at the spectacle of Catherine seated on the same bench with Hareton Earnshaw, leaning her hand on his shoulder; and confounded at his favourite's endurance of her proximity: it affected him too deeply to allow an observation on the subject that night. His emotion was only revealed by the immense sighs he drew, as he solemnly spread his large bible on the table, and overlaid it with dirty banknotes from his pocket-book, the produce of the day's transactions. At length, he summoned Hareton from his seat.

"Tak' these in to t' maister, lad," he said, "and bide there: I's gang up to my awn rahm. This hoile's neither mensful nor seemly for us: we mun side out and seearch another."

"Come, Catherine," I said, "we must 'side out' too: I've done my ironing, are you ready to go?"

"It is not eight o'clock!" she answered, rising unwillingly. "Hareton, I'll leave this book upon the chimneypiece, and I'll bring some more to-morrow."

"Ony books that yah leave, I shall tak' into th' hahse," said Joseph, "and it 'ull be mitch if yah find 'em agean; soa, yah may plase yourseln!"

Cathy threatened that his library should pay for hers; and, smiling as she passed Hareton, went singing up stairs: lighter of heart, I venture to say, than ever she had been under that roof before; except, perhaps, during her earliest visits to Linton.

The intimacy thus commenced, grew rapidly; though it encountered temporary interruptions. Earnshaw was not to be civilized with a wish, and my young lady was no philosopher, and no paragon of patience; but both their minds tending to the same point—one loving and desiring to esteem, and the other loving and desiring to be esteemed—they contrived in the end to reach it.

You see, Mr. Lockwood, it was easy enough to win Mrs. Heathcliff's heart. But now, I'm glad you did not try. The crown of all my wishes will be the union of those two. I shall envy no one on their wedding-day: there won't be a happier woman than myself in England!

CHAPTER XXXIII.

On the morrow of that Monday, Earnshaw being still unable to follow his ordinary employments, and therefore remaining about the house, I speedily found it would be impracticable to retain my charge beside me, as heretofore. She got down stairs before me, and out into the garden, where she had seen her cousin performing some easy work; and when I went to bid them come to breakfast, I saw she had persuaded him to clear a large space of ground from currant and gooseberry bushes, and they were busy planning together an importation of plants from the Grange.

I was terrified at the devastation which had been accomplished in a brief half hour; the black currant trees were the apple of Joseph's eye, and she had just fixed her choice of a flower bed in the midst of them.

"There! That will be all shown to the master," I exclaimed, "the minute it is discovered. And what excuse have you to offer for taking such liberties with the garden? We shall have a fine explosion on the head of it: see if we don't! Mr. Hareton, I wonder you should have no more wit, than to go and make that mess at her bidding!"

"I'd forgotten they were Joseph's," answered Earnshaw, rather puzzled; "but I'll tell him I did it."

We always ate our meals with Mr. Heathcliff. I held the mistress's post in making tea and carving; so I was indispensable at table. Catherine usually sat by me, but today she stole nearer to Hareton; and I presently saw she would have no more discretion in her friendship than she had in her hostility.

"Now, mind you don't talk with and notice your cousin too much," were my whispered instructions as we entered the room. "It will certainly annoy Mr. Heathcliff, and he'll be mad at you both."

"I'm not going to," she answered.

The minute after, she had sidled to him, and was sticking primroses in his plate of porridge.

He dared not speak to her there: he dared hardly look; and yet she went on teasing, till he was twice on the point of being provoked to laugh. I frowned, and then she glanced toward the master: whose mind was occupied on other subjects than his company, as his countenance evinced; and she grew serious for an instant, scrutinizing him with deep gravity. Afterwards she turned, and recommenced her nonsense; at last, Hareton uttered a smothered laugh. Mr. Heathcliff started; his eye rapidly surveyed our faces. Catherine met it with her accustomed look of nervousness and yet defiance, which he abhorred.

"It is well you are out of my reach," he exclaimed. "What fiend possesses you to stare back at me, continually, with those infernal eyes? Down with them! and don't remind me of your existence again. I thought I had cured you of laughing."

"It was me," muttered Hareton.

"What do you say?" demanded the master.

Hareton looked at his plate, and did not repeat the confession. Mr. Heathcliff looked at him a bit, and then silently resumed his breakfast and his interrupted musing. We had nearly finished, and the two young people prudently shifted wider asunder, so I anticipated no further disturbance during that sitting; when Joseph appeared at the door, revealing by his quivering lip and furious eyes, that the outrage committed on his precious shrubs was detected. He must have seen Cathy and her cousin about the spot before he examined it, for while his jaws worked like those of a cow chewing its cud, and rendered his speech difficult to understand, he began:—

"I mun hev my wage, and I mun goa! I *hed* aimed to dee, wheare I'd sarved fur sixty year; and I thowt I'd lug my books up into t' garret, and all my bits o' stuff, and they sud hev t' kitchen to theirseln; for t' sake·o' quietness. It wur hard to gie up my awn hearthstun, but I thowt I *could* do that! But, nah, shoo's taan my garden fro' me, and by th' heart, Maister, I cannot stand it! Yah may bend to th' yoak, and ye will—I noan used to 't, and an old man doesn't sooin get used to new barthens. I'd rayther arn my bite an' my sup wi' a hammer in th' road!"

"Now, now, idiot!" interrupted Heathcliff, "cut it short! What's your grievance? I'll interfere in no quarrels between you and Nelly. She may thrust you into the coalhole for anything I care."

"It's noan Nelly!" answered Joseph. "I sudn't shift for Nelly—Nasty ill nowt as shoo is. Thank God! *shoo* cannot stale t' sowl o' nob'dy! Shoo wer niver soa handsome, but what a body mud look at her 'bout winking. It's yon flaysome, grunoless quean, that's witched our lad, wi' her bold een and her forrard ways—till—Nay! it fair brusts my heart! He's forgetten all I've done for him, and made on him, and goan and riven up a whole row o' t' grandest currant trees, i' t' garden!" and here he lamented outright; unmanned by a sense of his bitter injuries, and Earnshaw's ingratitude and dangerous condition.

"Is the fool drunk?" asked Mr. Heathcliff. "Hareton, is it you he's finding fault with?"

"I've pulled up two or three bushes," replied the young man; "but I'm going to set 'em again."

"And why have you pulled them up?" said the master.

Catherine wisely put in her tongue.

"We wanted to plant some flowers there," she cried. "I'm the only person to blame, for I wished him to do it."

"And who the devil gave *you* leave to touch a stick about the place?" demanded her father-in-law, much surprised. "And who ordered *you* to obey her?" he added, turning to Hareton.

The latter was speechless; his cousin replied—

"You shouldn't grudge a few yards of earth for me to ornament, when you have taken all my land!"

"Your land, insolent slut! You never had any," said Heathcliff.

"And my money," she continued; returning his angry glare, and meantime biting a piece of crust, the remnant of her breakfast.

"Silence!" he exclaimed. "Get done, and begone!"

"And Hareton's land, and his money," pursued the reckless thing. "Hareton and I are friends now; and I shall tell him all about you!"

The master seemed confounded a moment: he grew pale, and rose up, eyeing her all the while, with an expression of mortal hate.

"If you strike me, Hareton will strike you," she said; "so you may as well sit down."

"If Hareton does not turn you out of the room, I'll strike him to hell," thundered Heathcliff. "Damnable witch! dare you pretend to rouse him against me? Off with her! Do you hear? Fling her into the kitchen! I'll kill her, Ellen Dean, if you let her come into my sight again!"

Hareton tried, under his breath, to persuade her to go.

"Drag her away!" he cried, savagely. "Are you staying to talk?" And he approached to execute his own command.

"He'll not obey you, wicked man, any more," said Catherine; "and he'll soon detest you as much as I do."

"Wisht! wisht!" muttered the young man, reproachfully. "I will not hear you speak so to him. Have done."

"But you won't let him strike me?" she cried.

"Come, then," he whispered, earnestly.

It was too late: Heathcliff had caught hold of her.

"Now, *you* go!" he said to Earnshaw. "Accursed

witch! this time she has provoked me when I could not bear it; and I'll make her repent it for ever!"

He had his hand in her hair; Hareton attempted to release her locks, entreating him not to hurt her that once. Heathcliff's black eyes flashed; he seemed ready to tear Catherine in pieces, and I was just worked up to risk coming to the rescue, when of a sudden his fingers relaxed; he shifted his grasp from her head to her arm, and gazed intently in her face. Then he drew his hand over her eyes, stood a moment to collect himself apparently, and turning anew to Catherine, said, with assumed calmness—"You must learn to avoid putting me in a passion, or I shall really murder you some time! Go with Mrs. Dean, and keep with her; and confine your insolence to her ears. As to Hareton Earnshaw, if I see him listen to you, I'll send him seeking his bread where he can get it! Your love will make him an outcast and a beggar. Nelly, take her; and leave me, all of you! Leave me!"

I led my young lady out: she was too glad of her escape to resist; the other followed, and Mr. Heathcliff had the room to himself till dinner. I had counselled Catherine to dine up stairs; but, as soon as he perceived her vacant seat, he sent me to call her. He spoke to none of us, ate very little, and went out directly afterwards, intimating that he should not return before evening.

The two new friends established themselves in the house during his absence; where I heard Hareton sternly check his cousin, on her offering a revelation of her father-in-law's conduct to his father. He said he wouldn't suffer a word to be uttered in his disparagement: if he were the devil, it didn't signify, he would stand by him; and he'd rather she would abuse himself, as she used to, than begin on Mr. Heathcliff. Catherine was waxing cross at this; but he found means to make her hold her tongue, by asking how she would like *him* to speak ill of her father? Then she comprehended that Earnshaw took the master's reputation home to himself; and was attached by ties stronger than reason could break—chains, forged by habit, which it would be cruel to attempt to loosen. She showed a good heart, thenceforth, in avoiding both complaints and expressions of antipathy concerning Heathcliff; and confessed to me her sorrow that she had endeavoured to raise a bad spirit be-

tween him and Hareton: indeed, I don't believe she has
ever breathed a syllable, in the latter's hearing, against her
oppressor since.

When this slight disagreement was over, they were friends
again, and as busy as possible in their several occupations of
pupil and teacher. I came in to sit with them, after I had
done my work; and I felt so soothed and comforted to watch
them, that I did not notice how time got on. You know,
they both appeared in a measure my children: I had long
been proud of one; and now, I was sure, the other would be
a source of equal satisfaction. His honest, warm, and intelligent nature shook off rapidly the clouds of ignorance and
degradation in which it had been bred; and Catherine's sincere commendations acted as a spur to his industry. His
brightening mind brightened his features, and added spirit
and nobility to their aspect: I could hardly fancy it the
same individual I had beheld on the day I discovered my
little lady at Wuthering Heights, after her expedition to the
Crags. While I admired and they laboured, dusk drew on,
and with it returned the master. He came upon us quite
unexpectedly, entering by the front way, and had a full view
of the whole three, ere we could raise our heads to glance
at him. Well, I reflected, there was never a pleasanter, or
more harmless sight; and it will be a burning shame to
scold them. The red fire-light glowed on their two bonny
heads, and revealed their faces animated with the eager
interest of children; for, though he was twenty-three and
she eighteen, each had so much of novelty to feel and learn,
that neither experienced nor evinced the sentiments of sober
disenchanted maturity.

They lifted their eyes together, to encounter Mr. Heathcliff: perhaps you have never remarked that their eyes are
precisely similar, and they are those of Catherine Earnshaw.
The present Catherine has no other likeness to her, except a
breadth of forehead, and a certain arch of the nostril ·that
makes her appear rather haughty, whether she will or not.
With Hareton the resemblance is carried farther: it is singular at all times, *then* it was particularly striking; because his senses were alert, and his mental faculties wakened
to unwonted activity. I suppose this resemblance disarmed
Mr. Heathcliff: he walked to the hearth in evident agitation;
but it quickly subsided as he looked at the young man: or, I

should say, altered its character; for it was there yet. He took the book from his hand, and glanced at the open page, then returned it without any observation; merely signing Catherine away: her companion lingered very little behind her, and I was about to depart also, but he bid me sit still.

"It is a poor conclusion, is it not?" he observed, having brooded a while on the scene he had just witnessed: "an absurd termination to my violent exertions? I get levers and mattocks to demolish the two houses, and train myself to be capable of working like Hercules, and when everything is ready and in my power, I find the will to lift a slate off either roof has vanished! My old enemies have not beaten me; now would be the precise time to revenge myself on their representatives: I could do it; and none could hinder me. But where is the use? I don't care for striking: I can't take the trouble to raise my hand! That sounds as if I had been labouring the whole time only to exhibit a fine trait of magnanimity. It is far from being the case: I have lost the faculty of enjoying their destruction, and I am too idle to destroy for nothing.

"Nelly, there is a strange change approaching: I'm in its shadow at present. I take so little interest in my daily life, that I hardly remember to eat and drink. Those two who have left the room are the only objects which retain a distinct material appearance to me; and that appearance causes me pain, amounting to agony. About *her* I won't speak; and I don't desire to think; but I earnestly wish she were invisible: her presence invokes only maddening sensations. *He* moves me differently: and yet if I could do it without seeming insane, I'd never see him again! You'll perhaps think me rather inclined to become so," he added, making an effort to smile, "if I try to describe the thousand forms of past associations, and ideas he awakens or embodies. But you'll not talk of what I tell you; and my mind is so eternally secluded in itself, it is tempting at last to turn it out to another.

"Five minutes ago, Hareton seemed a personification of my youth, not a human being: I felt to him in such a variety of ways, that it would have been impossible to have accosted him rationally. In the first place, his startling likeness to Catherine connected him fearfully with her. That, however, which you may suppose the most potent to arrest my ima-

gination, is actually the least: for what is not connected
with her to me? and what does not recall her? I cannot
look down to this floor, but her features are shaped on the
flags! In every cloud, in every tree—filling the air at night,
and caught by glimpses in every object by day—I am surrounded with her image! The most ordinary faces of men
and women—my own features—mock me with a resemblance.
The entire world is a dreadful collection of memoranda that
she did exist, and that I have lost her! Well, Hareton's
aspect was the ghost of my immortal love; of my wild endeavours to hold my right; my degradation, my pride, my
happiness, and my anguish—

"But it is frenzy to repeat these thoughts to you: only it
will let you know, why, with a reluctance to be always alone,
his society is no benefit; rather an aggravation of the constant torment I suffer: and it partly contributes to render
me regardless how he and his cousin go on together. I can
give them no attention, any more."

"But what do you mean by a *change*, Mr. Heathcliff?"
I said, alarmed at his manner: though he was neither in
danger of losing his senses, nor dying, according to my judgment: he was quite strong and healthy; and, as to his reason, from childhood he had a delight in dwelling on dark
things, and entertaining odd fancies. He might have had a
monomania on the subject of his departed idol; but on every
other point his wits were as sound as mine.

"I shall not know that till it comes," he said, "I'm only
half conscious of it now."

"You have no feeling of illness, have you?" I asked.

"No, Nelly, I have not," he answered.

"Then you are not afraid of death?" I pursued.

"Afraid? No!" he replied. "I have neither a fear nor
a presentiment, nor a hope of death. Why should I? With
my hard constitution and temperate mode of living, and un-
perilous occupations, I ought to, and probably *shall*, remain
above ground till there is scarcely a black hair on my head.
And yet I cannot continue in this condition! I have to
remind myself to breathe—almost to remind my heart to
beat! And it is like bending back a stiff spring; it is by
compulsion that I do the slightest act not prompted by one
thought; and by compulsion that I notice anything alive or
dead, which is not associated with one universal idea. I

have a single wish, and my whole being and faculties are yearning to attain it. They have yearned towards it so long, and so unwaveringly, that I'm convinced it *will* be reached —and *soon*—because it has devoured my existence: I am swallowed up in the anticipation of its fulfilment. My confessions have not relieved me; but they may account for some otherwise unaccountable phases of humour which I show. O, God! It is a long fight, I wish it were over!"

He began to pace the room, muttering terrible things to himself, till I was inclined to believe, as he said Joseph did, that conscience had turned his heart to an earthly hell. I wondered greatly how it would end. Though he seldom before had revealed this state of mind, even by looks, it was his habitual mood, I had no doubt: he asserted it himself; but not a soul, from his general bearing, would have conjectured the fact. You did not when you saw him, Mr. Lockwood: and at the period of which I speak, he was just the same as then; only fonder of continued solitude, and perhaps still more laconic in company.

CHAPTER XXXIV.

FOR some days after that evening, Mr. Heathcliff shunned meeting us at meals; yet he would not consent, formally, to exclude Hareton and Cathy. He had an aversion to yielding so completely to his feelings, choosing rather to absent himself; and eating once in twenty-four hours seemed sufficient sustenance for him.

One night, after the family were in bed, I heard him go down stairs, and out at the front door. I did not hear him re-enter, and in the morning I found he was still away. We were in April then: the weather was sweet and warm, the grass as green as showers and sun could make it, and the two dwarf apple trees near the southern wall in full bloom. After breakfast, Catherine insisted on my bringing a chair and sitting with my work under the fir trees at the end of the house; and she beguiled Hareton, who had perfectly recovered from his accident, to dig and arrange her little garden, which was shifted to that corner by the influence of Joseph's complaints. I was comfortably revelling in the spring fragrance around, and the beautiful soft blue overhead, when my young lady, who had run down near the gate to procure some primrose roots for a border, returned only half laden, and informed us that Mr. Heathcliff was coming in. "And he spoke to me," she added, with a perplexed countenance.

"What did he say?" asked Hareton.

"He told me to begone as fast as I could," she answered. "But he looked so different from his usual look that I stopped a moment to stare at him."

"How?" he inquired.

"Why, almost bright and cheerful. No, *almost* nothing —*very much* excited, and wild and glad!" she replied.

"Night-walking amuses him, then," I remarked, affecting a careless manner: in reality, as surprised as she was, and anxious to ascertain the truth of her statement; for to see the master looking glad would not be an every-day spectacle. I framed an excuse to go in. Heathcliff stood at the open door; he was pale, and he trembled: yet, certainly, he had a strange joyful glitter in his eyes, that altered the aspect of his whole face.

"Will you have some breakfast?" I said. "You must be hungry, rambling about all night!" I wanted to discover where he had been, but I did not like to ask directly.

"No, I'm not hungry," he answered, averting his head, and speaking rather contemptuously, as if he guessed I was trying to divine the occasion of his good humour.

I felt perplexed: I didn't know whether it were not a proper opportunity to offer a bit of admonition.

"I don't think it right to wander out of doors," I observed, "instead of being in bed: it is not wise, at any rate, this moist season. I dare say you'll catch a bad cold, or a fever: you have something the matter with you now!"

"Nothing but what I can bear," he replied; "and with the greatest pleasure, provided you'll leave me alone: get in, and don't annoy me."

I obeyed; and, in passing, I noticed he breathed as fast as a cat.

"Yes!" I reflected to myself, "we shall have a fit of illness. I cannot conceive what he has been doing."

That noon he sat down to dinner with us, and received a heaped-up plate from my hands, as if he intended to make amends for previous fasting.

" I've neither cold nor fever, Nelly," he remarked, in allusion to my morning's speech; " and I'm ready to do justice to the food you give me."

He took his knife and fork, and was going to commence eating, when the inclination appeared to become suddenly extinct. He laid them on the table, looked eagerly towards the window, then rose and went out. We saw him walking to and fro in the garden while we concluded our meal, and Earnshaw said he'd go and ask why he would not dine : he thought we had grieved him some way.

" Well, is he coming ?" cried Catherine, when her cousin returned.

" Nay," he answered; " but he's not angry : he seemed rarely pleased indeed; only I made him impatient by speaking to him twice; and then he bid me be off to you: he wondered how I could want the company of anybody else."

I set his plate to keep warm on the fender; and after an hour or two he re-entered, when the room was clear, in no degree calmer : the same unnatural—it was unnatural—appearance of joy under his black brows; the same bloodless hue, and his teeth visible, now and then, in a kind of smile; his frame shivering, not as one shivers with chill or weakness, but as a tight-stretched cord vibrates—a strong thrilling, rather than trembling.

I will ask what is the matter, I thought; or who should? And I exclaimed—

" Have you heard any good news, Mr. Heathcliff? You look uncommonly animated."

" Where should good news come from to me?" he said. " I'm animated with hunger; and, seemingly, I must not eat."

" Your dinner is here," I returned; " why won't you get it ?"

" I don't want it now," he muttered, hastily : " I'll wait till supper. And, Nelly, once for all, let me beg you to warn Hareton and the other away from me. I wish to be troubled by nobody : I wish to have this place to myself."

" Is there some new reason for this banishment?" I

inquired. " Tell me why you are so queer, Mr. Heathcliff? Where were you last night? I'm not putting the question through idle curiosity, but—"

" You are putting the question through very idle curiosity," he interrupted, with a laugh. " Yet, I'll answer it. Last night, I was on the threshold of hell. To-day, I am within sight of my heaven. I have my eyes on it: hardly three feet to sever me! And now you'd better go. You'll neither see nor hear anything to frighten you, if you refrain from prying."

Having swept the hearth and wiped the table, I departed; more perplexed than ever.

He did not quit the house again that afternoon, and no one intruded on his solitude; till, at eight o'clock, I deemed it proper, though unsummoned, to carry a candle and his supper to him. He was leaning against the ledge of an open lattice, but not looking out: his face was turned to the interior gloom. The fire had smouldered to ashes; the room was filled with the damp, mild air of the cloudy evening; and so still, that not only the murmur of the beck down Gimmerton was distinguishable, but its ripples and its gurgling over the pebbles, or through the large stones which it could not cover. I uttered an ejaculation of discontent at seeing the dismal grate, and commenced shutting the casements, one after another, till I came to his.

" Must I close this?" I asked, in order to rouse him; for he would not stir.

The light flashed on his features, as I spoke. Oh, Mr. Lockwood, I cannot express what a terrible start I got, by the momentary view! Those deep black eyes! That smile, and ghastly paleness! It appeared to me, not Mr. Heathcliff, but a goblin; and, in my terror, I let the candle bend towards the wall, and it left me in darkness.

" Yes, close it," he replied, in his familiar voice. " There, that is pure awkwardness! Why did you hold the candle horizontally? Be quick, and bring another."

I hurried out in a foolish state of dread, and said to Joseph—

" The master wishes you to take him a light, and ro kindle the fire." For I dare not go in myself again just then.

Joseph rattled some fire into the shovel, and went: but

he brought it back immediately, with the supper-tray in his other hand, explaining that Mr. Heathcliff was going to bed, and he wanted nothing to eat till morning. We heard him mount the stairs directly; he did not proceed to his ordinary chamber, but turned into that with the panelled bed: its window, as I mentioned before, is wide enough for anybody to get through; and it struck me that he plotted another midnight excursion, of which he had rather we had no suspicion.

"Is he a ghoul or a vampire?" I mused. I had read of such hideous, incarnate demons. And then I set myself to reflect how I had tended him in infancy, and watched him grow to youth, and followed him almost through his whole course; and what absurd nonsense it was to yield to that sense of horror. " But where did he come from, the little dark thing, harboured by a good man to his bane?" muttered superstition, as I dozed into unconsciousness. And I began, half dreaming, to weary myself with imagining some fit parentage for him; and, repeating my waking meditations, I tracked his existence over again, with grim variations; at last, picturing his death and funeral: of which, all I can remember is, being exceedingly vexed at having the task of dictating an inscription for his monument, and consulting the sexton about it; and, as he had no surname, and we could not tell his age, we were obliged to content ourselves with the single word, ' Heathcliff.' That came true: we were. If you enter the kirkyard, you'll read on his headstone, only that, and the date of his death.

Dawn restored me to common sense. I rose, and went into the garden, as soon as I could see, to ascertain if there were any footmarks under his window. There were none. " He has stayed at home," I thought, " and he'll be all right to-day!" I prepared breakfast for the household, as was my usual custom, but told Hareton and Catherine to get theirs ere the master came down; for he lay late. They preferred taking it out of doors, under the trees, and I set a little table to accommodate them.

On my re-entrance, I found Mr. Heathcliff below. He and Joseph were conversing about some farming business; he gave clear minute directions concerning the matter discussed, but he spoke rapidly and turned his head continually aside, and had the same excited expression, even more

U

exaggerated. When Joseph quitted the room he took his seat in the place he generally chose, and I put a basin of coffee before him. He drew it nearer, and then rested his arms on the table, and looked at the opposite wall, as I supposed, surveying one particular portion, up and down, with glittering, restless eyes, and with such eager interest that he stopped breathing during half a minute together.

"Come now," I exclaimed, pushing some bread against his hand, "eat and drink that, while it is hot: it has been waiting near an hour."

He didn't notice me, and yet he smiled. I'd rather have seen him gnash his teeth than smile so.

"Mr. Heathcliff! master!" I cried, "don't, for God's sake, stare as if you saw an unearthly vision."

"Don't, for God's sake, shout so loud," he replied. "Turn round, and tell me, are we by ourselves?"

"Of course," was my answer; "of course we are."

Still, I involuntarily obeyed him, as if I was not quite sure. With a sweep of his hand he cleared a vacant space in front among the breakfast things, and leant forward to gaze more at his ease.

Now, I perceived he was not looking at the wall; for when I regarded him alone, it seemed exactly that he gazed at something within two yards distance. And whatever it was, it communicated, apparently, both pleasure and pain in exquisite extremes: at least the anguished yet raptured expression of his countenance suggested that idea. The fancied object was not fixed: either his eyes pursued it with unwearied vigilance, and, even in speaking to me, were never weaned away. I vainly reminded him of his protracted abstinence from food: if he stirred to touch anything in compliance with my entreaties, if he stretched his hand out to get a piece of bread, his fingers clenched before they reached it, and remained on the table, forgetful of their aim.

I sat a model of patience, trying to attract his absorbed attention from its engrossing speculation; till he grew irritable, and got up, asking why I would not allow him to have his own time in taking his meals? and saying that on the next occasion, I needn't wait; I might set the things down and go. Having uttered these words he left the house, slowly sauntered down the garden path, and disappeared through the gate.

The hours crept anxiously by : another evening came. I did not retire to rest till late, and when I did, I could not sleep. He returned after midnight, and, instead of going to bed, shut himself into the room beneath. I listened, and tossed about, and, finally, dressed and descended. It was too irksome to lie there, harassing my brain with a hundred idle misgivings.

I distinguished Mr. Heathcliff's step, restlessly measuring the floor, and he frequently broke the silence by a deep inspiration, resembling a groan. He muttered detached words also; the only one I could catch was the name of Catherine, coupled with some wild term of endearment or suffering; and spoken as one would speak to a person present: low and earnest, and wrung from the depth of his soul. I had not courage to walk straight into the apartment; but I desired to divert him from his reverie, and therefore fell foul of the kitchen fire, stirred it, and began to scrape the cinders. It drew him forth sooner than I expected. He opened the door immediately, and said—

" Nelly, come here—is it morning ? Come in with your light."

" It is striking four," I answered. " You want a candle to take up stairs : you might have lit one at this fire."

" No, I don't wish to go up stairs," he said. " Come in, and kindle *me* a fire, and do anything there is to do about the room."

" I must blow the coals red first before I can carry any," I replied, getting a chair and the bellows.

He roamed to and fro, meantime, in a state approaching distraction ; his heavy sighs succeeding each other so thick as to leave no space for common breathing between.

" When day breaks I'll send for Green," he said; " I wish to make some legal inquiries of him while I can bestow a thought on those matters, and while I can act calmly. I have not written my will yet ; and how to leave my property I cannot determine. I wish I could annihilate it from the face of the earth."

" I would not talk so, Mr. Heathcliff," I interposed. " Let your will be a while : you'll be spared to repent of your many injustices yet ! I never expected that your nerves would be disordered : they are, at present, marvellously so, however ; and almost entirely through your own

U 2

fault. The way you've passed these three last days might knock up a Titan. Do take some food, and some repose. You need only look at yourself in a glass to see how you require both. Your cheeks are hollow, and your eyes bloodshot, like a person starving with hunger and going blind with loss of sleep."

"It is not my fault, that I cannot eat or rest," he replied. "I assure you it is through no settled designs. I'll do both, as soon as I possibly can. But you might as well bid a man struggling in the water rest within arm's length of the shore! I must reach it first, and then I'll rest. Well, never mind, Mr. Green: as to repenting of my injustices, I've done no injustice, and I repent of nothing. I'm too happy; and yet I'm not happy enough. My soul's bliss kills my body, but does not satisfy itself."

"Happy, master?" I cried. "Strange happiness! If you would hear me without being angry, I might offer some advice that would make you happier."

"What is that?" he asked. "Give it."

"You are aware, Mr. Heathcliff," I said, "that from the time you were thirteen years old, you have lived a selfish, unchristian life; and probably hardly had a bible in your hands during all that period. You must have forgotten the contents of the book, and you may not have space to search it now. Could it be hurtful to send for some one — some minister of any denomination, it does not matter which—to explain it, and show you how very far you have erred from its precepts; and how unfit you will be for its heaven, unless a change takes place before you die?"

"I'm rather obliged than angry, Nelly," he said, "for you remind me of the manner in which I desire to be buried. It is to be carried to the churchyard in the evening. You and Hareton may, if you please, accompany me: and mind, particularly, to notice that the sexton obeys my directions concerning the two coffins! No minister need come; nor need anything be said over me.—I tell you, I have nearly attained *my* heaven; and that of others is altogether unvalued and uncoveted by me."

"And supposing you persevered in your obstinate fast, and died by that means, and they refused to bury you in the precincts of the Kirk?" I said, shocked at his godless indifference. "How would you like it?"

"They won't do that," he replied: "if they did, you must have me removed secretly; and if you neglect it, you shall prove, practically, that the dead are not annihilated!"

As soon as he heard the other members of the family stirring he retired to his den, and I breathed freer. But in the afternoon, while Joseph and Hareton were at their work, he came into the kitchen again, and with a wild look, bid me come and sit in the house: he wanted somebody with him. I declined; telling him plainly that his strange talk and manner frightened me, and I had neither the nerve nor the will to be his companion alone.

"I believe you think me a fiend," he said, with his dismal laugh: "something too horrible to live under a decent roof." Then turning to Catherine, who was there, and who drew behind me at his approach, he added, half sneeringly — "Will *you* come, chuck? I'll not hurt you. No! to you, I've made myself worse than the devil. Well, there is *one* who won't shrink from my company! By God! she's relentless. Oh, damn it! It's unutterably too much for flesh and blood to bear—even mine."

He solicited the society of no one more. At dusk, he went into his chamber. Through the whole night, and far into the morning, we heard him groaning and murmuring to himself. Hareton was anxious to enter; but I bid him fetch Mr. Kenneth, and he should go in and see him. When he came, and I requested admittance and tried to open the door, I found it locked; and Heathcliff bid us be damned. He was better, and would be left alone; so the doctor went away.

The following evening was very wet: indeed it poured down till day-dawn; and, as I took my morning walk round the house, I observed the master's window swinging open, and the rain driving straight in. He cannot be in bed, I thought: those showers would drench him through. He must either be up or out. But I'll make no more ado, I'll go boldly and look."

Having succeeded in obtaining entrance with another key, I ran to unclose the panels, for the chamber was vacant; quickly pushing them aside, I peeped in. Mr. Heathcliff was there—laid on his back. His eyes met mine so keen and fierce, I started; and then he seemed to smile. I could not think him dead: but his face and throat were washed with rain; the bed-clothes dripped, and he was perfectly still. The lattice, flapping to and fro, had grazed one hand that rested on the sill; no blood trickled from the broken skin, and when I put my fingers to it, I could doubt no more: he was dead and stark!

I hasped the window; I combed his black long hair from his forehead; I tried to close his eyes: to extinguish, if possible, that frightful, life-like gaze of exultation, before any one else beheld it. They would not shut: they seemed to sneer at my attempts; and his parted lips and sharp, white teeth sneered too! Taken with another fit of cowardice, I cried out for Joseph. Joseph shuffled up and made a noise, but resolutely refused to meddle with him.

"Th' divil's harried off his soul," he cried, "and he may hev his carcass into t' bargin, for aught I care! Ech! what a wicked un he looks girnning at death!" and the old sinner grinned in mockery. I thought he intended to cut a caper round the bed; but suddenly composing himself, he fell on his knees, and raised his hands, and returned thanks that the lawful master and the ancient stock were restored to their rights.

I felt stunned by the awful event; and my memory unavoidably recurred to former times with a sort of oppressive sadness. But poor Hareton, the most wronged, was the only one who really suffered much. He sat by the corpse all night, weeping in bitter earnest. He pressed its hand, and kissed the sarcastic, savage face, that every one else shrank from contemplating; and bemoaned him with that strong grief which springs naturally from a generous heart, though it be tough as tempered steel.

Mr. Kenneth was perplexed to pronounce of what disorder the master died. I concealed the fact of his having swallowed nothing for four days, fearing it might lead to trouble; and then, I am persuaded, he did not abstain on purpose: it was the consequence of his strange illness, not the cause.

We buried him, to the scandal of the whole neighbourhood, as he wished. Earnshaw and I, the sexton, and six men to carry the coffin, comprehended the whole attendance. The six men departed when they had let it down into the grave: we stayed to see it covered. Hareton, with a streaming face, dug green sods, and laid them over the brown mould himself: at present it is as smooth and verdant as its companion mounds—and I hope its tenant sleeps as soundly. But the country folks, if you asked them, would swear on the bible that he *walks:* there are those who speak to having met him near the church, and on the moor, and even within this house. Idle tales, you'll say, and so say I. Yet that old man by the kitchen fire affirms he has seen two on 'em, looking out of his chamber window, on every rainy night since his death :—and an odd thing happened to me about a month ago. I was going to the Grange one evening —a dark evening, threatening thunder—and, just at the turn of the Heights, I encountered a little boy with a sheep and two lambs before him; he was crying terribly, and I supposed the lambs were skittish, and would not be guided.

" What is the matter, my little man?" I asked.

" There's Heathcliff and a woman, yonder, under t' Nab," he blubbered, " un' I darnut pass 'em."

I saw nothing; but neither the sheep nor he would go on; so I bid him take the road lower down. He probably raised the phantoms from thinking, as he traversed the moors alone, on the nonsense he had heard his parents and companions repeat. Yet still, I don't like being out in the dark, now; and I don't like being left by myself in this grim house: I cannot help it; I shall be glad when they leave it, and shift to the Grange.

" They are going to the Grange, then," I said.

" Yes," answered Mrs. Dean, " as soon as they are married, and that will be on New Year's day."

" And who will live here then?"

" Why Joseph will take care of the house, and, perhaps, a lad to keep him company. They will live in the kitchen, and the rest will be shut up."

" For the use of such ghosts as choose to inhabit it," I observed.

" No, Mr. Lockwood," said Nelly, shaking her head. " I believe the dead are at peace : but it is not right to speak of them with levity."

At that moment the garden gate swung to; the ramblers were returning.

" *They* are afraid of nothing," I grumbled, watching their approach through the window. " Together, they would brave Satan and all his legions."

As they stepped on to the door-stones, and halted to take

a last look at the moon—or, more correctly, at each other by her light—I felt irresistibly impelled to escape them again; and, pressing a remembrance into the hand of Mrs. Dean, and disregarding her expostulations at my rudeness, I vanished through the kitchen as they opened the house-door: and so should have confirmed Joseph in his opinion of his fellow-servant's gay indiscretions, had he not fortunately recognised me for a respectable character by the sweet ring of a sovereign at his feet.

My walk home was lengthened by a diversion in the direction of the kirk. When beneath its walls, I perceived decay had made progress, even in seven months: many a window showed black gaps deprived of glass; and slates jutted off, here and there, beyond the right line of the roof, to be gradually worked off in coming autumn storms.

I sought, and soon discovered, the three head-stones on the slope next the moor: the middle one, grey, and half buried in heath; Edgar Linton's only harmonized by the turf and moss creeping up its foot; Heathcliff's still bare.

I lingered round them, under that benign sky: watched the moths fluttering among the heath and hare-bells, listened to the soft wind breathing through the grass, and wondered how any one could ever imagine unquiet slumbers for the sleepers in that quiet earth.

THE END OF WUTHERING HEIGHTS.

AGNES GREY,

BY ACTON BELL.

AGNES GREY.

CHAPTER I.

THE PARSONAGE.

ALL true histories contain instruction; though, in some, the treasure may be hard to find, and when found, so trivial in quantity, that the dry, shrivelled kernel scarcely compensates for the trouble of cracking the nut. Whether this be the case with my history or not, I am hardly competent to judge. I sometimes think it might prove useful to some, and entertaining to others: but the world may judge for itself. Shielded by my own obscurity, and by the lapse of years, and a few fictitious names, I do not fear to venture; and will candidly lay before the public what I would not disclose to the most intimate friend.

My father was a clergyman of the north of England, who was deservedly respected by all who knew him; and, in his younger days, lived pretty comfortably on the joint income of a small incumbency and a snug little property of his own. My mother, who married him against the wishes of her friends, was a squire's daughter, and a woman of spirit. In vain it was represented to her, that if she became the poor parson's wife, she must relinquish her carriage and her lady's-maid, and all the luxuries and elegancies of affluence; which to her were little less than the necessaries of life. A carriage and a lady's-maid were great conveniences; but, thank

Heaven, she had feet to carry her, and hands to minister to her own necessities. An elegant house and spacious grounds were not to be despised; but she would rather live in a cottage with Richard Grey, than in a palace with any other man in the world.

Finding arguments of no avail, her father, at length, told the lovers they might marry if they pleased; but, in so doing, his daughter would forfeit every fraction of her fortune. He expected this would cool the ardour of both; but he was mistaken. My father knew too well my mother's superior worth, not to be sensible that she was a valuable fortune in herself; and if she would but consent to embellish his humble hearth, he should be happy to take her on any terms; while she, on her part, would rather labour with her own hands than be divided from the man she loved, whose happiness it would be her joy to make, and who was already one with her in heart and soul. So her fortune went to swell the purse of a wiser sister, who had married a rich nabob; and she, to the wonder and compassionate regret of all who knew her, went to bury herself in the homely village parsonage among the hills of ——. And yet, in spite of all this, and in spite of my mother's high spirit and my father's whims, I believe you might search all England through, and fail to find a happier couple.

Of six children, my sister Mary and myself were the only two that survived the perils of infancy and early childhood. I, being the younger by five or six years, was always regarded as the *child*, and the pet of the family: father, mother, and sister, all combined to spoil me—not by foolish indulgence, to render me fractious and ungovernable, but by ceaseless kindness, to make me too helpless and dependent—too unfit for buffeting with the cares and turmoils of life.

Mary and I were brought up in the strictest seclusion. My mother, being at once highly accomplished, well-informed, and fond of employment, took the whole charge of our education on herself, with the exception of Latin—which my father undertook to teach us—so that we never even went to school; and, as there was no society in the neighbourhood, our only intercourse with the world consisted in a stately tea-party, now and then, with the principal farmers and tradespeople of the vicinity (just to avoid being stigmatized as too proud to consort with our neighbours), and an annual visit to our paternal grandfather's; where himself, our kind grandmamma, a maiden aunt, and two or three elderly ladies and gentlemen, were the only persons we ever saw. Sometimes our mother would amuse us with stories and anecdotes of her younger days, which, while they entertained us amazingly, frequently awoke—in *me*, at least—a secret wish to see a little more of the world.

I thought she must have been very happy : but she never seemed to regret past times. My father, however, whose temper was neither tranquil nor cheerful by nature, often unduly vexed himself with thinking of the sacrifices his dear wife had made for him; and troubled his head with revolving endless schemes for the augmentation of his little fortune, for her sake and ours. In vain my mother assured him she was quite satisfied, and if he would but lay by a little for the children, we should all have plenty, both for time present and to come : but saving was not my father's forte. He would not run in debt (at least, my mother took good care he should not), but while he had money he must spend it : he liked to see his house comfortable, and his wife and daughters well clothed, and well attended; and besides, he was charitably disposed, and liked to give to the poor, according to his means: or, as some might think, beyond them.

At length, however, a kind friend suggested to him a means of doubling his private property at one stroke; and further increasing it, hereafter, to an untold amount. This friend was a merchant, a man of enterprising spirit and undoubted talent, who was somewhat straitened in his mercantile pursuits for want of capital; but generously proposed to give my father a fair share of his profits, if he would only entrust him with what he could spare; and he thought he might safely promise that whatever sum the latter chose to put into his hands, it should bring him in cent. per cent. The small patrimony was speedily sold, and the whole of its price was deposited in the hands of the friendly merchant; who as promptly proceeded to ship his cargo, and prepare for his voyage.

My father was delighted, so were we all, with our brightening prospects. For the present, it is true, we were reduced to the narrow income of the curacy; but my father seemed to think there was no necessity for scrupulously restricting

our expenditure to that; so, with a standing bill at Mr.
Jackson's, another at Smith's, and a third at Hobson's, we
got along even more comfortably than before: though my
mother affirmed we had better keep within bounds, for our
prospects of wealth were but precarious after all; and if my
father would only trust everything to her management, he
should never feel himself stinted: but he, for once, was incorrigible.

What happy hours Mary and I have passed, while sitting
at our work by the fire, or wandering on the heath-clad hills,
or idling under the weeping birch (the only considerable
tree in the garden), talking of future happiness to ourselves
and our parents, of what we would do, and see, and possess;
with no firmer foundation for our goodly superstructure,
than the riches that were expected to flow in upon us from
the success of the worthy merchant's speculations.   Our
father was nearly as bad as ourselves; only, that he affected
not to be so much in earnest: expressing his bright hopes
and sanguine expectations, in jests and playful sallies, that
always struck me as being exceedingly witty and pleasant.
Our mother laughed with delight to see him so hopeful and
happy: but still she feared he was setting his heart too
much upon the matter; and once, I heard her whisper as
she left the room, "God grant he be not disappointed!   I
know not how he would bear it."

Disappointed he was; and bitterly too.   It came like a
thunder-clap on us all, that the vessel which contained our
fortune had been wrecked, and gone to the bottom with all
its stores, together with several of the crew, and the unfor-
nate merchant himself.   I was grieved for him; I was
grieved for the overthrow of all our air-built castles: but,
with the elasticity of youth, I soon recovered the shock.

Though riches had charms, poverty had no terrors for an
inexperienced girl like me.   Indeed, to say the truth, there
was something exhilarating in the idea of being driven to
straits, and thrown upon our own resources.   I only wished
papa, mama, and Mary were all of the same mind as myself;
and then, instead of lamenting past calamities, we might all
cheerfully set to work to remedy them.   and the greater the
difficulties, the harder our present privations, the greater
should be our cheerfulness to endure the latter, and our
vigour to contend against the former.

Mary did not lament, but she brooded continually over the misfortune, and sank into a state of dejection from which no effort of mine could rouse her. I could not possibly bring her to regard the matter on its bright side as I did: and indeed I was so fearful of being charged with childish frivolity, or stupid insensibility, that I carefully kept most of my bright ideas and cheering notions to myself; well knowing they could not be appreciated.

My mother thought only of consoling my father, and paying our debts and retrenching our expenditure by every available means; but my father was completely overwhelmed by the calamity: health, strength, and spirits sank beneath the blow; and he never wholly recovered them. In vain my mother strove to cheer him, by appealing to his piety, to his courage, to his affection for herself and us. That very affection was his greatest torment: it was for our sakes he had so ardently longed to increase his fortune—it was our interest that had lent such brightness to his hopes, and that imparted such bitterness to his present distress. He now tormented himself with remorse at having neglected my mother's advice; which would at least, have saved him from the additional burden of debt—he vainly reproached himself for having brought her from the dignity, the ease, the luxury of her former station to toil with him through the cares and toils of poverty. It was gall and wormwood to his soul to see that splendid, highly accomplished woman, once so courted and admired, transformed into an active managing housewife, with hands and head continually occupied with household labours and household economy. The very willingness with which she performed these duties, the cheerfulness with which she bore her reverses, and the kindness which withheld her from imputing the smallest blame to him, were all perverted by this ingenious self-tormentor, into further aggravations of his sufferings. And thus the mind preyed upon the body, and disordered the system of the nerves, and they in turn increased the troubles of the mind, till by action and reaction his health was seriously impaired; and not one of us could convince him that the aspect of our affairs was not half so gloomy, so utterly hopeless, as his morbid imagination represented it to be.

The useful pony phaeton was sold, together with the stout

well-fed pony—the old favourite that we had fully determined should end its days in peace, and never pass from our hands; the little coach-house and stable were let; the servant boy, and the more efficient (being the more expensive) of the two maid-servants were dismissed. Our clothes were mended, turned, and darned to the utmost verge of decency; our food, always plain, was now simplified to an unprecedented degree —except my father's favourite dishes; our coals and candles were painfully economized—the pair of candles reduced to one, and that most sparingly used; the coals carefully hus-banded in the half empty grate: especially when my father was out on his parish duties, or confined to bed through ill-ness—then we sat with our feet on the fender, scraping the perishing embers together from time to time, and occasionally adding a slight scattering of the dust and fragments of coal, just to keep them alive. As for our carpets, they in time, were worn threadbare, and patched and darned even to a greater extent than our garments. To save the expense of a gardener, Mary and I undertook to keep the garden in order; and all the cooking and household work that could not easily be managed by one servant girl, was done by my mother and sister, with a little occasional help from me: only a little, because, though a woman in my own estimation, I was still a child in theirs; and my mother, like most active, managing women, was not gifted with very active daughters: for this reason—that being so clever and diligent herself, she was never tempted to trust her affairs to a deputy, but on the contrary, was willing to act and think for others as well as for number one; and whatever was the business in hand, she was apt to think that no one could do it so well as herself: so that whenever I offered to assist her, I received such an answer as—" No, love, you cannot indeed—there's nothing here you can do. Go and help your sister, or get her to take a walk with you—tell her she must not sit so much, and stay so constantly in the house as she does—she may well look thin and dejected."

" Mary, mama says I'm to help you; or get you to take a walk with me: she says you may well look thin and dejected, if you sit so constantly in the house."

" Help me you cannot, Agnes; and I cannot go out with you—I have far too much to do."

" Then let me help you."

" You cannot, indeed, dear child. Go and practise your music, or play with the kitten."

There was always plenty of sewing on hand; but I had not been taught to cut out a single garment, and except plain hemming and seaming, there was little I could do, even in that line; for they both asserted, that it was far easier to do the work themselves than to prepare it for me : and, besides, they liked better to see me prosecuting my studies, or amusing myself—it was time enough for me to sit bending over my work, like a grave matron, when my favorite little pussy was become a steady old cat. Under such circumstances, although I was not many degrees more useful than the kitten, my idleness was not entirely without excuse.

Through all our troubles, I never but once heard my mother complain of our want of money. As summer was coming on she observed to Mary and me, " What a desirable thing it would be for your papa to spend a few weeks at a watering place. I am convinced the sea air and the change of scene would be of incalculable service to him. But then you see there 's no money," she added with a sigh. We both wished exceedingly that the thing might be done, and lamented greatly that it could not. " Well, well!" said she, " it 's of no use complaining. Possibly something might be done to further the project after all. Mary, you are a beautiful drawer. What do you say to doing a few more pictures in your best style, and getting them framed, with the water-coloured drawings you have already done, and trying to dispose of them to some liberal picture-dealer, who has the sense to discern their merits ?"

" Mama, I should be delighted if you think they *could* be sold ; and for anything worth while."

" It 's worth while trying, however, my dear : do you procure the drawings, and I 'll endeavour to find a purchaser."

" I wish *I* could do something," said I.

" You, Agnes ! well, who knows ? You draw pretty well too : if you choose some simple piece for your subject, I dare say you will be able to produce something we shall all be proud to exhibit."

" But I have another scheme in my head, mama, and have had long, only I did not like to mention it."

" Indeed ! pray tell us what it is."

x

" I should like to be a governess."

My mother uttered an exclamation of surprise, and laughed. My sister dropped her work in astonishment, exclaiming, " *You* a governess, Agnes! What *can* you be dreaming off?"

" Well! I don't see anything so *very* extraordinary in it. I do not pretend to be able to instruct great girls; but surely I could teach little ones : and I should like it *so* much : I am so fond of children. Do let me, mama!"

" But, my love, you have not learned to take care of *yourself* yet; and young children require more judgment and experience to manage them than elder ones."

" But mama, I am above eighteen, and quite able to take care of myself, and others too. You do not know half the wisdom and prudence I possess, because I have never been tried."

Only think," said Mary, " what would you do in a house full of strangers, without me or mama to speak and act for you—with a parcel of children, besides yourself, to attend to; and no one to look to for advice ? You would not even know what clothes to put on."

" You think, because I always do as you bid me, I have no judgment of my own : but only try me—that is all I ask —and you shall see what I can do."

At that moment my father entered, and the subject of our discussion was explained to him.

" What, my little Agnes, a governess!" cried he, and, in spite of his dejection, he laughed at the idea.

" Yes, papa, don't *you* say anything against it : I should like it *so* much; and I am sure I could manage delightfully."

" But, my darling, we could not spare you." And a tear glistened in his eye as he added—" No, no! afflicted as we are, surely we are not brought to that pass yet."

" Oh, no!" said my mother. " There is no necessity, whatever, for such a step; it is merely a whim of her own. So you must hold your tongue, you naughty girl; for though you are so ready to leave *us*, you know very well we cannot part with *you*."

I was silenced for that day, and for many succeeding ones; but still I did not wholly relinquish my darling scheme. Mary got her drawing materials, and steadily set to work. I got mine too; but while I drew, I thought of other things.

How delightful it would be to be a governess! To go out into the world; to enter upon a new life; to act for myself; to exercise my unused faculties; to try my unknown powers; to earn my own maintenance, and something to comfort and help my father, mother, and sister, besides exonerating them from the provision of my food and clothing; to show papa what his little Agnes could do; to convince mama and Mary that I was not quite the helpless, thoughtless being they supposed. And then, how charming to be entrusted with the care and education of children! Whatever others said, I felt I was fully competent to the task: the clear remembrance of my own thoughts in early childhood would be a surer guide than the instructions of the most mature adviser. I had but to turn from my little pupils to myself at their age, and I should know, at once, how to win their confidence and affections: how to waken the contrition of the erring; how to embolden the timid, and console the afflicted; how to make Virtue practicable, Instruction desirable, and Religion lovely and comprehensible.

> "—— Delightful task!
> To teach the young idea how to shoot!"

To train the tender plants, and watch their buds unfolding day by day!

Influenced by so many inducements, I determined still to persevere; though the fear of displeasing my mother, or distressing my father's feelings, prevented me from resuming the subject for several days. At length, again, I mentioned it to my mother in private; and, with some difficulty, got her to promise to assist me with her endeavours. My father's reluctant consent was next obtained, and then, though Mary still sighed her disapproval, my dear, kind mother began to look out for a situation for me. She wrote to my father's relations, and consulted the newspaper advertisements—her own relations she had long dropped all communication with: a formal interchange of occasional letters was all she had ever had since her marriage, and she would not at any time have applied to them in a case of this nature. But so long and so entire had been my parents' seclusion from the world, that many weeks elapsed before a suitable situation could be procured. At last, to my great joy, it was decreed that I

x 2

should take charge of the young family of a certain Mrs.
Bloomfield; whom my kind, prim aunt Grey had known in
her youth, and asserted to be a very nice woman. Her husband was a retired tradesman, who had realized a very comfortable fortune; but could not be prevailed upon to give a
greater salary than twenty-five pounds to the instructress of
his children. I, however, was glad to accept this, rather
than refuse the situation—which my parents were inclined to
think the better plan.

But some weeks more were yet to be devoted to preparation. How long, how tedious those weeks appeared to me!
Yet they were happy ones in the main—full of bright hopes,
and ardent expectations. With what peculiar pleasure I
assisted at the making of my new clothes, and, subsequently,
the packing of my trunks! But there was a feeling of bitterness mingling with the latter occupation too; and when
it was done—when all was ready for my departure on the
morrow, and the last night at home approached—a sudden
anguish seemed to swell my heart. My dear friends looked
so sad, and spoke so very kindly, that I could scarcely keep
my eyes from overflowing: but I still affected to be gay.
I had taken my last ramble with Mary on the moors, my
last walk in the garden, and round the house; I had fed,
with her, our pet pigeons for the last time—the pretty
creatures that we had tamed to peck their food from our
hands: I had given a farewell stroke to all their silky backs
as they crowded in my lap. I had tenderly kissed my own
peculiar favourites, the pair of snow-white fantails; I had
played my last tune on the old familiar piano, and sung my
last song to papa: not the last, I hoped, but the last for,
what appeared to me, a very long time. And, perhaps, when
I did these things again, it would be with different feelings:
circumstances might be changed, and this house might never
be my settled home again. My dear little friend, the kitten,
would certainly be changed: she was already growing a fine
cat; and when I returned, even for a hasty visit at Christmas, would, most likely, have forgotten both her playmate
and her merry pranks. I had romped with her for the last
time, and when I stroked her soft bright fur, while she lay
purring herself to sleep in my lap, it was with a feeling of
sadness I could not easily disguise. Then, at bed-time,
when I retired with Mary to our quiet little chamber, where

already my drawers were cleared out and my share of the
bookcase was empty—and where, hereafter, she would have
to sleep alone, in dreary solitude, as she expressed it—my
heart sank more than ever: I felt as if I had been selfish
and wrong to persist in leaving her; and when I knelt once
more beside our little bed, I prayed for a blessing on her and
on my parents, more fervently than ever I had done before.
To conceal my emotion, I buried my face in my hands, and
they were presently bathed in tears. I perceived, on rising,
that she had been crying too: but neither of us spoke; and
in silence we betook ourselves to our repose, creeping more
closely together, from the consciousness that we were to
part so soon.

But the morning brought a renewal of hope and spirits.
I was to depart early; that the conveyance which took me
(a gig, hired from Mr. Smith, the draper, grocer, and tea-
dealer of the village), might return the same day. I rose,
washed, dressed, swallowed a hasty breakfast, received the
fond embraces of my father, mother, and sister, kissed the
cat,—to the great scandal of Sally, the maid,—shook hands
with her, mounted the gig, drew my veil over my face, and
then, but not till then, burst into a flood of tears. The gig
rolled on; I looked back; my dear mother and sister were
still standing at the door, looking after me, and waving their
adieux. I returned their salute, and prayed God to bless
them from my heart: we descended the hill, and I could see
them no more.

" It's a coldish mornin' for you, Miss Agnes," observed
Smith; " and a darksome un too; but we's, happen, get to
yon' spot afore there come much rain to signify."

" Yes, I hope so," replied I, as calmly as I could.

" It's comed a good sup last night too."

" Yes."

" But this cold wind will, happen, keep it off."

" Perhaps it will."

Here ended our colloquy. We crossed the valley, and
began to ascend the opposite hill. As we were toiling up,
I looked back again: there was the village spire, and the
old grey parsonage beyond it, basking in a slanting beam of
sunshine—it was but a sickly ray, but the village and surrounding hills were all in sombre shade, and I hailed the
wandering beam as a propitious omen to my home. With

clasped hands, I fervently implored a blessing on its inhabitants, and hastily turned away; for I saw the sunshine
was departing; and I carefully avoided another glance, lest
I should see it in gloomy shadow, like the rest of the landscape.

CHAPTER II.

FIRST LESSONS IN THE ART OF INSTRUCTION.

As we drove along, my spirits revived again, and I turned,
with pleasure, to the contemplation of the new life upon
which I was entering. But, though it was not far past the
middle of September, the heavy clouds and strong north-
easterly wind combined to render the day extremely cold
and dreary; and the journey seemed a very long one, for,
as Smith observed, the roads were " very heavy"; and, certainly, his horse was very heavy too: it crawled up the
hills, and crept down them, and only condescended to shake
its sides in a trot where the road was at a dead level or a
very gentle slope, which was rarely the case in those rugged
regions; so that it was nearly one o'clock before we reached
the place of our destination. Yet, after all, when we entered the lofty iron gateway, when we drove softly up the
smooth, well-rolled carriage road, with the green lawn on
each side, studded with young trees, and approached the
new but stately mansion of Wellwood, rising above its
mushroom poplar groves, my heart failed me, and I wished
it were a mile or two farther off. For the first time in my
life, I must stand alone: there was no retreating now. I
must enter that house, and introduce myself among its
strange inhabitants. But how was it to be done? True, I
was near nineteen; but, thanks to my retired life and the
protecting care of my mother and sister, I well knew that
many a girl of fifteen, or under, was gifted with a more
womanly address, and greater ease and self-possession, than
I was. Yet, if Mrs. Bloomfield were a kind, motherly
woman, I might do very well after all; and the children, of

course, I should soon be at ease with them—and Mr. Bloomfield, I hoped, I should have but little to do with.

"Be calm, be calm, whatever happens," I said within
myself; and truly I kept this resolution so well, and was so
fully occupied in steadying my nerves and stilling the rebellious flutter of my heart, that when I was admitted into the
hall, and ushered into the presence of Mrs. Bloomfield, I
almost forgot to answer her polite salutation; and it afterwards struck me, that the little I did say was spoken in the
tone of one half dead or half asleep. The lady, too, was
somewhat chilly in her manner, as I discovered when I had
time to reflect. She was a tall, spare, stately woman, with
thick black hair, cold grey eyes, and extremely sallow complexion.

With due politeness, however, she shewed me my bed-
room, and left me there to take a little refreshment. I was
somewhat dismayed at my appearance on looking in the
glass: the cold wind had swelled and reddened my hands,
uncurled and entangled my hair, and dyed my face of a pale
purple; add to this my collar was horridly crumpled, my
frock splashed with mud, my feet clad in stout new boots,
and as the trunks were not brought up, there was no
remedy;. so having smoothed my hair as well as I could, and
repeatedly twitched my obdurate collar, I proceeded to
clomp down the two flights of stairs, philosophising as I
went; and with some difficulty found my way into the room
where Mrs. Bloomfield awaited me.

She led me into the dining-room, where the family
luncheon had been laid out. Some beefsteaks and half cold
potatoes were set before me; and while I dined upon these,
she sat opposite, watching me (as I thought) and endeavouring to sustain something like a conversation—consisting
chiefly of a succession of commonplace remarks, expressed
with frigid formality: but this might be more my fault than
hers, for I really *could* not converse. In fact, my attention
was almost wholly absorbed in my dinner: not from raven-
ous appetite, but from distress at the toughness of the beefsteaks, and the numbness of my hands, almost palsied by
their five hours' exposure to the bitter wind. I would gladly
have eaten the potatoes and let the meat alone, but having
got a large piece of the latter on to my plate, I could not
be so impolite as to leave it; so, after many awkward and

unsuccessful attempts to cut it with the knife, or tear it with the fork, or pull it asunder between them, sensible that the awful lady was a spectator to the whole transaction, I at last desperately grasped the knife and fork in my fists, like a child of two years old, and fell to work with all the little strength I possessed. But this needed some apology—with a feeble attempt at a laugh, I said, " My hands are so be-numbed with the cold that I can scarcely handle my knife and fork."

" I dare say you would find it cold," replied she with a cool, immutable gravity that did not serve to re-assure me.

When the ceremony was concluded, she led me into the sitting-room again, where she rung and sent for the children.

" You will find them not very far advanced in their attain-ments," said she, " for I have had so little time to attend to their education myself, and we have thought them too young for a governess till now; but I think they are clever children, and very apt to learn, especially the little boy: he is, I think, the flower of the flock—a generous noble-spirited boy, one to be led, but not driven, and remarkable for always speaking the truth. He seems to scorn deception" (this was good news). " His sister Mary Ann will require watching," continued she, " but she is a very good girl upon the whole: though I wish her to be kept out of the nursery as much as possible, as she is now almost six years old, and might acquire bad habits from the nurses. I have ordered her crib to be placed in your room, and if you will be so kind as to overlook her washing and dressing, and take charge of her clothes, she need have nothing further to do with the nur-sery-maid."

I replied I was quite willing to do so; and at that moment my young pupils entered the apartment, with their two younger sisters. Master Tom Bloomfield was a well-grown boy of seven, with a somewhat wiry frame, flaxen hair, blue eyes, small turned up nose, and fair complexion. Mary Ann was a tall girl too, somewhat dark like her mother, but with a round full face and a high colour in her cheeks. The second sister was Fanny, a very pretty little girl; Mrs. Bloomfield assured me she was a remarkably gentle child, and required encouragement: she had not learned anything yet; but in a few days, she would be four years old, and then she might take her first lesson in the alphabet, and be promoted to the schoolroom. The remaining one was Harriet, a little broad, fat, merry, playful thing of scarcely two, that I coveted more than all the rest—but with her I had nothing to do.

I talked to my little pupils as well as I could, and tried to render myself agreeable; but with little success I fear, for their mother's presence kept me under an unpleasant restraint. They, however, were remarkably free from shyness. They seemed bold, lively children, and I hoped I should soon be on friendly terms with them—the little boy especially, of whom I had heard such a favourable character from his mama. In Mary Ann there was a certain affected simper, and a craving for notice, that I was sorry to observe. But her brother claimed all my attention to himself: he stood bolt upright between me and the fire, with his hands behind his back, talking away like an orator, occasionally interrupting his discourse with a sharp reproof to his sisters when they made too much noise.

" O Tom, what a darling you are !" exclaimed his mother. " Come and kiss dear mama; and then won't you show Miss Grey your schoolroom, and your nice new books ?"

"I won't kiss *you* mama; but I *will* show Miss Grey my schoolroom, and my new books."

" And *my* schoolroom, and *my* new books, Tom," said Mary Ann. "They're mine too."

" They're *mine*," replied he decisively. Come along, Miss Grey—I 'll escort you."

When the room and books had been shown, with some bickerings between the brother and sister that I did my utmost to appease or mitigate, Mary Ann brought me her doll, and began to be very loquacious on the subject of its fine clothes, its bed, its chest of drawers, and other appurtenances; but Tom told her to hold her clamour, that Miss Grey might see his rocking-horse, which, with a most important bustle, he dragged forth from its corner into the middle of the room, loudly calling on me to attend to it. Then, ordering his sister to hold the reins, he mounted, and made me stand for ten minutes, watching how manfully he used his whip and spurs. Meantime, however, I admired Mary Ann's pretty doll, and all its possessions; and then told Master Tom he was a capital rider, but I hoped he would not use his whip and spurs so much when he rode a real pony.

"Oh, yes, I will!" said he, laying on with redoubled ardour. "I'll cut into him like smoke! Eeh! my word! but he shall sweat for it."

This was very shocking : but I hoped in time to be able to work a reformation.

"Now you must put on your bonnet and shawl," said the little hero, "and I'll show you my garden."

"And *mine*," said Mary Ann.

Tom lifted his fist with a menacing gesture; she uttered a loud, shrill scream, ran to the other side of me, and made a face at him.

"Surely Tom, you would not strike your sister! I hope I shall *never* see you do that."

"You will sometimes : I'm obliged to do it now and then to keep her in order."

"But it is not your business to keep her in order, you know—that is for—"

"Well, now go and put on your bonnet."

"I don't know—it is so very cloudy and cold, it seems likely to rain;—and you know I have had a long drive."

"No matter—you *must* come; I shall allow of no excuses," replied the consequential little gentleman. And as it was the first day of our acquaintance, I thought I might as well indulge him. It was too cold for Mary Ann to venture, so she stayed with her mama; to the great relief of her brother, who liked to have me all to himself.

The garden was a large one, and tastefully laid out; besides several splendid dahlias, there were some other fine flowers still in bloom; but my companion would not give me time to examine them : I must go with him, across the wet grass, to a remote sequestered corner, the most important place in the grounds, because it contained *his* garden. There were two round beds, stocked with a variety of plants. In one there was a pretty little rose tree. I paused to admire its lovely blossoms.

"Oh, never mind that!" said he, contemptuously. "That's only *Mary Ann's* garden; look, THIS is mine."

After I had observed every flower, and listened to a disquisition on every plant, I was permitted to depart; but first, with great pomp, he plucked a polyanthus and presented it to me, as one conferring a prodigious favour. I observed, on the grass about his garden, certain apparatus of sticks and cord, and asked what they were.

" Traps for birds."

" Why do you catch them?"

" Papa says they do harm."

" And what do you do with them, when you catch them?"

" Different things. Sometimes I give them to the cat; sometimes I cut them in pieces with my penknife; but the next, I mean to roast alive."

" And why do you mean to do such a horrible thing?"

" For two reasons; first, to see how long it will live—and then, to see what it will taste like."

" But don't you know it is extremely wicked to do such things? Remember, the birds can feel as well as you; and think, how would you like it yourself?"

" Oh, that's nothing! I'm not a bird, and I can't feel what I do to them."

" But you will have to feel it some time, Tom: you have heard where wicked people go to when they die; and if you don't leave off torturing innocent birds, remember, you will have to go there, and suffer just what you have made them suffer."

" Oh, pooh! I sha'n't. Papa knows how I treat them, and he never blames me for it: he says it's just what *he* used to do when *he* was a boy. Last summer he gave me a nest full of young sparrows, and he saw me pulling off their legs and wings and heads, and never said anything; except that they were nasty things, and I must not let them soil my trousers: and uncle Robson was there too, and he laughed, and said I was a fine boy."

" But what would your mama say?"

" Oh, she doesn't care! she says it's a pity to kill the pretty singing birds, but the naughty sparrows, and mice and rats, I may do what I like with. So now, Miss Grey, you see it is *not* wicked."

" I still think it is, Tom; and perhaps your papa and mama would think so too, if they thought much about it. However," I internally added, "they may say what they please, but I am determined you shall do nothing of the kind, as long as I have power to prevent it."

He next took me across the lawn to see his mole-traps, and then into the stack-yard to see his weasel-traps: one o

which, to his great joy, contained a dead weasel; and then
into the stable to see, not the fine carriage horses, but a little
rough colt, which he informed me had been bred on purpose
for him, and he was to ride it as soon as it was properly
trained. I tried to amuse the little fellow, and listened to all
his chatter as complacently as I could; for I thought if he
had any affections at all, I would endeavour to win them;
and then, in time, I might be able to show him the error of
his ways: but I looked in vain for that generous, noble spirit,
his mother talked off; though I could see he was not without
a certain degree of quickness and penetration, when he chose
to exert it.

When we re-entered the house it was nearly tea-time.
Master Tom told me that, as papa was from home, he and
I and Mary Ann were to have tea with mama, for a treat;
for, on such occasions, she always dined at luncheon time
with them, instead of at six o'clock. Soon after tea, Mary
Ann went to bed, but Tom favoured us with his company
and conversation till eight. After he was gone, Mrs. Bloomfield further enlightened me on the subject of her children's
dispositions and acquirements, and on what they were to
learn, and how they were to be managed, and cautioned me
to mention their defects to no one but herself. My mother
had warned me before, to mention them as little as possible
to *her*, for people did not like to be told of their children's
faults, and so I concluded I was to keep silence on them
altogether. About half-past nine, Mrs. Bloomfield invited
me to partake a frugal supper of cold meat and bread. I
was glad when that was over, and she took her bed-room
candlestick and retired to rest; for though I wished to be
pleased with her, her company was extremely irksome to me;
and I could not help feeling that she was cold, grave, and
forbidding—the very opposite of the kind, warm-hearted
matron my hopes had depicted her to be.

———

CHAPTER III.

A FEW MORE LESSONS.

I ROSE next morning with a feeling of hopeful exhilaration, in spite of the disappointments already experienced; but I found the dressing of Mary Ann was no light matter, as her abundant hair was to be smeared with pomade, plaited in three long tails, and tied with bows of ribbon: a task my un-accustomed fingers found great difficulty in performing. She told me her nurse could do it in half the time, and, by keeping up a constant fidget of impatience, contrived to render me still longer. When all was done, we went into the school-room, where I met my other pupil, and chatted with the two till it was time to go down to breakfast. That meal being concluded, and a few civil words having been exchanged with Mrs. Bloomfield, we repaired to the school-room again, and commenced the business of the day. I found my pupils very backward, indeed; but Tom, though averse to every species of mental exertion, was not without abilities. Mary Ann could scarcely read a word, and was so careless and inattentive that I could hardly get on with her at all. However, by dint of great labour and patience, I managed to get something done in the course of the morning, and then accompanied my young charge out into the garden and adjacent grounds, for a little recreation before dinner. There we got along tolerably together, except that I found they had no notion of going with *me*: I must go with *them* wherever they chose to lead me. I must run, walk, or stand, exactly as it suited their fancy. This, I thought, was reversing the order of things; and I found it doubly dis-agreeable, as on this as well as subsequent occasions, they seemed to prefer the dirtiest places and the most dismal occupations. But there was no remedy; either I must follow them, or keep entirely apart from them, and thus appear neglectful of my charge. To-day, they manifested a particular attachment to a well at the bottom of the lawn, where they persisted in dabbling with sticks and pebbles for above half an hour. I was in constant fear that their mother would see them from the window, and blame me for allowing them thus to draggle their clothes and wet their feet and hands, instead of taking exercise; but no arguments, commands, or entreaties could draw them away. If *she* did not see them, some one else did—a gentleman on horseback had entered the gate and was proceeding up the road; at the distance of a few paces from us he paused, and calling to the children in a waspish penetrating tone, bade them " Keep out of that water." " Miss Grey," said he, " (I suppose it *is* Miss Grey) I am surprised that you should allow them to dirty their clothes in that manner! Don't you see how Miss Bloomfield has soiled her frock? and that Master Bloomfield's socks are quite wet? and both of them without gloves? Dear, dear! Let me *request* that in future you will keep them *decent* at least!" so saying, he turned away, and continued his ride up to the house. This was Mr. Bloomfield. I was surpised that he should nominate his children Master and Miss Bloomfield; and still more so, that he should speak so uncivilly to me, their governess, and a perfect stranger to himself. Presently the bell rung to summon us in I dined with the children at one, while he and his lady took their luncheon at the same table. His conduct there did not greatly raise him in my estimation. He was a man of ordinary stature —rather below than above—and rather thin than stout, apparently between thirty and forty years of age : he had a large mouth, pale, dingy complexion, milky blue eyes, and hair the colour of a hempen cord. There was a roast leg of mutton before him : he helped Mrs. Bloomfield, the children, and me, desiring me to cut up the children's meat; then, after twisting about the mutton in various directions, and eyeing it from different points, he pronounced it not fit to be eaten, and called for the cold beef.

" What is the matter with the mutton, my dear?" asked his mate.

" It is quite overdone. Don't you taste, Mrs. Bloomfield, that all the goodness is roasted out of it? And can't you see that all that nice, red gravy is completely dried away?"

" Well, I think the *beef* will suit you."

The beef was set before him, and he began to carve, but with the most rueful expressions of discontent.

" What is the matter with the *beef*, Mr. Bloomfield? I'm sure I thought it was very nice."

" And so it *was* very nice. A nicer joint could not be; but it is *quite* spoiled," replied he, dolefully.

" How so?"

" How so! Why, don't you see how it is cut? Dear—dear! it is quite shocking!"

" They must have cut it wrong in the kitchen then, for I'm sure I carved it quite properly here, yesterday."

" No *doubt* they cut it wrong in the kitchen—the savages! Dear—dear! Did ever any one see such a fine piece of beef so completely ruined? But remember that, in future, when a decent dish leaves this table, they shall not *touch* it in the kitchen. Remember *that*, Mrs. Bloomfield!"

Notwithstanding the ruinous state of the beef, the gentleman managed to cut himself some delicate slices, part of which he ate in silence. When he next spoke it was, in a less querulous tone, to ask what there was for dinner.

" Turkey and grouse," was the concise reply.

" And what besides?"

" Fish."

" What kind of fish?"

" I don't know."

" *You don't know?*" cried he, looking solemnly up from his plate, and suspending his knife and fork in astonishment.

" No. I told the cook to get some fish—I did not particularize what."

" Well, that beats everything! A lady professes to keep house, and doesn't even know what fish is for dinner! professes to order fish, and doesn't specify what!"

" Perhaps, Mr. Bloomfield, you will order dinner yourself in future."

Nothing more was said; and I was very glad to get out of the room with my pupils; for I never felt so ashamed and uncomfortable in my life for anything that was not my own fault.

In the afternoon we applied to lessons again; then went out again; then had tea in the schoolroom; then I dressed Mary Ann for dessert; and when she and her brother were gone down to the dining-room, I took the opportunity of beginning a letter to my dear friends at home: but the children came up before I had half completed it. At seven I had to put Mary Ann to bed; then I played with Tom till eight, when he too went; and I finished my letter and unpacked my clothes, which I had hitherto found no opportunity for doing, and, finally, went to bed myself.

But this is a very favourable specimen of a day's proceedings.

My task of instruction and surveillance, instead of becoming easier as my charges and I got better accustomed to each other, became more arduous as their characters unfolded. The name of governess, I soon found, was a mere mockery as applied to me: my pupils had no more notion of obedience than a wild, unbroken colt. The habitual fear of their father's peevish temper, and the dread of the punishments he was wont to inflict when irritated, kept them generally within bounds in his immediate presence. The girls, too, had some fear of their mother's anger; and the boy might occasionally be bribed to do as she bid him by the hope of reward: but I had no rewards to offer; and as for punishments, I was given to understand, the parents reserved that privilege to themselves; and yet they expected me to keep my pupils in order. Other children might be guided by the fear of anger, and the desire of approbation; but neither the one nor the other had any effect upon these.

Master Tom, not content with refusing to be ruled, must needs set up as a ruler, and manifested a determination to keep, not only his sisters, but his governess in order, by violent manual and pedal applications; and, as he was a tall, strong boy of his years, this occasioned no trifling inconvenience. A few sound boxes in the ear, on such occasions, might have settled the matter easily enough: but as, in that case, he might make up some story to his mother, which she would be sure to believe, as she had such unshaken faith in his veracity—though I had already discovered it to be by no means unimpeachable—I determined to refrain from striking him, even in self-defence; and, in his most violent moods, my only resource was to throw him on his back, and hold his hands and feet till the frenzy was somewhat abated. To the difficulty of preventing him from doing what he ought not, was added that of forcing him to do what he ought. Often he would positively refuse to learn, or to repeat his lessons, or even to look at his book. Here, again, a good birch rod might have been serviceable; but, as my powers were so limited, I must make the best use of what I had.

As there were no settled hours for study and play, I resolved to give my pupils a certain task, which, with moderate attention, they could perform in a short time; and till this was done, however weary I was, or however perverse they might be, nothing short of parental interference should induce me to suffer them to leave the schoolroom, even if I should sit with my chair against the door to keep them in. Patience, Firmness, and Perseverance, were my only weapons; and these I resolved to use to the utmost. I determined always strictly to fulfil the threats and promises I made; and, to that end, I must be cautious to threaten and promise nothing that I could not perform. Then, I would carefully refrain from all useless irritability and indulgence of my own ill temper: when they behaved tolerably, I would be as kind and obliging as it was in my power to be, in order to make the widest possible distinction between good and bad conduct; I would reason with them too in the simplest and most effective manner. When I reproved them, or refused to gratify their wishes, after a glaring fault, it should be more in sorrow than in anger: their little hymns and prayers I would make plain and clear to their understanding; when they said their prayers at night, and asked pardon for their offences, I would remind them of the sins of the past day, solemnly, but in perfect kindness, to avoid raising a spirit of opposition; penitential hymns should be said by the naughty; cheerful ones by the comparatively good; and every kind of instruction I would convey to them, as much as possible, by entertaining discourse—apparently with no other object than their present amusement in view.

By these means I hoped, in time, both to benefit the children and to gain the approbation of their parents; and also to convince my friends at home that I was not so wanting in skill and prudence as they supposed. I knew the difficulties I had to contend with were great; but I knew (at least I believed) unremitting patience and perseverance could overcome them; and night and morning I implored Divine assistance to this end. But either the children were so incorrigible, the parents so unreasonable, or myself so mistaken in my views, or so unable to carry them out, that my best intentions and most strenuous efforts seemed productive of no better result than sport to the children, dissatisfaction to their parents, and torment to myself.

The task of instruction was as arduous for the body as the mind. I had to run after my pupils to catch them, to carry

Y

or drag them to the table, and often forcibly to hold them there till the lesson was done. Tom I frequently put into a corner, seating myself before him in a chair, with a book which contained the little task that must be said or read, before he was released, in my hand. He was not strong enough to push both me and the chair away, so he would stand twisting his body and face into the most grotesque and singular contortions—laughable, no doubt, to an unconcerned spectator, but not to me—and uttering loud yells and doleful outcries, intended to represent weeping, but wholly without the accompaniment of tears. I knew this was done solely for the purpose of annoying me ; and, therefore, however I might inwardly tremble with impatience and irritation, I manfully strove to suppress all visible signs of molestation, and affected to sit with calm indifference, waiting till it should please him to cease this pastime, and prepare for a run in the garden, by casting his eye on the book and reading or repeating the few words he was required to say. Sometimes he would determine to do his writing badly ; and I had to hold his hand to prevent him from purposely blotting or disfiguring the paper. Frequently I threatened that, if he did not do better, he should have another line : then he would stubbornly refuse to write this line; and I, to save my word, had finally to resort to the expedient of holding his fingers upon the pen, and forcibly drawing his hand up and down, till, in spite of his resistance, the line was in some sort completed.

Yet Tom was by no means the most unmanageable of my pupils : sometimes, to my great joy, he would have the sense to see that his wisest policy was to finish his tasks, and go out and amuse himself till I and his sisters came to join him ; which frequently was not at all, for Mary Ann seldom followed his example in this particular : she apparently preferred rolling on the floor to any other amusement : down she would drop like a leaden weight ; and when I, with great difficulty, had succeeded in rooting her thence, I had still to hold her up with one arm, while with the other I held the book from which she was to read or spell her lesson. As the dead weight of the big girl of six became too heavy for one arm to bear, I transferred it to the other ; or, if both were weary of the burden, I carried her into a corner, and told her she might come out when she should find the use of her feet, and stand up : but she generally preferred lying there like a log till dinner or tea time, when, as I could not deprive her of her meals, she must be liberated, and would come crawling out with a grin of triumph on her round, red face. Often she would stubbornly refuse to pronounce some particular word in her lesson ; and now I regret the lost labour I have had in striving to conquer her obstinacy. If I had passed it over as a matter of no consequence, it would have been better for both parties, than vainly striving to overcome it as I did ; but I thought it my absolute duty to crush this vicious tendency in the bud : and so it was, if I could have done it ; and, had my powers been less limited, I might have enforced obedience ; but, as it was, it was a trial of strength between her and me, in which she generally came off victorious ; and every victory served to encourage and strengthen her for a future contest. In vain I argued, coaxed, entreated, threatened, scolded ; in vain I kept her in from play, or, if obliged to take her out, refused to play with her, or to speak kindly, or have anything to do with her ; in vain I tried to set before her the advantages of doing as she was bid, and being loved, and kindly treated in consequence, and the disadvantages of persisting in her absurd perversity. Sometimes, when she would ask me to do something for her, I would answer—

" Yes, I will, Mary Ann, if you will only say that word. Come ! you'd better say it at once, and have no more trouble about it."

" No."

" Then, of course, I can do nothing for you."

With me, at her age, or under, neglect and disgrace were the most dreadful of punishments ; but on her they made no impression. Sometimes, exasperated to the utmost pitch, I would shake her violently by the shoulder, or pull her long hair, or put her in the corner ; for which she punished me with loud, shrill, piercing screams, that went through my head like a knife. She knew I hated this, and when she had shrieked her utmost, would look into my face with an air of vindictive satisfaction, exclaiming—" *Now* then ! *that's* for you !" And then shriek again and again, till I was forced to stop my ears. Often these dreadful cries would bring Mrs. Bloomfield up to inquire what was the matter?

" Mary Ann is a naughty girl, ma'am."

" But what are these shocking screams?"

" She is screaming in a passion."

" I never heard such a dreadful noise! You might be killing her. Why is she not out with her brother?"

" I cannot get her to finish her lessons."

" But Mary Ann must be a *good* girl, and finish her lessons." This was blandly spoken to the child. " And I hope I shall *never* hear such terrible cries again!"

And fixing her cold, stony eyes upon me with a look that could not be mistaken, she would shut the door, and walk away. Sometimes I would try to take the little obstinate creature by surprise, and casually ask her the word while she was thinking of something else; frequently she would begin to say it, and then suddenly check herself, with a provoking look that seemed to say, " Ah! I'm too sharp for you; you sha'n't trick it out of me, either."

On another occasion, I pretended to forget the whole affair; and talked and played with her as usual, till night, when I put her to bed; then bending over her, while she lay all smiles and good humour, just before departing, I said, as cheerfully and kindly as before—

" Now, Mary Ann, just tell me that word before I kiss you good-night: you are a good girl now, and, of course, you will say it."

" No, I won't."

" Then I can't kiss you."

" Well, I don't care."

In vain I expressed my sorrow; in vain I lingered for some symptom of contrition; she really " didn't care," and I left her alone, and in darkness, wondering most of all at this last proof of insensate stubbornness. In *my* childhood I could not imagine a more afflictive punishment, than for my mother to refuse to kiss me at night: the very idea was terrible. More than the idea I never felt, for, happily, I never committed a fault that was deemed worthy of such a penalty; but once, I remember, for some transgression of my sister's, our mother thought proper to inflict it upon her: what *she* felt, I cannot tell; but my sympathetic tears and suffering for her sake, I shall not soon forget.

Another troublesome trait in Mary Ann, was her incorrigible propensity to keep running into the nursery, to play with her little sisters and the nurse. This was natural enough, but, as it was against her mother's express desire, I, of course, forbade her to do so, and did my utmost to keep her with me; but that only increased her relish for the nursery, and the more I strove to keep her out of it, the oftener she went, and the longer she stayed: to the great dissatisfaction of Mrs. Bloomfield, who, I well knew, would impute all the blame of the matter to me. Another of my trials was the dressing in the morning: at one time she would not be washed; at another she would not be dressed, unless she might wear some particular frock, that, I knew, her mother would not like her to have; at another she would scream, and run away if I attempted to touch her hair. So that, frequently, when, after much trouble and toil, I had, at length, succeeded in bringing her down, the breakfast was nearly half over; and black looks from " mama," and testy observations from " papa," spoken at me, if not to me, were sure to be my meed: for few things irritated the latter so much as want of punctuality at meal-times. Then, among the minor annoyances, was my inability to satisfy Mrs. Bloomfield with her daughter's dress; and the child's hair " was never fit to be seen." Sometimes, as a powerful reproach to me, she would perform the office of tire-woman herself, and then complain bitterly of the trouble it gave her.

When little Fanny came into the schoolroom, I hoped she would be mild and inoffensive at least; but a few days, if not a few hours, sufficed to destroy the illusion: I found her a mischievous, intractable little creature, given up to falsehood and deception, young as she was, and alarmingly fond of exercising her two favourite weapons of offence and defence; that of spitting in the faces of those who incurred her displeasure, and bellowing like a bull when her unreasonable desires were not gratified. As she, generally, was pretty quiet in her parents' presence, and they were impressed with the notion of her being a remarkably gentle child, her falsehoods were readily believed, and her loud uproars led them to suspect harsh and injudicious treatment on my part; and when, at length, her bad disposition became manifest, even to their prejudiced eyes, I felt that the whole was attributed to me.

" What a naughty girl Fanny is getting!" Mrs. Bloom-

field would say to her spouse. " Don't you observe, my
dear, how she is altered since she entered the schoolroom?
She will soon be as bad as the other two; and, I am sorry
to say, they have quite deteriorated of late."

" You may say that," was the answer. " I've been
thinking that same myself. I thought when we got them a
governess they'd improve; but, instead of that, they get
worse and worse: I don't know how it is with their learning; but their habits, I know, make no sort of improvement;
they get rougher, and dirtier, and more unseemly every day."

I knew this was all pointed at me; and these, and all
similar inuendoes, affected me far more deeply than any open
accusations would have done; for against the latter I should
have been roused to speak in my own defence: now, I judged
it my wisest plan to subdue every resentful impulse, suppress
every sensitive shrinking, and go on perseveringly, doing my
best; for, irksome as my situation was, I earnestly wished to
retain it. I thought, if I could struggle on with unremitting
firmness and integrity, the children would, in time, become
more humanized: every month would contribute to make
them some little wiser, and, consequently, more manageable;
for a child of nine or ten, as frantic and ungovernable as
these at six and seven would be a maniac.

I flattered myself I was benefiting my parents and sister
by my continuance here; for, small as the salary was, I still
was earning something, and, with strict economy, I could
easily manage to have something to spare for them, if they
would favour me by taking it. Then, it was by my own will
that I had got the place: I had brought all this tribulation
on myself, and I was determined to bear it; nay, more than
that, I did not even regret the step I had taken. I longed
to show my friends that, even now, I was competent to undertake the charge, and able to acquit myself honourably
to the end; and if ever I felt it degrading to submit so
quietly, or intolerable to toil so constantly, I would turn
towards my home, and say within myself—

" They may crush, but they shall not subdue me;
'Tis of thee that I think, not of them."

About Christmas I was allowed to visit home; but my
holiday was only of a fortnight's duration: " For," said Mrs.
Bloomfield, " I thought, as you had seen your friends so

lately, you would not care for a longer stay." I left her to think so still : but she little knew how long, how wearisome those fourteen weeks of absence had been to me; how intensely I had longed for my holidays, how greatly I was disappointed at their curtailment. Yet she was not to blame in this; I had never told her my feelings, and she could not be expected to divine them; I had not been with her a full term, and she was justified in not allowing me a full vacation.

CHAPTER IV.

THE GRANDMAMMA.

I SPARE my readers the account of my delight on coming home, my happiness while there—enjoying a brief space of rest and liberty in that dear, familiar place, among the loving and the loved—and my sorrow on being obliged to bid them, once more, a long adieu.

I returned, however, with unabated vigour to my work— a more arduous task than any one can imagine, who has not felt something like the misery of being charged with the care and direction of a set of mischievous turbulent rebels, whom his utmost exertions cannot bind to their duty ; while, at the same time, he is responsible for their conduct to a higher power, who exacts from him what cannot be achieved without the aid of the superior's more potent authority : which, either from indolence, or the fear of becoming un-popular with the said rebellious gang, the latter refuses to give. I can conceive few situations more harassing than that wherein, however you may long for success, however you may labour to fulfil your duty, your efforts are baffled and set at naught by those beneath you, and unjustly cen-sured and misjudged by those above.

I have not enumerated half the vexatious propensities of my pupils, or half the troubles resulting from my heavy responsibilities, for fear of trespassing too much upon the reader's patience ; as, perhaps, I have already done ; but my design, in writing the few last pages, was not to amuse, but to benefit those whom it might concern : he that has no

interest in such matters will doubtless have skipped them over
with a cursory glance, and, perhaps, a malediction against
the prolixity of the writer; but if a parent has, therefrom,
gathered any useful hint, or an unfortunate governess received thereby the slightest benefit, I am well rewarded for
my pains.

To avoid trouble and confusion, I have taken my pupils
one by one, and discussed their various qualities; but this
can give no adequate idea of being worried by the whole
three together; when, as was often the case, all were determined to "be naughty, and to tease Miss Grey, and put her
in a passion."

Sometimes, on such occasions, the thought had suddenly
occurred to me—"If *they* could see me now!" meaning, of
course, my friends at home; and the idea of how they would
pity me has made me pity myself—so greatly that I have
had the utmost difficulty to restrain my tears: but I have
restrained them, till my little tormentors were gone to dessert,
or cleared off to bed (my only prospects of deliverance), and
then, in all the bliss of solitude, I have given myself up to
the luxury of an unrestricted burst of weeping. But this
was a weakness I did not often indulge: my employments
were too numerous, my leisure moments too precious, to admit
of much time being given to fruitless lamentations.

I particularly remember one wild, snowy afternoon, soon
after my return in January; the children had all come up from
dinner, loudly declaring that they meant "to be naughty";
and they had well kept their resolution, though I had talked
myself hoarse, and wearied every muscle in my throat, in
the vain attempt to reason them out of it. I had got Tom
pinned up in a corner, whence, I told him, he should not
escape till he had done his appointed task. Meantime,
Fanny had possessed herself of my work-bag, and was rifling
its contents—and spitting into it besides. I told her to let
it alone, but to no purpose, of course. "Burn it, Fanny!"
cried Tom; and *this* command she hastened to obey. I
sprang to snatch it from the fire, and Tom darted to the
door. "Mary Ann, throw her desk out of the window!"
cried he; and my precious desk containing my letters and
papers, my small amount of cash, and all my valuables, was
about to be precipitated from the three-story window. I
flew to rescue it. Meanwhile Tom had left the room, and

was rushing down the stairs, followed by Fanny. Having secured my desk, I ran to catch them, and Mary Ann came scampering after. All three escaped me, and ran out of the house into the garden, where they plunged about in the snow, shouting and screaming in exultant glee.

What must I do? If I followed them, I should probably be unable to capture one, and only drive them farther away; if I did not, how was I to get them in? and what would their parents think of me, if they saw or heard the children rioting, hatless, bonnetless, gloveless, and bootless, in the deep, soft snow? While I stood in this perplexity, just without the door, trying, by grim looks and angry words, to awe them into subjection, I heard a voice behind me, in harshly piercing tones, exclaiming,—

"Miss Grey! Is it possible! What, in the devil's name, can you be thinking about?"

"I can't get them in, sir," said I, turning round, and beholding Mr. Bloomfield, with his hair on end, and his pale blue eyes bolting from their sockets.

"But I INSIST upon their being got in!" cried he, approaching nearer, and looking perfectly ferocious.

"Then sir, you must call them yourself, if you please, for they won't listen to me, " I replied, stepping back.

"Come in with you, you filthy brats; or I'll horsewhip you every one!" roared he; and the children instantly obeyed. "There, you see! they come at the first word!"

"Yes, when *you* speak."

"And it's very strange, that when you've the care of 'em, you've no better control over 'em than that!—Now there they are—gone up stairs with their nasty snowy feet! Do go after 'em and see them made decent, for Heaven's sake!"

That gentleman's mother was then staying in the house; and, as I ascended the stairs and passed the drawing-room door, I had the satisfaction of hearing the old lady declaiming aloud to her daughter-in-law to this effect (for I could only distinguish the most emphatic words),

"Gracious heavens!——never in all my life—— !——get their death as sure as——! Do you think my dear she's a *proper person?* Take my word for it——"

I heard no more; but that sufficed.

The senior Mrs. Bloomfield had been very attentive and

civil to me; and till now, I had thought her a nice, kind-hearted, chatty old body.   She would often come to me and talk in a confidential strain; nodding and shaking her head, and gesticulating with hands and eyes, as a certain class of old ladies are wont to do : though I never knew one that carried the peculiarity to so great an extent.   She would even sympathize with me for the trouble I had with the children, and express at times, by half sentences, interspersed with nods and knowing winks, her sense of the injudicious con-duct of their mama in so restricting my power, and neglect-ing to support me with her authority.   Such a mode of testifying disapprobation was not much to my taste; and I generally refused to take it in, or understand anything more than was openly spoken : at least, I never went farther than an implied acknowledgment that, if matters were otherwise ordered, my task would be a less difficult one, and I should be better able to guide and instruct my charge; but now I must be doubly cautious.   Hitherto, though I saw the old lady had her defects (of which one was a proneness to pro-claim her perfections), I had always been wishful to excuse them, and to give her credit for all the virtues she pro-fessed, and even imagine others yet untold.   Kindness, which had been the food of my life through so many years, had lately been so entirely denied me, that I welcomed with grateful joy the slightest semblance of it.   No wonder, then, that my heart warmed to the old lady, and always gladdened at her approach and regretted her departure.

But now, the few words luckily or unluckily heard in passing had wholly revolutionized my ideas respecting her : now I looked upon her as hypocritical and insincere, a flatterer, and a spy upon my words and deeds.   Doubtless it would have been my interest still to meet her with the same cheerful smile, and tone of respectful cordiality as before; but I could not, if I would : my manner altered with my feelings, and became so cold and shy that she could not fail to notice it.   She soon did notice it, and *her* manner altered too : the familiar nod was changed to a stiff bow, the gracious smile gave place to a glare of gorgon ferocity ; her vivacious loquacity was entirely transferred from me to "the darling boy and girls," whom she flattered and indulged more absurdly than ever their mother had done.

I confess I was somewhat troubled at this change : I

feared the consequences of her displeasure, and even made some efforts to recover the ground I had lost—and with better apparent success than I could have anticipated. At one time, I, merely in common civility, asked after her cough; immediately her long visage relaxed into a smile, and she favoured me with a particular history of that and her other infirmities, followed by an account of her pious resignation, delivered in the usual emphatic, declamatory style, which no writing can portray.

"But there's one remedy for all, my dear, and that's resignation," (a toss of the head) "resignation to the will of Heaven!" (an uplifting of the hands and eyes). "It has always supported me through all my trials, and always will do." (a succession of nods). "But then, it isn't everybody that can say that" (a shake of the head); "but I'm one of the pious ones, Miss Grey!" (a very significant nod and toss) "And, thank Heaven, I always was," (another nod) "and I glory in it!" (an emphatic clasping of the hands and shaking of the head). And with several texts of scripture, misquoted or misapplied, and religious exclamations so redolent of the ludicrous in the style of delivery and manner of bringing in, if not in the expressions themselves, that I decline repeating them, she withdrew; tossing her large head in high good-humour—with herself at least—and left me hoping that, after all, she was rather weak than wicked.

At her next visit to Wellwood House, I went so far as to say I was glad to see her looking so well. The effect of this was magical: the words, intended as a mark of civility, were received as a flattering compliment; her countenance brightened up, and from that moment she became as gracious and benign as heart could wish—in outward semblance at least. From what I now saw of her, and what I heard from the children, I knew that, in order to gain her cordial friendship, I had but to utter a word of flattery at each convenient opportunity: but this was against my principles; and for lack of this, the capricious old dame soon deprived me of her favour again, and I believe did me much secret injury.

She could not greatly influence her daughter-in-law against me, because, between that lady and herself, there was a mutual dislike—chiefly shewn by her in secret detractions and

calumniations; by the other, in an excess of frigid formality
in her demeanour; and no fawning flattery of the elder could
thaw away the wall of ice which the younger interposed between them. But with her son, the old lady had better success: he would listen to all she had to say, provided she
could soothe his fretful temper, and refrain from irritating
him by her own asperities; and I have reason to believe that
she considerably strengthened his prejudice against me. She
would tell him that I shamefully neglected the children, and
even his wife did not attend to them as she ought; and that
he must look after them himself, or they would all go to
ruin.

Thus urged, he would frequently give himself the trouble
of watching them from the windows during their play; at
times, he would follow them through the grounds, and too
often came suddenly upon them while they were dabbling in
the forbidden well, talking to the coachman in the stables, or
revelling in the filth of the farm-yard—and I, meanwhile,
wearily standing by, having previously exhausted my energy
in vain attempts to get them away. Often, too, he would
unexpectedly pop his head into the schoolroom while the
young people were at meals, and find them spilling their milk
over the table and themselves, plunging their fingers into their
own or each other's mugs, or quarrelling over their victuals
like a set of tiger's cubs. If I were quiet at the moment, I
was conniving at their disorderly conduct; if (as was frequently the case) I happened to be exalting my voice to en-
force order, I was using undue violence, and setting the girls
a bad example by such ungentleness of tone and language.

I remember one afternoon in spring, when, owing to the
rain, they could not go out; but, by some amazing good fortune, they had all finished their lessons, and yet abstained
from running down to tease their parents—a trick that annoyed me greatly, but which, on rainy days, I seldom could
prevent their doing; because, below, they found novelty and
amusement—especially when visitors were in the house; and
their mother, though she bid me keep them in the schoolroom, would never chide them for leaving it, or trouble herself to send them back. But this day they appeared satisfied
with their present abode, and what is more wonderful still,
seemed disposed to play together without depending on me
for amusement, and without quarrelling with each other.

Their occupation was a somewhat puzzling one: they were all squatted together on the floor by the window, over a heap of broken toys and a quantity of birds' eggs—or rather egg-shells, for the contents had luckily been abstracted. These shells they had broken up and were pounding into small fragments, to what end I could not imagine; but so long as they were quiet and not in positive mischief, I did not care; and, with a feeling of unusual repose, I sat by the fire, putting the finishing stitches to a frock for Mary Ann's doll; intending, when that was done, to begin a letter to my mother. Suddenly, the door opened, and the dingy head of Mr. Bloomfield looked in.

"All very quiet here! What are you doing?" said he. "No harm *to-day*, at least," thought I. But he was of a different opinion. Advancing to the window, and seeing the children's occupations, he testily exclaimed—"What in the world are you about?"

"We're grinding egg-shells, papa!" cried Tom.

"How *dare* you make such a mess, you little devils? Don't you see what confounded work you're making of the carpet?" (the carpet was a plain, brown drugget). "Miss Grey, did you know what they were doing?"

"Yes, sir."

"*You knew* it?"

"Yes."

"You *knew* it! and you actually sat there and permitted them to go on, without a word of reproof!"

"I didn't think they were doing any harm."

"Any harm! Why look there! Just look at that carpet, and see—was there ever anything like it in a Christian house before? No wonder your room is not fit for a pigsty—no wonder your pupils are worse than a litter of pigs!—no wonder—Oh! I declare, it puts me quite past my patience!" and he departed, shutting the door after him with a bang, that made the children laugh.

"It puts *me* quite past my patience too!" muttered I, getting up; and, seizing the poker, I dashed it repeatedly into the cinders, and stirred them up with unwonted energy; thus easing my irritation, under pretence of mending the fire.

After this, Mr. Bloomfield was continually looking in, to see if the schoolroom was in order; and, as the children were continually littering the floor with fragments of toys, sticks, stones, stubble, leaves, and other rubbish, which I could not prevent their bringing, or oblige them to gather up, and which the servants refused to "clean after them," I had to spend a considerable portion of my valuable leisure moments on my knees upon the floor, in painfully reducing things to order. Once I told them that they should not taste their supper till they had picked up everything from the carpet; Fanny might have hers when she had taken up a certain quantity, Mary Ann when she had gathered twice as many, and Tom was to clear away the rest. Wonderful to state, the girls did their part; but Tom was in such a fury that he flew upon the table, scattered the bread and milk about the floor, struck his sisters, kicked the coals out of the coal-pan, attempted to overthrow the table and chairs, and seemed inclined to make a Douglas-larder of the whole contents of the room: but I seized upon him, and, sending Mary Ann to call her mama, held him in spite of kicks, blows, yells, and execrations, till Mrs. Bloomfield made her appearance.

"What is the matter with my boy?" said she.

And when the matter was explained to her, all she did was to send for the nursery-maid to put the room in order, and bring Master Bloomfield his supper.

"There now," cried Tom, triumphantly, looking up from his viands with his mouth almost too full for speech. "There now, Miss Grey! you see I have got my supper in spite of you: and I haven't picked up a single thing!"

The only person in the house who had any real sympathy for me was the nurse; for she had suffered like afflictions, though in a smaller degree; as she had not the task of teaching, nor was she so responsible for the conduct of her charge.

"Oh, Miss Grey!" she would say, "you have some trouble with them childer!"

"I have indeed, Betty; and I dare say you know what it is."

"Ay, I do so! But I don't vex myself o'er 'em as you do. And then, you see, I hit 'em a slap sometimes; and them little uns—I gives 'em a good whipping now and then: there's nothing else will do for 'em, as what they say. Howsoever, I've lost my place for it."

"Have you, Betty? I heard you were going to leave."

"Eh, bless you, yes! Missis gave me warning a three-wik sin'. She told me afore Christmas how it mud be, if I hit 'em again; but I couldn't hold my hand off 'em at ñothing. I know not how *you* do, for Miss Mary Ann's worse by the half nor her sisters!"

CHAPTER V.

THE UNCLE.

BESIDES the old lady, there was another relative of the family, whose visits were a great annoyance to me—this was " Uncle Robson," Mrs. Bloomfield's brother; a tall, self-sufficient fellow, with dark hair and sallow complexion like his sister, a nose that seemed to disdain the earth, and little grey eyes, frequently half closed, with a mixture of real stupidity and affected contempt of all surrounding objects. He was a thick-set, strongly built man, but he had found some means of compressing his waist into a remarkably small compass; and that, together with the unnatural stiffness of his form, showed that the lofty-minded, manly Mr. Robson, the scorner of the female sex, was not above the foppery of stays. He seldom deigned to notice me; and, when he did, it was with a certain supercilious insolence of tone and manner that convinced me he was no gentleman: though it was intended to have a contrary effect. But it was not for that I disliked his coming, so much as for the harm he did the children—encouraging all their evil propensities, and undoing, in a few minutes, the little good it had taken me months of labour to achieve.

Fanny and little Harriet, he seldom condescended to notice; but Mary Ann was something of a favourite. He was continually encouraging her tendency to affectation (which I had done my utmost to crush), talking about her pretty face, and filling her head with all manner of conceited notions concerning her personal appearance (which I had instructed her to regard as dust in the balance compared with the cultivation of her mind and manners); and I never saw

a child so susceptible of flattery as she was. Whatever was
wrong, in either her or her brother, he would encourage by
laughing at, if not by actually praising : people little know
the injury they do to children by laughing at their faults, and
making a pleasant jest of what their true friends have endeavoured to teach them to hold in grave abhorrence.

Though not a positive drunkard, Mr. Robson habitually
swallowed great quantities of wine, and took with relish
an occasional glass of brandy and water. He taught his
nephew to imitate him in this to the utmost of his ability,
and to believe that the more wine and spirits he could take,
and the better he liked them, the more he manifested his
bold and manly spirit, and rose superior to his sisters. Mr.
Bloomfield had not much to say against it, for his favourite
beverage was gin and water; of which he took a considerable portion every day, by dint of constant sipping—and to
that, I chiefly attributed his dingy complexion and waspish
temper.

Mr. Robson likewise encouraged Tom's propensity to per-
secute the lower creation, both by precept and example. As
he frequently came to course or shoot over his brother-in-
law's grounds, he would bring his favourite dogs with him ;
and he treated them so brutally that, poor as I was, I would
have given a sovereign any day to see one of them bite
him, provided the animal could have done it with impunity.
Sometimes, when in a very complacent mood, he would go a
bird-nesting with the children : a thing that irritated and
annoyed me exceedingly; as, by frequent and persevering
attempts, I flattered myself I had partly shown them the
evil of this pastime, and hoped, in time, to bring them to
some general sence of justice and humanity ; but ten minutes
bird-nesting with uncle Robson, or even a laugh from him
at some relation of their former barbarities, was sufficient at
once to destroy the effect of my whole elaborate course of
reasoning and persuasion. Happily, however, during that
spring, they never, but once, got anything but empty nests,
or eggs—being too impatient to leave them till the birds
were hatched ; that once, Tom, who had been with his uncle
into the neighbouring plantation, came running in high glee
into the garden, with a brood of little callow nestlings in his
hands. Mary Ann and Fanny, whom I was just bringing
out, ran to admire his spoils, and to beg each a bird for

themselves. "No, not one!" cried Tom. "They're all mine: uncle Robson gave them to me—one, two, three, four, five—you sha'n't touch one of them! no, not one, for your lives!" continued he, exultingly; laying the nest on the ground, and standing over it with his legs wide apart, his hands thrust into his breeches-pockets, his body bent forward, and his face twisted into all manner of contortions in the ecstacy of his delight.

"But you shall see me fettle 'em off. My word, but I *will* wallop 'em! See if I don't now. By gum! but there's rare sport for me in that nest."

"But, Tom," said I, "I shall not allow you to torture those birds. They must either be killed at once or carried back to the place you took them from, that the old birds may continue to feed them."

"But you don't know where that is, madam: it's only me and uncle Robson that knows that."

"But if you don't tell me, I shall kill them myself—much as I hate it."

"You daren't. You daren't touch them for your life! because you know papa and mama, and uncle Robson, would be angry. Ha, ha! I've caught you there, miss!"

"I shall do what I think right in a case of this sort, without consulting any one. If your papa and mama don't happen to approve of it, I shall be sorry to offend them; but your uncle Robson's opinions, of course, are nothing to me."

So saying—urged by a sense of duty—at the risk of both making myself sick and incurring the wrath of my employers—I got a large flat stone, that had been reared up for a mouse-trap by the gardener, then, having once more vainly endeavoured to persuade the little tyrant to let the birds be carried back, I asked what he intended to do with them. With fiendish glee he commenced a list of torments; and while he was busied in the relation, I dropped the stone upon his intended victims and crushed them flat beneath it. Loud were the outcries, terrible the execrations, consequent upon this daring outrage; uncle Robson had been coming up the walk with his gun, and was just then pausing to kick his dog. Tom flew towards him, vowing he would make him kick me instead of Juno. Mr. Robson leant upon his

z

gun, and laughed excessively at the violence of his nephew's
passion, and the bitter maledictions and opprobrious epithets
he heaped upon me. " Well, you *are* a good un !" exclaimed
he, at length, taking up his weapon and proceeding towards
the house. " Damme, but the lad has some spunk in him,
too. Curse me, if ever I saw a nobler little scoundrel
than that. He's beyond petticoat government already : by
God! he defies mother, granny, governess, and all ! Ha,
ha, ha ! Never mind, Tom, I'll get you another brood to-
morrow."

" If you do, Mr. Robson, I shall kill them too," said I.

" Humph !" replied he, and having honoured me with
a broad stare—which, contrary to his expectations, I sustained without flinching—he turned away with an air of
supreme contempt, and stalked into the house. Tom next
went to tell his mama. It was not her way to say much on
any subject ; but, when she next saw me, her aspect and
demeanour were doubly dark and chill. After some casual
remark about the weather, she observed—

" I am sorry, Miss Grey, you should think it necessary to interfere with Master Bloomfield's amusements;
he was *very* much distressed about your destroying the
birds."

" When Master Bloomfield's amusements consist in injuring sentient creatures," I answered, " I think it my duty
to interfere."

" You seemed to have forgotten," said she, calmly, " that
the creatures were all created for our convenience."

I thought that doctrine admitted some doubt, but merely
replied—

" If they were, we have no right to torment them for our
amusement."

" I think," said she, " a child's amusement is scarcely
to be weighed against the welfare of a soulless brute."

" But, for the child's own sake, it ought not to be encouraged to have such amusements," answered I, as meekly as
I could, to make up for such unusual pertinacity. ' Blessed
are the merciful, for they shall obtain mercy.' "

" Oh ! of course ; but that refers to our conduct towards
each other."

" ' The merciful man shews mercy to his beast,' " I ventured to add.

" I think *you* have not shewn much mercy, ' replied she, with a short, bitter laugh; " killing the poor birds by whole-sale in that shocking manner, and putting the dear boy to such misery for a mere whim."

I judged it prudent to say no more. This was the nearest approach to a quarrel I ever had with Mrs. Bloomfield; as well as the greatest number of words I ever exchanged with her at one time, since the day of my first arrival.

But Mr. Robson and old Mrs. Bloomfield were not the only guests whose coming to Wellwood House annoyed me; every visitor disturbed me more or less; not so much be-cause they neglected me (though I did feel their conduct strange and disagreeable in that respect), as because I found it impossible to keep my pupils away from them, as I was repeatedly desired to do: Tom must talk to them, and Mary Ann must be noticed by them. Neither the one nor the other knew what it was to feel any degree of shame-faced-ness, or even common modesty. They would indecently and clamorously interrupt the conversation of their elders, tease them with the most impertinent questions, roughly collar the gentlemen, climb their knees uninvited, hang about their shoulders or rifle their pockets, pull the ladies' gowns, dis-order their hair, tumble their collars, and importunately beg for their trinkets.

Mrs. Bloomfield had the sense to be shocked and annoyed at all this, but she had not sense to prevent it: she expected me to prevent it. But how could I—when the guests, with their fine clothes and new faces, continually flattered and indulged them, out of complaisance to their parents—how could *I*, with my homely garments, everyday face, and honest words, draw them away? I strained every nerve to do so: by striving to amuse them, I endeavoured to attract them to my side; by the exertion of such authority as I possessed, and by such severity as I dared to use, I tried to deter them from tormenting the guests; and by reproaching their unmannerly conduct, to make them ashamed to repeat it. But they knew no shame; they scorned authority which had no terrors to back it; and as for kindness and affection, either they had no hearts, or such as they had were so strongly guarded, and so well concealed, that I, with all my efforts, had not yet discovered how to reach them.

But soon my trials in this quarter came to a close—sooner

z 2

than I either expected or desired; for one sweet evening
towards the close of May, as I was rejoicing in the near
approach of the holidays, and congratulating myself upon
having made some progress with my pupils (as far as their
learning went at least, for I *had* instilled *something* into their
heads, and I had at length, brought them to be a little—a
very little—more rational about getting their lessons done
in time to leave some space for recreation, instead of tormenting themselves and me all day long to no purpose),
Mrs. Bloomfield sent for me, and calmly told me that after
Midsummer my services would be no longer required. She
assured me that my character and general conduct were un-
exceptionable; but the children had made so little improvement since my arrival, that Mr. Bloomfield and she felt it
their duty to seek some other mode of instruction. Though
superior to most children of their years in abilities, they
were decidedly behind them in attainments; their manners
were uncultivated, and their tempers unruly. And this she
attributed to a want of sufficient firmness, and diligent, persevering care on my part.

Unshaken firmness, devoted diligence, unwearied perseverance, unceasing care, were the very qualifications on
which I had secretly prided myself; and by which I had
hoped in time to overcome all difficulties, and obtain success
at last. I wished to say something in my own justification:
but in attempting to speak, I felt my voice falter; and rather
than testify any emotion, or suffer the tears to overflow that
were already gathering in my eyes, I chose to keep silence,
and bear all like a self-convicted culprit.

Thus was I dismissed, and thus I sought my home. Alas!
what would they think of me? unable, after all my boasting
to keep my place, even for a single year, as governess to
three small children, whose mother was asserted by my own
aunt, to be a " very nice woman." Having been thus
weighed in the balance and found wanting, I need not hope
they would be willing to try me again. And this was an
unwelcome thought; for vexed, harassed, disappointed as I
had been, and greatly as I had learned to love and value my
home, I was not yet weary of adventure, nor willing to relax
my efforts. I knew that all parents were not like Mr. and
Mrs. Bloomfield, and I was certain all children were not
like theirs. The next family must be different, and any

change must be for the better. I had been seasoned by adversity, and tutored by experience, and I longed to redeem my lost honour in the eyes of those whose opinion was more than that of all the world to me.

CHAPTER VI.

THE PARSONAGE AGAIN.

For a few months I remained peaceably at home, in the quiet enjoyment of liberty and rest, and genuine friendship, from all of which I had fasted so long; and in the earnest prosecution of my studies, to recover what I had lost during my stay at Wellwood House, and to lay in new stores for future use. My father's health was still very infirm, but not materially worse than when I last saw him; and I was glad I had it in my power to cheer him by my return, and to amuse him with singing his favourite songs.

No one triumphed over my failure, or said I had better have taken his or her advice, and quietly stayed at home. All were glad to have me back again, and lavished more kindness than ever upon me, to make up for the sufferings I had undergone; but not one would touch a shilling of what I had so cheerfully earned and so carefully saved, in the hope of sharing it with them. By dint of pinching here, and scraping there, our debts were already nearly paid. Mary had had good success with her drawings; but our father had insisted upon *her* likewise keeping all the produce of her industry to herself. All we could spare from the supply of our humble wardrobe and our little casual expenses, he directed us to put into the savings bank; saying we knew not how soon we might be dependent on that alone for support: for he felt he had not long to be with us, and what would become of our mother and us when he was gone, God only knew!

Dear papa! if he had troubled himself less about the afflictions that threatened us in case of his death, I am convinced that dreaded event would not have taken place so

soon.   My mother would never suffer him to ponder on the
subject if she could help it.

" Oh, Richard !" exclaimed she, on one occasion, " if you
would but dismiss such gloomy subjects from your mind, you
would live as long as any of us : at least you would live to
see the girls married, and yourself a happy grandfather, with
a canty old dame for your companion."

My mother laughed, and so did my father : but his laugh
soon perished in a dreary sigh.

" *They* married—poor penniless things !" said he, " who
will take them I wonder !"

" Why nobody shall that isn't thankful for them.   Wasn't
I penniless when you took me ? and you *pretended*, at least,
to be vastly pleased with your acquisition.   But it's no
matter whether they get married or not : we can devise a
thousand honest ways of making a livelihood   And I wonder, Richard, you can think of bothering your head about
our *poverty* in case of your death ; as if *that* would be anything compared with the calamity of losing you—an affliction
that, you well know, would swallow up all others, and which
you ought to do your utmost to preserve us from : and there
is nothing like a cheerful mind for keeping the body in
health."

" I know, Alice, it is wrong to keep repining as I do, but
I cannot help it : you must bear with me."

" I *won't* bear with you, if I can alter you," replied my
mother : but the harshness of her words was outdone by the
earnest affection of her tone and pleasant smile, that made
my father smile again, less sadly and less transiently than
was his wont.

" Mama," said I, as soon as I could find an opportunity
of speaking with her alone, " my money is but little, and
cannot last long ; if I could increase it, it would lessen papa's
anxiety, on one subject at least.   I cannot draw like Mary,
and so the best thing I could do would be to look out for
another situation."

" And so you would actually try again, Agnes ?"

" Decidedly, I would."

" Why, my dear, I should have thought you had had
enough of it."

" I know," said I, " everybody is not like Mr. and Mrs.
Bloomfield—"

"Some are worse," interrupted my mother.

"But not many, I think," replied I, "and I'm sure all children are not like theirs; for I and Mary were not: we always did as you bid us, didn't we?"

"Generally: but then, I did not spoil you; and you were not perfect angels after all: Mary had a fund of quiet obstinacy, and you were somewhat faulty in regard to temper; but you were very good children on the whole."

"I know I was sulky sometimes, and I should have been glad to see these children sulky sometimes too; for then I could have understood them: but they never were, for they *could* not be offended, nor hurt, nor ashamed: they could not be unhappy in any way, except when they were in a passion."

"Well, if they *could* not, it was not their fault: you cannot expect stone to be as pliable as clay."

"No, but still it is very unpleasant to live with such unimpressible, incomprehensible creatures. You cannot love them; and if you could, your love would be utterly thrown away: they could neither return it, nor value, nor understand it. But, however, even if I should stumble on such a family again, which is quite unlikely, I have all this experience to begin with, and I should manage better another time; and the end and aim of this preamble is, let me try again."

"Well, my girl, you are not easily discouraged, I see: I am glad of that. But, let me tell you, you are a good deal paler and thinner than when you first left home; and we cannot have you undermining your health to hoard up money, either for yourself or others."

"Mary tells me I am changed too; and I don't much wonder at it, for I was in a constant state of agitation and anxiety all day long: but next time I am determined to take things coolly."

After some further discussion, my mother promised once more to assist me, provided I would wait and be patient; and I left her to broach the matter to my father, when and how she deemed it most advisable: never doubting her ability to obtain his consent. Meantime, I searched, with great interest, the advertising columns of the newspapers, and wrote answers to every "Wanted a Governess," that appeared at all eligible; but all my letters, as well as the replies, when I got any, were dutifully shown to my mother; and she, to my

chagrin, made me reject the situations one after another :
these were low people, these were too exacting in their
demands, and these too niggardly in their remuneration.

"Your talents are not such as every poor clergyman's
daughter possesses, Agnes," she would say, "and you must
not throw them away. Remember, you promised to be
patient : there is no need of hurry : you have plenty of time
before you, and may have many chances yet."

At length, she advised me to put an advertisement, myself, in the paper, stating my qualifications, &c.

"Music, singing, drawing, French, Latin, and German,"
said she, " are no mean assemblage : many will be glad to
have so much in one instructor ; and this time, you shall try
your fortune in a somewhat higher family—in that of some
genuine, thorough-bred gentleman ; for such are far more
likely to treat you with proper respect and consideration,
than those purse-proud tradespeople and arrogant upstarts.
I have known several among the higher ranks who treated
their governesses quite as one of the family ; though some,
I allow, are as insolent and exacting as any one else can be :
for there are bad and good in all classes."

The advertisement was quickly written and despatched.
Of the two parties who answered it, but one would consent
to give me fifty pounds, the sum my mother bade me name
as the salary I should require ; and here, I hesitated about
engaging myself, as I feared the children would be too old,
and their parents would require some one more showy, or
more experienced, if not more accomplished than I. But my
mother dissuaded me from declining it on that account : I
should do vastly well, she said, if I would only throw aside
my diffidence, and acquire a little more confidence in myself.
I was just to give a plain, true statement of my acquirements
and qualifications, and name what stipulations I chose to
make, and then await the result. The only stipulation I
ventured to propose, was that I might be allowed two
months holidays during the year to visit my friends, at Mid-
summer and Christmas. The unknown lady, in her reply,
made no objection to this, and stated that, as to my acquirements, she had no doubt I should be able to give satisfaction ;
but in the engagement of governesses, she considered those
things as but subordinate points ; as, being situated in the
neighbourhood of O———, she could get masters to supply

any deficiencies in that respect: but, in her opinion, next to unimpeachable morality, a mild and cheerful temper and obliging disposition were the most essential requisites.

My mother did not relish this at all, and now made many objections to my accepting the situation; in which my sister warmly supported her: but, unwilling to be baulked again, I overruled them all; and, having first obtained the consent of my father (who had, a short time previously, been apprised of these transactions), I wrote a most obliging epistle to my unknown correspondent, and, finally, the bargain was concluded.

It was decreed that, on the last day of January, I was to enter upon my new office, as governess in the family of Mr. Murray, of Horton Lodge, near O——, about seventy miles from our village: a formidable distance to me, as I had never been above twenty miles from home in all the course of my twenty years sojourn on earth; and as, moreover, every individual in that family and in the neighbourhood was utterly unknown to myself and all my acquaintances. But this rendered it only the more piquant to me. I had now, in some measure, got rid of the *mauvaise honte* that had formerly oppressed me so much; there was a pleasing excitement in the idea of entering these unknown regions, and making my way alone among its strange inhabitants. I now flattered myself I was going to see something of the world: Mr. Murray's residence was near a large town, and not in a manufacturing district, where the people had nothing to do but to make money; his rank, from what I could gather, appeared to be higher than that of Mr. Bloomfield; and, doubtless, he was one of those genuine thorough-bred gentry my mother spoke of, who would treat his governess with due consideration as a respectable, well-educated lady, the instructor and guide of his children, and not a mere upper servant. Then, my pupils being older, would be more rational, more teachable, and less troublesome than the last: they would be less confined to the schoolroom, and not require that constant labour and incessant watching; and, finally, bright visions mingled with my hopes, with which the care of children and the mere duties of a governess had little or nothing to do. Thus, the reader will see that I had no claim to be regarded as a martyr to filial piety, going forth to sacrifice peace and liberty for the sole purpose of laying up stores for the comfort and support of my parents: though, certainly, the comfort of my father, and the future support of my mother had a large share in my calculations; and fifty pounds appeared to me no ordinary sum. I must have decent clothes becoming my station; I must, it seemed, put out my washing, and also pay for my four annual journeys between Horton Lodge and home; but, with strict attention to economy, surely twenty pounds, or little more, would cover those expenses, and then there would be thirty for the bank, or little less: what a valuable addition to our stock! Oh, I *must* struggle to keep this situation, whatever it might be! both for my own honour among my friends and for the solid services I might render them by my continuance there.

CHAPTER VII.

HORTON LODGE.

THE 31st of January was a wild, tempestuous day: there was a strong north wind, with a continual storm of snow drifting on the ground and whirling through the air. My friends would have had me delay my departure, but fearful of prejudicing my employers against me by such want of punctuality at the commencement of my undertaking, I persisted in keeping the appointment.

I will not inflict upon my readers an account of my leaving home on that dark winter morning: the fond farewells, the long, long journey to O——, the solitary waitings in inns for coaches or trains—for there were some railways then—and, finally, the meeting at O—— with Mr. Murray's servant, who had been sent with the phaeton to drive me from thence to Horton Lodge. I will just state that the heavy snow had thrown such impediments in the way of both horses and steam-engines, that it was dark some hours before I reached my journey's end; and that a most bewildering storm came on at last, which made the few miles space between O—— and Horton Lodge a long and formidable passage. I sat resigned, with the cold, sharp snow drifting through my veil and filling my lap, seeing nothing, and wondering how the unfortunate horse and driver could make their way even as well as they did : and indeed it was but a toilsome, creeping style of progression, to say the best of it. At length we paused ; and, at the call of the driver, some one unlatched and rolled back upon their creaking hinges what appeared to be the park gates. Then we proceeded along a smoother road, whence, occasionally, I perceived some huge, hoary mass gleaming through the darkness, which I took to be a portion of a snow-clad tree. After a considerable time we paused again, before the stately portico of a large house with long windows descending to the ground.

I rose with some difficulty from under the superincumbent snow-drift, and alighted from the carriage, expecting that a kind and hospitable reception would indemnify me for the toils and hardships of the day. A gentlemanly person in black opened the door, and admitted me into a spacious hall lighted by an amber-coloured lamp suspended from the ceiling ; he led me through this, along a passage, and, opening the door of a back room, told me that was the schoolroom. I entered, and found two young ladies and two young gentlemen—my future pupils, I supposed. After a formal greeting, the elder girl, who was trifling over a piece of canvass and a basket of German wools, asked if I should like to go up stairs. I replied in the affirmative, of course.

" Matilda, take a candle, and show her her room," said she.

Miss Matilda, a strapping hoyden of about fourteen, with a short frock and trousers, shrugged her shoulders and made a slight grimace, but took a candle and proceeded before me, up the back stairs (a long, steep, double flight), and through a long, narrow passage, to a small but tolerably comfortable room. She then asked me if I would take some tea or coffee. I was about to answer No ; but remembering that I had taken nothing since seven o'clock that morning, and feeling faint in consequence, I said I would take a cup of tea. Saying she would tell " Brown," the young lady departed ; and by the time I had divested myself of my heavy, wet cloak, shawl, bonnet, &c., a mincing damsel came to say, the young ladies desired to know whether I would take my tea up there or in the schoolroom. Under the plea of fatigue, I chose to take it there. She withdrew; and, after a while, returned again with a small tea-tray, and placed it on the chest of drawers which served as a dressing-table. Having civilly thanked her, I asked at what time I should be expected to rise in the morning.

"The young ladies and gentlemen breakfast at half-past eight, ma'am," said she; "they rise early; but, as they seldom do any lessons before breakfast, I should think it will do if you rise soon after seven."

I desired her to be so kind as to call me at seven, and, promising to do so, she withdrew. Then, having broken my long fast on a cup of tea and a little thin bread and butter, I sat down beside the small, smouldering fire, and amused myself with a hearty fit of crying; after which, I said my prayers, and then, feeling considerably relieved, began to prepare for bed. Finding that none of my luggage was brought up, I instituted a search for the bell; and failing to discover any signs of such a convenience in any corner of the room, I took my candle and ventured through the long passage, and down the steep stairs, on a voyage of discovery. Meeting a well-dressed female on the way, I told her what I wanted; but not without considerable hesitation, as I was not quite sure whether it was one of the upper servants, or Mrs. Murray herself: it happened, however, to be the lady's maid. With the air of one conferring an unusual favour, she vouchsafed to undertake the sending up of my things; and when I had re-entered my room, and waited and wondered a long time (greatly fearing that she had forgotten or neglected to perform her promise, and doubting whether to keep waiting or go to bed, or go down again) my hopes, at length, were revived by the sound of voices and laughter, accompanied by the tramp of feet along the passage; and presently the luggage was brought in by a rough-looking maid and a man, neither of them very respectful in their demeanour to me. Having shut the door upon their retiring footsteps, and unpacked a few of my things, I betook myself to rest; gladly enough, for I was weary in body and mind.

It was with a strange feeling of desolation, mingled with a strong sense of the novelty of my situation, and a joyless kind of curiosity concerning what was yet unknown, that I awoke the next morning; feeling like one whirled away by enchantment, and suddenly dropped from the clouds into a remote and unknown land, widely and completely isolated from all he had ever seen or known before; or like a thistle-seed borne on the wind to some strange nook of uncongenial soil, where it must lie long enough before it can take root and germinate, extracting nourishment from what appears so alien to its nature : if, indeed, it ever can. But this gives no proper idea of my feelings at all; and no one that has not lived such a retired, stationary life as mine, can possibly imagine what they were : hardly even if he has known what it is to awake some morning and find himself in Port Nelson, in New Zealand, with a world of waters between himself and all that knew him.

I shall not soon forget the peculiar feeling with which I raised my blind and looked out upon the unknown world : a wide, white wilderness was all that met my gaze; a waste of

> " Deserts tossed in snow,
> And heavy-laden groves."

I descended to the schoolroom with no remarkable eager-ness to join my pupils, though not without some feeling of curiosity respecting what a further acquaintance would re-veal. One thing, among others of more obvious importance, I determined with myself—I must begin with calling them Miss and Master. It seemed to me a chilling and unnatural piece of punctilio between the children of a family and their instructor and daily companion : especially where the former were in their early childhood, as at Wellwood House; but even there, my calling the little Bloomfields by their simple names had been regarded as an offensive liberty : as their parents had taken care to show me, by carefully designating them *Master* and *Miss* Bloomfield, &c., in speaking to me. I had been very slow to take the hint, because the whole affair struck me as so very absurd; but now I determined to be wiser, and begin at once with as much form and cere-mony as any member of the family would be likely to require : and indeed, the children being so much older, there would be less difficulty; though the little words Miss and Master seemed to have a surprising effect in repressing all familiar, open-hearted kindness, and extinguishing every gleam of cordiality that might arise between us.

As I cannot, like Dogberry, find it in my heart to bestow *all* my tediousness upon the reader, I will not go on to bore him with a minute detail of all the discoveries and proceedings of this and the following day. No doubt he will be amply satisfied with a slight sketch of the different members of the family, and a general view of the first year or two of my sojourn among them.

To begin with the head: Mr. Murray was, by all accounts, a blustering, roystering country squire; a devoted fox-hunter, a skilful horse-jockey and farrier, an active, practical farmer, and a hearty *bon-vivant*. By all accounts, I say; for, except on Sundays, when he went to church, I never saw him from month to month: unless, in crossing the hall or walking in the grounds, the figure of a tall, stout gentleman, with scarlet cheeks and crimson nose, happened to come across me; on which occasions, if he passed near enough to speak, an unceremonious nod, accompanied by a "Morning, Miss Grey," or some such brief salutation, was usually vouchsafed. Frequently, indeed, his loud laugh reached me from afar; and oftener still I heard him swearing and blaspheming against the footmen, groom, coachman, or some other hapless dependent.

Mrs. Murray was a handsome, dashing lady of forty, who certainly required neither rouge nor padding to add to her charms; and whose chief enjoyments were, or seemed to be, in giving or frequenting parties, and in dressing at the very top of the fashion. I did not see her till eleven o'clock on the morning after my arrival; when she honoured me with a visit, just as my mother might step into the kitchen to see a new servant girl: yet not so, either, for my mother would have seen her immediately after her arrival, and not waited till the next day; and, moreover, she would have addressed her in a more kind and friendly manner, and given her some words of comfort as well as a plain exposition of her duties; but Mrs. Murray did neither the one nor the other. She just stepped into the schoolroom on her return from ordering dinner in the housekeeper's room, bade me good-morning, stood for two minutes by the fire, said a few words about the weather and the "rather rough" journey I must have had yesterday; petted her youngest child—a boy of ten—who had just been wiping his mouth and hands on her gown, after indulging in some savoury morsel from the housekeeper's stores; told me what a sweet, good boy he was; and then sailed out, with a self-complacent smile upon her face: thinking, no doubt, that she had done quite enough for the present, and had been delightfully condescending into the bargain. Her children evidently held the same opinion, and I alone thought otherwise.

After this she looked in upon me once or twice, during the absence of my pupils, to enlighten me concerning my duties towards them. For the girls, she seemed anxious only to render them as superficially attractive and showily accomplished as they could possibly be made, without present trouble or discomfort to themselves; and I was to act accordingly—to study and strive to amuse and oblige, instruct, refine, and polish, with the least possible exertion on their part, and no exercise of authority on mine. With regard to the two boys, it was much the same; only instead of accomplishments, I was to get the greatest possible quantity of Latin grammar and Valpy's Delectus into their heads, in order to fit them for school—the greatest possible quantity at least *without* trouble to themselves. John might be a " little high-spirited," and Charles might be a little " nervous and tedious—"

" But at all events, Miss Grey," said she, " I hope *you* will keep your temper, and be mild and patient throughout; especially with the dear little Charles: he is so extremely nervous and susceptible, and so utterly unaccustomed to anything but the tenderest treatment. You will excuse my naming these things to you; for the fact is, I have hitherto found all the governesses, even the very best of them, faulty in this particular. They wanted that meek and quiet spirit, which St. Matthew, or some of them, says is better than the putting on of apparel—you will know the passage to which I allude, for you are a clergyman's daughter. But I have no doubt you will give satisfaction in this respect as well as the rest. And remember, on all occasions, when any of the young people do anything improper, if persuasion and gentle remonstrance will not do, let one of the others come and tell me; for I can speak to them more plainly than it would be proper for you to do. And make them as happy as you can, Miss Grey, and I dare say you will do very well."

I observed that while Mrs. Murray was so extremely solicitous for the comfort and happiness of her children, and con-

tinually talking about it, she never once mentioned mine;
though they were at home surrounded by friends, and I an
alien among strangers; and I did not yet know enough of
the world, not to be considerably surprised at this anomaly.

Miss Murray, otherwise Rosalie, was about sixteen when I
came, and decidedly a very pretty girl; and in two years
longer, as time more completely developed her form and added
grace to her carriage and deportment, she became positively
beautiful; and that in no common degree. She was tall and
slender, yet not thin; perfectly formed, exquisitely fair, though
not without a brilliant, healthy bloom; her hair, which she
wore in a profusion of long ringlets, was of a very light
brown inclining to yellow; her eyes were pale blue, but
so clear and bright that few would wish them darker;
the rest of her features were small, not quite regular, and not
remarkably otherwise: but altogether you could not hesitate
to pronounce her a very lovely girl. I wish I could say as
much for mind and disposition as I can for her form and
face.

Yet think not I have any dreadful disclosures to make: she
was lively, light-hearted, and could be very agreeable, with
those who did not cross her will. Towards me, when I first
came she was cold and haughty, then insolent and overbear-
ing; but on a further acquaintance, she gradually laid aside
her airs, and in time became as deeply attached to me as it
was possible for *her* to be to one of my character and position: for she seldom lost sight, for above half an hour
at a time, of the fact of my being a hireling and a poor
curate's daughter. And yet, upon the whole, I believe she
respected me more than she herself was aware of; because I
was the only person in the house who steadily professed good
principles, habitually spoke the truth, and generally endeavoured to make inclination bow to duty: and this I say, not,
of course, in commendation of myself, but to show the unfortunate state of the family to which my services were, for
the present, devoted. There was no member of it in whom
I regretted this sad want of principle so much as Miss Murray
herself; not only because she had taken a fancy to me, but
because there was so much of what was pleasant and pre-
possessing in herself, that, in spite of her failings, I really
liked her—when she did not rouse my indignation, or ruffle
my temper by *too* great a display of her faults. These, how-

ever, I would fain persuade myself, were rather the effect
of her education than her disposition: she had never been
perfectly taught the distinction between right and wrong;
she had, like her brothers and sisters, been suffered, from
infancy, to tyrannize over nurses, governesses, and servants;
she had not been taught to moderate her desires, to control her temper or bridle her will, or to sacrifice her own
pleasure for the good of others. Her temper being naturally good, she was never violent or morose, but from constant indulgence and habitual scorn of reason, she was often
testy and capricious; her mind had never been cultivated:
her intellect, at best, was somewhat shallow; she possessed considerable vivacity, some quickness of perception,
and some talent for music and the acquisition of languages,
but till fifteen she had troubled herself to acquire nothing;
—then the love of display had roused her faculties, and induced her to apply herself, but only to the more showy accomplishments. And when I came it was the same : everything was neglected but French, German, music, singing,
dancing, fancy-work, and a little drawing—such drawing as
might produce the greatest show with the smallest labour,
and the principal parts of which were generally done by me.
For music and singing, besides my occasional instructions,
she had the attendance of the best master the country afforded; and in these accomplishments, as well as in dancing,
she certainly attained great proficiency. To music, indeed,
she devoted too much of her time : as, governess though I
was, I frequently told her; but her mother thought that if
she liked it, she *could* not give too much time to the acquisition of so attractive an art. Of fancy-work I knew nothing
but what I gathered from my pupil and my own observation;
but no sooner was I initiated, than she made me useful in
twenty different ways : all the tedious parts of her work were
shifted on to my shoulders ; such as stretching the frames,
stitching in the canvass, sorting the wools and silks, putting
in the grounds, counting the stitches, rectifying mistakes, and
finishing the pieces she was tired of.

At sixteen, Miss Murray was something of a romp, yet
not more so than is natural and allowable for a girl of that
age; but at seventeen, that propensity, like all other things,
began to give way to the ruling passion, and soon was swallowed up in the all absorbing ambition to attract and dazzle

A A

the other sex. But enough of her : now let us turn to her sister.

Miss Matilda Murray was a veritable hoyden, of whom little need be said. She was about two years and a half younger than her sister ; her features were larger, her complexion much darker. She might possibly make a handsome woman ; but she was far too big-boned and awkward ever to be called a pretty girl, and at present she cared little about it. Rosalie knew all her charms, and thought them even greater than they were, and valued them more highly than she ought to have done, had they been three times as great ; Matilda thought she was well enough, but cared little about the matter ; still less did she care about the cultivation of her mind, and the acquisition of ornamental accomplishments. The manner in which she learnt her lessons and practised her music, was calculated to drive any governess to despair. Short and easy as her tasks were, if done at all, they were slurred over, at any time and in any way ; but generally at the least convenient times, and in the way least beneficial to herself, and least satisfactory to me : the short half-hour of practising was horribly strummed through ; she, meantime, unsparingly abusing me, either for interrupting her with corrections, or for not rectifying her mistakes before they were made, or something equally unreasonable. Once or twice, I ventured to remonstrate with her seriously for such irrational conduct ; but on each of those occasions, I received such reprehensive expostulations from her mother, as convinced me that, if I wished to keep the situation, I must even let Miss Matilda go on in her own way.

When her lessons were over, however, her ill-humour was generally over too : while riding her spirited pony, or romping with the dogs or her brothers and sister, but especially with her dear brother John, she was as happy as a lark. As an animal, Matilda was all right, full of life, vigour, and activity ; as an intelligent being, she was barbarously ignorant, indocile, careless, and irrational ; and, consequently, very distressing to one who had the task of cultivating her understanding, reforming her manners, and aiding her to acquire those ornamental attainments which, unlike her sister, she despised as much as the rest. Her mother was partly aware of her deficiencies, and gave me many a lecture as to how I should try to form her tastes, and endeavour to rouse and cherish her dormant vanity; and, by insinuating, skilful flattery, to win her attention to the desired objects —which I would not do; and how I should prepare and smooth the path of learning till she could glide along it without the least exertion to herself: which I could not, for nothing can be taught to any purpose without some little exertion on the part of the learner.

As a moral agent, Matilda was reckless, headstrong, violent, and unamenable to reason. One proof of the deplorable state of her mind was, that from her father's example she had learned to swear like a trooper. Her mother was greatly shocked at the "unlady-like trick," and wondered "how she had picked it up." "But you can soon break her of it, Miss Grey," said she: "it is only a habit; and if you will just gently remind her every time she does so, I am sure she will soon lay it aside." I not only "gently reminded" her, I tried to impress upon her how wrong it was, and how distressing to the ears of decent people; but all in vain: I was only answered by a careless laugh, and, "Oh, Miss Grey, how shocked you are! I'm so glad!" Or, "Well! I can't help it; papa shouldn't have taught me: I learned it all from him; and may be a bit from the coachman."

Her brother John, *alias* Master Murray, was about eleven when I came; a fine, stout, healthy boy, frank and good-natured in the main, and might have been a decent lad had he been properly educated; but now he was as rough as a young bear, boisterous, unruly, unprincipled, untaught, unteachable—at least, for a governess under his mother's eye. His masters at school might be able to manage him better —for to school he was sent, greatly to my relief, in the course of a year; in a state, it is true, of scandalous ignorance as to Latin, as well as the more useful though more neglected things: and this, doubtless, would all be laid to the account of his education having been entrusted to an ignorant female teacher, who had presumed to take in hand what she was wholly incompetent to perform. I was not delivered from his brother till full twelve months after, when he also was despatched in the same state of disgraceful ignorance as the former.

Master Charles was his mother's peculiar darling. He was little more than a year younger than John, but much smaller, paler, and less active and robust; a pettish, cowardly, capricious, selfish little fellow, only active in doing mischief, and only clever in inventing falsehoods: not simply to hide his faults, but, in mere malicious wantonness, to bring odium upon others. In fact, Master Charles was a very great nuisance to me: it was a trial of patience to live with him peaceably; to watch over him was worse; and to teach him, or pretend to teach him, was inconceivable. At ten years old, he could not read correctly the easiest line in the simplest book; and as, according to his mother's principle, he was to be told every word, before he had time to hesitate or examine its orthography, and never even to be informed, as a stimulant to exertion, that other boys were more forward than he, it is not surprising that he made but little progress during the two years I had charge of his education. His minute portions of Latin grammar, &c., were to be repeated over to him, till he chose to say he knew them, and then he was to be helped to say them; if he made mistakes in his little easy sums in arithmetic, they were to be shown him at once, and the sum done for him, instead of his being left to exercise his faculties in finding them out himself; so that, of course, he took no pains to avoid mistakes, but frequently set down his figures at random, without any calculation at all.

I did not invariably confine myself to these rules: it was against my conscience to do so; but I seldom could venture to deviate from them in the slightest degree, without incurring the wrath of my little pupil, and subsequently of his mama; to whom he would relate my transgressions, maliciously exaggerated, or adorned with embellishments of his own; and often, in consequence, was I on the point of losing or resigning my situation. But, for their sakes at home, I smothered my pride and suppressed my indignation, and managed to struggle on till my little tormentor was despatched to school; his father declaring that home education was "no go for him, it was plain: his mother spoiled him outrageously, and his governess could make no hand of him at all."

A few more observations about Horton Lodge and its ongoings, and I have done with dry description for the present. The house was a very respectable one; superior to Mr. Bloomfield's, both in age, size, and magnificence: the garden was not so tastefully laid out; but instead of the smooth-shaven lawn, the young trees guarded by palings, the grove of upstart poplars, and the plantation of firs, there was a wide park, stocked with deer, and beautified by fine old trees. The surrounding country itself was pleasant, as far as fertile fields, flourishing trees, quiet green lanes, and smiling hedges with wild flowers scattered along their banks, could make it; but it was depressingly flat to one born and nurtured among the rugged hills of ——.

We were situated nearly two miles from the village church, and, consequently, the family carriage was put in requisition every Sunday morning, and sometimes oftener. Mr. and Mrs. Murray generally thought it sufficient to show themselves at church once in the course of the day; but frequently the children preferred going a second time to wandering about the grounds all the day with nothing to do. If some of my pupils chose to walk and take me with them, it was well for me; for otherwise, my position in the carriage was, to be crushed into the corner farthest from the open window, and with my back to the horses: a position which invariably made me sick; and, if I were not actually obliged to leave the church in the middle of the service, my devotions were disturbed with a feeling of languor and sickliness, and the tormenting fear of its becoming worse; and a depressing headache was generally my companion throughout the day, which would otherwise have been one of welcome rest, and holy, calm enjoyment.

"It's very odd, Miss Grey, that the carriage should always make you sick: it never makes *me*," remarked Miss Matilda.

"Nor me either," said her sister; "but I dare say it would, if I sat where she does—such a nasty, horrid place, Miss Grey; I wonder how you can bear it!"

I am obliged to bear it, since no choice is left me—I might have answered; but in tenderness for their feelings I only replied—"Oh! it is but a short way, and if I am not sick in church, I don't mind it."

If I were called upon to give a description of the usual divisions and arrangements of the day, I should find it a very difficult matter. I had all my meals in the schoolroom with my pupils, at such times as suited their fancy: sometimes they would ring for dinner before it was half cooked; sometimes they would keep it waiting on the table for above an hour, and then be out of humour because the potatoes were cold, and the gravy covered with cakes of solid fat; sometimes they would have tea at four; frequently, they would storm at the servants because it was not in precisely at five; and when these orders were obeyed, by way of encouragement to punctuality, they would keep it on the table till seven or eight.

Their hours of study were managed in much the same way: my judgment or convenience was never once consulted. Sometimes Matilda and John would determine "to get all the plaguy business over before breakfast," and send the maid to call me up at half-past five, without any scruple or apology; sometimes, I was told to be ready precisely at six, and, having dressed in a hurry, came down to an empty room, and after waiting a long time in suspense, discovered that they had changed their minds, and were still in bed; or, perhaps, if it were a fine summer morning, Brown would come to tell me that the young ladies and gentlemen had taken a holiday, and were gone out; and then, I was kept waiting for breakfast till I was almost ready to faint: they having fortified themselves with something before they went.

Often they would do their lessons in the open air; which I had nothing to say against: except that I frequently caught cold by sitting on the damp grass, or from exposure to the evening dew, or some insidious draught, which seemed to have no injurious effect on them. It was quite right that they should be hardy; yet, surely, they might have been taught some consideration for others who were less so. But I must not blame them for what was, perhaps, my own fault; for I never made any particular objections to sitting where they pleased; foolishly choosing to risk the consequences, rather than trouble them for my convenience. Their indecorous manner of doing their lessons was quite as remarkable as the caprice displayed in their choice of time and place. While receiving my instructions, or repeating what they had learned, they would lounge upon the sofa, lie on the rug, stretch, yawn, talk to each other, or look out of the window; whereas, I could not so much as stir the fire, or pick up the handkerchief I had dropped, without being rebuked for inattention by one of my pupils, or told that "mama would not like me to be so careless."

The servants, seeing in what little estimation the governess was held by both parents and children, regulated their behaviour by the same standard. I have frequently stood up for them, at the risk of some injury to myself, against the tyranny and injustice of their young masters and mistresses; and I always endeavoured to give them as little trouble as possible: but they entirely neglected my comfort, despised my requests, and slighted my directions. All servants, I am convinced, would not have done so; but domestics in general, being ignorant and little accustomed to reason and reflection, are too easily corrupted by the carelessness and bad example of those above them; and these, I think, were not of the best order to begin with.

I sometimes felt myself degraded by the life I led, and ashamed of submitting to so many indignities; and sometimes I thought myself a fool for caring so much about them, and feared I must be sadly wanting in christian humility, or that charity which "suffereth long and is kind, seeketh not her own, is not easily provoked, beareth all things, endureth all things." But, with time and patience, matters began to be slightly ameliorated: slowly, it is true, and almost imperceptibly; but I got rid of my male pupils (that was no trifling advantage), and the girls, as I intimated before concerning one of them, became a little less insolent, and began to show some symptoms of esteem. "Miss Grey was a queer creature: she never flattered, and did not praise them half enough; but whenever she did speak favourably of them, or anything belonging to them, they could be quite sure her approbation was sincere. She was very obliging, quiet, and peaceable in the main, but there were some things that put her out of temper: they did not much care for that, to be sure, but still it was better to keep her in tune; as when she was in a good humour she would talk to them, and be very agreeable and amusing sometimes, in her way; which was quite different to mama's, but still very well for a change. She had her own opinions on every subject, and kept steadily to them—very tiresome opinions they often were; as she was always thinking of what was right and what was wrong, and had a strange reverence for matters connected with religion, and an unaccountable liking to good people."

CHAPTER VIII.

THE "COMING OUT."

At eighteen, Miss Murray was to emerge from the quiet obscurity of the schoolroom into the full blaze of the fashionable
world—as much of it, at least, as could be had out of London; for her papa could not be persuaded to leave his rural
pleasures and pursuits, even for a few weeks' residence in
town. She was to make her debut on the third of January,
at a magnificent ball, which her mama proposed to give to all
nobility and choice gentry of O—— and its neighbourhood
for twenty miles round. Of course, she looked forward to it
with the wildest impatience, and the most extravagant anticipations of delight.

"Miss Grey," said she, one evening, a month before the
all important day, as I was perusing a long and extremely
interesting letter of my sister's—which I had just glanced at
in the morning to see that it contained no very bad news,
and kept till now, unable before to find a quiet moment for
reading it,—"Miss Grey, do put away that dull, stupid
letter, and listen to me! I'm sure my talk must be far more
amusing than that."

She seated herself on the low stool at my feet; and I,
suppressing a sigh of vexation, began to fold up the epistle.

"You should tell the good people at home not to bore
you with such long letters," said she; "and above all, do
bid them write on proper note-paper, and not on those great
vulgar sheets. You should see the charming little lady-like
notes mama writes to her friends."

"The good people at home," replied I, "know very well
that the longer their letters are, the better I like them. I
should be very sorry to receive a charming little lady-like
note from any of them; and I thought you were too much
of a lady yourself, Miss Murray, to talk about the ' vulgarity'
of writing on a large sheet of paper."

"Well, I only said it to tease you. But now I want to
talk about the ball, and to tell you that you positively must
put off your holidays till it is over."

"Why so?—I shall not be present at the ball."

"No, but you will see the rooms decked out before it

begins, and hear the music, and, above all, see me in my splendid new dress. I shall be so charming, you'll be ready to worship me—you really must stay."

" I should like to see you very much; but I shall have many opportunities of seeing you equally charming, on the occasion of some of the numberless balls and parties that are to be, and I cannot disappoint my friends by postponing my return so long."

" Oh, never mind your friends! Tell them we won't let you go."

" But, to say the truth, it would be a disappointment to myself: I long to see them as much as they to see me— perhaps more."

" Well, but it is such a short time."

" Nearly a fortnight by my computation; and, besides, I cannot bear the thoughts of a Christmas spent from home: and, moreover, my sister is going to be married."

" Is she—when?"

" Not till next month; but I want to be there to assist her in making preparations, and to make the best of her company while we have her."

" Why didn't you tell me before?"

" I've only got the news in this letter, which you stigmatise as dull and stupid, and won't let me read."

" To whom is she to be married?"

" To Mr. Richardson, the vicar of a neighbouring parish."

" Is he rich?"

" No; only comfortable."

" Is he handsome?"

" No, only decent."

" Young?"

" No; only middling."

" O mercy! what a wretch! What sort of a house is it?"

" A quiet little vicarage, with an ivy-clad porch, an old fashioned garden, and—"

"Oh stop!—you'll make me sick. How *can* she bear it?"

" I expect she'll not only be able to bear it, but to be very happy. You did not ask me if Mr. Richardson were a good, wise, or amiable man; I could have answered Yes, to all these questions—at least so Mary thinks, and I hope she will not find herself mistaken."

" But—miserable creature! how can she think of spending

her life there, cooped up with that nasty old man; and *no* hope of change?"

"He is not old: he's only six or seven and thirty; and she herself is twenty-eight, and as sober as if she were fifty."

· "Oh! that's better then—they're well matched: but do they call him the 'worthy vicar'?"

"I don't know; but if they do, I believe he merits the epithet."

"Mercy, how shocking! and will she wear a white apron, and make pies and puddings?"

"I don't know about the white apron, but I dare say she will make pies and puddings now and then; but that will be no great hardship, as she has done it before."

"And will she go about in a plain shawl, and a large straw bonnet, carrying tracts and bone soup to her husband's poor parishioners?"

"I'm not clear about that; but I dare say she will do her best to make them comfortable in body and mind, in accordance with our mother's example."

CHAPTER IX.

THE BALL.

"Now, Miss Grey," exclaimed Miss Murray, immediately I entered the schoolroom, after having taken off my outdoor garments, upon returning from my four weeks' recreation, "Now—shut the door, and sit down, and I'll tell you all about the ball."

"No,—damn it, no!" shouted Miss Matilda. "Hold your tongue, can't ye? and let me tell her about my new mare—*such* a splendour, Miss Grey! a fine blood mare—"

"Do be quiet, Matilda; and let me tell my news first."

"No, no, Rosalie; you'll be such a damned long time over it—she shall hear me first.—I'll be hanged if she doesn't!"

"I'm sorry to hear, Miss Matilda, that you've not got rid of that shocking habit yet."

" Well, I can't help it: but I'll never say a wicked word again, if you'll only listen to me, and tell Rosalie to hold her confounded tongue."

Rosalie remonstrated, and I thought I should have been torn in pieces between them; but Miss Matilda having the loudest voice, her sister at length gave in, and suffered her to tell her story first: so I was doomed to hear a long account of her splendid mare, its breeding and pedigree, its paces, its action, its spirit, &c., and of her own amazing skill and courage in riding it; concluding with an assertion that she could clear a five-barred gate " like winking," that papa said she might hunt next time the hounds met, and mama had ordered a bright scarlet hunting-habit for her.

" Oh, Matilda! what stories you are telling!" exclaimed her sister.

" Well," answered she, no whit abashed, " I know I *could* clear a five-barred gate, if I tried, and papa *will* say I may hunt, and mama *will* order the habit when I ask it "

" Well, now get along," replied Miss Murray; " and do, dear Matilda, try to be a little more lady-like. Miss Grey, I wish you *would* tell her not to use such shocking words; she *will* call her horse a mare: it is so *inconceivably* shock-ing! and then she uses such dreadful expressions in de-scribing it: she *must* have learned it from the grooms. It nearly puts me into fits when she begins."

" I learned it from papa, you ass! and his jolly friends," said the young lady, vigorously cracking a hunting-whip, which she habitually carried in her hand. " I'm as good a judge of horseflesh as the best of 'em."

" Well, now get along, you shocking girl! I really shall take a fit if you go on in such a way. And now, Miss Grey, attend to me; I'm going to tell you about the ball. You must be dying to hear about it, I know. Oh, *such* a ball! You never saw or heard, or read, or dreamt of anything like it in all your life! The decorations, the entertainment, the supper, the music were indescribable! and then the guests! There were two noblemen, three baronets, and five titled ladies, and other ladies and gentlemen innumerable. The ladies, of course, were of no consequence to me, except to put me in a good humour with myself, by showing how ugly and awkward most of them were; and the best, mama told me,—the most transcendent beauties among them, were nothing to me. As for *me*, Miss Grey—I'm so *sorry* you didn't see me! I was *charming*—wasn't I, Matilda?"

" Middling."

" No, but I really *was*—at least so mama said—and Brown and Williamson. Brown said she was sure no gentleman could set eyes on me without falling in love that minute; and so I may be allowed to be a little vain. I know you think me a shocking, conceited, frivolous girl; but, then, you know, I don't attribute it *all* to my personal attractions: I give some praise to the hairdresser, and some to my exquisitely lovely dress—you must see it to-morrow—white gauze over pink satin—and so *sweetly* made! and a necklace and brace-let of beautiful, large pearls! "

" I have no doubt you looked very charming: but should that delight you so very much ?"

" Oh, no !—not that alone : but, then, I was so much ad-mired; and I made so *many* conquests in that one night—you'd be astonished to hear—"

" But what good will they do you ?"

" What good ! Think of any woman asking that !"

" Well, I should think one conquest would be enough; and too much, unless the subjugation were mutual."

" Oh, but you know I never agree with you on those points. Now, wait a bit, and I'll tell you my principal ad-mirers—those who made themselves very conspicuous that night and after : for I've been to two parties since. Unfor-tunately the two noblemen, Lord G—— and Lord F——, were married, or I might have condescended to be particularly gracious to *them* ; as it was, I did not : though Lord F——, who hates his wife, was evidently much struck with me. He asked me to dance with him twice—he is a charming dancer, by-the-bye, and so am I : you can't think how well I did—I was astonished at myself. My lord was very complimentary too—rather too much so in fact—and I thought proper to be a little haughty and repellent; but I had the pleasure of see-ing his nasty, cross wife ready to perish with spite and vexa-tion—"

" Oh, Miss Murray ! you don't mean to say that such a thing could really give you pleasure ! However wrong or —"

" Well, I know its very wrong;—but never mind ! I mean to be good some time—only don't preach now, there's a good creature. I haven't told you half yet. Let me see.

Oh! I was going to tell you how many unmistakeable admirers I had :—Sir Thomas Ashby was one,—Sir Hugh Meltham and Sir Broadley Wilson are old codgers, only fit companions for papa and mama. Sir Thomas is young, rich, and gay ; but an ugly beast, nevertheless : however, mama says I should not mind that after a few months' acquaintance. Then, there was Henry Meltham, Sir Hugh's younger son ; rather good-looking, and a pleasant fellow to flirt with : but *being* a younger son, that is all he is good for ; then there was young Mr. Green, rich enough, but of no family, and a great stupid fellow, a mere country booby ; and then, our good rector, Mr. Hatfield : an *humble* admirer he ought to consider himself ; but I fear he has forgotten to number humility among his stock of christian virtues."

" Was Mr. Hatfield at the ball ?"

" Yes, to be sure. Did you think he was too good to go ?"

" I thought he might consider it unclerical."

" By *no* means. He did not profane his cloth by dancing ; but it was with difficulty he could refrain, poor man : he looked as if he were dying to ask my hand just for *one* set ; and— oh ! by-the-bye—he's got a new curate : that seedy old fellow Mr. Bligh has got his long-wished-for living at last, and is gone."

" And what is the new one like ?".

" Oh, *such* a beast ! Weston his name is. I can give you his description in three words,—an insensate, ugly, stupid blockhead. That's four, but no matter—enough of *him* now."

Then she returned to the ball, and gave me a further account of her deportment there, and at the several parties she had since attended ; and further particulars respecting Sir Thomas Ashby and Messrs. Meltham, Green, and Hatfield, and the ineffaceable impression she had wrought upon each of them.

" Well, which of the four do you like best ?" said I, suppressing my third or fourth yawn.

" I detest them all !" replied she, shaking her bright ringlets in vivacious scorn.

" That means, I suppose, I like them all—but which most ? "

" No, I really detest them all ; but Harry Meltham is the handsomest and most amusing, and Mr. Hatfield the cleverest,

Sir Thomas the wickedest, and Mr. Green the most stupid.
But the one I'm to have, I suppose, if I'm doomed to have
any of them, is Sir Thomas Ashby."

" Surely not, if he's so wicked, and if you dislike him?"

" Oh, I don't mind his being wicked : he's all the better
for that; and as for disliking him—I shouldn't greatly object
to being Lady Ashby of Ashby Park, if I must marry   But
if I could be always young, I would be always single.   I
should like to enjoy myself thoroughly, and coquet with all
the world, till I am on the verge of being called an old maid;
and then, to escape the infamy of that, after having made ten
thousand conquests, to break all their hearts save one, by
marrying some high-born, rich, indulgent husband, whom,
on the other hand, fifty ladies were dying to have."

" Well, as long as you entertain these views, keep single
by all means, and never marry at all : not even to escape the
infamy of old-maidenhood."

CHAPTER X.

THE CHURCH.

" WELL, Miss Grey, what do you think of the new curate?"
asked Miss Murray, on our return from church the Sunday
after the recommencement of our duties.

" I can scarcely tell," was my reply : " I have not even
heard him preach."

" Well, but you saw him, didn't you?"

" Yes, but I cannot pretend to judge of a man's character
by a single, cursory glance at his face."

" But isn't he ugly?"

" He did not strike me as being particularly so; I don't
dislike that cast of countenance : but the only thing I particularly noticed about him was his style of reading; which
appeared to me good—infinitely better, at least, than Mr.
Hatfield's.   He read the Lessons as if he were bent on giving
full effect to every passage : it seemed as if the most careless
person could not have helped attending, nor the most igno-

rant have failed to understand; and the prayers he read as if
he were not reading at all, but praying earnestly and sincerely from his own heart."

" Oh, yes, that's all he is good for: he can plod through
the service well enough; but he has not a single idea beyond
it."

" How do you know?"

" Oh! I know perfectly well; I am an excellent judge in
such matters. Did you see how he went out of church?
stumping along—as if there were nobody there but himself—
never looking to the right hand or the left, and evidently
thinking of nothing but just getting out of the church, and,
perhaps, home to his dinner: his great stupid head could contain no other idea."

" I suppose you would have had him cast a glance into
the squire's pew," said I, laughing at the vehemence of her
hostility.

" Indeed! I should have been highly indignant if he had
dared to do such a thing!" replied she, haughtily tossing her
head; then, after a moment's reflection, she added—" Well,
well! I suppose he's good enough for his place: but, I'm
glad I'm not dependent on *him* for amusement—that's all.
Did you see how Mr. Hatfield hurried out to get a bow from
me, and be in time to put us into the carriage?"

" Yes," answered I; internally adding, " and I thought it
somewhat derogatory to his dignity as a clergyman to come
flying from the pulpit in such eager haste to shake hands
with the squire, and hand his wife and daughters into their
carriage: and, moreover, I owe him a grudge for nearly shutting me out of it;" for, in fact, though I was standing before
his face, close beside the carriage steps, waiting to get in, he
would persist in putting them up and closing the door, till
one of the family stopped him by calling out that the governess was not in yet; then, without a word of apology, he departed, wishing them good-morning, and leaving the footman
to finish the business.

Nota bene.—Mr. Hatfield never spoke to me, neither did
Sir Hugh or Lady Meltham, nor Mr. Harry or Miss Meltham,
nor Mr. Green or his sisters, nor any other lady or gentleman
who frequented that church: nor, in fact, any one that visited
at Horton Lodge.

Miss Murrray ordered the carriage again, in the afternoon,

for herself and her sister: she said it was too cold for them to enjoy themselves in the garden: and besides, she believed Harry Meltham would be at church. "For," said she, smiling slyly at her own fair image in the glass, "he has been a most exemplary attendant at church these last few Sundays: you would think he was quite a good christian. And you may go with us, Miss Grey: I want you to see him; he is so greatly improved since he returned from abroad—you can't think! And besides, then you will have an opportunity of seeing the beautiful Mr. Weston again, and of hearing him preach."

I did hear him preach, and was decidedly pleased with the evangelical truth of his doctrine, as well as the earnest simplicity of his manner, and the clearness and force of his style. It was truly refreshing to hear such a sermon, after being so long accustomed to the dry, prosy discourses of the former curate, and the still less edifying harangues of the rector. Mr. Hatfield would come sailing up the aisle, or rather sweeping along like a whirlwind, with his rich silk gown flying behind him and rustling against the pew doors, mount the pulpit like a conqueror ascending his triumphal car; then sinking on the velvet cushion in an attitude of studied grace, remain in silent prostration for a certain time; then mutter over a Collect, and gabble through the Lord's Prayer, rise, draw off one bright lavender glove, to give the congregation the benefit of his sparkling rings, lightly pass his fingers through his well-curled hair, flourish a cambric handkerchief, recite a very short passage, or, perhaps, a mere phrase of scripture, as a head-piece to his discourse, and, finally, deliver a composition which, as a composition, might be considered good, though far too studied and too artificial to be pleasing to me: the propositions were well laid down, the arguments logically conducted; and yet, it was sometimes hard to listen quietly throughout, without some slight demonstrations of disapproval or impatience.

His favourite subjects were church discipline, rites and ceremonies, apostolical succession, the duty of reverence and obedience to the clergy, the atrocious criminality of dissent, the absolute necessity of observing all the forms of godliness, the reprehensible presumption of individuals who attempted to think for themselves in matters connected with religion, or to be guided by their own interpretations of Scripture, and, occasionally (to please his wealthy parishioners), the necessity of deferential obedience from the poor to the rich—supporting his maxims and exhortations throughout with quotations from the Fathers : with whom he appeared to be far better acquainted than with the Apostles and Evangelists, and whose importance he seemed to consider, at least, equal to theirs. But now and then he gave us a sermon of a different order—what some would call a very good one; but sunless and severe: representing the Deity as a terrible taskmaster, rather than a benevolent father. Yet, as I listened, I felt inclined to think the man was sincere in all he said : he must have changed his views, and become decidedly religious; gloomy, and austere, yet still devout. But such illusions were usually dissipated, on coming out of church, by hearing his voice in jocund colloquy with some of the Melthams or Greens, or, perhaps, the Murrays themselves; probably laughing at his own sermon, and hoping that he had given the rascally people something to think about; perchance, exulting in the thoughts that old Betty Holmes would now lay aside the sinful indulgence of her pipe, which had been her daily solace for upwards of thirty years, that George Higgins would be frightened out of his Sabbath evening walks, and Thomas Jackson would be sorely troubled in his conscience, and shaken in his sure and certain hope of a joyful resurrection at the last day.

Thus, I could not but conclude that Mr. Hatfield was one of those who "bind heavy burdens, and grievous to be borne, and lay them upon men's shoulders, while they themselves will not move them with one of their fingers"; and who " make the word of God of none effect by their traditions, teaching for doctrines the commandments of men." I was well pleased to observe that the new curate resembled him, as far as I could see, in none of these particulars.

" Well, Miss Grey, what do you think of him now?" said Miss Murray, as we took our places in the carriage after service.

" No harm still," replied I.

" No harm!" repeated she, in amazement. " What do you mean ?"

" I mean, I think no worse of him than I did before."

" No worse! I should think not indeed—quite the contrary ! Is he not greatly improved ?"

B B

"Oh, yes; very much indeed," replied I; for I had now discovered that it was Harry Meltham she meant, not Mr. Weston. That gentleman had eagerly come forward to speak to the young ladies: a thing he would hardly have ventured to do had their mother been present; he had likewise politely handed them into the carriage. He had not attempted to shut me out, like Mr. Hatfield; neither, of course, had he offered me his assistance (I should not have accepted it, if he had), but as long as the door remained open he had stood smirking and chatting with them, and then lifted his hat and departed to his own abode: but I had scarcely noticed him all the time. My companions, however, had been more observant; and, as we rolled along, they discussed between them not only his looks, words, and actions, but every feature of his face, and every article of his apparel.

"You sha'n't have him all to yourself, Rosalie," said Miss Matilda at the close of this discussion; "I like him: I know he'd make a nice, jolly companion for me."

"Well, you're quite welcome to him, Matilda," replied her sister, in a tone of affected indifference.

"And I'm sure," continued the other, "he admires me quite as much as he does you; doesn't he, Miss Grey?"

"I don't know; I'm not acquainted with his sentiments."

"Well, but he *does* though."

"My *dear* Matilda! nobody will ever admire you till you get rid of your rough, awkward manners."

"Oh, stuff! Harry Meltham likes such manners; and so do papa's friends."

"Well, you *may* captivate old men, and younger sons; but nobody else, I am sure, will ever take a fancy to you."

"I don't care: I'm not always grubbing after money, like you and mama. If my husband is able to keep a few good horses and dogs, I shall be quite satisfied; and all the rest may go to the devil!"

"Well, if you use such shocking expressions, I'm sure no real gentleman will ever venture to come near you. Really, Miss Grey, you should not let her do so."

"I can't possibly prevent it, Miss Murray."

"And you're quite mistaken, Matilda, in supposing that Harry Meltham admires you: I assure you he does nothing of the kind."

Matilda was beginning an angry reply; but, happily, our

journey was now at an end; and the contention was cut short by the footman opening the carriage door, and letting down the steps for our descent.

CHAPTER XI.

THE COTTAGERS.

As I had now only one regular pupil—though she contrived to give me as much trouble as three or four ordinary ones, and though her sister still took lessons in German and drawing—I had considerably more time at my own disposal than I had ever been blessed with before, since I had taken upon me the governess's yoke; which time, I devoted partly to correspondence with my friends, partly to reading, study, and the practice of music, singing, &c., partly to wandering in the grounds or adjacent fields, with my pupils if they wanted me, alone if they did not.

Often, when they had no more agreeable occupation at hand, the Misses Murray would amuse themselves with visiting the poor cottagers on their father's estate, to receive their flattering homage, or to hear the old stories or gossiping news of the garrulous old women; or, perhaps, to enjoy the purer pleasure of making the poor people happy with their cheering presence and their occasional gifts, so easily bestowed, so thankfully received. Sometimes, I was called upon to accompany one or both of the sisters in these visits; and sometimes I was desired to go alone, to fulfil some promise which they had been more ready to make than to perform; to carry some small donation, or read to one who was sick or seriously disposed : and thus I made a few acquaintances among the cottagers; and, occasionally, I went to see them on my own account.

I generally had more satisfaction in going alone than with either of the young ladies; for they, chiefly owing to their defective education, comported themselves towards their inferiors in a manner that was highly disagreeable for me to witness. They never, in thought, exchanged places with them; and, consequently, had no consideration for their feelings, regarding them as an order of beings entirely different from themselves. They would watch the poor creatures at their meals, making uncivil remarks about their food, and their manner of eating; they would laugh at their simple notions and provincial expressions, till some of them scarcely durst venture to speak; they would call the grave elderly men and women old fools and silly old blockheads to their faces; and all this without meaning to offend. I could see that the people were often hurt and annoyed by such conduct, though their fear of the "grand ladies" prevented them from testifying any resentment; but *they* never perceived it. They thought that, as these cottagers were poor and untaught, they must be stupid and brutish; and as long as they, their superiors, condescended to talk to them, and to give them shillings and half crowns, or articles of clothing, they had a right to amuse themselves, even at their expense; and the people must adore them as angels of light, condescending to minister to their necessities, and enlighten their humble dwellings.

I made many and various attempts to deliver my pupils from these delusive notions without alarming their pride—which was easily offended, and not soon appeased—but with little apparent result; and I know not which was the more reprehensible of the two : Matilda was more rude and boisterous; but from Rosalie's womanly age and lady-like exterior, better things were expected : yet she was as provokingly careless and inconsiderate as a giddy child of twelve.

One bright day in the last week of February, I was walking in the park, enjoying the threefold luxury of solitude, a book, and pleasant weather; for Miss Matilda had set out on her daily ride, and Miss Murray was gone in the carriage with her mama to pay some morning calls. But it struck me that I ought to leave these selfish pleasures, and the park with its glorious canopy of bright blue sky, the west wind sounding through its yet leafless branches, the snow-wreaths still lingering in its hollows, but melting fast beneath the sun, and the graceful deer browsing on its moist herbage already assuming the freshness and verdure of spring—and go to the cottage of one Nancy Brown, a widow, whose son was at work all day in the fields, and who was afflicted with an inflammation in the eyes; which had for some time incapacitated her from reading : to her own great grief, for she was a woman of a serious, thoughtful turn of mind. I accordingly went, and found her alone, as usual, in her little, close, dark cottage, redolent of smoke and confined air, but as tidy and clean as she could make it. She was seated beside her little fire (consisting of a few red cinders and a bit of stick), busily knitting, with a small sackcloth cushion at her feet, placed for the accommodation of her gentle friend the cat; who was seated thereon with her long tail half encircling her velvet paws, and her half-closed eyes dreamily gazing on the low, crooked fender.

" Well, Nancy, how are you to-day?"

" Why, middling, miss, i' myseln—my eyes is no better, but I'm a deal easier i' my mind nor I have been," replied she, rising to welcome me with a contented smile: which I was glad to see, for Nancy had been somewhat afflicted with religious melancholy. I congratulated her upon the change. She agreed that it was a great blessing, and expressed herself " right down thankful for it" ; adding, " If it please God to spare my sight, and make me so as I can read my Bible again, I think I shall be as happy as a queen."

" I hope he will, Nancy," replied I ; " and, meantime, I'll come and read to you now and then, when I have a little time to spare."

With expressions of grateful pleasure, the poor woman moved to get me a chair ; but, as I saved her the trouble, she busied herself with stirring the fire, and adding a few more sticks to the decaying embers ; and then, taking her well-used Bible from the shelf, dusted it carefully, and gave it me. On my asking if there was any particular part she should like me to read, she answered,

" Well, Miss Grey, if it's all the same to you, I should like to hear that chapter in the First Epistle of St. John, that says, ' God is love, and he that dwelleth in love dwelleth in God, and God in him.'

With a little searching, I found these words in the fourth chapter. When I came to the seventh verse she interrupted me, and, with needless apologies for such a liberty, desired me to read it very slowly, that she might take it all in, and dwell on every word ; hoping I would excuse her, as she was but a simple body."

"The wisest person," I replied, " might think over each of these verses for an hour, and be all the better for it ; and I would rather read them slowly than not."

Accordingly, I finished the chapter as slowly as need be, and at the same time as impressively as I could; my auditor listened most attentively all the while, and sincerely thanked me when I had done. I sat still about half a minute to give her time to reflect upon it; when, somewhat to my surprise, she broke the pause by asking me how I liked Mr. Weston?

" I don't know," I replied, a little startled by the suddenness of the question; " I think he preaches very well."

" Ay, he does so; and talks well too."

" Does he?"

" He does. May-be, you haven't seen him—not to talk to him much, yet?"

" No, I never see any one to talk to—except the young ladies of the hall."

" Ah; they're nice, kind young ladies; but they can't talk as he does."

" Then he comes to see you, Nancy?"

" He does, miss; and I'se thankful for it. He comes to see all us poor bodies a deal ofter nor Maister Bligh, or th' Rector ever did; an' it's well he does, for he's always welcome: we can't say as much for th' Rector—there is 'at says they're fair feared on him. When he comes into a house, they say he's sure to find summut wrong, and begin a calling 'em as soon as he crosses th' doorstuns: but may-be he thinks it his duty-like to tell 'em what's wrong. And very oft, he comes o' purpose to reprove folk for not coming to church, or not kneeling an' standing when other folk does, or going to th' Methody chapel, or summut o' that sort: but I can't say 'at he ever fund much fault wi' me. He came to see me once or twice, afore Maister Weston come, when I was so ill troubled in my mind; and as I had only very poor health besides, I made bold to send for him—and he came right enough. I was sore distressed, Miss Grey—thank God, it's owered now—but when I took my Bible, I could get no comfort of it at all. That very chapter 'at you've just been reading troubled me as much as aught—' He that loveth not, knoweth not God.' It seemed fearsome to me; for I felt that I loved neither God nor man as I should do, and could not, if I tried over so. And th' chapter afore, where it says—' He that is born of God cannot commit sin.' And another place where it says—' Love is the fulfilling of the law.' And many—many others, miss: I should fair weary you out, if I was to tell them all. But all seemed to condemn me, and to shew me 'at I was not in the right way; and as I knew not how to get into it, I sent our Bill to beg Maister Hatfield to be as kind as look in on me some day; and when he came, I telled him all my troubles."

"And what did he say, Nancy?"

"Why, miss, he seemed to scorn me. I might be mista'en—but he like gave a sort of a whistle, and I saw a bit of a smile on his face; and he said, 'Oh it's all stuff'! You've been among the Methodists, my good woman." But I telled him I'd never been near the Methodies. And then he said——

"'Well,' says he, 'you must come to church, where you'll hear the scriptures properly explained, instead of sitting poring over your Bible at home.'

"But I telled him I always used coming to church when I had my health; but this very cold winter weather I hardly durst venture so far—and me so bad wi' th' rheumatiz and all.

"But he says, 'It'll do your rheumatiz good to hobble to church: there's nothing like exercise for the rheumatiz. You can walk about the house well enough; why can't you walk to church? The fact is,' says he, 'you're getting too fond of your ease. It's always easy to find excuses for shirking one's duty.'

"But then, you know, Miss Grey, it wasn't so. However, I telled him I'd try. 'But please, sir,' says I, "if I do go to church, what the better shall I be? I want to have my sins blotted out, and to feel that they are remembered no more against me, and that the love of God is shed abroad in my heart; and if I can get no good by reading my Bible an' saying my prayers at home, what good shall I get by going to church?'"

"'The church,' says he, 'is the place appointed by God for His worship. It's your duty to go there as often as you can. If you want comfort, you must seek it in the path of duty'—an' a deal more he said, but I cannot remember all his fine words. However, it all came to this, that I was to come to church as oft as ever I could, and bring my prayer-book with me, an' read up all the sponsers after the clerk, an' stand, an' kneel, an' sit, an' do all as I should, and take the Lord's supper at every opportunity, an' hearken his sermons, and Maister Bligh's, an' it 'ud be all right: if I went on doing my duty, I should get a blessing at last.

"'But if you get no comfort that way,' says he, 'it's all up.'

"'Then sir,' says I, 'should you think I'm a reprobate?'

"'Why,' says he—he says, 'if you do your best to get to heaven and can't manage it, you must be one of those that seek to enter in at the strait gate and shall not be able.'

"An' then he asked me if I'd seen any of the ladies o' th' Hall about that mornin'; so I telled him where I'd seen the young misses go on th' moss-lane;—an' he kicked my poor cat right across th' floor, an' went off after 'em as gay as a lark: but I was very sad. That last word o' his fair sunk into my heart, an' lay there like a lump o' lead, till I was weary to bear it.

"Howsever, I follered his advice: I thought he meant it all for th' best, though he *had* a queer way with him. But you know, miss, he's rich an' young, and such like cannot right understand the thoughts of a poor old woman such as me. But, howsever, I did my best to do all as he bade me —but may-be I'm plaguing you, miss, wi' my chatter."

"Oh no, Nancy! Go on, and tell me all."

"Well, my rheumatiz got better—I know not whether wi' going to church or not, but one frosty Sunday I got this cold i' my eyes. Th' inflammation didn't come on all at once like, but bit by bit—but I wasn't going to tell you about my eyes, I was talking about my trouble o' mind;— and to tell the truth, Miss Grey, I don't think it was anyways eased by coming to church—nought to speak on, at least: I like got my health better; but that didn't mend my soul. I hearkened and hearkened the ministers, and read an' read at my prayer-book; but it was all like sounding brass, and a tinkling cymbal: the sermons I couldn't understand, an' th' prayer-book only served to shew me how wicked I was, that I could read such good words an' never be no better for it, and oftens feel it a sore labour an' a heavy task beside, instead of a blessing and a privilege as all good Christians does. It seemed like as all were barren an' dark to me. And then, them dreadful words, 'Many shall seek to enter in, and shall not be able.' They like as they fair dried up my sperrit.

"But one Sunday, when Maister Hatfield gave out about the sacrament, I noticed where he said, ' If there be any of you that cannot quiet his own conscience, but requireth further comfort or counsel, let him come to me, or some other discreet and learned minister of God's word, and open his grief !' So, next Sunday morning, afore service, I just looked into the vestry, an' began a talking to th' Rector again. I hardly could fashion to take such a liberty, but I thought when my soul was at stake I shouldn't stick at a trifle. But he said he hadn't time to attend to me then.

" ' And, indeed,' says he, ' I've nothing to say to you but what I've said before. Take the sacrament of course, and go on doing your duty ; and if that won't serve you, nothing will. So don't bother me any more.'

" So then, I went away. But I heard Maister Weston— Maister Weston was there, miss—this was his first Sunday at Horton, you know, an' he was i' th' vestry in his surplice, helping th' Rector on with his gown."

" Yes, Nancy."

" And I heard him ask Maister Hatfield who I was; an' he says, ' Oh, she's a canting old fool.'

" And I was very ill grieved, Miss Grey ; but I went to my seat, and I tried to do my duty as aforetime : but I like got no peace. An' I even took the sacrament; but I felt as though I were eating and drinking to my own damnation all th' time. So I went home, sorely troubled.

" But next day, afore I'd gotten fettled up—for indeed, miss, I'd no heart to sweeping an' fettling, an' washing pots ; so I sat me down i' th' muck—who should come in but Maister Weston ! I started aiding stuff then, an' sweeping an' doing ; and I expected he'd begin a calling me for my idle ways, as Maister Hatfield would a' done ; but I was mista'en: he only bid me good-mornin' like, in a quiet dacent way. So I dusted him a chair, an' fettled up th' fireplace a bit ; but I hadn't forgotten th' Rector's words, so says I, ' I wonder, sir, you should give yourself that trouble, to come so far to see a " canting old fool," such as me.'

" He seemed taken aback at that ; but he would fain persuade me 'at the Rector was only in jest ; and when that wouldn't do, he says, ' Well Nancy, you shouldn't think so much about it : Mr. Hatfield was a little out of humour just then : you know we're none of us perfect—even Moses spoke unadvisedly with his lips. But now sit down a minute, if you can spare the time, and tell me all your doubts and fears; and I'll try to remove them.'

"So I sat me down anent him. He was quite a stranger you know, Miss Grey, and even *younger* nor Maister Hatfield, I believe; an' I had thought him not so pleasant looking as him, and rather a bit crossish, at first, to look at; but he spake so civil like—and when th' cat, poor thing, jumped on to his knee, he only stroked her, and gave a bit of a smile: so I thought that was a good sign; for once, when she did so to th' Rector, he knocked her off, like as it might be in scorn and anger, poor thing. But you can't expect a cat to know manners like a Christian, you know, Miss Grey."

"No; of course not, Nancy. But what did Mr. Weston say then?"

"He said naught; but he listened to me as steady an' patient as could be, an' never a bit o' scorn about him; so I went on, an' telled him all, just as I've telled you—an' more too.

"'Well,' says he, 'Mr. Hatfield was quite right in telling you to persevere in doing your duty; but in advising you to go to church and attend to the service, and so on, he didn't mean that was the whole of a Christian's duty: he only thought you might there learn what more was to be done, and be led to take delight in those exercises, instead of finding them a task and a burden. And if you had asked him to explain those words that trouble you so much, I think he would have told you, that if many shall seek to enter in at the strait gate and shall not be able, it is their own sins that hinder them; just as a man with a large sack on his back might wish to pass through a narrow doorway, and find it impossible to do so unless he would leave his sack behind him. But you, Nancy, I dare say, have no sins that you would not gladly throw aside, if you knew how?'

"'Indeed sir, you speak truth,' said I.

"'Well,' says he, 'you know the first and great commandment—and the second which is like unto it—on which two commandments hang all the law and the prophets? You say you cannot love God; but it strikes me, that if you rightly consider who and what He is, you cannot help it. He is your father, your best friend : every blessing, every-

thing good, pleasant, or useful comes from Him; and everything evil, everything you have reason to hate, to shun, or
to fear comes from satan—*His* enemy as well as ours. And
for *this* cause was God manifest in the flesh, that He might
destroy the works of the devil : in one word God IS LOVE ;
and the more of love we have within us, the nearer we are to
Him, and the more of His spirit we possess.'

" ' Well sir,' I said, ' if I can always think on these things,
I think I might well love God : but how can I love my neighbours, when they vex me, and be so contrairy and sinful as
some on 'em is ? '

" ' It may seem a hard matter,' says he, ' to love our
neighbours, who have so much of what is evil about them,
and whose faults so often awaken the evil that lingers within
ourselves; but remember, that *He* made them, and *He* loves
them ; and whosoever loved him that begat, loveth him that
is begotten also. And if God so loveth us, that He gave
His only begotten Son to die for us, we ought also to love
one another. But if you cannot feel positive affection for
those who do not care for you, you can at least try to do to
them as you would they should do unto you : you can endeavour to pity their failings and excuse their offences, and
to do all the good you can to those about you. And if you
accustom yourself to this, Nancy, the very effort itself will
make you love them in some degree—to say nothing of the
goodwill your kindness would beget in them, though they
might have little else that is good about them. If we love
God and wish to serve him, let us try to be like Him, to do
His work, to labour for His glory—which is the good of
man—to hasten the coming of His kingdom, which is the
peace and happiness of all the world : however powerless we
may seem to be, in doing all the good we can through life,
the humblest of us may do much towards it; and let us dwell
in love, that He may dwell in us and we in Him. The more
happiness we bestow, the more we shall receive, even here ;
and the greater will be our reward in heaven when we rest
from our labours.' I believe, miss, them is his very words,
for I've thought e'm ower many a time. An' then he took
that Bible, an' read bits here and there, an' explained 'em as
clear as the day : and it seemed like as a new light broke in
on my soul; an' I felt fair a glow about my heart, an' only

wished poor Bill an' all the world could ha' been there, an' heard it all, and rejoiced wi' me.

" After he was gone, Hannah Rogers, one o' th' neighbours, came in and wanted me to help her to wash. I telled her I couldn't just then, for I hadn't set on th' potaties for th' dinner, nor washed up th' breakfast stuff yet. So then she began a calling me for my nasty idle ways. I was a little bit vexed at first, but I never said nothing wrong to her: I only telled her, like all in a quiet way, 'at I'd had th' new parson to see me; but I'd get done as quick as ever I could, an' then come an' help her. So then she softened down; and my heart like as it warmed towards her, an' in a bit we was very good friends. An' so it is, Miss Grey, 'a soft answer turneth away wrath; but grievous words stir up anger.' It isn't only in them you speak to, but in yourself."

" Very true, Nancy, if we could always remember it."

" Ay, if we could !"

" And did Mr. Weston ever come to see you again?"

" Yes, many a time ; and since my eyes has been so bad, he's sat an' read to me by the half hour together: but you know, miss, he has other folks to see, and other things to do —God bless him ! An' that next Sunday he preached *such* a sermon ! His text was, ' Come unto me all ye that labour and are heavy laden, and I will give you rest,' and them two blessed verses that follows. You wasn't there, miss, you was with your friends then—but it made me *so* happy ! And I *am* happy now, thank God! an' I take a pleasure, now, in doing little bits o' jobs for my neighbours—such as a poor old body 'a 'ts half blind can do; and they take it kindly of me, just as he said. You see, miss, I'm knitting a pair o' stockings now ;—they're for Thomas Jackson : he's a queerish old body, an' we've had many a bout at threaping, one anent t'other ; an' at times we've differed sorely. So I thought I couldn't do better nor knit him a pair o' warm stockings ; an' I've felt to like him a deal better, poor old man, sin' I began. It's turned out just as Maister Weston said."

" Well, I'm very glad to see you so happy, Nancy, and so wise: but I must go now ; I shall be wanted at the Hall," said I, and bidding her good-bye, I departed, promising to come again when I had time, and feeling nearly as happy as herself.

At another time, I went to read to a poor labourer who was in the last stage of consumption. The young ladies had been to see him, and somehow a promise of reading had been extracted from them; but it was too much trouble, so they begged *me* to do it instead. I went, willingly enough; and there too I was gratified with the praises of Mr. Weston, both from the sick man and his wife. The former told me that he derived great comfort and benefit from the visits of the new parson, who frequently came to see him, and was "another guess sort of man," to Mr. Hatfield; who before the other's arrival at Horton had now and then paid him a visit; on which occasions he would always insist upon having the cottage door kept open, to admit the fresh air for his own convenience, without considering how it might injure the sufferer; and having opened his Prayer-book and hastily read over a part of the Service for the sick, would hurry away again: if he did not stay to administer some harsh rebuke to the afflicted wife, or to make some thoughtless, not to say heartless, observation, rather calculated to increase than diminish the troubles of the suffering pair.

"Whereas," said the man, "Maister Weston 'ull pray with me quite in a different fashion, an' talk to me as kind as owt; an' oft read to me too, an' sit beside me just like a brother."

"Just for all the world!" exclaimed his wife; "an' about a three wik sin', when he seed how poor Jem shivered wi' cold, an' what pitiful fires we kept. he axed if wer stock o' coals was nearly done. I telled him it was, an' we was ill set to get more: but you know mum I didn't think o' him helping us; but howsever, he sent us a sack o' coals next day; un' we've had good fires ever sin : un' a great blessing it is, this winter time. But that's his way, Miss Grey: when he comes into a poor body's house a seein' sick folk, he like notices what they most stand i' need on; an' if he thinks they can't readily get it therseln, he never says nowt about it, but just gets it for 'em. An' it isn't everybody 'at 'ud do that, 'at has as little as he has: for you know, mum, he's now't at all to live on but what he gets fra' th' rector, an' that's little enough they say."

I remembered then, with a species of exultation, that he had frequently been styled a vulgar brute by the amiable

Miss Murray, because he wore a silver watch, and clothes not quite so bright and fresh as Mr. Hatfield's.

In returning to the lodge I felt very happy, and thanked God that I had now something to think about; something to dwell on as a relief from the weary monotony, the lonely drudgery, of my present life: for I *was* lonely. Never, from month to month, from year to year, except during my brief intervals of rest at home, did I see one creature to whom I could open my heart, or freely speak my thoughts with any hope of sympathy, or even comprehension: never one, unless it were poor Nancy Brown, with whom I could enjoy a single moment of real social intercourse, or whose conversation was calculated to render me better, wiser, or happier than before; or who, as far as I could see, could be greatly benefited by mine. My only companions had been unamiable children, and ignorant, wrong-headed girls; from whose fatiguing folly, unbroken solitude was often a relief most earnestly desired and dearly prized. But to be restricted to such associates was a serious evil, both in its immediate effects and the consequences that were likely to ensue. Never a new idea or stirring thought came to me from without; and such as rose within me were, for the most part, miserably crushed at once, or doomed to sicken and fade away, because they could not see the light.

Habitual associates are known to exercise a great influence over each other's minds and manners. Those whose actions are for ever before our eyes, whose words are ever in our ears, will naturally lead us, albeit against our will, slowly, gradually, imperceptibly, perhaps, to act and speak as they do. I will not presume to say how far this irresistible power of assimilation extends; but if one civilized man were doomed to pass a dozen years amid a race of intractable savages, unless he had power to improve them, I greatly question whether, at the close of that period, he would not have become, at least, a barbarian himself. And I, as I could not make my young companions better, feared exceedingly that they would make me worse—would gradually bring my feelings, habits, capacities, to the level of their own; without, however, imparting to me their light-heartedness and cheerful vivacity.

Already, I seemed to feel my intellect deteriorating, my

heart petrifying, my soul contracting; and I trembled lest
my very moral perceptions should become deadened, my
distinctions of right and wrong confounded, and all my
better faculties be sunk, at last, beneath the baneful influence of such a mode of life. The gross vapours of
earth were gathering round me, and closing in upon my
inward heaven; and thus it was that Mr. Weston rose at
length upon me, appearing like the morning star in my
horizon, to save me from the fear of utter darkness; and I
rejoiced that I had now a subject for contemplation that was
above me, not beneath. I was glad to see that all the world
was not made up of Bloomfields, Murrays, Hatfields,
Ashbys, &c.; and that human excellence was not a mere
dream of the imagination. When we hear a little good and
no harm of a person, it is easy and pleasant to imagine
more: in short, it is needless to analyze all my thoughts;
but Sunday was now become a day of peculiar delight to
me (I was now almost broken-in to the back corner in the
carriage), for I liked to hear him—and I liked to see him,
too; though I knew he was not handsome, or even what is
called agreeable, in outward aspect: but, certainly, he was
not ugly.

In stature he was a little, a very little, above the middle
size; the outline of his face would be pronounced too square
for beauty, but to me it announced decision of character; his
dark brown hair was not carefully curled, like Mr. Hatfield's,
but simply brushed aside over a broad, white forehead; the
eyebrows, I suppose, were too projecting, but from under
those dark brows there gleamed an eye of singular power,
brown in colour, not large, and somewhat deepset, but
strikingly brilliant, and full of expression; there was character, too, in the mouth, something that bespoke a man of
firm purpose and a habitual thinker; and when he smiled—
but I will not speak of that yet, for, at the time I mention, I
had never seen him smile: and, indeed, his general appearance did not impress me with the idea of a man given to
such a relaxation, nor of such an individual as the cottagers
described him. I had early formed my opinion of him; and,
in spite of Miss Murray's objurgations, was fully convinced
that he was a man of strong sense, firm faith, and ardent
piety, but thoughtful and stern: and when I found that,
to his other good qualities, was added that of true bene-

volence and gentle, considerate kindness, the discovery, perhaps, delighted me the more, as I had not been prepared to expect it.

———

CHAPTER XII.

THE SHOWER.

THE next visit I paid to Nancy Brown was in the second week in March: for, though I had many spare minutes during the day, I seldom could look upon an hour as entirely my own; since, where everything was left to the caprices of Miss Matilda and her sister, there could be no order or regularity. Whatever occupation I chose, when not actually busied about them or their concerns, I had, as it were, to keep my loins girded, my shoes on my feet, and my staff in my hand; for not to be immediately forthcoming when called for, was regarded as a grave and inexcusable offence: not only by my pupils and their mother, but by the very servant, who came in breathless haste to call me, exclaiming, " You're to go to the schoolroom *directly*, mum—the young ladies is WAITING!!" Climax of horror! actually waiting for their governess!!!

But this time I was pretty sure of an hour or two to myself; for Matilda was preparing for a long ride, and Rosalie was dressing for a dinner party at Lady Ashby's: so I took the opportunity of repairing to the widow's cottage, where I found her in some anxiety about her cat, which had been absent all day. I comforted her with as many anecdotes of that animal's roving propensities as I could recollect. " I'm feared o' th' gamekeepers," said she, " that's all 'at I think on. If th' young gentlemen had been at home, I should a' thought they'd been setting their dogs at her, 'an' worried her, poor thing, as they did *many* a poor thing's cat; but I haven t that to be feared on now." Nancy's eyes were better, but still far from well: she had been trying to make a Sunday shirt for her son, but told me she could only bear to do a little bit at it now and then, so that it progressed but slowly, though the poor lad wanted it sadly. So I proposed to help her a little, after I had read to her, for I had plenty of time that evening, and need not return till dusk. She thankfully accepted the offer. " An' you'll be a bit o' company for me too, miss," said she ; " I like as I feel lonesome without my cat." But when I had finished reading, and done the half of a seam, with Nancy's capacious brass thimble fitted on to my finger by means of a roll of paper, I was disturbed by the entrance of Mr. Weston, with the identical cat in his arms. I now saw that he could smile, and very pleasantly too.

" I've done you a piece of good service, Nancy," he began ; then seeing me, he acknowledged my presence by a slight bow. I should have been invisible to Hatfield, or any other gentleman of those parts. " I've delivered your cat," he continued, " from the hands, or rather the gun, of Mr. Murray's gamekeeper."

" God bless you, sir!" cried the grateful old woman, ready to weep for joy as she received her favourite from his arms.

" Take care of it," said he, " and don't let it go near the rabbit warren, for the gamekeeper swears he'll shoot it if he sees it there again : he would have done so to-day, if I had not been in time to stop him. I believe it is raining, Miss Grey," added he, more quietly, observing that I had put aside my work, and was preparing to depart. " Don't let me disturb you—I sha'n't stay two minutes."

" You'll *both* stay while this shower gets owered," said Nancy, as she stirred the fire, and placed another chair beside it ; " what ! there's room for all."

" I can see better here, thank you, Nancy," replied I, taking my work to the window, where she had the goodness to suffer me to remain unmolested, while she got a brush to remove the cat's hairs from Mr. Weston's coat, carefully wiped the rain from his hat, and gave the cat its supper, busily talking all the time : now thanking her clerical friend for what he had done ; now wondering how the cat had found out the warren ; and now lamenting the probable consequences of such a discovery. He listened with a quiet, good-natured smile, and at length took a seat in compliance with her pressing invitations, but repeated that he did not mean to stay.

" I have another place to go to," said he, " and I see'

C C

(glancing at the book on the table) " some one else has been reading to you."

" Yes, sir ; Miss Grey has been as kind as read me a chapter ; an' now she's helping me with a shirt for our Bill—but I'm feared she'll be cold there. Won't you come to th' fire, miss ?"

" No, thank you, Nancy, I'm quite warm. I must go as soon as this shower is over."

" Oh, miss ! You said you could stop while dusk !" cried the provoking old woman, and Mr. Weston seized his hat.

" Nay, sir," exclaimed she, " pray don't go now, while it rains so fast."

" But it strikes me I'm keeping your visitor away from the fire."

" No, you're not, Mr. Weston," replied I, hoping there was no harm in a falsehood of that description.

" No, sure !" cried Nancy. "What, there's lots o' room !"

" Miss Grey," said he, half jestingly, as if he felt it necessary to change the present subject, whether he had anything particular to say or not, " I wish you would make my peace with the squire, when you see him. He was by when I rescued Nancy's cat, and did not quite approve of the deed. I told him I thought he might better spare all his rabbits than she her cat, for which audacious assertion he treated me to some rather ungentlemanly language ; and I fear I retorted a trifle too warmly."

" Oh, lawful sir! I hope you didn't fall out wi' th' maister for sake o' my cat! he cannot bide answering again—can th' maister."

"Oh! it's no matter, Nancy : I don't care about it, really ; I said nothing *very* uncivil ; and I suppose Mr. Murray is accustomed to use rather strong language when he's heated."

" Ay, sir : it's a pity !"

" And now, I really must go. I have to visit a place a mile beyond this ; and you would not have me to return in the dark : besides, it has nearly done raining now—so good-evening, Nancy.—Good-evening, Miss Grey."

" Good-evening, Mr. Weston ; but don't depend upon me for making your peace with Mr. Murray, for I never see him —to speak to."

" Don't you? it can't be helped then," replied he in dolorous resignation : then with a peculiar half smile, he added,

" But never mind ; I imagine the squire has more to apologize for than I." And left the cottage.

I went on with my sewing as long as I could see, and then bade Nancy good-evening ; checking her too lively gratitude by the undeniable assurance that I had only done for her what she would have done for me, if she had been in my place and I in hers. I hastened back to Horton Lodge, where having entered the schoolroom, I found the tea-table all in confusion, the tray flooded with slops, and Miss Matilda in a most ferocious humour.

" Miss Grey, whatever have you been about? I've had tea half an hour ago, and had to make it myself, and drink it all alone ! I wish you *would* come in sooner ! "

" I've been to see Nancy Brown. I thought you would not be back from your ride."

" How could I ride in the rain, I should like to know ? That damned pelting shower was vexatious enough—coming on when I was just in full swing : and then to come and find nobody in to tea !—and you know I can't make the tea as I like it."

" I didn't think of the shower," replied I (and, indeed, the thought of its driving her home had never entered my head).

" No, of course ; you were under shelter yourself, and you never thought of other people."

I bore her coarse reproaches with astonishing equanimity, even with cheerfulness ; for I was sensible that I had done more good to Nancy Brown than harm to her : and perhaps some other thoughts assisted to keep up my spirits, and impart a relish to the cup of cold, overdrawn tea, and a charm to the otherwise unsightly table ; and—I had almost said— to Miss Matilda's unamiable face. But she soon betook herself to the stables, and left me to the quiet enjoyment of my solitary meal.

CHAPTER XIII.

THE PRIMROSES.

MISS MURRAY now always went twice to church, for she so loved admiration that she could not bear to lose a single opportunity of obtaining it ; and she was so sure of it wherever she showed herself, that whether Harry Meltham and Mr. Green were there or not, there was certain to be somebody present who would not be insensible to her charms : besides the Rector, whose official capacity generally obliged him to attend. Usually, also, if the weather permitted, both she and her sister would walk home; Matilda because she hated the confinement of the carriage ; she, because she disliked the privacy of it, and enjoyed the company that generally enlivened the first mile of the journey in walking from the church to Mr. Green's park gates : near which commenced the private road to Horton Lodge, which lay in the opposite direction ; while the highway conducted in a straightforward course to the still more distant mansion of Sir Hugh Meltham. Thus there was always a chance of being accompanied, so far, either by Harry Meltham, with or without Miss Meltham, or Mr. Green, with perhaps one or both of his sisters, and any gentlemen visitors they might have.

Whether I walked with the young ladies or rode with their parents, depended upon their own capricious will : if they chose to " take" me, I went; if, for reasons best known to themselves, they chose to go alone, I took my seat in the carriage. I liked walking better, but a sense of reluctance to obtrude my presence on any one who did not desire it, always kept me passive on these and similar occasions; and I never inquired into the causes of their varying whims. Indeed, this was the best policy—for to submit and oblige was the governess's part, to consult their own pleasure was that of the pupils. But when I did walk, this first half of the journey was generally a great nuisance to me. As none of the before-mentioned ladies and gentlemen ever noticed me, it was disagreeable to walk beside them, as if listening to what they said or wishing to be thought one of them, while they talked over me, or across; and if their eyes, in speaking, chanced to fall on me, it seemed as if they looked on vacancy

—as if they either did not see me, or were very desirous to make it appear so. It was disagreeable, too, to walk behind, and thus appear to acknowledge my own inferiority; for, in truth, I considered myself pretty nearly as good as the best of them, and wished them to know that I did so, and not to imagine that I looked upon myself as a mere domestic, who knew her own place too well to walk besides such fine ladies and gentlemen as they were—though her young ladies might choose to have her with them, and even condescend to converse with her when no better company were at hand. Thus —I am almost ashamed to confess it—but indeed I gave myself no little trouble in my endeavours (if I did keep up with them) to appear perfectly unconscious or regardless of their presence, as if I were wholly absorbed in my own reflections or the contemplation of surrounding objects; or if I lingered behind, it was some bird or insect, some tree or flower, that attracted my attention, and having duly examined that, I would pursue my walk alone, at a leisurely pace, until my pupils had bidden adieu to their companions, and turned off into the quiet, private road.

One such occasion I particularly well remember : it was a lovely afternoon about the close of March; Mr. Green and his sisters had sent their carriage back empty, in order to enjoy the bright sunshine and balmy air in a sociable walk home along with their visitors, Captain Somebody and Lieutenant Somebody else (a couple of military fops), and the Misses Murray, who, of course, contrived to join them. Such a party was highly agreeable to Rosalie; but not finding it equally suitable to my taste, I presently fell back, and began to botanize and entomologize along the green banks and budding hedges, till the company was considerably in advance of me. And I could hear the sweet song of the happy lark; then my spirit of misanthropy began to melt away beneath the soft, pure air, and genial sunshine : but sad thoughts of early childhood, and yearnings for departed joys, or for a brighter future lot, arose instead. As my eyes wandered over the steep banks covered with young grass and green-leaved plants, and surmounted by budding hedges, I longed intensely for some familiar flower that might recall the woody dales or green hillsides of home : the brown moorlands, of course, were out of the question. Such a discovery would make my eyes gush out with water, no doubt; but that was one of my greatest enjoyments now. At length, I descried, high up between the twisted roots of an oak, three lovely primroses, peeping so sweetly from their hidingplace that the tears already started at the sight; but they grew so high above me, that I tried in vain to gather one or two, to dream over and to carry with me: I could not reach them, unless I climbed the bank, which I was deterred from doing by hearing a footstep at that moment behind me, and was, therefore, about to turn away, when I was startled by the words, "Allow me to gather them for you, Miss Grey," spoken in the grave, low tones of a well-known voice. Immediately the flowers were gathered, and in my hand. It was Mr. Weston, of course—who else would trouble himself to do so much for *me?*"

I thanked him; whether warmly or coldly, I cannot tell: but certain I am that I did not express half the gratitude I felt. It was foolish, perhaps, to feel any gratitude at all; but it seemed to me, at that moment, as if this were a remarkable instance of his good nature: an act of kindness which I could not repay, but never should forget: so utterly unaccustomed was I to receive such civilities, so little prepared to expect them, from any one within fifty miles of Horton Lodge. Yet this did not prevent me from feeling a little uncomfortable in his presence; and I proceeded to follow my pupils at a much quicker pace than before; though, perhaps, if Mr. Weston had taken the hint and let me pass without another word, I might have repented it an hour after: but he did not. A somewhat rapid walk for me, was but an ordinary pace for him.

"Your young ladies have left you alone," said he.

"Yes; they are occupied with more agreeable company."

"Then don't trouble yourself to overtake them."

I slackened my pace; but next moment regretted having done so: my companion did not speak; and I had nothing in the world to say, and feared he might be in the same predicament. At length, however, he broke the pause by asking, with a certain quiet abruptness peculiar to himself, if I liked flowers.

"Yes; very much," I answered, "wild flowers especially."

"*I* like wild flowers," said he, "others I don't care about, because I have no particular associations connected with them—except one or two. What are your favourite flowers?"

" Primroses, blue-bells, and heath-blossoms."

" Not violets?"

" No; because, as you say, I have no particular associations connected with them; for there are no sweet violets among the hills and valleys round my home."

" It must be a great consolation to you to have a home, Miss Grey," observed my companion after a short pause: " however remote, or however seldom visited, still it is something to look to."

" It is so much that I think I could not live without it," replied I, with an enthusiasm of which I immediately repented; for I thought it must have sounded essentially silly.

" Oh, yes; you could," said he, with a thoughtful smile. " The ties that bind us to life are tougher than you imagine, or than any one can who has not felt how roughly they may be pulled without breaking. You might be miserable without a home, but even *you* could live; and not *so* miserably as you suppose. The human heart is like Indian-rubber: a little swells it, but a great deal will not burst it. If ' little more than nothing will disturb it, little less than all things will suffice' to break it. As in the outer members of our frame, there is a vital power inherent in itself, that strengthens it against external violence. Every blow that shakes it will serve to harden it against a future stroke; as constant labour thickens the skin of the hand, and strengthens its muscles instead of wasting them away: so that a day of arduous toil that might excoriate a lady's palm, would make no sensible impression on that of a hardy ploughman.

" I speak from experience—partly my own. There was a time when I thought as you do—at least, I was fully persuaded that home and its affections were the only things that made life tolerable: that, if deprived of these, existence would become a burden hard to be endured; but now I have no home—unless you would dignify my two hired rooms at Horton by such a name;—and not twelve months ago, I lost the last and dearest of my early friends; and yet, not only I live, but I am not wholly destitute of hope and comfort, even for this life: though I must acknowledge that I can seldom enter even an humble cottage at the close of day, and see its inhabitants peaceably gathered around their cheerful hearth, without a feeling *almost* of envy at their domestic enjoyment."

"You don't know what happiness lies before you yet," said I: "you are now only in the commencement of your journey."

"The best of happiness," replied he, "is mine already—the power and the will to be useful."

We now approached a style communicating with a footpath that conducted to a farm-house, where, I suppose, Mr. Weston purposed to make himself "useful"; for he presently took leave of me, crossed the style, and traversed the path with his usual firm, elastic tread, leaving me to ponder his words as I continued my course alone. I had heard before that he had lost his mother not many months before he came. She then was the last and dearest of his early friends; and he had *no home.* I pitied him from my heart : I almost wept for sympathy. And this, I thought, accounted for the shade of premature thoughtfulness that so frequently clouded his brow, and obtained for him the reputation of a morose and sullen disposition with the charitable Miss Murray and all her kin. " But," thought I, " he is not so miserable as I should be under such a deprivation : he leads an active life; and a wide field for useful exertion lies before him. He can *make* friends; and he can make a home too, if he pleases; and, doubtless, he will please some time. God grant the partner of that home may be worthy of his choice, and make it a happy one—such a home as he deserves to have ! And how delightful it would be to——" But no matter what I thought.

I began this book with the intention of concealing nothing; that those who liked might have the benefit of perusing a fellow-creature's heart : but we have *some* thoughts that all the angels in heaven are welcome to behold, but not our brother-men—not even the best and kindest amongst them.

By this time the Greens had taken themselves to their own abode, and the Murrays had turned down the private road, whither I hastened to follow them. I found the two girls warm in an animated discussion on the respective merits of the two young officers; but on seeing me Rosalie broke off in the middle of a sentence to exclaim, with malicious glee—

" Oh, ho, Miss Grey ! you're come at last, are you ? No *wonder* you lingeerd so long behind ; and no *wonder* you always stand up so vigorously for Mr. Weston when I abuse him. Ah, ha! I see it all now!"

" Now, come Miss Murray, don't be foolish," said I, attempting a good-natured laugh; " you know such nonsense can make no impression on me."

But she still went on talking such intolerable stuff—her sister helping her with appropriate fictions coined for the occasion—that I thought it necessary to say something in my own justification.

" What folly all this is!" I exclaimed. " If Mr. Weston's road happened to be the same as mine for a few yards, and if he chose to exchange a word or two in passing, what is there so remarkable in that? I assure you, I never spoke to him before; except once."

Where? where? and when?" cried they eagerly.

" In Nancy's cottage."

" Ah, ha! you've met him there, have you?" exclaimed Rosalie, with exultant laughter. " Ah! now, Matilda, I've found out why she's so fond of going to Nancy Brown's! she goes there to flirt with Mr. Weston."

" Really that is not worth contradicting!—I only saw him there once, I tell you—and how could I know he was coming?"

Irritated as I was at their foolish mirth and vexatious imputations, the uneasiness did not continue long: when they had had their laugh out, they returned again to the captain and lieutenant; and, while they disputed and commented upon them, my indignation rapidly cooled; the cause of it was quickly forgotten, and I turned my thoughts into a pleasanter channel. Thus we proceeded up the park, and entered the hall; and as I ascended the stairs to my own chamber, I had but one thought within me: my heart was filled to overflowing with one single earnest wish. Having entered the room, and shut the door, I fell upon my knees and offered up a fervent but not impetuous prayer: " Thy will be done," I strove to say throughout; but, " Father, all things are possible with Thee, and may it be Thy will," was sure to follow. That wish—that prayer—both men and women would have scorned me for—" But Father, *Thou* wilt *not* despise!" I said, and felt that it was true. It seemed to me that another's welfare was at least as ardently implored for as my own; nay, even *that* was the principal object of my heart's desire. I might have been deceiving myself; but that idea gave me confidence to ask, and power to hope I did not ask in vain. As for the primroses, I kept two of them in a glass in my room until they were completely withered, and the housemaid threw them out; and the petals of the other I pressed between the leaves of my Bible—I have them still, and mean to keep them always.

CHAPTER XIV.

THE RECTOR.

THE following day was as fine as the preceding one. Soon after breakfast Miss Matilda, having galloped and blundered through a few unprofitable lessons, and vengeably thumped the piano for an hour, in a terrible humour with both me and it, because her mama would not give her a holiday, had betaken herself to her favourite places of resort, the yards, the stables, and the dog-kennels; and Miss Murray was gone forth to enjoy a quiet ramble with a new fashionable novel for her companion, leaving me in the schoolroom hard at work upon a water-colour drawing which I had promised to do for her, and which she insisted upon my finishing that day.

At my feet lay a little rough terrier. It was the property of Miss Matilda; but she hated the animal, and intended to sell it, alleging that it was quite spoiled. It was really an excellent dog of its kind; but she affirmed it was fit for nothing, and had not even the sense to know its own mistress.

The fact was, she had purchased it when but a small puppy, insisting at first that no one should touch it but herself; but, soon becoming tired of so helpless and troublesome a nursling, she had gladly yielded to my entreaties to be allowed to take charge of it; and I, by carefully nursing the little creature from infancy to adolescence, of course, had obtained its affections: a reward I should have greatly valued and looked upon as far outweighing all the trouble I had had with it, had not poor Snap's grateful feelings exposed him to many a harsh word and many a spiteful kick and pinch from his owner, and were he not now in danger of being " put away," in consequence, or transferred to some rough, stony-hearted master. But how could I help it? I could not make the dog hate me, by cruel treatment; and she would not propitiate him by kindness.

However, while I thus sat, working away with my pencil, Mrs. Murray came, half-sailing, half-bustling, into the room.

" Miss Grey," she began,—" dear! how can you sit at your drawing such a day as this?" (She thought I was doing it for my own pleasure.) " I *wonder* you don't put on your bonnet and go out with the young ladies."

" I think, ma'am, Miss Murray is reading; and Miss Matilda is amusing herself with her dogs."

" If you would try to amuse Miss Matilda yourself a little more, I think she would not be *driven* to seek amusement in the companionship of dogs and horses, and grooms, so much as she is; and if you would be a little more cheerful and conversable with Miss Murray, she would not so often go wandering in the fields with a book in her hand. However, I don't want to vex you," added she, seeing, I suppose, that my cheeks burned and my hand trembled with some un-amiable emotion. " Do, pray, try not to be so touchy,—there's no speaking to you else. And tell me if you know where Rosalie is gone: and why she likes to be so much alone?"

" She says she likes to be alone when she has a new book to read."

" But why can't she read it in the park or the garden?—why should she go into the fields and lanes? And how is it that that Mr. Hatfield so often finds her out? She told me last week he'd walked his horse by her side all up Moss Lane; and now I'm sure it was he I saw from my dressing-room window, walking so briskly past the park gates, and on towards the field where she so frequently goes. I wish you would go and see if she is there; and just gently remind her that it is not proper for a young lady of her rank and prospects to be wandering about by herself in that manner, exposed to the attentions of any one that presumes to address her; like some poor neglected girl that has no park to walk in, and no friends to take care of her: and tell her that her papa would be extremely angry if he knew of her treating Mr. Hatfield in the familiar manner that I fear she does;

and—oh! if you—if *any* governess had but half a mother's
watchfulness—half a mother's anxious care, I should be
saved this trouble; and you would see at once the necessity
of keeping your eye upon her, and making your company
agreeable to —— Well, go—go; there's no time to be lost,"
cried she, seeing that I had put away my drawing materials,
and was waiting in the door-way for the conclusion of her
address.

According to her prognostications, I found Miss Murray
in her favourite field just without the park; and, unfortunately, not alone; for the tall, stately figure of Mr. Hatfield was slowly sauntering by her side.

Here was a poser for me. It was my duty to interrupt
the *tête-à-tête:* but how was it to be done? Mr. Hatfield
could not be driven away by so insignificant a person as I;
and to go and place myself on the other side of Miss Murray,
and intrude my unwelcome presence upon her without noticing her companion, was a piece of rudeness I could not be
guilty of: neither had I the courage to cry aloud from the top
of the field that she was wanted elsewhere. So I took the
intermediate course of walking slowly, but steadily towards
them; resolving, if my approach failed to scare away the beau,
to pass by and tell Miss Murray her mama wanted her.

She certainly looked very charming as she strolled, lingering along under the budding horse-chestnut trees that
stretched their long arms over the park-palings, with her
closed book in one hand, and in the other a graceful sprig of
myrtle, which served her as a very pretty plaything; her
bright ringlets escaping profusely from her little bonnet, and
gently stirred by the breeze, her fair cheek flushed with
gratified vanity, her smiling blue eyes, now slyly glancing
towards her admirer, now gazing downward at her myrtle
sprig. But Snap, running before me, interrupted her in the
midst of some half-pert, half-playful repartee, by catching
hold of her dress and vehemently tugging thereat; till Mr.
Hatfield, with his cane, administered a resounding thwack
upon the animal's skull, and sent it yelping back to me,
with a clamorous outcry that afforded the reverend gentleman great amusement; but seeing me so noon, he thought, I
suppose, he might as well be taking his departure; and as I
stooped to caress the dog, with ostentatious pity to shew my
disapproval of his severity, I heard him say,—

" When shall I see you again, Miss Murray?"

" At church, I suppose," replied she, " unless your business chances to bring you here again, at the precise moment when I happen to be walking by."

" I could always manage to have business here, if I knew precisely when and where to find you."

" But if I would, I could not inform you, for I am so immethodical, I never can tell to-day what I shall do to-morrow."

" Then give me that, meantime, to comfort me," said he, half jestingly and half in earnest, extending his hand for the sprig of myrtle.

" No, indeed, I sha'n't."

" Do! *pray* do! I shall be the most miserable of men if you don't. You cannot be so cruel as to deny me a favour so easily granted and yet so highly prized!" pleaded he as ardently as if his life depended on it.

By this time, I stood within a very few yards of them, impatiently waiting his departure.

" There then! take it and go," said Rosalie.

He joyfully received the gift, murmured something that made her blush and toss her head, but with a little laugh that shewed her displeasure was entirely affected; and then with a courteous salutation withdrew.

" Did you ever see such a man, Miss Grey?" said she, turning to me; " I'm so *glad* you came! I thought I never *should* get rid of him; and I was so terribly afraid of papa seeing him."

" Has he been with you long?"

" No, not long, but he's so extremely impertinent: and he's always hanging about, pretending his business or his clerical duties require his attendance in these parts, and really watching for poor me, and pouncing upon me wherever he sees me."

" Well, your mama thinks you ought not to go beyond the park or garden without some discreet, matronly person like me to accompany you, and keep off all intruders. She descried Mr. Hatfield hurrying past the park gates, and forthwith despatched me with instructions to seek you up and to take care of you, and likewise to warn —"

" Oh, mama's so tiresome! As if I couldn't take care of myself. She bothered me before about Mr. Hatfield; and

I told her she might trust me: I never should forget my
rank and station for the most delightful man that ever
breathed. I wish he would go down on his knees to-
morrow, and implore me to be his wife, that I might just
show her how mistaken she is in supposing that I could
ever——Oh, it provokes me so! To think that I could be
such a fool as to fall in *love!* It is quite beneath the dignity of a woman to do such a thing. Love! I detest the
word! as applied to one of our sex, I think it a perfect
insult. A preference I *might* acknowledge; but never for
one like poor Mr. Hatfield, who has not seven hundred a
year to bless himself with. I like to talk to him, because
he's so clever and amusing—I wish Sir Thomas Ashby were
half as nice; besides, I must have *somebody* to flirt with,
and no one else has the sense to come here; and when
we go out, mama won't let me flirt with anybody but Sir
Thomas—if he's there; and if he's *not* there, I'm bound
hand and foot, for fear somebody should go and make up
some exaggerated story, and put it into his head that I'm
engaged, or likely to be engaged, to somebody else; or,
what is more probable, for fear his nasty old mother should
see or hear of my ongoings, and conclude that I'm not a fit
wife for her excellent son: as if the said son were not the
greatest scamp in Christendom; and as if any woman of
common decency were not a world too good for him."

" Is it really so, Miss Murray? and does your mama
know it, and yet wish you to marry him?"

" To-be-sure, she does! She knows more against him than
I do, I believe: she keeps it from me lest I should be discouraged; not knowing how little I care about such things.
For it's no great matter, really: he'll be all right when he's
married, as mama says; and reformed rakes make the best
husbands, *everybody* knows. I only wish he were not so ugly
—*that's* all *I* think about: but then there's no choice here
in the country; and papa *will not* let us go to London—"

" But I should think Mr. Hatfield would be far better."

" And so he would, if he were lord of Ashby Park—there's
not a doubt of it: but the fact is, I *must* have Ashby Park,
whoever shares it with me."

" But Mr. Hatfield thinks you like him all this time; you
don't consider how bitterly he will be disappointed when he
finds himself mistaken."

" *No*, indeed! It will be a proper punishment for his presumption—for ever *daring* to think I could like him. I should enjoy nothing so much as lifting the veil from his ·eyes."

" The sooner you do it the better then."

" No ; I tell you, I like to amuse myself with him. Besides, he doesn'‚t really think I like him. I take good care of that : you don't know how cleverly I manage. He may presume to think he can *induce* me to like him ; for which I shall punish him as he deserves."

" Well, mind you don't give too much reason for such presumption—that's all," replied I.

But all my exhortations were in vain : they only made her somewhat more solicitous to disguise her wishes and her thoughts from me. She talked no more to me about the Rector ; but I could see that her mind, if not her heart, was fixed upon him still, and that she was intent upon obtaining another interview : for though, in compliance with her mother's request, I was now constituted the companion of her rambles for a time, she still persisted in wandering in the fields and lanes that lay in the nearest proximity to the road ; and, whether she talked to me or read the book she carried in her hand, she kept continually pausing to look round her, or gaze up the road to see if any one was coming ; and if a horseman trotted by, I could tell by her unqualified abuse of the poor equestrian, whoever he might be, that she hated him *because* he was not Mr. Hatfield.

" Surely," thought I, " she is not so indifferent to him as she believes herself to be, or would have others to believe her ; and her mother's anxiety is not so wholly causeless as she affirms."

Three days passed away, and he did not make his appearance. On the afternoon of the fourth, as we were walking beside the park palings in the memorable field, each furnished with a book (for I always took care to provide myself with something to be doing when she did not require me to talk), she suddenly interrupted my studies by exclaiming—

" Oh, Miss Grey ! do be so kind as to go and see Mark Wood, and take his wife half a crown from me—I should have given or sent it a week ago, but quite forgot. There !" said she, throwing me her purse, and speaking very fast—
" Never mind getting it out now, but take the purse and

give them what you like : I would go with you, but I want
to finish this volume. I'll come and meet you when I've
done it. Be quick, will you—and—oh, wait ; hadn't you
better read to him a bit ? Run to the house and get some
sort of a good book. Anything will do."

I did as I was desired ; but, suspecting something from
her hurried manner and the suddenness of the request, I
just glanced back before I quitted the field, and there was
Mr. Hatfield about to enter at the gate below. By sending
me to the house for a book, she had just prevented my meeting him on the road.

" Never mind !" thought I, " there'll be no great harm
done. Poor Mark will be glad of the half-crown, and perhaps of the good book too ; and if the Rector does steal Miss
Rosalie's heart, it will only humble her pride a little ; and
if they do get married at last, it will only save her from a
worse fate ; and she will be quite a good enough partner for
him, and he for her."

Mark Wood was the consumptive labourer whom I mentioned before. He was now rapidly wearing away. Miss
Murray, by her liberality, obtained literally the blessing of
him that was ready to perish ; for though the half-crown
could be of very little service to him, he was glad of it for
the sake of his wife and children, so soon to be widowed and
fatherless. After I had sat a few minutes, and read a little
for the comfort and edification of himself and his afflicted
wife, I left them ; but I had not proceeded fifty yards before
I encountered Mr. Weston, apparently on his way to the
same abode. He greeted me in his usual quiet, unaffected
way, stopped to inquire about the condition of the sick man
and his family, and with a sort of unconscious, brotherly disregard to ceremony, took from my hand the book out of
which I had been reading, turned over its pages, made a few
brief but very sensible remarks, and restored it ; then told
me about some poor sufferer he had just been visiting, talked
a little about Nancy Brown, made a few observations upon
my little rough friend the terrier, that was frisking at his
feet, and finally upon the beauty of the weather, and departed.

I have omitted to give a detail of his words, from a notion
that they would not interest the reader as they did me, and
not because I have forgotten them. No ; I remember them

well; for I thought them over and over again in the course of that day and many succeeding ones, I know not how often; and recalled every intonation of his deep, clear voice, every flash of his quick, brown eye, and every gleam of his pleasant, but too transient smile. Such a confession will look very absurd, I fear; but no matter: I have written it: and they that read it will not know the writer.

While I was walking along, happy within, and pleased with all around, Miss Murray came hastening to meet me; her buoyant step, flushed cheek, and radiant smiles showing that she, too, was happy, in her own way. Running up to me, she put her arm through mine, and without waiting to recover breath, began—

" Now, Miss Grey, think yourself highly honoured, for I'm come to tell you my news before I've breathed a word of it to any one else."

" Well, what is it?"

" Oh, *such* news! In the first place, you must know that Mr. Hatfield came upon me just after you were gone. I was in *such* a way for fear papa or mama should see him; but you know I couldn't call you back again, and so I—oh, dear! I can't tell you all about it now, for there's Matilda, I see, in the park, and I must go and open my budget to her. But, however, Hatfield was most uncommonly audacious, unspeakably complimentary, and unprecedentedly tender— tried to be so, at least—he didn't succeed very well in *that*, because it's ·not his vein. I'll tell you all he said another time."

" But what did *you* say—I'm more interested in that?"

" I'll tell you that, too, at some future period. I happened to be in a very good humour just then; but, though I was complaisant and gracious enough, I took care not to compromise myself in any possible way. But, however, the conceited wretch chose to interpret my amiability of temper his own way, and at length presumed upon my indulgence so far—what do you think?—he actually—made me an offer!"

" And you——"

" I proudly drew myself up, and with the greatest coolness expressed my astonishment at such an occurrence, and hoped he had seen nothing in my conduct to justify his expectations. You should have *seen* how his countenance fell! He went perfectly white in the face. I assured him that I esteemed him and all that, but could not possibly accede to his proposals; and if I did, papa and mama could never be brought to give their consent.'

" 'But if they could,' said he, ' would yours be wanting?'

" 'Certainly, Mr. Hatfield,' I replied, with a cool decision which quelled all hope at once. Oh, if you had seen how dreadfully mortified he was—how crushed to the earth by his disappointment! really, I almost pitied him myself.

" One more desperate attempt, however, he made. After a silence of considerable duration, during which he struggled to be calm, and I to be grave—for I felt a strong propensity to laugh—which would have ruined all—he said, with the ghost of a smile—

" 'But tell me plainly, Miss Murray, if I had the wealth of Sir Hugh Meltham, or the prospects of his eldest son, would you still refuse me? answer me truly, upon your honour.'

" 'Certainly,' said I. 'That would make no difference whatever.'

" It was a great lie, but he looked so confident in his own attractions still, that I determined not to leave him one stone upon another. He looked me full in the face; but I kept my countenance so well that he could not imagine I was saying anything more than the actual truth.

" 'Then it's all over, I suppose,' he said, looking as if he could have died on the spot with vexation and the intensity of his despair. But he was angry as well as disappointed. There was he, suffering so unspeakably, and there was I, the pitiless cause of it all, so utterly impenetrable to all the artillery of his looks and words, so calmly cold and proud, he could not but feel some resentment; and with singular bitterness he began—

" 'I certainly did not expect this, Miss Murray. I might say something about your past conduct, and the hopes you have led me to foster, but I forbear, on condition——'

" 'No conditions, Mr. Hatfield!' said I, now truly indignant at his insolence.

" 'Then let me beg it as a favour,' he replied, lowering his voice at once, and taking a humbler tone: 'let me entreat that you will not mention this affair to any one whatever. If you will keep silence about it, there need be no unpleasant-

ness on either side—nothing, I mean, beyond what is quite
unavoidable: for my own feelings I will endeavour to keep to
myself, if I cannot annihilate them—I will try to forgive, if
I cannot forget the cause of my sufferings. I will not suppose, Miss Murray, that you know how deeply you have
injured me. I would not have you aware of it; but if, in
addition to the injury you have already done me—pardon
me, but whether innocently or not, you *have* done it—and if
you add to it by giving publicity to this unfortunate affair,
or naming it *at all*, you will find that I too can speak, and
though you scorned my love, you will hardly scorn my——'

" He stopped, but he bit his bloodless lip, and looked so
terribly fierce that I was quite frightened. However, my
pride upheld me still, and I answered disdainfully,—

" ' I do not know what motive you suppose I could have for
naming it to any one, Mr. Hatfield; but if I were disposed
to do so, you would not deter me by threats; and it is
scarcely the part of a gentleman to attempt it.'

" ' Pardon me, Miss Murray,' said he, ' I have loved you
so intensely—I do still adore you so deeply, that I would not
willingly offend you; but though I never have loved, and
never *can* love any woman as I have loved you, it is equally
certain that I never was so ill-treated by any. On the contrary, I have always found your sex the kindest and most
tender and obliging of God's creation, till now. (Think of
the conceited fellow saying that!) And the novelty and
harshness of the lesson you have taught me to-day, and the
bitterness of being disappointed in the only quarter on which
the happiness of my life depended, must excuse any appearance of asperity. If my presence is disagreeable to you,
Miss Murray,' he said, (for I was looking about me to show
how little I cared for him, so he thought I was tired of him,
I suppose),—' if my presence is disagreeeble to you, Miss
Murray, you have only to promise me the favour I named,
and I will relieve you at once. There are many ladies—
some even in this parish—who would be delighted to accept
what you have so scornfully trampled under your feet. They
would be naturally inclined to hate one whose surpassing love-
liness has so completely estranged my heart from them and
blinded me to their attractions; and a single hint of the truth
from me to one of these, would be sufficient to raise such a
talk against you as would seriously injure your prospects,

and diminish your chance of success with any other gentleman, you or your mama might design to entangle.'

" 'What do you mean, sir?' said I, ready to stamp with
passion.

" 'I mean that this affair from beginning to end appears
to me like a case of arrant flirtation, to say the least of it—
such a case as you would find it rather inconvenient to have
blazoned through the world: especially with the additions
and exaggerations of your female rivals, who would be too
glad to publish the matter, if I only gave them a handle to
it. But I promise you, on the faith of a gentleman, that no
word or syllable that could tend to your prejudice shall ever
escape my lips, provided you will——'

" 'Well, well, I won't mention it,' said I. 'You may rely
upon my silence, if that can afford you any consolation.'

" 'You promise it?'

" 'Yes,' I answered, 'for I wanted to get rid of him
now.'

" 'Farewell, then!' said he, in a most doleful heart-sick
tone; and with a look where pride vainly struggled against
despair, he turned and went away: longing, no doubt, to get
home, that he might shut himself up in his study and cry—
if he doesn't burst into tears before he gets there.''

"But you have broken your promise already," said I,
truly horrified at her perfidy.

"Oh! it's only to you; I know you won't repeat it."

"Certainly, I shall not: but you say you are going to tell
your sister; and she will tell your brothers when they come
home, and Brown immediately, if you do not tell her yourself; and Brown will blazon it, or be the means of blazoning
it throughout the country."

"No, indeed, she won't. We shall not tell her at all, unless
it be under the promise of the strictest secrecy."

"But how can you expect her to keep her promises better
than her more enlightened mistress?"

"Well, well she sha'n't hear it then," said Miss Murray,
somewhat snappishly.

"But you will tell your mama, of course," pursued I;
" and she will tell your papa."

"Of course, I shall tell mama, that is the very thing that
pleases me so much. I shall now be able to convince her
how mistaken she was in her fears about me."

" Oh, *that's* it, is it ? I was wondering what it was that delighted you so much."

" Yes; and another thing is, that I've humbled Mr. Hatfield so charmingly; and another—why, you must allow me some share of female vanity: I don't pretend to be without that most essential attribute of our sex—and if you had seen poor Hatfield's intense eagerness in making his ardent declaration, and his flattering proposal, and his agony of mind, that no effort of pride could conceal, on being refused, you would have allowed I had some cause to be gratified."

" The greater his agony, I should think, the less your cause for gratification."

" Oh, nonsense !" cried the young lady, shaking herself with vexation. " You either can't understand me or you won't. If I had not confidence in your magnanimity, I should think you envied me. But you will, perhaps, comprehend this cause of pleasure—which is as great as any— namely, that I am delighted with myself for my prudence, my self-command, my heartlessness, if you please. I was not a bit taken by surprise, not a bit confused, or awkward, or foolish; I just acted and spoke as I ought to have done, and was completely my own mistress throughout. And here was a man, decidedly good-looking—Jane and Susan Green call him bewitchingly handsome—I suppose they're two of the ladies he pretends would be so glad to have him; but, however, he was certainly a very clever, witty, agreeable companion—not what *you* call clever, but just enough to make him entertaining; and a man one needn't be ashamed of anywhere, and would not soon grow tired of; and to confess the truth, I rather liked him—better even, of late, than Harry Meltham—and he evidently idolized me; and yet, though he came upon me all alone and unprepared, I had the wisdom, and the pride, and the strength to refuse him—and so scornfully and coolly as I did : I have good reason to be proud of that !"

" And are you equally proud of having told him that his having the wealth of Sir Hugh Meltham would make no difference to you when that was not the case; and of having promised to tell no one of his misadventure, apparently without the slightest intention of keeping your promise ? "

" Of course! what else could I do ? You would not have had me—but I see, Miss Grey, you're not in a good temper.

Here's Matilda; I'll see what she and mama have to say about it."

She left me, offended at my want of sympathy, and thinking, no doubt, that I envied her. I did not—at least, I firmly believed I did not. I was sorry for her; I was amazed, disgusted at her heartless vanity; I wondered why so much beauty should be given to those who made so bad a use of it, and denied to some who would make it a benefit to both themselves and others.

But, God knows best, I concluded. There are, I suppose, some men as vain, as selfish, and as heartless as she is, and, perhaps, such women may be useful to punish them.

CHAPTER XV.

THE WALK.

" O DEAR! I wish Hatfield had not been so precipitate!" said Rosalie next day at four P.M., as, with a portentous yawn, she laid down her worsted-work and looked listlessly towards the window. There's no inducement to go out now; and nothing to look forward to. The days will be so long and dull when there are no parties to enliven them; and there are none this week, or next either, that I know of."

" Pity you were so cross to him," observed Matilda, to whom this lamentation was addressed. " He'll never come again: and I suspect you liked him after all. I hoped you would have taken him for your beau, and left dear Harry to me."

" Humph! my beau must be an Adonis indeed, Matilda, the admired of all beholders, if I am to be contented with him alone. I'm sorry to lose Hatfield, I confess; but the first decent man, or number of men, that come to supply his place, will be more than welcome. It's Sunday to-morrow— I do wonder how he'll look, and whether he'll be able to go through the service. Most likely he'll pretend he's got a cold and make Mr. Weston do it all."

" Not he!" exclaimed Matilda, somewhat contemptuously. " Fool as he is, he's not so soft as that comes to."

Her sister was slightly offended; but the event proved
Matilda was right: the disappointed lover performed his
pastoral duties as usual. Rosalie, indeed, affirmed he looked
very pale and dejected: he might be a little paler; but the
difference, if any, was scarcely perceptible. As for his dejection, I certainly did not hear his laugh ringing from the
vestry as usual, nor his voice loud in hilarious discourse;
though I did hear it uplifted in rating the sexton in a
manner that made the congregation stare; and, in his transits to and from the pulpit and the communion-table there
was more of solemn pomp, and less of that irreverent, self-
confident, or rather self-delighted imperiousness with which
he usually swept along—that air that seemed to say, "You
all reverence and adore me, I know; but if any one does not,
I defy him to the teeth!" But the most remarkable change
was, that he never once suffered his eyes to wander in the
direction of Mr. Murray's pew, and did not leave the church
till we were gone.

Mr. Hatfield had doubtless received a very severe blow;
but his pride impelled him to use every effort to conceal the
effects of it. He had been disappointed in his certain hope
of obtaining not only a beautiful, and, to him, highly attractive wife, but one whose rank and fortune might give
brilliance to far inferior charms: he was likewise, no doubt,
intensely mortified by his repulse, and deeply offended at the
conduct of Miss Murray throughout. It would have given
him no little consolation to have known how disappointed
she was to find him apparently so little moved, and to see
that he was able to refrain from casting a single glance at
her throughout both services; though, she declared, it showed
he was thinking of her all the time, or his eyes would have
fallen upon her, if it were only by chance: but if they had
so chanced to fall, she would have affirmed it was because
they could not resist the attraction. It might have pleased
him too, in some degree, to have seen how dull and dissatisfied
she was throughout that week (the greater part of it, at
least), for lack of her usual source of excitement; and how
often she regretted having "used him up so soon," like a
child that, having devoured its plum-cake too hastily, sits
sucking its fingers, and vainly lamenting its greediness.

At length, I was called upon, one fine morning, to accompany her in a walk to the village. Ostensibly she went to

get some shades of Berlin wool, at a tolerably respectable shop that was chiefly supported by the ladies of the vicinity : really—I trust there is no breach of charity in supposing, that she went with the idea of meeting either with the Rector himself, or some other admirer by the way; for as we went along, she kept wondering, " what Hatfield would do or say if we met him," &c., &c., as we passed Mr. Green's park-gates, she " wondered whether he was at home —great stupid blockhead;" as Lady Meltham's carriage passed us, she " wondered what Mr. Harry was doing this fine day" : and then began to abuse his elder brother for being " such a fool as to get married and go and live in London."

" Why," said I, " I thought you wanted to live in London yourself."

" Yes, because it's so dull here : but then he makes it still duller by taking himself off; and if he were not married I might have him instead of that odious Sir Thomas."

Then, observing the prints of a horse's feet on the somewhat miry road, she " wondered whether it was a gentleman's horse," and finally concluded it was, for the impressions were too small to have been made by a " great, clumsy cart-horse"; and then she " wondered who the rider could be," and whether we should meet him coming back, for she was sure he had only passed that morning; and lastly, when we entered the village and saw only a few of its humble inhabitants moving about, she " wondered why the stupid people couldn't keep in their houses ; she was sure she didn't want to see their ugly faces, and dirty, vulgar clothes—it wasn't for that she came to Horton !"

Amid all this, I confess, I wondered too, in secret, whether we should meet, or catch a glimpse of somebody else ; and as we passed his lodgings I even went so far as to wonder whether he was at the window. On entering the shop, Miss Murray desired me to stand in the doorway while she transacted her business, and tell her if any one passed. But alas! there was no one visible besides the villagers, except Jane and Susan Green coming down the single street, apparently returning from a walk.

" Stupid things !" muttered she, as she came out after having concluded her bargain. " Why couldn't they have their dolt of a brother with them? even *he* would be better than nothing."

She greeted them, however, with a cheerful smile, and protestations of pleasure at the happy meeting equal to their own. They placed themselves one on each side of her, and all three walked away chatting and laughing as young ladies do when they get together, if they be but on tolerably intimate terms. But I, feeling myself to be one too many, left them to their merriment and lagged behind, as usual on such occasions: I had no relish for walking beside Miss Green or Miss Susan like one deaf and dumb, who could neither speak nor be spoken to.

But this time I was not long alone. It struck me, at first, as very odd, that just as I was thinking about Mr. Weston he should come up and accost me; but afterwards, on due reflection, I thought there was nothing odd about it, unless it were the fact of his speaking to me; for on such a morning and so near his own abode, it was natural enough that he should be about; and as for my thinking of him, I had been doing that, with little intermission, ever since we set out on our journey; so there was nothing remarkable in that.

" You are alone again, Miss Grey," said he.

" Yes."

" What kind of people are those ladies—the Misses Green ?"

" I really don't know."

" That's strange—when you live so near and see them so often !"

" Well, I suppose they are lively, good-tempered girls; but I imagine you must know them better than I do, yourself, for I never exchanged a word with either of them."

" Indeed ! They don't strike me as being particularly reserved."

" Very likely they are not so to people of their own class; but they consider themselves as moving in quite a different sphere from me !"

He made no reply to this ; but after a short pause, he said—

" I suppose it's these things, Miss Grey, that make you think you could not live without a home ?"

" Not exactly. The fact is I am too socially disposed to be able to live contentedly without a friend ; and as the only friends I have, or am likely to have, are at home, if it—or

rather, if they were gone—I will not say I could not live—
but I would rather not live in such a desolate world."

"But why do you say the only friends you are likely
to have? Are you so unsociable that you cannot make
friends?"

"No, but I never made one yet; and in my present position there is no possibility of doing so, or even of forming a
common acquaintance. The fault may be partly in myself,
but I hope not altogether."

"The fault is partly in society, and partly, I should think,
in your immediate neighbours: and partly, too, in yourself;
for many ladies, in your position, would make themselves be
noticed and accounted of. But your pupils should be companions for you in some degree; they cannot be many years
younger than yourself."

"Oh, yes, they are good company sometimes; but I cannot
call them friends, nor would they think of bestowing such a
name on me—they have other companions better suited to
their tastes."

"Perhaps you are too wise for them. How do you amuse
yourself when alone—do you read much?"

"Reading is my favourite occupation, when I have leisure
for it and books to read."

From speaking of books in general, he passed to different
books in particular, and proceeded by rapid transitions from
topic to topic, till several matters, both of taste and opinion,
had been discussed considerably within the space of half an
hour, but without the embellishment of many observations
from himself; he being evidently less bent upon communicating his own thoughts and predilections, than on discovering
mine. He had not the tact, or the art, to effect such a purpose by skilfully drawing out my sentiments or ideas through
the real or apparent statement of his own, or leading the
conversation by imperceptible gradations to such topics as he
wished to advert to: but such gentle abruptness, and such
single-minded straightforwardness could not possibly offend
me.

"And why should he interest himself at all in my moral
and intellectual capacities? what is it to him what I think or
feel?" I asked myself. And my heart throbbed in answer
to the question.

But Jane and Susan Green soon reached their home. As

they stood parleying at the park-gates, attempting to persuade Miss Murray to come in, I wished Mr. Weston would go, that she might not see him with me when she turned round; but, unfortunately, his business, which was to pay one more visit to poor Mark Wood, led him to pursue the same path as we did, till nearly the close of our journey. When, however, he saw that Rosalie had taken leave of her friends and I was about to join her, he would have left me and passed on at a quicker pace; but, as he civilly lifted his hat in passing her, to my surprise, instead of returning the salute with a stiff, ungracious bow, she accosted him with one of her sweetest smiles, and, walking by his side, began to talk to him with all imaginable cheerfulness and affability; and so we proceeded all three together.

After a short pause in the conversation, Mr. Weston made some remark addressed particularly to me, as referring to something we had been talking of before; but, before I could answer, Miss Murray replied to the observation and enlarged upon it: he rejoined; and, from thence to the close of the interview, she engrossed him entirely to herself. It might be partly owing to my own stupidity, my want of tact and assurance; but I felt myself wronged: I trembled with apprehension; and I listened with envy to her easy, rapid flow of utterance, and saw with anxiety the bright smile with which she looked into his face from time to time: for she was walking a little in advance, for the purpose (as I judged) of being seen as well as heard. If her conversation was light and trivial, it was amusing, and she was never at a loss for something to say, or for suitable words to express it in. There was nothing pert or flippant in her manner now, as when she walked with Mr. Hatfield; there was only a gentle, playful kind of vivacity, which I thought must be peculiarly pleasing to a man of Mr. Weston's disposition and temperament.

When he was gone she began to laugh, and muttered to herself. " I thought I could do it !"

" Do what?" I asked.

" Fix that man."

" What in the world do you mean?"

" I mean that he will go home and dream of me. I have shot him through the heart!"

" How do you know?"

" By many infallible proofs : more especially the look he gave me when he went away. It was not an impudent look —I exonerate him from that—it was a look of reverential, tender adoration. Ha, ha ! he's not quite such a stupid blockhead as I thought him !"

I made no answer, for my heart was in my throat, or something like it, and I could not trust myself to speak. " Oh God, avert it !" I cried, internally—" for his sake, not for mine ! "

Miss Murray made several trivial observations as we passed up the park, to which (in spite of my reluctance to let one glimpse of my feelings appear) I could only answer by mono-syllables. Whether she intended to torment me, or merely to amuse herself, I could not tell—and did not much care; but I thought of the poor man and his one lamb, and the rich man with his thousand flocks; and I dreaded I knew not what for Mr. Weston, independently of my own blighted hopes.

Right glad was I to get into the house, and find myself alone once more in my own room. My first impulse was to sink into the chair beside the bed ; and laying my head on the pillow, to seek relief in a passionate burst of tears : there was an imperative craving for such an indulgence ; but, alas! I must restrain and swallow back my feelings still : there was the bell—the odious bell for the schoolroom dinner; and I must go down with a calm face, and smile, and laugh, and talk nonsense—yes, and eat, too, if possible, as if all was right, and I was just returned from a pleasant walk.

<hr>

CHAPTER XVI.

THE SUBSTITUTION.

NEXT Sunday was one of the gloomiest of April days—a day of thick, dark clouds, and heavy showers. None of the Murrays were disposed to attend church in the afternoon, excepting Rosalie : she was bent upon going as usual; so she ordered the carriage, and I went with her : nothing

loth, of course, for at church I might look without fear of
scorn or censure upon a form and face more pleasing to me
than the most beautiful of God's creations; I might listen
without disturbance to a voice more charming than the
sweetest music to my ears; I might seem to hold communion with that soul in which I felt so deeply interested,
and imbibe its purest thoughts and holiest aspirations, with
no alloy to such felicity except the secret reproaches of my
conscience, which would too often whisper that I was deceiving my own self, and mocking God with the service of a
heart more bent upon the creature than the creator.

Sometimes such thoughts would give me trouble enough;
but sometimes I could quiet them with thinking—it is not
the man, it is his goodness that I love. "Whatsoever things
are pure, whatsoever things are lovely, whatsoever things
are honest and of good report, think on these things." We
do well to worship God in His works; and I know none of
them in which so many of His attributes—so much of His
own spirit shines, as in this His faithful servant; whom to
know and not to appreciate, were obtuse insensibility in me,
who have so little else to occupy my heart.

Almost immediately after the conclusion of the service,
Miss Murray left the church. We had to stand in the porch,
for it was raining, and the carriage was not yet come. I
wondered at her coming forth so hastily, for neither young
Meltham nor Squire Green was there; but I soon found
it was to secure an interview with Mr. Weston as he came
out, which he presently did. Having saluted us both, he
would have passed on, but she detained him; first with
observations upon the disagreeable weather, and then with
asking if he would be so kind as to come some time to-
morrow to see the granddaughter of the old woman who
kept the porter's lodge, for the girl was ill of a fever, and
wished to see him. He promised to do so.

"And at what time will you be most likely to come, Mr.
Weston? The old woman will like to know when to expect
you—you know such people think more about having their
cottages in order when decent people come to see them than
we are apt to suppose."

Here was a wonderful instance of consideration from the
thoughtless Miss Murray. Mr. Weston named an hour in
the morning at which he would endeavour to be there. By

this time the carriage was ready, and the footman was waiting, with an open umbrella, to escort Miss Murray through
the churchyard. I was about to follow; but Mr. Weston
had an umbrella too, and offered me the benefit of its shelter,
for it was raining heavily.

"No, thank you, I don't mind the rain," I said. I always
lacked common sense when taken by surprise.

"But you don't *like* it, I suppose?—an umbrella will do you
no harm at any rate," he replied, with a smile that showed he
was not offended; as a man of worse temper or less penetration would have been at such a refusal of his aid. I could
not deny the truth of his assertion, and so went with him
to the carriage; he even offered me his hand on getting in:
an unnecessary piece of civility, but I accepted that too,
for fear of giving offence. One glance he gave, one little
smile at parting—it was but for a moment; but therein I
read, or thought I read, a meaning that kindled in my
heart a brighter flame of hope than had ever yet arisen.

"I would have sent the footman back for you, Miss Grey,
if you'd waited a moment—you needn't have taken Mr. Weston's umbrella," observed Rosalie, with a very unamiable cloud
upon her pretty face.

"I would have come without an umbrella, but Mr. Weston
offered me the benefit of his, and I could not have refused it
more than I did without offending him," replied I, smiling
placidly; for my inward happiness made that amusing, which
would have wounded me at another time.

The carriage was now in motion. Miss Murray bent forwards, and looked out of the window as we were passing Mr.
Weston. He was pacing homewards along the causeway,
and did not turn his head.

"Stupid ass!" cried she, throwing herself back again in
the seat. "You don't know *what* you've lost by not looking
this way!"

"What has he lost?"

"A bow from me, that would have raised him to the
seventh heaven!"

I made no answer. I saw she was out of humour, and
I derived a secret gratification from the fact, not that she
was vexed, but that she thought she had reason to be so. It
made me think my hopes were not entirely the offspring of
my wishes and imagination.

"I mean to take up Mr. Weston instead of Mr. Hatfield," said my companion, after a short pause, resuming something of her usual cheerfulness. "The ball at Ashby Park takes place on Tuesday, you know; and mama thinks it very likely that Sir Thomas will propose to me then : such things are often done in the privacy of the ball-room, when gentlemen are most easily ensnared, and ladies most enchanting. But if I am to be married so soon, I must make the best of the present time : I am determined Hatfield shall not be the only man who shall lay his heart at my feet, and implore me to accept the worthless gift in vain."

"If you mean Mr. Weston to be one of your victims," said I, with affected indifference, "you will have to make such overtures yourself, that you will find it difficult to draw back when he asks you to fulfil the expectations you have raised."

"I don't suppose he will ask me to *marry* him—nor should I desire it : that would be *rather* too much presumption! but I intend him to feel my power. He has felt it already, indeed : but he shall *acknowledge* it too ; and what visionary hopes he may have, he must keep to himself, and only amuse me with the result of them—for a time."

"Oh! that some kind spirit would whisper those words in his ear!" I inwardly exclaimed. I was far too indignant to hazard a reply to her observation aloud ; and nothing more was said about Mr. Weston that day, by me or in my hearing. But next morning, soon after breakfast, Miss Murray came into the schoolroom where her sister was employed at her studies, or rather her lessons, for studies they were not, and said, "Matilda, I want you to take a walk with me about eleven o'clock."

"Oh, I can't, Rosalie! I have to give orders about my new bridle and saddle-cloth, and speak to the rat-catcher about his dogs : Miss Grey must go with you."

"No, I want *you*," said Rosalie ; and calling her sister to the window she whispered an explanation in her ear ; upon which the latter consented to go.

I remembered that eleven was the hour at which Mr. Weston proposed to come to the porter's lodge ; and remembering that, I beheld the whole contrivance. Accordingly, at dinner, I was entertained with a long account of how Mr. Weston had overtaken them as they were walking along the road; and how they had had a long walk and talk with him, and really found him quite an agreeable companion; and how he must have been, and evidently was, delighted with them and their amazing condescension, &c. &c.

CHAPTER XVII.

CONFESSIONS.

As I am in the way of confessions, I may as well acknowledge that, about this time, I paid more attention to dress than ever I had done before. This is not saying much; for hitherto I had been a little neglectful in that particular : but now, also, it was no uncommon thing to spend as much as two minutes in the contemplation of my own image in the glass; though I never could derive any consolation from such a study. I could discover no beauty in those marked features, that pale hollow cheek, and ordinary dark brown hair; there might be intellect in the forehead, there might be expression in the dark grey eyes : but what of that?—a low Grecian brow, and large black eyes devoid of sentiment would be esteemed far preferable. It is foolish to wish for beauty. Sensible people never either desire it for themselves or care about it in others. If the mind be but well cultivated, and the heart well disposed, no one ever cares for the exterior. So said the teachers of our childhood; and so say we to the children of the present day. All very judicious and proper, no doubt; but are such assertions supported by actual experience?

We are naturally disposed to love what gives us pleasure, and what more pleasing than a beautiful face—when we know no harm of the possessor at least? A little girl loves her bird—Why? Because it lives and feels; because it is helpless and harmless? A toad, likewise, lives and feels, and is equally helpless and harmless; but though she would not hurt a toad, she cannot love it like the bird, with its graceful form, soft feathers, and bright, speaking eyes. If a woman is fair and amiable, she is praised for both qualities, but espe-

cially the former, by the bulk of mankind : if, on the other
hand, she is disagreeable in person and character, her plain-
ness is commonly inveighed against as her greatest crime, because, to common observers, it gives the greatest offence;
while if she is plain and good, provided she is a person of
retired manners and secluded life, no one ever knows of her
goodness, except her immediate connections. Others, on the
contrary, are disposed to form unfavourable opinions of her
mind and disposition, if it be but to excuse themselves for
their instinctive dislike of one so unfavoured by nature; and
vice versa with her whose angel form conceals a vicious heart,
or sheds a false, deceitful charm over defects and foibles that
would not be tolerated in another. They that have beauty,
let them be thankful for it, and make a good use of it, like
any other talent; they that have it not, let them console themselves, and do the best they can without it: certainly, though
liable to be overestimated, it is a gift of God, and not to be
despised. Many will feel this, who have felt that they could
love, and whose hearts tell them that they are worthy to be
loved again; while yet they are debarred, by the lack of this,
or some such seeming trifle, from giving and receiving that
happiness they seem almost made to feel and to impart. As
well might the humble glow-worm despise that power of
giving light, without which the roving fly might pass her
and repass her a thousand times, and never rest beside her:
she might hear her winged darling buzzing over and around
her; he vainly seeking her, she longing to be found, but with
no power to make her presence known, no voice to call him,
no wings to follow his flight;—the fly must seek another
mate, the worm must live and die alone.

Such were some of my reflections about this period. I
might go on prosing more and more, I might dive much
deeper, and disclose other thoughts, propose questions the
reader might be puzzled to answer, and deduce arguments
that might startle his prejudices, or, perhaps, provoke his
ridicule, because he could not comprehend them; but I forbear.

Now, therefore, let us return to Miss Murray. She accompanied her mama to the ball on Tuesday; of course,
splendidly attired, and delighted with her prospects and her
charms. As Ashby Park was nearly ten miles distant from
Horton Lodge, they had to set out pretty early, and I in-

E E

tended to have spent the evening with Nancy Brown, whom
I had not seen for a long time; but my kind pupil took care
I should spend it neither there nor anywhere else beyond the
limits of the schoolroom, by giving me a piece of music to
copy, which kept me closely occupied till bed-time.   About
eleven next morning, as soon as she had left her room, she
came to tell me her news.   Sir Thomas had, indeed, proposed
to her at the ball: an event which reflected great credit on
her mama's sagacity, if not upon her skill in contrivance.   I
rather incline to the belief that she had first laid her plans,
and then predicted their success.   The offer had been accepted, of course, and the bridegroom elect was coming that
day to settle matters with Mr. Murray.

Rosalie was pleased with the thoughts of becoming mistress of Ashby Park; she was elated with the prospect of the
bridal ceremony and its attendant splendour and eclat, the
honeymoon spent abroad, and the subsequent gaieties she
expected to enjoy in London and elsewhere; she appeared
pretty well pleased too, for the time being, with Sir Thomas
himself, because she had so lately seen him, danced with him,
and been flattered by him; but, after all, she seemed to
shrink from the idea of being so soon united: she wished
the ceremony to be delayed some months, at least; and I
wished it too.   It seemed a horrible thing to hurry on the
inauspicious match, and not to give the poor creature time
to think and reason on the irrevocable step she was about
to take.   I made no pretension to "a mother's watchful,
anxious care," but I was amazed and horrified at Mrs. Murray's heartlessness, or want of thought for the real good of
her child; and, by my unheeded warnings and exhortations,
I vainly strove to remedy the evil.   Miss Murray only laughed
at what I said; and I soon found that her reluctance to an
immediate union arose chiefly from a desire to do what execution she could among the young gentlemen of her acquaintance, before she was incapacitated from further mischief of
the kind.   It was for this cause that, before confiding to me
the secret of her engagement, she had extracted a promise
that I would not mention a word on the subject to any one.
And when I saw this, and when I beheld her plunge more
recklessly than ever into the depths of heartless coquetry, I
had no more pity for her.   "Come what will," I thought,
" she deserves it.   Sir Thomas cannot be too bad for her;

and the sooner she is incapacitated from deceiving and injuring others the better."

The wedding was fixed for the first of June. Between that and the critical ball was little more than six weeks; but, with Rosalie's accomplished skill and resolute exertion, much might be done, even within that period: especially as Sir Thomas spent most of the interim in London; whither he went up, it was said, to settle affairs with his lawyer, and make other preparations for the approaching nuptials. He endeavoured to supply the want of his presence by a pretty constant fire of billets-doux; but these did not attract the neighbours' attention, and open their eyes, as personal visits would have done; and old Lady Ashby's haughty, sour spirit of reserve withheld her from spreading the news, while her indifferent health prevented her coming to visit her future daughter-in-law; so that, altogether, this affair was kept far closer than such things usually are.

Rosalie would sometimes shew her lover's epistles to me, to convince me what a kind, devoted husband he would make. She showed me the letters of another individual, too, the unfortunate Mr. Green, who had not the courage, or as she expressed it, the "spunk," to plead his cause in person, but whom one denial would not satisfy: he must write again and again. He would not have done so if he could have seen the grimaces his fair idol made over his moving appeals to her feelings, and heard her scornful laughter, and the opprobrious epithets she heaped upon him for his perseverance.

" Why don't you tell him, at once, that you are engaged?" I asked.

" Oh, I don't want him to know that," replied she. " If he knew it, his sisters and everybody would know it, and then there would be an end of my—ahem! And, besides, if I told him that, he would think my engagement was the only obstacle, and that I would have him if I were free; which I could not bear that any man should think, and he, of all others, the least. ·Besides, I don't care for his letters," she added, contemptuously; " he may write as often as he pleases, and look as great a calf as he likes when I meet him; it only amuses me."

Meantime, young Meltham was pretty frequent in his visits to the house or transits past it; and, judging by Matilda's execrations and reproaches, her sister paid more attention to

him than civility required : in other words, she carried on as
animated a flirtation as the presence of her parents would
admit.   She made some attempts to bring Mr. Hatfield once
more to her feet ; but finding them unsuccessful, she repaid
his haughty indifference with still loftier scorn, and spoke of
him with as much disdain and detestation as she had formerly
done of his curate.   But, amid all this, she never for a moment lost sight of Mr. Weston.   She embraced every opportunity of meeting him, tried every art to fascinate him, and
pursued him with as much perseverance as if she really loved
him and no other, and the happiness of her life depended
upon eliciting a return of affection.   Such conduct was completely beyond my comprehension.   Had I seen it depicted
in a novel, I should have thought it unnatural ; had I heard
it described by others, I should have deemed it a mistake or
an exaggeration ; but when I saw it with my own eyes, and
suffered from it too, I could only conclude that excessive
vanity, like drunkenness, hardens the heart, enslaves the faculties, and perverts the feelings ; and that dogs are not the
only creatures which, when gorged to the throat, will yet
gloat over what they cannot devour, and grudge the smallest
morsel to a starving brother.
     She now became extremely beneficent to the poor cot-
tagers.   Her acquaintance among them was more widely
extended, her visits to their humble dwellings were more
frequent and excursive than they had ever been before.
Hereby, she earned among them the reputation of a condescending and very charitable young lady ; and their en-
comiums were sure to be repeated to Mr. Weston: whom also,
she had, thus, a daily chance of meeting in one or other of
their abodes, or in her transits to and fro ; and often, likewise, she could gather, through their gossip, to what places
he was likely to go at such and such a time, whether to
baptize a child, or to visit the aged, the sick, the sad, or the
dying; and most skilfully she laid her plans accordingly.   In
these excursions she would sometimes go with her sister—
whom, by some means, she had persuaded or bribed to enter
into her schemes—sometimes alone, never, now, with me ; so
that I was debarred the pleasure of seeing Mr. Weston, or hearing his voice even in conversation with another : which would
certainly have been a very great pleasure, however hurtful or
however fraught with pain.   I could not even see him at
church : for Miss Murray, under some trivial pretext, chose

to take possession of that corner in the family pew which had been mine ever since I came; and, unless I had the presumption to station myself between Mr. and Mrs. Murray, I must sit with my back to the pulpit, which I accordingly did.

Now, also, I never walked home with my pupils: they said their mama thought it did not look well to see three people out of the family walking, and only two going in the carriage; and, as they greatly preferred walking in fine weather, I should be honoured by going with the seniors. "And, besides," said they, "you can't walk as fast as we do; you know you're always lagging behind." I knew these were false excuses, but I made no objections, and never contradicted such assertions, well knowing the motives which dictated them. And in the afternoons, during those six memorable weeks, I never went to church at all. If I had a cold, or any slight indisposition, they took advantage of that to make me stay at home; and often they would tell me they were not going again that day, themselves, and then pretend to change their minds, and set off without telling me: so managing their departure that I never discovered the change of purpose till too late. Upon their return home, on one of these occasions, they entertained me with an animated account of a conversation they had had with Mr. Weston as they came along. "And he asked if you were ill, Miss Grey," said Matilda; "but we told him you were quite well, only you didn't want to come to church—so he'll think you're turned wicked."

All chance meetings on week-days were likewise carefully prevented; for, lest I should go to see poor Nancy Brown or any other person, Miss Murray took good care to provide sufficient employment for all my leisure hours. There was always some drawing to finish, some music to copy, or some work to do, sufficient to incapacitate me from indulging in anything beyond a short walk about the grounds, however she or her sister might be occupied.

One morning, having sought and waylaid Mr. Weston, they returned in high glee to give me an account of their interview. "And he asked after you again," said Matilda, in spite of her sister's silent but imperative intimation that she should hold her tongue. "He wondered why you were never with us, and thought you must have delicate health, as you came out so seldom."

" He didn't, Matilda—what nonsense you're talking !"

" Oh, Rosalie, what a lie ! He did, you know ; and you said—Don't, Rosalie—hang it !—I won't be pinched so ! And, Miss Grey, Rosalie told him you were quite well, but you were always so buried in your books that you had no pleasure in anything else."

" What an idea he must have of me !" I thought.

" And," I asked, " does old Nancy ever inquire about me ? "

" Yes ; and we tell her you are so fond of reading and drawing that you can do nothing else."

" That is not the case though ; if you had told her I was so busy I *could* not come to see her, it would have been nearer the truth."

" I don't think it would," replied Miss Murray, suddenly kindling up ; " I'm sure you have plenty of time to yourself now, when you have so little teaching to do."

It was no use beginning to dispute with such indulged, unreasoning creatures ; so I held my peace. I was accustomed, now, to keeping silence when things distasteful to my ear were uttered ; and now, too, I was used to wearing a placid smiling countenance when my heart was bitter within me. Only those who have felt the like can imagine my feelings, as I sat with an assumption of smiling indifference, listening to the accounts of those meetings and interviews with Mr. Weston, which they seemed to find such pleasure in describing to me ; and hearing things asserted of him which, from the character of the man, I knew to be exaggerations and perversions of the truth, if not entirely false—things derogatory to him, and flattering to them—especially to Miss Murray—which I burned to contradict, or, at least, to show my doubts about, but dared not ; lest, in expressing my disbelief, I should display my interest too. Other things I heard, which I felt or feared were indeed too true : but I must still conceal my anxiety respecting him, my indignation against them, beneath a careless aspect ; others, again, mere hints of something said or done, which I longed to hear more of, but could not venture to inquire. So passed the weary time. I could not even comfort myself with saying, " She will soon be married ; and then there may be hope."

Soon after her marriage the holidays would come ; and

when I returned from home, most likely, Mr. Weston would be gone, for I was told that he and the Rector could not agree (the Rector's fault, of course), and he was about to remove to another place.

No—besides my hope in God, my only consolation was in thinking that, though he knew it not, I was more worthy of his love than Rosalie Murray, charming and engaging as she was; for I could appreciate his excellence, which she could not: I would devote my life to the promotion of his happiness; she would destroy his happiness for the momentary gratification of her own vanity. "Oh, if he could but know the difference!" I would earnestly exclaim. "But no! I would not have him see my heart: yet, if he could but know her hollowness, her worthless, heartless frivolity, he would then be safe, and I should be—*almost* happy, though I might never see him more!"

I fear, by this time, the reader is well nigh disgusted with the folly and weakness I have so freely laid before him. I never disclosed it then, and would not have done so had my own sister or my mother been with me in the house. I was a close and resolute dissembler—in this one case at least. My prayers, my tears, my wishes, fears, and lamentations, were witnessed by myself and Heaven alone.

When we are harassed by sorrows or anxieties, or long oppressed by any powerful feelings which we must keep to ourselves, for which we can obtain and seek no sympathy from any living creature, and which yet we cannot, or will not wholly crush, we often naturally seek relief in poetry—and often find it, too—whether in the effusions of others, which seem to harmonize with our existing case, or in our own attempts to give utterance to those thoughts and feelings in strains less musical, perchance, but more appropriate, and therefore more penetrating and sympathetic, and, for the time, more soothing, or more powerful to rouse and to unburden the oppressed and swollen heart. Before this time, at Wellwood House and here, when suffering from home-sick melancholy, I had sought relief twice or thrice at this secret source of consolation; and now I flew to it again, with greater avidity than ever, because I seemed to need it more. I still preserve those relics of past sufferings and experience, like pillars of witness set up in travelling through the vale of life, to mark particular occurrences.

The footsteps are obliterated now; the face of the country
may be changed; but the pillar is still there, to remind me
how all things were when it was reared.   Lest the reader
should be curious to see any of these effusions, I will favour
him with one short specimen : cold and languid as the lines
may seem, it was almost a passion of grief to which they
owed their being.

> O, they have robbed me of the hope
>   My spirit held so dear ;
> They will not let me hear that voice
>   My soul delights to hear.
>
> They will not let me see that face
>   I so delight to see ;
> And they have taken all thy smiles,
>   And all thy love from me.
>
> Well, let them seize on all they can ;—
>   One treasure still is mine,—
> A heart that loves to think on thee,
>   And feels the worth of thine.

Yes ! at least, they could not deprive me of that : I could
think of him day and night; and I could feel that he was
worthy to be thought of.   Nobody knew him as I did ; nobody could appreciate him as I did ; nobody could love him
as I—could, if I might : but there was the evil.   What business had I to think so much of one that never thought of
me ?   Was it not foolish ? was it not wrong ?   Yet, if I
found such deep delight in thinking of him, and if I kept
those thoughts to myself, and troubled no one else with
them, where was the harm of it ?   I would ask myself.   And
such reasoning prevented me from making any sufficient effort
to shake off my fetters.

But, if those thoughts brought delight, it was a painful,
troubled pleasure, too near akin to anguish ; and one that
did me more injury than I was aware of.   It was an indulgence that a person of more wisdom or more experience
would doubtless have denied herself.   And yet, how dreary
to turn my eyes from the contemplation of that bright object
and force them to dwell on the dull, grey, desolate prospect

around: the joyless, hopeless, solitary path that lay before me. It was wrong to be so joyless, so desponding; I should have made God my friend, and to do His will the pleasure and the business of my life; but faith was weak, and passion was too strong.

In this time of trouble I had two other causes of affliction. The first may seem a trifle, but it cost me many a tear: Snap, my little dumb, rough-visaged, but bright-eyed, warm-hearted companion, the only thing I had to love me, was taken away, and delivered over to the tender mercies of the village ratcatcher, a man notorious for his brutal treatment of his canine slaves. The other was serious enough: my letters from home gave intimation that my father's health was worse. No boding fears were expressed, but I was grown timid and despondent, and could not help fearing that some dreadful calamity awaited us there. I seemed to see the black clouds gathering round my native hills, and to hear the angry muttering of a storm that was about to burst, and desolate our hearth.

CHAPTER XVIII.

MIRTH AND MOURNING.

THE 1st of June arrived at last; and Rosalie Murray was transmuted into Lady Ashby. Most splendidly beautiful she looked in her bridal costume. Upon her return from church, after the ceremony, she came flying into the school-room, flushed with excitement, and laughing, half in mirth, and half in reckless desperation, as it seemed to me.

" Now, Miss Grey, I'm Lady Ashby!" she exclaimed. " It's done! my fate is sealed: there's no drawing back now. I'm come to receive your congratulations and bid you good-bye; and then I'm off for Paris, Rome, Naples, Switzerland, London—oh, dear! what a deal I shall see and hear before I come back again. But don't forget me: I sha'n't forget you, though I've been a naughty girl. Come, why don't you congratulate me?"

" I cannot congratulate you," I replied, " till I know
whether this change is really for the better : but I sincerely
hope it is; and I wish you true happiness and the best of
blessings."

" Well, good-bye—the carriage is waiting, and they're
calling me."

She gave me a hasty kiss, and was hurrying away; but,
suddenly returning, embraced me with more affection than I
thought her capable of evincing, and departed with tears in
her eyes. Poor girl! I really loved her then; and forgave
her from my heart all the injury she had done me—and others
also: she had not half known it, I was sure; and I prayed
God to pardon her too.

During the remainder of that day of festal sadness, I was
left to my own devices. Being too much unhinged for any
steady occupation, I wandered about with a book in my hand
for several hours, more thinking than reading, for I had
many things to think about. In the evening, I made use of
my liberty to go and see my old friend Nancy once again;
to apologise for my long absence (which must have seemed
so neglectful and unkind) by telling her how busy I had
been; and to talk, or read, or work for her, whichever might
be most acceptable, and also, of course, to tell her the news
of this important day : and perhaps to obtain a little information from her in return, respecting Mr. Weston's expected
departure. But of this she seemed to know nothing, and I
hoped, as she did, that it was all a false report. She was
very glad to see me ; but, happily, her eyes were now so
nearly well that she was almost independent of my services.
She was deeply interested in the wedding; but while I
amused her with the details of the festive day, the splendours
of the bridal party and of the bride herself, she often sighed
and shook her head, and wished good might come of it; she
seemed, like me, to regard it rather as a theme for sorrow
than rejoicing. I sat a long time talking to her about that
and other things—but *no one came.*

Shall I confess that I sometimes looked towards the door
with a half expectant wish to see it open and give entrance
to Mr. Weston, as had happened once before! and that,
returning through the lanes and fields, I often paused to look
round me, and walked more slowly than was at all necessary
—for, though a fine evening, it was not a hot one—and,

finally, felt a sense of emptiness and disappointment at
having reached the house without meeting or even catching
a distant glimpse of any one, except a few labourers returning from their work?

Sunday, however, was approaching: I should see him
then; for now that Miss Murray was gone, I could have my
old corner again. I should see him, and by look, speech,
and manner, I might judge whether the circumstance of her
marriage had very much afflicted him. Happily, I could
perceive no shadow of a difference: he wore the same aspect
as he had worn two months ago—voice, look, manner, all
alike unchanged: there was the same keen-sighted, unclouded truthfulness in his discourse, the same forcible clearness in his style, the same earnest simplicity in all he said
and did, that made itself, not marked by the eye and ear, but
felt upon the hearts of his audience.

I walked home with Miss Matilda; but *he did not join us.*
Matilda was now sadly at a loss for amusement, and wofully
in want of a companion: her brothers at school, her sister
married and gone, she too young to be admitted into society;
for which, from Rosalie's example, she was in some degree
beginning to acquire a taste—a taste at least for the company of certain classes of gentlemen; at this dull time of
year—no hunting going on, no shooting even—for, though
she might not join in that, it was *something* to see her father
or the gamekeeper go out with the dogs, and to talk with
them on their return about the different birds they had
bagged. Now, also, she was denied the solace which the
companionship of the coachman, groom, horses, greyhounds,
and pointers might have afforded; for her mother having,
notwithstanding the disadvantages of a country life, so satisfactorily disposed of her elder daughter, the pride of her
heart, had begun seriously to turn her attention to the
younger; and being truly alarmed at the roughness of her
manners, and thinking it high time to work a reform, had
been roused at length to exert her authority, and prohibited
entirely the yards, stables, kennels, and coach-house. Of
course, she was not implicitly obeyed; but, indulgent as she
had hitherto been, when once her spirit was roused, her
temper was not so gentle as she required that of her governesses to be, and her will was not to be thwarted with impunity. After many a scene of contention between mother

and daughter, many a violent outbreak which I was ashamed
to witness, in which the father's authority was often called
in to confirm with oaths and threats the mother's slighted
prohibitions—for even *he* could see that " Tilly, though she
would have made a fine lad, was not quite what a young lady
ought to be"—Matilda at length found that her easiest plan
was to keep clear of the forbidden regions; unless she could
now and then steal a visit without her watchful mother's
knowledge.

Amid all this, let it not be imagined that I escaped without many a reprimand, and many an implied reproach, that
lost none of its sting from not being openly worded; but
rather wounded the more deeply, because, from that very
reason, it seemed to preclude self-defence. Frequently, I
was told to amuse Miss Matilda with other things, and to
remind her of her mother's precepts and prohibitions. I did
so to the best of my power: but she would not be amused
against her will, and could not against her taste; and though
I went beyond mere reminding, such gentle remonstrances
as I could use were utterly ineffectual.

" *Dear* Miss Grey! it is the *strangest* thing. I suppose
you can't help it, if it's not in your nature—but I *wonder*
you can't win the confidence of that girl, and make your
society at *least* as agreeable to her as that of Robert or
Joseph!"

" They can talk the best about the things in which she is
most interested," I replied.

" Well! that is a strange confession, *however*, to come
from her *governess!* Who is to form a young lady's tastes,
I wonder, if the governess doesn't do it! I *have* known
governesses who have so completely identified themselves
with the reputation of their young ladies for elegance and
propriety in mind and manners, that they would *blush* to
speak a word against them; and to hear the slightest blame
imputed to their pupils was worse than to be censured in
their own persons,—and I really think it very natural, for
my part."

" Do you, ma'am?"

" Yes, of course: the young lady's proficiency and elegance is of more consequence to the governess than her own,
as well as to the world. If she wishes to prosper in her vocation she must devote all her energies to her business: all

her ideas and all her ambition will tend to the accomplish-
ment of that one object. When we wish to decide upon the
merits of a governess, we naturally look at the young ladies
she professes to have educated, and judge accordingly. The
judicious governess knows this: she knows that, while she
lives in obscurity herself, her pupil's virtues and defects will
be open to every eye; and that, unless she loses sight of
herself in their cultivation, she need not hope for success.
You see, Miss Grey, it is just the same as any other trade or
profession: they that wish to prosper must devote themselves body and soul to their calling; and if they begin to
yield to indolence or self-indulgence they are speedily dis-
tanced by wiser competitors: there is little to choose between a person that ruins her pupils by neglect, and one that
corrupts them by her example. You will excuse my dropping these little hints: you know it is all for your own
good. Many ladies would speak to you much more strongly;
and many would not trouble themselves to speak at all, but
quietly look out for a substitute. That, of course, would be
the *easiest* plan: but I know the advantages of a place like
this to a person in your situation; and I have no desire to
part with you, as I am sure you would do very well if you
will only think of these things and try to exert yourself a
little more: then, I am convinced, you would *soon* acquire
that delicate tact which alone is wanting to give you a
proper influence over the mind of your pupil."

I was about to give the lady some idea of the fallacy of
her expectations; but she sailed away as soon as she had
concluded her speech. Having said what she wished, it was
no part of her plan to await my answer: it was my business
to hear, and not to speak.

However, as I have said, Matilda at length yielded, in
some degree, to her mother's authority (pity it had not been
exerted before); and being thus deprived of almost every
source of amusement, there was nothing for it but to take
long rides with the groom and long walks with the governess,
and to visit the cottages and farm-houses on her father's
estate, to kill time in chatting with the old men and women
that inhabited them. In one of these walks, it was our
chance to meet Mr. Weston. This was what I had long desired; but now, for a moment, I wished either he or I were
away: I felt my heart throb so violently that I dreaded lest

some outward signs of emotion should appear; but I think he hardly glanced at me, and I was soon calm enough. After a brief salutation to both, he asked Matilda if she had lately heard from her sister.

" Yes," replied she. " She was at Paris when she wrote, and very well, and very happy."

She spoke the last word emphatically, and with a glance impertinently sly. He did not seem to notice it, but replied, with equal emphasis, and very seriously—

" I hope she will continue to be so."

" Do you think it likely?" I ventured to inquire: for Matilda had started off in pursuit of her dog, that was chasing a leveret.

" I cannot tell," replied he. " Sir Thomas may be a better man than I suppose; but, from all I have heard and seen, it seems a pity that one so young and gay, and—and *interesting,* to express many things by one word—whose greatest, if not her only fault, appears to be thoughtlessness— no trifling fault to be sure, since it renders the possessor liable to almost every other, and exposes him to so many temptations: but it seems a pity that she should be thrown away on such a man. It was her mother's wish, I suppose?"

"Yes; and her own too, I think, for she always laughed at my attempts to dissuade her from the step."

" You did attempt it? Then, at least, you will have the satisfaction of knowing that it is no fault of yours, if any harm should come of it. As for Mrs. Murray, I don't know how she can justify her conduct: if I had sufficient acquaintance with her, I'd ask her."

" It seems unnatural: but some people think rank and wealth the chief good; and, if they can secure that for their children, they think they have done their duty."

" True: but is it not strange that persons of experience, who have been married themselves, should judge so falsely?"

Matilda now came panting back, with the lacerated body of the young hare in her hand.

"Was it your intention to kill that hare, or to save it, Miss Murray?" asked Mr. Weston, apparently puzzled at her gleeful countenance.

" I pretended to want to save it," she answered, honestly enough, " as it was so glaringly out of season; but I was better pleased to see it killed. However, you can both witness that I couldn t help it : Prince was determined to have her ; and he clutched her by the back, and killed her in a minute ! Wasn't it a noble chase ? "

" Very ! for a young lady after a leveret."

There was a quiet sarcasm in the tone of his reply which was not lost upon her ; she shrugged her shoulders, and, turning away with a significant " Humph !" asked me how I had enjoyed the fun. I replied that I saw no fun in the matter ; but admitted that I had not observed the transaction very narrowly.

" Didn't you see how it doubled—just like an old hare ? and didn't you hear it scream ?"

" I'm happy to say I did not."

" It cried out just like a child."

" Poor little thing ! What will you do with it ?"

" Come along—I shall leave it in the first house we come to. I don't want to take it home, for fear papa should scold me for letting the dog kill it."

Mr. Weston was now gone, and we too went on our way ; but as we returned, after having deposited the hare in a farm-house, and demolished some spice-cake and currant wine in exchange, we met him returning also from the execution of his mission, whatever it might be. He carried in his hand a cluster of beautiful bluebells which he offered to me ; observing, with a smile, that though he had seen so little of me for the last two months, he had not forgotten that bluebells were numbered among my favourite flowers. It was done as a simple act of good-will, without compliment or remarkable courtesy, or any look that could be construed into " reverential, tender adoration," (*vide* Rosalie Murray) ; but still, it was something to find my unimportant saying so well remembered : it was something that he had noticed so accurately the time I had ceased to be visible.

" I was told," said he, " that you were a perfect bookworm, Miss Grey : so completely absorbed in your studies that you were lost to every other pleasure."

" Yes, and it's quite true !" cried Matilda.

" No, Mr. Weston ; don't believe it : it's a scandalous libel. These young ladies are too fond of making random assertions at the expense of their friends ; and you ought to be careful how you listen to them."

" I hope *this* assertion is groundless, at any rate."

"Why? Do you particularly object to ladies' studying?"

"No; but I object to any one so devoting himself or herself to study, as to lose sight of everything else. Except under peculiar circumstances, I consider very close and constant study as a waste of time, and an injury to the mind as well as the body."

"Well, I have neither the time nor the inclination for such transgressions."

We parted again.

Well! what is there remarkable in all this? Why have I recorded it? Because, reader, it was important enough to give me a cheerful evening, a night of pleasing dreams, and a morning of felicitous hopes. Shallow-brained cheerfulness, foolish dreams, unfounded hopes, you would say; and I will not venture to deny it: suspicions to that effect arose too frequently in my own mind. But our wishes are like tinder: the flint and steel of circumstances are continually striking out sparks, which vanish immediately, unless they chance to fall upon the tinder of our wishes; then, they instantly ignite, and the flame of hope is kindled in a moment.

But alas! that very morning, my flickering flame of hope was dismally quenched by a letter from my mother, which spoke so seriously of my father's increasing illness, that I feared there was little or no chance of his recovery; and, close at hand as the holidays were, I almost trembled lest they should come too late for me to meet him in this world. Two days after, a letter from Mary told me his life was despaired of, and his end seemed fast approaching. Then, immediately, I sought permission to anticipate the vacation, and go without delay. Mrs. Murray stared, and wondered at the unwonted energy and boldness with which I urged the request, and thought there was no occasion to hurry; but finally gave me leave: stating, however, that there was "no need to be in such agitation about the matter—it might prove a false alarm after all; and if not—why, it was only in the common course of nature: we must all die some time; and I was not to suppose myself the only afflicted person in the world;" and concluding with saying I might have the phaeton to take me to O——. "And instead of *repining*, Miss Grey, be thankful for the *privileges* you enjoy. There's many a poor clergyman whose family would be plunged into ruin by the event of his death; but *you*, you see, have influential friends ready to continue their patronage, and to show you every consideration."

I thanked her for her "consideration," and flew to my room to make some hurried preparations for my departure. My bonnet and shawl being on, and a few things hastily crammed into my largest trunk, I descended. But I might have done the work more leisurely, for no one else was in a hurry; and I had still a considerable time to wait for the phaeton. At length it came to the door, and I was off: but, oh, what a dreary journey was that! how utterly different from my former passages homewards! Being too late for the last coach to ———, I had to hire a cab for ten miles, and then a car to take me over the rugged hills. It was half-past ten before I reached home. They were not in bed.

My mother and sister both met me in the passage—sad—silent—pale! I was so much shocked and terror-stricken that I could not speak, to ask the information I so much longed yet dreaded to obtain.

"Agnes!" said my mother, struggling to repress some strong emotion.

"Oh, Agnes!" cried Mary, and burst into tears.

"How is he?" I asked, gasping for the answer.

"Dead!"

It was the reply I had anticipated: but the shock seemed none the less tremendous.

CHAPTER XIX.

THE LETTER.

My father's mortal remains had been consigned to the tomb; and we, with sad faces and sombre garments, sat lingering over the frugal breakfast-table, revolving plans for our future life. My mother's strong mind had not given way beneath even this affliction: her spirit, though crushed, was not broken. Mary's wish was that I should go back to Horton Lodge, and that our mother should come and live with her and Mr. Richardson at the vicarage: she affirmed that he

F F

wished it no less than herself, and that such an arrangement could not fail to benefit all parties; for my mother's society and experience would be of inestimable value to them, and they would do all they could to make her happy. But no arguments or entreaties could prevail : my mother was determined not to go. Not that she questioned, for a moment, the kind wishes and intentions of her daughter; but she affirmed that so long as God spared her health and strength, she would make use of them to earn her own livelihood, and be chargeable to no one; whether her dependence would be felt as a burden or not. If she could afford to reside as a lodger in —— vicarage, she would choose that house before all others as the place of her abode; but not being so circumstanced, she would never come under its roof, except as an occasional visitor : unless sickness or calamity should render her assistance really needful, or until age or infirmity made her incapable of maintaining herself.

"No, Mary," said she, "if Richardson and you have anything to spare, you must lay it aside for your family; and Agnes and I must gather honey for ourselves. Thanks to my having had daughters to educate, I have not forgotten my accomplishments. God willing, I will check this vain repining,"—she said, while the tears coursed one another down her cheeks in spite of her efforts; but she wiped them away, and resolutely shaking back her head, continued, "I will exert myself, and look out for a small house commodiously situated in some populous but healthy district, where we will take a few young ladies to board and educate—if we can get them—and as many day pupils as will come, or as we can manage to instruct. Your father's relations and old friends will be able to send us some pupils, or to assist us with their recommendations, no doubt : I shall not apply to my own. What say you to it, Agnes? will you be willing to leave your present situation and try?"

"Quite willing, mama; and the money I have saved will do to furnish the house. It shall be taken from the bank directly."

"When it is wanted : we must get the house, and settle all preliminaries first."

Mary offered to lend the little she possessed; but my mother declined it, saying, that we must begin on an economical plan; and she hoped that the whole or part of mine, added to what we could get by the sale of the furniture, and what little our dear papa had contrived to lay aside for her since the debts were paid, would be sufficient to last us till Christmas; when, it was hoped, something would accrue from our united labours. It was finally settled that this should be our plan; and that inquiries and preparations should immediately be set on foot; and while my mother busied herself with these, I should return to Horton Lodge at the close of my four weeks' vacation, and give notice for my final departure when things were in train for the speedy commencement of our school.

We were discussing these affairs on the morning I have mentioned, about a fortnight after my father's death, when a letter was brought in for my mother, on beholding which the colour mounted to her face—lately pale enough with anxious watchings and excessive sorrow. "From my father!" murmured she, as she hastily tore off the cover. It was many years since she had heard from any of her own relations before. Naturally wondering what the letter might contain, I watched her countenance while she read it, and was somewhat surprised to see her bite her lip and knit her brows as if in anger. When she had done, she somewhat irreverently cast it on the table, saying with a scornful smile—

"Your grandpapa has been so kind as to write to me. He says he has no doubt I have long repented of my 'unfortunate marriage,' and if I will only acknowledge this, and confess I was wrong in neglecting his advice, and that I have justly suffered for it, he will make a lady of me once again— if that be possible after my long degradation—and remember my girls in his will. Get my desk, Agnes, and send these things away : I will answer the letter directly. But first, as I may be depriving you both of a legacy, it is just that I should tell you what I mean to say. I shall say that he is mistaken in supposing that I can regret the birth of my daughters (who have been the pride of my life, and are likely to be the comfort of my old age), or the thirty years I have passed in the company of my best and dearest friend; —that, had our misfortunes been three times as great as they were (unless they had been of my bringing on), I should still the more rejoice to have shared them with your father,

and administered what consolation I was able ; and, had his
sufferings in illness been ten times what they were, I could
not regret having watched over and laboured to relieve
them ;—that, if he had married a richer wife, misfortunes
and trials would no doubt have come upon him still ; while I
am egotist enough to imagine that no other woman could
have cheered him through them so well : not that I am superior to the rest, but I was made for him, and he for me ; and
I can no more repent the hours, days, years of happiness
we have spent together, and which neither could have had
without the other, than I can the privilege of having been
his nurse in sickness, and his comfort in affliction.

" Will this do, children ?—or shall I say we are all very
sorry for what has happened during the last thirty years,
and my daughters wish they had never been born ; but
since they have had that misfortune, they will be thankful
for any trifle their grandpapa will be kind enough to bestow ? "

Of course, we both applauded our mother's resolution :
Mary cleared away the breakfast things ; I brought the desk ;
the letter was quickly written and despatched ; and, from
that day, we heard no more of our grandfather, till we saw
his death announced in the newspaper a considerable time
after—all his worldly possessions, of course, being left to our
wealthy, unknown cousins.

CHAPTER XX.

THE FAREWELL.

A HOUSE in A——, the fashionable watering-place, was
hired for our seminary ; and a promise of two or three pupils
was obtained to commence with. I returned to Horton
Lodge about the middle of July, leaving my mother to conclude the bargain for the house, to obtain more pupils, to sell
off the furniture of our old abode, and to fit out the new one.

We often pity the poor, because they have no leisure to
mourn their departed relatives, and necessity obliges them to

labour through their severest afflictions; but is not active employment the best remedy for overwhelming sorrow—the surest antidote for despair? It may be a rough comforter: it may seem hard to be harassed with the cares of life when we have no relish for its enjoyments; to be goaded to labour when the heart is ready to break, and the vexed spirit implores for rest only to weep in silence: but is not labour better than the rest we covet? and are not those petty, tormenting cares less hurtful than a continual brooding over the great affliction that oppresses us? Besides, we cannot have cares, and anxieties, and toil, without hope—if it be but the hope of fulfilling our joyless task, accomplishing some needful project, or escaping some further annoyance. At any rate, I was glad my mother had so much employment for every faculty of her action-loving frame. Our kind neighbours lamented that she, once so exalted in wealth and station, should be reduced to such extremity in her time of sorrow; but I am persuaded that she would have suffered thrice as much had she been left in affluence, with liberty to remain in that house, the scene of her early happiness and late affliction, and no stern necessity to prevent her from incessantly brooding over and lamenting her bereavement.

I will not dilate upon the feelings with which I left the old house, the well-known garden, the little village church—then doubly dear to me, because my father, who, for thirty years, had taught and prayed within its walls, lay slumbering now beneath its flags—and the old bare hills, delightful in their very desolation, with the narrow vales between, smiling in green wood and sparkling water—the house where I was born, the scene of all my early associations, the place where throughout life my earthly affections had been centred;—and left them to return no more! True, I was going back to Horton Lodge, where, amid many evils, one source of pleasure yet remained: but it was pleasure mingled with excessive pain; and my stày, alas! was limited to six weeks. And even of that precious time, day after day slipped by and I did not see him: except at church, I never saw him for a fortnight after my return. It seemed a long time to me: and, as I was often out with my rambling pupil, of course hopes would keep rising, and disappointments would ensue; and, then, I would say to my own heart, " Here is a convincing proof—if you would but have the sense to see it, or the

candour to acknowledge it—that he does not care for you.
If he only thought *half* as much about you as you do about
him, he would have contrived to meet you many times ere
this : you must know that, by consulting your own feelings.
Therefore, have done with this nonsense : you have no ground
for hope : dismiss, at once, these hurtful thoughts and foolish
wishes from your mind, and turn to your own duty, and the
dull blank life that lies before you. You might have *known*
such happiness was not for you."

But I saw him at last. He came suddenly upon me as I
was crossing a field in returning from a visit to Nancy Brown,
which I had taken the opportunity of paying while Matilda
Murray was riding her matchless mare. He must have heard
of the heavy loss I had sustained : he expressed no sympathy, offered no condolence; but almost the first words he
uttered were,—" How is your mother ?" And this was no
matter of course question, for I never told him that I *had* a
mother : he must have learned the fact from others, if he
knew it at all; and, besides, there was sincere goodwill, and
even deep, touching, unobtrusive sympathy in the tone and
manner of the inquiry. I thanked him with due civility, and
told him she was as well as could be expected. " What will
she do ?" was the next question. Many would have deemed
it an impertinent one, and given an evasive reply; but such
an idea never entered my head, and I gave a brief but plain
statement of mother's plans and prospects.

" Then you will leave this place shortly ?" said he.

" Yes, in a month."

He paused a minute, as if in thought. When he spoke
again, I hoped it would be to express his concern at my departure; but it was only to say—" I should think you will
be willing enough to go ?"

" Yes—for some things," I replied.

" For *some* things only—I wonder what should make you
regret it !"

I *was* annoyed at this in some degree; because it embarrassed me : I had only one reason for regretting it; and that
was a profound secret, which he had no business to trouble
me about.

" Why," said I—" why should you suppose that I dislike
the place ?"

" You told me so yourself," was the decisive reply. " You

said, at least, that you could not live contentedly without a friend; and that you had no friend here, and no possibility of making one—and besides, I know you *must* dislike it."

" But, if you remember rightly, I said, or meant to say, I could not live contentedly without a friend in the *world*: I was not so unreasonable as to require one always near me. I think I could be happy in a house full of enemies, if——" but no; that sentence must not be continued—I paused, and hastily added—" And besides, we cannot well leave a place where we have lived for two or three years, without some feeling of regret."

" Will you regret to part with Miss Murray, your sole remaining pupil and companion ? "

" I dare say I shall in some degree : it was not without sorrow I parted with her sister."

" I can imagine that."

" Well, Miss Matilda is quite as good—better in one respect."

" What is that ?"

" She's honest."

" And the other is not ?"

" I should not call her *dis*honest; but it must be confessed, she's a little artful."

" *Artful* is she ?—I saw she was giddy and vain—and now," he added, after a pause, " I can well believe she was artful too; but so excessively so as to assume an aspect of extreme simplicity and unguarded openness. Yes," continued he, musingly, " that accounts for some little things that puzzled me a trifle before."

After that, he turned the conversation to more general subjects. He did not leave me till we had nearly reached the park gates : he had certainly stepped a little out of his way to accompany me so far, for he now went back and disappeared down Moss-lane, the entrance of which we had passed some time before. Assuredly I did not regret this circumstance : if sorrow had any place in my heart, it was that he was gone at last—that he was no longer walking by my side, and that that short interval of delightful intercourse was at an end. He had not breathed a word of love, or dropped one hint of tenderness or affection, and yet I had been supremely happy. To be near him, to hear him talk as he did talk; and to feel that he thought me worthy to be so spoken to—

capable of understanding and duly appreciating such discourse—was enough.

"Yes, Edward Weston, I could, indeed, be happy in a house full of enemies, if I had but one friend, who truly, deeply, and faithfully loved me; and if that friend were you —though we might be far apart—seldom to hear from each other, still more seldom to meet—though toil, and trouble, and vexation might surround me, still—it would be too much happiness for me to dream of! Yet, who can tell," said I within myself, as I proceeded up the park,—"who can tell what this one month may bring forth? I have lived nearly three-and-twenty years, and I have suffered much, and tasted little pleasure yet: is it likely my life all through will be so clouded? Is it not possible that God may hear my prayers, disperse these gloomy shadows, and grant me some beams of heaven's sunshine yet? Will he entirely deny to me those blessings which are so freely given to others, who neither ask them nor acknowledge them when received? May I not still hope and trust? I did hope and trust for a while: but, alas, alas! the time ebbed away: one week followed another, and, excepting one distant glimpse and two transient meetings—during which scarcely anything was said—while I was walking with Miss Matilda, I saw nothing of him: except, of course, at church.

And now, the last Sunday was come, and the last service. I was often on the point of melting into tears during the sermon—the last I was to hear from him: the best I should hear from any one, I was well assured. It was over—the congregation were departing; and I must follow. I had then seen him, and heard his voice too, probably for the last time. In the churchyard, Matilda was pounced upon by the two Misses Green. They had many inquiries to make about her sister, and I know not what besides. I only wished they would have done, that we might hasten back to Horton Lodge: I longed to seek the retirement of my own room, or some sequestered nook in the grounds, that I might deliver myself up to my feelings—to weep my last farewell, and lament my false hopes and vain delusions. Only this once and then adieu to fruitless dreaming—thenceforth, only sober, solid, sad reality should occupy my mind. But while I thus resolved, a low voice close beside me, said—"I suppose you are going this week, Miss Grey?" "Yes," I replied. I was very much startled; and had I been at all hysterically inclined, I certainly should have committed myself in some way then. Thank God, I was not.

" Well," said Mr. Weston, " I want to bid you good-bye —it is not likely I shall see you again before you go."

" Good-bye, Mr. Weston," I said. Oh, how I struggled to say it calmly! I gave him my hand. He retained it a few seconds in his.

" It is possible we may meet again," said he; " will it be of any consequence to you whether we do or not?"

" Yes, I should be very glad to see you again."

I *could* say no less. He kindly pressed my hand, and went. Now, I was happy again—though more inclined to burst into tears than ever. If I had been forced to speak at that moment, a succession of sobs would have inevitably ensued; and as it was, I could not keep the water out of my eyes. I walked along with Miss Murray, turning aside my face, and neglecting to notice several successive remarks, till she bawled out that I was either deaf or stupid; and then (having recovered my self-possession), as one awakened from a fit of abstraction, I suddenly looked up and asked what she had been saying.

CHAPTER XXI.

THE SCHOOL.

I LEFT Horton Lodge, and went to join my mother in our new abode at A——. I found her well in health, resigned in spirit, and even cheerful, though subdued and sober, in her general demeanour. We had only three boarders and half a dozen day-pupils to commence with; but by due care and diligence we hoped ere long to increase the number of both.

I set myself with befitting energy to discharge the duties of this new mode of life. I call it *new*, for there was, indeed, a considerable difference between working with my mother in a school of our own, and working as a hireling among strangers, despised and trampled upon by old and

young: and for the first few weeks I was by no means unhappy. "It is possible we may meet again," and "will it
be of any consequence to you whether we do or not?"—
Those words still rang in my ear and rested on my heart:
they were my secret solace and support. "I shall see him
again.—He will come; or he will write." No promise, in
fact, was too bright or too extravagant for hope to whisper
in my ear. I did not believe half of what she told me: I
pretended to laugh at it all; but I was far more credulous
than I myself supposed; otherwise, why did my heart leap
up when a knock was heard at the front door, and the maid,
who opened it, came to tell my mother a gentleman wished
to see her? and why was I out of humour for the rest of the
day, because it proved to be a music-master come to offer his
services to our school? and what stopped my breath for a
moment, when the postman having brought a couple of letters, my mother said, "Here Agnes, this is for you," and
threw one of them to me? and what made the hot blood rush
into my face when I saw it was directed in a gentleman's
hand? and why—oh! why did that cold, sickening sense of
disappointment fall upon me, when I had torn open the cover
and found it was *only* a letter from Mary, which, for some
reason or other, her husband had directed for her?

Was it then come to this—that I should be *disappointed*
to receive a letter from my only sister: and because it was
not written by a comparative stranger? Dear Mary! and
she had written it so kindly—and thinking I should be so
pleased to have it!—I was not worthy to read it! And I
believe, in my indignation against myself, I should have put
it aside till I had schooled myself into a better frame of
mind, and was become more deserving of the honour and
privilege of its perusal: but there was my mother looking
on, and wishful to know what news it contained; so I read it
and delivered it to her, and then went into the schoolroom to
attend to the pupils: but amidst the cares of copies and sums
—in the intervals of correcting errors here, and reproving
derelictions of duty there, I was inwardly taking myself to
task with far sterner severity. "What a fool you must be,"
said my head to my heart, or my sterner to my softer self;
—"how could you ever dream that he would write to *you?*
What grounds have you for such a hope—or that he will see
you, or give himself any trouble about you—or even think of

you again?" "What grounds?"—and then Hope set before
me that last, short interview, and repeated the words I had
so faithfully treasured in my memory. "Well, and what was
there in that?—Who ever hung his hopes upon so frail a
twig? What was there in those words that any common
acquaintance might not say to another? Of course, it was
possible you might meet again: he might have said so if you
had been going to New Zealand; but that did not imply any
intention of seeing you—and then, as to the question that
followed, any one might ask that: and how did you answer?
—Merely with a stupid, commonplace reply, such as you
would have given to Master Murray, or anyone else you had
been on tolerably civil terms with." "But, then," persisted
Hope, "the tone and manner in which he spoke." "Oh,
that is nonsense! he always speaks impressively; and at that
moment there were the Greens and Miss Matilda Murray
just before, and other people passing by, and he was obliged
to stand close beside you, and to speak very low, unless he
wished everybody to hear what he said; which—though it
was nothing at all particular—of course, he would rather
not." But then, above all, that emphatic, yet gentle pressure
of the hand, which seemed to say, ' *Trust me ;*' and many
other things besides—too delightful, almost too flattering,
to be repeated even to one's self. "Egregious folly—too
absurd to require contradiction—mere inventions of the imagination, which you ought to be ashamed of. If you would
but consider your own unattractive exterior, your unamiable
reserve, your foolish diffidence—which must make you appear cold, dull, awkward, and perhaps ill-tempered too ;—if
you had but rightly considered these from the beginning, you
would never have harboured such presumptuous thoughts :
and now that you have been so foolish, pray repent and
amend, and let us have no more of it!"

I cannot say that I implicitly obeyed my own injunctions:
but such reasoning as this became more and more effective as
time wore on, and nothing was seen or heard of Mr. Weston;
until at last, I gave up hoping, for even my heart acknowledged it was all in vain. But still, I would think of him: I
would cherish his image in my mind; and treasure every word,
look, and gesture that my memory could retain; and brood
over his excellences and his peculiarities, and, in fact, all I had
seen, heard, or imagined respecting him.

"Agnes, this sea air and change of scene do *you* no good, I think: I never saw you look so wretched. It must be that you sit too much, and allow the cares of the schoolroom to worry you. You must learn to take things easy, and to be more active and cheerful; you must take exercise whenever you can get it, and leave the most tiresome duties to me: they will only serve to exercise my patience, and, perhaps, try my temper a little."

So said my mother, as we sat at work one morning during the Easter holidays. I assured her that my employments were not at all oppressive; that I was well; or, if there was anything amiss, it would be gone as soon as the trying months of spring were over: when summer came I should be as strong and hearty as she could wish to see me: but inwardly her observation startled me. I knew my strength was declining, my appetite had failed, and I was grown listless and desponding;—and if, indeed, he could never care for me, and I could never see him more—if I was forbidden to minister to his happiness—forbidden, for ever, to taste the joys of love, to bless and to be blessed—then, life must be a burden, and if my heavenly Father would call me away, I should be glad to rest. But it would not do to die and leave my mother. Selfish, unworthy daughter, to forget her for a moment! Was not her happiness committed in a great measure to my charge?— and the welfare of our young pupils too? Should I shrink from the work that God had set before me, because it was not fitted to my taste? Did not He know best what I should do, and where I ought to labour? and should I long to quit His service before I had finished my task, and expect to enter into His rest without having laboured to earn it? "No; by His help I will arise and address myself diligently to my appointed duty. If happiness in this world is not for me, I will endeavour to promote the welfare of those around me, and my reward shall be hereafter." So said I in my heart; and from that hour I only permitted my thoughts to wander to Edward Weston—or at least to dwell upon him now and then—as a treat for rare occasions: and, whether it was really the approach of summer, or the effect of these good resolutions, or the lapse of time, or all together, tranquillity of mind was soon restored; and bodily health and vigour began likewise, slowly, but surely, to return.

Early in June, I received a letter from Lady Ashby, late

Miss Murray. She had written to me twice or thrice before, from the different stages of her bridal tour, always in good spirits, and professing to be very happy. I wondered every time that she had not forgotten me, in the midst of so much gaiety and variety of scene. At length, however, there was a pause; and it seemed she had forgotten me, for upwards of seven months passed away and no letter. Of course, I did not break my heart about *that*, though I often wondered how she was getting on; and when this last epistle so unexpectedly arrived, I was glad enough to receive it. It was dated from Ashby Park, where she was come to settle down at last, having previously divided her time between the continent and the metropolis. She made many apologies for having neglected me so long, assured me she had not forgotten me, and had often intended to write, &c. &c., but had always been prevented by something. She acknowledged that she had been leading a very dissipated life, and I should think her very wicked and very thoughtless; but, notwithstanding that, she thought a great deal, and, among other things, that she should vastly like to see me. "We have been several days here already," wrote she. "We have not a single friend with us, and are likely to be very dull. You know I never had a fancy for living with my husband like two turtles in a nest, were he the most delightful creature that ever wore a coat; so do take pity upon me and come. I suppose your Mid-summer holidays commence in June, the same as other people's, therefore you cannot plead want of time; and you must and shall come—in fact, I shall die if you don't. I want you to visit me as a *friend*, and stay a long time. There is nobody with me, as I told you before, but Sir Thomas and old Lady Ashby: but you needn't mind them —they'll trouble us but little with their company. And you shall have a room to yourself, whenever you like to retire to it, and plenty of books to read when my company is not sufficiently amusing. I forget whether you like babies; if you do, you may have the pleasure of seeing mine—the most charming child in the world, no doubt; and all the more so, that I am not troubled with nursing it—I was deter-mined I wouldn't be bothered with that. Unfortunately, it is a girl, and Sir Thomas has never forgiven me: but, how-ever, if you will only come, I promise you shall be its gover-ness as soon as it can speak; and you shall bring it up in

the way it should go, and make a better woman of it than
its mama. And you shall see my poodle, too: a splendid
little charmer imported from Paris; and two fine Italian
paintings of great value—I forget the artist. Doubtless you
will be able to discover prodigious beauties in them, which
you must point out to me, as I only admire by hearsay; and
many elegant curiosities besides, which I purchased at Rome
and elsewhere; and, finally, you shall see my new home—
the splendid house and grounds I used to covet so greatly.
Alas! how far the promise of anticipation exceeds the pleasure of possession! There's a fine sentiment! I assure you
I am become quite a grave old matron: pray come, if it be
only to witness the wonderful change. Write by return of
post, and tell me when your vacation commences, and say
that you will come the day after, and stay till the day before
it closes—in mercy to,

Yours affectionately,
Rosalie Ashby."

I showed this strange epistle to my mother, and consulted
her on what I ought to do. She advised me to go; and I
went—willing enough to see Lady Ashby, and her baby too,
and to do anything I could to benefit her, by consolation or
advice; for I imagined she must be unhappy, or she would
not have applied to me thus—but feeling, as may readily be
conceived, that, in accepting the invitation, I made a great
sacrifice for her, and did violence to my feelings in many
ways, instead of being delighted with the honourable distinction of being entreated by the baronet's lady to visit her
as a friend. However, I determined my visit should be only
for a few days at most; and I will not deny that I derived
some consolation from the idea that, as Ashby Park was not
very far from Horton, I might possibly see Mr. Weston, or,
at least, hear something about him.

CHAPTER XXII.

THE VISIT.

ASHBY PARK was certainly a very delightful residence. The mansion was stately without, commodious and elegant within; the park was spacious and beautiful, chiefly on account of its magnificent old trees, its stately herds of deer, its broad sheet of water, and the ancient woods that stretched beyond it: for there was no broken ground to give variety to the landscape, and but very little of that undulating swell which adds so greatly to the charm of park scenery. And so, this was the place Rosalie Murray had so longed to call her own, that she must have a share of it, on whatever terms it might be offered—whatever price was to be paid for the title of mistress, and whoever was to be her partner in the honour and bliss of such a possession! Well! I am not disposed to censure her now.

She received me very kindly; and, though I was a poor clergyman's daughter, a governess, and a schoolmistress, she welcomed me with unaffected pleasure to her home; and—what surprised me rather—took some pains to make my visit agreeable. I could see, it is true, that she expected me to be greatly struck with the magnificence that surrounded her; and, I confess, I was rather annoyed at her evident efforts to reassure me, and prevent me from being overwhelmed by so much grandeur—too much awed at the idea of encountering her husband and mother-in-law, or too much ashamed of my own humble appearance. I was not ashamed of it at all; for, though plain, I had taken good care not to be shabby or mean, and should have been pretty considerably at my ease, if my condescending hostess had not taken such manifest pains to make me so; and, as for the magnificence that surrounded her, nothing that met my eyes struck me or affected me half so much as her own altered appearance. Whether from the influence of fashionable dissipation, or some other evil, a space of little more than twelve months had had the effect that might be expected from as many years, in reducing the plumpness of her form, the freshness of her complexion, the vivacity of her movements, and the exuberance of her spirits.

I wished to know if she was unhappy; but I felt it was not my province to inquire: I might endeavour to win her confidence; but, if she chose to conceal her matrimonial cares from me, I would trouble her with no obtrusive questions. I, therefore, at first, confined myself to a few general inquiries about her health and welfare, and a few commendations on the beauty of the park, and of the little girl that should have been a boy: a small delicate infant of seven or eight weeks old, whom its mother seemed to regard with no remarkable degree of interest or affection, though full as much as I expected her to show.

Shortly after my arrival, she commissioned her maid to conduct me to my room and see that I had everything I wanted: it was a small, unpretending, but sufficiently comfortable apartment. When I descended thence—having divested myself of all travelling encumbrances, and arranged my toilet with due consideration for the feelings of my lady hostess—she conducted me herself to the room I was to occupy when I chose to be alone, or when she was engaged with visitors, or obliged to be with her mother-in-law, or otherwise prevented, as she said, from enjoying the pleasure of my society. It was a quiet, tidy little sitting-room; and I was not sorry to be provided with such a harbour of refuge.

"And sometime," said she, " I will show you the library: I never examined its shelves, but, I dare say, it is full of wise books; and you may go and burrow among them whenever you please. And now you shall have some tea—it will soon be dinner time, but, I thought as you were accustomed to dine at one, you would perhaps like better to have a cup of tea about this time, and to dine when we lunch; and then, you know, you can have your tea in this room, and that will save you from having to dine with Lady Ashby and Sir Thomas: which would be rather awkward—at least, not awkward, but rather—a—you know what I mean. I thought you mightn't like it so well—especially as we may have other ladies and gentlemen to dine with us occasionally."

"Certainly," said I, " I would much rather have it as you say; and, if you have no objection, I should prefer having all my meals in this room."

"Why so?"

"Because, I imagine, it would be more agreeable to Lady Ashby and Sir Thomas."

" Nothing of the kind."

" At any rate, it would be more agreeable to me."

She made some faint objections, but soon conceded; and I could see that the proposal was a considerable relief to her.

" Now, come into the drawing-room," said she. " There's the dressing bell; but I won't go yet: it's no use dressing when there's no one to see you; and I want to have a little discourse."

The drawing-room was certainly an imposing apartment, and very elegantly furnished; but I saw its young mistress glance towards me as we entered, as if to notice how I was impressed by the spectacle, and accordingly I determined to preserve an aspect of stony indifference, as if I saw nothing at all remarkable. But this was only for a moment: immediately conscience whispered, " Why should I disappoint her to save my pride? No—rather let me sacrifice my pride to give her a little innocent gratification." And I honestly looked round, and told her it was a noble room, and very tastefully furnished. She said little, but I saw she was pleased.

She showed me her fat French poodle, that lay curled up on a silk cushion, and the two fine Italian paintings: which, however, she would not give me time to examine, but, saying I must look at them some other day, insisted upon my admiring the little jewelled watch she had purchased in Geneva; and then she took me round the room to point out sundry articles of *vertu* she had brought from Italy: an elegant little time-piece, and several busts, small graceful figures, and vases, all beautifully carved in white marble. She spoke of these with animation, and heard my admiring comments with a smile of pleasure : that soon, however, vanished, and was followed by a melancholy sigh; as if in consideration of the insufficiency of all such baubles to the happiness of the human heart, and their woful inability to supply its insatiate demands.

Then, stretching herself upon a couch, she motioned me to a capacious easy-chair that stood opposite—not before the fire, but before a wide open window; for it was summer, be it remembered : a sweet, warm evening in the latter half of June. I sat for a moment in silence, enjoying the still, pure air, and the delightful prospect of the park that lay before

me, rich in verdure and foliage, and basking in yellow sunshine, relieved by the long shadows of declining day. But I
must take advantage of this pause : I had inquiries to make,
and, like the substance of a lady's postscript, the most important must come last. So I began with asking after Mr.
and Mrs. Murray, and Miss Matilda and the young gentlemen.

I was told that papa had the gout, which made him
very ferocious; and that he would not give up his choice
wines, and his substantial dinners and suppers, and had
quarrelled with his physician, because the latter had dared to
say that no medicine could cure him while he lived so freely;
that mama and the rest were well. Matilda was still wild
and reckless, but she had got a fashionable governess, and
was considerably improved in her manners, and soon to be
introduced to the world; and John and Charles (now at
home for the holidays) were, by all accounts, "fine, bold,
unruly, mischievous boys."

"And how are the other people getting on?" said I—
"the Greens, for instance?"

"Ah! Mr. Green is heart-broken, you know," replied she,
with a languid smile : "he hasn't got over his disappointment yet, and never will, I suppose. He's doomed to be an
old bachelor; and his sisters are doing their best to get married."

"And the Melthams?"

"Oh, they're jogging on as usual, I suppose: but I know
very little about any of them — except Harry," said she,
blushing slightly, and smiling again. "I saw a great deal
of him while we were in London; for, as soon as he heard
we were there, he came up under pretence of visiting his
brother, and either followed me, like a shadow, wherever I
went, or met me, like a reflection, at every turn. You
needn't look so shocked, Miss Grey; I was very discreet, I
assure you : but, you know, one can't help being admired.
Poor fellow! He was not my only worshipper; though he was
certainly the most conspicuous, and, I think, the most devoted
among them all. And that detestable—ahem—and Sir
Thomas chose to take offence at him—or my profuse expenditure, or something—I don't exactly know what—and hurried me down to the country at a moment's notice; where
I'm to play the hermit, I suppose, for life."

And she bit her lip, and frowned vindictively upon the fair domain she had once so coveted to call her own.

"And Mr. Hatfield," said I, "what is become of him?"

Again, she brightened up, and answered gaily—

"Oh! he made up to an elderly spinster, and married her, not long since; weighing her heavy purse against her faded charms, and expecting to find that solace in gold which was denied him in love, ha, ha!"

"Well, and I think that's all—except Mr. Weston: what is he doing?"

"I don't know I'm sure. He's gone from Horton."

"How long since? and where is he gone to?"

"I know nothing about him," replied she, yawning— "except that he went about a month ago—I never asked where," (I would have asked whether it was to a living or merely another curacy, but thought it better not,) "and the people made a great rout about his leaving," continued she, "much to Mr. Hatfield's displeasure; for Hatfield didn't like him, because he had too much influence with the common people, and because he was not sufficiently tractable and submissive to him—and for some other unpardonable sins, I don't know what. But now I positively must go and dress: the second bell will ring directly, and if I come to dinner in this guise, I shall never hear the end of it from Lady Ashby. It's a strange thing one can't be mistress in one's own house! Just ring the bell, and I'll send for my maid, and tell them to get you some tea. Only think of that intolerable woman—"

"Who—your maid?"

"No; my mother-in-law—and my unfortunate mistake! Instead of letting her take herself off to some other house, as she offered to do when I married, I was fool enough to ask her to live here still, and direct the affairs of the house for me; because, in the first place, I hoped we should spend the greater part of the year in town, and in the second place, being so young and inexperienced, I was frightened at the idea of having a houseful of servants to manage, and dinners to order, and parties to entertain, and all the rest of it, and I thought she might assist me with her experience; never dreaming that she would prove a usurper, a tyrant, an incubus, a spy, and everything else that's detestable. I wish she was dead!"

She then turned to give her orders to the footman, who
had been standing bolt upright within the door for the last
half minute, and had heard the latter part of her animadver-
sions; and, of course, made his own reflections upon them,
notwithstanding the inflexible, wooden countenance he
thought proper to preserve in the drawing-room. On my
remarking afterwards that he must have heard her, she replied—

" Oh, no matter ! I never care about the footmen; they're
mere automatons : it's nothing to them what their superiors
say or do; they won't dare to repeat it; and as to what
they think—if they presume to think at all—of course, nobody cares for that. It would be a pretty thing indeed, if
we were to be tongue-tied by our servants !"

So saying, she ran off to make her hasty toilet, leaving me
to pilot my way back to my sitting-room, where, in due
time, I was served with a cup of tea. After that, I sat
musing on Lady Ashby's past and present condition; and on
what little information I had obtained respecting Mr. Weston,
and the small chance there was of ever seeing or hearing
anything more of him throughout my quiet, drab-colour life:
which, henceforth, seemed to offer no alternative between
positive rainy days, and days of dull grey clouds without
downfall. At length, however, I began to weary of my
thoughts, and to wish I knew where to find the library my
hostess had spoken of; and to wonder whether I was to remain there doing nothing till bedtime.

As I was not rich enough to possess a watch, I could not
tell how time was passing, except by observing the slowly
lengthening shadows from the window; which presented a
side view, including a corner of the park, a clump of trees,
whose topmost branches had been colonized by an innumerable company of noisy rooks, and a high wall with a
massive wooden gate: no doubt communicating with the
stable-yard, as a broad carriage-road swept up to it from the
park. The shadow of this wall soon took possession of the
whole of the ground as far as I could see, forcing the golden
sunlight to retreat inch by inch, and at last take refuge in
the very tops of the trees. Ere long, even they were left in
shadow—the shadow of the distant hills, or of the earth
itself; and, in sympathy for the busy citizens of the rookery,
I regretted to see their habitation, so lately bathed in glorious

light, reduced to the sombre, worky-day hue of the lower
world, or of my own world within. For a moment, such
birds as soared above the rest might still receive the lustre
on their wings, which imparted to their sable plumage the
hue and brilliance of deep red gold; at last, that too departed.
Twilight came stealing on; the rooks became more quiet; I
became more weary, and wished I were going home to-
morrow. At length it grew dark; and I was thinking of
ringing for a candle, and betaking myself to bed, when my
hostess appeared, with many apologies for having neglected
me so long, and laying all the blame upon that " nasty old
woman," as she called her mother-in-law.

"If I didn't sit with her in the drawing-room while Sir
Thomas is taking his wine," said she, " she would never forgive me; and, then, if I leave the room the instant he
comes—as I have done once or twice—it is an unpardonable
offence against her dear Thomas. *She* never shewed such
disrespect to *her* husband; and as for affection, wives never
think of that now-a-days, she supposes : but things were
different in *her* time—as if there was any good to be done
by staying in the room, when he does nothing but grumble
and scold when he's in a bad humour, talk disgusting nonsense when he's in a good one, and go to sleep on the sofa
when he's too stupid for either; which is most frequently
the case now, when he has nothing to do but to sot over his
wine."

" But could you not try to occupy his mind with something better; and engage him to give up such habits ? I'm
sure you have powers of persuasion, and qualifications for
amusing a gentleman, which many ladies would be glad to
possess."

" And so you think I would lay myself out for his amusement! No; that's not *my* idea of a wife. It's the husband's part to please the wife, not hers to please him ; and if
he isn't satisfied with her as she is—and thankful to possess
her too—he isn't worthy of her, that's all. And as for persuasion, I assure you I shan't trouble myself with that : I've
enough to do to bear with him as he is, without attempting
to work a reform. But I'm sorry I left you so long alone,
Miss Grey. How have you passed the time ?"

" Chiefly in watching the rooks."

" Mercy, how dull you must have been! I really must

show you the library; and you must ring for everything you want, just as you would in an inn, and make yourself comfortable. I have selfish reasons for wishing to make you happy, because I want you to stay with me, and not fulfil your horrid threat of running away in a day or two."

"Well, don't let me keep you out of the drawing-room any longer to-night, for at present I am tired, and wish to go to bed."

<hr />

CHAPTER XXIII.

THE PARK.

I CAME down a little before eight, next morning, as I knew by the striking of a distant clock. There was no appearance of breakfast. I waited above an hour before it came, still vainly longing for access to the library; and, after that lonely repast was concluded, I waited again about an hour and a half in great suspense and discomfort, uncertain what to do. At length, Lady Ashby came to bid me good-morning. She informed me she had only just breakfasted, and now wanted me to take an early walk with her in the park. She asked how long I had been up, and on receiving my answer, expressed the deepest regret, and again promised to show me the library. I suggested she had better do so at once, and then there would be no further trouble either with remembering or forgetting. She complied, on condition that I would not think of reading, or bothering with the books now; for she wanted to show me the gardens, and take a walk in the park with me, before it became too hot for enjoyment: which, indeed, was nearly the case already. Of course, I readily assented; and we took our walk accordingly.

As we were strolling in the park, talking of what my companion had seen and heard during her travelling experience, a gentleman on horseback rode up and passed us. As he turned, in passing, and stared me full in the face, I had a good opportunity of seeing what he was like. He was tall,

thin, and wasted, with a slight stoop in the shoulders, a pale
face, but somewhat blotchy, and disagreeably red about the
eyelids, plain features, and a general appearance of languor
and flatness, relieved by a sinister expression in the mouth
and the dull, soulless eyes.

"I detest that man!" whispered Lady Ashby, with bitter
emphasis, as he slowly trotted by.

"Who is it?" I asked, unwilling to suppose that she
should so speak of her husband.

"Sir Thomas Ashby," she replied, with dreary composure.

"And do you *detest* him, Miss Murray?" said I, for I was
too much shocked to remember her name at the moment.

"Yes, I do, Miss Grey, and despise him too ; and if you
knew him you would not blame me."

"But you knew what he was before you married him."

"No; I only thought so : I did not half know him really.
I know you warned me against it, and I wish I had listened
to you: but it's too late to regret that now. And besides,
mama ought to have known better than either of us, and she
never said anything against it—quite the contrary. And
then I thought he adored me, and would let me have my
own way : he did pretend to do so at first, but now he does
not care a bit about me. Yet I should not care for that: he
might do as he pleased, if I might only be free to amuse
myself and to stay in London, or have a few friends down
here : but *he will* do as he pleases, and I must be a prisoner
and a slave. The moment he saw I could enjoy myself without him, and that others knew my value better than himself,
the selfish wretch began to accuse me of coquetry and extra-
vagance; and to abuse Harry Meltham, whose shoes he was
not worthy to clean. And then, he must needs have me
down in the country, to lead the life of a nun, lest I should
dishonour him or bring him to ruin ; as if he had not been
ten times worse every way, with his betting book, and his
gaming table, and his opera girls, and his Lady This and
Mrs. That—yes, and his bottles of wine, and glasses of
brandy and water too! Oh, I would give ten thousand
worlds to be Miss Murray again! It is *too* bad to feel life,
health, and beauty wasting away, unfelt and unenjoyed, for
such a brute as that!" exclaimed she, fairly bursting into
tears in the bitterness of her vexation.

Of course, I pitied her exceedingly ; as well for her false

idea of happiness and disregard of duty, as for the wretched
partner with whom her fate was linked. I said what I could
to comfort her, and offered such counsels as I thought she
most required: advising her, first, by gentle reasoning, by
kindness, example, and persuasion to try to ameliorate her
husband; and then, when she had done all she could, if she
still found him incorrigible, to endeavour to abstract herself
from him—to wrap herself up in her own integrity, and
trouble herself as little about him as possible. I exhorted
her to seek consolation in doing her duty to God and man,
to put her trust in Heaven, and solace herself with the care
and nurture of her little daughter; assuring her she would
be amply rewarded by witnessing its progress in strength
and wisdom, and receiving its genuine affection.

"But I can't devote myself entirely to a child," said she:
"it may die—which is not at all improbable."

"But, with care, many a delicate infant has become a
strong man or woman."

"But it may grow so intolerably like its father that I
shall hate it."

"That is not likely; it is a little girl, and strongly resembles its mother."

"No matter; I should like it better if it were a boy—only
that its father will leave it no inheritance that he can possibly squander away. What pleasure can I have in seeing a
girl grow up to eclipse me, and enjoy those pleasures that I
am for ever debarred from? But supposing I could be so
generous as to take delight in this, still it is *only* a child;
and I can't centre all my hopes in a child: that is only one
degree better than devoting oneself to a dog. And as for
all the wisdom and goodness you have been trying to instil
into me—that is all very right and proper I dare say, and if
I were some twenty years older, I might fructify by it: but
people must enjoy themselves when they're young; and if
others won't let them—why, they must hate them for it!"

"The best way to enjoy yourself is to do what is right
and hate nobody. The end of Religion is not to teach us
how to die, but how to live; and the earlier you become wise
and good, the more of happiness you secure. And now, Lady
Ashby, I have one more piece of advice to offer you, which
is, that you will not make an enemy of your mother-in-law
Don't get into the way of holding her at arm's length, and

regarding her with jealous distrust. I never saw her, but I have heard good as well as evil respecting her; and I imagine that, though cold and haughty in her general demeanour, and even exacting in her requirements, she has strong affections for those who can reach them; and, though so blindly attached to her son, she is not without good principles, or incapable of hearing reason. If you would but conciliate her a little, and adopt a friendly, open manner—and even confide your grievances to her—*real* grievances, such as you have a right to complain of—it is my firm belief that she would, in time, become your faithful friend, and a comfort and support to you, instead of the incubus you describe her."

But I fear my advice had little effect upon the unfortunate young lady; and, finding I could render myself so little serviceable, my residence at Ashby Park became doubly painful. But still, I must stay out that day and the following one, as I had promised to do so: though, resisting all entreaties and inducements to prolong my visit further, I insisted upon departing the next morning; affirming that my mother would be lonely without me, and that she impatiently expected my return. Nevertheless, it was with a heavy heart that I bade adieu to poor Lady Ashby and left her in her princely home. It was no slight additional proof of her unhappiness, that she should so cling to the consolation of my presence, and earnestly desire the company of one whose general tastes and ideas were so little congenial to her own—whom she had completely forgotten in her hours of prosperity, and whose presence would be rather a nuisance than a pleasure, if she could but have half her heart's desire.

CHAPTER XXIV.

THE SANDS.

OUR school was not situated in the heart of the town: on entering A—— from the north-west there is a row of respectable looking houses, on each side of the broad, white road, with narrow slips of garden ground before them, Venetian

blinds to the windows, and a flight of steps leading to each
trim, brass-handled door.   In one of the largest of these
habitations dwelt my mother and I, with such young ladies
as our friends and the public chose to commit to our charge.
Consequently, we were a considerable distance from the sea,
and divided from it by a labyrinth of streets and houses.
But the sea was my delight; and I would often gladly pierce
the town to obtain the pleasure of a walk beside it, whether
with the pupils, or alone or with my mother during the vacations.   It was delightful to me at all times and seasons, but
especially in the wild commotion of a rough sea-breeze, and
in the brilliant freshness of a summer morning.

I awoke early on the third morning after my return from
Ashby Park—the sun was shining through the blind, and I
thought how pleasant it would be to pass through the quiet
town and take a solitary ramble on the sands while half the
world was in bed.   I was not long in forming the resolution,
nor slow to act upon it.   Of course I would not disturb my
mother, so I stole noiselessly down stairs, and quietly unfastened the door.   I was dressed and out, when the
church clock struck a quarter to six.   There was a feeling of
freshness and vigour in the very streets; and when I got free
of the town, when my foot was on the sands and my face
towards the broad, bright bay, no language can describe the
effect of the deep, clear azure of the sky and ocean, the bright
morning sunshine on the semi-circular barrier of craggy cliffs
surmounted by green swelling hills, and on the smooth, wide
sands, and the low rocks out at sea—looking, with their
clothing of weeds and moss, like little grass-grown islands—
and above all, on the brilliant, sparkling waves.   And then,
the unspeakable purity and freshness of the air! there was
just enough heat to enhance the value of the breeze, and just
enough wind to keep the whole sea in motion, to make the
waves come bounding to the shore, foaming and sparkling,
as if wild with glee.   Nothing else was stirring—no living
creature was visible besides myself.   My footsteps were the
first to press the firm, unbroken sands;—nothing before had
trampled them since last night's flowing tide had obliterated
the deepest marks of yesterday, and left it fair and even, except where the subsiding water had left behind it the traces
of dimpled pools, and little running streams.

Refreshed, delighted, invigorated, I walked along, forgetting all my cares, feeling as if I had wings to my feet, and could go at least forty miles without fatigue, and experiencing a sense of exhilaration to which I had been an entire stranger since the days of early youth. About half-past six, however, the grooms began to come down to air their master's horses—first one, and then another, till there were some dozen horses and five or six riders: but that need not trouble me, for they would not come as far as the low rocks which I was now approaching. When I had reached these, and walked over the moist, slippery sea-weed (at the risk of floundering into one of the numerous pools of clear, salt water that lay between them), to a little mossy promontory with the sea splashing round it, I looked back again to see who next was stirring. Still, there were only the early grooms with their horses, and one gentleman with a little dark speck of a dog running before him, and one water-cart coming out of the town to get water for the baths. In another minute or two, the distant bathing machines would begin to move; and then the elderly gentlemen of regular habits, and sober quaker ladies would be coming to take their salutary morning walks. But however interesting such a scene might be, I could not wait to witness it, for the sun and the sea so dazzled my eyes in that direction, that I could but afford one glance; and then I turned again to delight myself with the sight and the sound of the sea dashing against my promontory—with no prodigious force, for the swell was broken by the tangled sea-weed and the unseen rocks beneath; otherwise I should soon have been deluged with spray. But the tide was coming in; the water was rising; the gulfs and lakes were filling; the straits were widening; it was time to seek some safer footing; so I walked, skipped, and stumbled back to the smooth, wide sands, and resolved to proceed to a certain bold projection in the cliffs, and then return.

Presently, I heard a snuffling sound behind me, and then a dog came frisking and wriggling to my feet. It was my own Snap—the little dark, wire-haired terrier! When I spoke his name, he leapt up in my face and yelled for joy. Almost as much delighted as himself, I caught the little creature in my arms, and kissed him repeatedly. But how came he to be there? He could not have dropped from the sky, or come all that way alone: it must be either his master, the rat-catcher, or somebody else that had brought him; so, repressing my extravagant caresses, and endeavouring to repress his likewise, I looked round, and beheld—Mr. Weston!

"Your dog remembers you well, Miss Grey," said he, warmly grasping the hand I offered him without clearly knowing what I was about. "You rise early."

"Not often so early as this," I replied, with amazing composure, considering all the circumstances of the case.

"How far do you purpose to extend your walk?"

"I was thinking of returning—it must be almost time, I think."

He consulted his watch—a gold one now—and told me it was only five minutes past seven.

"But doubtless, you have had a long enough walk," said he, turning towards the town, to which I now proceeded leisurely to retrace my steps; and he walked beside me.

"In what part of the town do you live?" asked he. "I never could discover."

Never could discover? Had he endeavoured to do so then? I told him the place of our abode. He asked how we prospered in our affairs. I told him we were doing very well,—that we had had a considerable addition to our pupils after the Christmas vacation, and expected a still further increase at the close of this.

"You must be an accomplished instructor," he observed.

"No, it is my mother," I replied; "she manages things so well, and is so active, and clever, and kind."

"I should like to know your mother. Will you introduce me to her some time, if I call?"

"Yes, willingly."

"And will you allow me the privilege of an old friend, of looking in upon you now and then?"

"Yes, if—I suppose so."

This was a very foolish answer, but the truth was, I considered that I had no right to invite any one to my mother's house without her knowledge; and if I had said, "yes, if my mother does not object," it would appear as if by his question I understood more than was expected; so, *supposing* she would not, I added, "I suppose so." but of course I should have said something more sensible and more polite, if I had had my wits about me. We continued our walk for a minute in silence; which, however, was shortly relieved (no small relief to me),

by Mr. Weston commenting upon the brightness of the
morning and the beauty of the bay, and then upon the advantages A—— possessed over many other fashionable places of
resort:

"You don't ask what brings me to A——," said he.
"You can't suppose I'm rich enough to come for my own
pleasure."

"I heard you had left Horton."

"You didn't hear, then, that I had got the living of
F—— ?"

F—— was a village about two miles distant from A——.

"No," said I; "we live so completely out of the world,
even here, that news seldom reaches me through any quarter;
except through the medium of the —— *Gazette.* But I hope
you like your new parish; and that I may congratulate you
on the acquisition?"

"I expect to like my parish better a year or two hence,
when I have worked certain reforms I have set my heart upon
—or, at least, progressed some steps towards such an achieve-
ment. But you may congratulate me now; for I find it very
agreeable to *have* a parish all to myself, with nobody to interfere with me—to thwart my plans or cripple my exertions:
and besides, I have a respectable house in a rather pleasant
neighbourhood, and three hundred pounds a year; and, in fact,
I have nothing but solitude to complain of, and nothing but
a companion to wish for.

He looked at me as he concluded; and the flash of his dark
eyes seemed to set my face on fire: greatly to my own discomfiture, for to evince confusion at such a juncture was intolerable. I made an effort, therefore, to remedy the evil, and
disclaim all personal application of the remark by a hasty, ill-
expressed reply, to the effect that, if he waited till he was well
known in the neighbourhood, he might have numerous opportunities for supplying his want among the residents of F——
and its vicinity, or the visitors of A——, if he required so
ample a choice: not considering the compliment implied by
such an assertion, till his answer made me aware of it.

"I am not so presumptuous as to believe that," said he,
"though you tell it me; but if it were so, I am rather particular in my notions of a companion for life, and perhaps I
might not find one to suit me among the ladies you mention."

"If you require perfection, you never will."

"I do not—I have no right to require it, as being so far from perfect myself."

Here the conversation was interrupted by a water-cart lumbering past us, for we were now come to the busy part of the sands; and, for the next eight or ten minutes, between carts and horses, and asses, and men, there was little room for social intercourse, till we had turned our backs upon the sea, and begun to ascend the precipitous road leading into the town. Here my companion offered me his arm, which I accepted, though not with the intention of using it as a support.

"You don't often come on to the sands, I think," said he, "for I have walked there many times, both morning and evening, since I came, and never seen you till now; and several times, in passing through the town, too, I have looked about for your school—but I did not think of the —— Road; and once or twice I made inquiries, but without obtaining the requisite information."

When we had surmounted the acclivity, I was about to withdraw my arm from his, but by a slight tightening of the elbow was tacitly informed that such was not his will, and accordingly desisted. Discoursing on different subjects, we entered the town, and passed through several streets. I saw that he was going out of his way to accompany me, notwithstanding the long walk that was yet before him; and, fearing that he might be inconveniencing himself from motives of politeness, I observed—

"I fear I am taking you out of your way, Mr. Weston—I believe the road to F—— lies quite in another direction."

"I'll leave you at the end of the next street," said he.

"And when will you come to see mama?"

"To-morrow—God willing."

The end of the next street was nearly the conclusion of my journey. He stopped there, however, bid me good-morning, and called Snap, who seemed a little doubtful whether to follow his old mistress or his new master, but trotted away upon being summoned by the latter.

"I won't offer to restore him to you, Miss Grey," said Mr. Weston, smiling, "because I like him."

"Oh, I don't want him," replied I, "now that he has a good master; I'm quite satisfied."

"You take it for granted that I am a good one, then?"

The man and the dog departed, and I returned home, full
of gratitude to Heaven for so much bliss, and praying that
my hopes might not again be crushed.

CHAPTER XXV.

CONCLUSION.

" WELL, Agnes, you must not take such long walks again
before breakfast," said my mother, observing that I drank
an extra cup of coffee and ate nothing—pleading the heat
of the weather, and the fatigue of my long walk as an excuse. I certainly did feel feverish, and tired too.

" You always do things by extremes : now, if you had
taken a *short* walk every morning, and would continue to
do so, it would do you good."

" Well, mama, I will."

" But this is worse than lying in bed or bending over your
books : you have quite put yourself into a fever."

" I won't do it again," said I.

I was racking my brains with thinking how to tell her
about Mr. Weston, for she must know he was coming to-
morrow. However, I waited till the breakfast things were
removed, and I was more calm and cool; and then, having
sat down to my drawing, I began—

" I met an old friend on the sands to-day, mama."

" An old friend ! Who could it be ?"

" Two old friends, indeed. One was a dog ;" and then
I reminded her of Snap, whose history I had recounted before, and related the incident of his sudden appearance and
remarkable recognition ; " and the other," continued I,
" was Mr. Weston, the curate of Horton."

" Mr. Weston ! I never heard of him before."

" Yes, you have : I've mentioned him several times, I
believe : but you don't remember."

" I've heard you speak of Mr. Hatfield."

" Mr. Hatfield was the Rector, and Mr. Weston the Curate :
I used to mention him sometimes in contradistinction to Mr.
Hatfield, as being a more efficient clergyman. However, he

was on the sands this morning with the dog—he had bought
it, I suppose, from the ratcatcher; and he knew me as well
as it did—probably through its means: and I had a little
conversation with him, in the course of which, as he asked
about our school, I was led to say something about you and
your good management; and he said he should like to know
you, and asked if I would introduce him to you, if he should
take the liberty of calling to-morrow; so I said I would.
Was I right?"

"Of course. What kind of a man is he?"

"A very *respectable* man, I think : but you will see him
to-morrow. He is the new vicar of F——, and as he has
only been there a few weeks, I suppose he has made no
friends yet, and wants a little society."

The morrow came. What a fever of anxiety and expectation I was in from breakfast till noon—at which time he
made his appearance! Having introduced him to my mother,
I took my work to the window, and sat down to await the
result of the interview. They got on extremely well together; greatly to my satisfaction, for I had felt very anxious
about what my mother would think of him. He did not
stay long that time : but when he rose to take leave, she said
she should be happy to see him, whenever he might find it
convenient to call again; and when he was gone, I was gratified by hearing her say,—

"Well! I think he's a very sensible man. But why did
you sit back there, Agnes," she added, "and talk so little?"

"Because you talked so well, mama, I thought you required no assistance from me : and, besides, he was your
visitor, not mine."

After that, he often called upon us—several times in the
course of a week. He generally addressed most of his conversation to my mother : and no wonder, for she *could* converse. I almost envied the unfettered, vigorous fluency of
her discourse, and the strong sense evinced by everything
she said—and yet, I did not ; for, though I occasionally regretted my own deficiencies for his sake, it gave me very
great pleasure to sit and hear the two beings I loved and
honoured above every one else in the world, discoursing together so amicably, so wisely, and so well. I was not always
silent, however ; nor was I at all neglected. I was quite as
much noticed as I would wish to be : there was no lack of

kind words and kinder looks, no end of delicate attentions, too fine and subtle to be grasped by words, and therefore indescribable—but deeply felt at heart.

Ceremony was quickly dropped between us: Mr. Weston came as an expected guest, welcome at all times, and never deranging the economy of our household affairs. He even called me "Agnes": the name had been timidly spoken at first, but, finding it gave no offence in any quarter, he seemed greatly to prefer that appellation to "Miss Grey"; and so did I. How tedious and gloomy were those days in which he did not come! And yet not miserable; for I had still the remembrance of the last visit and the hope of the next to cheer me. But when two or three days passed without my seeing him, I certainly felt very anxious—absurdly, unreasonably so; for, of course, he had his own business and the affairs of his parish to attend to. And I dreaded the close of the holidays, when *my* business also would begin, and I should be sometimes unable to see him, and sometimes—when my mother was in the schoolroom — obliged to be with him alone : a position I did not at all desire, in the house; though to meet him out of doors, and walk beside him, had proved by no means disagreeable.

One evening, however, in the last week of the vacation, he arrived—unexpectedly : for a heavy and protracted thunder-shower during the afternoon had almost destroyed my hopes of seeing him that day; but now the storm was over, and the sun was shining brightly.

"A beautiful evening, Mrs. Grey!" said he, as he entered. "Agnes, I want you to take a walk with me to—" (he named a certain part of the coast—a bold hill on the land side, and towards the sea a steep precipice, from the summit of which a glorious view is to be had). "The rain has laid the dust, and cooled and cleared the air, and the prospect will be magnificent. Will you come?"

"Can I go, mama?"

"Yes; to be sure."

I went to get ready, and was down again in a few minutes; though, of course, I took a little more pains with my attire than if I had merely been going out on some shopping expedition alone. The thunder-shower had certainly had a most beneficial effect upon the weather, and the evening was most delightful. Mr. Weston would have me to take his arm : he

H H

said little during our passage through the crowded streets, but walked very fast, and appeared grave and abstracted. I wondered what was the matter, and felt an indefinite dread that something unpleasant was on his mind; and vague surmises, concerning what it might be, troubled me not a little, and made me grave and silent enough. But these fantasies vanished upon reaching the quiet outskirts of the town; for as soon as we came within sight of the venerable old church, and the —— hill, with the deep blue sea beyond it, I found my companion was cheerful enough.

"I'm afraid I've been walking too fast for you, Agnes," said he: "in my impatience to be rid of the town, I forgot to consult your convenience; but now, we'll walk as slowly as you please. I see, by those light clouds in the west, there will be a brilliant sunset, and we shall be in time to witness its effect upon the sea, at the most moderate rate of progression."

When we had got about half-way up the hill, we fell into silence again; which, as usual, he was the first to break.

"My house is desolate yet, Miss Grey," he smilingly observed, "and I am acquainted now with all the ladies in my parish, and several in this town too; and many others I know by sight and by report; but not one of them will suit me for a companion: in fact, there is only one person in the world that will; and that is yourself; and I want to know your decision?"

"Are you in earnest, Mr. Weston?"

"In earnest! How could you think I should jest on such a subject?"

He laid his hand on mine that rested on his arm: he must have felt it tremble—but it was no great matter now.

"I hope I have not been too precipitate," he said, in a serious tone. "You must have known that it was not my way to flatter and talk soft nonsense, or even to speak the admiration that I felt; and that a single word or glance of mine meant more than the honied phrases and fervent protestations of most other men."

I said something about not liking to leave my mother, and doing nothing without her consent.

"I settled everything with Mrs. Grey, while you were putting on your bonnet," replied he. "She said I might have her consent, if I could obtain yours; and I asked her, in case I should be so happy, to come and live with us—for I was sure you would like it better. But she refused, saying she could now afford to employ an assistant, and would continue the school till she could purchase an annuity sufficient to maintain her in comfortable lodgings; and, meantime, she would spend her vacations alternately with us and your sister, and should be quite contented if you were happy. And so now I have overruled your objections on her account. Have you any other?

" No—none."

" You love me then?" said he, fervently pressing my hand.

" Yes."

———

Here I pause. My diary, from which I have compiled these pages, goes but little farther. I could go on for years; but I will content myself with adding, that I shall never forget that glorious summer evening, and always remember with delight that steep hill, and the edge of the precipice where we stood together, watching the splendid sun-set mirrored on the restless world of waters at our feet—with hearts filled with gratitude to Heaven, and happiness and love—almost too full for speech.

A few weeks after that, when my mother had supplied herself with an assistant, I became the wife of Edward Weston; and never have found cause to repent it, and am certain that I never shall. We have had trials, and we know that we must have them again; but we bear them well together, and endeavour to fortify ourselves and each other against the final separation—that greatest of all afflictions to the survivor. But, if we keep in mind the glorious heaven beyond, where both may meet again, and sin and sorrow are unknown, surely that too may be borne: and, meantime, we endeavour to live to the glory of Him who has scattered so many blessings in our path.

Edward, by his strenuous exertions, has worked surprising reforms in his parish, and is esteemed and loved by its inhabitants—as he deserves; for whatever his faults may be as a man (and no one is entirely without), I defy anybody to blame him as a pastor, a husband, or a father.

Our children, Edward, Agnes, and little Mary, promise

H H 2

well; their education, for the time being, is chiefly committed to me; and they shall want no good thing that a mother's care can give. Our modest income is amply sufficient for our requirements; and by practising the economy we learnt in harder times, and never attempting to imitate our richer neighbours, we manage not only to enjoy comfort and contentment ourselves, but to have every year something to lay by for our children, and something to give to those who need it.

And now I think I have said sufficient.

THE END OF AGNES GREY.

SELECTIONS

FROM THE LITERARY REMAINS OF

ELLIS AND ACTON BELL.

SELECTIONS,

&c. &c.

IT would not have been difficult to compile a volume out
of the papers left by my sisters, had I, in making the
selection, dismissed from my consideration the scruples
and the wishes of those whose written thoughts these
papers held. But this was impossible: an influence,
stronger than could be exercised by any motive of ex-
pediency, necessarily regulated the selection. I have, then,
culled from the mass only a little poem here and there.
The whole makes but a tiny nosegay, and the colour and
perfume of the flowers are not such as fit them for festal
uses.

It has been already said that my sisters wrote much in
childhood and girlhood. Usually, it seems a sort of injustice to expose in print the crude thoughts of the unripe
mind, the rude efforts of the unpractised hand; yet I
venture to give three little poems of my sister Emily's,
written in her sixteenth year, because they illustrate a point
in her character.

At that period she was sent to school. Her previous
life, with the exception of a single half-year, had been
passed in the absolute retirement of a village parsonage,
amongst the hills bordering Yorkshire and Lancashire.
The scenery of these hills is not grand—it is not romantic;

it is scarcely striking. Long low moors, dark with heath, shut in little valleys, where a stream waters, here and there, a fringe of stunted copse. Mills and scattered cottages chase romance from these valleys; it is only higher up, deep in amongst the ridges of the moors, that Imagination can find rest for the sole of her foot: and even if she finds it there, she must be a solitude-loving raven—no gentle dove. If she demand beauty to inspire her, she must bring it inborn: these moors are too stern to yield any product so delicate. The eye of the gazer must *itself* brim with a " purple light," intense enough to perpetuate the brief flower-flush of August on the heather, or the rare sunset-smile of June; out of his heart must well the freshness, that in latter spring and early summer brightens the bracken, nurtures the moss, and cherishes the starry flowers that spangle for a few weeks the pasture of the moor-sheep. Unless that light and freshness are innate and self-sustained, the drear prospect of a Yorkshire moor will be found as barren of poetic as of agricultural interest: where the love of wild nature is strong, the locality will perhaps be clung to with the more passionate. constancy, because from the hill-lover's self comes half its charm.

My sister Emily loved the moors. Flowers brighter than the rose bloomed in the blackest of the heath for her; out of a sullen hollow in a livid hill-side her mind could make an Eden. She found in the bleak solitude many and dear delights; and not the least and best loved was—liberty.

Liberty was the breath of Emily's nostrils; without it, she perished. The change from her own home to a school, and from her own very noiseless, very secluded, but unrestricted and inartificial mode of life, to one of disciplined routine (though under the kindliest auspices), was what she failed in enduring. Her nature proved here too strong for her fortitude. Every morning when she woke, the vision of home and the moors rushed on her, and darkened and saddened the day that lay before her. Nobody knew what ailed her but me—I knew only too well. In this struggle her health was quickly broken: her white face, attenuated form, and failing strength threatened rapid decline. I felt in my heart she would die if she did not go home, and with this conviction obtained her recall. She had only been three months at school; and it was some years before the experiment of sending her from home was again ventured on. After the age of twenty, having meantime studied alone with diligence and perseverance, she went with me to an establishment on the Continent: the same suffering and conflict ensued, heightened by the strong recoil of her upright, heretic and English spirit from the gentle Jesuitry of the foreign and Romish system. Once more she seemed sinking, but this time she rallied through the mere force of resolution : with inward remorse and shame she looked back on her former failure, and resolved to conquer in this second ordeal. She did conquer: but the victory cost her dear. She was never happy till she carried her hard-won knowledge back to the remote English village, the old parsonage-house, and desolate Yorkshire hills. A very few years more, and she looked her last on those hills, and breathed her last in that house, and under the aisle of that obscure village church found her last lowly resting-place. Merciful was the decree that spared her when she was a stranger in a strange land, and guarded her dying bed with kindred love and congenial constancy.

The following pieces were composed at twilight, in the schoolroom, when the leisure of the evening play-hour brought back in full tide the thoughts of home.

POEMS BY ELLIS BELL.

I.

A LITTLE while, a little while,
  The weary task is put away,
And I can sing and I can smile,
  Alike, while I have holiday.

Where wilt thou go my harassed heart—
  What thought, what scene invites thee now?
What spot, or near or far apart,
  Has rest for thee, my weary brow?

There is a spot, 'mid barren hills,
  Where winter howls, and driving rain;
But, if the dreary tempest chills,
  There is a light that warms again.

The house is old, the trees are bare,
  Moonless above bends twilight's dome;
But what on earth is half so dear—
  So longed for—as the hearth of home?

The mute bird sitting on the stone,
  The dank moss dripping from the wall,
The thorn-trees gaunt, the walks o'ergrown,
  I love them—how I love them all!

Still—as I mused—the naked room,
  The alien firelight died away;
And from the midst of cheerless gloom,
  I passed to bright, unclouded day.

A little and a lone green lane
  That opened on a common wide;
A distant, dreamy, dim, blue chain
  Of mountains, circling every side.

A heaven so clear, an earth so calm,
  So sweet, so soft, so hushed an air;
And—deepening still the dream-like charm—
  Wild moor-sheep feeding everywhere.

That was the scene, I knew it well;
    I knew the turfy pathway's sweep,
That, winding o'er each billowy swell,
    Marked out the tracks of wándering sheep.

Could I have lingered but an hour,
    It well had paid a week of toil;
But Truth has banished Fancy's power:
    Restraint and heavy task recoil.

Even as I stood with raptured eye,
    Absorbed in bliss so deep and dear,
My hour of rest had fleeted by,
    And back came labour, bondage, care.

————

II.

THE BLUEBELL.

THE Bluebell is the sweetest flower
    That waves in summer air:
Its blossoms have the mightiest power
    To soothe my spirit's care.

There is a spell in purple heath
    Too wildly, sadly dear;
The violet has a fragrant breath,
    But fragrance will not cheer.

The trees are bare, the sun is cold,
    And seldom, seldom seen;
The heavens have lost their zone of gold,
    And earth her robe of green.

And ice upon the glancing stream
    Has cast its sombre shade;
And distant hills and valleys seem
    In frozen mist arrayed.

The Bluebell cannot charm me now,
    The heath has lost its bloom;
The violets in the glen below,
    They yield no sweet perfume.

But, though I mourn the sweet Bluebell,
  'Tis better far away;
I know how fast my tears would swell
  To see it smile to-day.

For, oh! when chill the sunbeams fall
  Adown that dreary sky,
And gild yon dank and darkened wall
  With transient brilliancy;

How do I weep, how do I pine
  For the time of flowers to come,
And turn me from that fading shine,
  To mourn the fields of home!

III.

LOUD without the wind was roaring
  Through th' autumnal sky; ·
Drenching wet, the cold rain pouring,
  Spoke of winter nigh.
    All too like that dreary eve,
    Did my exiled spirit grieve.
Grieved at first, but grieved not long,
  Sweet—how softly sweet!—it came;
Wild words of an ancient song,
  Undefined, without a name.

" It was spring, and the skylark was singing:"
  Those words they awakened a spell;
They unlocked a deep fountain, whose springing,
  Nor absence, nor distance can quell.

In the gloom of a cloudy November,
  They uttered the music of May;
They kindled the perishing ember
  Into fervour that could not decay.

Awaken, o'er all my dear moorland,
  West-wind, in thy glory and pride!
O! call me from valley and lowland,
  To walk by the hill-torrent's side!

It is swelled with the first snowy weather;
　The rocks they are icy and hoar,
And sullenly waves the long heather,
　And the fern leaves are sunny no more.

There are no yellow stars on the mountain;
　The bluebells have long died away,
From the brink of the moss-bedded fountain;
　From the side of the wintry brae.

But lovelier than corn-fields all waving
　In emerald, and vermeil, and gold,
Are the heights where the north-wind is raving,
　And the crags where I wandered of old.

It was morning : the bright sun was beaming;
　How sweetly it brought back to me,
The time when nor labour nor dreaming
　Broke the sleep of the happy and free.

But blithely we rose as the dawn-heaven
　Was melting to amber and blue,
And swift were the wings to our feet given,
　As we traversed the meadows of dew.

For the moors ! For the moors, where the short grass
　Like velvet beneath us should lie !
For the moors ! For the moors, where each high pass
　Rose sunny against the clear sky !

For the moors, where the linnet was trilling
　Its song on the old granite stone;
Where the lark, the wild sky-lark, was filling
　Every breast with delight like its own !

What language can utter the feeling
　Which rose, when in exile afar,
On the brow of a lonely hill kneeling,
　I saw the brown heath growing there ?

It was scattered and stunted, and told me
　That soon even that would be gone :
It whispered, " The grim walls enfold me,
　I have bloomed in my last summer's sun."

But not the loved music whose waking
  Makes the soul of the Swiss die away,
Has a spell more adored and heartbreaking
  Than, for me, in that blighted heath lay.

The spirit which bent 'neath its power,
  How it longed—how it burned to be free!
If I could have wept in that hour,
  Those tears had been heaven to me.

Well—well; the sad minutes are moving,
  Though loaded with trouble and pain;
And some time the loved and the loving
  Shall meet on the mountains again!

———

The following little piece has no title; but in it the Genius
of a solitary region seems to address his wandering and wayward votary, and to recall within his influence the proud
mind which rebelled at times even against what it most
loved.

SHALL earth no more inspire thee,
  Thou lonely dreamer, now?
Since passion may not fire thee,
  Shall nature cease to bow?

Thy mind is ever moving,
  In regions dark to thee;
Recall its useless roving,
  Come back, and dwell with me.

I know my mountain breezes
  Enchant and soothe thee still;
I know my sunshine pleases,
  Despite thy wayward will.

When day with evening blending,
  Sinks from the summer sky,
I've seen thy spirit bending
  In fond idolatry.

I've watched thee every hour,
  I know my mighty sway:
I know my magic power
  To drive thy griefs away.

Few hearts to mortals given,
    On earth so wildly pine;
Yet few would ask a heaven
    More like this earth than thine.

Then let my winds caress thee;
    Thy comrade let me be:
Since nought beside can bless thee,
    Return—and dwell with me.

Here again is the same mind in converse with a like abstraction. The Night-Wind, breathing through an open window, has visited an ear which discerned language in its whispers.

THE NIGHT-WIND.

In summer's mellow midnight,
    A cloudless moon shone through
Our open parlour-window,
    And rose-trees wet with dew.

I sat in silent musing;
    The soft wind waved my hair;
It told me heaven was glorious,
    And sleeping earth was fair.

I needed not its breathing
    To bring such thoughts to me;
But still it whispered lowly,
    " How dark the woods will be!

" The thick leaves in my murmur
    " Are rustling like a dream,
" And all their myriad voices
    " Instinct with spirit seem."

I said, " Go, gentle singer,
    " Thy wooing voice is kind:
" But do not think its music
    " Has power to reach my mind.

" Play with the scented flower,
    " The young tree's supple bough,
" And leave my human feelings
    " In their own course to flow."

" The wanderer would not heed me;
　" Its kiss grew warmer still.
" O come !" it sighed so sweetly;
　" I 'll win thee 'gainst thy will.

" Were we not friends from childhood?
　" Have I not loved thee long?
" As long as thou, the solemn night,
　" Whose silence wakes my song?

" And when thy heart is resting
　" Beneath the church-aisle stone,
" *I* shall have time for mourning,
　" And *thou* for being alone."

———

In these stanzas a louder gale has roused the sleeper on
her pillow: the wakened soul struggles to blend with the
storm by which it is swayed:—

Ay—there it is ! it wakes to-night
　Deep feelings I thought dead;
Strong in the blast—quick gathering light—
　The heart's flame kindles red.

" Now I can tell by thine altered cheek,
　" And by thine eyes' full gaze,
" And by the words thou scarce dost speak,
　" How wildly fancy plays.

" Yes—I could swear that glorious wind
　" Has swept the world aside,
" Has dashed its memory from thy mind
　" Like foam-bells from the tide:

" And thou art now a spirit pouring
　" Thy presence into all:
" The thunder of the tempest's roaring,
　" The whisper of its fall:

" An universal influence,
　" From thine own influence free;
" A principle of life—intense—
　" Lost to mortality.

" Thus truly, when that breast is cold,
  " Thy prisoned soul shall rise;
" The dungeon mingle with the mould—
  " The captive with the skies.
" Nature's deep being, thine shall hold,
" Her spirit all thy spirit fold,
  " Her breath absorb thy sighs.
" Mortal! though soon life's tale is told;
  " Who once lives, never dies!"

LOVE AND FRIENDSHIP.

LOVE is like the wild rose-briar;
  Friendship like the holly-tree.
The holly is dark when the rose-briar blooms,
  But which will bloom most constantly?

The wild rose-briar is sweet in spring,
  Its summer blossoms scent the air;
Yet wait till winter comes again,
  And who will call the wild-briar fair?

Then, scorn the silly rose-wreath now,
  And deck thee with the holly's sheen,
That, when December blights thy brow,
  He still may leave thy garland green.

THE ELDER'S REBUKE.

" LISTEN! When your hair, like mine,
  " Takes a tint of silver gray;
" When your eyes, with dimmer shine,
  " Watch life's bubbles float away:
" When you, young man, have borne like me
" The weary weight of sixty-three,
" Then shall penance sore be paid
  " For those hours so wildly squandered;
" And the words that now fall dead
  " On your ear, be deeply pondered—
" Pondered and approved at last:
" But their virtue will be past!

" Glorious is the prize of Duty,
  " Though she be ' a serious power ';
" Treacherous all the lures of Beauty,
  " Thorny bud and poisonous flower !

" Mirth is but a mad beguiling
  " Of the golden-gifted time ;
" Love—a demon-meteor, wiling
  " Heedless feet to gulfs of crime.

" Those who follow earthly pleasure,
  " Heavenly knowledge will not lead ;
" Wisdom hides from them her treasure,
  " Virtue bids them evil-speed !

" Vainly may their hearts, repenting,
  " Seek for aid in future years ;
" Wisdom, scorned, knows no relenting ;
  " Virtue is not won by fears."

Thus spake the ice-blooded elder gray ;
The young man scoffed as he turned away,
Turned to the call of a sweet lute's measure,
Waked by the lightsome touch of pleasure :
Had he ne'er met a gentler teacher,
Woe had been wrought by that pitiless preacher.

THE WANDERER FROM THE FOLD.

How few, of all the hearts that loved,
  Are grieving for thee now ;
And why should mine to-night be moved
  With such a sense of woe ?

Too often thus, when left alone,
  Where none my thoughts can see,
Comes back a word, a passing tone
  From thy strange history.

Sometimes I seem to see thee rise,
  A glorious child, again ;
All virtues beaming from thine eyes
  That ever honoured men :

Courage and truth, a generous breast
  Where sinless sunshine lay :
A being whose very presence blest
  Like gladsome summer-day.

O, fairly spread thy early sail,
  And fresh, and pure, and free,
Was the first impulse of the gale
  Which urged life's wave for thee !

Why did the pilot, too confiding,
  Dream o'er that ocean's foam,
And trust in Pleasure's careless guiding
  To bring his vessel home?

For well he knew what dangers frowned,
  What mists would gather, dim ;
What rocks, and shelves, and sands, lay round
  Between his port and him.

The very brightness of the sun,
  The splendour of the main,
The wind which bore him wildly on
  Should not have warned in vain.

An anxious gazer from the shore—
  I marked the whitening wave,
And wept above thy fate the more
  Because—I could not save.

It recks not now, when all is over :
  But yet my heart will be
A mourner still, though friend and lover
  Have both forgotten thee!

WARNING AND REPLY.

IN the earth—the earth—thou shalt be laid,
  A grey stone standing over thee ;
Black mould beneath thee spread,
  And black mould to cover thee.

" Well—there is rest there,
　" So fast come thy prophecy;
" The time when my sunny hair
　" Shall with grass roots entwined be."

But cold—cold is that resting-place,
　Shut out from joy and liberty,
And all who loved thy living face
　Will shrink from it shudderingly.

" Not so. *Here* the world is chill,
　" And sworn friends fall from me :
" But *there*—they will own me still,
　" And prize my memory."

Farewell, then, all that love,
　All that deep sympathy :
Sleep on : Heaven laughs above,
　Earth never misses thee.

Turf-sod and tombstone drear
　Part human company ;
One heart breaks only—here,
　But that heart was worthy thee !

LAST WORDS.

I KNEW not 'twas so dire a crime
　To say the word, Adieu;
But this shall be the only time
　My lips or heart shall sue.

The wild hill-side, the winter morn,
　The gnarled and ancient tree,
If in your breast they waken scorn,
　Shall wake the same in me.

I can forget black eyes and brows,
　And lips of falsest charm,
If you forget the sacred vows
　Those faithless lips could form.

If hard commands can tame your love,
　Or strongest walls can hold,
I would not wish to grieve above
　A thing so false and cold.

And there are bosoms bound to mine
　With links both tried and strong;
And there are eyes whose lightning shine
　Has warmed and blest me long:

Those eyes shall make my only day,
　Shall set my spirit free,
And chase the foolish thoughts away
　That mourn your memory.

THE LADY TO HER GUITAR.

For him who struck thy foreign string,
　I ween this heart has ceased to care;
Then why dost thou such feelings bring
　To my sad spirit—old Guitar?

It is as if the warm sunlight
　In some deep glen should lingering stay,
When clouds of storm, or shades of night
　Have wrapt the parent orb away.

It is as if the glassy brook
　Should image still its willows fair,
Though years ago the woodman's stroke
　Laid low in dust their Dryad-hair.]

Even so, Guitar, thy magic tone
　Hath moved the tear and waked the sigh;
Hath bid the ancient torrent moan,
　Although its very source is dry.

THE TWO CHILDREN.

Heavy hangs the rain-drop
　From the burdened spray;
Heavy broods the damp mist
　On uplands far away.

Heavy looms the dull sky,
  Heavy rolls the sea;
And heavy throbs the young heart
  Beneath that lonely tree.

Never has a blue streak
  Cleft the clouds since morn;
Never has his grim fate
  Smiled since he was born.

Frowning on the infant,
  Shadowing childhood's joy;
Guardian-angel knows not
  That melancholy boy.

Day is passing swiftly
  Its sad and sombre prime;
Boyhood sad is merging
  In sadder manhood's time:

All the flowers are praying
  For sun, before they close,
And he prays too—unconscious—
  That sunless human rose.

Blossom—that the west-wind
  Has never wooed to blow,
Scentless are thy petals,
  Thy dew is cold as snow!

Soul—where kindred kindness,
  No early promise woke,
Barren is thy beauty,
  As weed upon a rock.

Wither—soul and blossom!
  You both were vainly given:
Earth reserves no blessing
  For the unblest of heaven!

———

Child of delight, with sun-bright hair,
  And sea-blue, sea-deep eyes!
Spirit of bliss! What brings thee here,
  Beneath these sullen skies?

Thou shouldst live in eternal spring,
    Where endless day is never dim;
Why, Seraph, has thine erring wing
    Wafted thee down to weep with him?

" Ah! not from heaven am I descended,
    " Nor do I come to mingle tears;
" But sweet is day, though with shadows blended;
    " And, though clouded, sweet are youthful years.

" I—the image of light and gladness—
    " Saw and pitied that mournful boy,
" And I vowed—if need were—to share his sadness,
    " And give to him my sunny joy.

" Heavy and dark the night is closing;
    " Heavy and dark may its biding be:
" Better for all from grief reposing,
    " And better for all who watch like me—

" Watch in love by a fevered pillow,
    " Cooling the fever with pity's balm;
" Safe as the petrel on tossing billow,
    " Safe in mine own soul's golden calm!

" Guardian-angel he lacks no longer;
    " Evil fortune he need not fear:
" Fate is strong, but love is stronger;
    " And *my* love is truer than angel-care."

THE VISIONARY.

ILENT is the house: all are laid asleep:
One alone looks out o'er the snow-wreaths deep;
Watching every cloud, dreading every breeze
That whirls the wildering drift, and bends the groaning trees.

Cheerful is the hearth, soft the matted floor;
Not one shivering gust creeps through pane or door;
The little lamp burns straight, its rays shoot strong and far:
I trim it well, to be the wanderer's guiding-star.

Frown, my haughty sire! chide, my angry dame!
Set your slaves to spy; threaten me with shame:

But neither sire nor dame, nor prying serf shall know,
What angel nightly tracks that waste of frozen snow.

What I love shall come like visitant of air,
Safe in secret power from lurking human snare;
What love's me, no word of mine shall e'er betray,
Though for faith unstained my life must forfeit pay.

Burn, then, little lamp; glimmer straight and clear—
Hush! a rustling wing stirs, methinks, the air:
He for whom I wait, thus ever comes to me;
Strange Power! I trust thy might; trust thou my constancy.

———

ENCOURAGEMENT.

I do not weep; I would not weep;
   Our mother needs no tears:
Dry thine eyes, too; 'tis vain to keep
   This causeless grief for years.

What though her brow be changed and cold,
   Her sweet eyes closed for ever?
What though the stone—the darksome mould
   Our mortal bodies sever?

What though her hand smooth ne'er again
   Those silken locks of thine?
Nor, through long hours of future pain,
   Her kind face o'er thee shine?

Remember still, she is not dead;
   She sees us, sister, now;
Laid, where her angel spirit fled,
   'Mid heath and frozen snow.

And, from that world of heavenly light
   Will she not always bend
To guide us in our lifetime's night,
   And guard us to the end?

Thou knowest she will; and thou mayst mourn
   That *we* are left below:
But not that she can ne'er return
   To share our earthly woe.

STANZAS.

OFTEN rebuked, yet always back returning
  To those first feelings that were born with me,
And leaving busy chase of wealth and learning
  For idle dreams of things which cannot be:

To-day, I will seek not the shadowy region,
  Its unsustaining vastness waxes drear;
And visions rising, legion after legion,
  Bring the unreal world too strangely near.

I'll walk, but not in old heroic traces,
  And not in paths of high morality,
And not among the half-distinguished faces,
  The clouded forms of long-past history.

I'll walk where my own nature would be leading:
  It vexes me to choose another guide:
Where the grey flocks in ferny glens are feeding;
  Where the wild wind blows on the mountain side.

What have those lonely mountains worth revealing?
  More glory and more grief than I can tell:
The earth that wakes *one* human heart to feeling
  Can centre both the worlds of Heaven and Hell.

———

The following are the last lines my sister Emily ever
wrote.

No coward soul is mine,
No trembler in the world's storm-troubled sphere:
  I see Heaven's glories shine,
And faith shines equal, arming me from fear.

O God within my breast,
Almighty, ever-present Deity!
  Life—that in me has rest,
As I—undying Life—have power in thee!

Vain are the thousand creeds
That move men's hearts: unutterably vain;
  Worthless as withered weeds,
Or idlest froth amid the boundless main,

To waken doubt in one
Holding so fast by thine infinity;
So surely anchored on
The stedfast rock of immortality.

With wide-embracing love
Thy spirit animates eternal years,
Pervades and broods above,
Changes, sustains, dissolves, creates, and rears

Though earth and man were gone,
And suns and universes ceased to be,
And Thou were left alone,
Every existence would exist in Thee.

There is not room for Death,
Nor atom that his might could render void:
Thou—Thou art Being and Breath,
And what Thou art may never be destroyed.

POEMS BY ACTON BELL.

In looking over my sister Anne's papers, I find mournful
evidence that religious feeling had been to her but too
much like what it was to Cowper; I mean, of course, in
a far milder form.   Without rendering her a prey to
those horrors that defy concealment, it subdued her mood
and bearing to a perpetual pensiveness: the pillar of a
cloud glided constantly before her eyes: she ever waited
at the foot of a secret Sinai, listening in her heart to
the voice of a trumpet sounding long and waxing louder.
Some, perhaps, would rejoice over these tokens of sincere
though sorrowing piety in a deceased relative; I own, to
me they seem sad, as if her whole innocent life had been
passed under the martyrdom of an unconfessed physical
pain: their effect, indeed, would be too distressing, were

it not combated by the certain knowledge that in her last moments this tyranny of a too tender conscience was overcome; this pomp of terrors broke up, and, passing away, left her dying hour unclouded. Her belief in God did not then bring to her dread, as of a stern Judge,— but hope, as in a Creator and Saviour: and no faltering hope was it, but a sure and stedfast conviction; on which, in the rude passage from Time to Eternity, she threw the weight of her human weakness, and by which she was enabled to bear what was to be borne, patiently— serenely—victoriously.

DESPONDENCY.

I HAVE gone backward in the work;
    The labour has not sped;
Drowsy and dark my spirit lies,
    Heavy and dull as lead.

How can I rouse my sinking soul
    From such a lethargy?
How can I break these iron chains
    And set my spirit free?

There have been times when I have mourned
    In anguish o'er the past,
And raised my suppliant hands on high,
    While tears fell thick and fast;

And prayed to have my sins forgiven,
    With such a fervent zeal,
An earnest grief, a strong desire
    As now I cannot feel.

And I have felt so full of love,
    So strong in spirit then,
As if my heart would never cool,
    Or wander back again.

And yet, alas ! how many times
  My feet have gone astray !
How oft have I forgot my God !
  How greatly fallen away !

My sins increase—my love grows cold,
  And Hope within me dies :
Even Faith itself is wavering now ;
  Oh, how shall I arise ?

I cannot weep, but I can pray,
  Then let me not despair :
Lord Jesus, save me, lest I die !
  Christ, hear my humble prayer !

A PRAYER.

My God (oh, let me call Thee mine,
  Weak, wretched sinner though I be),
My trembling soul would fain be Thine ;
  My feeble faith still clings to Thee.

Not only for the Past I grieve,
  The Future fills me with dismay ;
Unless Thou hasten to relieve,
  Thy suppliant is a castaway.

I cannot say my faith is strong,
  I dare not hope my love is great,
But strength and love to Thee belong ;
  Oh, do not leave me desolate !

I know I owe my all to Thee ;
  Oh, *take* the heart I cannot give !
Do Thou my Strength—my Saviour be,
  And *make* me to Thy glory live.

IN MEMORY OF A HAPPY DAY IN FEBRUARY.

Blessed be Thou for all the joy
  My soul has felt to-day !
Oh, let its memory stay with me,
  And never pass away !

I was alone, for those I loved
  Were far away from me;
The sun shone on the withered grass,
  The wind blew fresh and free.

Was it the smile of early spring
  That made my bosom glow?
'Twas sweet; but neither sun nor wind
  Could cheer my spirit so.

Was it some feeling of delight
  All vague and undefined?
No; 'twas a rapture deep and strong,
  Expanding in the mind.

Was it a sanguine view of life,
  And all its transient bliss,
A hope of bright prosperity?
  Oh, no! it was not this.

It was a glimpse of truth divine
  Unto my spirit given,
Illumined by a ray of light
  That shone direct from heaven.

I felt there was a God on high,
  By whom all things were made;
I saw His wisdom and His power
  In all His works displayed.

But most throughout the moral world,
  I saw His glory shine;
I saw His wisdom infinite,
  His mercy all divine.

Deep secrets of His providence,
  In darkness long concealed,
Unto the vision of my soul
  Were graciously revealed.

But while I wondered and adored
  His Majesty divine,
I did not tremble at His power:
  I felt that God was mine.

I knew that my Redeemer lived;
  I did not fear to die;
Full sure that I should rise again
  To immortality.

I longed to view that bliss divine,
  Which eye hath never seen;
Like Moses, I would see His face
  Without the veil between.

CONFIDENCE.

OPPRESSED with sin and woe,
  A burdened heart I bear,
Opposed by many a mighty foe;
  But I will not despair.

With this polluted heart,
  I dare to come to Thee,
Holy and mighty as Thou art,
  For Thou wilt pardon me.

I feel that I am weak,
  And prone to every sin;
But Thou who giv'st to those who seek,
  Will give me strength within.

Far as this earth may be
  From yonder starry skies;
Remoter still am I from Thee:
  Yet Thou will not despise.

I need not fear my foes,
  I need not yield to care;
I need not sink beneath my woes,
  For Thou wilt answer prayer.

In my Redeemer's name,
  I give myself to Thee;
And, all unworthy as I am,
  My God will cherish me.

My sister Anne had to taste the cup of life as it is mixed for the class termed " Governesses."

The following are some of the thoughts that now and then solace a governess :—

LINES WRITTEN FROM HOME.

THOUGH bleak these woods, and damp the ground,
    With fallen leaves so thickly strewn,
And cold the wind that wanders round
    With wild and melancholy moan;

There *is* a friendly roof, I know,
    Might shield me from the wintry blast;
There is a fire whose ruddy glow
    Will cheer me for my wanderings past.

And so, though still where'er I go
    Cold stranger glances meet my eye;
Though, when my spirit sinks in wo,
    Unheeded swells the unbidden sigh;

Though solitude, endured too long,
    Bids youthful joys too soon decay,
Makes mirth a stranger to my tongue,
    And overclouds my noon of day;

When kindly thoughts that would have way,
    Flow back, discouraged, to my breast,
I know there is, though far away,
    A home where heart and soul may rest.

Warm hands are there, that, clasped in mine,
    The warmer heart will not belie;
While mirth and truth, and friendship shine
    In smiling lip and earnest eye.

The ice that gathers round my heart
    May there be thawed; and sweetly, then,
The joys of youth, that now depart,
    Will come to cheer my soul again.

Though far I roam, that thought shall be
　My hope, my comfort everywhere;
While such a home remains to me,
　My heart shall never know despair.

———

THE NARROW WAY.

BELIEVE not those who say
　The upward path is smooth,
Lest thou shouldst stumble in the way,
　And faint before the truth.

It is the only road
　Unto the realms of joy;
But he who seeks that blest abode,
　Must all his powers employ.

Bright hopes and pure delight
　Upon his course may beam,
And there, amid the sternest heights,
　The sweetest flowerets gleam.

On all her breezes borne,
　Earth yields no scents like those;
But he that dares not grasp the thorn,
　Should never crave the rose.

Arm—arm thee for the fight!
　Cast useless loads away;
Watch through the darkest hours of night;
　Toil through the hottest day.

Crush pride into the dust,
　Or thou must needs be slack;
And trample down rebellious lust,
　Or it will hold thee back.

Seek not thy honour here;
　Waive pleasure and renown;
The world's dread scoff undaunted bear,
　And face its deadliest frown.

To labour and to love,
  To pardon and endure,
To lift thy heart to God above,
  And keep thy conscience pure;

Be this thy constant aim,
  Thy hope, thy chief delight;
What matter who should whisper blame,
  Or who should scorn or slight?

What matter, if thy God approve,
  And if, within thy breast,
Thou feel the comfort of His love,
  The earnest of His rest?

DOMESTIC PEACE.

WHY should such gloomy silence reign,
  And why is all the house so drear,
When neither danger, sickness, pain,
  Nor death, nor want have entered here?

We are as many as we were
  That other night, when all were gay
And full of hope, and free from care;
  Yet, is there something gone away.

The moon without, as pure and calm,
  Is shining, as that night she shone;
But now, to us, she brings no balm,
  For something from our hearts is gone.

Something whose absence leaves a void—
  A cheerless want in every heart;
Each feels the bliss of all destroyed,
  And mourns the change—but each apart.

The fire is burning in the grate
  As redly as it used to burn;
But still the hearth is desolate,
  Till mirth, and love, and *peace* return.

K K

'T was *peace* that flowed from heart to heart,
  With looks and smiles that spoke of heaven,
And gave us language to impart
  The blissful thoughts itself had given.

Domestic peace ! best joy of earth,
  When shall we all thy value learn ?
White angel—to our sorrowing hearth,
  Return—oh, graciously return !

THE THREE GUIDES.

(First published in Fraser's Magazine.)

Spirit of Earth ! thy hand is chill :
  I've felt its icy clasp ;
And, shuddering, I remember still
  That stony-hearted grasp.
Thine eye bids love and joy depart :
  Oh, turn its gaze from me !
It presses down my shrinking heart ;
  I will not walk with thee !

" Wisdom is mine," I've heard thee say :
  " Beneath my searching eye,
" All mist and darkness melt away,
  " Phantoms and fables fly.
" Before me truth can stand alone,
  " The naked, solid truth ;
" And man matured by worth will own,
  " If I am shunned by youth.

" Firm is my tread, and sure though slow :
  " My footsteps never slide ;
" And he that follows me shall know
  " I am the surest guide."
Thy boast is vain ; but were it true
  That thou couldst safely steer
Life's rough and devious pathway through,
  Such guidance I should fear.

How could I bear to walk for aye,
  With eyes to earthward prone,
O'er trampled weeds and miry clay,
  And sand and flinty stone ;

Never the glorious view to greet
  Of hill, and dale, and sky;
To see that Nature's charms are sweet,
  Or feel that Heaven is nigh?

If in my heart arose a spring,
  A gush of thought divine,
At once stagnation thou wouldst bring
  With that cold touch of thine.
If, glancing up, I sought to snatch
  But one glimpse of the sky,
My baffled gaze would only catch
  Thy heartless, cold grey eye.]

If to the breezes wandering near,
  I listened eagerly,
And deemed an angel's tongue to hear
  That whispered hope to me,
That heavenly music would be drowned
  In thy harsh, droning voice;
Nor inward thought, nor sight, nor sound,
  Might my sad soul rejoice.

Dull is thine ear, unheard by thee
  The still small voice of Heaven;
Thine eyes are dim and cannot see
  The helps that God has given.
There is a bridge o'er every flood
  Which thou canst not perceive;
A path through every tangled wood,
  But thou wilt not believe.

Striving to make thy way by force,
  Toil-spent and bramble-torn,
Thou'lt fell the tree that checks thy course
  And burst through brier and thorn:
And, pausing by the river's side,
  Poor reasoner! thou wilt deem,
By casting pebbles in its tide,
  To cross the swelling stream.

Right through the flinty rock thou'lt try
  Thy toilsome way to bore,
Regardless of the pathway nigh
  That would conduct thee o'er.   K K 2

Not only art thou then, unkind,
    And freezing cold to me,
But unbelieving, deaf, and blind;
    I will not walk with thee

Spirit of Pride! thy wings are strong,
    Thine eyes like lightning shine;
Ecstatic joys to thee belong,
    And powers almost divine.
But 'tis a false, destructive blaze
    Within those eyes I see;
Turn hence their fascinating gaze,
    I will not follow thee.

" Coward and fool!" thou mayst reply,
    " Walk on the common sod;
" Go, trace with timid foot and eye
    " The steps by others trod.
" 'Tis best the beaten path to keep,
    " The ancient faith to hold;
" To pasture with thy fellow-sheep,
    " And lie within the fold.

" Cling to the earth, poor grovelling worm;
    " 'Tis not for thee to soar
" Against the fury of the storm,
    " Amid the thunder's roar!
" There's glory in that daring strife
    " Unknown, undreamt by thee;
" There's speechless rapture in the life
    " Of those who follow me."

Yes, I have seen thy votaries oft,
    Upheld by thee their guide,
In strength and courage mount aloft
    The steepy mountain-side;
I've seen them stand against the sky,
    And gazing from below,
Beheld thy lightning in their eye,
    Thy triumph on their brow.

Oh, I have felt what glory, then,
    What transport must be theirs!
So far above their fellow-men,
    Above their toils and cares;

Inhaling Nature's purest breath,
    Her riches round them spread,
The wide expanse of earth beneath,
    Heaven's glories overhead!

But I have seen them helpless, dash'd,
    Down to a bloody grave,
And still thy ruthless eye has flash'd,
    Thy strong hand did not save;
I've seen some o'er the mountain's brow
    Sustain'd a while by thee,
O'er rocks of ice and hills of snow
    Bound fearless, wild, and free.

Bold and exultant was their mien,
    While thou didst cheer them on;
But evening fell,—and then, I ween,
    Their faithless guide was gone.
Alas! how fared thy favourites then,—
    Lone, helpless, weary, cold?
Did ever wanderer find again
    The path he left of old?

Where is their glory, where the pride
    That swell'd their hearts before?
Where now the courage that defied
    The mightiest tempest's roar?
What shall they do when night grows black,
    When angry storms arise?
Who now will lead them to the track
    Thou taught'st them to despise?

Spirit of Pride, it needs not this
    To make me shun thy wiles,
Renounce thy triumph and thy bliss,
    Thy honours and thy smiles!
Bright as thou art, and bold, and strong,
    That fierce glance wins not me,
And I abhor thy scoffing tongue—
    I will not follow thee!

Spirit of Faith! be thou my guide,
    O clasp my hand in thine,
And let me never quit thy side;
    Thy comforts are divine!

Earth calls thee blind, misguided one,—
  But who can shew like thee
Forgotten things that have been done,
  And things that are to be ?

Secrets conceal'd from Nature's ken,
  Who like thee can declare ?
Or who like thee to erring men
  God's holy will can bear ?
Pride scorns thee for thy lowly mien,—
  But who like thee can rise
Above this toilsome, sordid scene,
  Beyond the holy skies ?

Meek is thine eye and soft thy voice,
  But wondrous is thy might,
To make the wretched soul rejoice,
  To give the simple light !
And still to all that seek thy way
  This magic power is given,—
E'en while their footsteps press the clay,
  Their souls ascend to heaven.

Danger surrounds them,—pain and woe
  Their portion here must be,
But only they that trust thee know
  What comfort dwells with thee ;
Strength to sustain their drooping pow'rs,
  And vigour to defend,—
Thou pole-star of my darkest hours,
  Affliction's firmest friend !

Day does not always mark our way,
  Night's shadows oft appal,
But lead me, and I cannot stray,—
  Hold me, I shall not fall ;
Sustain me, I shall never faint,
  How rough soe'er may be
My upward road,—nor moan, nor plaint
  Shall mar my trust in thee.

Narrow the path by which we go,
  And oft it turns aside
From pleasant meads where roses blow,
  And peaceful waters glide ;

Where flowery turf lies green and soft,
    And gentle gales are sweet,
To where dark mountains frown aloft,
    Hard rocks distress the feet,—

Deserts beyond lie bleak and bare,
    And keen winds round us blow;
But if thy hand conducts me there,
    The way is right, I know.
I have no wish to turn away;
    My spirit does not quail,—
How can it while I hear thee say,
    " Press forward and prevail!"

Even above the tempest's swell
    I hear thy voice of love,—
Of hope and peace, I hear thee tell,
    And that blest home above;
Through pain and death I can rejoice,
    If but thy strength be mine,—
Earth hath no music like thy voice,
    Life owns no joy like thine!

Spirit of Faith, I'll go with thee!
    Thou, if I hold thee fast,
Wilt guide, defend, and strengthen me,
    And bear me home at last;
By thy help all things I can do,
    In thy strength all things bear,—
Teach me, for thou art just and true,
    Smile on me, thou art fair !

————

I have given the last memento of my sister Emily; this is
the last of my sister Anne:—

I HOPED, that with the brave and strong,
    My portioned task might lie;
To toil amid the busy throng,
    With purpose pure and high.

But God has fixed another part
  And He has fixed it well;
I said so with my bleeding heart,
  When first the anguish fell.

Thou, God, hast taken our delight,
  Our treasured hope away:
Thou bid'st us now weep through the night
  And sorrow through the day.

These weary hours will not be lost,
  These days of misery,
These nights of darkness, anguish-tost,
  Can I but turn to Thee.

With secret labour to sustain
  In humble patience every blow;
To gather fortitude from pain,
  And hope and holiness from woe.

Thus let me serve Thee from my heart,
  Whate'er may be my written fate:
Whether thus early to depart,
  Or yet a while to wait.

If Thou shouldst bring me back to life,
  More humbled I should be;
More wise—more strengthened for the strife—
  More apt to lean on Thee.

Should death be standing at the gate
  Thus should I keep my vow:
But, Lord! whatever be my fate,
  Oh, let me serve Thee now !

These lines written, the desk was closed, the pen laid aside,
for ever.

London: Printed by STEWART and MURRAY, Old Bailey.